ROBERT'S RULES OF ORDER
NEWLY REVISED

ROBERT'S RULES OF ORDER
NEWLY REVISED

11TH EDITION

GENERAL HENRY M. ROBERT
U.S. Army

A New and Enlarged Edition by
SARAH CORBIN ROBERT
HENRY M. ROBERT III
WILLIAM J. EVANS
DANIEL H. HONEMANN
THOMAS J. BALCH

with the assistance of
DANIEL E. SEABOLD
SHMUEL GERBER

DA CAPO PRESS
A Member of the Perseus Books Group

Cataloging-in-Publication Data is available from
the Library of Congress
ISBN 978-0-306-82021-2 (hardcover) 3 4 5 6 7 8 9-16 15 14
        978-0-306-82020-5 (paperback) 13 14-16 15
        978-0-306-82022-9 (leatherbound) 1 2 3 4 5 6 7 8 9 10-16 15 14 13
Library of Congress Control Number: 2011932260

For questions and answers and further information on parliamentary
procedure visit www.robertsrules.com

Da Capo Press is a member of the Perseus Books Group.

Find us on the World Wide Web at www.dacapopress.com

Da Capo Press books are available at special discounts for bulk purchases
in the U.S. by corporations, institutions, and other organizations. For
more information, please contact the Special Markets Department at the
Perseus Books Group, 2300 Chestnut Street, Suite 200, Philadelphia,
PA 19103, or call (800) 810-4145, ext. 5000, or e-mail special.markets@
perseusbooks.com.

Text design by Rachel Hegarty
Set in 9.5-point Galliard by Eclipse Publishing Services

Eighth printing of the 11th edition, April 2013

*Where there is no law, but every man
does what is right in his own eyes, there
is the least of real liberty.*

—HENRY M. ROBERT

*It is difficult to find another branch of
knowledge where a small amount of study
produces such great results in increased
efficiency in a country where the people
rule, as in parliamentary law.*

—HENRY M. ROBERT

THE EDITIONS OF THIS MANUAL

First Edition	February 1876	POCKET MANUAL OF RULES OF ORDER FOR DELIBERATIVE ASSEMBLIES
Second Edition	July 1876	
Third Edition	1893	(Cover short title: ROBERT'S RULES OF ORDER)

Fourth Edition (Completely reworked and 75 percent enlarged by original author)	1915	ROBERT'S RULES OF ORDER REVISED
Fifth Edition	1943	
Sixth Edition ("Seventy-Fifth Anniversary")	1951	

Seventh Edition (Enlarged more than twofold and totally recast to be made self-explanatory)	1970	ROBERT'S RULES OF ORDER NEWLY REVISED
Eighth Edition	1981	
Ninth Edition	1990	
Tenth Edition ("Millennium")	2000	
ELEVENTH EDITION (Significantly re-edited with expanded and updated treatment of many topics)	2011	

Inclusive of Robert's Rules of Order and Robert's Rules of Order Revised More Than Five and a Half Million Copies in Print

ABBREVIATIONS IN THIS BOOK

(13)   A boldface number, usually enclosed in parentheses, refers to a section number (here section 13). Section numbers appear at the top of each page, preceded by the symbol §.

cf.   Compare to ("confer")

e.g.   For example ("exempli gratia")

ff.   And the pages immediately following the given page

l., ll.   Line, lines

p., pp.   Page, pages

tinted p.   The pages toward the end of this book with "Charts, Tables, and Lists," which are separately paginated and are marked with gray on their outer edges, are referred to as "tinted pages."

Also see pages 119–20, "Notes on Example Format Throughout the Book."

CONTENTS

—
I
—

THE DELIBERATIVE ASSEMBLY:
ITS TYPES AND THEIR RULES

—
II
—

THE CONDUCT OF BUSINESS
IN A DELIBERATIVE ASSEMBLY

III

DESCRIPTION OF MOTIONS
IN ALL CLASSIFICATIONS

IV

MEETING AND SESSION

—
V
—

THE MAIN MOTION

—
VI
—

SUBSIDIARY MOTIONS

VII

PRIVILEGED MOTIONS

VIII

INCIDENTAL MOTIONS

IX

MOTIONS THAT BRING A QUESTION AGAIN BEFORE THE ASSEMBLY

—
X
—

RENEWAL OF MOTIONS;
DILATORY AND IMPROPER MOTIONS

—
XI
—

QUORUM; ORDER OF BUSINESS
AND RELATED CONCEPTS

XII

ASSIGNMENT OF THE FLOOR; DEBATE

XIII

VOTING

XIV

NOMINATIONS AND ELECTIONS

XV

OFFICERS; MINUTES AND OFFICERS' REPORTS

XVI

BOARDS AND COMMITTEES

——

XVII

——

MASS MEETINGS; ORGANIZATION
OF A PERMANENT SOCIETY

XVIII

BYLAWS

XIX

CONVENTIONS

XX

DISCIPLINARY PROCEDURES

CHARTS, TABLES, AND LISTS
Tinted pages following page 670

PREFACE

to the Eleventh Edition

This Eleventh Edition of *Robert's Rules of Order Newly Revised* (RONR) is issued one hundred thirty-five years after the 1876 publication, by then-Major (later Brigadier General) Henry M. Robert, of the first in the series of books familiarly known as "Robert's Rules of Order." A complete list of the editions is shown on page vi, and their history is told in the Introduction.

This Eleventh Edition in the entire series is the fifth edition of the second complete reworking of the subject matter first published in 1970. It is the only book in print containing the completely developed body of rules understood as "Robert's Rules of Order."

In the decade since the publication of the Tenth Edition at the turn of the millennium, three important resources have been added to supplement RONR.

First, for some time there has been a felt tension between the need for a parliamentary manual lengthy enough to provide rules as comprehensive and unambiguous as possible so as to cover the great number and variety of parliamentary issues that may arise in a deliberative assembly, on the one hand, and the desirability of a book simple and straightforward enough to allow the ordinary meeting-goer easily to learn and use the basic rules that are sufficient for most meetings, on the other hand.

When this book last underwent complete revision in 1970, a concerted effort was made to enhance the value of the work for the study of parliamentary law—to the extent consistent with its primary purpose as a reference manual. For those who will brave it, it is written to serve as a self-explanatory text that can be read through, with topics presented in an order that will best convey an overall understanding of the subject matter. Nevertheless, it is recognized that this project may be a bigger challenge than many newcomers to parliamentary procedure will find themselves at first able or willing to take on.

In 2005, to meet the need for a simple and short book, *Robert's Rules of Order Newly Revised In Brief* was first published. A new edition of *In Brief*, updated and revised so as to mesh with this Eleventh Edition, has now been published. This Eleventh Edition of RONR, the complete rule book, now contains 669 pages of text, plus tables and index. All of its content has to be included because it *may* be needed and has at some time come up as a question of procedure somewhere. This book is designed as a reference providing, as nearly as possible, an answer to any question of parliamentary procedure that may arise.

To gain an introductory familiarity with meeting rules, however, many people will find it useful to start with the *In Brief* book. In only twenty minutes, the average reader can learn the bare essentials, and with about an hour's reading can cover all the basics. Additional chapters give suggestions on how most efficiently to use this Eleventh Edition of RONR as a reference manual and guidance to those chosen as convention delegates or alternates, or as president, vice-president, secretary, or treasurer of an organization. Helpful tables at the end give both the chair and the ordinary member the proper wording to use in handling the most common motions and conducting a meeting.

It cannot be stressed too strongly, however, that *In Brief* is an introductory supplement to, not a replacement for, this book. Only this book is comprehensive enough to be suitable for adoption as the rule book governing an assembly, and it covers many essential matters—from the content of bylaws to disciplinary procedures—that are hardly touched on in the shorter work.

Second, an electronic version of RONR, as well as of *In Brief*, was made available through collaboration with American Legal Publishing, and a new version to accompany the new editions of both is being published. Its search feature is especially useful, and it contains much helpful additional material, such as instructions for tellers in counting ballots and for timekeepers, sample forms, explanation of secondary amendments, and much more.

Third, the Robert's Rules Association—the organization of the original author's descendants that oversees the management and regular updating of the work—sponsors a website at www.robertsrules.com. On its "Question and Answer Forum," one may post queries and conduct discussion about any aspect of parliamentary procedure.

The website also includes "RONR Official Interpretations" on issues of parliamentary law arising between editions that RONR's authors deem useful to address. Since the publication of the first edition of *Robert's Rules* in 1876, General Robert and, since his death, his successors have been receiving and replying to questions of parliamentary law. As the Introduction notes concerning the 1915 revision, "The reorganization, expansion, and clarification represented by *Robert's Rules of Order Revised* was largely the outgrowth of hundreds of letters received by the author over the years, submitting questions of parliamentary law arising in organizations and not covered in the earlier editions." Traditionally, the ongoing process by which the authorship responds to inquiries in the years between editions has been an integral part of the continuing task of clarifying and periodically revising the work; RONR Official Interpretations continues this practice in a modern format.

RONR Official Interpretations are not technically binding on an organization that has adopted *Robert's Rules of Order Newly Revised* as its parliamentary authority, but they are nonetheless definitive interpretations of the work by the current authors and should therefore be treated as highly persuasive. It is thus advisable for presiding officers, or the parliamentarians who advise them, to consult them for guidance on matters they address.

This Eleventh Edition of RONR contains important additions to, and clarifications of, the rules in the Tenth Edition. The process of arriving at additional content through the technique of interpretation continues, as situations occurring in assemblies point to a need for more fully developed rules applying to particular cases. In the preparation of this edition, the entire text of the work has been subjected to a thorough review, seeking to ferret out any remaining inconsistencies or ambiguities in concept or statement.

Some of the most significant changes,* with the pages on which their principal content may be found, are:

1. A thorough revision of Chapter XX, Disciplinary Procedures, including more detailed treatment of removal of officers and trials as well

---

*These brief summary references may not themselves be cited as rules; they serve only to direct readers to the pages in the book where principal treatment of the changed rules may be found. (Pages for conforming changes are not generally included in this list.)

as expanded provisions on remedies for abuse of authority by the chair in a meeting and on handling disruptions by members.

2. Revision of the content of modified parliamentary rules in small boards and in committees, together with recognition that a small assembly may wish to employ these less formal procedures [9–10, 16, 487–88, 500–501].

3. Provision that a board may adopt its own special rules of order and standing rules so long as they do not conflict with the society's rules [486].

4. A new subsection on "electronic meetings," with substantially expanded treatment of the topic [97–99].

5. Recognition of "one person, one vote" as a fundamental principle of parliamentary law [407].

6. Addition of a definition of a member "in good standing" [6].

7. Clarification of the rules governing the ways in which business can go over from one session to a later one, including making clear, with the inclusion of unfinished business and unfinished special orders, that there are five such ways (instead of the four explicitly identified as such in earlier editions) [90–91].

8. Clarification of the nature of the notice required for special meetings, and the relation between it and the motions in order at the special meeting [91–93].

9. A new subsection on challenging the announced result of elections [444–46]; a substantial revision of the section on *Motions Relating to Methods of Voting and the Polls* [283–86]; and more precise rules on the retention of tally sheets and ballots [411, 418–19, 422], on the remedy for violation of the right to vote [252–53], and on time limits for recounting, challenging, and changing a vote, as well as for seeking to retake it by another method [408–9].

10. New provisions on precedent [251–52].

11. Recognition of "Is there any debate?" as a less formal alternative to "Are you ready for the question?" and clarification of the proper procedure with regard to the use of these questions, or use of the question, "Are there any amendments?" depending on whether the motion is debatable or amendable [38, 44, 120, 386].

12. Establishment of *Request for Information* as the preferred name for the motion *Point of Information*, in an effort to reduce the common misunderstanding or misuse of this motion to give information rather than request it [294–95].

13. Clarification of the relation between acts of an executive board and its parent assembly [482–83, 577].
14. Revision of the rules concerning the suspending effect of *Reconsider* and addition of a new sub-subsection on reconsideration of a motion that is no longer in order because of intervening action [318, 321–22].
15. More precise delineation of the motions in order in the absence of a quorum [347–48] and in a convention before adoption of the Credentials Committee report, as well as what rules apply before adoption of the Standing Rules of the Convention [615, 618, 641].
16. Clarification of what rights members have to inspect records of the assembly, boards, and committees [460].
17. Provision permitting notice to be sent by electronic communication, such as e-mail or fax, to members who consent [89].

For a more extensive list of changes in the Eleventh Edition, see www.robertsrules.com.

The authors wish to acknowledge their indebtedness to Hofstra University for providing facilities at its campus on Long Island, New York, to Mark Corsey of Eclipse Publishing Services, and for the editorial assistance of Robert Pigeon and Jonathan Crowe, Editors, and Fred Francis, Managing Editor, of Da Capo Press, a member of the Perseus Books Group.

Henry M. Robert III
Daniel H. Honemann
Thomas J. Balch
Daniel E. Seabold
Shmuel Gerber

INTRODUCTION

This book embodies a codification of the present-day general parliamentary law (omitting provisions having no application outside legislative bodies). The book is also designed as a manual to be adopted by organizations or assemblies as their parliamentary authority. When the manual has been thus adopted, the rules within it, together with any special rules of procedure that may also be adopted, are binding upon the body and constitute that body's rules of order.

Parliamentary law originally was the name given to the rules and customs for carrying on business in the English Parliament that were developed through a continuing process of decisions and precedents somewhat like the growth of the common law. These rules and customs, as brought to America with the settling of the New World, became the basic substance from which the practice of legislative bodies in the United States evolved. Out of early American legislative procedure and paralleling it in further development has come the *general parliamentary law*, or *common parliamentary law*, of today, which is adapted to the needs of organizations and assemblies of widely differing purposes and conditions. In legislative bodies, there is often recourse to the general parliamentary law in situations not covered by the rules or precedents of the particular body—although some of the necessary procedure in such a case must be proper to that type of assembly alone.

The kind of gathering in which parliamentary law is applicable is known as a *deliberative assembly*. This expression was used by Edmund Burke to describe the English Parliament, in a speech to the electorate at Bristol in 1774; and it became the basic term for a body of persons meeting (under conditions detailed on pp. 1–2) to discuss and determine upon common action.

Acting under the general parliamentary law, any deliberative assembly can formally adopt written rules of procedure which, as fully explained on pages 15ff., can confirm, add to, or deviate from parliamentary law itself. As indicated above, the term *rules of order*, in its proper sense, refers to any written parliamentary rules so adopted, whether they are contained in a manual or have been specially composed by the adopting body. The term *parliamentary procedure*, although frequently used synonymously with *parliamentary law*, refers in this book to parliamentary law as it is followed in any given assembly or organization, *together with* whatever rules of order the body may have adopted.

Thomas Jefferson speaks of "the Parliamentary branch of the law." From this country's beginning, it has been an underlying assumption of our culture that what has been authoritatively established as parliamentary law is in the nature of a body of law—in the sense of being binding within all assemblies except as they may adopt special rules varying from the general parliamentary law. But since there has not always been complete agreement as to what constitutes parliamentary law, no society or assembly should attempt to transact business without having adopted some standard manual on the subject as its authority in all cases not covered by its own special rules.

Early Origins of the English Parliament

The holding of assemblies of the elders, fighting men, or people of a tribe, community, or city to make decisions or render opinions on important matters is doubtless a custom older than history. The ancient Athenian historian Thucydides (c. 460–400 B.C.), in his *History of the Peloponnesian War* (between Athens and Sparta), cites numerous cases of determinations by the peoples of cities being decided in assembly by vote. In one passage (Book I, 86–87), describing the assembly at Sparta in which, in the beginning, the Peloponnesian alliance reached the decision to declare war on Athens, he records a specific instance of what we now know as a voice vote (referred to, however, as a decision "by acclamation"), where the device that developed in modern parliamentary times as a *Division of the Assembly* (see pp. 280–82) was resorted to, in its original form. His account of the incident reads, in part, as follows:

> ... Sthenelaïdas, one of the ephors* at this time, came forward last and spoke to the Lacedaemonians in the following way: ... [delivering a brief indictment summarizing a pattern of conduct by the

---

*In Sparta during that period, the *ephors* were a board of five "overseers" elected annually who were the top governing officials in the city.

Athenians that, he argued, constituted a breach of a thirty year treaty of truce which he found totally unacceptable].

After making this sort of speech, he himself as ephor put the question to the assembly of the Lacedaemonians. And he stated that he could not distinguish which shout was the louder (for they decide by acclamation, not by vote) but said, because he wanted them to become more eager for war by revealing their opinions openly, "Lacedaemonians, those of you who think that the treaty has been broken, and the Athenians are aggressors, stand over there," pointing out the place to them, "and those who do not think so, on the other side." They stood up and separated, and there were many more who thought the treaty had been broken.

According to a widely held view, our own tradition of parliamentary process may be traced to ways of life in Anglo-Saxon tribes before their migration to the island of Britain starting in the fifth century A.D. Among these peoples on the continent of Europe, the tribe was the largest regularly existing political unit. From analogy with the customs of other Germanic tribes, it is supposed that freemen were accustomed to come together in the "Village-moot," to make "bye-laws" for their village and to administer justice. These groups also chose men to represent them at the "Hundred-moot," of the district, which acted as a court of appeal and arbitrated intervillage disputes. Still higher in authority, and similarly constituted, was the "Folk-moot," which was also the citizen army of the tribe.

The same institutions, it is believed, were carried into Anglo-Saxon England, where the Folk-moot became the "Shire-moot." There is little historical knowledge of events in the island of Britain during the two hundred years after the first Anglo-Saxon invasions early in the fifth century. When a picture of Anglo-Saxon England in its formative stages does emerge, the Shire-moot—later called the "Shire Court"—is found to be an instrument of local government subject to crown supervision, under a king advised by a national assembly known as the "witan," or "witenagemot." Originally established in each of the separate early English kingdoms and supposed to include all freemen who held land, the witenagemot in the united and Christianized England normally met at the call of the king and was composed of such major landholders, ealdormen, king's officers, bishops, and abbots as he might wish to summon. Although the witenagemot was not in practice a democratic institution, the king's authority was held to derive from its consent, and it might exert influence in the choice of a new king.

The Norman Conquest in 1066 brought England under tight military control by a French-speaking administration, but the structure of Anglo-Saxon governmental machinery was left largely intact.

The Norman kings assembled councils composed of court officials, barons, and prelates—of whom the number present depended on the importance of the business to be discussed. In its fullest form this assembly was known as the "Great Council," and was looked upon as constitutionally a continuation of the witenagemot. Under the feudal system, it was the duty of each baron to advise the king on any matter on which he might request the baron's opinion. The early Great Councils were feudal assemblies summoned by the king for the purpose of obtaining such advice.

The conversion of the Great Council into what we now know as Parliament came about during the thirteenth and early fourteenth centuries. The word *parliament* was in use slightly earlier to describe any important meeting held for the purpose of discussion. This word was first officially applied to certain Great Councils of a particular character in the time of Henry III (reigned 1216–1272). The distinguishing feature of the early parliaments was the fact that the barons of the Council were invited not only to express their opinions individually on matters laid before them by the king, but to discuss, *with each other*, the overall "state of the realm"—the business "of king and kingdom" rather than only "the king's business." The earliest parliament clearly identifiable as of this character was held in 1258.

A second important change in the English national assembly began soon afterward with the introduction into Parliament of representatives of the shires (knights) and of the towns or boroughs (burgesses)—that is, taken together, representatives of the *communities*, or *Commons*. Although a number of precedents for such a step had been set earlier, the first national parliament in which the Commons were included was that held by Edward I in 1275. Initially, the primary purpose in summoning the Commons was usually to obtain their approval for measures of taxation, and they were included in Parliament only on occasions when such support was desired. After 1311, however, the Commons were in attendance at every parliament. Separation of Parliament into the two branches which later became known as the House of Lords and the House of Commons took place by degrees and was completed shortly after 1340.

Development of Procedure in Parliament

"The proceedings of parliament in ancient times, and for a long while," Thomas Jefferson wrote more than four and a half centuries later (in the preface to his famous *Manual*, discussed below), "were crude, multiform, and embarrassing. They have been however constantly advancing towards uniformity and accuracy. ..."*

Many of the advances in the parliamentary system alluded to by Jefferson occurred from the latter part of the sixteenth century through the seventeenth century. This was a period of prolonged internal conflict over the prerogatives of Parliament—as opposed to those of the king—which stimulated an increased interest in procedure, especially in the House of Commons. During this same time, the Journal of the House of Commons, which was first undertaken by the clerk of the House on his own initiative in 1547, became established as a source of precedent on matters of procedure. The first recorded instance of such use of this Journal was in 1580 or 1581. The Journal was given official status as a document of the Commons about 1623.

Roughly concurrent with the initiation of the Journal of the House of Commons was the development of a body of writing on its procedure. The earliest formal treatment of the Commons' procedure in English was written between 1562 and 1566 by Sir Thomas Smyth and was published in 1583, six years after the author's death, as part of a larger work, *De Repvblica Anglorvm: The manner of Gouvernement or policie of the realme of England.* Activity by other authors in writing treatises on parliamentary precedents and practices followed. In 1689, the small book *Lex Parliamentaria* (London), variously attributed to George Petyt or George Philips, listed as references thirty-five earlier parliamentary works or sources. The book—a pocket manual prepared for the convenience of members of Parliament—includes entries from the Journal of the House of Commons relating to procedure, of which the following examples illustrate the gradual evolution of parliamentary law and are readily recognized as early wordings of present-day principles and rules:

- *One subject at a time*: 1581. When a Motion has been made that Matter must receive a Determination by the Question, or be laid aside

---

*Thomas Jefferson, preface to *A Manual of Parliamentary Practice for the Use of the Senate of the United States* (1801; reprint, Old Saybrook, Ct.: Applewood Books, 1993), p. xv.

by the general Sense of the House, before another be entertain'd. (p. 158.)

- *Alternation between opposite points of view in assignment of the floor*: 1592. It was made a Rule, That the Chairman shall ask the Parties that would speak, on which side they would speak ... and the Party that speaketh against the last Speaker, is to be heard first. (p. 209.)

- *Requirement that the chair always call for the negative vote*: 1604. [I]t is no full Question without the Negative part be put, as well as the Affirmative. (p. 161.)

- *Decorum and avoidance of personalities in debate*: 1604. He that digresseth from the Matter, to fall upon the Person, ought to be suppressed by the Speaker. ... No reviling or nipping words must be used. (p. 157.)

- *Confinement of debate to the merits of the pending question*: 1610. A Member speaking, and his speech, seeming impertinent, and there being much hissing and spitting, it was conceived for a Rule, that Mr. Speaker may stay impertinent Speeches. (p. 156.)

- *Division of a question*: 1640. If a Question upon a Debate contains more Parts than one, and Members seem to be for one Part, and not for the other; it may be moved, that the same may be divided into two, or more Questions: as Dec. 2, 1640, the Debate about the Election of two Knights was divided into two Questions. (p. 169.)

The Parliamentary Process Brought to America

The same period when the procedure of the House of Commons was undergoing its new development was also the time during which permanent English colonies were established in the Western Hemisphere, beginning with Virginia in 1607. The founding of this colony was soon followed by the institution of the first representative assembly in America, authorized for Virginia by the governor acting for the London Company in 1619. This body consisted of a House of Burgesses as an elected lower chamber and a small Governor's Council as an upper chamber. As additional colonies were founded, similar assemblies were established in them, and succeeding generations of English settlers brought along the parliamentary processes they had known in the old country.

Into each legislature—into county, town, and parish meeting—the colonists transplanted the rules and customs of Parliament, as far as these rules and customs were applicable under the particular company charter,

proprietary grant, or similar instrument by which the colony was established. This new type of self-government, through general parliamentary
principles operating under specifications contained in a written basic document, represented a phase in the development of parliamentary law that
was peculiar to America, since in England the Constitution was unwritten. Thus, each colony acquired the beginning of a body of experience
later to go into the framing of individual state constitutions. The manner
in which these rules and customs were adapted to meet the situation
within each colony may account for the local variance in parliamentary
tradition which persisted among people in America long after the founding of the United States, and that would eventually be one of the conditions that led to the writing of *Robert's Rules of Order.*

When policies of the mother country in the 1700s had gradually
changed with the growth of the British Empire in such a way as to set
the stage for the American Revolution, representatives of the different
colonies considered common resistance to the actions of Parliament. In
these deliberations, the colonists were able to function effectively by depending on procedures originally developed in Parliament itself!

The First Continental Congress, convening in Philadelphia on
September 5, 1774, was made up of delegates largely unacquainted with
the representatives of colonies other than their own, and most of the advance planning among the colonies had been by correspondence. Thus,
the accomplishments of the first two days of the Congress are worth
mentioning as an indication of the grounding and experience of the
members in parliamentary methods, and of the thoroughness of their
preparation. By September 7 the Continental Congress had: (1) examined the credentials of, and certified as delegates, the accredited representatives; (2) completed its own organization by adopting four "rules
of conduct to be observed in debating and determining the questions";
and (3) made progress toward carrying out its purposes to the extent
of adopting resolutions for the appointing of committees to study
the colonies' rights and to examine statutes affecting their trade and
manufactures.

Under existing rules and customs, the Second Continental Congress
carried on the war; it also directed the framing of, and adopted, the Declaration of Independence. In assemblies in each state, through similar
proceedings somewhat modified by local tradition, colonial charters were
amended to conform to an independent status, or new state constitutions
were drafted. Many of the provisions thus codified had been gradually

arrived at by the separate colonies over periods of more than a hundred years. These state constitutions in turn—stemming from a common experience with English law and adapting that law to the new conditions—provided the material from which the Constitution of the United States was produced at the Constitutional Convention in 1787, in the face of seemingly deep and discouraging disagreements.

By the close of the eighteenth century, the stages through which the parent English parliamentary methods had passed in America may be summarized as follows:

- the use, within each colony, of such parliamentary rules as were applicable under its individual charter or other authorization for the establishment of the colony;
- the application of these same practices in intercolonial gatherings when representatives of the colonies met to act in their common interest; and
- the use of parliamentary procedure as an instrument for implementing the processes of representative government under a written constitution.

Jefferson's *Manual*

Despite this progress, the parliamentary system of the young United States needed further codification. As presiding officer of the Senate while serving as Vice-President of the United States (1797–1801), Thomas Jefferson saw this need, which he described—with respect to the situation in the Senate—in this way:

> The Constitution of the United States ... authorizes each branch of [the Congress] "to determine the rules of its own proceedings." The Senate have accordingly formed some rules for their own government; but these going only to few cases, they have referred to the decision of their President, without debate and without appeal, all questions of order arising either under their own rules or where they have provided none. This places under the discretion of the President [of the Senate] a very extensive field of decision ... which, irregularly exercised, would have a powerful effect on the proceedings and determinations. ... The President must feel ... the necessity of recurring ... to some known system of rules. ...

But to what system ... is he to recur, as supplementary to [the rules] of the Senate?*

Parliament, Jefferson concluded, provided the most practical model for the Congress. It had "served as a prototype to most of" the existing state legislatures. It was "the model which we have all studied, while we are little acquainted with the modifications of it in our several states. ... Its rules are probably as wisely constructed for governing the debates of a deliberative body, and obtaining its true sense, as any which can become known to us. ... (p. xiv.)

"Considering therefore the law of proceedings in the Senate as composed of the precepts of the constitution, the regulations of the Senate, and, where these are silent, of the rules of Parliament,"** Jefferson compiled his *Manual of Parliamentary Practice*, published in 1801. In it, he extensively cited about fifty English works and documents on parliamentary law and related subjects. Among his sources, however, Jefferson in his preface to the *Manual* (p. xv) acknowledges primary indebtedness to *Precedents of Proceedings in the House of Commons* by John Hatsell, who was clerk of the House of Commons from 1768 to 1820. First published in 1781, Hatsell's work is today the best authority on eighteenth-century procedure in the House of Commons.

The position of Jefferson's *Manual* is unchallenged as the first to define and interpret parliamentary principles for our democratic republic and to offer a basic pattern of rules and a measure of uniformity for the legislative processes of the United States. The authority of the *Manual* became established through its adoption by state legislatures and by other groups. The House of Representatives also adopted Jefferson's *Manual*; however, differences between the House and the Senate would cause the House to develop and become governed by a separate body of rules and practices largely superseding Jefferson's work.

Cushing's *Manual*

Within a few decades after Jefferson wrote his *Manual*, the formation of societies of various kinds—political, cultural, scientific, charitable,

---

*Jefferson, *Manual*, pp. xiii, xiv.

**Ibid., p. xiv.

and religious—began to create an increasing need for a body of rules adapted to the requirements of nonlegislative organizations. It seems to have been early recognized that such societies have a deliberative character which calls for the application of essentially the same principles of decision as in a legislative body. Yet certain differences in their conditions—as compared with those of the legislative body—must be taken into account in the formulation of any system of rules suitable for the occasional meeting or the nonlegislative organization. For example:

- Congress and most state legislatures are composed of two Houses, with sessions (p. 82) usually lasting from several months to nearly a year; but sessions of an ordinary local society rarely last longer than one meeting of two or three hours.
- The members of a legislative body are generally paid to attend its daily meetings and can be legally compelled to do so, so that the quorum—in Congress, for example—is a majority of the members; but the quorum in a voluntary society must be much less if the organization is to be able to function.
- The business of a legislative body is vastly greater in volume and more complex than that of the typical ordinary society, so that most of the work in legislative bodies is done in standing committees, whereas in a local society it is handled by the assembly or, if necessary, is assigned to special committees.

The first author who attempted to meet the procedural needs of the country's growing number of voluntary societies was Luther S. Cushing (1803–1856), Clerk of the Massachusetts House of Representatives and a noted jurist. His small volume, *Manual of Parliamentary Practice: Rules of Proceeding and Debate in Deliberative Assemblies*—which became known as "Cushing's Manual"—was published in 1845, with a section of further notes being added in 1847. This work, the author said, was intended for "assemblies of every description, but more especially for those which are not legislative in their character."* Cushing accordingly omitted from his manual rules applicable only to lawmaking bodies, but

---

*Luther Cushing, *Manual of Parliamentary Practice: Rules of Proceeding and Debate in Deliberative Assemblies*, 7th ed. (Boston: Taggard & Thompson, 1847), p. 4.

he included those that he considered suitable for both legislative and lay assemblies.

Among Cushing's observations and conclusions with respect to non-legislative assemblies in particular were the following:

1. The general parliamentary rules in Jefferson's *Manual* formed "the basis of the common parliamentary law of this country." (p. 4.)
2. Through modifications by state legislatures, "a system of parliamentary rules [had] been established in each state, different in some particulars from those of every other state." (p. 13.)
3. Some ordinary meetings were conducted "not merely according to the general parliamentary law" but also following the system of the individual state. (p. 14.)
4. For such societies to be considered bound by the parliamentary practice of a particular state legislature in this way, Cushing held, was "erroneous." (p. 14.)
5. The "occasional assembly" or ordinary organization was properly subject only to the common parliamentary law and to such rules as the body would specially adopt for itself. (p. 14.)

In adherence to the last proposition, Cushing confined his book to what he considered "common parliamentary law," and prescribed that on all other necessary matters of procedure, each organization or assembly should adopt rules of its own (*rules of order*)—much as Congress and legislatures do.

Although Cushing's *Manual* was concisely written, was well received, and became a classic accepted as standard, it was to prove insufficient to the needs of the assemblies for which it was intended. The devising of an adequate supplementary system of rules of order by each assembly for its own use—as envisioned by Cushing—was to prove a task beyond the capacity of the average organization. In the years following the Civil War, the confusion that still existed in parliamentary practice among the multiplying number of lay associations and meetings became a matter of concern to Henry Martyn Robert.

Genesis of *Robert's Rules of Order*

Henry Martyn Robert* (1837–1923) was an engineering officer in the regular army—finally attaining the rank of Brigadier General as chief of his corps—who was active in church organizations and civic and educational work wherever he was stationed, as much as military duties allowed him time. He was the son of Dr. Joseph Thomas Robert (1807–1884), successively a physician, Baptist minister, and educator, who became the first president of what is now Morehouse College. Henry Robert's interest in parliamentary law—as he often related—had been precipitated in 1863 at New Bedford, Massachusetts, where he had been transferred from more strenuous war duty after a recurrence of tropical fever. Without warning, he was asked to preside over a meeting—said to have related to the defense of the city in the event of Confederate attack from the sea and to have lasted for fourteen hours—and did not know how. But he felt that the worst thing he could do would be to decline. "My embarrassment was supreme," he wrote. "I plunged in, trusting to Providence that the assembly would behave itself. But with the plunge went the determination that I would never attend another meeting until I knew something of ... parliamentary law."**

Afterward, in a small book on another subject he found a few pages of "rules for deliberative assemblies." From these he copied information "showing four or five motions according to rank" (see pp. 61–62), "two or three ... that could not be debated and some that could not be amended" and carried it on a slip of paper in his wallet for several years afterward. With this, he hoped he would be safe.

In 1867 Robert was promoted to Major and ordered to San Francisco, which was then a turbulent community made up of people recently arrived from every state. As he and his wife worked with persons from

---

*Named by his parents after Henry Martyn (1781–1812), English Anglican missionary to India who translated extensive portions of the Bible into Eastern languages, and perished from the rigors of his missionary efforts. Martyn's journals and letters were published posthumously under the editorship of Samuel Wilberforce (1805–1873), noted Anglican bishop, in 1837, the year Henry Robert was born.

**Henry Martyn Robert, notes for a lecture in Cincinnati, c. 1916, in Henry M. Robert Papers, Library of Congress. Further quotations of remarks by General Robert are from the same source, except as noted.

different parts of the country in several organizations seeking to improve social conditions there, they found themselves in the midst of a strange situation. Remarking on it many years later, in a lecture in Cincinnati, he stated that "Friction as to what constituted parliamentary law was indeed no uncommon thing." Each member of these organizations had brought from his home state different and often strong convictions as to what were correct parliamentary rules, and a presiding officer usually followed the customs of the locality from which he came. Under these conditions, confusion and misunderstanding had reached a point where issues of procedure consumed time that should have gone into the real work of the societies.

Robert doubted that these organizations would be able to function efficiently until there could be better agreement as to what constituted parliamentary law. In his words:

> So I inquired at the largest book store for the best books on the subject. *Cushing's Manual* was handed me and also *Wilson's Digest*, a book containing about 2400 decisions made in the English Parliament and our Congress. Then I sent for the *Congressional Manual*, which contained *Jefferson's Manual*—...[,] The Rules of the House of Representatives and Barclay's *Digest of Rules and Practice of the House*. ...
>
> A careful reading of these books showed that it was not an easy matter to decide what was parliamentary law. ... For instance, both Jefferson and Cushing gave an equal rank to the motions for the Previous Question, and to Postpone Definitely, and Indefinitely, and to Commit; the House of Representatives makes them rank thus: Previous Question, Postpone Definitely, Commit, Amend, and Postpone Indefinitely at the foot of the list; and the Senate does not allow the Previous Question and instead of placing Indefinitely Postpone at the foot, it puts it at the head of the list. Also if a motion to strike out a paragraph is lost, the paragraph can afterwards be amended according to the rules and practice of both Houses of Congress, but it could not be amended according to Jefferson and Cushing and the practice of the English Parliament. In Congress the question would be stated and put on striking out the paragraph whereas according to the other authorities it should be put on whether the paragraph shall stand as a part of the resolution.

Again, as to debate: The U.S. Senate allowed each member to speak twice on the same day to the same question without any limit as to time; all the other authorities allowed only one speech from each member on any question, and the House of Representatives also limited that speech to one hour. Also in Congress certain motions are undebatable, whereas the other authorities did not allude to such a thing as an undebatable motion, except that Cushing said in a note that legislative bodies usually, to quote, "provide that certain questions, as for example, to Adjourn, to Lay on the Table, for the Previous Question, or as to the Order of Business, shall be decided without debate."

These examples will … show the difficulties in the way of [anyone] … who was anxious to know enough [parliamentary law] to enable him to cooperate with others in effective work in lines in which he was interested.

Robert decided to prepare a few rules of order—expected to run to about sixteen pages—which he hoped would be suitable for the societies to which he and his wife belonged. If these organizations adopted such rules, "each member could know what motions could be debated and amended, which ones required a two-thirds vote, and what was the order of precedence."* When a few sheets had been printed, he began to try them out. The reception was encouraging, but the pamphlet was never completed. He came to the conclusion that the real problem would not be solved by "a half dozen societies having a system of parliamentary law of their own."

At about this time (1871), Robert was transferred to duty based in Portland, Oregon. Although he was obliged to lay aside parliamentary studies because of heavier responsibilities, such contact with organizations as he had time for strengthened ideas which had begun to crystallize in San Francisco: (1) In the country at large, the average society would find it difficult to have an adequate set of rules of order prepared specially for its own use, as Cushing had apparently expected it to do. Few ordinary organizations had, in fact, done so. (2) Even if a society were in a position to work out a satisfactory set of rules, this would only create

---

*That is, which motions can be made when which others are pending (see pp. 60–62).

further multiplicity. *The need was the reverse—to enable civic-minded people to belong to several organizations or to move to new localities without constantly encountering different parliamentary rules.* (3) Conditions in ordinary societies, different as the purposes of those societies might be, were sufficiently similar from a parliamentary point of view to be guided by practically the same rules of order. (4) As far as any trend could be seen, it appeared that the best presiding officers were following the practice of the U.S. House of Representatives on basic points, such as the order of precedence of motions, which motions could be debated, and so on. The practice of the House was then approaching an established form after marked evolution during the preceding decades—during which it had become considerably different from the "old common parliamentary law" as laid down by Jefferson and Cushing.

Robert thus became convinced of the need for a new kind of parliamentary manual, "*based, in its general principles, upon the rules and practice of Congress, and adapted, in its details, to the use of ordinary societies. Such a work should give, not only the methods of organizing and conducting the meetings, the duties of the officers and the names of the ordinary motions, but in addition, should state in a systematic manner, in reference to each motion, its object and effect; whether it can be amended or debated; if debatable, the extent to which it opens the main question to debate; the circumstances under which it can be made, and what other motions can be made when it is pending.*"*

Writing such a manual as Robert envisioned would amount to weaving into a single whole a statement of existing parliamentary law and a set of proposed rules of order. His idea was that the book should be written in a form suitable for adoption by any society, without interfering with the organization's right to adopt any special rules it might require. In the manual, rules taken from the practice of the House should be used except in specific cases where analysis showed that some other rule was better for the conditions in an ordinary organization—which did not, for example, have the enormous volume of business to be handled, the sharp division along party lines, or the extended length of congressional

---

*Henry M. Robert, preface to *Pocket Manual of Rules of Order for Deliberative Assemblies*, 1st ed. (Chicago: S.C. Griggs & Company, 1876), p. 3, carried with but slight variation in several succeeding editions (emphasis added).

sessions with daily meetings. Sometimes the Senate practice might be preferable, such as allowing each member to speak twice to the same question on the same day.

Robert had no time to begin writing until January 1874 in Milwaukee, when a severe winter tied up army engineering services along Lake Michigan for about three months. By October he had a revised manuscript of the rules of order proper, for which he was ready to seek a publisher. This manuscript, which would have made up the complete book as he originally conceived it, became the first part of the work that was finally published. When early efforts to obtain a publisher failed, he decided to have 4,000 copies made by a job printer at his own expense and under his direction. Since Robert's military duties often would not permit him to correct proofs promptly, the printer could only spare enough type to set and print sixteen pages at a time—the type then being distributed and used again for the next sixteen pages.

The printing slowly progressed in this manner through most of the year 1875. Soon after it began, Robert—having concluded, at least partly through his wife's influence, that more information should be added for the benefit of persons with no experience in meetings—wrote and added a second part, to which he gave the title "Organization and Conduct of Business." Because of its purpose and the nature of its contents, Part II was written in a simpler style, and it contained such repetition of material from Part I as the author thought would be useful to the intended reader. By the end of 1875, the printing of the two parts of the *Pocket Manual of Rules of Order for Deliberative Assemblies* (176 pages) was completed.

Even then, with his 4,000 "ready-printed" copies, the author was able to obtain a contract with a publisher only by making unusual concessions. In the face of the latter's skepticism as to the demand for such a work, Robert agreed to pay for binding the 4,000 copies and to bear the expense of giving 1,000 copies of the book to parliamentarians, educators, legislators, and church leaders throughout the country. The first edition of the manual accordingly was published by S. C. Griggs and Company of Chicago on February 19, 1876. The publisher placed on the cover the title *Robert's Rules of Order*. That first edition is now long a rare book.

Robert expected the 3,000 copies available for sale to last two years, during which he planned to prepare a revision on the basis of comments and suggestions from users. But the edition—received with immediate and enthusiastic acclaim—was sold out in four months. Six weeks after the original publication, work was begun on a second edition, with sixteen more pages, which was ready at the end of July 1876.

The following year, the portions of the second 1876 edition comprising the elementary Part II, "Organization and Conduct of Business," and the "Table of Rules Relating to Motions"—which, with continuing development, has been found in all editions but was originally a new and unique feature of the *Pocket Manual*—were also offered separately in paperback under the title *Parliamentary Guide* (price twenty-five cents). The *Guide* did not remain long in print, however, as the demand apparently was for the complete *Robert's Rules of Order* (then priced at seventy-five cents). The latter volume gained another twenty-six pages through changes and additions made by the author in a third edition issued in 1893.

In 1896, when the Griggs firm went out of business, the then recently formed Scott, Foresman and Company purchased the former publisher's list and thus acquired the publishing rights to *Robert's Rules of Order*. The designation "Robert's Rules of Order," the short title printed on the cover of the *Pocket Manual*, properly refers only to the three earliest editions, the last of which was superseded in 1915. At that time, the three editions of the *Pocket Manual* had totaled more than a half million copies.

Subsequent Revisions

Robert's Rules of Order Revised, the first complete revision, was the product of three years of the original author's full-time effort, beginning in 1912, with his second wife, Isabel Hoagland Robert, a former teacher, acting as his secretary and editorial assistant. (His first wife, Helen Thresher Robert, who influenced him to include the elementary portion in the first edition, had died in 1895.) The revision was published on May 5, 1915. Shortly afterward, General Robert wrote that much more work had been put into it than into the three previous editions combined. The 1915 revision, expanded by 75 percent from the 1893 edition, had less than one fourth of its content taken directly from that edition. The reorganization, expansion, and clarification represented by *Robert's Rules of Order Revised* was largely the outgrowth of hundreds of letters received by the author over the years, submitting questions of parliamentary law arising in organizations and not covered in the earlier editions.

Upon General Robert's death in 1923, his only son, Henry M. Robert, Jr.—a professor of mathematics, and later economics, at the United States Naval Academy, who also taught parliamentary law at Columbia University during each summer session—took over the author's office under a trust that his father had established. In that capacity, Henry Jr. continued his father's practice of replying to parliamentary questions from users of the book. It had been the original author's wish that after his death his son should further revise the manual as developments might dictate. Henry Jr. looked forward to doing this following his retirement from the Naval Academy, but he died in 1937 before that time came.

The trusteeship of *Robert's Rules of Order Revised* then passed to Henry Jr.'s widow, Sarah Corbin Robert—like Isabel, a former teacher. At General Robert's request, she had served as a critical reader in the preparation of his last two books, the elementary text, *Parliamentary Practice* (1921), and the work he considered his definitive explanatory effort, *Parliamentary Law* (1923). She had also substituted in teaching her husband's courses at Columbia when Henry Jr. had to give up doing so because of an increased workload at the Naval Academy.

In 1943, changes that General Robert had recorded between 1915 and the time of his death, for inclusion in the next revision of the manual, were incorporated within the 1915 pagination with Isabel and Sarah Robert serving as editors. Under their authorship, additional front and end matter was inserted and further in-page changes were made for the Seventy-fifth Anniversary Edition of 1951. Under the title of *Robert's Rules of Order Revised*, the manual thus remained in basically the 1915 typesetting until 1970, by which time a combined total of 2.65 million copies of all editions issued until then had been in use.

About 1960, work was begun on a second complete revision of the book under the direction of Sarah Corbin Robert. She was joined in this project by her son, Henry M. Robert III, and by William J. Evans, a Baltimore lawyer, with James W. Cleary later serving as an editorial adviser to the publisher. This undertaking had a twofold goal: (1) a thorough overhauling of the parliamentary content dictated by two generations' use of the then-existing work, and (2) the new development of a reference book that would both be suitable for adoption by organizations as their parliamentary authority, and at the same time be as readable and as near to completely self-explanatory as possible—equally useful to a presiding officer, organization member, parliamentarian, and instructor in parliamentary procedure. Achieving this dual goal to the authors' best ability proved to be a task whose magnitude was only dimly perceived at the outset. The resulting general revision of the book was published as *Robert's Rules of Order Newly Revised* on the ninety-fourth anniversary of the publication of the first edition, February 19, 1970. As the original author stated that more work had been put into the 1915 revision than into the three previous editions combined, so it is believed that more work went into the production of the 1970 edition of *Robert's Rules of Order Newly Revised* than into all six editions brought out previously.

An additional key figure in guiding the authorship affairs of the book since that time, particularly in their commercial aspect, has been John Robert Redgrave, a great-grandson of the original author and the business representative of The Robert's Rules Association, which replaced the first trust after the death of General Robert's last surviving child.

Consistent with the earlier practice of publishing partial revisions containing in-page changes within the same pagination, a 1981 edition prepared by Henry M. Robert III and William J. Evans made a number of clarifications throughout the work. These changes were the result of experience in using the book in the eleven-year period following the 1970 revision. Some of the more important areas of clarification related to the *Previous Question*, the motion to *Lay on the Table*, the nature of a board as a form of assembly, the rule prohibiting interruption of actual voting, and the rules governing amendment at the expiration of the allotted time under different kinds of orders limiting debate or setting a time for voting. The 1981 edition was issued additionally in paperback format by Scott, Foresman and Company in 1984. This was the first time that a current edition of the complete manual had been offered in paperback.

In 1990, the same process was carried further with the issuance of a ninth edition of the work, again authored by Henry M. Robert III and William J. Evans, with Daniel H. Honemann, also a Baltimore attorney, then joining to assist them. Under new technology applied to that edition, however, a complete resetting of the book became for the first time an easy matter. This fact permitted a greater variety of changes and the incorporation of more additional material than would otherwise have been feasible. Two of the most significant of the revisions were the reinsertion, in improved form, of a subsection on hints to inexperienced presiding officers found in earlier editions, and a new treatment of some standard principles of interpretation of bylaws and other documents.

The Tenth Edition was published as the Millennium Edition of the year 2000. It was the work of four coauthors, with Henry M. Robert III, William J. Evans, and Daniel H. Honemann joined by Thomas J. Balch, a member of the Illinois bar residing in Virginia. A listing of the more important areas of revision in the 2000 edition appears in its preface. Among them were clarification of the role of "established custom" in relation to written rules, and greater specification of the cases in which an action is null and void so that a *Point of Order* that would otherwise be untimely may be raised and, correlatively, those circumstances in which the rules may not be suspended.

This Eleventh Edition responds anew to the ever-continuing need for further refinement of interpretation and for answering newly arising questions. With the passing of William Evans, this edition is the work of Henry M. Robert III, Daniel H. Honemann, and Thomas J. Balch, with the assistance of Daniel E. Seabold, a professor of mathematics at Hofstra University in Hempstead, New York, and Shmuel Gerber, an editor on the staff of a New York–area newspaper.

All editions of the work issued after the death of the original author have thus been prepared by persons who either knew and worked with him or are connected to such persons in a direct continuity of professional association.

An accompanying development since the appearance of the 1990 edition relates to the publisher. For most of the twentieth century, the name of Robert's Rules of Order was synonymous with that of Scott, Foresman and Company. As changes in the economics of publishing have dictated the sale and division of companies since 1990, however, the publishing rights in the book successively passed to HarperCollins, to Addison, Wesley, Longman, and then to Perseus Books, which, through its Da Capo Press division, is the official publisher today.

Influence of Robert

The crux of *Robert's Rules of Order*'s initial contribution was in making it possible for assemblies and societies to free themselves from confusion and dispute over rules governing the use of the different motions of parliamentary law. In this respect the book filled the need that the author accurately stated in the quotation from his preface found on page xliii of this introduction.

In basing his rules on the practice of the U.S. House of Representatives in the manner already described, Robert stated that this practice—except where obviously unsuited to ordinary societies—had come to determine the actual common parliamentary law of the country, just as the practice of the House of Commons had done in England. Within any assembly or organization, however, it was his idea that the authority of his rules should rest on formal adoption of his manual by the particular body. But the book was soon cited increasingly as an authority apart from individual adoption—in such a manner as to constitute acknowledgment of its rules as parliamentary law itself. Thus Robert—by offering a codification of the rules and practices of the House of Representatives adapted to ordinary societies—gave formal direction to a movement toward establishing a more complete common parliamentary law, built upon congressional practice. In this way, Robert had a central role in bringing the parliamentary law of the United States to a stability and a stage of development that led former House parliamentarian Clarence Cannon to describe it as a "system of procedure adapted to the wants of deliberative assemblies generally and which, though variously interpreted in minor details by different writers, is now in the main standardized and authoritatively established."*

In an often quoted statement, the original author said: "The great lesson for democracies to learn is for the majority to give to the minority a full, free opportunity to present their side of the case, and then for the minority, having failed to win a majority to their views, gracefully to submit and to recognize the action as that of the entire organization, and cheerfully to assist in carrying it out, until they can secure its repeal."** But this same man, as he headed many engineering boards in the later phases of his professional career, became known for guiding them to produce reports that were unanimously concurred in by the board members. His record as a leader in civic, social-service, and church activities was similar. He was loath to settle for less.

---

* *Encyclopaedia Britannica*, 1958 ed., s.v. "Rules of Order."

**Henry M. Robert, *Parliamentary Law* (1923; reprint, New York: Irvington Publications, 1975), p. 4.

This was not the contradiction that it may at first seem. Robert was surely aware of the early evolutionary development of parliamentary procedure in the English House of Lords resulting in a movement from "consensus," in its original sense of unanimous agreement, toward a decision by majority vote as we know it today. This evolution came about from a recognition that a requirement of unanimity or near unanimity can become a form of tyranny in itself. In an assembly that tries to make such a requirement the norm, a variety of misguided feelings—reluctance to be seen as opposing the leadership, a notion that causing controversy will be frowned upon, fear of seeming an obstacle to unity—can easily lead to decisions being taken with a pseudoconsensus which in reality implies elements of default, which satisfies no one, and for which no one really assumes responsibility. Furthermore, what is apparently taken to be the sense of the meeting may well be little more than a "least common denominator" of such generality as to contribute little to the solution of the practical problem involved, thereby leaving such matters to officers or staff or the meeting's organizers to work out according to their own intentions. Robert saw, on the other hand, that the evolution of majority vote in tandem with lucid and clarifying debate—resulting in a decision representing the view of the deliberate majority—far more clearly ferrets out and demonstrates the will of an assembly. It is through the application of genuine persuasion and parliamentary technique that General Robert was able to achieve decisions in meetings he led which were so free of divisiveness within the group.

PRINCIPLES UNDERLYING PARLIAMENTARY LAW

The rules of parliamentary law found in this book will, on analysis, be seen to be constructed upon a careful balance of the rights of persons or subgroups within an organization's or an assembly's total membership. That is, these rules are based on a regard for the rights:

- of the majority,
- of the minority, especially a strong minority—greater than one third,
- of individual members,
- of absentees, and
- of all these together.

The means of protecting all of these rights in appropriate measure forms much of the substance of parliamentary law, and the need for this protection dictates the degree of development that the subject has undergone.

Parliamentary procedure enables the overall membership of an organization—expressing its general will through the assembly of its members—both to establish and empower an effective leadership as it wishes, and at the same time to retain exactly the degree of direct control over its affairs that it chooses to reserve to itself.

Ultimately, it is the majority taking part in the assembly who decide the general will, but only following upon the opportunity for a deliberative process of full and free discussion. Only two thirds or more of those present and voting may deny a minority or any member the right of such discussion.

In this connection, there is an underlying assumption of a *right* that *exists* even though it may not always be prudent or helpful for it to be exercised. Each individual or subgroup has the right to make the maximum effort to have his, her, or its position declared the will of the assembly to the extent that can be tolerated in the interests of the entire body.

Another important principle is that, as a protection against instability—arising, for example, from such factors as slight variations in attendance—the requirements for changing a previous action are greater than those for taking the action in the first place.

Fundamentally, under the rules of parliamentary law, a deliberative body is a free agent—free to do what it wants to do with the greatest measure of protection to itself and of consideration for the rights of its members.

The application of parliamentary law is the best method yet devised to enable assemblies of any size, with due regard for every member's opinion, to arrive at the general will on the maximum number of questions of varying complexity in a minimum amount of time and under all kinds of internal climate ranging from total harmony to hardened or impassioned division of opinion.

CHAPTER

I

THE DELIBERATIVE ASSEMBLY:
ITS TYPES AND THEIR RULES

§1. THE DELIBERATIVE ASSEMBLY

Nature of the Deliberative Assembly

A *deliberative assembly*—the kind of gathering to which parliamentary law is generally understood to apply—has the following distinguishing characteristics:

- It is a group of people, having or assuming freedom to act in concert, meeting to determine, in full and free discussion, courses of action to be taken in the name of the entire group.
- The group meets in a single room or area or under equivalent conditions of opportunity for simultaneous aural communication among all participants.*

---

*A group that attempts to conduct the deliberative process in writing— such as by postal mail, electronic mail (e-mail), or facsimile transmission (fax)—does not constitute a deliberative assembly. When making decisions by such means, many situations unprecedented in parliamentary law will arise, and many of its rules and customs will not be applicable (see also pp. 97–99).

- Persons having the right to participate—that is, the members—are ordinarily free to act within the assembly according to their own judgment.
- In any decision made, the opinion of each member present has equal weight as expressed by vote—through which the voting member joins in assuming direct personal responsibility for the decision, should his or her vote be on the prevailing side.
- Failure to concur in a decision of the body does not constitute withdrawal from the body.
- If any members are absent—as is usually the case in any formally organized assembly such as a legislative body or the assembly of an ordinary society—the members present at a regular or properly called meeting act for the entire membership, subject only to such limitations as may be established by the body's governing rules (see "quorum of members," however, p. 21; also **40**).

The rules in this book are principally applicable to meeting bodies possessing all of the foregoing characteristics. Certain of these parliamentary rules or customs may sometimes also find application in other gatherings which, although resembling the deliberative assembly in varying degrees, do not have all of its attributes as listed above.

The distinction should be noted between the *assembly* (that is, the *body of people* who assemble) and the *meeting* (which is the *event* of their being assembled to transact business). The relation between these terms, however, is such that their application may coincide; a "mass meeting," for example, is described below as one type of assembly. The term *meeting* is also distinguished from *session*, according to definitions stated in **8**. A session may be loosely described as a single complete course of an assembly's engagement in the conduct of business, and may consist of one or more meetings.

A *member* of an assembly, in the parliamentary sense, as mentioned above, is a person entitled to full participation in its proceedings, that is, as explained in **3** and **4**, the right to *attend meetings*, to *make motions*, to *speak in debate*, and to *vote*. No member can be individually deprived of these basic rights of membership—or of any basic rights concomitant to them, such as the right to make nominations or to give previous notice of a motion—except through disciplinary proceedings. Some organized societies define additional classes of "membership" that do not entail all of these rights. Whenever the term *member* is used in this book, it refers to full participating membership in the assembly unless otherwise specified. Such members are also described as "voting members" when it is necessary to make a distinction.

A deliberative assembly that has not adopted any rules is commonly understood to hold itself bound by the rules and customs of the *general parliamentary law*—or *common parliamentary law* (as discussed in the Introduction)—to the extent that there is agreement in the meeting body as to what these rules and practices are. Most assemblies operate subject to one or more classes of written rules, however, that the particular body—or, sometimes, a higher authority under which it is constituted—has formally adopted. Taken as a whole, such rules may relate to the establishment of the organization or society of which the assembly is the meeting body, they may interpret or supplement the general parliamentary law, or they may involve provisions not directly related to the transaction of business. The classes of rules that an assembly or an organization may adopt and the position that the rules in this book assume within such a body's overall system of rules are initially explained in **2**. Aside from rules of parliamentary procedure and the particular rules of an assembly, the actions of any deliberative body are also subject to applicable procedural rules prescribed by local, state, or

1   national law and would be null and void if in violation of such law.*

The basic principle of decision in a deliberative assembly is that, to become the act or choice of the body, a proposition 5 must be adopted by a *majority vote*; that is, direct approval—implying assumption of responsibility for the act—must be registered by more than half of the members present and voting on the particular matter, in a regular or properly called meeting of the body (see also pp. 400–401). Modifications 10 of the foregoing principle that impose a requirement of more than a majority vote arise: (a) where required by law; (b) where provided by special rule of a particular organization or assembly as dictated by its own conditions; or (c) where required under the general parliamentary law in the case of 15 certain steps or procedures that impinge on the normal rights of the minority, of absentees, or of some other group within the assembly's membership.

When a decision is to be based on more than a majority, the requirement most commonly specified is a *two-thirds* 20 *vote*—that is, the expressed approval of at least two thirds of those present and voting. Under certain circumstances, whatever the vote required, there may be an additional requirement of *previous notice*, which means that notice of the proposal to be brought up—at least briefly describing its 25 substance—must be announced at the preceding meeting or must be included in the "call" of the meeting at which it is to be considered (see also pp. 121–24). The call of a meeting is a written notice of the time and place, which is sent to all members of the organization a reasonable time in advance. 30 Other bases for decision which find use in certain cases are

---

*If the assembly is itself a lawmaking body, its actions are subject to applicable law of a higher authority—as, for example, the acts of a state legislature in the United States, which must not be in conflict with the constitution of that state, with national law, or with the national constitution.

defined in **44**, such as a *majority of the entire membership*— that is, more than half of all the members.

Whenever the rules of an assembly require a majority vote, a two-thirds vote, or any other basis for decision, it must be understood that, unless otherwise specified in the rules (as in the case of certain procedural actions), such a vote is effective only if taken when the necessary minimum number of members, known as a quorum, is present (see p. 21; also **40**).

Types of Deliberative Assembly

The deliberative assembly may exist in many forms. Among the principal types that it is convenient to distinguish for the purposes of parliamentary law are: (1) the *mass meeting*; (2) the *assembly of an organized society*, particularly when meeting at the local or lowest subdivisional level; (3) the *convention*; (4) the *legislative body*; and (5) the *board*. A brief introductory explanation of the five principal types of deliberative assembly is given below.

THE MASS MEETING.   The mass meeting is the simplest form of assembly in principle, although not the one most frequently encountered. A mass meeting is a meeting of an unorganized group that is announced as open to everyone (or everyone within a specified sector of the population) interested in a particular problem or purpose defined by the meeting's sponsors, and that is called with a view to appropriate action to be decided on and taken by the meeting body. A series of connected meetings making up a session may be held on such a basis. The class of persons invited might be, for example, supporters of a given political party, homeowners residing within a certain city, persons opposed to a tax increase, or any similar group. Admittance may be limited to the invited category if desired. Everyone who attends a mass meeting has the

1 right to participate in the proceedings as a member of the
assembly, upon the understanding that he is in general sympathy with the announced object of the meeting.

It should be noted that a large attendance is not an
5 essential feature of the mass meeting, although it may usually be desired. A series of meetings held for the purpose of
organizing a society are in the nature of mass meetings until
the society has been formed.

Mass meetings are particularly treated in **53**.

10

THE LOCAL ASSEMBLY OF AN ORGANIZED
SOCIETY. The assembly at the meetings of an organized
permanent society existing as a local club or local branch is
the type of assembly with which the average person is most
15 likely to have direct experience. As the highest authority
within such a society or branch (subject only to the provisions
of the *bylaws* or other basic document establishing the organization), this body acts for the total membership in the
transaction of its business. Such an assembly's membership
20 is limited to persons who are recorded on the rolls of the
society as voting members and who are *in good standing.**
The bylaws of an organized local society (see pp. 12–15)
usually provide that it shall hold regular meetings at stated
intervals—such as weekly, monthly, quarterly, or sometimes
25 even annually—and also usually provide a procedure for
calling special meetings as needed (see pp. 91–93). Each of

---

*Members in good standing are those whose rights as members of the
assembly are not under suspension as a consequence of disciplinary proceedings or by operation of some specific provision in the bylaws. A member
may thus be in good standing even if in arrears in payment of dues (see
pp. 406, 571–72). If only some of an individual's rights as a member of the
assembly are under suspension (for example, the rights to make motions and
speak in debate), other rights of assembly membership may still be exercised
(for example, the rights to attend meetings and vote).

these meetings in such an organization normally is a separate session (**8**).

THE CONVENTION.   A convention is an assembly of *delegates* (other than a permanently established public law-making body) chosen, normally for one session only, as representatives of constituent units or subdivisions of a much larger body of people in whose name the convention sits and acts.

The most common type of convention is that of an organized state or national society—held, for example, annually or biennially—in which the delegates are selected by, and from among the members of, each local branch. A convention is sometimes also called for the purpose of forming an association or federation; or, like a mass meeting, it may be convened to draw interested parties or representatives of interested organizations together in acting upon a common problem. The ordinary convention seldom lasts longer than a week. In principle, however, there is no limit on the length of the convention session. A constitutional convention, for example—convoked to draft a proposed new state constitution—may continue for weeks or months.

The voting membership of a convention consists of persons who hold proper credentials as delegates or as persons in some other way entitled to such membership, which must be certified and reported to the convention by its Credentials Committee. Whenever the term "majority of the entire membership" is used in this book, it means, in the case of a convention of delegates, a majority of the total number of convention members entitled to vote, as set forth in the official roll of voting members of the convention (pp. 403–4, 617).

The conclusion of the convention session normally dissolves the assembly. In the case of a state or national society,

1 when another convention convenes a year or two later, it is a
   new assembly.

   Conventions are particularly treated in **58**, **59**, and **60**.

5   THE LEGISLATIVE BODY.   The term *legislative body*
   refers to a constitutionally established public lawmaking body
   of representatives chosen by the electorate for a fixed term of
   office—such as Congress or a state legislature. Such a body
   typically (though not always) consists of two assemblies, or
10 "houses." Its sessions may last for months, during which it
   meets daily and its members are paid to devote their full
   time to its work and can be legally compelled to attend its
   meetings.

   Each state or national legislative assembly generally has
15 its own well-developed body of rules, interpretations, and
   precedents, so that the exact procedure for a particular legislative house can be found only in its own manual.

   In this connection, however, it should be noted that certain smaller public bodies may serve a lawmaking function yet
20 not assume the character of a full-scale legislative assembly,
   and instead may somewhat resemble a board or the assembly of a society. An example of such a body might be a city
   council that meets weekly or monthly and whose members
   continue their own full-time occupations during their term
25 of service.

       THE BOARD.   A board, in the general sense of the
   term, is an administrative, managerial, or quasi-judicial body
   of elected or appointed persons that differs from several of
30 the other principal types of deliberative assembly as follows:

   a) boards are frequently smaller than most other assemblies;
      and
   b) while a board may or may not function autonomously, its
35   operation is determined by responsibilities and powers

delegated to it or conferred on it by authority outside   *1*
itself.

A board may be assigned a particular function on behalf
of a national, state, or local government, as a village board   *5*
that operates like a small city council, a board of education,
or a board of examiners. In a nonstock corporation that has
no assembly or body of persons constituting a general voting
membership, as a university or foundation, the board of
directors, managers, trustees, or governors is the supreme   *10*
governing body of the institution. Similarly, in a stock corporation, although the board of directors is elected by stock-
holders who hold an annual meeting, it constitutes the
highest authority in the management of the corporation. A
board within an organized society, on the other hand, is an   *15*
instrumentality of the society's full assembly, to which it is
subordinate. Boards are discussed in greater detail in **49**.

Applicability of Modified Parliamentary Rules in Small Boards and in Committees

20

The distinction between a *board* and a *committee* must be
briefly noted here for an understanding of what follows.
A board of any size is a form of assembly as just explained.
Committees, on the other hand, are bodies that are often,   *25*
but not necessarily, very small, and that are subordinate
instruments of an assembly or are accountable to a higher
authority in some way not characteristic of an assembly. Large
boards generally follow parliamentary procedure in the same
way as any other assembly. In small boards, and in commit-   *30*
tees, most parliamentary rules apply, but certain modifications
permitting greater flexibility and informality are commonly
allowed. Whenever reference is made in this book to "small
boards," the size implied will depend somewhat on conditions, but such boards are usually to be understood as   *35*

1   consisting of not more than about a dozen persons. The dis-
    tinguishing characteristics of boards and committees are
    discussed in **49** and **50**.

5

§2. RULES OF AN ASSEMBLY
OR ORGANIZATION

        An organized society requires certain rules to establish its
10 basic structure and manner of operation. In addition, a need
    for formally adopted rules of procedure arises in any assembly,
    principally because there may be disagreement or a lack of
    understanding as to what is parliamentary law regarding
    points that can affect the outcome of substantive issues.
15   Experience has shown that some of the rules of a society
    should be made more difficult to change, or to suspend—
    that is, to set aside for a specific purpose—than others. Upon
    this principle, the rules which an established organization may
    have are commonly divided into classes—some of which are
20 needed by every society, while others may be required only
    as conditions warrant. Within this framework under the gen-
    eral parliamentary law, an assembly or society is free to adopt
    any rules it may wish (even rules deviating from parliamentary
    law) provided that, in the procedure of adopting them, it
25 conforms to parliamentary law or its own existing rules. The
    only limitations upon the rules that such a body can thus
    adopt might arise from the rules of a parent body (as those
    of a national society restricting its state or local branches), or
    from national, state, or local law affecting the particular type
30 of organization.
        The various kinds of rules which a society may formally
    adopt include the following: Corporate Charter, Constitution
    and/or Bylaws, Rules of Order (which include a standard
    work on parliamentary law adopted as the society's Parlia-
35 mentary Authority, and any Special Rules of Order), and

Standing Rules. Each of these types of rules is discussed   *1*
below. (For a more complete treatment of constitution
and/or bylaws, see **56** and **57**.)

In matters not governed by any adopted rule, a society
may be guided by established custom, also discussed below.   *5*

Corporate Charter

The Corporate Charter (in different states variously called
the *Certificate of Incorporation, Articles of Incorporation,*   *10*
Articles of Association, etc.) is a legal instrument that sets
forth the name and object of the society and whatever other
information is needed for incorporating the society under the
laws of the particular state—or under federal law in the case
of a few special types of organizations. Incorporation is some-   *15*
times necessary or may be advisable, depending upon the
differing laws of each state, if the organization is to hold property, inherit a legacy, make legally binding contracts, hire
employees, be in a position to sue or be sued as a society, protect its officers and members from personal liability, or the   *20*
like. Apart from this consideration, in general, a society need
not be incorporated unless incorporation is dictated by a law
relating to the society's contemplated activities.

A corporate charter should be drafted by an attorney and
must then be processed in accordance with the legal pro-   *25*
cedure for incorporation in the state (or under federal law if
applicable). Any later amendments (that is, changes in the
charter) are subject to the requirements of law and any
limitations placed in the charter itself.

In an incorporated organization, the corporate charter   *30*
supersedes all its other rules, none of which can legally contain anything in conflict with the charter. Nothing in the
charter can be suspended by the organization itself unless
the charter so provides. For these reasons, a corporate charter
generally should contain only what is necessary to obtain it,   *35*

1 and to establish the desired status of the organization under law—leaving as much as possible to the bylaws or to lower-ranking rules if appropriate in accordance with the principles explained below and in **56.***

5

Constitution; Bylaws

In general, the constitution or the bylaws—or both—of a society are the documents that contain its own basic rules

10 relating principally to itself as an organization, rather than to the parliamentary procedure that it follows. In the ordinary case, it is now the recommended practice that all of a society's rules of this kind be combined into a single instrument, usually called the "bylaws," although in some societies called the

15 "constitution"—or the "constitution and bylaws," even when it is only one document. The term *bylaws*, as used in this book, refers to this single, combination-type instrument—by whatever name the particular organization may describe it—which:

20

1) should have essentially the same form and content whether or not the society is incorporated (except for the omission or inclusion of articles on the name and object as noted below);

25 2) defines the primary characteristics of the organization—in such a way that the bylaws serve as the fundamental instrument establishing an unincorporated society, or conform to the corporate charter if there is one;

---

*The word *charter* may also refer to a certificate issued by a national or state organization, granting the right to form a particular local or subordinate unit. While such a charter is not an instrument of incorporation and is usually quite general in its terms, it supersedes any rules the subordinate body may adopt, because it carries with it the requirement that the subordinate unit adopt no rules that conflict with those of the grantor.

3) prescribes how the society functions; and

4) includes all rules that the society considers so important that they (a) cannot be changed without previous notice to the members and the vote of a specified large majority (such as a two-thirds vote), and (b) cannot be suspended (with the exception of clauses that provide for their own suspension under specified conditions, or clauses in the nature of rules of order as described on p. 17, ll. 22–25; see also pp. 263–65, 580–82).

While the number of articles in the bylaws will be determined by the size and activities of the organization, the general nature of the subjects covered will be indicated by the following list of articles, typical of those found in the bylaws of the average unincorporated society: (1) Name of the organization; (2) its Object; (3) Members; (4) Officers; (5) Meetings; (6) Executive Board (if needed); (7) Committees; (8) Parliamentary Authority (that is, the name of the manual of parliamentary procedure that the organization is to follow; see below); and (9) Amendment of Bylaws (prescribing the procedure for making changes in the bylaws). If the society is incorporated, its name and its object are usually set forth in the corporate charter, in which case the first two articles listed above should be omitted from the bylaws. The appropriate content of bylaws is discussed in detail in **56**.

It formerly was common practice to divide the basic rules of an organization into two documents, in order that one of them—the *constitution*—might be made more difficult to amend than the other, to which the name *bylaws* was applied. In such a case, the constitution would generally contain the most essential provisions relating to the first five items listed in the preceding paragraph (leaving additional details to the bylaws), and would prescribe the procedure for amending the constitution. Such an arrangement may still be found in cases where a national, state, or local law applying to the

1   particular type of organization requires a constitution separate
from the bylaws, or in older organizations that have had little
occasion to change their existing rules. Unless the constitution is made more difficult to amend than the bylaws, how-
5   ever, no purpose is served by separating these two sets of
rules. In an incorporated society there generally should not
be a constitution separate from the bylaws, since in such a
case the constitution would duplicate much of the corporate
charter. Although it is not improper, in an unincorporated
10   society, to have both a constitution and bylaws as separate
documents (provided that the constitution is made more difficult to amend), there are decided advantages in keeping all
of the provisions relating to each subject under one heading
within a single instrument—which results in fewer problems
15   of duplication or inconsistency, and gives a more understand-
able and workable body of rules.

Except for the corporate charter in an incorporated society, the bylaws (as the single, combination-type instrument
is called in this book) comprise the highest body of rules in
20   societies as normally established today. Such an instrument
supersedes all other rules of the society, except the corporate
charter, if there is one. In organizations that have both a constitution and bylaws as separate documents, however, the
constitution is the higher of the two bodies of rules and
25   supersedes the bylaws.

The bylaws, by their nature, necessarily contain whatever
limitations are placed on the powers of the assembly of a
society (that is, the members attending a particular one of its
meetings) with respect to the society as a whole. Similarly, the
30   provisions of the bylaws have direct bearing on the rights of
members within the organization—whether present or absent
from the assembly. It is a good policy for every member on
joining the society to be given a copy of the bylaws, printed
together with the corporate charter, if there is one, and any
35   special rules of order or standing rules that the society may

have adopted as explained below. A member should become
familiar with the contents of these rules if he looks toward
full participation in the society's affairs.

Rules of Order

The term *rules of order* refers to written rules of parliamentary procedure formally adopted by an assembly or an
organization. Such rules relate to the orderly transaction of
business in meetings and to the duties of officers in that connection. The object of rules of order is to facilitate the smooth
functioning of the assembly and to provide a firm basis for
resolving questions of procedure that may arise.

In contrast to bylaws, rules of order derive their proper
substance largely from the general nature of the parliamentary
process rather than from the circumstances of a particular
assembly. Consequently, although the tone of application of
rules of order may vary, there is little reason why most
of these rules themselves should not be the same in all ordinary societies and should not closely correspond to the common parliamentary law. The usual and preferable method by
which an ordinary society now provides itself with suitable
rules of order is therefore to place in its bylaws a provision
prescribing that the current edition of a specified and generally accepted manual of parliamentary law shall be the organization's *parliamentary authority*, and then to adopt only
such *special rules of order* as it finds needed to supplement or
modify rules contained in that manual. However, if the bylaws
of a society do not designate a parliamentary authority, one
may be adopted by the same vote as is required to adopt a
special rule of order, although it is preferable to amend the
bylaws. In a mass meeting or a meeting of a body not yet
organized, adoption of a parliamentary authority (or individual rules of order) may take place at the beginning of the
meeting by majority vote.

1 Special rules of order supersede any rules in the parliamentary authority with which they may conflict.* The average society that has adopted a suitable parliamentary authority seldom needs special rules of order, however, with the fol-
5 lowing notable exceptions:

- It is sometimes desirable to adopt a rule establishing the society's own order of business (see p. 25).
- A rule relating to the length or number of speeches
10 permitted each member in debate is often found necessary.
- A society with a small assembly—such as one having a dozen or fewer members—may wish to adopt a rule that its meetings will be governed by some or all of the some-
15 what less formal procedures applicable to small boards (see pp. 487–88).

 Special rules of order are usually adopted in the form of *resolutions* (pp. 33, 105–9), but when they are printed, the
20 enacting words ("*Resolved*, That") are dropped.
 When a society or an assembly has adopted a particular parliamentary manual—such as this book—as its authority, the rules contained in that manual are binding upon it in all cases where they are not inconsistent with the bylaws (or con-
25 stitution) of the body, any of its special rules of order, or any provisions of local, state, or national law applying to the particular type of organization. What another manual may have to say in conflict with the adopted parliamentary authority then has no bearing on the case. In matters on which an
30 organization's adopted parliamentary authority is silent, provisions found in other works on parliamentary law may be

---

*However, when the parliamentary authority is prescribed in the bylaws, and that authority states that a certain rule can be altered only by a provision in the bylaws, no special rule of order can supersede that rule.

persuasive—that is, they may carry weight in the absence of
overriding reasons for following a different course—but they
are not binding on the body.

Although it is unwise for an assembly or a society to attempt to function without formally adopted rules of order, a
recognized parliamentary manual may be cited under such
conditions as persuasive. Or, by being followed through long-
established custom in an organization, a particular manual
may acquire a status within the body similar to that of an
adopted parliamentary authority.

Any special rules of order should be adopted separately
from the bylaws and should be printed in the same booklet
with, but under a heading separate from, the bylaws. Although rules in the nature of special rules of order are sometimes placed within the bylaws—as occurs most frequently
when a society prescribes its own order of business—such an
arrangement is less desirable, since it may lead to cases of
uncertainty as to whether a particular rule can be suspended.

Rules of order—whether contained in the parliamentary
authority or adopted as special rules of order—can be suspended by a two-thirds vote as explained in **25** (with the
exceptions there specified). Rules clearly identifiable as in
the nature of rules of order that are placed within the bylaws
can (with the same exceptions) also be suspended by a two-
thirds vote; but, except for such rules and for clauses that provide for their own suspension, as stated above, rules in the
bylaws cannot be suspended.

Adoption or amendment of special rules of order that are
separate from the bylaws requires either (a) previous notice
(pp. 121–24) and a two-thirds vote or (b) a vote of a majority
of the entire membership. After the bylaws of a society have
been initially adopted when the organization is formed, the
adoption or amendment of special rules of order placed
within the bylaws is subject to the procedure for amending
the bylaws (see **57**).

Standing Rules

Standing rules, as understood in this book except in the case of conventions, are rules (1) which are related to the details of the administration of a society rather than to parliamentary procedure, and (2) which can be adopted or changed upon the same conditions as any ordinary act of the society. An example of such a rule might be one setting the hour at which meetings are to begin, or one relating to the maintenance of a guest register. Standing rules generally are not adopted at the time a society is organized, but individually if and when the need arises. Like special rules of order, standing rules may be printed under a separate heading in the booklet containing the bylaws, and in such a case, any enacting words such as "*Resolved*, That" should be dropped. A standing rule can be adopted by a majority vote without previous notice, provided that it does not conflict with or amend any existing rule or act of the society. (For the vote required for rescinding or amending such a rule, see p. 306, ll. 24–31.) A standing rule remains in effect until rescinded or amended, but if it has its application only within the context of a meeting, it can be suspended at any particular session (although not for future sessions) by a majority vote. Rules that have any application outside a meeting context, however, cannot be suspended.

Standing rules in conventions differ from ordinary standing rules in some respects, as explained on pages 618–20. Some assemblies, particularly legislative bodies, also apply the name *standing rules* to their rules of order. Whatever names an assembly may apply to its various rules, the vote required to adopt, amend, or suspend a particular rule is determined by the nature of its content according to the definitions given above.

Custom

1

In some organizations, a particular practice may sometimes come to be followed as a matter of established custom so that it is treated practically as if it were prescribed by a rule. If there is no contrary provision in the parliamentary authority or written rules of the organization, the established custom should be adhered to unless the assembly, by a majority vote, agrees in a particular instance to do otherwise. However, if a customary practice is or becomes in conflict with the parliamentary authority or any written rule, and a *Point of Order* (**23**) citing the conflict is raised at any time, the custom falls to the ground, and the conflicting provision in the parliamentary authority or written rule must thereafter be complied with. If it is then desired to follow the former practice, a special rule of order (or, in appropriate circumstances, a standing rule or a bylaw provision) can be added or amended to incorporate it.

5

10

15

CHAPTER
II

THE CONDUCT OF BUSINESS
IN A DELIBERATIVE ASSEMBLY

1 §3. BASIC PROVISIONS AND PROCEDURES

The basic parliamentary concepts and practices are inter-
connected in such a way that a complete statement of the
5 rules that relate to any one of them frequently involves reference to several other concepts. This section contains an initial
explanation of a number of these topics, which are given a
more detailed treatment later in this book.

In reading all that follows throughout this manual, it
10 should be borne in mind that—as in any treatment of any
subject—a statement of a rule generally cannot include all
possible exceptions to the rule. Whenever a particular statement appears to conflict with a more general statement elsewhere in the book, therefore, the particular statement
15 governs in the matter to which it states that it applies (see also
p. 589).

Minimum Composition of a Deliberative Assembly

QUORUM OF MEMBERS.   The minimum number of members who must be present at the meetings of a deliberative assembly for business to be validly transacted is the *quorum* of the assembly. The requirement of a quorum is a protection against totally unrepresentative action in the name of the body by an unduly small number of persons. In both houses of Congress, the quorum is a majority of the members, by the United States Constitution. Such a quorum is appropriate in legislative bodies but too large in most voluntary societies. In an ordinary society, therefore, a provision of the bylaws should specify the number of members that shall constitute a quorum, which should approximate the largest number that can be depended on to attend any meeting except in very bad weather or other extremely unfavorable conditions. In the absence of such a provision in a society or assembly whose real membership can be accurately determined at any time—that is, in a body having an enrolled membership composed only of persons who maintain their status as members in a prescribed manner—the quorum is a majority of the entire membership, by the common parliamentary law. In the meetings of a convention, unless the bylaws of the organization provide otherwise, the quorum is a majority of the delegates who have been registered at the convention as in attendance, irrespective of whether some may have departed. In a mass meeting, or in a regular or properly called meeting of an organization whose bylaws do not prescribe a quorum and whose membership is loosely determined (as, for example, in many church congregations or alumni associations), there is no minimum number of members who must be present for the valid transaction of business, or—as it is usually expressed—the quorum consists of those who attend the meeting. (The rules relating to the quorum are more fully stated in **40**.)

1   MINIMUM OFFICERS.   The minimum essential officers for the conduct of business in a deliberative assembly are
a *presiding officer*, who conducts the meeting and sees that
the rules are observed, and a *secretary*, or *clerk*, who makes a
5 written record of what is done—usually called "the minutes."
If the officers are members of the assembly—as they usually
are in ordinary societies—they are counted in determining
whether a quorum is present.

The presiding officer should be placed so that, even when
10 he is seated—on a high stool if necessary when behind a
lectern—he can see the entire hall and all present can see him
(see also pp. 448–49). The presiding officer's official place or
station (usually in the center of the platform or stage, if there
is one) is called "the chair." During meetings, whoever is pre-
15 siding is said to be "in the chair" (whether standing or seated
at the time), and he is also referred to as "the chair." The
phrase "the chair" thus applies both to the person presiding
and to his station in the hall from which he presides. The secretary's desk should be placed so that papers can easily be
20 passed to him from the chair during the meeting.

The duties of the presiding officer, the secretary, and
other officers that an assembly or society may have are described in **47**.

25
Pattern of Formality

Customs of formality that are followed by the presiding
officer and members under parliamentary procedure serve to
maintain the chair's necessary position of impartiality and
30 help to preserve an objective and impersonal approach, especially when serious divisions of opinion arise.

CUSTOMS OBSERVED BY MEMBERS.   The presi-
dent or chief officer of an organized society, who normally
35 presides at its meetings, is then addressed as "Mr. President"

or "Madam President" (whether a married or unmarried 1
woman), "Mr. [or Madam] Moderator," or by whatever may
be his or her official title. In the lower house of a legislative
body, this officer is most commonly "Mr. [or Madam]
Speaker." A vice-president is addressed as "Mr. President" or 5
"Madam President" while actually presiding. (A possible
exception may arise where the usual form would make the
meaning unclear—for example, when the vice-president is in
the chair while the president is also on the platform. In such
an instance, the vice-president should be addressed as "Mr. 10
[or Madam] Vice-President.") A person presiding at a meeting who has no regular title or whose position is only temporary is addressed as "Mr. [or Madam] Chairman" by
long-established usage. Several variations of this form—such
as "chairperson" or "chair"—are now frequently encoun- 15
tered, however, and may be in use as the general practice in
particular assemblies. Even in a small meeting, the presiding
officer of an assembly should not be addressed or referred
to by name. (The only exceptions that might arise in an
assembly* would be in cases of a testimonial nature, such as 20
in the presentation of a gift to a president who is about to go
out of office.) With nearly the same strictness of observance,
he should not be addressed by the personal pronoun "you"—
although occasional exceptions may occur in ordinary societies if brief administrative consultation takes place during a 25
meeting. As a general rule, when additional reference to the
presiding officer is necessary in connection with addressing
him by his official title, members speak of him as "the
chair"—as in, "Mr. President, do I understand the chair to
state ... ?" 30

Members address only the chair, or address each
other through the chair. In the parliamentary transaction of

---

*As distinguished from a small committee, where some relaxation of this
rule may be appropriate, depending on the conditions.

1 business—within a latitude appropriate to the conditions of
the particular body—members generally should try to avoid
mentioning another member's name whenever the person involved can be described in some other way, as in, "Mr. Pres-
5 ident, may I ask the member to explain ...," or, "Mr.
Chairman, I hope that the gentleman who last spoke will
think of the probable consequences ..." With a very limited
number of particular exceptions, and except in committees
and small boards, a member never speaks while seated;* and
10 with a slightly larger number of exceptions, a member does
not speak without first having *obtained the floor* as described
on pages 29–31.

CUSTOMS OBSERVED BY THE PRESIDING
15 OFFICER.   The presiding officer speaks of himself only in
the third person—that is, he never uses the personal pronoun
"I." In actual parliamentary proceedings he always refers to
himself as "the chair"—as in, "The chair rules that ..." At
other times during meetings—such as when he makes a
20 report to the members in the capacity of an administrative
officer of the organization rather than as presiding officer of
the assembly—he may, if he wishes, describe himself by his
official title, as in, "Your President is pleased to report ..."
Strictly speaking, the chair does not mention a member's
25 name and does not address an individual member as "you,"
except in connection with certain disciplinary procedures (see
p. 646). Instead he may say, for example, "The chair must ask
the member to confine his remarks to the merits of the pending question." In practice in an ordinary lay assembly, how-
30 ever, there are a number of occasions where the chair often
refers to members by name, such as when assigning the *floor*
(that is, the exclusive right to be heard at that time, as

---

*A member who is unable to stand is permitted to speak while seated.

explained on pp. 29–31), or when announcing the members *1*
of a committee.

(For more complete explanations of the general forms observed by the presiding officer and members in an assembly,
see **42** and **43**.) *5*

Call to Order; Order of Business

When the time of a meeting has arrived, the presiding
officer opens it, after he has determined that a quorum is *10*
present, by *calling the meeting to order*. He takes the chair
(that is, occupies the presiding officer's station in the hall),
waits or signals for quiet, and, while standing, announces in
a clear voice, "The meeting will come to order," or, "The
meeting will be in order." (For the procedure to be followed *15*
when a quorum of members do not appear, see pp. 347–48.)
The call to order may be immediately followed by religious
or patriotic exercises or other opening ceremonies.

The initial procedures in a mass meeting or in one called
to form a society are described in **53** and **54**. Sessions (**8**) of *20*
permanently organized bodies usually follow an established
order of business that specifies the sequence in which certain
general types or classes of business are to be brought up or
permitted to be introduced. If the assembly has no binding
order of business, any member who obtains the floor (see *25*
pp. 29–31) can introduce any legitimate matter he desires
(within the objects of the organization as defined in its bylaws) at any time when no business is before the assembly for
consideration. A society may follow the order of business
given in the manual that the bylaws of the organization des- *30*
ignate as its parliamentary authority, or it may have adopted
its own particular order of business. Although an organization
has no binding order of business until it has either adopted
its own or has adopted a parliamentary authority that specifies

1 one, the following order of business (which is fully explained
   in **41**) has come to be regarded as usual or standard for one-
   meeting sessions of ordinary societies:

5 1) Reading and Approval of Minutes*
   2) Reports of Officers, Boards, and Standing (that is, per-
      manently established) Committees
   3) Reports of Special (Select or Ad Hoc) Committees (that
      is, committees appointed to exist only until they have
10   completed a specified task)
   4) Special Orders (that is, matters which have previously
      been assigned a type of special priority, as explained in **14**
      and **41**)
   5) Unfinished Business and General Orders (that is, matters
15   which have come over from the preceding meeting or
      which have been scheduled for the present meeting)
   6) New Business (that is, matters initiated in the present
      meeting)

20   In a meeting where an established order of business is
   being followed, the chair calls for the different classes of business in the prescribed order.
       A mass meeting usually requires no order of business,
   since, referring to the headings listed above, there is nothing
25 but new business to be brought up (unless the meeting is one
   within a series).

---

*The order of business is separate and distinct from the procedure of
calling a meeting to order, which is not a part of the order of business. A
meeting opens by being called to order even when it has no established order
of business. Additional "calls to order" may occur during the order of business
at various times not specified in advance, if the assembly takes a recess (**8, 20**)
or adjourns to a future time (**8, 22**) before the order of business is completed.
For these reasons, it is not proper to list a "call to order" as the first item in
an order of business or agenda, as is often incorrectly done.

A convention commonly adopts its own order of busi- *1*
ness—which often specifies the exact hours at which certain
important questions are to be taken up. The order of business
of a convention is known as the *program*, or the *agenda*,
depending on whether it is interwoven with, or separate *5*
from, the overall schedule of convention meetings, events,
etc. (see **41, 59**).

A legislative body usually has a more elaborate order of
business suited to its own needs.

10

Means by Which Business Is Brought Before the Assembly

MOTIONS.   Business is brought before an assembly by
the *motion* of a member. A motion may itself bring its subject *15*
to the assembly's attention, or the motion may follow upon
the presentation of a report or other communication.

A motion is a formal proposal by a member, in a meeting,
that the assembly take certain action. The proposed action
may be of a substantive nature, or it may express a certain *20*
view or direct that a particular investigation be conducted and
the findings be reported to the assembly for possible further
action, or the like.

The basic form of motion—the only one whose introduction brings business before the assembly—is a *main motion*. *25*
There are also many other separate parliamentary motions
that have evolved for specific purposes. While all of these
motions propose some form of action and while all of them
are said to be brought "before the assembly" when they are
placed under consideration, most of them do not *bring* *30*
business before it in the sense described above—as a main
motion does. Many of these motions involve procedural steps
relating to a main motion already being considered.

The main motion sets a pattern from which all other motions are derived. In the remainder of this chapter, rules and *35*

1 explanations relating to "motions" have the main motion as
their frame of reference. The manner in which a main motion
is brought before the assembly is explained on pages 32ff.

5   MOTIONS GROWING OUT OF REPORTS OR
COMMUNICATIONS.   After the presentation of the report of an officer, a board, or a committee, one or more
motions to carry out recommendations contained in the
report may be introduced. (For the procedures in such cases,
10 see **41** and **51**.)
        A motion may also grow out of the presentation of a
written communication to the assembly. This may be in the
form of a letter or memorandum from a member who is not
present, from a superior body (such as a state or national
15 executive board to a local chapter), or from an outside source.
A communication normally is addressed to the president or
secretary and is read aloud by the secretary—unless the presiding officer properly should read it because of special importance of the content or source.
20   It is not customary to make a motion to *receive* a communication or a committee report, which means only to permit or cause such a paper to be read. This is an example of a
case in the ordinary routine of business where the formality
of a motion is dispensed with. It should be noted that a mo-
25 tion "to receive" a communication after it has been read is
meaningless and should therefore be avoided.
        The reading of a communication does not in itself for-
mally bring a question before the assembly. After the reading,
or at the time provided by the order of business, a motion
30 can be offered proposing appropriate action. If no member
feels that anything needs to be done, the matter is dropped
without a motion.

        BUSINESS THAT COMES UP WITHOUT A MO-
35 TION, BECAUSE OF PREVIOUS ACTION.   Business

may come up automatically at a certain time or at a certain
point in the order of business, if it has previously been postponed (**14**) or otherwise made a general or special order
(**41**). In such cases, the business is announced at the proper
time by the chair, and, if it has already been introduced in
the form of a motion, no additional motion is made at
that time.

Obtaining and Assigning the Floor

Before a member in an assembly can make a motion or
speak in *debate*—the parliamentary name given to any form
of discussion of the merits of a motion—he must *obtain the
floor*; that is, he must be *recognized* by the chair as having the
exclusive right to be heard at that time. (For the parliamentary motions that can be made without obtaining the floor,
see tinted pp. 40–41.) The chair must recognize any member
who seeks the floor while entitled to it.

To claim the floor, a member rises at his place when no
one else has the floor (or goes to a microphone in a large
hall), faces the chair, and says, "Mr. President," or "Mr.
Chairman," or "Madam Chairman," or whatever is the chair's
proper title.* If the member is entitled to the floor at the
time, the chair recognizes him—normally by announcing, as
applicable, the person's name or title, or the place or unit
that he represents. This member then has the floor** and can

---

*In small boards and in committees, members generally need not rise to
obtain the floor. See p. 487.

**The expression "privileges of the floor," sometimes used in legislative
bodies or conventions, has nothing to do with having the floor, but means
merely that a person is permitted to enter the portion of the hall floor otherwise restricted to members and necessary staff. It carries no right to speak or
any other right of membership, except as may be determined by rules or action
of the body.

1 remain standing and speak in debate or make a motion as
  permitted under the rules in this book depending on the parliamentary situation at the time. If only one person is seeking
  the floor in a small meeting where all present know and can
5 clearly see one another, the chair can recognize the member
  merely by nodding to him. On the other hand, if a speech is
  prearranged, or if several members are attempting to claim
  the floor at once in a large meeting, presiding officers often
  use the formal wording, "The chair recognizes Mr. Smith."
10 When the names of the members are not generally known, a
  person addressing the chair to claim the floor should state his
  name and any necessary identification as soon as the presiding
  officer turns toward him, as "Edward Wells, Delegate, Cres-
  cent County." The chair then assigns the floor by repeating
15 the member's name or identification. When the member fin-
  ishes speaking, he *yields* the floor by resuming his seat.

  If two or more rise at about the same time, the general
  rule is that, all other things being equal, the member who
  rose and addressed the chair first *after the floor was yielded* is
20 entitled to be recognized. A member cannot establish "prior
  claim" to the floor by rising before it has been yielded. In
  principle, it is out of order to rise or be standing while another
  person has the floor—except for the purpose of making one
  of the motions or taking one of the parliamentary steps that
25 can legitimately interrupt at such a time (tinted pp. 40–41).
  In a very large assembly, if members must walk some distance
  to microphones, it may be necessary to vary from the preceding rule as dictated by conditions in the particular hall.
  Some arrangements used in large assemblies are outlined on
30 page 383.

  While a motion is open to debate, there are three important cases where the floor should be assigned to a person who
  may not have been the first to rise and address the chair (but
  who did so before anyone had actually been recognized).
35 These cases are as follows:

1) If the member who made the motion claims the floor and *1*
has not already spoken on the question, he is entitled to
be recognized in preference to other members.

2) No one is entitled to the floor a second time in debate on
the same motion on the same day as long as any other *5*
member who has not spoken on this motion desires the
floor.

3) In cases where the chair knows that persons seeking
the floor have opposite opinions on the question (and the
member to be recognized is not determined by [1] or [2] *10*
above), the chair should let the floor alternate, as far
as possible, between those favoring and those opposing
the measure. To accomplish this, the chair may say, for
example, "Since the last speaker spoke in favor of the motion, who wishes to speak in opposition to the motion?" *15*
or "Since the last speaker opposed the motion, who
wishes to speak in its favor?"

A member cannot rise for the purpose of claiming *preference in being recognized* (as this right is called in all of the *20*
above cases) after the chair has recognized another member.
If at any time the chair makes a mistake, however, and assigns
the floor to the wrong person—when preference in recognition was timely claimed or in any other case—his attention
can be called to it by raising a *Point of Order* (**23**), and he *25*
should immediately correct the error.

The preceding rules usually are adequate for assigning the
floor in most business meetings. In great assemblies or conventions, or in bodies that must handle a heavy agenda (**41**)
or complex issues, additional situations often occur where the *30*
best interests of the assembly require the floor to be assigned
to a claimant who was not the first to rise and address the
chair. (For the rules governing these cases, see **42**.)

§4. THE HANDLING OF A MOTION

The handling of a motion varies in certain details according to conditions. In the ordinary case, especially under new business, there are six essential steps—three by which the motion is *brought before the assembly*, and three in the *consideration* of the motion.

How a Motion Is Brought Before the Assembly

The three steps by which a motion is normally brought before the assembly are as follows:

1) A member *makes* the motion. (The words *move* and *offer* also refer to this step. A person is said to "make a motion," but he uses the word "move" when he does so. He is also said "to move" a particular proposal, as in "to move a postponement.")
2) Another member *seconds* the motion.
3) The chair *states the question on the motion*. (The step of stating the question on the motion should not be confused with *putting the question*, which takes place later and means putting the motion to a vote.)

Neither the making nor the seconding of a motion places it before the assembly; only the chair can do that, by the third step (stating the question). When the chair has stated the question, the motion is *pending*, that is, "on the floor." It is then open to debate (if it is a main motion or one of several other *debatable* parliamentary motions, which are described in later chapters). If the assembly decides to do what a motion proposes, it *adopts* the motion, or the motion is *carried*; if the assembly expressly decides against doing what the motion proposes, the motion is *lost*, or *rejected*.

MAKING A MOTION. To make a main motion, a *1*
member must obtain the floor, as explained above, when
no other question is pending and when business of the kind
represented by the motion is in order. The member then
makes his motion, in simple cases by saying, "I move that ... *5*
[announcing what he proposes in a wording intended to become the assembly's official statement of the action taken]."
For more important or complex questions, or when greater
formality is desired, he presents the motion in the form of a
resolution. The usual wording then is, "I move the adoption *10*
of the following resolution: '*Resolved*, That ...'"; or, "I offer
the following resolution: '*Resolved*, That ...'" (For additional
information on the proper form for main motions and resolutions, see **10**.)

A resolution or a long or complicated motion should be *15*
prepared in advance of the meeting, if possible, and should
be put into writing before it is offered. The mover then passes
it to the chair as soon as he has offered it. If conditions make
it impractical for a member offering a written resolution to
read it himself, he should sign it and pass or send it to the *20*
chair ahead of time (in a large meeting, often by page or mes-
senger), or he can deliver it to the secretary before the meeting. In such a case the member offers his resolution by saying,
"I move the adoption of the resolution relating to ... , which
I have sent to the chair [or "have delivered to the Secre- *25*
tary"]," identifying it by its subject matter; or, when moving
its adoption, the member may identify the resolution by its
designated title, number, letter, or the like. The chair then
says, "The resolution offered by Mrs. A is as follows: ..." or,
"The Secretary will read the resolution offered by Mrs. A," *30*
and the chair (or the secretary) reads the resolution in full. If
the text of the resolution or motion has been distributed to
the members in advance, however, it need not be read when
moved.

1   As soon as a member has made a motion, he resumes his
seat. He will have the right to speak first in debate, if he
wishes, after the chair has stated the question. If the motion
has not been heard or is not clear, another member can ask
5   that it be repeated, which the chair can request the maker or
the secretary to do, or can do himself.

Under parliamentary procedure, strictly speaking, discussion of any subject is permitted only with reference to a pending motion. When necessary, a motion can be prefaced by a
10   few words of explanation, which must not become a speech;
or a member can first request information, or he can indicate
briefly what he wishes to propose and can ask the chair to assist him in wording an appropriate motion. In general, however, when a member has obtained the floor while no motion
15   is pending—unless it is for a special purpose, such as to ask a
question—he makes a motion immediately. Any desired im-
provements upon the member's proposal can be accomplished by several methods after the motion has been made
(for a summary, see pp. 114–16). For a member to begin to
20   discuss a matter while no question is pending, without
promptly leading to a motion, implies an unusual circumstance and requires permission of the assembly (see
p. 299) in addition to obtaining the floor. In larger assemblies, this rule requires firm enforcement. In smaller
25   meetings, it may sometimes be relaxed with constructive
effect if the members are not accustomed to working under
the standard rule. Unless the assembly has specifically authorized that a particular subject be discussed while no motion is
pending, however, such a discussion can be entered into only
30   at the sufferance of the chair or until a point of order is made;
and in the latter case, the chair must immediately require that
a motion be offered or the discussion cease. The general rule
against discussion without a motion is one of parliamentary
procedure's powerful tools for keeping business "on track,"
35   and an observance of its spirit can be an important factor

in making even a very small meeting rapidly moving and   *1*
interesting.*

SECONDING A MOTION.   After a motion has been
made, another member who wishes it to be considered says,   *5*
"I second the motion," or, "I second it," or even, "Second!"—without obtaining the floor, and in small assemblies
without rising.** In large assemblies, and especially in those
where nonmembers may be seated in the hall, the seconder
should stand, and without waiting to be recognized should   *10*
state his name (with other identification, if appropriate) and
say, "Mr. President [or "Mr. Chairman"], I second the motion." In some organizations, especially labor unions, the
word "support" is used in place of "second."

If no member seconds the motion, the chair must be sure   *15*
that all have heard it before proceeding to other business. In
such a case the chair normally asks, "Is there a second to the
motion?" In a large hall he may repeat the motion before
doing so. Or, if a resolution was submitted in writing and read
by the chair or the secretary rather than by the mover (as de-   *20*
scribed on p. 33), the chair may say, "Miss A has moved the
adoption of the resolution just read. Is there a second to
the resolution?"; or, if the text of the resolution has been distributed to the members in advance and was moved without

---

*In the very early development of parliamentary procedure, a presiding
officer was expected to distill from the debate the essence of a motion and, in
conclusion, take a vote on that motion. It was found in the House of Lords
in England that, when there was no definite motion pending, it was not possible to tell whether debate was germane, and the debate itself often became
discursive and lengthy. In addition, the presiding officer might not digest the
debate into a motion in a way satisfactory to most of the members. In such a
case, there was little opportunity to put the motion in proper form before
voting, since the chair's formulation of it occurred at the conclusion.

**Motions need not be seconded in a small board or a committee.

1 being read, the chair may say, for example, "Miss A has moved
the adoption of the resolution relating to ... , as printed. Is
there a second to the resolution?" If there still is no second,
the chair says, "The motion [or "resolution"] is not sec-
5 onded"; or, "Since there is no second, the motion is not before this meeting." Then he immediately says, "The next item
of business is ..."; or, if appropriate, "Is there any further
business?"

A second merely implies that the seconder agrees that the
10 motion should *come before the meeting* and not that he necessarily favors the motion. A member may second a motion
(even if using the word "support" as indicated above) because
he would like to see the assembly go on record as *rejecting*
the proposal, if he believes a vote on the motion would have
15 such a result. A motion made by direction of a board or duly
appointed committee of the assembly requires no second
from the floor (provided the subordinate group is composed
of more than one person), since the motion's introduction
has been directed by a majority vote within the board or com-
20 mittee and is therefore desired by at least two assembly members or elected or appointed persons to whose opinion the
assembly is presumed to give weight regarding the board's or
committee's concerns. (For rules governing the appointment
of non–assembly members to committees, see pp. 174–75,
25 492–93, 496.)

The requirement of a second is for the chair's guidance
as to whether he should state the question on the motion,
thus placing it before the assembly. Its purpose is to prevent
time from being consumed by the assembly's having to
30 dispose of a motion that only one person wants to see
introduced.

In handling routine motions, less attention is paid to the
requirement of a second. If the chair is certain that a motion
meets with wide approval but members are slow in seconding

it, he can state the question without waiting for a second.   *1*
However, until debate has begun in such a case—or, if there
is no debate, until the chair begins to take the vote and any
member has voted—a point of order (see **23**) can be raised
that the motion has not been seconded; and then the chair   *5*
must proceed formally and ask if there is a second. Such a
point of order should not be made only for the sake of form,
if it is clear that more than one member wishes to take up the
motion. After debate has begun or, if there is no debate, after
any member has voted, the lack of a second has become im-   *10*
material and it is too late to make a point of order that the
motion has not been seconded. If a motion is considered and
adopted without having been seconded—even in a case where
there was no reason for the chair to overlook this requirement—the absence of a second does not affect the validity of   *15*
the motion's adoption.

(For lists of certain parliamentary motions that do not
require a second, see tinted pp. 40–41.)

THE STATING OF THE QUESTION BY THE   *20*
CHAIR.   When a motion that is in order has been made and
seconded, the chair formally places it before the assembly by
stating the question; that is, he states the exact motion and
indicates that it is open to debate (and certain other parliamentary processes to be explained in **5** and **6**) in the manner   *25*
indicated below as appropriate to the case:

- The basic form used by the chair in stating the question
  on an ordinary motion is, "It is moved and seconded that
  [or "to"] ... [repeating the motion]." The chair then nor-   *30*
  mally turns toward the maker of the motion to see if he
  wishes to be assigned the floor. If the maker does not
  claim the floor and, after a pause, no one else does, the
  chair may ask, "Are you ready for the question?" (or, less

1 formally, "Is there any debate?")* For example, "It is
moved and seconded that the Society allocate fifty dollars
for ..."; or, "... that fifty dollars be allocated ..."; or, "It
is moved and seconded to allocate fifty dollars for ... The
5 chair recognizes Mr. A."

- In the case of a resolution, the chair may state the question
by saying, "It is moved and seconded to adopt the following resolution [or, "... that the following resolution be
adopted"]: '*Resolved*, That ... [reading the resolution].'"

10 - If the chair, in stating the question on a written resolution
or motion, wishes the secretary to read it, he may state
the question as follows: "It is moved and seconded to
adopt the resolution which the Secretary will now read."
The secretary reads the resolution, after which the chair
15 continues: "The question is on the adoption of the resolution just read."

- If a written resolution was not read by the mover but was
read by the chair or the secretary before being seconded,
the chair may state the question thus: "It is moved and
20 seconded to adopt the resolution just read."

- The chair at his discretion may also use the form given
immediately above in cases where the member offering a
resolution has read it clearly and the chair is confident that
all members have understood it. In such a case, however,
25 any member has the right to have the motion or resolution read again when the question is stated.

- Similarly, if the text of a resolution has been distributed
to the members in advance, the chair may state the ques-

---

*For a parliamentary motion that is not debatable but is amendable (see
list on tinted p. 43), only "Are you ready for the question?" or "Are there
any amendments?" are applicable phrases. For a parliamentary motion that
is neither debatable nor amendable (see list on tinted p. 42), the chair omits
any such query and instead puts the motion to a vote immediately after stating it.

tion without reading it in full, instead identifying the res-   *1*
olution by its subject or designated title, number, letter,
or the like, as by saying, "It is moved and seconded to
adopt the resolution relating to ..., as printed." In such a
case, too, any member has the right to have the motion   *5*
or resolution read by the chair or the secretary.

In principle, the chair must state the question on a motion
immediately after it has been made and seconded, unless he
is obliged to rule that the motion is out of order or unless, in   *10*
his opinion, the wording is not clear.

Rules and explanations relating to the conditions under
which various motions are out of order will be found particularly in **5**, **6**, and **7**; in **10** (pp. 110–13); and in the first
three of the "Standard Descriptive Characteristics" given in   *15*
the sections on each of the parliamentary motions (**11–37**).
When a member who has legitimately obtained the floor
offers a motion which is not in order, the chair may be able,
in certain instances, to suggest an alternative motion which
would be in order and would carry out the desired intent to   *20*
the satisfaction of the maker. If the chair is obliged to rule
that the motion is out of order, he should say, "The chair
rules that the motion is out of order [or "not in order"] because ... [briefly stating the reason]." (He should not say,
"You are out of order," nor, "Your motion is out of order."   *25*
To state that a *member* is out of order implies that the member is guilty of a breach of decorum or other misconduct in a
meeting; and even in such a case, the chair does not normally
address the member in the second person. See pp. 24–25; also
61.) If the chair rules that a motion is out of order, his deci-   *30*
sion is subject to an appeal to the judgment of the assembly.
(For procedure regarding *Appeal*, see **24**.)

If a motion is offered in a wording that is not clear or that
requires smoothing before it can be recorded in the minutes,
it is the duty of the chair to see that the motion is put into   *35*

1 suitable form—preserving the content to the satisfaction of
the mover—*before* the question is stated. The chair should
not admit a motion that the secretary would have to para-
phrase for the record. The chair—either on his own initiative
5 or at the secretary's request—can require any main motion,
amendment (**10**, **12**), or instructions to a committee to be
in writing before he states the question.

Until the chair states the question, the maker has the right
to modify his motion as he pleases or to withdraw it entirely.
10 After the question has been stated by the chair, the motion
becomes the property of the assembly, and then its maker can
do neither of these things without the assembly's consent (see
pp. 295–98); but while the motion is pending the assembly
can change the wording of the motion by the process of
15 *amendment* (**12**) before acting upon it.

After a motion has been made but before the chair states
it or rules that it is out of order, no debate is in order. At such
a time, however, any member can quickly rise and, without
waiting to be recognized, can say, "Mr. President, I would
20 like to ask the maker of the motion if he will accept the following modification: ... [or, "... if he would be willing to
change the words ... to ... "]." The maker then answers, "Mr.
President, I accept [or "do not accept," or "cannot accept"]
the modification"; or, he can respond by making a different
25 modification: "Mr. President, I will modify the motion as
follows: ..."

If the maker of a motion modifies it before the question
is stated, a person who has seconded it has the right to withdraw his second; but if a modification is accepted *as suggested*
30 *by another member*—either before or after the motion has
been seconded—the suggester has in effect seconded the
modified motion, so that no other second is necessary. Under
any circumstances where a second is withdrawn but it is clear
that another member favors consideration of the motion in
35 its modified form, the chair treats the motion as seconded. If

the maker makes any change in his motion and it remains, in   *1*
effect, seconded, or (if necessary) is then seconded, the chair
says, "It is moved and seconded ...," stating the question
on the modified motion just as if it had been so moved originally. If a modification is suggested and the maker declines   *5*
to make any change, the chair says, "The modification is not
accepted," and (provided that the motion has been seconded)
he states the question on it as it was moved by the maker.

Modifications of a motion that are suggested before the
question is stated should usually be limited to changes that   *10*
are likely to be generally acceptable to the members present—
or, in other words, changes that probably would not occasion
debate if proposed as amendments while the motion was
pending.

In a similar manner, before the question on a motion has   *15*
been stated, any member who believes that the maker will
immediately withdraw the motion if a certain fact is pointed
out to him can quickly rise and say (without waiting for
recognition), "Mr. Chairman, I would like to ask if the member would be willing to withdraw his motion in view of ...   *20*
[stating the reasons for the suggested withdrawal]." The
maker responds, "I withdraw [or "decline to withdraw"] the
motion." If the maker withdraws his motion, the chair says,
"The motion is withdrawn," and proceeds to the next business. If the purpose of the withdrawal was to deal with a more   *25*
urgent matter first, the chair immediately recognizes the
appropriate member to bring it up. If the maker is unwilling
to withdraw his motion, the chair says, "The member declines
to withdraw the motion," and (if the motion has been seconded) he then states the question.   *30*

Strictly speaking, before the question is stated no comment should accompany suggestions that a motion be modified or withdrawn. In ordinary meetings, however, time can
often be saved by brief informal consultation—which the
chair can permit at his discretion, provided that he is careful   *35*

1   to see that this privilege is not abused or allowed to run into
    debate. The chair can frequently maintain the necessary con-
    trol over such informal consultation by standing while it takes
    place (in contrast to the rule that he should normally be
5   seated during debate unless it would obstruct his view of the
    members; see p. 451).

The Consideration of a Main Motion: Basic Steps

10   Once a main motion has been brought before the assem-
    bly through the three steps described above, there are three
    further basic steps by which the motion is considered in the
    ordinary and simplest case (unless it is adopted by *unanimous*
    consent, as explained on pp. 54–56). These normal steps are
15 as follows:

    1) Members *debate* the motion (unless no member claims
       the floor for that purpose).
    2) The chair *puts the question* (that is, puts it to a vote).
20 3) The chair *announces the result* of the vote.

        In addition, while the motion is open to debate, the as-
    sembly may wish to take a number of actions as a part of the
    motion's consideration—which can themselves be the subject
25 of certain parliamentary motions, as explained in **5** and **6**. In
    the following description of the three principal steps in the
    consideration of a main motion, it is assumed that none of
    these other motions are introduced.

30   DEBATE ON THE QUESTION.   Immediately after
    stating the question, the chair should turn toward the maker
    of the motion to see if he wishes to be assigned the floor first
    in debate—to which the maker has the right if he claims it
    before anyone else has been recognized, even though others
35 may have risen and addressed the chair first.

A member who desires to speak in debate must obtain the floor as described on pages 29–31. The chair in assigning the floor should be guided by the principles explained in the same pages, and in **42**. In the debate, each member has the right to speak twice on the same question on the same day,* but cannot make a second speech on the same question so long as any member who has not spoken on that question desires the floor. A member who has spoken twice on a particular question on the same day has *exhausted his right to debate* that question for that day.

Without the permission of the assembly, no one can speak longer than permitted by the rules of the body—or, in a nonlegislative assembly that has no rule of its own relating to the length of speeches, longer than ten minutes.

Debate must be confined to the merits of the pending question. Speakers must address their remarks to the chair, maintain a courteous tone, and—especially in reference to any divergence of opinion—should avoid injecting a personal note into debate. To this end, they must never attack or make any allusion to the motives of members. As already noted, speakers should refer to officers only by title and should avoid the mention of other members' names as much as possible.

Except in committees and small boards, the presiding officer should not enter into discussion of the merits of pending questions (unless, in rare instances, he leaves the chair until the pending business has been disposed of, as described on pp. 394–95). While members are speaking in debate, the presiding officer should remain seated unless the view between him and the members would be obstructed. In the latter case, he should step back slightly while a member is speaking. Although the presiding officer should give close attention to each speaker's remarks during debate, he cannot

*For procedures where greater freedom of debate is desired, see **15** and **52**.

interrupt the person who has the floor so long as that person does not violate any of the assembly's rules and no disorder arises. The presiding officer must never interrupt a speaker simply because he knows more about the matter than the speaker does.

The presiding officer cannot close debate so long as any member who has not exhausted his right to debate desires the floor, except by order of the assembly, which requires a two-thirds vote (**15, 16, 43**).

(For additional rules and information related to debate, see **43**.)

PUTTING THE QUESTION.   When the debate appears to have closed, the chair may ask, "Are you ready for the question?" or "Is there any further debate?" If no one then rises to claim the floor, the chair proceeds to put the question—that is, he puts it to a vote after once more making clear the exact question the assembly is called upon to decide. If the chair's wording of the question is erroneous, a point of order may be made until any member has actually voted. Except as it may be corrected in response to such a point of order, the exact wording the chair uses in putting the question is definitive, and the wording in the minutes should be the same. Where there is any possibility of confusion, the chair, before calling for the vote, should make sure that the members understand the effect of an "aye" vote and of a "no" vote. In putting the question, the chair should stand (except in a small board or a committee) and should especially project his voice to be sure that all are aware that the vote is being taken. The vote on a motion is normally taken by *voice* (or *viva voce*),* unless, under certain conditions, it is taken by *rising* or—sometimes in committees, or in small boards, or other very small assemblies—by a *show of hands*. In putting

---

*Pronounced VIE-vuh VOE-see.

the question by any of these methods, the chair calls first for   1
the affirmative vote, and all who wish to vote in favor of the
motion so indicate in the manner specified; then he calls for
the negative vote. The chair must always call for the negative
vote, no matter how nearly unanimous the affirmative vote   5
may appear, except that this rule is commonly relaxed in the
case of noncontroversial motions of a complimentary or courtesy nature; but even in such a case, if any member objects,
the chair must call for the negative vote. A further exception
arises when the negative vote is intrinsically irrelevant, as, for   10
example, when "a vote of one fifth of the members present"
is required, and the number who have voted in the affirmative is clearly greater than one fifth of those present (see
p. 403). The chair should not call for abstentions in taking
a vote, since the number of members who respond to such a   15
call is meaningless. To "abstain" means not to vote at all, and
a member who makes no response if "abstentions" are called
for abstains just as much as one who responds to that effect
(see also p. 407).

The three methods of putting the question stated in the   20
preceding paragraph, as well as the forms used when a vote
taken by rising or by a show of hands is counted, are described below. Other methods of taking a formal vote (as distinguished from adopting a motion by unanimous consent,
pp. 54–56) are used only when expressly ordered by the as-   25
sembly or prescribed by its rules; they are described in **45**.

Form for Taking a Voice Vote. A vote by voice is the regular method of voting on any motion that does not require
more than a majority vote for its adoption (see p. 4; **44**). In
taking a voice vote, the chair puts the question by saying,   30
"The question is on the adoption of the motion to [or "that"]
... [repeating or clearly identifying the motion]. Those in
favor of the motion, say *aye.* [Pausing for response.] ... Those
opposed, say *no.*" (Alternative forms are: "All those in favor
..."; "All in favor ..."; or the wording formerly prescribed in   35

1   Congress, "As many as are in favor ...") In the case of a resolution, the question may be put as follows: "The question is
on the adoption of the following resolution: [reading it].
Those in favor of adopting the resolution that was just read,
5   say *aye.* ... Those opposed, say *no.*" If the resolution has been
read very recently and there appears to be no desire to have
it read again, the chair may use this form: "The question is
on the adoption of the resolution last read. Those in favor of
adopting the resolution, say *aye.* ... Those opposed, say *no.*"
10   However, if there has been any debate or amendment since
the resolution was last read, any member can demand that it
be read again when the question is put, if the chair does not
do so on his own.*

     Form for Taking a Rising (Division) Vote. The simple
15   rising vote (in which the number of members voting on each
side is not counted) is used principally in cases where a voice
vote has been taken with an inconclusive result, and as the
normal method of voting on motions requiring a two-thirds
vote for adoption (see *Chair's Announcement of the Voting*
20   *Result,* etc., below). When only a majority is required, however, time may sometimes be saved by taking a rising vote initially, if the chair believes in advance that a voice vote *will be*
inconclusive. In all such cases the vote can be taken in a form

---

*In the case of any resolution, motion, or paper placed before the assem-
bly that has not been read even once, the chair normally should not put it to
a vote or seek its approval or adoption without reading it (or having it read
by the secretary) unless permission is first obtained by unanimous consent.
In a case where the full text has been distributed to the members in advance
and it is customary for the reading to be omitted, the chair may initially pre-
sume that there is no objection to omitting the reading (but any member still
has the right to demand that it be read). Such a case typically involves adoption of an agenda; approval of the minutes; or, in a convention, the rules proposed by the Committee on Standing Rules or the program proposed by the
Program Committee. (See also p. 38, l. 27 to p. 39, l. 6.)

like this: "Those in favor of the motion to invite Mr. Jones to   *1*
be guest speaker at our next meeting will rise. [Or, "stand."]
... Be seated. ... Those opposed will rise. ... Be seated."

If a rising vote remains inconclusive, the chair or the
assembly can order the vote to be counted (see p. 52; **30**;   *5*
p. 410). The form then used is, for example: "The question
is on the motion to limit all speeches at this meeting to two
minutes. Those in favor of the motion will rise and remain
standing until counted. ... Be seated. Those opposed will rise
and remain standing until counted. ... Be seated."   *10*

Form for Taking a Vote by Show of Hands. As an alternative to voting by voice, a vote by show of hands can be used
as the basic voting method in small boards or in committees,
and it is so used in some assemblies. An inconclusive voice
vote is also sometimes verified by this method. For either   *15*
of these purposes, the use of voting by show of hands in
assemblies should be limited to very small meetings where
every member can clearly see every other member present. In
voting by this method, the question can be put, for example,
as follows: "The question is on the motion that the bill for   *20*
building repairs be paid as rendered. All those in favor of the
motion will raise the right hand. ... Lower hands. [Or, nodding, "Thank you."] Those opposed will raise the right hand.
... Lower hands."

25

CHAIR'S ANNOUNCEMENT OF THE VOTING
RESULT; VERIFICATION PROCEDURES AND CASES
WHERE THE CHAIR VOTES. The chair, remaining
standing, announces the result of the vote immediately after
putting the question—that is, as soon as he has paused to per-   *30*
mit response to his call for the negative vote. A majority vote
in the affirmative adopts any motion unless it is one of the particular motions that require a larger vote under parliamentary
law or the rules of the organization. (For the parliamentary
motions that require a two-thirds vote, see tinted pp. 44–45).   *35*

Under all of the voting methods described above except a counted rising vote (or a counted show of hands), the result is determined by the chair's judgment as to the prevailing side—which it is his duty, in doubtful cases, to verify beyond reasonable doubt, and to the satisfaction of the members, by the procedures described below.

In voting by any of these methods (including a counted rising vote), a member has the right to change his vote up to the time the result is announced. After that, he can make the change only by unanimous permission of the assembly. (See p. 408, and see pp. 54–56 regarding the granting of such permission by unanimous consent.)

Content of Complete Announcement.   In general (that is, as applying to main motions and other types of motions explained in later chapters), the chair's announcement of the result of the vote should include the following:

1) Report of the voting itself, stating which side "has it"— that is, which side is more numerous—or, in the case of a motion requiring a two-thirds vote for adoption, whether there are two thirds in the affirmative. If the vote has been counted, the chair should first give the count before announcing the prevailing side.
2) Declaration that the motion is adopted or lost.
3) Statement indicating the effect of the vote, or ordering its execution, if needed or appropriate.

The three points listed immediately above generally complete the chair's announcement of the voting result. However, whenever it is stated in this book that a certain procedural motion relating to a vote that has been taken is in order immediately after the result of a vote has been announced (see, for example, p. 408), that interval begins as soon as the chair has pronounced the first two points.

Form of Announcement of Voting Result and the Business 1
That Follows. The three points generally covered by the
chair's announcement of the voting result as listed above are
normally spoken without separation into distinct elements;
and, where applicable, they are immediately followed without 5
pause by announcement of the next item of business, or (in
the case of "secondary" motions, which are described in the
next chapter) by the stating of the next motion that consequently comes up for consideration.

Standard forms, as shown in the bulleted list below, can 10
be given only for the part of the announcement covered by
the first two points listed above. The form of the third
point—which is usually needed only for a vote that has
caused a motion to be *adopted*—is determined by the particular motion. For example, after declaring that the motion is 15
adopted, the chair might indicate its effect by saying, "The
Secretary will send to the bank a certified copy of the resolution naming Mr Thomas and Ms. Watkins as signatories";
or, "The question is postponed to the next meeting of the
Society." 20

Immediately after completing the announcement of the
voting result, to announce the next business in order,
the chair might say, for example, "The next item of business
is the report of the Treasurer," or, "Is there any further new
business?" or, to state the question on the motion that comes 25
up next as a result of the vote, "The question is now on the
main motion as amended."

The full sequence of announcing the voting result and the
business that follows is frequently illustrated in the subsections *Form and Example* in the sections covering the differ- 30
ent parliamentary motions in chapters VI–IX, and on pages
120–21 as applied to the main motion.

Depending on the voting method and the vote required
for adoption of the motion, the chair makes the standard

portion of the announcement, covering the first two numbered points as listed on page 48, as follows:

- *For a voice vote:* "… The ayes have it and the motion is adopted [or "agreed to" or "carried"]. …"* Or, "… The noes have it and the motion is lost. …"
- *For a rising vote (uncounted) or a vote by show of hands:* "… The affirmative has it and the motion is adopted. …" Or, "… The negative has it and the motion is lost. …"
- *For a rising vote or a show of hands on which a count has been ordered:* "… There are 32 in the affirmative and 30 in the negative. The affirmative has it and the motion is adopted. …" Or, "… There are 29 in the affirmative and 33 in the negative. The negative has it and the motion is lost. …"
- *For a motion requiring a two-thirds vote for adoption (where an uncounted rising vote is conclusive):* "… There are two thirds in the affirmative and the motion is adopted. …" Or, "… There are less than two thirds in the affirmative and the motion is lost. …"
- *For a motion requiring a two-thirds vote for adoption (where a count of the vote is taken):* "… There are 51 in the affirmative and 23 in the negative. There are two thirds in the affirmative and the motion is adopted. …" Or, "… There are 48 in the affirmative and 26 in the negative. There are less than two thirds in the affirmative and the motion is lost. …"
- *When the chair votes where his vote will affect the result* (see below): "… There are 35 in the affirmative and 35 in the negative. The chair votes in the affirmative, making

---

*The ellipsis points (dots) before and after each form indicate that it follows immediately after the putting of the question, and is immediately followed by the remainder of the announcement of the result, as described above.

36 in the affirmative and 35 in the negative, so that the
affirmative has it and the motion is adopted. ..." Or,
"... There are 39 in the affirmative and 38 in the negative.
The chair votes in the negative, making 39 in the affirmative and 39 in the negative, so that there is less than a
majority in the affirmative and the motion is lost. ..."

- *When the chair votes where his vote will affect the result
  on a motion requiring a two-thirds vote for adoption:*
  "... There are 59 in the affirmative and 30 in the negative.
  The chair votes in the affirmative, making 60 in the affirmative and 30 in the negative, so that there are two thirds
  in the affirmative and the motion is adopted. ..." Or,
  "... There are 60 in the affirmative and 30 in the negative.
  The chair votes in the negative, making 60 in the affirmative and 31 in the negative, so that there are less than
  two thirds in the affirmative and the motion is lost. ..."

Verifying an Inconclusive Vote. A voice vote—or, in
larger meetings, even a vote by show of hands—may sometimes be inconclusive, either because the voting is close or
because a significant number of members have failed to vote.
If the chair feels that members may question a somewhat
close result of which he is reasonably convinced, he can first
say, "The ayes [or "the noes"] *seem* to have it." The chair
then pauses, and any member who doubts the result is thus
invited to demand verification of the vote by a *division*, as explained below. If no member makes such a demand or states
that he doubts the result, the chair continues, "The ayes have
it ...," as shown above. If the chair is in actual doubt in the
case of such a vote, however, he should not announce a result,
but should immediately retake the vote—strictly speaking,
always as a rising vote. (Regarding use of a show of hands as
a method of verifying an inconclusive voice vote, however,
see below.) If it appears when those in the affirmative rise that
the vote will be close enough to require a count, the chair

1 should count the vote, or direct the secretary to do so,
or (in a large assembly) appoint a convenient number of
tellers—preferably an even number equally divided between
members known to be in favor of the motion and those op-
5 posed to it. If, after a vote has been retaken as an uncounted
rising vote, the chair finds himself still unable to determine
the result, he should take the vote a third time as a *counted*
rising vote.

Division of the Assembly.   Whether or not the chair pauses
10 to say, "The ayes seem to have it ...," any member (without
a second) has the right to require that a voice vote (or even a
vote by show of hands) be retaken as a rising vote, so long as
he does not use the procedure as a dilatory tactic when there
clearly has been a full vote and there can be no reasonable
15 doubt of the result. A vote retaken by rising at the demand
of a member is called a *Division of the Assembly*, or simply
"a division." A member can demand a division from the moment the negative votes have been cast until the result of
the vote has been announced or immediately thereafter (see
20 pp. 408–9). To do so, the member, without obtaining the
floor, calls out the single word "Division!" or "I call for [or
"demand"] a division," or "I doubt the result of the vote."
The chair must then immediately take the rising vote. Either
the chair on his own initiative or the assembly by a majority
25 vote can order such a vote to be counted. If a division appears
doubtfully close and the chair does not order a count, a member, as soon as the chair has announced the result, can rise
and address the chair, and is entitled to preference in recognition for the purpose of moving that the vote be counted. If
30 such a motion is made and is seconded, the chair puts the
question (by a voice vote) on whether a count shall be ordered. If a count is ordered, the chair takes the doubtfully
close division again by a counted rising vote. (For additional
information regarding *Division of the Assembly* and motions
35 relating to voting, see **29** and **30**.)

Verification by Show of Hands. In very small assemblies   1
where everyone present can clearly see everyone else, an inconclusive voice vote may sometimes be verified satisfactorily
by a show of hands if no member objects. A show of hands is
not a division, however, and it is not always as effective in   5
causing a maximum number of members to vote when some
have not done so. In small meetings, a voice vote can be retaken by a show of hands at the initiative of the chair; or, during the same time that it is in order to demand a division, any
member can call out, "Mr. President, may we have a show of   10
hands?" In either case, any other member still has the right
to demand a division, which requires the chair to take a rising
vote. The chair can also immediately take a rising vote in response to a request for a show of hands.

Chair's Vote As Part of the Announcement, Where It Affects   15
the Result. If the presiding officer is a member of the assembly or voting body, he has the same voting *right* as any other
member. Except in a small board or a committee, however—
unless the vote is secret (that is, unless it is by ballot; **45**)—
the chair protects his impartial position by exercising his   20
voting right only when his vote would affect the outcome, in
which case he can either vote and thereby change the result,
or he can abstain. If he abstains, he simply announces the result with no mention of his own vote. In a counted rising vote
(or a count of hands) on a motion requiring a majority   25
vote for adoption, the outcome will be determined by the
chair's action in cases where, without his vote, there is (a) a
tie, or (b) one more in the affirmative than in the negative.*
Since a majority in the affirmative is necessary to adopt the
motion in the case mentioned, a final result in the form of a   30
tie rejects it. When there is a tie without the chair's vote, the

---

*For a discussion of the conditions under which the chair's vote affects
the result in the case of motions requiring a two-thirds vote for adoption, see
page 406.

chair can vote in the affirmative, and such a vote adopts the motion; but if the chair abstains from voting, the motion is lost. When there is one more in the affirmative than in the negative without the chair's vote, the motion is adopted if the chair abstains; but if he votes in the negative, the result is thereby tied and the motion is lost.

(For additional information regarding the procedures used in voting, see **44** and **45**.)

Adoption of a Motion or Action Without a Motion, by Unanimous Consent

In cases where there seems to be no opposition in routine business or on questions of little importance, time can often be saved by the procedure of *unanimous consent*, or as it was formerly also called, *general consent*. Action in this manner is in accord with the principle that rules are designed for the protection of the minority and generally need not be strictly enforced when there is no minority to protect. Under these conditions, the method of unanimous consent can be used either to adopt a motion without the steps of stating the question and putting the motion to a formal vote, or it can be used to take action without even the formality of a motion. To obtain unanimous consent in either case, the chair states that "If there is no objection ... [or, "Without objection ..."]," the action that he mentions will be taken; or he may ask, "Is there any objection to ... ?" He then pauses, and if no member calls out, "I object," the chair announces that, "Since there is no objection ...," the action is decided upon. If any member objects, the chair must state the question on the motion, allow any desired debate (unless it is an "undebatable" parliamentary motion—see **6** and tinted pp. 42–43), and put the question in the regular manner. Or—if no motion has been made—the chair must first ask, "Is there a motion to ... [stating the proposed action]"; or he must at least put the question, assuming such a motion. If an objection is made with reasonable promptness, even though the chair may have already announced the result as one of "no objection," he must disregard such an announcement and proceed to state the question in the usual manner.

"Unanimous consent" does not necessarily imply that every member present is in favor of the proposed action; it may only mean that the opposition, feeling that it is useless to oppose or discuss the matter, simply acquiesces. Similarly, when a member responds to the chair's inquiry, "Is there any objection … ?" with "I object," he may not necessarily oppose the motion itself, but may believe that it is wise to take a formal vote under the circumstances. In other words, the objection is raised, not to the proposed action, but to the action's being taken without a formal vote. No member should hesitate to object if he feels it is desirable to do so, but he should not object merely for dilatory purposes. If a member is uncertain of the effect of an action proposed for unanimous consent, he can call out, "I reserve the right to object," or, "Reserving the right to object, …" After brief consultation he can then object or withdraw his reservation.

The correction and approval of minutes (pp. 354–55) is an example of business that is normally handled by unanimous consent. As a second example, assume that a speaker whose time has expired in debate on a motion asks for two additional minutes. If the chair thinks that all members will approve, he may handle the matter as follows:

> CHAIR: If there is no objection, the member's time will be extended two minutes … [pause]. Since there is no objection, the member's time is extended two minutes.

Or:

> CHAIR: Is there any objection to the member's time being extended two minutes? … [pause]. The chair hears no objection, and it is so ordered.

1 Or, particularly if no objection is anticipated:

> CHAIR: Without objection, the member's time is extended two minutes.

5

In cases where unanimous consent is already apparent, the chair may sometimes assume it. For example, if everyone is obviously absorbed in listening to a speaker who seems near the end of his remarks, the chair may allow him to conclude *10* without interruption, although his time has expired.

Whenever it is stated in this book that a certain action or the adoption of a certain motion "requires a two-thirds vote," the same action can, in principle, also be taken by unanimous consent. If much hinges on the outcome, however, it is usu-*15* ally better to take a formal vote. Action by unanimous consent requires the presence of a quorum, just as for the transaction of business by any other method.

Relation of Other Motions to the Main Motion
20

As already noted, the foregoing initial description of the handling of motions refers principally to the *main motion*—the basic form of motion by which business is brought up and by which the assembly takes substantive action. As also stated *25* above, the consideration of a main motion can involve a number of other procedures not yet described—which are nevertheless in the nature of action by the assembly and are themselves properly the subject of motions. In the same way there are a number of "privileged" motions, which are not *30* associated with the main question but can nevertheless be introduced while it is pending because they relate to certain urgent matters that may arise and warrant immediate determination at such a time. Except for interrupting consideration of the main motion, motions of this type have no direct effect *35* on its disposition. Finally, there are motions by which business

can be brought before the assembly under a number of special   *1*
circumstances involving an earlier question. For each of the
permissible processes in all of these categories, there has
evolved a particular motion with its own name and rules governing its use—resembling or differing from the main motion   *5*
in varying degrees. All such derived forms of motions, proposing procedural steps specifically defined under parliamentary law, are loosely referred to for descriptive purposes in this
book as "parliamentary" motions.

The next chapter contains a brief statement of the purpose   *10*
of each of the parliamentary motions, together with an explanation of the classes into which all motions are divided.
The main motion is more fully treated in **10**, as are each of
the other motions in **11–37**.

CHAPTER

III

DESCRIPTION OF MOTIONS
IN ALL CLASSIFICATIONS

1 §5. BASIC CLASSIFICATIONS;
ORDER OF PRECEDENCE OF MOTIONS

Classes of Motions

5 As noted in Chapter II, the word *motion* refers to a formal proposal by a member, in a meeting, that the assembly take certain action. Before a subject can be considered, it must be placed before the assembly in the form of a motion. From the basic type of motion known as the main motion, as also
10 noted in the preceding chapter, many other specific motions have been derived and have become defined under parliamentary law.

For convenience in description, motions may be classified as shown at the top of the next page. (As indicated to the
15 right of the list, the motions in the second, third, and fourth classes—subsidiary, privileged, and incidental motions taken together—are also called "secondary motions.")*

---

*Secondary motions must not be confused with secondary *amendments*, a much more specialized concept explained on pages 135–36.

1. Main motions   *1*
    a. Original main motions
    b. Incidental main motions
2. Subsidiary motions ⎫
3. Privileged motions ⎬ Secondary   *5*
4. Incidental motions ⎭ motions
5. Motions that bring a question again before the assembly

Secondary Motions as an Underlying Concept   *10*

NATURE OF SECONDARY MOTIONS.   The con-
cept of *secondary motions* serves as a starting point for the
division of motions into the classes shown. It also throws light
on the *order of precedence of motions*, which, as explained
below, is a basic element of the rules under which these   *15*
motions are used in the transaction of business.

Secondary motions may be seen as related to the following fundamental principle of parliamentary law: *Only one question can be considered at a time; once a motion is before the
assembly, it must be adopted or rejected by a vote, or the assembly* *20*
must take action disposing of the question in some other way,
before any other business (except certain matters called "privi-
leged questions") can be introduced. By this principle, a main
motion can be made only when no other motion is pending.
Thus, however, the need for a number of particular *secondary*   *25*
motions arises.

A secondary motion is one whose relationship to the main
question, or whose procedural character or urgency, is such
that:
                                                                   30
1) it can be made and considered while a main motion is
    pending (or, occasionally, it is applicable just before or
    after a related main question is pending)—without vio-
    lating the principle of taking up only one question at a
    time; and   *35*

1 2) when the secondary motion has been made and has been
admitted by the chair as *in order* (that is, as being legitimately able to come before the assembly at the time
according to the rules affecting its use), it must be acted
5 upon or disposed of before direct consideration of the
main question can be continued.

Secondary motions generally are made and seconded and
are stated by the chair, as a main motion would be—except
10 that certain of them are in order while another member has
the floor, and most of the motions in this latter group do not
require a second (see tinted pp. 40–41).

When a secondary motion is placed before the assembly,
it becomes the immediately pending question; the main mo-
15 tion remains pending while the secondary motion is also
pending. A main motion is the *immediately pending question*
whenever it is pending with no secondary motion. Whenever
the chair has occasion to inform the assembly as to what is
the immediately pending question, however, he does not use
20 this phrase, but employs the parliamentary form, "The question is on the motion to …" The latter form is used even
when more than one motion is pending.

TAKING OF PRECEDENCE BY ONE MOTION
25 OVER ANOTHER.   If two motions "A" and "B" are related under rules of parliamentary procedure in such a way
that motion "B" can be made while motion "A" is pending
and, when stated by the chair, can thus temporarily replace
"A" as the immediately pending question, motion "B" *takes*
30 *precedence* over* (or *takes precedence of*) motion "A," and
motion "A" *yields to*** motion "B." A secondary motion thus

---

*Pronounced pree-SEED-n's.

**The word *yield* as used in this sense has no connection with *yielding
the floor* as explained on page 30.

takes precedence over the main motion; and a main motion takes precedence over nothing and yields to all applicable secondary motions. *1*

Certain secondary motions also take precedence over others, so that it is possible for more than one secondary motion to be pending at a time (together with the main motion). In such a case, the motion most recently stated by the chair (among those that have not been voted on) is the immediately pending question. *5*

10

ORDER OF PRECEDENCE OF MOTIONS; RANK. The rules under which secondary motions take precedence over one another have been gradually evolved through experience. While these rules are proper to each of the specific motions, they follow patterns that are related to the division of secondary motions into the classes of *subsidiary, privileged,* and *incidental* motions. *15*

Viewed apart from incidental motions and with modifications under particular conditions explained on page 65, the main motion, the seven subsidiary motions, and the five privileged motions fall into a definite *order of precedence*, which gives a particular *rank* to each of these thirteen motions. The main motion—which does not take precedence over anything—ranks lowest. Each of the other twelve motions has its proper position in the order, taking precedence over the motions that rank below it and yielding to those that rank above it. The privileged motions rank above all other motions. The manner in which the order of precedence of motions operates is illustrated in the summaries of subsidiary and privileged motions given in the next section (see also the chart on tinted pp. 3–5). *20* *25* *30*

The incidental motions each have a certain relationship to the order of precedence of motions; but this relationship can be fully discussed only in terms of the rules governing the individual motions. Other factors also affect the conditions *35*

1   under which these motions are in order, as described on pages
69–74. When a particular incidental motion is in order, it
takes precedence over the main motion and any other
motions that may be pending. Incidental motions have no
5   rank among themselves, and none of them can be assigned a
position in the order of precedence of motions.

    The rank of the motions in the fifth classification as listed
at the beginning of this chapter—that is, the *motions that
bring a question again before the assembly*—is discussed in the
10   description of these motions beginning on page 74.

§6. DESCRIPTION OF CLASSES
15   AND INDIVIDUAL MOTIONS

Main Motions

    A *main motion* is a motion whose introduction brings
business before the assembly. As already noted, a main motion
20   can be made only when no other motion is pending, and it
ranks lowest in the order of precedence of motions.

    It is usual to distinguish between *original main motions*
and *incidental main motions*—which differ principally in the
nature of their subject matter. The difference in the rules gov-
25   erning the use of main motions in these two subclasses is only
slight. It should be noted that incidental main motions form
a category completely separate from *incidental motions*—the
fourth general class of motions. (The distinction between
original main motions and incidental main motions is fully
30   discussed on pp. 100–102.)

Subsidiary Motions

    Subsidiary motions assist the assembly in treating or dis-
35   posing of a main motion (and sometimes other motions).

MANNER OF LISTING THE MOTIONS. Each of *1* the subsidiary motions is briefly described below in terms of the type of situation where it is of use, in a manner that may convey a suggestion of how the order of precedence of motions was arrived at. In the case of the subsidiary motions *5* only, their distinguishing characteristics as a class are explained *after* this description of the individual motions, since these characteristics will be more easily understood if the material is read in that order. The subsidiary motions are listed below in reverse order of rank—which is the chronological order in *10* which they would be moved if all of them became pending at one time. Each of the motions listed takes precedence over— that is, ranks above—the main motion, and also any or all of the motions listed before it.

15

LISTING OF INDIVIDUAL SUBSIDIARY MO-TIONS. The subsidiary motions, briefly described by function, are as follows:

1) If an embarrassing main motion has been brought before *20* the assembly, a member can propose to dispose of this question without bringing it to a direct vote, by moving to *Postpone Indefinitely* (**11**).

2) If a main motion might be more suitable or acceptable in an altered form, a proposal to change its wording (either *25* to clarify or, within limits, to modify the meaning) before the main motion is voted on can be introduced by moving to *Amend* (**12**).

3) But it may be that much time would be required to amend the main motion properly, or that additional in- *30* formation is needed, so that it would be better to turn the motion or resolution over to a committee for study or redrafting before the assembly considers it further. Such action can be proposed by moving to *Commit* the main question—or *Refer* it to a committee (**13**). *35*

1   4) If the assembly might prefer to consider the main motion
       later in the same meeting or at another meeting, this can
       be proposed by moving to *Postpone to a Certain Time*—
       also called the motion to *Postpone Definitely*, or simply to
5   *Postpone* (**14**).

    5) If it is desired to continue consideration of a motion but
       debate is consuming too much time, a member can move
       to place a limit on the debate; on the other hand, if special
       circumstances make it advisable to permit more or longer
10   speeches than under the usual rules, a motion to do so
       can be made; or, it may sometimes be desirable to com-
       bine the elements of limitation and extension, as in limit-
       ing the length of speeches but allowing more speeches
       per member. All such modifications of the normal limits
15   of debate on a pending motion are proposed by means of
       the motion to *Limit or Extend Limits of Debate* (**15**).

    6) If it is desired to close debate and amendment of a pend-
       ing motion so that it will come to an immediate vote, this
       can be proposed by moving the *Previous Question* (**16**).

20 7) If there is reason for the assembly to lay the main motion
       aside temporarily without setting a time for resuming its
       consideration, but with the provision that it can be taken
       up again whenever a majority so decides, this can be pro-
       posed by the motion to *Lay on the Table* (**17**).

25

    CHARACTERISTICS OF SUBSIDIARY MOTIONS
    AS A CLASS.   Subsidiary motions as a class are distinguished
    by having *all five* of the following characteristics: (1) They are
    always *applied* to another motion while it is pending, to aid
30 in treating or disposing of it; the adoption of one of
    them always *does something to* this other motion—that is,
    changes its status in some way—without adopting or ex-
    pressly rejecting it. (2) They can be applied to *any* main
    motion. (Regarding other applications, see below.) (3) They
35 fit into an order of precedence, as already explained, so that

no subsidiary motion can be moved when a motion of higher rank is already pending. (4) They are out of order when another member has the floor. (5) They are in order during the entire time that a motion to which they can be applied is pending, except as may be precluded by a previously adopted motion to *Limit or Extend Limits of Debate* or for the *Previous Question* that is in effect. (In this respect, they differ from the incidental motions; cf. p. 69, ll. 26–35 and p. 198, ll. 4–6.)

CASES WHERE ONE SUBSIDIARY MOTION CAN BE APPLIED TO ANOTHER.   The subsidiary motion to *Amend* is applicable to many other motions in addition to the main motion. All of the subsidiary motions can be amended except *Postpone Indefinitely*, the *Previous Question*, and *Lay on the Table* (which, by the nature of what they propose, do not lend themselves to amendment). When the motion to *Amend* is applied to another subsidiary motion, its rank is modified so that it takes precedence over the motion to which it is applied, even if that motion ranks higher than *Amend* in the regular order of precedence of motions. For example, suppose that a motion to *Postpone* the main question to a certain time is immediately pending. In such a case, motions to *Limit or Extend Limits of Debate*, for the *Previous Question*, and to *Lay on the Table* are in order; motions to *Postpone Indefinitely*, to *Amend*, and to *Commit*, on the other hand, may have become pending before the motion to *Postpone Definitely* was moved, but none of these three motions can now be made—*except* that it is in order to move to amend the motion to *Postpone*, while it is immediately pending.

Debate can also be limited or extended on any debatable motion* that is immediately pending (or on a specified series

*See explanation in 7; rules governing the individual motions, **11–37**; Table of Rules Relating to Motions, tinted pages 6–29; and lists, tinted pages 42–43.

of pending motions including the immediately pending question, **15**); and, similarly, debate and amendment can be closed on a motion or series of motions that are debatable and amendable, or amendment can be closed on motions that can be amended but not debated (**16**). The four lowest-ranking subsidiary motions can be debated (except that *Amend* is undebatable when it is applied to an undebatable motion). Debate of the three highest-ranking subsidiary motions is not permitted, since that would defeat their purpose. From these rules, it follows that the motion to *Limit or Extend Limits of Debate* can be applied to any of the four subsidiary motions of lower rank (but not to the two that rank above it), while the *Previous Question* can be applied to any of the five subsidiary motions that rank below it (but not to the one subsidiary motion that ranks above it).

INCIDENTAL MAIN MOTIONS CORRESPONDING TO SUBSIDIARY MOTIONS. For each of the first five subsidiary motions (that is, for all except the *Previous Question* and *Lay on the Table*), there is a corresponding incidental main motion (p. 101) of the same name that can be made when no other motion is pending.

(Each of the subsidiary motions is fully discussed in **11–17**.)

Privileged Motions

CHARACTERISTICS OF PRIVILEGED MOTIONS AS A CLASS. Unlike subsidiary or incidental motions, *privileged motions* do not relate to the pending business, but have to do with special matters of immediate and overriding importance which, without debate, should be allowed to interrupt the consideration of anything else. Like subsidiary motions, however, the five privileged motions fit into an order of precedence. All of them take precedence over

motions of any other class (except in certain instances where *1*
the immediately pending question may be a motion to
Amend, a motion for the *Previous Question*, or an incidental
motion that was moved while a still higher-ranking privileged
motion was immediately pending). The privileged motions *5*
as a class are also known as "privileged questions," which
should not be confused with "questions of privilege," as described in connection with the second motion listed below.

LISTING OF INDIVIDUAL PRIVILEGED MO- *10*
TIONS.   The privileged motions are listed below in ascend-
ing order of rank. Each of the succeeding motions takes
precedence over any or all of the motions listed before it.

1) If the adopted program or order of business is not being *15*
   followed, or if consideration of a question has been set
   for the present time and is now in order but the matter is
   not being taken up, a single member, by making a *Call
   for the Orders of the Day* (**18**), can require such a schedule
   to be enforced—unless the assembly decides by a two- *20*
   thirds vote (**25**) to set the orders of the day aside.
2) If a pressing situation is affecting a right or privilege of
   the assembly or of an individual member (for example,
   noise, inadequate ventilation, introduction of a confidential subject in the presence of guests, etc.), a member can *25*
   Raise a Question of Privilege (**19**), which permits him to
   interrupt pending business to state an urgent request or
   motion. If the matter is not simple enough to be taken
   care of informally, the chair then makes a ruling as to
   whether it is admitted as a question of privilege and *30*
   whether it requires consideration before the pending business is resumed.
3) A short intermission in a meeting, even while business is
   pending, can be proposed by moving to *Recess* (**20**) for a
   specified length of time. *35*

4) A member can propose to close the meeting entirely by moving to *Adjourn* (**21**). This motion can be made and the assembly can adjourn even while business is pending, provided that the time for the next meeting is established by a rule of the society or has been set by the assembly. (In such a case, the pending business and any other business that is unfinished at the time of adjournment, as well as any questions that have been temporarily disposed of, either fall to the ground or are carried over to the next meeting, depending on the circumstances; see pp. 236–37.)

5) Under certain conditions while business is pending, the assembly—before adjourning or postponing the pending business—may wish to fix a date and hour, and sometimes the place, for another meeting, or (in an established society) for another meeting before the next regular meeting. In cases of this kind, the motion to *Fix the Time to Which to Adjourn* (**22**) can be made—even while a matter is pending—unless another meeting is already scheduled for later within the same session. This is the highest ranking of all motions.

INCIDENTAL MAIN MOTIONS CORRESPONDING TO PRIVILEGED MOTIONS.   For the motions to *Recess*, to *Adjourn*,* and to *Fix the Time to Which to Adjourn*, there are corresponding incidental main motions of the same names (p. 101). Questions of privilege can also be brought up while no motion is pending, and at such times they are moved just as any main motion.

---

*The distinction between the main and the privileged motions to adjourn is different from any other case where an incidental main motion corresponds to a secondary motion of the same name, since a motion "to adjourn" can retain "privileged" characteristics even when no question is pending (see **21**).

(Each of the privileged motions is fully discussed in 18–22.)   *1*

Incidental Motions   *5*

CHARACTERISTICS OF INCIDENTAL MOTIONS AS A CLASS.   *Incidental motions* relate, in different ways, to the pending business or to business otherwise at hand—some of them with varying degrees of resemblance to subsidiary motions, but none of them possessing all five of the   *10* characteristics listed on pages 64–65. As a class, incidental motions deal with questions of procedure *arising out of*: (1) commonly, another pending motion; but also (2) sometimes, another motion or item of business

15

a) that it is desired to introduce,
b) that has been made but has not yet been stated by the chair, or
c) that has just been pending.

20

An incidental motion is said to be *incidental to* the other motion or matter out of which it arises. With but few exceptions, incidental motions are related to the main question in such a way that they must be decided immediately, before business can proceed. Most incidental motions are undebatable.   *25*
Each of the incidental motions is applicable only in its own type of special circumstance—which may be a particular characteristic present in the motion to which it is incidental, or a particular point in time or possible occurrence during the assembly's involvement with the other motion or matter.   *30* This is an important respect in which incidental motions differ from subsidiary motions, since subsidiary motions—in principle and with certain qualifications already noted (p. 64, l. 34 to p. 65, l. 8)—are applicable to any main motion over the entire time that it is pending.   *35*

1   LISTING OF INDIVIDUAL INCIDENTAL MO-
TIONS. The order in which the incidental motions are
listed below, unlike that in which the subsidiary and privileged
motions are presented above, has no relation to what other
5   motions they may take precedence over or yield to (see discussion beginning on p. 72). The incidental motions arise as
follows:

1) Although the presiding officer has the responsibility of
10   enforcing the rules, any member who believes he has no-
ticed a case where the chair is failing to do so can, at the
time the breach occurs, call attention to it by making a
Point of Order (**23**); the effect is to require the chair to
make a ruling on the question involved.
15 2) Although the duty of ruling on all questions of parliamentary procedure affecting the assembly's proceedings rests
with the chair, any two members, by moving and seconding an *Appeal* (**24**) immediately after the chair has made
such a ruling, can require him to submit the matter to a
20   vote of the assembly.
3) When it is desired that the assembly take up a question or
do something that would be in violation of a rule that applies, it can be proposed in some cases to *Suspend the Rules*
(**25**) to permit accomplishment of the desired purpose.
25 4) If an original main motion has been made and a member
believes that it would do harm for the motion even to be
discussed in the meeting, he can raise an *Objection to the
Consideration of the Question* (**26**), provided he does so
before debate has begun or any subsidiary motion (other
30   than a motion to *Lay on the Table*) has been stated; the
assembly then votes on whether the main motion shall be
considered (and if there is a two-thirds vote against consideration, the motion is dropped).
5) If a pending main motion (or a pending amendment)
35   contains two or more parts capable of standing as separate

questions, the assembly can vote to treat each part accordingly in succession; such a course is proposed by the motion for *Division of a Question* (**27**).

6) If the main motion is in the form of a resolution or document containing several paragraphs or sections which (although not separate questions) could be most efficiently handled by opening each paragraph or section to amendment one at a time (before the whole is finally voted on), such a procedure can be proposed by the motion for *Consideration by Paragraph or Seriatim* (**28**).

7) If a member doubts the accuracy of the chair's announcement of the result of a voice vote (or even a vote by show of hands)—or doubts that a representative number of persons voted—he can demand a *Division of the Assembly* (**29**); a single member thus has the power to require a standing vote, but not to order a count, which only the chair or the assembly can do (see next item).

8) A member can move that a vote be taken (a) by ballot, (b) by roll call, or (c) by a counted standing vote, especially if a division of the assembly has appeared inconclusive and the chair neglects to order a count. This grouping also includes a motion (d) that the polls be closed or reopened in a ballot vote. All these motions are grouped under the heading of *Motions Relating to Methods of Voting and the Polls* (**30**).

9) If the bylaws or rules of the organization do not prescribe how nominations are to be made, and if the assembly has taken no action to do so prior to an election, any member can move while the election is pending (a) to specify one of various methods by which the candidates shall be nominated; or, if the need arises, (b) to close nominations, or (c) to reopen them; these are the *Motions Relating to Nominations* (**31**).

10) A member may *Request to Be Excused from a Duty* (**32**) if he wishes to be relieved from an obligation imposed upon

1   him by the bylaws or by virtue of some position or office
       he holds.

11) There are several other types of *Requests and Inquiries*
       (**33**) which a member can make in connection with busi-
5   ness that someone desires to introduce, or which is pend-
       ing or has just been pending. These include:

   a) *Parliamentary Inquiry* (a request for the chair's opin-
       ion on a matter of parliamentary procedure as it re-
       lates to the business at hand—not involving a ruling).

10   b) *Request for Information* or, as it is also called, *Point of
       Information* (an inquiry as to facts affecting the busi-
       ness at hand—directed to the chair or, through the
       chair, to a member).

   c) *Request for Permission (or Leave) to Withdraw or Mod-
15   ify a Motion* (after it has been stated by the chair).

   d) *Request to Read Papers.*

   e) *Request for Any Other Privilege.*

       The first two types of inquiry are responded to by the
       chair, or by a member at the direction of the chair;
20   the other requests can be granted only by the assembly.

CONDITIONS UNDER WHICH INCIDENTAL
MOTIONS TAKE PRECEDENCE OVER, OR YIELD
TO, OTHER MOTIONS.   Incidental motions take prece-
25   dence over other motions according to the following principle: *An incidental motion is in order only when it is
legitimately incidental to another pending motion, or when it
is legitimately incidental in some other way to business at
hand* (see p. 69); *it then takes precedence over any other motions
30 that are pending.* Each incidental motion has its own rules
that determine the conditions under which it is incidental—
that is, the motions or situations to which it can be applied,
and the circumstances or stage of consideration at which this
can be done. Usually, but not always, an incidental motion is
35   legitimately incidental to another *pending* motion only while
the other motion is immediately pending.

As stated above, incidental motions have no rank among themselves and cannot be assigned positions within the order of precedence of motions, although they have individual relationships to that order which are described in the sections dealing with these motions (**23–33**). With the exception of a *Division of the Assembly*, incidental motions yield to the privileged motions and generally yield to the motion to *Lay on the Table*, unless the incidental motion arose out of a motion of higher rank than the one to which it would otherwise yield (see also second paragraph below). By the principle stated in the preceding paragraph, an incidental motion yields to any motion legitimately incidental to itself—as all motions do. For example, a motion for a *Division of a Question*, or one to *Suspend the Rules*, would yield to a *Point of Order* arising in connection with itself.

Whenever it is stated in this book that "incidental motions" or "all incidental motions" take precedence over a certain motion, or that a certain motion yields to "all applicable incidental motions," it must be understood that the incidental motions referred to are only those that are legitimately incidental at the time they are made. For example, "Incidental motions always take precedence over the main motion"; but an *Objection to the Consideration of a Question* is legitimate only against an *original* main motion, and the objection is no longer in order after consideration of the question has begun—even though an original main motion is immediately pending (**26**). Similarly, "A *Point of Order* takes precedence over any pending question (of no matter how high a rank) out of which it arises"—but it does so only at the time the breach of order occurs.

In connection with motions that can be incidental to motions of any rank (such as *Point of Order*, *Appeal*, *Suspend the Rules*, *Motions Relating to Voting*, and certain types of *Requests and Inquiries*), whenever it is stated that one of these motions yields to "all motions" above a certain rank, the incidental motion nevertheless does not yield to any motion

1   ranking below the one out of which it arises. For example, "A *Point of Order* yields to the motion to *Lay on the Table*, and to all privileged motions." This statement is true without qualification if the point of order is in connection with a mo-

5   tion ranking lower than *Lay on the Table* (that is, a main motion or any other subsidiary motion); but a point of order arising from a motion to *Recess* would yield only to the two higher-ranking privileged motions—to *Adjourn* and to *Fix the Time to Which to Adjourn*.

10   While a series consisting of a main motion and a number of subsidiary or privileged motions is being considered, it is possible for some of the incidental motions—such as a *Point of Order*, an *Appeal*, or a *Division of the Assembly*—to arise more than once, in connection with different motions in the

15   series.

    INCIDENTAL MAIN MOTIONS CORRESPONDING TO INCIDENTAL MOTIONS. Counterparts of some of the incidental motions may occur as incidental main

20   motions. For example, a *standing rule* (**2**) can be suspended for the duration of a session (**8**); and a motion for such a suspension, made when no business is pending, is an incidental main motion. Similarly, a motion prescribing how nominations shall be made is an incidental main motion if it is moved

25   while no election is pending.

    (Each of the incidental motions is fully discussed in **23–33**.)

    Motions That Bring a Question Again
    Before the Assembly

30

    BASIS OF THIS CLASSIFICATION. Four motions are grouped in this book as *motions that bring a question again before the assembly* since, either by their adoption or by their introduction, they allow the assembly to consider again

35   the merits of a question that has previously been disposed of in some way. All of the motions that bring a question again

before the assembly are usually made—and, like main   *1*
motions, three of them can only be made—while no business
is pending. The existence of these motions as a separate category may be seen as related to the following principles of
parliamentary law: *5*

a) *During the meeting or series of connected meetings (called
    a "session," 8) in which the assembly has decided a question,
    the same or substantially the same question cannot be
    brought up again, except through special procedures.*   *10*
b) *While a question is temporarily disposed of (by any of sev-
    eral methods described in this and later chapters) but is
    not finally settled, no similar or conflicting motion whose
    adoption would restrict the assembly in acting on the first
    question can be introduced.*   *15*
c) *To change what the assembly has adopted requires something
    more (in the way of a vote or previous notice to the members)
    than was necessary to adopt it in the first place.*

The motions that bring a question again before the assembly   *20*
enable the assembly, without violating the above principles,
to reopen a completed question during the same session, or
to take up one that has been temporarily disposed of, or to
change something previously adopted and still in force.

25

LISTING OF INDIVIDUAL MOTIONS IN THIS
CLASS.   The order in which these motions are listed below
has no relation to the order of precedence of motions. The
first three of these motions are either main motions or have
the same low rank as main motions, and the fourth has special   *30*
characteristics relating to rank (see pp. 78–79, 317–18). The
motions that bring a question again before the assembly,
briefly described by function, are as follows:

1) If it is desired to resume consideration of a main motion   *35*
    (along with any series of motions that may be *adhering*

to it—see p. 118) which lies on the table, it can be proposed by means of the motion to *Take from the Table* (**34**) that the motion or series become pending again. (A main motion is said to lie on the table if it was laid on the table earlier in the present session, or in the last previous session with no more than a quarterly time interval having intervened [see pp. 89–90], and it has not yet been finally disposed of.)

2) If it is desired to cancel or countermand an entire main motion, resolution, order, or rule that has been adopted and that has continuing force and effect, such action can be proposed by means of the motion to *Rescind* (or *Repeal*, or *Annul*, **35**); and by another form of the same parliamentary motion—that is, the motion to *Amend Something Previously Adopted* (**35**)—it can be proposed to modify the wording or text previously adopted, or to substitute a different version.

3) If a question has been referred, or a task has been assigned, to a committee that has not yet made its final report, and it is desired to take the matter out of the committee's hands, either so that the assembly itself can consider or act upon it or so that it can be dropped, such action can be proposed by means of the motion to *Discharge a Committee* (**36**).

4) If, in the same session that a motion has been voted on but no later than the same day or the next day on which a business meeting is held, new information or a changed situation makes it appear that a different result might reflect the true will of the assembly, a member who voted with the prevailing side can, by moving to *Reconsider* (**37**) the vote, propose that the question come before the assembly again as if it had not previously been voted on.

RELATIONSHIPS AMONG MOTIONS IN THIS CLASS.   The motions that bring a question again before the

assembly have a number of differences among themselves, *1*
and they may be variously subgrouped depending on the
point of view, as follows:

- The motions to *Take from the Table* and to *Reconsider*— *5*
  and the motion to *Discharge a Committee*, in certain applications—are classed only with the motions that bring a
  question again before the assembly and cannot be satisfactorily placed in any other class. The motion that takes
  the form either to *Rescind* or to *Amend Something Previ-* *10*
  ously Adopted—and the motion to *Discharge a Committee*,
  in its other applications—are incidental main motions having special characteristics, as explained in the next item
  below.

- The motion to *Rescind* or to *Amend Something Previously* *15*
  Adopted is an incidental main motion because (a) it brings
  business before the assembly by its *introduction* and
  (b) when it is voted on, business thereby ceases to be
  pending. By contrast, two other motions in this class—
  Take from the Table and *Reconsider* (as applied to a main *20*
  motion)—do not bring a question again before the
  assembly by their introduction, but by their *adoption*,
  which automatically causes a main question to *become*
  pending. The remaining motion, *Discharge a Committee*,
  either shares this same characteristic with the motions to *25*
  Take from the Table and to *Reconsider*, or else it is in effect
  a particular case of the incidental main motion to *Rescind*
  or to *Amend Something Previously Adopted*—depending
  on whether the matter to be taken out of the committee's
  hands was in the form of a pending motion referred by *30*
  means of the subsidiary motion to *Commit*, or was a task
  assigned to the committee by means of a main motion
  (see pp. 168, 313–14).

- From another point of view, the motion to *Discharge*
  a Committee—even when applied to cause a previously *35*

referred motion to become pending again—is similar to the motion to *Rescind* or to *Amend Something Previously Adopted* in regard to the rules governing its use. Both of these motions have special requirements for their adoption—that is, both require either notice or more than a majority vote (see pp. 306–7, 312).

• Again, the motion to *Discharge a Committee* (as applied to a *motion* that was referred) and the motion to *Take from the Table* have the common feature of proposing that the assembly take up a matter still "within its control" (see pp. 90–91, 340–41) that was *temporarily* disposed of. On the other hand, the motion to *Rescind* or to *Amend Something Previously Adopted* and the motion to *Reconsider* are both applied to a motion that has been finally voted on. However, the latter motions differ from each other in that the motion to *Rescind* or to *Amend Something Previously Adopted* can be applied only to a motion on which the vote was affirmative, and it proposes a specified change in a decision that may have been made at any time previously. By contrast, the motion to *Reconsider* can, with certain exceptions, be applied to a vote that was either affirmative or negative, within a limited time after that vote, and it proposes no specific change in a decision but simply proposes that the original question be reopened.

• The motion to *Reconsider* can be applied to several of the subsidiary, privileged, or incidental motions; and in certain cases when so applied, it assumes the character of a secondary motion—that is, a motion that can be made and considered while other motions are pending. It is the only one of the four motions in this class that can be applied to a secondary motion alone—that is, without also being applied to a related main motion. Because of the time limit on making the motion to *Reconsider*, the *making* of this motion takes precedence over all others (even the

highest-ranking motion in the regular order of precedence *1*
of motions, *Fix the Time to Which to Adjourn*); but its consideration has only the rank of the motion proposed to
be reconsidered. The motion to *Reconsider* thus cannot
always be taken up at the time it is made. This feature of *5*
the motion is one of its unique characteristics.

(Each of the motions that bring a question again before
the assembly is fully discussed in **34–37**.)

10

§7. STANDARD DESCRIPTIVE
CHARACTERISTICS OF MOTIONS

Many of the most important rules governing the use of *15*
the individual motions described in this chapter reduce to
eight *standard descriptive characteristics.* In addition to containing basic rules of procedure for each motion, these characteristics serve as points of comparison showing how the
motion resembles or differs from a main motion. *20*
The standard descriptive characteristics of a motion are
the following:

1. Over what motions, if any, it takes precedence (that is,
   what motions can be pending without causing this mo- *25*
   tion to be out of order); also, to what motions it yields
   (that is, what motions can be made and considered while
   this motion is pending). (The main motion, ranking lowest, takes precedence over no other motion and yields to
   all subsidiary motions, all privileged motions, and all *30*
   applicable incidental motions.)
2. To what motions or to what type of situation it is
   applicable; also, what motions, particularly subsidiary
   motions, are applicable to it, if any. (The main motion is
   applicable to no other motion; and all subsidiary motions, *35*

and certain incidental motions under various conditions, are applicable to it.)

3. Whether it is in order when another has the floor. (A main motion is not.)

4. Whether it requires a second. (A main motion does. Whenever it is stated in this book that a certain motion "must" be seconded, or "requires" a second, the precise meaning is as explained on pp. 35–37, and the requirement does not apply when the motion is made by direction of a board or committee.)

5. Whether it is debatable—that is, whether debate on its merits is permitted while it is immediately pending. (A main motion is.)

6. Whether it is amendable. (A main motion is.)

7. What vote is required for its adoption. (A main motion requires a majority vote, except as noted on pp. 103–4.)

8. Whether it can be reconsidered. (A main motion can.)

The standard descriptive characteristics of the main motion are more fully stated in **10**, and those of the other parliamentary motions are given in **11–37**. In addition, key facts with regard to Standard Descriptive Characteristics 1 and 2 are shown in Chart I, tinted pages 3–5, and with regard to Standard Descriptive Characteristics 3 through 8 are shown in Chart II, tinted pages 6–29.

Additional background for the detailed treatment of the motions in **10–37** is provided by the discussion of the topics "meeting" and "session" in **8** and **9**.

CHAPTER
IV

MEETING AND SESSION

§8. MEETING, SESSION, RECESS, ADJOURNMENT

Explanation of Terms

In an assembly, as alluded to above on pages 2 and 25, each event of the members' being assembled to transact business constitutes a separate *meeting*; but the complete unit of engagement in proceedings by the assembly is a *session*, which (in the general case covering all types of assemblies) consists of one or more connected meetings. The term *session* is a fundamental concept entering into many important parliamentary rules.

In parliamentary law and as understood in this book, the terms defined below have distinct meanings:

- A *meeting* of an assembly is a single official gathering of its members in one room or area to transact business for a length of time during which there is no cessation of proceedings and the members do not separate, unless for a short *recess,* as defined below. (For modification of the "one-room-or-area" requirement when the bylaws authorize electronic meetings, see pp. 97–99.) Depending on the business to be transacted, a meeting may last from a few minutes to several hours.

- A *session* of an assembly, unless otherwise defined by the bylaws or governing rules of the particular organization or body, is a meeting or series of connected meetings devoted to a single order of business, program, agenda, or announced purpose, in which—when there is more than one meeting—each succeeding meeting is scheduled with a view to continuing business at the point where it was left off at the previous meeting (see also discussion of distinction between recess and adjournment, p. 85).

- A *recess,* strictly speaking, is a short intermission or break within a meeting that does not end the meeting or destroy its continuity as a single gathering, and after which proceedings are immediately resumed at the point where they were interrupted. During the recess, members may leave the hall or room in which the meeting is being held, but they are expected to remain nearby. A recess frequently has a purpose connected with the business of the meeting itself—such as to count ballots, to permit consultation among members, or the like. (For the motion to *Recess,* see **20**.)

- A meeting is said to *stand at ease* if the chair, without objection, simply permits a brief pause, without a declaration of recess. In such a case there is technically no interruption of the meeting, and members remain in their places. Quiet conversation among neighboring members may take place, but it must cease immediately when the chair declares the meeting again in order or any member objects to continuing to stand at ease.

- An *adjournment* (that is, the act of the assembly's adjourning) terminates a meeting; it may also end the session. If another meeting to continue the same business or order of business has been set for a definite time (or to be "at the call of the chair"), the adjournment does not end the session. (See also pp. 93–94 for the use of the word *adjournment* as applied to an *adjourned meeting*; for the motion to *Adjourn* see **21**.)

• The term *adjournment sine die** (or *adjournment without day*) usually refers to the close of a session of several meetings: (a) where the adjournment dissolves the assembly— as in a series of mass meetings or in an annual or biennial convention for which the delegates are separately chosen for each convention; or (b) where, unless called into special session, the body will not be convened again until a time prescribed by the bylaws or constitution—as in the case of a session of a legislature. In cases where the words *sine die* are applicable, they may be, but are not always, mentioned in the motion to adjourn or the chair's declaration of the adjournment.

Interrelation of the Concepts

NUMBER OF MEETINGS IN A SESSION. The length of a session or the number of meetings included within it varies depending on the type of assembly.

In a permanent society whose bylaws provide for regular weekly, monthly, or quarterly meetings that go through an established order of business in a single afternoon or evening, each "meeting" of this kind normally completes a separate session—unless the assembly at such a meeting schedules an *adjourned meeting* as explained on pages 93–94. This rule is the common parliamentary law and holds except where the bylaws provide otherwise. Although any society has the right to define, in its bylaws, what shall constitute a session of the

---

*Pronounced SIGN-ee- DYE-ee.

1   organization, it is usually unwise in ordinary societies to adopt
    a rule making regular sessions last over a long period of time.
    Such a rule would make it possible for the hands of the or-
    ganization to be tied during that time, since the same ques-
5   tion cannot be brought up again during the same session after
    it is too late to reconsider (**37**) a vote that has finally disposed
    of a motion without adopting it (that is, a vote that has
    rejected or indefinitely postponed it or has sustained an ob-
    jection to its consideration; see **11**, **26**).
10   In the case of a state or national organization that holds
    annual or biennial conventions, each convention constitutes
    a session of the organization—having one agenda or pro-
    gram—which may be broken up into separate meetings in the
    morning, afternoon, and evening, or into many meetings held
15 over several days. In Congress a session may comprise hun-
    dreds of almost daily meetings, sometimes continuing for
    nearly a year.

    DEPARTURE FROM PARLIAMENTARY MEAN-
20 INGS IN ORDINARY SPEECH.   Because of the fact that
    a meeting and a session usually coincide in ordinary local so-
    cieties or branches, these two terms often tend to become
    confused or used interchangeably in everyday speech. When-
    ever either word is used, the context should be noted in the
25 light of the explanations in this section. A similar situation
    exists regarding the terms *recess, adjournment,* and *adjourn-
    ment sine die.* It is common, especially in conventions, to hear
    the word *recess* also applied to a longer break that *does* termi-
    nate a meeting and that consequently should be understood
30 as an adjournment, as in "to recess until tomorrow." On the
    other hand, assemblies sometimes "adjourn" or provide in
    the program or agenda for an "adjournment" when only a
    short recess is intended. The use of the word *recess* to describe
    the interval between regular sessions of an organization or
35 assembly, as in "the summer recess of Congress," is a collo-

quialism that has no relationship to the parliamentary meaning of the term. *1*

COMPARATIVE EFFECTS OF RECESS AND ADJOURNMENT WITHIN A SESSION. The distinction between *recess* and *adjournment* may in some cases become thin so that it must be judged in the individual context. For example, according to the definitions given above, a break in the proceedings of a convention for lunch may be more in the nature of a recess, or of an adjournment, depending *10* on the time and the extent of dispersion of the members that is required for them to be served. From the viewpoint of the effect of a recess or an adjournment on the procedure the next time the assembly is called to order, the difference is that at the conclusion of a recess there never are any "opening" *15* proceedings, but business is always immediately resumed where it was left off, just as if there had been no recess. At the beginning of any meeting (after the first meeting in a session), on the other hand, the resumption of business at the point where it was left off may be, but is not necessarily, pre- *20* ceded by brief opening ceremonies and the reading of minutes. Normally in a session lasting several days, the minutes are read at the beginning of the first meeting each day; and the beginning of a later meeting the same day may be virtually indistinguishable from the conclusion of a recess.* *25*

HOW MEETINGS TO CONTINUE A SESSION ARE SCHEDULED. When a meeting adjourns without ending the session, this necessarily means that the time for another meeting to continue the same business or order of business *30* has already been set (or that provision has been made for such

---

*If the assembly recesses rather than adjourns, that may preclude certain motions to *Suspend the Rules* (see "Renewal of the Motion," p. 262) and to *Reconsider and Enter on the Minutes* (see p. 334, ll. 11–16).

1 a meeting to be held "at the call of the chair"). The time or
provision for this next meeting of the session may have been
established by one of the following methods (which are listed
in order of frequency of occurrence): (a) through a program
5 adopted at the beginning of a convention; (b) by the adoption in the present meeting of a motion (main or privileged,
depending on when it is moved) to fix the time to which to
adjourn; or (c) by a specification in the motion to adjourn, *if*
that motion was made as a main motion while no other ques-
10 tion was pending.

ORDINARY PRACTICE IN ADJOURNING.   In ordi-
nary practice a meeting is closed by adopting a motion simply
"to adjourn"; or under certain conditions the chair can declare
15 the adjournment without a motion, as explained on pages
240–41. The society meets again at the time provided in its
bylaws or other rules, or as already established by the adoption
of an earlier motion. If it does not expect to convene until the
next "regular meeting" prescribed by rule or bylaw, the chair
20 declares that the meeting "is adjourned," and such an adjournment closes the session. On the other hand, if another meeting
in the same session has been scheduled by any of the methods
listed in the preceding paragraph, the chair announces the time
as he declares the adjournment, saying, for example, that the
25 "meeting is adjourned until 4 P.M. tomorrow."

In the event of fire, riot, or other extreme emergency, if
the chair believes taking time for a vote on adjourning would
be dangerous to those present, he should declare the meeting
adjourned—to a suitable time and place for an adjourned
30 meeting (if he is able), or to meet at the call of the chair.

Significance of Session

The principal significance of the session as a complete unit
35 of an assembly's engagement in proceedings lies in the free-

dom of each new session, as contrasted with the limitations   *1*
placed upon a session in progress by decisions it has made.
Some of the consequences of this characteristic of the session
are described in the following paragraphs.

5

FREEDOM OF EACH NEW SESSION.   As a general
rule, one session cannot place a question beyond the reach of
a majority at a later session except through the process
of adopting a special rule of order or an amendment to the
bylaws (either of which requires more than a majority vote;   *10*
see immediately below). It is improper, for example, to postpone anything beyond the next regular session—which would
be an attempt to prevent that session from considering the
question. The principle stated applies in qualified form to
cases in which a majority rescinds or amends something   *15*
adopted at an earlier session, or discharges a committee from
further consideration of a question referred to it at an earlier
session—which a majority can do provided that previous no
tice was given. (See p. 306, l. 24 to p. 307, l. 12 and p. 312,
ll. 3–15 for the vote required for these actions without previ-   *20*
ous notice.)

RELATION OF A SESSION'S FREEDOM TO THE
RULES OF AN ORGANIZATION.   The application of
the same principle to the case of *standing rules* (which, as the   *25*
term is understood in this book, do not deal with parliamentary procedure; see **2**) is as follows: Although a standing rule
can be adopted by a majority vote at any session and continues in force until it is rescinded or amended, such a rule does
not interfere materially with the freedom of a later session,   *30*
since it can be suspended for the duration of any session (but
not for longer) by a majority vote.
   Bylaws, on the other hand—and *special rules of order*,
which *do* deal with parliamentary procedure—contain the
provisions that are expected to have stability from session to   *35*

1　session, and to represent the judgment of the whole society
as distinguished from the members voting at any particular
session. These rules therefore require both previous notice
and a two-thirds vote for amendment (with a vote of a major-
5　ity of the entire membership as an allowable alternative); and
rules of order require a two-thirds vote for suspension, while
bylaws normally cannot be suspended (see **2, 25**).

RELATION OF A SESSION'S FREEDOM TO THE
10　RENEWABILITY OF MOTIONS.　The conditions under
which a motion can be *renewed*—that is, can be introduced
as if new after having previously been made and disposed of
without adoption—are closely related to the freedom of each
new session, and to the distinction between a meeting and a
15　session. As stated in **38** and on page 84, the same or substantially the same question cannot be brought up a second time
during the same session except by means of the parliamentary
motions that bring a question again before the assembly. At
any later session, on the other hand, any motion that is still
20　applicable can normally be renewed unless it has *come over
from the previous session* (by one of the five processes mentioned on pp. 90–91 under *Regular Meeting*, below) as *not
finally disposed of* (see also **38**, where the renewal of motions
is fully discussed).

25

RELATION OF A SESSION'S FREEDOM TO LIMI-
TATION ON APPOINTMENT AS CHAIRMAN PRO
TEM.　If the assembly is to elect a chairman pro tem to hold
office beyond the current session (in the event of illness or
30　disability of both the regular presiding officer and his alternate), notice must be given at the preceding meeting or in
the call of the meeting that elects him. One session cannot
interfere with the freedom of each new session to choose its
own chairman pro tem except by an election held with previ-
35　ous notice (pp. 121–24).

§9. PARTICULAR TYPES
OF BUSINESS MEETINGS

Regular Meeting

The term *regular meeting* (or *stated meeting*) refers to the periodic business meeting of a permanent society, local branch, or board, held at weekly, monthly, quarterly, or similar intervals, for which the day (as, "the first Tuesday of each month") should be prescribed by the bylaws and the hour and place should be fixed by a standing rule. If, instead, an organization follows the practice of scheduling the dates of its regular meetings by resolution, notice must be sent to all members in advance of each regular meeting, and the number of days' notice required should be prescribed by the bylaws (p. 576).

When notice is required to be sent, unless a different standard is specified that requirement is met if written notice is sent to each member either:

a) by postal mail to the member's last known address; or
b) by a form of electronic communication, such as e-mail or fax, by which the member has agreed to receive notice.

Each regular meeting normally completes a separate session, as explained on pages 83–84 (see *Adjourned Meeting*, pp. 93–94 below, however). Some societies have frequent meetings for social or cultural purposes at which business may be transacted, and also hold a session every month or quarter especially for business. In such societies, the term *regular meeting* applies particularly to the regular business session.

Important rules relating to the continuance of a question from one session to the next depend on whether *no more than a quarterly time interval* intervenes between the two sessions. In this book, it is understood that no more than a quarterly time interval intervenes between two sessions if the second session begins at any time during or before the third calendar month after the calendar month in which the first session ends. For example, with reference to a session held in January, no more than a quarterly time interval has elapsed since the previous session if that session ended on or after October 1st of the preceding calendar year; and no more than a quarterly time interval will elapse before the next session if that session will begin on or before April 30th of the current year.

If two business sessions are separated by *more than a quarterly time interval*—or if the term of a specified portion of the membership expires before the start of the later session (as may happen in an elected legislative assembly or in a board)—then business can go over from the earlier session to the later one only by means of referral to a committee (**13**).

If two consecutive regular business sessions are separated by *no more than a quarterly time interval*, then—provided that there is no specified portion of the membership whose term expires before the start of the later session—there are several ways in which business can go over from the earlier session to the later one:*

1) by being postponed to, or otherwise set as a general or special order for, the later session (see **14, 41**);
2) by being laid on the table (**17**) at the earlier session and not taken from the table (**34**) before that session adjourns;

---

*It should be noted that if some, but not all, of an organization's regular business sessions are separated by no more than quarterly time intervals, it is only between meetings which are that close together that a question can go over from one session to the next by any means other than referral to a committee. If a society holds regular monthly business meetings from September through May, for example, but does not meet during the summer, a question can be postponed until the next meeting at any of the meetings from September through April, but such a question cannot be postponed at the May meeting until the September meeting.

3) by going over to the later session as unfinished business or as an unfinished special order (see pp. 236–37, 356–59);
4) by being the subject of a motion to *Reconsider* (**37**) that is not finally disposed of at the earlier session; and
5) by being referred to a committee (**13**) that can report at the later session.

The only way for business to be carried over directly from one session to some later regular session *beyond* the next regular business session is by being referred to a committee that will report at that later session.

When a question is carried over from one session to another by any of the above processes, it remains *within the control of the assembly* as a question that has been *temporarily, but not finally, disposed of.*

Any business that falls within the objects of the society as defined in its bylaws (or, in the case of a board, any business within the authority of the board) can be transacted at any regular meeting (provided that the parliamentary rules relating to action already taken, or to matters not finally disposed of and remaining within the control of the assembly, are complied with in cases where they apply; compare pp. 110–13; see also **35** and **38**).

Special Meeting

A *special meeting* (or *called meeting*) is a separate session of a society held at a time different from that of any regular meeting, and convened only to consider one or more items of business specified in the call of the meeting. Notice of the time, place, and purpose of the meeting, clearly and specifically describing the subject matter of the motions or items of business to be brought up, must be sent to all members a reasonable number of days in advance. The reason for special

meetings is to deal with matters that may arise between regular meetings and that require action by the society before
the next regular meeting, or to dedicate an entire session to
one or more particular matters.* As in the case of a regular
meeting, the session of a special meeting in an ordinary society is normally concluded in a single meeting, unless the
assembly at the special meeting schedules an adjourned meeting (see below).

Special meetings can properly be called only (a) as authorized in the bylaws (see p. 576); or (b) when authorized by
the assembly itself, as part of formal disciplinary procedures,
for purposes of conducting a trial and determining a punishment (see footnote, p. 661). A section of the bylaws that
authorizes the calling of special meetings should prescribe:

1) by whom such a meeting is to be called—which provision
   is usually in the form of a statement that the president (or,
   in large organizations, the president with the approval of
   the board) can call a special meeting, and that he shall call
   a special meeting at the written request of a specific number of members; and
2) the number of days' notice required. Unless otherwise
   provided in the bylaws, the number of days is computed
   by counting all calendar days (including holidays and
   weekends), excluding the day of the meeting but including the day the notice is sent.

The president directs the secretary to send the notice of the
special meeting to all members at the society's expense in
compliance with the bylaws no later than the required num-

---

*When a special meeting intervenes between two regular meetings, that
does not affect the rules governing whether and how business can go over
from the earlier regular meeting to the later regular meeting.

ber of days in advance, making sure that it contains all the necessary information.

The only business that can be transacted at a special meeting is that which has been specified in the call of the meeting. This rule, however, does not preclude the consideration of privileged motions, or of any subsidiary, incidental, or other motions that may arise in connection with the transaction of such business or the conduct of the meeting. If, at a special meeting, action is taken relating to business not mentioned in the call, that action, to become valid, must be ratified (see pp. 124–25) by the organization at a regular meeting (or at another special meeting properly called for that purpose).

The requirement that business transacted at a special meeting be specified in the call should not be confused with a requirement that previous notice of a motion be given. Although the call of a special meeting must state the purpose of the meeting, it need not give the exact content of individual motions that will be considered. When a main motion related to business specified in the call of a special meeting is pending, it is as fully open to germane amendment as if it had been moved at a regular meeting.

Adjourned Meeting

An *adjourned meeting* is a meeting in continuation of the session of the immediately preceding regular or special meeting. The name *adjourned meeting* means that the meeting is scheduled for a particular time (and place, if it is not otherwise established) by the assembly's "adjourning to" or "adjourning until" that time and place. If a regular meeting or a special meeting is unable to complete its work, an adjourned meeting can be scheduled for later the same day or some other convenient time before the next regular meeting, by the adoption (as applicable) of a main or a privileged motion to fix the time to which to adjourn, or a main motion to

1 adjourn until the specified time (see **21**, **22**). In such a case, the adjourned meeting is sometimes spoken of as "an adjournment of" the regular or special meeting. This usage should not be confused with the act of adjourning.

5 　　When common expressions such as "regular [or "stated"] meeting," "special [or "called"] meeting," and "annual meeting" (see below) are used in the bylaws, rules, or resolutions adopted by an organization, the word *meeting* is understood to mean *session* in the parliamentary sense, and therefore *10* covers all adjourned meetings.

　　An adjourned meeting takes up its work at the point where it was interrupted in the order of business or in the consideration of the question that was postponed to the adjourned meeting, except that the minutes of the preceding *15* meeting are first read.

Annual Meeting

　　The term *annual meeting* is used in two senses.

20 　　Certain types of societies may hold only one business meeting of the general membership each year, perhaps leaving the management of the organization's affairs in the meantime to a board. Such a meeting is then the annual meeting of the society.

25 　　In local organizations that hold regular business meetings throughout the year, however, the bylaws may provide that one of these regular meetings held at a specified time each year shall be known as the annual meeting. The only difference between this kind of annual meeting and the other *30* regular meetings is that the annual reports of officers and standing committees, the election of officers, and any other items of business that the bylaws may prescribe for the annual meeting are in order, besides the ordinary business that may come up. The minutes of the previous regular meeting are *35* read and approved as usual at the annual meeting, and the

minutes of the annual meeting are read and approved at the   *1*
next regular meeting. Minutes of one annual meeting should
not be held for action until the next one a year later.

Business that is required to be attended to "at the annual
meeting" can be taken up at any time (when it is in order)   *5*
during the session of the annual meeting, or, in other words,
either at that meeting as originally convened or at any
adjournment of it. If such an item of business has actually
been taken up as required during the session of the annual
meeting, it may also be postponed beyond that session in ac-   *10*
cordance with the regular rules for the motion to *Postpone*
(see **14**, especially p. 185).

Executive Session

15

An *executive session* in general parliamentary usage has
come to mean any meeting of a deliberative assembly, or a
portion of a meeting, at which the proceedings are secret.
This term originally referred to the consideration of executive
business—that is, presidential nominations to appointive   *20*
offices, and treaties—behind closed doors in the United
States Senate. The practice of organizations operating under
the lodge system is equivalent to holding all regular meetings
in executive session. In any society, certain matters relating
to discipline (**61, 63**), such as trials, must be handled only in   *25*
executive session. A meeting enters into executive session only
when required by rule or established custom, or upon the
adoption of a motion to do so. A motion to go into executive session is a question of privilege (**19**), and therefore is
adopted by a majority vote.   *30*

Whenever a meeting is being held in executive session,
only members of the body that is meeting, special invitees,
and such employees or staff members as the body or its rules
may determine to be necessary are allowed to remain in the
hall. Thus, in the case of a board or committee meeting being   *35*

held in executive session, all persons—whether or not they are members of the organization—who are not members of the board or committee (and who are not otherwise specifically invited or entitled to attend) are excluded from the meeting.

A member of a society can be punished under disciplinary procedure if he violates the secrecy of an executive session. Anyone else permitted to be present is honor-bound not to divulge anything that occurred. The minutes, or record of proceedings, of an executive session must be read and acted upon only in executive session, unless that which would be reported in the minutes—that is, the action taken, as distinct from that which was said in debate—was not secret, or secrecy has been lifted by the assembly. When the minutes of an executive session must be considered for approval at an executive session held solely for that purpose, the brief minutes of the latter meeting are, or are assumed to be, approved by that meeting.

Public Session

A deliberative assembly or committee is normally entitled to determine whether nonmembers may attend or be excluded from its meetings (even when not in executive session). Many public and semipublic bodies, however, are governed by sunshine laws—that is, their meetings must be open to the public. Normally, such laws have no application to private, nongovernmental bodies.

In meetings of many public bodies, such as school boards, the public may attend. Similarly, in some private organizations such as church councils, parishioners may be permitted to attend. These attendees are not members of the meeting body and ordinarily have no right to participate. Some bodies, especially public ones, may invite nonmembers to express their views, but this is done under the control of the presiding

officer subject to any relevant rules adopted by the body and *1*
subject to appeal by a member. Often, by rule or practice,
time limits are placed on speakers and relevance is closely
monitored.

5

Electronic Meetings

EXTENSION OF PARLIAMENTARY LAW TO ELEC-
TRONIC MEETINGS.   Except as authorized *in the bylaws*,
the business of an organization or board can be validly trans- *10*
acted only at a regular or properly called *meeting*—that is, as
defined on pages 81–82, a single official gathering in one
room or area—of the assembly of its members at which a quorum is present.

Among some organizations, there is an increasing prefer- *15*
ence, especially in the case of a relatively small board or other
assembly, to transact business at *electronic meetings*—that is,
at meetings at which, rather than all participating members
being physically present in one room or area as in traditional
(or "face-to-face") meetings, some or all of them communi- *20*
cate with the others through electronic means such as the
Internet or by telephone. A group that holds such alternative
meetings does not lose its character as a deliberative assembly
(see pp. 1–2) so long as the meetings provide, at a minimum,
conditions of opportunity for simultaneous aural communi- *25*
cation among all participating members equivalent to those
of meetings held in one room or area. Under such conditions,
an electronic meeting that is properly authorized in the bylaws is treated as though it were a meeting at which all the
members who are participating are actually present. *30*

If electronic meetings are to be authorized, it is advisable
to adopt additional rules pertaining to their conduct (see
Additional Rules for the Conduct of Electronic Meetings,
below).

TYPES OF ELECTRONIC MEETINGS.   Various provisions for electronic meetings are possible, so that more than the minimum standard of an audioconference may be required. Thus, if the bylaws provide for meeting by videoconference (but not merely by "teleconference" or "audioconference"), the meeting must be conducted by a technology that allows all participating members to see each other, as well as to hear each other, at the same time. Provision may also be made for the use of additional collaborative technology to aid in the conduct of a meeting.

It is important to understand that, regardless of the technology used, the opportunity for simultaneous aural communication is essential to the deliberative character of the meeting. Therefore, a group that attempts to conduct the deliberative process in writing (such as by postal mail, e-mail, "chat rooms," or fax)—which is not recommended—does not constitute a deliberative assembly. Any such effort may achieve a consultative character, but it is foreign to the deliberative process as understood under parliamentary law.

ELECTRONIC MEETINGS IN COMMITTEES.   As in the case of a board or any assembly, committees that are expressly established by the bylaws can hold a valid electronic meeting only if authorized in the bylaws to do so. A committee that is not expressly established by the bylaws, however, may instead be authorized by a standing rule of the parent body or organization, or by the motion establishing the particular committee, to hold electronic meetings.

ADDITIONAL RULES FOR THE CONDUCT OF ELECTRONIC MEETINGS.   If an organization authorizes its assembly, boards, or committees to hold electronic meetings, such a provision should indicate whether members who are not present in person have the *right* to participate by electronic means, or whether the body may choose to allow

or disallow such participation; and, conversely, whether there *1*
is required to be a central location for members who wish to
attend meetings in person. The notice of an electronic meeting must include an adequate description of how to participate in it (for example, the telephone number to call for a *5*
teleconference must be provided). Various additional rules
(in the bylaws, special rules of order, standing rules, or instructions to a committee, as appropriate) may also be necessary or advisable regarding the conduct of electronic
meetings, such as rules relating to: *10*

- the type of equipment or computer software required for
  participation in meetings, whether the organization must
  provide such equipment or software, and contingencies
  for technical difficulties or malfunctions; *15*
- methods for determining the presence of a quorum;
- the conditions under which a member may raise a point
  of order doubting the presence of a quorum, and the conditions under which the continued presence of a quorum
  is presumed if no such point of order is raised; *20*
- methods for seeking recognition and obtaining the floor;
- means by which motions may be submitted in writing
  during a meeting; and
- methods for taking and verifying votes.

25

In addition, depending on the character of the organization,
it may be advisable to adopt provisions for ensuring that nonmembers cannot participate in meetings (unless properly invited to do so), especially during any meeting or portion of a
meeting held in executive session. *30*

§10. THE MAIN MOTION

As explained in **3–6**, a *main motion* is a motion whose introduction brings business before the assembly; such a motion can be made only while no other motion is pending.

Distinction Between Original Main and Incidental Main Motions

The division of main motions into *original* and *incidental* main motions was mentioned in **6** and is discussed below.

An *original main motion* is a main motion that introduces a substantive question as a new subject. This is the motion most often used, and is the basic device by which a matter is presented to the assembly for possible action, as "... that the Club contribute $50 to the centennial celebration"; or "... that the Society go on record as favoring the Popular Run route for the proposed new beltway"; or "... to adopt the following resolution: '*Resolved*, That the Northridge Improvement Association oppose a municipal tax increase at this time.'" It may be more suitable for an original main motion

to be made orally, or to be submitted in writing, depending *1*
on its length, complexity, or importance. (See *Making a
Motion*, p. 33, where many of the statements apply especially
to original main motions.)

An *incidental main motion* is a main motion that is inci- *5*
dental to or relates to the business of the assembly, or its past
or future action. Such a motion is distinguished by the following characteristics:

1) It proposes an action specifically defined under parlia- *10*
   mentary law and described by a particular parliamentary
   term. There are thus a definite number of incidental main
   motions somewhat as in the case of the secondary motions (subsidiary, privileged, and incidental) and the
   motions that bring a question again before the assembly. *15*
2) It does *not* mark the beginning of a particular involvement of the assembly in a substantive matter, as an original main motion does. (Like all main motions, however,
   it can be made only when nothing is pending, and it
   brings business before the assembly.) Action that can be *20*
   proposed by the incidental main motions may relate:
   (a) to further steps in dealing with a substantive matter
   in which the assembly's involvement has begun earlier; or
   (b) to procedure, without direct reference to a particular
   substantive item of business. *25*

An incidental main motion involving a subject already
entered into might be a motion to *adopt* recommendations
which a committee has prepared upon instructions (not relating to a referred *motion*), or a motion to *ratify* action taken *30*
at a meeting when no quorum was present. An example of
an incidental main motion relating to procedure without reference to an item of business would be a motion to take a
recess, made when no business is pending, or a motion to
place a special *limit* on the length of speeches throughout a *35*

1 meeting. In each of the examples just mentioned, the itali-
cized word—*adopt, ratify, limit, recess*—is the parliamentary
term that describes the motion.

An incidental main motion is usually made orally. The
5 chief difference in the rules governing original and incidental
main motions is that an *Objection to the Consideration of a
Question* (**26**) can be applied only to original main and not
to incidental main motions. The reason is that, in the case of
an incidental main motion dealing with a subject previously
10 entered into, the involvement has already begun and it is
too late to object; and in the case of an incidental main motion involving only procedure, an objection to its consideration has no legitimate purpose. In conventions, incidental
main motions are not referred to a resolutions committee
15 (pp. 633ff.).

Most of the incidental main motions closely correspond
to secondary (subsidiary, privileged, or incidental) motions
described by the same or similar names—as in the last two of
the four examples above. (Compare the subsidiary motion to
20 *Limit or Extend Limits of Debate*, **15**, and the privileged motion to *Recess*, **20**.) Referring to the Table of Rules Relating
to Motions on tinted pages 6–29, most of the motions listed
as "main"—with the exception of No. 1 (original main motion)—are incidental main motions in their usual application.
25 The motions to *adopt* and to *ratify* are briefly discussed at the
end of this chapter.

Standard Descriptive Characteristics

30 A main motion:

1. Takes precedence of nothing—that is, it cannot be moved
when any other question is pending. It yields to all subsidiary, all privileged, and all applicable incidental mo-
35 tions; that is, any subsidiary or privileged motion, and any
incidental motion that is applicable in the particular case

at the particular time, can be moved while a main motion *1*
is pending.

2. Can be applied to no other motion. All subsidiary motions can be applied to it. If it is postponed to a certain
time or laid on the table, it carries with it any subsidiary *5*
motions that may also be pending. If it is referred to a
committee, the only subsidiary motions that it carries with
it to the committee are pending amendments (so that a
motion to *Postpone Indefinitely*, if pending, is dropped).
An *Objection to the Consideration of a Question* can be *10*
applied only to an original main motion, not to an incidental main motion.

3. Is out of order when another has the floor.

4. Must be seconded.

5. Is debatable. *15*

6. Is amendable.

7. Requires a majority vote, except:
   a) when the motion proposes an action for which the
      bylaws or special rules of order prescribe a require-
      ment of more than a majority vote (such as a two- *20*
      thirds vote, or previous notice [pp. 121–24], or both).
      For example, the bylaws of some organizations require
      greater than a majority vote for motions proposing
      admission to membership, the purchase or sale of real
      estate, etc.; *25*
   b) when adoption of the motion would have the effect
      of suspending a rule of order or a parliamentary right
      of members, in which case it requires a two-thirds
      vote—as, for example, a motion to place a special limit
      on the length or number of speeches per member dur- *30*
      ing a meeting or a session; or
   c) when adoption of the motion would have the effect
      of changing something already adopted, as in a mo-
      tion to postpone an event previously scheduled by
      vote of the assembly, or to discharge a committee *35*
      (from an uncompleted task previously assigned to it

by means of a main motion, before the committee is
ready to report)—in which case the vote required
is as stated on pages 306–7 under Standard Characteristic 7 of the motion that takes the form either to
Rescind or to *Amend Something Previously Adopted.*

8. Can be reconsidered. (See, however, Standard Characteristic 8 of the motion that takes the form either to *Rescind*
or to *Amend Something Previously Adopted,* p. 307; with
reference to the adoption of bylaws, see p. 559, ll. 25–27,
and p. 592, ll. 18–19.)

The Framing of Main Motions

WORDING OF A MAIN MOTION.   If a main motion
is adopted, it becomes the officially recorded statement of an
action taken by the assembly. A motion should therefore be
worded in a concise, unambiguous, and complete form appropriate to such a purpose. It cannot employ language that
is not allowed in debate (**43**). A member making a motion
embodying something that has just been said by the chair or
another member in informal consultation during a meeting
should avoid statements such as "I so move," and should
himself recite the complete motion that he offers.

Motions to "reaffirm" a position previously taken by
adopting a motion or resolution are not in order. Such a motion serves no useful purpose because the original motion is
still in effect; also, possible attempts to amend a motion to
reaffirm would come into conflict with the rules for the motion to *Amend Something Previously Adopted* (**35**); and if such
a motion to reaffirm failed, it would create an ambiguous situation.

A motion whose only effect is to propose that the assembly *refrain* from doing something should not be offered if
the same result can be accomplished by offering no motion
at all. It is incorrect, for example, to move "that no response
be made" to a request for a contribution to a fund, or "that

our delegates be given no instructions," unless some purpose   *1*
would be served by adoption of such a motion. This could
be the case, for example, if the membership of an organization wishes to make certain that a subordinate body, such as
its executive board, will not take such action at a later date,   *5*
or if the motion expresses an opinion or reason as to why no
action should be taken.

It is preferable to avoid a motion containing a negative
statement even in cases where the effect of the motion is to
propose that something be done, since members may become   *10*
confused as to the effect of voting for or against such a motion. Rather than moving, for example, that the association
go on record as "not in favor of the proposed public bond
issue," it should be moved that the association "oppose" or
"declare its opposition to" the bond issue. In this connection,   *15*
it should be noted that voting down a motion or resolution
that would express a particular opinion is not the same as
adopting a motion expressing the opposite opinion, since—
if the motion is voted down—neither opinion has been expressed. A member may be in complete agreement with the   *20*
views contained in such a resolution yet feel that his organization should not speak out on the matter, and he might
therefore vote against the resolution.

MOTIONS SUBMITTED IN WRITING; RESOLU-   *25*
TIONS.   As previously stated, a main motion—particularly
an original main motion—is frequently offered as a *resolution*,
either because of its importance or because of its length or
complexity. Any resolution—and any long or complicated motion, whether cast as a resolution or not—should always be   *30*
submitted in writing as described on page 33. In preparing an
important written motion or resolution (which should be
done in advance of the meeting if possible), it is often advisable
to consult with members who can be of assistance in perfecting it, and also with those whose support is likely to be neces-   *35*
sary for its adoption. If such a motion is not offered as a

resolution, it can simply be written out in the form in which it would be moved orally (beginning with the word "That"); for example, "That the Merchants' Association sponsor an essay contest open to high school students of the city, to be conducted according to the following specifications: ...." If put in the form of a resolution, the preceding example would be written, "*Resolved*, That the Merchants' Association sponsor an essay contest ...." In a resolution, the name of the adopting organization can also be made a part of the enacting words, as in "*Resolved by the International Benevolent Association in convention assembled*, That ...."

The form in which a main motion is written does not determine in any way what must be referred to a "resolutions committee," nor does it affect the form of the motions reported by such a committee (see, for example, "platform," pp. 636–37).

An example of a simple resolution expressing an opinion or position of an organized society is given on page 100, lines 19–21. If the resolution is offered in a mass meeting (or in any meeting where there is no established organization whose act the adopted resolution would become), it may begin, "*Resolved*, That it is the sense of this meeting that ..." A resolution can consist of more than one resolving clause, as in the following example:

> *Resolved*, That it is the sense of this meeting that the existing zoning ordinance should undergo a general revision; and
> *Resolved*, That the Secretary be requested to send a copy of this resolution, and of the report already presented at this meeting, to the Mayor and to each member of the City Council.

USE OF A PREAMBLE.   It is usually inadvisable to attempt to include reasons for a motion's adoption within the

motion itself. To do so may encumber the motion and may
weigh against its adoption—since some members who approve of the action it proposes may dislike voting for it if it
states reasons with which they disagree. When special circumstances make it desirable to include a brief statement of
background, the motion should be cast in the form of a
resolution, with the background or reasons incorporated in
a *preamble* that is placed before the resolving clauses. A
preamble consists of one or more clauses beginning
"Whereas, ..." *It should be emphasized that neither rule nor
custom requires a resolution to have a preamble, and one should
not be used merely for the sake of form.* In general, the use of a
preamble should be limited to cases where it provides little-
known information without which the point or the merits of
a resolution are likely to be poorly understood, where unusual
importance is attached to making certain reasons for an action
a matter of record, or the like.

An example of a resolution with an appropriate preamble
might be the following:

> Whereas, A privately conducted survey by experts
> engaged by the Association reveals conditions constitut-
> ing a serious fire hazard throughout the lower office-
> building area bordering the waterfront;
> *Resolved*, That a committee of seven consisting of
> [names of four], and three others to be named by the
> chair, be appointed to draw up recommendations
> whereby the Association may bring to bear all possible
> influence to secure proper enforcement of city fire regu-
> lations and any revision of them that may be found to
> be appropriate.

To avoid detracting from the force of the resolution itself,
a preamble generally should contain no more clauses than
are strictly necessary. In cases where an elaborate resolution

1 (consisting of several preamble clauses and several resolving clauses) cannot be avoided, however, the following skeleton example will serve as a guide:

5   Whereas, The ... [text of the first preamble clause];
           . . . .
           Whereas, ... [text of the next to the last preamble clause]; and
           Whereas, ... [text of the last preamble clause];
10   *Resolved*, That ... [stating action to be taken];
           Resolved, That ... [stating further action to be taken]; and
           Resolved, That ... [stating still further action to be taken].

15
       In the consideration of a resolution having a preamble, the preamble is always amended last, since changes in the resolving clauses may require changes in the preamble. In moving the adoption of a resolution, the preamble is not usually men-
20 tioned, since it is included in the resolution. When the *Previous Question* (**16**) is ordered on the resolution before the preamble has been considered for amendment, however, the *Previous Question* does not apply to the preamble, which becomes open to debate and amendment unless the *Previous*
25 *Question* is then separately ordered on it also.

       DETAILS OF FORM AND VARIATIONS IN RESOLUTIONS.   The following details regarding the usual form for writing resolutions, and the variations that are used,
30 should be noted:
       If there is a preamble, each clause, written as a separate paragraph, begins with the word "Whereas" followed by a comma, and the next word should begin with a capital letter. The preamble, regardless of how many paragraphs it has,
35 should never contain a period. Each of its paragraphs should close with a semicolon, followed, in the case of the next to

the last paragraph, by the word "and" (which is optional for the preceding paragraphs also). The last paragraph of the preamble should close with a semicolon, after which a connecting expression such as "therefore" or "therefore, be it" or "now, therefore, be it" is sometimes added. When one of these phrases is included, no punctuation should follow it, and it should always be placed at the end of the preamble paragraph, never at the beginning of the resolving paragraph, thus:

> Whereas, The ... [text of the preamble]; now, therefore, be it
> *Resolved*, That ... [stating action to be taken].

A resolution is often more forceful with a minimum of connecting words, however, as in the earlier examples above.

The word *"Resolved"* is underlined or printed in italics, and is followed by a comma and the word "That"—which begins with a capital "T." If there is more than one resolving clause, each of them should be a separate paragraph. Unless the paragraphs are numbered as in the alternative form described below, each paragraph begins with the words *"Resolved*, That," just as the first resolving clause. Each resolving paragraph may close with a semicolon (followed by the word "and" at least in the case of the next to the last, as in the example already shown); or each resolving paragraph may end with a period. A resolving paragraph should not contain a period within its structure, though observance of this rule is becoming less strict. As an alternative form, separate paragraphs, except the first, may be numbered and begin with the word "That"—as follows:

> *Resolved*, That ...
> 2. That ...
> 3. That ...

(For the format used in a *platform*, see pp. 636–37.)

1 ORDERS (INSTRUCTIONS TO EMPLOYEES). In organizations with employees, the assembly or the board can give instructions to an employee in the form of an *order*, which is written just as a resolution except that the word "*Ordered*" *5* is used in place of the word "*Resolved.*" An example would be: "*Ordered*, That the steward obtain impoundment of all unauthorized vehicles found parked on the club premises."

SERIES OF RESOLUTIONS OFFERED BY A SIN-
10 GLE MAIN MOTION. If a single composite proposal for taking a number of actions in reference to a particular subject has too many elements to be conveniently written into one resolution (even of several clauses), it can be set forth in a series of separate resolutions that can be numbered and *15* offered by means of a single main motion, thus: "Mr. President, I move the adoption of [or "I offer"] the following resolutions: ..." Such a series of resolutions can include orders as described above. In the case of a series of resolutions relating to a single subject, if members desire one or more of *20* the resolutions to be considered separately, the motion for *Division of a Question* (**27**) must be made and adopted by a majority vote. Sometimes a series of independent resolutions relating to completely different subjects is offered by a single main motion in the same way. In the latter case—where the *25* subjects are independent—any resolution in the series must be taken up and voted on separately at the demand of a single member. Such a demand can be made even when another has the floor, at any time until the vote has been taken on adopting the series. A member wishing to make this demand rises *30* and says, for example, "Mr. President, I call for a separate vote on Resolution No. 2."

Main Motions That Are Not in Order

35 Below are stated a number of characteristics or conditions that cause a particular main motion to be out of order, and—

where applicable—the alternative courses that are open for accomplishing the desired result:

1) No main motion is in order that conflicts with the corporate charter, constitution, or bylaws (although a main motion to amend them may be in order; see **35, 57**); and to the extent that procedural rules applicable to the organization or assembly are prescribed by federal, state, or local law, no main motion is in order that conflicts with such rules.

2) No main motion is in order that presents substantially the same question as a motion that was finally disposed of earlier in the same session by being rejected, postponed indefinitely (**11**), or subjected to an *Objection to the Consideration of a Question* (**26**) that was sustained. A main motion that was thus disposed of can, however, be renewed (**38**)—that is, the same question can be introduced again as if new—at any later session; or, a motion to reconsider the vote that disposed of it can be made for a limited time during the same session, and if such a motion to *Reconsider* (**37**) is adopted, the previously disposed of main motion will thereby become pending.*

3) Apart from a motion to *Rescind* or to *Amend Something Previously Adopted* (**35**), no main motion is in order that conflicts with a motion previously adopted at any time and still in force.** If a main motion that interferes with a desired action has been adopted, a motion to reconsider (**37**) the vote on it can be made for a limited time during the same session; and if it is reconsidered, it can be voted

---

*Upon the reconsideration of a vote that postponed a main motion indefinitely, both the main motion *and* the motion to *Postpone Indefinitely* will become pending, the motion to *Postpone Indefinitely* becoming the immediately pending question.

**Unless an adopted main motion specifies a time for the termination of its effect, it continues in force until it is rescinded.

1 down or amended as desired, in the reconsideration.
   Although reconsideration is the preferable procedure in
   such a case when possible, an adopted main motion, at
   any time before or after it is too late to reconsider it, can
5 be changed by means of the motion to *Amend Something
   Previously Adopted,* or it can be rescinded and the desired
   new motion can then be introduced.

4) No main motion is in order that would conflict with or
   that presents substantially the same question as one which
10 has been *temporarily but not finally disposed of*—whether
   in the same or an earlier session—and which remains
   within the control of the assembly (see pp. 90–91, 340–41).
   If a motion that has been temporarily disposed of interferes with the desired introduction of another main mo-
15 tion, it can be brought before the assembly again (at which
   point the earlier motion can possibly be amended to en-
   compass the idea of the desired new motion), as follows:

   a) if it is in the hands of a committee, the committee can
      be discharged from further consideration of the ques-
20   tion, or the vote that referred it to the committee can
      be reconsidered (so long as such reconsideration is
      permissible) and reversed (see **13**, **36**, **37**);

   b) if it is due to come up at a later time, or at a later point
      in the order of business, as a general order, a special
25   order, or unfinished business, the rules can be sus-
      pended and it can be taken up out of its proper order,
      or any intervening items of business can be individually
      laid on the table or postponed as they arise, or the vote
      that established the general order or special order can
30   be reconsidered (so long as such reconsideration is per-
      missible) and reversed (see **41**, especially pp. 363–64);

   c) if it lies on the table, it can be taken from the table
      (see **17**, **34**); or

   d) if it is the subject of a motion to *Reconsider* (**37**) that
35   has been made but not finally disposed of, the motion

to *Reconsider* can be adopted.* Such a motion to *Reconsider*—if it is not already pending—can be brought before the assembly for this purpose as follows: (1) if it has not yet been taken up, it can be *called up* by any member when no other question is pending, or (2) if it has been taken up and temporarily disposed of, it can be brought before the assembly again by whichever of the processes mentioned in (b) or (c) above is applicable.

5) A main motion that proposes action outside the scope of the organization's object as defined in the bylaws or corporate charter is out of order unless the assembly by a two-thirds vote authorizes its introduction.

Many of the alternative courses for obtaining a result that cannot be directly reached through a main motion, as described in items (2), (3), and (4) above, involve parliamentary motions having special requirements (such as a two-thirds vote or previous notice, pp. 121–24) for their adoption. The rules relating to the motions to *Suspend the Rules* (**25**), *Take from the Table* (**34**), *Rescind or Amend Something Previously Adopted* (**35**), *Discharge a Committee* (**36**), and *Reconsider* (**37**), and the rules relating to the renewal of motions (**38**), should be read in connection with the application of these methods.

Treatment of Main Motions

The basic procedure by which main motions are introduced and considered is described in detail in **4**. Additional

---

*Rejection of the motion to *Reconsider* will not cause the main motion to be brought before the assembly again, but will cause the vote that had previously disposed of the main motion to become final.

points to be noted in connection with the handling of main motions are as follows:

PROCEDURES BY WHICH THE PROPOSAL CONTAINED IN A MAIN MOTION CAN BE IMPROVED UPON BEFORE ACTION IS TAKEN. As previously noted (pp. 34–35), it is a general parliamentary rule that a subject must be brought up in the form of a motion (embodying a specific proposal) before it can be discussed in a meeting of an assembly. A motion should be as well thought out as possible before it is introduced. At the same time, it will frequently happen that the assembly—although desiring to take some kind of action on the subject that a main motion has brought to its attention—wishes to make some change in the proposal before voting on its adoption. There are several means by which such a result can be accomplished, depending on the conditions and the degree or scope of the changes desired. The courses that are open in such cases are summarized below:

1) After a main motion has been made and before the question has been stated by the chair, any member can quickly rise and, with little or no explanatory comment, informally suggest one or more modifications in the motion, which at this point the maker can accept or reject as he wishes (see pp. 40–41). Application of this method should generally be limited to minor changes about which there is unlikely to be a difference of opinion.

2) After the question has been stated by the chair—although the assembly, and not the maker of the motion, then has control over its wording—the maker can request unanimous consent to modify the motion (see pp. 295–98). If any member then objects, however, the desired modification must be introduced in the form of a motion to *Amend*, as noted below.

3) By means of the subsidiary motion to *Amend* (**12**), members can propose changes to be made in the wording and,
within limits, the meaning of a pending main motion before it is voted on. These amendments must be seconded,
are debatable, and are adopted by a majority vote. Such
proposed amendments can take the form of either:

   a) changes to particular words or paragraphs in the main
motion—of which several specific types are permitted
under the rules for the motion to *Amend*; or

   b) a motion to *substitute* an entire new text of the
main motion in place of the pending version (see
pp. 153–62).

Whatever amendments are adopted, the main motion is
then voted on in its amended form.

4) If proper recasting of a main motion will require time or
study, the subsidiary motion to *Commit* (**13**), which is
adopted by a majority vote, can be used to refer the main
motion to a committee. When this committee reports, it
normally recommends appropriate amendments for the
assembly's consideration. Such a committee can be a special committee, appointed only for the particular case, or
it can be one of a number of standing committees that
may be permanently established within the organization
(see **50**). Some assemblies provide in their rules for the
automatic referral of all main motions dealing with certain
classes of subjects to specified standing committees as
soon as they are introduced. Bills are handled in this manner in most legislative bodies. In conventions, the rules
of the organization often require that all resolutions not
reviewed by some other committee be submitted to a
Resolutions Committee before coming before the general
voting body (see pp. 633–34). Where an assembly is large
and has a volume of business, it is usually desirable to have
every main question go to a committee before final action
is taken.

5) If the general problem posed by a main motion might be better dealt with by an alternative measure that cannot conveniently be proposed as an amendment in the form of a substitute (see above), a member speaking in debate can urge rejection of the pending main motion, saying that if it is voted down he will offer a different main motion which he can describe briefly and which deals with the general problem in a substantially different way (see, however, p. 111, no. 2). Or, with the same explanation, he may move to postpone the main motion indefinitely (**11**). If the pending motion is thereafter voted down, or indefinitely postponed, the chair immediately recognizes this member again for the purpose of making his alternative motion, even if another member rises to claim the floor first and addresses the chair.

INTRODUCTION OF SUBSIDIARY OR INCIDENTAL MOTIONS AS A PART OF—OR PRIVILEGED MOTIONS AS AN INTERRUPTION OF—THE CONSIDERATION OF A MAIN MOTION. While a main motion is pending, as described in **5** and **6**, one or more subsidiary motions or incidental motions can be introduced and disposed of as an integral part of the main motion's consideration, or the introduction of one or more privileged motions can interrupt its consideration. A member may speak in debate on the main motion and conclude by offering a secondary motion.

Such motions are usually made during the period while the main motion is open to debate, although certain incidental motions can also arise before or after this stage in its handling. The precise times and circumstances when each of these motions is in order are determined by the first three of the motion's standard descriptive characteristics. If the assembly's treatment of a particular main motion involves a number of these other motions, they may occur in such a way that each one of them is disposed of before the next is intro-

duced, or—depending on the circumstances—several of them   *1*
may become pending at one time by operation of the order
of precedence of motions (see pp. 59–62).

In the latter case, when a motion that takes precedence
over all pending questions is made, that motion is disposed   *5*
of first, and then "the question recurs" on the next-most-
recently-moved motion; that is (as far as applicable in the
existing parliamentary situation), its consideration is resumed
at the point where the higher-ranking motion interrupted it.
This motion is again open to debate and amendment if it is a   *10*
debatable and amendable motion. In this manner, the motions in the series of pending questions are voted on in the
reverse of the order in which they were made—with the main
motion being voted on last—unless the result of the vote on
one of the other motions causes consideration of the remain-   *15*
der of the series to be halted.

This principle may be illustrated by a somewhat more
complicated example than may ordinarily occur in practice.
Referring to the explanation of subsidiary, privileged, and incidental motions in **6**, assume that the following series of mo-   *20*
tions is pending and that the motions have been moved in
the order shown:

1) a main motion;
2) a motion to postpone the main question indefinitely;   *25*
3) an amendment to the main motion;
4) a motion to refer the main question (with the pending
   amendment) to a committee;
5) a motion to postpone the pending questions to a certain
   time;   *30*
6) a motion to vote on the postponement by ballot;
7) a motion to lay the pending questions on the table; and
8) a motion to take a recess.

In such a case, the motion to *Recess* is voted on first, then the   *35*
motion to *Lay on the Table*, and so on, proceeding upward

1 through the list above. If any one of the motions (8), (7), (5), (4), or (2) is adopted, however, consideration of the remaining motions stops. These processes, and others that may be employed in or interrupt a main motion's consideration,
5 are explained initially in **6** and are further illustrated in the examples in **11–33**.

A subsidiary or incidental motion *adheres* to a main question if it is related to the main question in such a way that—once introduced—it must be decided before the main
10 question can be decided. Adhering motions thus remain connected with the main question if that question is interrupted or temporarily disposed of, and remain to be decided first if and when the main question is taken up again. In the example in the preceding paragraph, motions (2) through (7) adhere
15 to the main motion—except that motion (2), to *Postpone Indefinitely*, would cease to adhere to it if motion (4), to *Commit*, were adopted (see Standard Descriptive Characteristic 2, p. 103). Motion (8) in the example does not adhere to the main question.
20

MAIN MOTIONS BROUGHT UP BY MEANS OF A CALL FOR THE ORDERS OF THE DAY OR BY RAISING A QUESTION OF PRIVILEGE.   Under the process by which a main motion is normally introduced, as already
25 explained, it can be moved only while no motion is pending. Certain questions may come before the assembly with the status of main motions after having interrupted other business, however, if they are brought up by means of either of the two lowest-ranking *privileged* motions. To *Call for the Orders of*
30 *the Day* (**18**) and to *Raise a Question of Privilege* (**19**) each have privileged rank and can therefore interrupt pending business. As a result of the application of one of these devices to interrupt a pending question, an *order of the day* (that is, another question previously set as due to come up automat-
35 ically at the time) may be taken up, or an urgent motion

relating to the privileges of the assembly or of a member   *1*
may be admitted as a *question of privilege* to be entertained
immediately. But when such an order of the day or question
of privilege has thus become pending, it is treated exactly
as any other main motion. (The description of the first   *5*
two privileged motions on p. 67 and the sections on them
referred to above should be read in connection with this
paragraph.)

Notes on Example Format Throughout the Book   *10*

Below for the main motion, and in each of the succeeding sections covering the different motions of parliamentary law (**11–37**), is a subsection headed *Form and Example*
giving a script showing the words to be spoken by a member   *15*
making the motion and by the chair in stating and putting
the question on it. In these subsections and throughout this
book as applicable, the following methods of notation are
used:

20

- The examples generally show the presiding officer addressed as "Mr. President" or "Madam President." While
this form corresponds to the chair's designation in most
organized societies, the presiding officer should be addressed by whatever is his or her official title in the par-   *25*
ticular organization or assembly. Where he or she has no
special title, or in a meeting of an unorganized body such
as a mass meeting, the form "Mr. Chairman" or "Madam
Chairman" should be used (see also pp. 22–24).
- The phrase "obtaining the floor" in parentheses before   *30*
words spoken by a member indicates that this member
must first obtain the floor in the manner explained on
pages 29–31.
- The word "Second" in parentheses after words spoken in
making a motion indicates that, except in cases where it   *35*

1   is proposed on behalf of a board or a committee, another
     member must second the motion as described on pages
     35–37, and that it is assumed that this is done.

5   **Form and Example**

     The example below illustrates the handling of a main mo-
     tion in a case that involves only the basic forms of the six prin-
     cipal steps—three in bringing the motion before the assembly
10   (p. 32) and three in its consideration (p. 42).

     Assume that the chair has just asked if there is any new
     business (see p. 360).

     MEMBER A (obtaining the floor): I move that the Society contribute
15   $100 to the Centennial Celebration. (Second.)

     CHAIR: It is moved and seconded that the Society contribute $100
     to the Centennial Celebration. [Proceeding as shown on pp. 37–39.]

     The chair immediately turns toward Member A (who re-
20   sumed his seat after making his motion) to see if he wishes
     the floor first in debate (see p. 31, ll. 1–3). Member A is
     already rising to claim the floor. The chair recognizes him:

     CHAIR: Mr. A.

25

     Member A explains the reasons why the contribution
     should be made, followed by others who also speak in debate
     after having obtained the floor. When debate appears to have
     ended, the chair makes sure that no one else wishes to speak,
30   as by asking, "Are you ready for the question?" or "Is there
     any further debate?" and then puts the question—that is, puts
     the motion to a vote—as follows:

     CHAIR: The question is on the motion that the Society contribute
35   $100 to the Centennial Celebration. Those in favor of the motion, say

aye. [Pausing for response.] ... Those opposed, say *no.* ... The ayes have   *1*
it and the motion is agreed to. The Treasurer will issue the appropriate
check and the Secretary will prepare a covering letter forwarding the contribution to the Chairman of the Centennial Commission. Is there further new business?   *5*

If the assembly is taking up business under the heading
of Special Orders in the order of business, or that of Unfinished Business and General Orders (rather than New Business
as in the above example), the chair, instead of saying, "Is there   *10*
further new business," announces, "The next item of business
is ... [immediately proceeding to state the question]" (see pp.
357–60).

(See **4** for variations in the steps illustrated above. For examples of the use of subsidiary and incidental motions in the   *15*
handling of main motions and the application of privileged
motions while a main motion is pending, see **11–33**.)

Previous Notice of Motions
                                                                                       20
The term *previous notice* (or *notice*), as applied to neces-
sary conditions for the adoption of certain motions, has a
particular meaning in parliamentary law. A requirement of
previous notice means that announcement that the motion
will be introduced—indicating its exact content as described   *25*
below—must be included in the call of the meeting (p. 4) at
which the motion will be brought up, or, as a permissible
alternative, if no more than a quarterly time interval (see
pp. 89–90) will have elapsed since the preceding meeting, the
announcement must be made at the preceding meeting. The   *30*
call of a meeting is generally sent to all members a reasonable
time in advance, which may be prescribed in the bylaws. In
organizations that meet less often than at quarterly time intervals (see pp. 89–90), or that meet as a convention of delegates, the bylaws should require the secretary to issue a call.   *35*

1   Motions that have the effect of changing or nullifying previous action of the assembly—such as the motion to *Rescind* or to *Amend Something Previously Adopted* (**35**), the motion to *Discharge a Committee* (**36**), or a motion to postpone an

5   event already scheduled—require previous notice if they are to be adopted by only a majority vote. Accordingly, it is ordinarily desirable to give previous notice if there is a possibility of serious disagreement. The adoption or amendment of special rules of order requires either (a) previous notice *and* a

10   two-thirds vote or (b) a vote of a majority of the entire membership—as does the amendment of bylaws if they do not prescribe the procedure for their amendment, which they should do (see also Table of Rules Relating to Motions, tinted pp. 6–29). Bylaws sometimes also provide a requirement of

15   notice for original main motions dealing with certain subjects (compare Standard Characteristic 7[a], p. 103).

        Subject to any rules of the organization that provide how notice shall be given, it can be given as follows:

        If previous notice is given *at a meeting*, it can be given

20   orally unless the rules of the organization require it to be in writing—which is often the case with notice of amendments to bylaws. Unless the rules require the full text of the motion, resolution, or bylaw amendment to be submitted in the notice, only the purport need be indicated; but such a statement

25   of purport must be accurate and complete—as in "to raise the annual dues to $20"—since it will determine what amendments are in order when the motion is considered. The notice becomes invalid if the motion is amended beyond the scope of the notice (see also **35, 57**).

30   When no question is pending, a member desiring to give a notice is entitled to preference in recognition (but see pp. 378–82 for circumstances in which others may have a higher priority for such preference). But if the member wishing to give the notice is unable to obtain the floor while no

35   business is pending (as may sometimes happen, for example, in a convention that is following an adopted agenda or pro-

gram, **41**, or in cases where a meeting of an ordinary society　*1*
adjourns before completing its regular order of business), the
notice, if necessary, can interrupt pending business or any
other pending motion; the notice is also in order when
another person has been assigned the floor but has not yet　*5*
begun to speak, and is in order even after it has been voted
to adjourn, provided that the chair has not yet declared the
meeting adjourned (see also pp. 238–40).

A notice can be given and taken note of in a meeting as
follows:　*10*

MEMBER A (obtaining the floor): I give notice that at the next meeting I will move to rescind the resolution adopted April 17, 20___, relating
to …

CHAIR: Notice has been given that at the next meeting … [repeating　*15*
the substance of the notice].

The secretary then records the notice in the minutes. If
the member desiring to give the notice is unable to obtain
the floor, the following variations in form can be used as　*20*
appropriate to the case:

MEMBER A (rising and addressing the chair immediately after the chair
has recognized another member, Mr. Y, and before the latter has begun
to speak—or remaining standing if he has just sought the floor unsuc-　*25*
cessfully): Mr. President!

CHAIR: For what purpose does the member rise [or, if Member A has
remained standing after seeking the floor, "For what purpose does the
member address the chair"]?

MEMBER A: I wish to give notice of the following amendment to the　*30*
bylaws: "To amend Article II, Section 3, by …"

CHAIR: Notice has been given of the following amendment to the
bylaws: … Mr. Y has the floor.

Instead of being given at a meeting, a notice can also be　*35*
sent to every member with the call of the meeting at which

1 the matter is to come up for action, except where the rules of
the organization provide otherwise. In such a case, the member desiring to give the notice writes to the secretary alone,
requesting that the notice be sent with the call of the next
5 meeting; and the secretary should then do this at the expense
of the organization.

Motion to Adopt and Motion to Ratify

10   A motion to *adopt* (or *accept* or *agree to*) an officer's or a
committee's report or recommendations which the assembly
(by means of a main motion) directed the officer or committee to prepare is an incidental main motion. A motion to
adopt or accept a report or the recommendations of a stand-
15 ing committee prepared on the committee's own initiative
and dealing with a subject that was not expressly referred to
the committee, however, is an original main motion.

A motion to adopt a resolution, bylaws, or any other document can be amended by adding, "and that it be printed
20 and that members be furnished with copies," or, "that it [or
"they"] go into effect at the close of this annual meeting,"
or anything of a similar nature (see also **51**; for the adoption
of bylaws, see **56** and p. 569, l. 36 to p. 570, l. 2).

The motion to *ratify* (also called *approve* or *confirm*) is an
25 incidental main motion that is used to confirm or make valid
an action already taken that cannot become valid until approved by the assembly. Cases where the procedure of ratification is applicable include:

30 • action improperly taken at a regular or properly called
meeting at which no quorum was present;
• action taken at a special meeting with regard to business
not mentioned in the call of that meeting;
• action taken by officers, committees, delegates, or subor-
35 dinate bodies in excess of their instructions or authority;

- action taken by a local unit that requires approval of the *1*
  state or national organization; or
- action taken by a state or national society subject to approval by its constituent units.

5

An assembly can ratify only such actions of its officers,
committees, delegates, or subordinate bodies as it would have
had the right to authorize in advance. It cannot make valid a
voice-vote election when the bylaws require elections to be
by ballot; nor can it ratify anything done in violation of pro- *10*
cedural rules prescribed by national, state, or local law, or in
violation of its own bylaws, except that provision for a quorum in the bylaws does not prevent it from ratifying action
taken at a meeting when no quorum was present.

A motion to ratify can be amended by substituting a mo- *15*
tion of censure, and vice versa, when the action involved
has been taken by an officer or other representative of the
assembly.

Since the motion to ratify (or to censure) is a main motion, it is debatable and opens the entire question to debate. *20*

CHAPTER VI

SUBSIDIARY MOTIONS

*See 6, pages 62ff., for a list of these motions and a
description of their characteristics as a class.*

§11. POSTPONE INDEFINITELY
(To drop the main motion without a direct vote on it)

Postpone Indefinitely is a motion that the assembly decline
to take a position on the main question. Its adoption kills the
main motion (for the duration of the session) and avoids a
direct vote on the question. It is useful in disposing of a badly
chosen main motion that cannot be either adopted or expressly rejected without possibly undesirable consequences.

Standard Descriptive Characteristics

The subsidiary motion to *Postpone Indefinitely*:

1. Takes precedence over nothing except the main question
   to which it is applied. It is the lowest-ranking subsidiary motion and yields to all other subsidiary motions, to
   all privileged motions, and to all applicable incidental
   motions.
2. Can be applied only to the main question and can therefore be made only while a main question is immediately

pending. Motions to *Limit or Extend Limits of Debate* and   1
for the *Previous Question* can be applied to it without
affecting the main question. It cannot be committed
(although the motion to *Commit* can be made while it is
pending; see below). It cannot be definitely postponed or   5
laid on the table alone, but when it is pending, the main
question can be definitely postponed or laid on the table,
and in such a case, the motion to *Postpone Indefinitely* is
also postponed to the specified time or carried to the table.

3. Is out of order when another has the floor.   10
4. Must be seconded.
5. Is debatable; and, unlike the case of any other subsidiary
    motion, debate on the motion to *Postpone Indefinitely* can
    go fully into the merits of the main question.
6. Is not amendable.   15
7. Requires a majority vote.
8. An affirmative vote on the motion to *Postpone Indefinitely*
    can be reconsidered.* A negative vote on it cannot be
    reconsidered, and after such a vote this motion cannot
    be renewed as to the same main motion, for two reasons: 20
    (a) by the negative vote on *Postpone Indefinitely*, the effort
    to prevent the issue raised by the main motion from com-
    ing to a head is already lost; and (b) the opponents of the
    main motion will be given another chance to kill it by di-
    rect rejection when the vote on the main motion is taken.   25

Further Rules and Explanation

EFFECT ON THE PENDING MOTION.   The effect
of postponing a question indefinitely is to suppress it   30

---

*Upon the reconsideration of a vote that postponed a main motion in-
definitely, both the main motion *and* the motion to *Postpone Indefinitely* will
become pending, the motion to *Postpone Indefinitely* becoming the immediately pending question.

throughout the current session. In a convention or conference consisting of several meetings, the suppression continues
throughout the entire series of meetings, and in ordinary societies, throughout the weekly, monthly, or other meeting, as
the case may be. Consequently, the adoption of the motion
to *Postpone Indefinitely* is in effect an indirect rejection of the
main motion.

EFFECT OF REFERRAL (OF THE MAIN MOTION)
ON A PENDING MOTION TO POSTPONE INDEFI-
NITELY.   If a main motion is referred to a committee while
Postpone Indefinitely is pending, the latter motion is ignored
and does not go to the committee, since the adoption of the
motion to *Commit* indicates that the assembly is not in favor
of postponing indefinitely.

OCCASIONAL SPECIAL USE.   The motion to *Post-*
pone Indefinitely is sometimes employed by strategists to test
their strength on a motion they oppose. Making this motion
enables members who have exhausted their right of debate
on the main question to speak further because, as explained
under Standard Characteristic 5, the motion to *Postpone*
Indefinitely, though technically a new question, necessarily
involves debate of the main question. Its effect, therefore, is
to give the opponents of the pending measure a chance to
kill it without risking its adoption, as they would be doing if
the vote were taken on the main motion itself. If opponents
of the main question carry the indefinite postponement, the
main question is suppressed for the session; if they fail, they
still have a vote on the main question and, having learned
their strength by the vote on the indefinite postponement,
can form an opinion as to the advisability of continuing their
effort.

Form and Example

Assume that the following resolution is pending in a meeting of a local unit of a state professional society: "*Resolved*, That the Ferndale Unit endorse the State President of the Society, James Thornton, for the office of United States Senator." Debate creates a delicate situation. Members are loyal to their state president, but in questions of public office they wish to support the nominee of their choice. Yet, for them to vote *no* on the endorsement might appear to be a repudiation of their state president. Furthermore, a vote on this question either in the affirmative or in the negative might tend to create an unfortunate division within the local unit.

MEMBER A (obtaining the floor): I move that the resolution be postponed indefinitely. (Second.)

CHAIR: It is moved and seconded that the resolution pertaining to the endorsement of James Thornton for United States Senator be postponed indefinitely. The chair recognizes Mr. A.

Debate on the subsidiary motion to *Postpone Indefinitely* will likely involve also the advisability of the resolution itself. When debate ceases, however, the subsidiary motion is voted on first.

CHAIR: The question is on the motion to postpone indefinitely the resolution, "*Resolved*, That the Ferndale Unit endorse the State President of the Society, James Thornton, for the office of United States Senator." As many as are in favor of postponing the resolution indefinitely, say *aye*. … Those opposed, say *no*. … The ayes have it and the resolution is postponed indefinitely.

If the motion to *Postpone Indefinitely* is lost, the chair announces the result and immediately states the question on the main motion. The wording in this case is:

1   CHAIR: The noes have it. The motion to postpone indefinitely is lost.
The question is on the resolution, "*Resolved*, That ..." [Continues as for
any main motion.]

5   ## §12. AMEND

The subsidiary motion to *Amend* is a motion to modify
the wording—and within certain limits the meaning—of a
pending motion before the pending motion itself is acted
10   upon.

Less frequently, it may become desirable to apply a similar
process to something already adopted—as bylaws, a program,
or a resolution. It should be noted that the motion then used
is not the subsidiary motion to *Amend*, but a main motion
15   having particular characteristics. This section deals only with
Amend as a subsidiary motion. (For the motion to *Amend
Something Previously Adopted*, see **35**.)

Amend is probably the most widely used of the subsidiary
motions, although the full procedure for its most effective ap-
20   plication is not generally well understood by the meeting-
going public at large. The ordinary member's becoming at
home with the formal amendment process is the keystone of
the power of the general membership to keep details of the
direction of an organization under its control to the extent it
25   wishes to do so. To understand how the process works, it is
important to realize that, when an assembly "takes action,"
all it ever actually does itself is to *adopt a statement*—directing
that a certain action be carried out, or expressing a certain
view or aspiration. The precise wording of the statement can
30   become crucial when it deals, for example, with a complex
matter or an expressed position on a publicly controversial
issue. To enable an assembly to work through internal disagreements about the precise wording of a statement in an
orderly manner, the rules governing the subsidiary motion to
35   *Amend* include extensive detailed specifications stating the

types of change in language structure through which modifications are to be achieved.

Adoption of a subsidiary motion to *Amend* does *not* adopt the motion thereby amended; that motion remains pending in its modified form. Rejection of a motion to *Amend* leaves the pending motion worded as it was before the amendment was voted on.

Neither the member who offers an amendment nor the maker of the main motion *amends* or "makes an amendment"; only the assembly can do that. A member's vote on an amendment does not obligate him to vote in a particular way on the motion to which the amendment applies; he is free to vote as he pleases on the main motion, whether it is amended or not.

An amendment must always be *germane*—that is, closely related to or having bearing on the subject of the motion to be amended. This means that no new subject can be introduced under pretext of being an amendment (see pp. 136–38).

Standard Descriptive Characteristics

The subsidiary motion to *Amend*:

1. a) *When applied to a main motion:* It takes precedence over the main motion and over the subsidiary motion to *Postpone Indefinitely.* It yields to all subsidiary motions other than *Postpone Indefinitely* and *Amend*, and it also yields to a motion to *Amend* that is applied to it; and it yields to all privileged motions and all applicable incidental motions.

   b) *When applied to other than a main motion:* It takes precedence over the motion that it proposes to amend. It yields to any privileged or subsidiary motion (other than *Amend*) to which the motion that it proposes to amend would yield, and it also yields to motions to

Amend, to *Limit or Extend Limits of Debate*, or for the *Previous Question* that are applied to it; and it yields to all applicable incidental motions.

2. Can be applied to any main motion (but in the case of some incidental main motions only in a limited manner); also can be applied, in different limited ways, to any other motion that legitimately contains a variable factor; for example, can be applied to change the duration of a proposed recess or the hour to which a pending question is to be postponed. (For lists of motions that cannot be amended, see tinted pp. 42–43.)

Amend can be applied to itself (that is, to a pending *primary* amendment), so that a *secondary amendment** (or "amendment to an amendment") will result, but it cannot be applied to a secondary amendment (see Standard Characteristic 6, below; and *Degrees of Amendment*, p. 135).

The sections in this book dealing with each individual motion contain under Standard Characteristic 6 a statement of whether *Amend* is applicable to that particular motion, and if applicability is limited, in what manner.

Motions to *Limit or Extend Limits of Debate* and for the *Previous Question* can be applied to a pending primary amendment or secondary amendment; and these motions affect only the immediately pending amendment unless otherwise specified. A *Division of the Question* can be applied to the motion to *Amend*; the motion for *Consideration by Paragraph or Seriatim* can also be applied to it. The motion to *Amend* cannot have motions to *Commit*, *Postpone Definitely*, or *Lay on the Table* applied to it alone, but when a primary amendment or a primary and a

---

*Secondary amendments must not be confused with secondary *motions*, a much more general concept explained on pages 59ff.

secondary amendment are pending, the main question can be committed, postponed, or laid on the table, and the amendments then undergo the same process with the main question. The motion to *Amend* cannot be postponed indefinitely.

3. Is out of order when another has the floor.

4. Must be seconded.

5. Is debatable whenever the motion to which it is applied is debatable. Such debate must be confined to the desirability of the amendment, however, and must not extend to the merits of the motion to be amended, except as may be necessary to determine whether the amendment is advisable. *Amend* is undebatable whenever the motion to be amended is undebatable.

6. Is generally amendable. This characteristic, however, creates two degrees of amendment—primary and secondary—and a secondary amendment cannot be amended (see *Degrees of Amendment*, p. 135).

7. Requires a majority vote, regardless of the vote required to adopt the question to be amended. This is true even in cases where adoption of the amendment would result in changing the vote required to adopt the question being amended, as from a two-thirds vote to a majority vote or vice versa (see, e.g., Standard Characteristic 7 of *Postpone to a Certain Time*, p. 182, and the example on p. 190).

8. Can be reconsidered.

Further Rules and Explanation (with Forms)

CLASSIFICATION AS TO FORM. There are three basic processes of amendment, the third of which is an indivisible combination of the first two. For each of these processes, some of the rules are different depending on whether it is applied with reference to a few words or to a

1 whole paragraph or section; so that each process has two
forms, as follows:

1. First process: to *insert*, or to *add*.
5   a. To *insert words*, or, if they are placed at the end of the
sentence or passage being amended, to *add words*.
       b. To *insert a paragraph*, or, if it is placed at the end, to
add a paragraph.
2. Second process: to *strike out*.*
10   a. To strike out words.
       b. To strike out a paragraph.
3. Third process: an indivisible combination of processes (1)
and (2) having the following forms:
       a. To *strike out and insert* (which applies to words).
15   b. To *substitute*; that is, in effect, to strike out a paragraph, or the entire text of a resolution or main mo-
tion, and insert another in its place.** (Note that
substitute is a technical parliamentary term that is not
applied to anything less than a complete paragraph of
20   one or more sentences, so that this term is not applicable to Form 3[a].)

Forms 1(a), 2(a), and 3(a), relating to *words*, can be applied to change the wording within a single sentence, or occasionally within two or more consecutive sentences that

---

*It should be noted that the application of the word "delete" to any form
of amendment is not a preferred parliamentary usage, but the shortened
expression "to strike" is acceptable.

**A motion to strike out a paragraph from one place and insert it in a
different place is also possible. Such a motion is not a motion to *substitute*; it
is similar to the second of the two types of motions to *strike out and insert
(applying to words)* discussed on page 149, line 19 to page 150, line 2. The
wording of the paragraph cannot be materially amended by a motion of this
type or by any secondary amendments to it. However, once such a motion
has been adopted, the transferred paragraph may be amended by any of the
usual forms.

make up a *part* of a single paragraph. Forms 1(b), 2(b), and *1* 3(b), relating to a *paragraph*, can also be applied to a section, article, or larger unit.

The rules for each of the different forms of amendment are given in separate subsections beginning on page 139. *5*

DEGREES OF AMENDMENT.   As noted in Standard Characteristics 2 and 6, above, a subsidiary motion to *Amend* can, in general, be amended, so that two degrees of amendment—primary and secondary—are possible. A primary *10* amendment applies directly to the pending resolution, main motion, or other motion (except *Amend*) to be amended. A secondary amendment applies to a pending primary amendment; it proposes a change in the primary amendment or, in certain cases, in a paragraph that the primary amendment *15* proposes to strike out of the pending resolution or motion (see p. 147, l. 24 to p. 148, l. 13; p. 154, ll. 10–20).

The terms *amendment of the first degree* and *amendment of the second degree*, or *amendment to the main question* and *amendment to the amendment*, are correct expressions, but *20* the terms *primary amendment* and *secondary amendment* are preferred. An amendment of the third degree is not permitted. To accomplish the same purpose, a member can say, while a secondary amendment is pending, that if it is voted down, he will offer another secondary amendment—which *25* he can then indicate briefly—in its place.

No more than one primary amendment and one secondary amendment are permitted to be pending at a time,* but any number of each can be considered in succession—so long as they do not again raise questions already decided. (See *30* *Filling Blanks*, pp. 162–67, however, for a special method of

---

*For exceptions relating to indivisible conforming amendments and multiple amendments proposed by a single motion, see pages 273–74, 275, and 520–23.

1   amending highly variable factors, such as times, amounts,
    names, or numbers, by which several alternative proposals can
    be pending at the same time.)

5   DETERMINING THE GERMANENESS OF AN
    AMENDMENT.   As already stated, an amendment must be
    germane to be in order. To be *germane*, an amendment must
    in some way involve the same question that is raised by the
    motion to which it is applied. When a secondary amendment
10 proposes a change in the primary amendment, it must be ger-
    mane *to that primary amendment*—not just to the motion
    the primary amendment would change. When a secondary
    amendment proposes a change in a paragraph that a primary
    amendment proposes to strike out, either by a motion to
15 strike out a paragraph or by a motion to substitute, it must
    be germane to that paragraph. An amendment cannot intro-
    duce an independent question; but an amendment can be
    hostile to, or even defeat, the spirit of the original motion
    and still be germane.
20   Aside from these principles, there is no single, all-inclusive
    test for determining when a proposed amendment is germane
    and when it is not. A method by which the germaneness of
    an amendment can often be verified, however, grows out
    of the following general rules of parliamentary law:
25
    1) During the session in which the assembly has decided a
        question, another main motion raising the same or sub-
        stantially the same question cannot be introduced.
    2) While a motion has been temporarily disposed of (as ex-
30   plained on pp. 90–91), no other motion can be admitted
        that might conflict with one of the possible final decisions
        on the first motion.

    By these rules, if a proposed amendment is related to the
35 main motion in such a way that, after the adoption, rejection,

or temporary disposal of the present main motion, the essen- 1
tial idea of the amendment could not be introduced as an
independent resolution during the same session, the amendment is germane and should be admitted, since there will not,
or may not, be any opportunity to present it later. This test 5
cannot be reliably used to determine that an amendment is
out of order, since it is sometimes possible for an amendment
to be germane even if, regardless of action on the present
main motion, the idea embodied in the amendment could be
introduced independently later in the same session. 10

As an example of a germane amendment, assume that a
motion is pending "that the Society authorize the purchase
of a new desk for the Secretary." It would be germane and in
order to amend by inserting after "desk" the words "and
matching chair," since both relate to providing the secretary 15
with the necessary furniture. On the other hand, an amendment to add to the motion the words "and the payment
of the President's expenses to the State Convention" is not
germane.

Or assume that the following is the pending motion: 20
"that the City Council commend Officer George for his action in ..." An amendment to strike out "commend" and insert "censure," although antagonistic to the original intent,
is germane and *in order* because both ideas deal with the
council's opinion of the officer's action. Also, since a motion 25
to censure the officer for the same act could not be introduced independently in the same session after the adoption
of a motion to commend him, the amendment to change
commend to *censure* is germane under the rule given above.
It should be noted that *censure* is different from *not commend* 30
(see *Improper Amendments*, below).

There are borderline cases where a presiding officer will
find it difficult to judge the germaneness of an amendment.
Whenever in doubt, he should admit the amendment or, in
important cases, refer the decision to the assembly: "The chair 35

1 is in doubt and will ask the assembly to decide whether the
amendment is germane. [Debate, if any, provided that debate
is in order.] The question is on whether the amendment is
germane to the resolution [or "to the primary amendment"].
5 Those of the opinion that the amendment *is* germane, say
aye. ... Those of the opinion that it is *not* germane, say *no*. ...,
etc." (See also example under *Point of Order*, pp. 254–55.)

IMPROPER AMENDMENTS.   The following types of
10 amendment are out of order:

1) One that is not germane to the question to be amended.
2) One that merely makes the adoption of the amended
question equivalent to a rejection of the original motion.
15 Thus, in the motion that "our delegates be instructed to
vote in favor of the increase in Federation dues," an
amendment to insert "not" before "be" is out of order
because an affirmative vote on not giving a certain instruction is identical with a negative vote on giving the
20 same instruction. But it *would* be in order to move to
insert "not" before "to" ("instructed not to vote in
favor"), since this would change the main motion into
one to give different instructions.
3) One that would cause the question as amended to be out
25 of order.*
4) One that proposes to change one of the forms of amendment listed on page 134 into another form. A pending
primary amendment to "strike out 'oak' before 'furniture,'" for example, cannot be converted into the form
30 *strike out and insert* by moving to add "and insert
'maple.'"
5) One that would have the effect of converting one parliamentary motion into another. For example, a motion to

---

*For an exception, see page 146, ll. 5–9.

"postpone the question until 2 P.M." cannot be amended
by "striking out 'until 2 P.M.' and inserting 'indefinitely,'"
since this would convert it into a different kind of
motion.

6) One that strikes out the word "*Resolved*" or other enacting words.

NOTE ON AMENDMENT OF PREAMBLE. When
a resolution has a preamble (one or more clauses beginning
"Whereas"), the preamble is not opened to amendment until
after amendment of the resolving clauses has been completed.
After any amendment of the preamble, a single vote is taken
on the question of adopting the entire resolution or paper
(see also pp. 278–79).

RULES FOR THE DIFFERENT FORMS OF
AMENDMENT. Because *Amend* can be moved in different forms, rules pertaining to each form of the motion are
given separately below, with examples. The general guidelines
for consideration of primary and secondary amendments that
are presented under *Form and Example: 1(a), 1(b)*, pages
141–46, are applicable also to the other forms.

It should be noted that many of the rules governing the
different forms of amendment are particular applications of
the following principle: After the assembly has voted that certain words (or a certain paragraph) shall, or shall not, form
part of a pending resolution, it is not in order to make
another motion to *Amend* that raises the same question of
content and effect. Common sense should guide the presiding officer in interpreting the rules, both to give freedom for
improvement of the main motion finally to be voted on, and
at the same time to protect the assembly from motions for
amendment that present questions it has already decided.

1(a). To Insert, or to Add, Words. A motion to insert
words must specify the exact place of insertion by naming the

1   word before or after which, or the words between which, the insertion is to be made—whichever will better locate and point out the effect of the change. For long or printed copies, the line number and paragraph number should be designated.

5   In the consideration of a motion to *insert* certain words, or (if they are to be placed at the end of the passage being amended) to *add* certain words, any necessary perfecting of the new words should be done by secondary amendment *before* the vote is taken on inserting or adding as proposed by

10   the primary amendment. Otherwise there may be no opportunity to perfect the inserted or added words, for reasons explained in the next paragraph.

After words have been inserted or added, they cannot be changed or struck out, except through a reconsideration of

15   the vote (see **37**), or through an amendment presenting a new question in the form of a motion:

1) To strike out the entire paragraph into which the words were inserted.

20   2) To strike out a portion of the paragraph, including all or a part of the words inserted and enough other words to make a different question from the one decided by the insertion.

3) To substitute an entire paragraph for the one into which

25   the words were inserted.

4) To strike out a portion of the paragraph (including all or a part of the words inserted) and insert other words, in a way that presents a new question.

30   If a motion to insert certain words in a particular place is voted down, it is still in order—provided that it will present an essentially new question—to make a motion:

1) To insert only a part of the same words.

35   2) To insert all or a part of the same words together with some others.

3) To insert the same words *in place of* others (motion to *strike out and insert*).
4) To insert the same words in another place where the effect will be different.

A motion to insert, or to add, words can have applied to it secondary amendments in any of the three forms relating to words—inserting or adding; striking out; or striking out and inserting.

1(b). To Insert, or to Add, a Paragraph.   The rules for the insertion or addition of a paragraph are essentially the same as those given above, except that after a paragraph has been inserted, words can still be added to it (that is, placed at the end of the paragraph only) provided that they do not conflict with or modify anything in the paragraph as already inserted. When a paragraph is to be inserted or added, any necessary perfecting should first be done by secondary amendments. After its insertion or addition, the paragraph cannot be struck out except in connection with other paragraphs that make the question materially different. If a motion to insert or add a paragraph is voted down, its rejection does not preclude any other motion except one that presents essentially the same question. If a rejected paragraph is rewritten or shortened in such a way that its effect is changed, it becomes a different paragraph under the rules for amendment.

Form and Example: 1(a), 1(b). To Insert, or to Add (Words or a Paragraph).   Typical forms in which a motion to insert, or to add, may be made are: "I move to amend the resolution by inserting the word 'waterfront' before the word 'property'"; "I move to insert 'plus expenses' after '$100'"; "I move to insert 'permanent' between 'all' and 'employees'"; "I move to insert in Line 5 of the second paragraph, the word 'preferred' before 'stocks'"; "I move to insert after Paragraph 3 the following paragraph: ..."; "I move to amend by adding the words, 'at a cost not to exceed $2,000'"; "I move to add the following paragraph: ..."

1   In stating the question on each motion in any series involving amendments, and again when putting the motion to
a vote, the chair should take care that the members understand which motion is under immediate consideration, as well
5   as the effect of adopting or rejecting it.

Therefore, when stating the question on an amendment,
the chair may find it advisable to employ three steps:

1) State the question as for any other motion: "It is moved
10   and seconded to ..."
2) Read the main motion (or the portion affected by the
   amendment) as it would stand if the amendment were
   adopted: "If the amendment is adopted, the main motion
   will read ..."
15 3) Make clear once more that it is the *amendment* that is
   under immediate consideration: "The question is on ..."

Assume that the main motion "That the Society purchase the property adjoining the present Headquarters" is
20 pending.

MEMBER A (obtaining the floor): I move to add the words "and convert it into a parking lot." (Second.)

CHAIR: It is moved and seconded to add the words "and convert it
25 into a parking lot." If the amendment is adopted, the main motion will
read, "That the Society purchase the property adjoining the present
Headquarters and convert it into a parking lot." The question is on
adding the words "and convert it into a parking lot."

30 Similarly, when putting to a vote the question on an
amendment, if debate or consideration of other motions has
intervened since the amendment was stated, the chair may
find it advisable to employ a comparable set of three steps:

35 1) Repeat the amendment: "The question is on ..."

2) Read the main motion (or the portion affected by the amendment) as it would stand if the amendment were adopted: "If the amendment is adopted, the main motion will read …"

3) Take the vote in such a way as to make clear it is the *amendment* that is to be voted on: "Those in favor of …, say *aye*. [Pausing for response.] … Those opposed, say *no*."

CHAIR: The question is on adding the words "and convert it into a parking lot." If the amendment is adopted, the main motion will read, "That the Society purchase the property adjoining the present Headquarters and convert it into a parking lot." Those in favor of adding the words "and convert it into a parking lot," say *aye*. [Pausing for response.] … Those opposed, say *no*.

After taking the vote, the chair announces the result of the vote on the amendment, and then states the question that consequently becomes immediately pending.

CHAIR: The ayes have it and the amendment is adopted. The question is now on the main motion as amended, "That the Society purchase the property adjoining the present Headquarters and convert it into a parking lot."

Should the amendment fail, the chair's announcement of the result would be as follows:

CHAIR: The noes have it and the amendment is lost. The question is now on the main motion, "That the Society purchase the property adjoining the present Headquarters."

At this point, regardless of whether the amendment is adopted or rejected, the resolution is again open to debate, and it is in order to offer a different amendment.

1   In some cases—depending on the length of the resolution and the amendment, the nature of the subject matter,
the conditions of the assembly, etc.—the question may be
clearer to the members if the chair restates only the amend-
5   ment, rather than employing the three steps outlined above.
On the other hand, in circumstances of particular complexity,
when confusion is otherwise likely, the chair may find it advisable to employ *four* steps: first, to reread the entire main
motion or resolution (or the paragraph or portion that the
10   amendment would affect); second, to read the proposed
amendment; third, to read the motion, resolution, or affected
portion as it would stand if the amendment were adopted;
and fourth, to make it clear once more that it is the *amendment* that is to be voted on.

15   As an example of *secondary amendment by inserting*, assume that there are pending: (1) a resolution, "*Resolved*, That
the Society purchase the property adjoining the present
Headquarters"; and (2) (immediately pending) a primary
amendment, "to add the words, 'and convert it into a parking
20   lot.'" (Details as to probable costs of proposed phases of the
project are assumed to be known.)

MEMBER X (obtaining the floor): I move to insert in the pending
amendment the word "landscaped" before "parking lot." (Second.)

25   CHAIR: It is moved and seconded to amend by inserting in the primary
amendment the word "landscaped" before "parking lot." If the word is
inserted, the primary amendment will be, "to add to the resolution for
the purchase of the property, the words 'and convert it into a *landscaped*
parking lot.'" The question is on inserting the word "landscaped."

30

It should be noted that in the preceding example the chair
gives the *primary* amendment as it would read if the secondary amendment were adopted.

Debate, if any, must be confined to the issue: *If* the con-
35   version to a parking lot is to be included in the project at this

time, should the lot be landscaped? When this debate has
ended, the chair puts the secondary amendment to a vote,
announces the result, and states the question before the
assembly, as follows:

CHAIR: The question is on inserting in the primary amendment the
word "landscaped" before "parking lot." If the word is inserted, the primary amendment will be, "To add to the resolution for the purchase of
the adjoining property, the words, 'and convert it into a *landscaped*
parking lot.'" It should be noted that this vote will not decide whether
a parking lot is to be part of the project. This vote will determine only
whether the parking lot will be landscaped *if* it is constructed. A vote of
aye is *for* landscaping. A vote of *no* is *against* landscaping. Those in favor
of inserting the word "landscaped" in the amendment, say *aye*. ... Those
opposed, say *no*. ... The ayes have it and the word is inserted. The question is now on the primary amendment as amended, which is, "to add
to the resolution the words, 'and convert it into a landscaped parking
lot.'" If the amendment is adopted, the resolution will read, "*Resolved*,
That the Society purchase the property adjoining the present Headquarters, *and convert it into a landscaped parking lot.*" Adoption of this
amendment will mean that if the property is purchased by the Society,
there will be a parking lot—which will be landscaped. The question is on
the amendment.

Debate and voting on the question proceed as described
above.

Amendments are sometimes so simple or acceptable that
they may be adopted by *unanimous consent* (see pp. 54–56).
For example, assume that while a main motion is pending,
"That the Properties Committee be directed to secure estimates for the necessary building repairs," a member moves
"to amend by inserting the words 'at least three' before
'estimates.'" If the chair senses that there is general approval,
he may say, "If there is no objection, the words 'at least three'
will be inserted. The wording would then be 'to secure at

1   least three estimates.' [Pause.] Since there is no objection,
the words are inserted."

2(a). To Strike Out Words.   A motion to strike out words
must specify their location when it is not otherwise clear.

5   When a motion to strike out certain words is made, it can
be applied only to consecutive words; but the words to be
struck out may become separated as a result of secondary
amendments, in which case the primary amendment is voted
on in a form in which it could not have been moved directly.

10   To strike out separated words, the best method is to make a
motion to strike out the entire clause or sentence containing
the separated words and insert a new clause or sentence as
desired. Separated words can also be struck out by separate
motions.

15   If a motion to strike out certain words is adopted, the
same words cannot be inserted again unless the place or
the wording is so changed as to make a new proposition. If a
motion to strike out certain words fails, it is still in order—
subject to the requirement that the words involved must be

20   consecutive—to move:

1) To strike out only a part of the same words.
2) To strike out all or a part of the same words together with
   some others.

25   3) To strike out all or a part of the same words and insert
   different ones.
4) To strike out all or a part of the same words together with
   some others and insert different words.

30   It is important to note that: *The motion to amend by striking out certain words can be amended only by striking out words
from the primary amendment.* The effect of such a secondary
amendment is that words struck out of the primary amendment will remain in the main motion regardless of whether

35   the primary amendment is adopted or rejected. For example,

assume that the following are pending: (1) a main motion directing the secretary to write to Congressmen Altman, Brock, Crowley, Davidson, and Edwards; (2) a primary amendment to strike out "Brock, Crowley, Davidson"; and (3) a secondary amendment to strike out "Crowley" from the primary amendment. If the secondary amendment is adopted, the primary amendment then becomes "to strike out 'Brock' and 'Davidson'" from the main motion—so that Crowley's name will remain in the main motion regardless of the outcome of the vote on the primary amendment, which no longer affects him. As a consequence of the rule stated at the beginning of this paragraph, a primary amendment to strike out a single word cannot be amended.

When a motion is made to strike out a sentence that might desirably be retained with some changes, the form of secondary amendment allowed for motions to strike out certain words may not be readily applicable. In such a case, a member can say in debate on the primary amendment that he believes the sentence should be reworded in a way which he can then state, and that if the motion to strike out the present sentence is adopted he will move to insert his new version. If the motion to strike out is lost, he can also move to strike out the present sentence and insert his new version.

2(b). To Strike Out a Paragraph. There is an essential difference between the motion to strike out a paragraph and the motion to strike out certain words, which lies in the rules and effect of secondary amendment. When it is moved to *strike out an entire paragraph*, the paragraph that would be struck out is opened to improvement by *secondary amendment in any of the three forms relating to words* (inserting or adding; striking out; or striking out and inserting) before the vote is taken on the primary amendment. If the primary amendment to strike out is voted down, the paragraph then remains in the resolution *with any changes that were made by secondary amendment.* The following differences in the effect

1 of a *secondary amendment to strike out*—dependent on
whether the primary amendment to strike out involves only
certain words or a paragraph—should be particularly noted:

5   • If the primary amendment is to strike out certain *words*,
then words struck out of the primary amendment will remain *in* the resolution regardless of the final vote on the
primary amendment (as explained under *Strike Out
Words*, above).

10 • But if the primary amendment is to strike out a *paragraph*, then words struck out of that paragraph in the
process of secondary amendment are *out of* the resolution
regardless of the final vote on the primary amendment.

15   After a paragraph has been struck out, it cannot be inserted again unless the wording (or, possibly, the place) is
changed in a way that presents an essentially new question.
After a motion to strike out a particular paragraph has been
voted down, any amendment presenting a materially new
20 question involving the same paragraph, or any part of it, is
still in order.

   *Form and Example: 2(a), 2(b). To Strike Out (Words or a
Paragraph).*   The motion to strike out may be made in such
forms as "I move to strike out the word 'concrete' before
25 'pavement' in Line 5"; or "I move to strike out the third paragraph of the platform statement." Variations similar to those
given for inserting or adding (p. 141) are applicable.

   Assume that the following main motion is pending: "That
the Bowling League establish a division open to the juniors
30 and seniors of Southwood High School."

   MEMBER A (obtaining the floor): I move to amend by striking out
the words "juniors and." (Second.)

   CHAIR: It is moved and seconded to amend by striking out the words
35 "juniors and." If the amendment is adopted, the main motion will be to

"establish a division open to the seniors of Southwood High School." *1*
The question is on striking out the words "juniors and."

From this point, the procedure is similar to that already
illustrated for inserting or adding. *5*

3(a). To Strike Out and Insert (applying to words). The
motion to strike out and insert is especially applicable in situations where it may be impossible to secure the desired result without making the act of "striking out" inseparable from
that of "inserting"—as may happen if some members are *10*
unwilling to vote for the one unless assured of the other. The
two parts of this motion cannot be separated, either by secondary amendment or by a *Division of the Question.*

To avoid confusion with the form of amendment known
as *Substitute* (p. 153, #3[b]), which applies to paragraphs or *15*
longer elements, the word *substitute* should not be used in
connection with the motion to *strike out and insert*, which
applies to words.

Motions to strike out and insert fall into two types:

20

• those by which a different wording is inserted in the same
  place; and
• those by which the same wording struck out of one place
  is inserted in a different place.

25

The two parts of the motion to strike out and insert must
not represent two independent questions, unless the mover
receives unanimous consent to make such a combined motion; rather, the two parts must be germane to each other.
Thus, in motions of the first type mentioned in the previous *30*
paragraph—to strike words out of and insert words into the
same place—the words to be inserted must in some way be
related to, or address the same issue as, the words to be struck
out; and in motions of the second type—to strike words out
of one place and insert words into a different place—the *35*

1   words to be inserted must not be materially different from
the words to be struck out.

The first type of the motion to strike out and insert—the
kind that proposes to insert a different wording in the same
5   place—is perhaps more common.

When such a primary amendment is offered, the chair
states the question on it and lets debate of its merits begin in
the usual way. For purposes of secondary amendment, however, this type of motion is treated as if resolved into its two
10   elements, with secondary amendment of each element following the rules that would apply to two separate motions
for primary amendment—one to strike out (amendable only
by striking out) and another to insert (amendable in any of
three forms relating to words). A single secondary amend-
15   ment involving both elements of a primary amendment to
strike out and insert is not in order. If a motion to strike out
and insert involves enough words that several secondary
amendments—particularly to the words to be struck out—
might be possible, it is often best to take any amendments to
20   the words to be struck out first, because members who wish
to perfect the words to be inserted by secondary amendment
may need to know exactly what language those words will replace, to be able to perfect them effectively. Amendments to
the words to be inserted are then taken up after amendments
25   to the words to be struck out have been disposed of. But the
chair should make a judgment depending on the conditions
as to whether the assembly wishes to follow this procedure
or will find it helpful. In any event, the primary amendment
remains open to debate at all times while it is pending with
30   no secondary amendment pending, and this debate goes into
the merits of both parts of the motion viewed as a single
whole.

While a primary amendment to strike out and insert certain words is pending, if an admissible secondary amendment

to the words to be struck out is introduced and no amend- *1*
ments to the words to be inserted have been proposed, the
chair simply proceeds to entertain the secondary amendment,
letting debate on the primary amendment resume after the
secondary amendment has been dealt with. But the first time *5*
that a secondary amendment to the words to be inserted is
offered—assuming a number of amendments to the words to
be struck out might be possible—the chair has the option, as
described in the preceding paragraph, of saying: "The chair
believes it would be better to follow the procedure of taking *10*
any amendments to the words to be struck out first, as
permitted under the rules. Accordingly, before entertaining
the amendment just offered, the chair will ask: Are there any
amendments [or "any further amendments"] to the words
to be struck out?" When it appears that no one else wishes to *15*
propose an amendment to the words to be struck out, the
chair then says: "The primary amendment as amended is open
to debate, and secondary amendments to the words to be inserted are now in order." After reasonable opportunity to
offer any amendments of the latter type has been given, sec- *20*
ondary amendments to either element are in order. When
these and any further debate have concluded, the vote is taken
on the motion to strike out and insert as it stands after secondary amendment.

After a motion to strike out and insert has been adopted, *25*
what has been struck out and what has been inserted are subject to the same rules regarding further amendment, as if the
striking out and the inserting had been done by separate motions: The inserted matter cannot be struck out, and the matter that has been struck out cannot be inserted again, except *30*
through a reconsideration of the vote on the amendment, or
through changes in the wording or the place in a way that
presents a new question (under the rules already given for
Insert, or Add, and for *Strike Out*).

If a motion to strike out and insert is voted down, it is still in order:

- to make either of the separate motions to *strike out*, or to *insert*, the same words that would have been struck out or inserted by the combined motion that was lost; or
- to make another motion to *strike out and insert*—provided that the change in either the wording to be struck out or the wording to be inserted presents a question materially different from the one that was voted down.

When a primary amendment to strike out a passage of any length or complexity and insert a new version is pending and some members would prefer to insert something different or keep something closer to the original, it may be difficult or impossible to reach the desired end by secondary amendment. Situations of this kind can occur especially when the amendment relates to one or more complete sentences that do not constitute an entire paragraph. In such a case, a member should speak against the pending primary amendment and say that if it is rejected he will offer a new motion to strike out the same passage and insert the version he desires—which he should then state. He should present his case as strongly as possible, because if the first proposed version is inserted, it cannot be changed afterward except in connection with a different question.

As already explained in connection with the rules for the motion to *strike out*, the motion to *strike out and insert* can be used to obtain the effect of striking out or modifying separated words. To do this, a member can move to strike out of the resolution a passage long enough to include all of the words to be removed or changed, and insert the revised passage. If several changes in a paragraph are desired, it is usually

better to rewrite the paragraph and offer the new version as *1*
a *substitute*, as explained below.

    Form and Example: 3(a). To Strike Out and Insert (applying to words). As an example of a motion to strike out and insert, assume that the following resolution is pending: *5* "*Resolved*, That the Citizens' Association endorse the Rockville site for the new Community College."

    MEMBER A (obtaining the floor): I move to amend by striking out "Rockville" and inserting "Chatham." (Second.) *10*

    CHAIR: It is moved and seconded to strike out "Rockville" and insert "Chatham." If the amendment is adopted, the resolution will be to "endorse the Chatham site for the new Community College." The question is on striking out "Rockville" and inserting "Chatham."

15

Debate on the amendment is limited to the relative advantages of the two sites. After the amendment is debated, the chair puts it to vote, as in the case already illustrated for *Insert or Add*. Debate on the resolution can go into the question of whether the association should express approval of *20* any site.

    3(b). To Substitute. A motion to *Amend* by striking out an entire paragraph, section, or article—or a complete main motion or resolution—and inserting a different paragraph or other unit in its place is called a motion to *substitute*, and the *25* paragraph or resolution to be inserted is said to be offered (or proposed) as "a substitute." A substitute can be offered for a paragraph or a main motion of only one sentence, and in such a case the paragraph proposed as a substitute can contain several sentences. (For the replacement of sentences *within* a *30* paragraph, see below.) A substitute offered for a main motion or resolution, or for a paragraph within a resolution, is a primary amendment and can therefore be moved only when no other amendment is pending. If a motion proposes to replace

1   one or more paragraphs that are involved in a pending pri-
    mary amendment, it is a secondary amendment to which the
    term *substitute* is also applicable.*

        A primary amendment to *substitute* is treated similarly to
5   a motion to *strike out and insert* as described on pages
    149–53. It is open to debate at all times while it is pending
    with no secondary amendment pending; and such debate may
    go fully into the merits of both the original text and the sub-
    stitute, since this is necessary to determine the desirability of
10 the primary amendment. But for purposes of secondary
    amendment, the motion to substitute is looked upon as re-
    solved into its two elements, the paragraph to be struck out
    and the paragraph to be inserted. In contrast to the rules for
    striking out and inserting *words*, however, when a motion to
15 *substitute* is under consideration the paragraph to be struck
    out as well as the paragraph to be inserted can be perfected
    by secondary amendment in any of the three basic forms (in-
    serting or adding; striking out; or striking out and inserting),
    since this is the procedure when either of the separate mo-
20 tions to *insert* or to *strike out* is applied to the paragraph.

        As in the case of a motion to strike out and insert words,
    the chair has the option of accepting only amendments to the
    paragraph to be struck out first, and then only amendments
    to the proposed substitute, thereafter accepting either type
25 of secondary amendment. Following this procedure is likely
    to be more often indicated in the case of a motion to substi-
    tute, particularly if a substantive issue hangs on such a mo-
    tion, as in the example given below. After all secondary
    amendments have been disposed of and after any further de-
30 bate on the motion to substitute, the vote is taken on whether
    to make this substitution.

---

*It is thus possible to introduce a proposed "substitute for a substitute,"
which cannot be amended, since it is a secondary amendment.

For replacing an unbroken *part* of a paragraph when the part to be replaced consists of (or contains) one or more complete sentences, there is an option between offering the amendment as a motion to strike out the part and insert the new matter (that is, as a motion to *strike out and insert*), or moving it in the form of a substitute for the entire paragraph with only the desired part changed. Either of these motions, as applied to the same case, will present substantially the same question when it is made, but the effect of each of them is different as to permissible secondary amendment. If much of the paragraph is involved in such a case, it is generally better to offer the desired amendment in the form of a substitute. If this method is used, however, secondary amendment can also involve the portion of the paragraph in which no change was proposed initially.

In taking the vote on whether to make the substitution, the chair should first read both the paragraph of the original text and the proposed substitute—*as they stand at the time* as amended. Even if the entire resolution or main motion is replaced, adopting the motion to *substitute* only *amends* the resolution, which remains pending as amended.

After a paragraph, section, or version of a resolution has been substituted for another, the substituted paragraph or resolution cannot be amended except by *adding* something that does not modify the paragraph's existing content—as is true of any paragraph that has been inserted. The paragraph that has been replaced cannot be inserted again unless a material change in the wording (or possibly, the place) makes a new question—as is true of any paragraph that has been struck out.

If a motion to substitute is lost, the assembly has decided only that the paragraph proposed as a substitute shall not replace the one specified. The same proposed new paragraph can still replace a different one, or can simply be inserted. On the other hand, the paragraph that was retained in the

1   resolution can be further amended, or struck out (if it is not
the entire resolution); or it still can be replaced by a different
substitute.

When a question is being considered *by paragraph or*
5   *seriatim* (**28**), it is in order to move a substitute for any paragraph or section at the time that the paragraph or section is
opened to amendment. But it is not in order to move a substitute for the entire document until all of the paragraphs
or sections have been individually considered and the point
10   is reached when the chair announces that the entire paper is
open to amendment.

If a resolution is referred to a committee while a primary
amendment—or a primary and a secondary amendment—are
pending, the committee can report by recommending a sub-
15   stitute for the resolution, even though the substitute cannot
become pending until the other amendments have been
voted on in their normal order. Thus, when a committee has
so reported, the chair first states the question on the secondary amendment that was pending when the resolution was
20   committed, puts the secondary amendment to vote, and then
continues with the primary amendment to which it applied.
As soon as this primary amendment is disposed of, the chair
states the question on the substitute recommended by the
committee, and proceeds as he would with any other motion
25   to substitute.

In a similar way, if a resolution is referred to a committee
while a substitute and a secondary amendment (either to the
original or to the substitute) are pending, the committee can
report in favor of either version, with any desired recommen-
30   dation as to secondary amendment; or the committee can recommend rejection of the pending substitute and propose a
new substitute in its place. In all such cases, the chair starts
with the parliamentary situation as it was when the resolution
was committed; he then proceeds as with any motion to sub-
35   stitute, and states the question on any new amendment (rec-

ommended by the committee) as soon as it is in order for that amendment to be pending under the usual rules.

The motion to *substitute* often provides a convenient and timesaving method for handling a poorly framed resolution, or for introducing a different and better approach to the real question raised by a main motion. While changes by separate amendments are in progress, a member who feels that he has a better solution by substitution can indicate its features briefly and announce his intention of offering the substitute as soon as no other amendment is pending. If the member wishing to propose the substitute thinks it appropriate, he can try to bring the pending amendments to an immediate vote by moving the *Previous Question* (**16**) on them.

An amendment in the form of a substitute can also be used to defeat or work against the purpose of the measure originally introduced. Such a stratagem can be utilized with a view either to converting the measure into a weakened form before its final adoption, or to substituting a version that is likely to be rejected in the final vote. It should be noted that a vote in favor of substituting an entire resolution or main motion is ordinarily a vote to kill any provisions of the original version that are not included in the substitute.

Properly applied, the rules for the treatment of motions to *substitute* automatically operate in fairness to both sides when there is disagreement as to the preferability of the original or the substitute. Under the procedure of initially accepting amendments to each element of the primary amendment exclusively—which is generally indicated whenever such disagreement exists—the proponents of the original version are first given the opportunity to amend their proposition into a more acceptable form in the light of conditions revealed by the introduction of the substitute. When this process is correctly handled as described on pages 150–51 and 154, it tends to ensure that the provisions of the version first offered receive appropriate consideration, without impeding free

1   debate of the proposal to substitute. By the requirement that
internal amendment of the substitute be done before the vote
on the motion to make the substitution, the members are
protected from having to decide whether to reject the original
5   version without knowing what may finally replace it.

Form and Example: 3(b). To Substitute.   As an example
of a motion to substitute, assume that the following resolution is pending: "*Resolved*, That the Parish Federation undertake the construction and equipping of a new service wing
10   for the Parish House, to be financed as far as possible by a
mortgage on the present building."

Debate points strongly to a need for further investigation,
but many members are determined to secure immediate authorization. The meeting seems evenly divided, and the out-
15   come is unpredictable.

MEMBER A (obtaining the floor): I move to substitute for the pending
resolution the following: "*Resolved*, That the Parish Board be directed
to engage appropriate professional consultants to make a survey of, and
20   prepare a complete report on, the need, probable cost, feasible methods
of financing, and maintenance of a new service wing for the Parish
House." (Second.)

CHAIR: It is moved and seconded to amend by substituting for the
pending resolution the following: [reading the substitute submitted by
25   Member A]. The motion to substitute proposes that the resolution just
read shall come before the assembly in place of the pending resolution.
[Debate.]

MEMBER L (who favors the *pending* resolution and is, therefore, opposed to the motion to substitute—obtaining the floor): I move to
30   amend the proposed substitute by adding the words "within twenty
days." (Second.)

CHAIR: The chair believes it will be preferable to take any amendments to the pending resolution first, as permitted under the rules.
Such amendments, if adopted, will affect the wording in which the pend-
35   ing resolution will come to a final vote if the motion to substitute

fails.* Accordingly, before entertaining the amendment just offered, the   *1*
chair will call for any amendments to the pending resolution, which he
will first reread. The pending resolution is as follows: "*Resolved*, That the
Parish Federation undertake the construction and equipping of a new
service wing for the Parish House, to be financed as far as possible by a   *5*
mortgage on the present building." Are there any amendments to the
pending resolution?

    MEMBER X (obtaining the floor): I move to amend the pending res-
olution by striking out everything after the word "undertake" and inserting the words "a campaign to raise funds for the construction and   *10*
equipping of a new service wing for the Parish House." (Second.)

    The chair states the question on this amendment, making
its effect clear, and, after debate, puts it to vote. For purposes
of the example, assume that the proponents of the original   *15*
resolution differ on the amendment, some voting for it,
others opposing it. Also, since the adoption of this amendment presumably would make the pending resolution *less*
objectionable to those who feel that the proposed project is
presently ill advised and who therefore hope that the substi-   *20*
tution will be made, most of those members probably vote
for the amendment. Assume that it is adopted. The chair announces the result as follows:

    CHAIR: The ayes have it and the amendment is adopted. The pending   *25*
resolution now reads, "*Resolved*, That the Parish Federation undertake a
campaign to raise funds for the construction and equipping of a new service wing for the Parish House." The question is on the motion to substitute. (Further debate on the relative merits of the pending resolution
and the proposed substitute.)   *30*

    MEMBER L (who favors the *pending* resolution—obtaining the floor):
I move to amend the substitute by adding "within twenty days." (Second.)

---

    *If the members are familiar with the procedure for handling motions
to substitute, the chair may omit the sentence preceding the asterisk.

1   CHAIR: Before entertaining the amendment just offered, the chair will
again ask: Are there any further amendments to the pending resolution?
[Pause.] There being none, it is moved and seconded to amend the proposed substitute by adding the words "within twenty days." If the amend-
5 ment is adopted, the substitute will read, "*Resolved*, That the Parish Board
be directed to engage appropriate professional consultants to make a survey of, and prepare a complete report on, the need, probable cost, feasible
methods of financing, and maintenance of a new service wing for the
Parish House within twenty days." The question is on amending the pro-
10 posed substitute by adding the words "within twenty days."

Brief debate shows that the proposed survey could not be
properly carried out in twenty days. Assume that this amendment is voted down.

15

MEMBER B (who is in favor of the motion to substitute, but fears it
will fail unless some time limit is specified—obtaining the floor): I move
to amend the substitute by adding "within sixty days." (Second.)

20   The chair states the question on this amendment
and (after brief debate) puts it to vote. Assume that the
amendment is adopted. In announcing the result, the chair
continues:

25   CHAIR: The ayes have it and the amendment is adopted. The proposed substitute now reads, "*Resolved*, That the Parish Board be directed
to engage ... for the Parish House within sixty days." Are you ready for
the question on the motion to substitute?

30   After further amendment of the proposed substitute, the
chair says:

CHAIR: Are there any further amendments to the proposed substitute? [Pause.] There being none, it is now in order to offer amendments
35 *either* to the pending resolution *or* to the proposed substitute.

When all debate and secondary amendment has concluded, the chair puts to vote the motion to substitute. Both resolutions are read, usually by the chair—the pending resolution first, then the resolution proposed as a substitute.

CHAIR: The question is on the motion to substitute. The chair will read the pending resolution first, then the resolution proposed as a substitute. The pending resolution is: "*Resolved*, That the Parish Federation undertake a campaign to raise funds for the construction and equipping of a new service wing for the Parish House." The resolution proposed as a substitute is: "*Resolved*, That the Parish Board be directed to engage appropriate professional consultants to make a survey of, and prepare a complete report on, the need, probable cost, ... within sixty days." The question is: Shall the resolution last read be substituted for the pending resolution? Those in favor of the motion to substitute, say *aye*. ... Those opposed, say *no*. ...

The chair announces the result of the vote and states the question on whichever resolution is left pending, as follows:

CHAIR: The ayes have it and the motion to substitute is adopted. The question is now on the resolution: [reading the resolution directing the employment of professional consultants].

Or:

CHAIR: The noes have it and the motion to substitute is lost. The question is now on the resolution: [reading the resolution for a fund-raising campaign].

Regardless of which resolution is now pending, there may be further debate. If the motion to substitute has been adopted, the resolution now pending is in the position of a paragraph that has been inserted, and it can no longer be amended except by *adding* nonmodifying matter. On the

1   other hand, if the motion to substitute has been lost, the res-
     olution for the fund drive can be further amended; but in de-
     termining whether an amendment now offered presents a
     new question and can therefore be admitted, account must
5   be taken of any motions to amend that were voted on before
     the motion to substitute was introduced, or while it was
     pending.

     FRIENDLY AMENDMENTS.   The term "friendly
10   amendment" is often used to describe an amendment offered
     by someone who is in sympathy with the purposes of the main
     motion, in the belief that the amendment will either improve
     the statement or effect of the main motion, presumably to
     the satisfaction of its maker, or will increase the chances of
15   the main motion's adoption. Regardless of whether or not
     the maker of the main motion "accepts" the amendment, it
     must be opened to debate and voted on formally (unless
     adopted by unanimous consent) and is handled under the
     same rules as amendments generally (see also pp. 295–98).
20

     ### Filling Blanks

     Filling blanks, although not a form of amendment in it-
     self, is a closely related device by which an unlimited number
25   of alternative choices for a particular specification in a main
     motion or primary amendment can be pending at the same
     time. In effect, it permits an exception to the rule (p. 135,
     ll. 27–30) that only one primary and one secondary amend-
     ment can be pending at a time, and in certain cases it has dis-
30   tinct advantages.
     In amending by the ordinary method, a maximum of
     three alternatives can be pending at once, and the last one
     moved must be voted on first. In filling blanks, the number
     of alternatives is not limited; members have an opportunity
35   to weigh all choices before voting and to vote on them in a

fair and logical order. Among cases adapted to such treatment are main motions or primary amendments containing names of persons or places, dates, numbers, or amounts.

CREATING A BLANK.   A blank to be filled can be created in one of three ways:

a) A member can offer a motion or an amendment containing a blank: for example, "*Resolved*, That Lodge No. 432 build a new headquarters at a cost not to exceed $_____"; or an amendment to a main motion can propose "to add 'provided that estimates be received on or before _____.'"

b) A member can move that a blank be created. For example, assume that the pending resolution is: "*Resolved*, That Lodge No. 432 build a new headquarters at a cost not to exceed $300,000." Any member can move "to create a blank by striking out of the pending resolution the sum '$300,000.'" If such a motion is adopted, the specification struck out to create the blank automatically becomes one of the proposals for filling it—as "$300,000" in the example. Although the motion to create a blank may appear to resemble a motion to amend by striking out and inserting, it is in fact an incidental motion (see p. 69). It is not in order to create a blank in a motion on which the *Previous Question* has been ordered. The motion to create a blank requires a second, but it is neither debatable nor amendable; it can also be made and voted on while a primary or a secondary amendment relating to the subject specification is pending. For example, assuming the same pending resolution as above, the identical motion to create a blank by striking out "$300,000" can be made while a primary amendment "to strike out '$300,000' and insert '$350,000'" is also pending. Adoption of the motion to create a blank in such a case (before the amendment is

1 voted on) causes both specifications—the one in the pending resolution and the corresponding one in the amendment—to become proposals for filling the blank; as "$300,000" and "$350,000" in the example.

5 c) The chair can suggest the creation of a blank, as follows: "The chair suggests creating a blank by striking out '$300,000.' If there is no objection, a blank will be created. [Pause.] There is no objection; the blank is created." If a member objects, the chair puts the question to a vote, *10* treating the question just as he would treat a motion to create a blank made as described above.

When a blank exists or has been created, any number of members can suggest, without a second, a different name, *15* place, number, date, or amount for filling it. No member can suggest more than one proposal for filling the blank, except when the blank can be filled with more than one name, as may happen, for example, in a motion to appoint members of a committee. In such a case, a member can suggest additional *20* names—after all other members have had an opportunity to suggest one—but no more than allowed for in the blank. Thus, the suggestion of more than one name at a time by a single member can be entertained only if no objection is made.

Proposals to fill a blank in a debatable motion are debat-*25* able. Each proposal is treated as an independent original to be voted on separately until one is approved by a majority.

FILLING A BLANK WITH NAMES.   The following principles apply to the process of filling a blank with one or *30* more names:

a) The procedure for filling a blank with one name is practically the same as for making nominations. The chair repeats each name as it is proposed, and finally takes a vote *35* on each in that same order, until one receives a majority.

b) If the blank is to be filled with more than one name and   *1*
no more are suggested than are required, the names can
be inserted by unanimous consent.

c) If more names are suggested than are required, the chair
takes a vote on each in the order of its proposal until   *5*
enough to fill the blank have received a majority vote.
The names remaining in the list as proposed are ignored,
since the assembly has decided which names shall fill the
blank.

d) If the number of names is not specified, the chair takes a   *10*
vote on each name suggested; and all names approved by
a majority vote are inserted.

FILLING A BLANK WITH AMOUNTS OF MONEY.
Sometimes the particular nature of the blank determines the   *15*
order in which proposals for filling it should be put to vote.
Typical instances of this kind are blanks to be filled with
amounts of money. In such cases it is advisable, whenever a
logical order is apparent, to arrange the proposed entries so
that *the one least likely to be acceptable will be voted on first*, and   *20*
so on. New supporters may then be gained with each suc-
ceeding vote until a majority in favor of one entry is reached.

As an example of the procedure for filling a blank with an
amount of money, assume that a resolution to build a new
headquarters "at a cost not to exceed \$_____" is pending,   *25*
and that it is proposed to fill the blank with the following
amounts: \$350,000, \$250,000, \$400,000, and \$300,000.
The character of this measure—to *spend* money—indicates
that the amounts should be arranged and voted on in order
from the highest to lowest. If \$400,000 is rejected, the vote   *30*
is taken next on \$350,000; and if that is not adopted, the
chair puts the question on \$300,000. If that amount is
adopted, no vote is taken on \$250,000, and the chair imme-
diately says, "The amount of \$300,000 fills the blank. The
question is now on the resolution: '*Resolved*, That ... at a cost   *35*

1   not to exceed $300,000.'" Note that if the smallest sum had
been voted on first, it might have been adopted, with the result that those who preferred the added advantages possible
through a larger expenditure would have been cut off from
5   considering larger sums.

On the other hand, suppose that the motion or resolution
is "to sell the headquarters for an amount not less than
$_____." In the case of such a motion—to *accept* a sum of
money in *settlement*—the amounts being considered should
10 be arranged and voted on in order from the smallest to the
largest. Thus, those who are willing to sell for the smallest
amount, and some additional members, will be willing to sell
for the next larger sum, and so on, until the smallest sum for
which the majority is willing to sell is reached.
15

FILLING A BLANK WITH PLACES, DATES, OR
NUMBERS.   When a blank is to be filled with a place, date,
or number, a choice of methods for arranging and voting on
the proposals can be made as follows:
20

a) Voting on the suggestions in the order in which they are
offered, as when filling a blank with names.
b) Voting on the proposals in the order of their probable ac-
ceptability, beginning with the least popular choice, as
25   when filling a blank with an amount.
c) (If there is no clear-cut reason why either increasing or
decreasing order would be preferable), voting first on the
largest number, longest time, or most distant date, and
so on.
30

The particular circumstances must determine the order to be
used.

If an amount has been struck out in order to create a
blank, that amount is voted on in its proper place in the log-
35 ical sequence among the other amounts. If a name has been

struck out to create a blank, however, it comes first in the *1* order of names to be voted on.

The suggestions for filling a blank can be voted on by any of the regular methods (pp. 44ff., 409ff.). Voting by ballot or roll call is seldom used except in the case of names, however, *5* unless there is keen competition—for example, among several cities seeking a convention. When names are being voted on, the ballot has an advantage in more truly revealing the will of the voting body; frequently when the vote is by voice, members vote for those nominated first. *10*

It should be noted that the vote that fills a blank does not decide the main question. When the blank is filled, the chair must immediately state the question on the adoption of the completed motion.

The *Previous Question* cannot be ordered to stop the mak- *15* ing of suggestions for filling a blank. The same result may be accomplished, however, by a motion to *Close Suggestions* which is identical to a motion to *Close Nominations* (**31**). It may be adopted by a two-thirds vote and is in order if a rea- sonable opportunity to make suggestions has been given. *20*

Normally, blanks should be filled before voting on the motion itself; but if a large majority is confident that the meas- ure will be rejected in any case, time may be saved by ordering the *Previous Question* on *all* applicable pending questions be- fore the blank is filled. This brings the assembly to an imme- *25* diate vote on suggestions already made to fill the blank, if any, and on the main motion or on the amendment containing the blank. If by chance the motion is nevertheless adopted, the blank should be filled and the motion completed before any new subject (except a privileged one) is introduced. *30*

(For further examples of both creating and filling a blank, see p. 171, ll. 2–4; p. 172, ll. 16–18; p. 173, l. 31 to p. 174, l. 9; pp. 178–79; p. 272, ll. 11–15; p. 288, ll. 12–20.)

§13. COMMIT OR REFER

The subsidiary motion to *Commit* or *Refer* is generally used to send a pending question to a relatively small group of selected persons—a committee—so that the question may be carefully investigated and put into better condition for the assembly to consider.

The motion to *Commit* also has three *variations* whose object is not to turn the main question over to a smaller group, but to permit the assembly's full meeting body to consider it with the greater freedom of debate that is allowed in committees—that is, with no limit on the number of times a member can speak. These forms of the motion are:

a) to "go into a committee of the whole";
b) to "go into quasi committee of the whole" (or, to "consider as if in committee of the whole"); and
c) to "consider informally."

"Informal consideration" is the simplest of the three methods and is usually the best in ordinary societies whose meetings are not large (see pp. 540–41).

The term *recommit* is applied to a motion that proposes to refer a question a second time, either to the same committee that previously considered it or to a different one.

All of the rules in this section, except when stated to the contrary, apply equally to variations (a), (b), and (c) above, and to a motion to recommit.

When a motion proposes to assign a task or refer a matter to a committee when no question is pending, such a motion is not the subsidiary motion to *Commit*, but is a main motion. It is an incidental main motion if the assignment or referral is pursuant to a subject on which the assembly has already taken some action; but it is an original main motion if the matter to be assigned or referred relates to a new subject.

Standard Descriptive Characteristics   *1*

The subsidiary motion to *Commit* or *Refer*:

1. Takes precedence over the main motion, over the sub-   5
   sidiary motions to *Postpone Indefinitely* and to *Amend*,
   and over the incidental motions for *Division of a Question*
   and for *Consideration by Paragraph or Seriatim*. It also
   takes precedence over a debatable appeal (or a point of
   order which has been referred by the chair to the judg-   10
   ment of the assembly and that is debatable when so referred, p. 249, ll. 7–12) under either of the following
   conditions: (a) if the appeal or question of order does not
   adhere to the main question; or (b) if no other motions
   except those named in the preceding sentence are pend-   15
   ing or involved in the appeal or question of order. It yields
   to the subsidiary motions to *Postpone Definitely*, to *Limit*
   or Extend Limits of Debate, for the *Previous Question*, and
   to *Lay on the Table*; to a motion to *Amend* that is applied
   to it; to all privileged motions; and to all applicable inci- 20
   dental motions.
2. Can be applied to main motions, with any amendments
   that may be pending; can be thus applied to *orders of the*
   day (**18**, **41**) or *questions of privilege* (**19**) while they are
   actually pending as main motions, and such an application 25
   is independent of, and does not affect, any other matter
   that they may have interrupted; can be applied to debatable appeals (or points of order referred by the chair to
   the judgment of the assembly that are debatable when so
   referred, p. 249, ll. 7–12), but if such an appeal adheres   30
   (p. 118) to the main question (that is, if the appeal must
   be decided before the main question is decided), the
   motion to *Commit* can be applied to the appeal only
   in connection with the main question, which also goes
   to the committee (see also p. 177); and can be applied to   35

nonadhering debatable appeals separately, without affecting the status of any other questions that may be pending.
It cannot be applied to an undebatable appeal. It cannot
be applied to the motion to *Reconsider* alone—that is,
it cannot be applied to a motion to reconsider a main
question; and if a main question is committed while a motion to reconsider an amendment is pending, such a
motion to *Reconsider* is thereafter ignored. It cannot be
applied to any subsidiary motion, except that its application to a main question also affects any motions to *Amend*
that may be pending, as noted above. It cannot be moved
after the adoption of a motion to close debate on the
main question at a definite hour or to limit the total time
allowed for debate; but it remains in order if only a limitation on the length of speeches is in force (see **15**). Motions to *Amend*, to *Limit or Extend Limits of Debate*, and
for the *Previous Question* can be applied to it without affecting the main question. The motion to *Commit* cannot
be definitely postponed or laid on the table alone, but
when it is pending the main question can be definitely
postponed or laid on the table, and in such a case, the
motion to *Commit* is also postponed or carried to
the table. It cannot be postponed indefinitely.

3. Is out of order when another has the floor.

4. Must be seconded.

5. Is debatable. The debate can extend only to the desirability of committing the main question and to the appropriate details of the motion to *Commit*, as explained below,
however, and not to the merits of the main question.

6. Is amendable as follows: in the case of a standing committee, as to the committee to which the main question
is to be referred; in the case of a special committee, as to
the committee's composition and manner of selection;
and in the case of any form of committee, as to any
instructions the committee is to follow. It can be amended

so as to change from any one of the five forms of the mo-   *1*
tion (listed on p. 173, l. 35 to p. 174, l. 4) to another, or
a blank can be created (pp. 162–67) and the suggested
forms voted on in the order given on pages 173–74.

7. Requires a majority vote.   *5*

8. An affirmative vote on the motion to *Commit* can be reconsidered if the committee has not begun consideration
of the question. Thereafter, if the assembly wishes to take
the question out of the hands of the committee, the motion to *Discharge a Committee* (**36**) must be used. A neg-   *10*
ative vote on the motion to *Commit* can be reconsidered
only until such time as progress in business or debate has
been sufficient to make it essentially a new question.
Thereafter, the motion can be renewed (see pp. 339–40).

   15

Further Rules and Explanation

NECESSARY DETAILS OF THE MOTION. The
motion to *Commit* usually should include all necessary
details: *20*

- If the main question is to be considered in a committee
  of the whole, or in quasi committee of the whole ("as if
  in committee of the whole"), or if it is to be considered
  informally, the motion should specify which of these   *25*
  methods is to be used.
- If the main question is to be sent to a standing committee
  (see **50**), the motion should specify the name of the
  committee.
- If the main question is to go to a special (select, or ad   *30*
  hoc) committee (see **50**), the motion should specify the
  number of committee members, and the method of their
  selection unless the method is prescribed by the bylaws;
  or, if preferred, the motion can name the members of the
  special committee. (The word *special*, or *select*, or *ad hoc*,   *35*

is not generally used in a motion to refer to a special committee; the motion is worded, for example, "to refer the question to a committee of five to be appointed by ..." See also forms of the motion on pp. 178–79.)

- Instructions to the committee can also be included in the motion to *Commit*, whether the committee is to be a standing or a special one, or a committee of the whole. These instructions, which are binding on the committee, may involve such matters as when the committee should meet, how it should consider the question, whether it should employ an expert consultant, and when it should report. The committee can be given "full power" to act for the society in a specific case and can be authorized to spend money or even to add to its own membership.

Although these details can be changed by ordinary amendments, they can often be handled more efficiently by treating them as in filling blanks (pp. 162–67, 178–79).

DILATORY MOTION TO COMMIT. The chair should rule out of order, as dilatory, any motion to *Commit* that is obviously absurd or unreasonable—such as one that (because of the time involved or any other reason) would have the effect of defeating the purpose of the main question.

ALTERNATIVE PROCEDURES WHEN THE MOTION IS INCOMPLETE. When a motion to *Commit* merely lacks essential details—for example, when the motion is made simply "to refer the main question to a committee"—the chair should not rule it out of order. Instead, these two courses are open:

a) Members can offer suggestions or formal amendments to complete the required details, or the chair can call for them.

b) The chair can put the motion to *Commit* to vote at once   *1*
    in its simple form.

The second alternative is appropriate if no one is seeking
recognition and the chair believes that the motion to *Commit*   *5*
is not likely to be adopted, in which case time spent in completing the details would be wasted. Opponents of the motion to *Commit* may try to bring about the same result (that
is, obtaining an immediate vote on the referral) by moving
the *Previous Question* on it (see **16**). If the necessary two   *10*
thirds (of those voting) vote to order the *Previous Question*
on an incomplete motion to *Commit*, the motion is almost
certain to be rejected, whatever details might be added.
    In the event that any of the above procedures results in
the adoption of an incomplete motion "to refer the question   *15*
to a committee," the details must be completed as described
in the following paragraphs. In such a case, no new subject
(except a privileged one) can be introduced until the assembly
has decided all of these related questions. In completing the
details, the member who made the motion to commit has no   *20*
preference in recognition, since he or she could have included
any desired specifications in that motion.

COMPLETING AN INCOMPLETE MOTION TO
COMMIT.   In completing a motion that simply refers "the   *25*
main question to a committee"—either while the motion to
Commit is pending or after it is adopted—the chair first asks,
"To what committee shall the question be referred?" If only
one suggestion is made, he assumes that this is the will of the
assembly, and he states that it is inserted into the motion to   *30*
Commit. But if different proposals are made, either in the
form of primary and secondary amendments or simply as suggestions, the chair treats them as proposals to fill a blank
(pp. 162–67) and puts them to vote in the following order
until one receives a majority: (1) committee of the whole;   *35*

(2) quasi committee of the whole (or "as if in committee of the whole"); (3) consider informally; (4) standing committees, in the order in which they are proposed; and (5) special (select, or ad hoc) committees, the one containing the largest number of members being voted on first. A proposal to recommit to the same standing or special committee that previously considered the question should be voted on before other proposals for standing or special committees are voted on.

If it is decided that the committee is to be a special one, the chair then asks—unless the rules provide the method—"How shall the committee be appointed?" Again, if only one suggestion is made, it is inserted by unanimous consent, but if different methods are suggested or moved, they are voted on in the following order: (1) election by ballot; (2) nominations from the floor ("open nominations") with viva-voce election; (3) nominations by the chair; and (4) appointment by the chair (see also pp. 492ff.). The first of these methods of selection that receives a majority vote is then inserted into the motion to *Commit* and the remainder are ignored.

If the motion to *Commit* lacks any other detail, the chair proceeds in a similar fashion to obtain completion of the motion. As soon as it is completed, if it is a *pending* motion to *Commit*, the chair states the question on it, thus opening it to additional debate during which any member can move—or the chair himself can suggest—that it be amended by adding instructions. By a majority vote, instructions can also be added to a motion to *Commit* that is being completed after its adoption.

NAMING MEMBERS TO A SPECIAL COMMITTEE. A standing or special committee may include, or even have as its chairman, one or more persons who are not members of the assembly or the society; but if the chair appoints the committee, the names of all such nonmembers being

appointed must be submitted to the assembly for approval, 1
unless the bylaws or the motion to appoint the committee
specifically authorizes the presiding officer to appoint nonmembers (see also pp. 492–93, 495–96). When a motion to
refer to a special committee has been adopted, no business 5
except privileged matters can intervene until selection of the
committee members is completed—except that if the chair is
to appoint the committee, he can, if he wishes and time permits, state that he will announce the names of its members
later. In such a case, however, the committee must be left with 10
reasonable time to accomplish its purpose after the names of
its members have been announced for the record and any
non–society members have been approved as necessary under
the rule stated at the beginning of this paragraph in a meeting
of the assembly. The committee cannot act before such an 15
announcement of its membership is made, unless otherwise
authorized by vote of the assembly.

Although it is not necessary to place on a special committee the member who made the motion to *Commit*, it is usual
to do so when such a person is interested and qualified. For 20
a discussion of the appropriate size and personnel of committees under various circumstances, see pages 497–98.

DESIGNATING THE COMMITTEE CHAIRMAN.
If the chair appoints or nominates the committee, he has the 25
duty to select its chairman—which he does by naming that
person to the committee first—and the committee cannot
elect another. The chair should not state the name of any
committee member until he has decided his preference for
chairman. The chair should specifically mention as chairman 30
the first committee member he names, but if he neglects to
state this fact, the designation nevertheless is automatic unless
the first-named member immediately declines the chairmanship (which the member can do, and remain on the committee). If the first-named member declines to serve as chairman, 35

1   the chair then names his next choice for this position. If the
committee's task is heavy and will require some time to complete, it often is advisable to appoint a vice-chairman. The
anomalous title "co-chairman" should be avoided, as it causes
5   impossible dilemmas in attempts to share the functions of a
single position.

If the committee is named by a power other than the chair
(such as the assembly or the executive board), the body that
elects the committee members has the power, at the time the
10 appointments are made, to designate any one of them as
chairman. If a chairman is not designated when the committee is appointed, the committee has the right to elect its own
chairman. In the latter case, the first-named member has the
duty of calling the committee together and of acting as tem-
15 porary chairman until the committee elects a chairman. Since
such a committee may confirm its first-named member in the
chairmanship, it is important that this person be qualified and
dependable.

20   FREEDOM OF ACTION AFTER REFERRAL.   Once
a committee to which a resolution or other main motion has
been referred commences its deliberations, the committee is
free to consider, and recommend for adoption, any amendment to the resolution or motion so referred, without regard
25 to whether or not the assembly, prior to the referral, considered the same or a similar amendment and either adopted or
rejected it. When the committee reports, even if to the same
meeting that made the referral, the matter stands before the
assembly as if introduced for the first time, and the assembly
30 itself, therefore, is also free to consider any such amendment,
whether considered by the committee or not.*

---

*The provisions of this paragraph do not apply, however, with respect to
informal consideration (pp. 168, 540–41).

EFFECT ON MOTIONS ADHERING TO THE RE-
FERRED QUESTION.   If the motion to *Postpone Indefi-*
nitely is pending when a main motion is referred to a
committee, the motion for indefinite postponement is
dropped from further consideration. Pending amendments
and any adhering debatable appeals (**24**), on the other hand,
go to the committee with the main motion, and are reported
with it. If, at the time a main motion is committed, a motion
to reconsider an adhering subsidiary or incidental motion is
pending or has been made but not yet taken up, the motion
to *Reconsider* is thereafter ignored.

SUBSEQUENT INSTRUCTIONS.   After a question
has been referred to a committee and at any time before the
committee submits its report, even at another session, the
assembly by a majority vote can give the committee additional
instructions in reference to the referred question.

VACANCIES IN A COMMITTEE.   The power to ap-
point a committee includes the power to fill any vacancy that
may arise in it. The resignation of a member of a committee
should be addressed to the appointing power, and it is the responsibility of that power to fill the resulting vacancy (see also
pp. 467–68). Unless the bylaws or other governing rules provide otherwise (see pp. 497, 653), the appointing authority
has the power to remove or replace members of the committee: If a single person, such as the president, has the power
of appointment, he has the power to remove or replace a
member so appointed; but if the assembly has the power
of selection, removal or replacement can take place only
under rules applicable to the motions to *Rescind* or *Amend*
Something Previously Adopted (see p. 497). Committee members are presumed to serve until their successors are
appointed.

1   PROCEDURE WHEN A COMMITTEE REPORTS.
For the procedure when a committee submits its report on a
referred question, see **51**; see also pages 156–57.

5   **Form and Example**

The motion to *Commit* or *Refer* may be made in many
forms. The following are typical: "I move to refer the motion
to a committee"; "I move to recommit the resolution"; "I
10   move that the motion be referred to the Social Committee";
"I move that the resolution be referred to a committee of
three to be appointed by the chair" [or "nominated by the
chair," or "elected from open nominations"]; "I move that
the question be referred to the Executive Board with full
15   power"; "I move to refer the resolution to a committee of
seven, the chairman to be Mr. Brownley, six members to be
elected by ballot from open nominations, and the committee
to be instructed to report at the April meeting"; "I move that
the Club now resolve itself into [or "go into"] a committee
20   of the whole to consider the resolution"; "I move that the
resolution be considered in quasi committee of the whole"
[or "considered as if in committee of the whole"]; and "I
move that the motion be considered informally."

Assume that a resolution is pending which, after debate,
25   apparently requires careful amendment before the assembly
will be willing to act on it. However, the assembly is pressed
for time.

MEMBER A (obtaining the floor): I move that the resolution be re-
30   ferred to a committee to be appointed by the chair. (Second.)

CHAIR: It is moved and seconded that the resolution be referred to
a committee to be appointed by the chair. [Pause.] Are you ready for the
question? [No response.] Of how many members shall the committee
consist?

35   MEMBER B (obtaining the floor): I move to amend the motion to

commit by inserting after the word "committee" the words "of three."   *1*
(Second.)

CHAIR: It is moved and seconded to amend the motion by inserting
after the word "committee" the words "of three."

MEMBER C (obtaining the floor): I move to amend the amendment   *5*
by striking out "three" and inserting "seven." (Second.)

CHAIR: If there is no objection, the chair suggests that the number
of committee members be decided upon by the method of filling blanks.
[Pause.] There is no objection and it is so ordered. It has been suggested
that the committee be composed of seven and also three members. Are   *10*
there additional suggestions?

MEMBER D (calling from his seat): I suggest five.

CHAIR: Five is also suggested. Are there other suggestions? [No response.] If not, the different numbers of members suggested for the proposed committee are seven, five, and three. These will be voted on in   *15*
descending order. Those in favor of seven members, say *aye*. ... Those
opposed, say *no*. ... The noes have it and the number seven is not
adopted. Those in favor of five members, say *aye*. ... Those opposed, say
no. ... The ayes have it and the number five is chosen for the committee
membership. The question is now on the motion "to refer the resolution   *20*
to a committee of five to be appointed by the chair." [Pause. No response.] Those in favor of referring the resolution to such a committee,
say *aye*. ... Those opposed, say *no*. ... The ayes have it and the motion is
adopted. The chair appoints Mr. Johnson as chairman, Dr. Donaldson,
Mrs. Applegarth, Mr. Frank, Miss Dillon.   *25*

§14. POSTPONE TO A CERTAIN TIME
(OR DEFINITELY)

30

The subsidiary motion to *Postpone to a Certain Time* (or
Postpone Definitely, or *Postpone*) is the motion by which action
on a pending question can be put off, within limits, to a definite day, meeting, or hour, or until after a certain event. (The
expression "to defer" should be avoided, since it is often   *35*

1   subject to vague usage.) This motion can be moved regardless
of how much debate there has been on the motion it proposes to postpone. A question may be postponed either so
that it may be considered at a more convenient time, or be-
5   cause debate has shown reasons for holding off a decision
until later. This motion should not be confused with *Postpone
Indefinitely*, which, as explained earlier (**11**), does not actually
postpone the pending question, but kills it.
     When a motion proposes to postpone a matter that is not
10   pending—for example, the hearing of a committee's report—
such a motion is not the subsidiary motion to *Postpone*, but
is an incidental main motion (**10**). If the effect would be to
change action already taken by the assembly, as, for example,
"to postpone for three weeks the dinner scheduled for Octo-
15   ber 15," such a motion is a particular case of the motion to
Amend Something Previously Adopted (**35**).

Standard Descriptive Characteristics

20   The subsidiary motion to *Postpone to a Certain Time*:

1. Takes precedence over the main motion; over the subsidiary motions to *Postpone Indefinitely*, to *Amend*, and
to *Commit*; and over the incidental motions for *Division
25   of the Question* and for *Consideration by Paragraph or
Seriatim*. It also takes precedence over a debatable appeal
(or a point of order which has been referred by the chair
to the judgment of the assembly and which is debatable
when so referred, p. 249, ll. 21–24) under either of the
30   following conditions: (a) if the appeal does not adhere to
the main question; or (b) if no other motions except those
named in the preceding sentence are pending or involved
in the appeal or question of order. It takes precedence
over a debatable motion to *Reconsider* when it is in order
35   to apply it to that motion under the conditions stated in

Standard Characteristic 2 below. It yields to the subsidiary   *1*
motions to *Limit or Extend Limits of Debate*, for the
Previous Question, or to *Lay on the Table*; to a motion to
Amend that is applied to it; to all privileged motions; and
to all applicable incidental motions.   *5*

2. Can be applied to main motions, with any motions
to *Postpone Indefinitely*, *Amend*, or *Commit* that may be
pending; can be thus applied to *orders of the day*
(pp. 185–88; **41**) or *questions of privilege* (**19**) while they
are actually pending as main motions, and such an appli-   *10*
cation is independent of, and does not affect, any other
matter that they may have interrupted; can be applied to
debatable appeals (or points of order referred by the chair
to the judgment of the assembly that are debatable when
so referred, p. 249, ll. 21–24), but if such an appeal ad-   *15*
heres (p. 118) to the main question (that is, if the appeal
must be decided before the main question is decided), the
motion to *Postpone* can be applied to the appeal only in
connection with the main question, which is thus also
postponed (see also p. 188); can be applied to nonadher-   *20*
ing debatable appeals separately, without affecting the status of any other questions that may be pending; and
can be applied to an immediately pending, debatable motion to *Reconsider* (**37**) when it is in order to postpone
the question or series of adhering questions containing   *25*
the motion(s) to be reconsidered, in which case all such
questions and adhering motions are postponed with the
motion to *Reconsider*. It cannot be applied to an undebatable appeal or to an undebatable motion to *Reconsider*;
and it cannot be applied to any subsidiary motion, except   *30*
that its application to a main question also affects any motions to *Postpone Indefinitely*, *Amend*, or *Commit* that
may be pending, as noted above. It cannot be moved after
the adoption of a motion to close debate on the main
question at a definite hour or of a motion to limit the total   *35*

time allowed for debate; but it remains in order if only a limitation on the length of speeches is in force (see **15**). Motions to *Amend*, to *Limit or Extend Limits of Debate*, and for the *Previous Question* can be applied to it without affecting the main question. The motion to *Postpone* cannot be laid on the table alone, but when it is pending the main question can be laid on the table, carrying to the table also the motion to *Postpone*. It cannot be postponed indefinitely or committed.

3. Is out of order when another has the floor.

4. Must be seconded.

5. Is debatable; but debate is limited in that is must not go into the merits of the main question any more than is necessary to enable the assembly to decide whether the main question should be postponed and to what time.

6. Is amendable as to the time to which the main question is to be postponed, and as to making the postponed question a *special order* (see pp. 185–88; **41**).

7. Requires a majority vote in its simple and usual form. If (as originally moved or as a result of amendment) it makes a question a *special order*, however, the motion to *Postpone* then requires a two-thirds vote, because it suspends any rules that will interfere with the question's consideration at the time specified. An amendment to the motion to *Postpone* requires only a majority vote, even if it would add a provision to make the postponed question a special order and would consequently change to two thirds the vote necessary for adoption of the motion to *Postpone*.

8. An affirmative vote on the motion to *Postpone* can be reconsidered. A negative vote on the motion to *Postpone* can be reconsidered only until such time as progress in business or debate has been sufficient to make it essentially a new question. Thereafter, the motion can be renewed (see pp. 339–40).

Further Rules and Explanation   *1*

LIMITS ON POSTPONEMENT AND THEIR RELA-
TION TO MEETING AND SESSION.   Rules limiting the
time to which a question can be postponed are related to   *5*
the terms *meeting* and *session* (**8**), as follows:

In a case where more than a quarterly time interval (see
pp. 89–90) will elapse between meetings (for example, in an
annual convention of delegates or in a local society that holds
only an annual meeting), a question cannot be postponed be-   *10*
yond the end of the present session. In cases where no more
than a quarterly time interval (see pp. 89–90) will elapse between sessions, a question can be postponed until, but not
beyond, the next regular business session. For example, in a
society that holds regular business meetings on the same day   *15*
of each week, a question cannot, at one meeting, be postponed for longer than a week.

If it is desired to postpone a question to a time between
regular meetings, it is necessary first to provide for an *ad-*
journed meeting, which is a continuation of the session sched-   *20*
uling it; then the question can be postponed to that meeting.
If a motion to postpone a question to a regular meeting is
already pending, the privileged motion to *Fix the Time to*
Which to Adjourn (**22**) can be used to set an adjourned meeting, and the motion to *Postpone* can then be amended so that   *25*
the proposed postponement will be to the adjourned meeting. Some societies have frequent sessions for social or cultural purposes at which business may be transacted, and also
hold a session every month or quarter especially for business.
In such societies these rules apply particularly to the regular   *30*
business sessions, to which questions can be postponed from
the previous regular business session or from any intervening
meeting.

When the time to which a question has been postponed
arrives and the question is taken up, it can be postponed again   *35*

1   if the additional delay will not interfere with the proper han-
    dling of the postponed motion.

       Neither the motion to *Postpone to a Certain Time* nor any
    amendment to it is in order if the effect would be the same
5   as that of the motion to *Postpone Indefinitely*—that is, if it
    would kill the measure. For example, a motion to postpone
    until tomorrow a pending question of accepting an invitation
    to a banquet tonight cannot be recognized as a motion to
    Postpone to a Certain Time. The chair must either rule this
10 motion out of order or, if the motion to *Postpone Indefinitely*
    is in order at the time, he can state the motion as such at his
    discretion. The same would apply to a motion to postpone a
    question from one regular business session to the next in cases
    where the next business session will not be held within a quar-
15 terly time interval (see pp. 89–90).

       RULE AGAINST POSTPONEMENT OF A CLASS OF
    SUBJECTS.   As already noted, the subsidiary motion to
    Postpone can be applied only to a question that is actually
20 pending; but an individual item of business that is not pend-
    ing can, when appropriate, be postponed by means of a main
    motion.

       It is not in order, either through a subsidiary motion or a
    main motion, to postpone a class of business composed of
25 several items or subjects, such as reports of officers or reports
    of committees (see *Order of Business*, **41**); but each report
    can be postponed separately as it is announced or called for.*
    If it is desired to reach an item immediately but it falls at a
    later point in the regular order of business, the assembly, by
30 a two-thirds vote or by unanimous consent (pp. 54–56), can
    adopt either a motion to "suspend the rules and take up" the
    desired question, or a motion "to pass" one or more items

---

*It should be noted that a similar rule applies to the subsidiary motion
to *Lay on the Table* (see pp. 211, 215–16, 363).

or classes of subjects in the order of business. After a question
taken up out of its proper order by either of these methods
has been disposed of, the regular order of business is resumed
at the point where it was left off (see motion to *Suspend the
Rules*, **25**).

POSTPONEMENT OF A SUBJECT THAT THE BY-
LAWS SET FOR A PARTICULAR SESSION.   A matter
that the bylaws require to be attended to at a specified session,
such as the election of officers, cannot, in advance and
through a main motion, be postponed to another session. It
can be taken up at any time when it is in order during the
specified session (that is, either as originally convened or at
any adjournment of it); and it can be postponed to an adjourned meeting in the manner explained above, after first
adopting, if necessary, a motion to *Fix the Time to Which to
Adjourn*. The adjourned meeting, as already stated, is a continuation of the same session. The procedure of postponing
such a matter to an adjourned meeting is sometimes advisable, as in an annual meeting for the election of officers on a
stormy night when, although a quorum is present, the attendance is abnormally small. If the matter has actually been
taken up during the specified session as required, it also may
be postponed beyond that session in accordance with the regular rules for the motion to *Postpone*. It is usually unwise to
do so, however, unless completing it during the session
proves impossible or impractical.

PRIORITY OF POSTPONED ITEMS AND ITS RELA-
TION TO ORDER OF BUSINESS AND ORDERS OF
THE DAY.   When a question is due to come up after postponement, it may be subject to a priority that depends on the
form in which the motion to *Postpone* was adopted. Rules affecting the postponement of more than one item of business
to the same or conflicting times are closely related to *order of*

1   *business* and *orders of the day* (**41**), according to principles that
    may be summarized as follows:

    A postponed question becomes an *order of the day* for the
    time to which it is postponed. An order of the day cannot be
5   taken up before the time for which it is set, except by recon-
    sidering (**37**) the vote that established the order, or by sus-
    pending the rules by a two-thirds vote. Orders of the day
    consist of *general orders* and *special orders*. Special orders have
    precedence over general orders. If a question is postponed
10 without making it a special order, it is a general order for the
    time to which it is postponed.

    An order of the day can be made for a definite session,
    day, or meeting, or for a particular hour. When set for *a ses-
    sion, day, or meeting*, special orders and general orders usually
15 have their established places in the order of business. Special
    orders that are not set for a particular hour normally are taken
    up after reports of special committees are heard. General or-
    ders are taken up after unfinished business is disposed of but
    are grouped with it under the heading, "Unfinished Business
20 and General Orders." The effect of setting an order of the
    day for a particular *hour* depends on whether it is a general
    order or a special order.

    The effect of postponing a question to a specified hour
    or until after a particular event in a meeting (making it a
25 *general order for that hour*) is: (1) to ensure that the question
    cannot come up before the predetermined time except by a
    two-thirds vote or through a reconsideration of the postpone-
    ment; and (2) to provide that it will come up at the time
    named, or later, depending on certain circumstances. Such
30 an order of the day cannot interrupt pending questions, and
    (except by a two-thirds vote) it cannot come up before gen-
    eral orders have been reached in the order of business, even
    if the time named has arrived or passed; but it is automatically
    taken up at the time named or as soon thereafter as general
35 orders have been reached and any of the following matters,

all of which have precedence over it, have been disposed   *1*
of: (1) a question pending at the time named; (2) a special
order for a particular hour that comes into conflict; (3) a motion to *Reconsider* that is called up (**37**); or (4) any other general order made before it was made, unless such other general   *5*
order was set for a time that has not yet arrived.

Any number of questions can be postponed to the same
time (provided that they are not made special orders for the
same or obviously conflicting hours). Such questions, or
other postponed questions that come into conflict, are taken   *10*
up in the order in which they were postponed. If a matter
that has been postponed to a meeting, or to an hour during
a meeting, is not disposed of before adjournment, it becomes
a part of unfinished business, unless it was a special order (in
which case it becomes an unfinished special order).   *15*

Making a question a special order for a certain time
(which can be done only by a two-thirds vote unless in connection with the adoption of an agenda or program, **41, 59**)
suspends any rules that may interfere with consideration of
the question at the time specified—except those relating: *20*
(a) to adjournment or recess; (b) to questions of privilege;
(c) to special orders made before this special order was made;
or (d) to *the* special order for a meeting, as explained below.
As previously stated, if a matter is made *a* special order for a
definite day or meeting without naming an hour, it is taken   *25*
up, along with any unfinished special orders, under that heading in the order of business; and it thus has precedence over
unfinished business and general orders. But if a matter is
made a special order for a particular *hour*, it will interrupt or
have precedence over any other business then pending or set   *30*
for the same time, except: (1) another special order made before it was; or (2) *the* special order for a meeting.

A matter can be made *the* special order for a meeting if it
is desired to reserve an entire meeting, or as much of it as
necessary, for the consideration of a single subject. At the   *35*

1 appointed meeting, the chair announces the special order as
the pending business immediately after the minutes have been
disposed of. At the time that a matter is made *the* special order
for a meeting, any other special orders that were made earlier
5 and are likely to come into conflict with *the* special order
should be adjusted to different times. If this has been neglected, however, *the* special order for a meeting has precedence over any other form of special order.

10   EFFECT ON MOTIONS ADHERING TO A POST-
PONED QUESTION.   When a main motion is postponed,
motions to *Postpone Indefinitely, Amend,* and *Commit* may
be pending, and debate may have been limited or closed. All
such adhering or attached motions are postponed with the
15 main question, and when consideration of that question is resumed at the specified time, the business is in the same condition as it was immediately before the postponement, with
the following exception: If the consideration is not resumed
until the next session, any limitation on or curtailment of de-
20 bate is exhausted and therefore ignored. Similarly, when a
main motion is postponed, it also carries with it any adhering
debatable appeals (**24**)—that is, debatable appeals that are
related to the main question in such a way that they must be
decided before the main question is acted upon. The main
25 question cannot be postponed while an undebatable appeal
is pending.
     Except for the effect of an unexhausted order limiting or
closing debate, as explained in the preceding paragraph, when
a question is taken up *on a different day* from the one on
30 which it was postponed, the right of members to debate it
begins over again, as if the question had not previously been
debated; that is, each person can again speak twice to each
debatable question, regardless of whether he may have already
done so before the postponement (see **43**).

Form and Example

The form used in making this motion depends on the desired object:

a) Simply to postpone the question to the next meeting, when it will have precedence over new business: "I move to postpone the motion [or "that the question be postponed"] to the next meeting."

b) To specify an hour before which the question will not be taken up (unless by a two-thirds vote or through reconsideration), and when it will come up automatically as soon as no business is pending and any remaining matters that have precedence over it have been disposed of: "I move that the resolution be postponed until 3 P.M." [or "… until 9 P.M. at the meeting scheduled for February 15"].

c) To postpone consideration of a motion until after a certain event in a meeting, when it will immediately be taken up (unless a special order intervenes)· "I move to postpone the question until after the address by our guest speaker."

d) To ensure that the question will come up at the next meeting and will not be crowded out by other matters: "I move that the question be postponed to the next meeting and be made a special order." (Two-thirds vote required for adoption.)

e) To ensure that the matter will come up at precisely a certain hour, even if it interrupts pending business: "I move that the resolution be postponed and be made a special order for 3 P.M. tomorrow." (Two-thirds vote required for adoption.)

f) To postpone a subject—such as a revision of the bylaws— to an adjourned meeting at which the entire time can be devoted to it if necessary, a motion to *Fix the Time to Which to Adjourn* should first be made and adopted, and

1   then the motion to *Postpone* should be made in this form:
"I move that the question be postponed and made *the*
special order for the adjourned meeting set for next Tuesday evening." (Two-thirds vote required for adoption.)

5   Assume that a controversial resolution is pending at a convention and that many of the delegates who are most interested and best informed on the subject will not be able to be
present until tomorrow.

10   MEMBER A (obtaining the floor): I move to postpone the resolution
until eleven o'clock tomorrow morning. (Second.)
     CHAIR: It is moved and seconded that the resolution be postponed
until eleven o'clock tomorrow morning. [Pause.]
15   MEMBER B (after obtaining the floor and stating that in his opinion
further consideration of the resolution should under no circumstances
be delayed *beyond* 11 A.M. the next day): I move to amend the motion
to postpone, by adding "and make it a special order." (Second.)
     CHAIR: It is moved and seconded to amend the motion to postpone
20   the resolution until eleven o'clock tomorrow morning by adding "and
make it a special order." [Debate, if any.] The question is on amending
the motion to postpone by adding "and make it a special order." Those
in favor of the amendment, say *aye*. ... Those opposed, say *no*. ... The
ayes have it and the amendment is adopted. The question now is on the
25   motion, as amended, to postpone the resolution until eleven o'clock tomorrow morning and make it a special order. This motion now requires
a two-thirds vote. [Pause.] Are you ready for the question? [Pause. No
further debate.] Those in favor of the motion to postpone the resolution
until eleven o'clock tomorrow morning and make it a special order, will
30   rise. ... Be seated. Those opposed, rise. ... Be seated. There are two thirds
in the affirmative and the motion is adopted. The resolution is a special
order for 11 A.M. tomorrow. The next item of business is ...

     If the amendment to make a special order is rejected, the
35   chair proceeds in the usual manner to take a voice vote on

the *unamended* motion to postpone. If the motion to post- 1
pone is not adopted, he again states the question on the resolution. But if the resolution *has* been made a special order
for the following day at 11 A.M., as in the above example, then
at the appointed time the chair says: 5

CHAIR: It is now eleven o'clock. The following resolution was made
a special order for this time. "*Resolved*, That ..." The question is on the
adoption of the resolution. ...

10

§15. LIMIT OR EXTEND LIMITS OF DEBATE

The subsidiary motion to *Limit or Extend Limits of
Debate* is one of the two motions by means of which an
assembly can exercise special control over debate on a pend- 15
ing question or on a series of pending questions. (The other
motion serving such a purpose is the *Previous Question*, **16**.
Neither of these motions is allowed in committees; see **50**.)

The motion to *Limit or Extend Limits of Debate* can *limit*
debate by: (1) reducing the number or length of speeches 20
permitted, without including specific provision for closing debate; or (2) requiring that, at a certain later hour or after
debate for a specified length of time, debate shall be closed.
It can *extend the limits* of debate by allowing more and longer
speeches than under the regular rules (see pp. 387–90). It 25
cannot impose an immediate closing of debate, which requires a different motion—the *Previous Question*.

When an assembly adopts a motion to *Limit or Extend
Limits of Debate*, it is said to adopt an "order" taking such
action. (The word *order* as applied in this sense should not 30
be confused with the technical terms *order of the day*, *general
order*, and *special order* as used in **3**, **14**, and **41**.) When an
order limiting or extending the limits of debate finally ceases
to be in force as relates to all the motions it affected, the order
is said to be "exhausted" (see pp. 195–96). 35

If a motion proposing to change the regular limits of debate (for any length of time or during the consideration of one or more particular subjects) is made while no question is pending, such a motion is not the subsidiary motion to *Limit or Extend Limits of Debate*, but is an incidental main motion (although it requires a two-thirds vote for its adoption, just as the subsidiary motion does).

Standard Descriptive Characteristics

The subsidiary motion to *Limit or Extend Limits of Debate*:

1. Takes precedence over all debatable motions. It yields to the subsidiary motions for the *Previous Question* and to *Lay on the Table*; to a motion to *Amend* that is applied to it; to all privileged motions; and to all applicable incidental motions.
2. Can be applied to any immediately pending debatable motion, to an entire series of pending debatable motions, or to any consecutive part of such a series beginning with the immediately pending question. (It therefore can be made only while a debatable motion is immediately pending. If a series of debatable questions is pending and an undebatable incidental motion is immediately pending, the latter must be disposed of before any motion to *Limit or Extend Limits of Debate* can be made.) Motions to *Amend* and (for the purpose of stopping amendment) the motion for the *Previous Question* can be applied to it without affecting the main question. The motion to *Limit or Extend Limits of Debate* cannot be laid on the table alone, but when it is pending the main question can be laid on the table, carrying to the table also the motion to *Limit or Extend Limits of Debate*.
3. Is out of order when another has the floor.

4. Must be seconded.

5. Is not debatable.

6. Is amendable, but any amendment, like the motion itself, is undebatable.

7. Requires a two-thirds vote—because it suspends the rules, and because limiting debate takes away the basic rights of all members to full discussion and may restrict a minority's right to present its case.

8. An affirmative vote on the motion to *Limit or Extend Limits of Debate* can be reconsidered, without debate, at any time before the order limiting or extending limits of debate is exhausted (see pp. 195–96). If the order has been partially carried out, only the unexecuted part can be subject to reconsideration. A negative vote on the motion to *Limit or Extend Limits of Debate* can be reconsidered only until such time as progress in business or debate has been sufficient to make it essentially a new question. Thereafter, the motion can be renewed (see pp. 339–40).

Further Rules and Explanation

EFFECT ON PENDING AND SUBSEQUENT MOTIONS.   This motion's effect upon other pending and subsequent motions depends on the nature of its specific provisions, and is closely related to its position in the order of precedence of motions (**5**), as follows:

If a series of debatable questions is pending and a motion to *Limit or Extend Limits of Debate* does not specify the motions to which it is to apply, then only the immediately pending question is affected. An order *limiting* debate applies not only to the motion(s) on which the limitation is ordered, but also to any debatable subsidiary motions, motions to *Reconsider*, or debatable appeals that may become pending *subsequently* while the order is in force. An order *extending*

1   *limits* of debate, on the other hand, does not affect any mo-
     tion that was not pending when the order was adopted.
         While a motion to *Limit or Extend Limits of Debate* is
     pending, its precedence prevents the making of subsidiary
5   motions of lower rank (*Postpone Indefinitely, Amend, Com-
     mit, Postpone to a Certain Time*). After a limitation or exten-
     sion on debate has been ordered, however, its effect on which
     subsidiary motions can be made depends on whether the
     order *provides for closing debate* and, if so, whether it also
10   *specifies the hour at which the vote shall be taken.*
         If, as in *Form and Example* (c) below, the limitation or ex-
     tension that has been ordered does not provide for *closing* de-
     bate, it has no effect on what subsidiary motions can be made.
     On the other hand, after the adoption of an order that does
15   provide for closing debate—by requiring that, at a certain later
     hour or after debate for a specified length of time, debate shall
     be closed—motions to *Commit* or to *Postpone to a Certain
     Time* cannot be made, since these motions would be in con-
     flict with the purpose of that order.* If motions to *Commit*
20   or to *Postpone* were already part of a series that was pending
     when an order scheduling the close of debate was adopted,
     the remaining questions may be postponed or committed at
     the time the motions for such action come to a vote.
         After the expiration of the allotted time under any order
25   that—as in *Form and Example* (b)—provides for closing de-
     bate without specifying when the vote shall be taken, amend-
     ments and motions to *Postpone Indefinitely* and *Lay on the
     Table* remain in order, but they are then undebatable. If, how-
     ever, the order that provides for closing debate also specifies
30   the hour at which the vote shall be taken—as in (a) and (d)

---

*If debate on a pending question while such a limitation is in effect
nonetheless reveals an arguably valid reason for committal or postponement,
the vote adopting the order can be reconsidered, or a motion can be made to
establish a different limit.

under *Form and Example* below—then, after that hour has   *1*
passed, the main motion is treated as if the *Previous Question*
had been ordered: no further debate on any pending question
is allowed, no further amendments can be offered, and all
pending questions must be voted on immediately.   *5*

Regardless of the form of an order to limit or extend
limits of debate, the main question and any adhering motions
can be laid on the table while the order is in effect.

If it is desired to move a subsidiary motion that is prohibited under an adopted order to limit debate, the vote   *10*
adopting the order can be reconsidered, or a motion can be
made to establish a different limit. Unlike the case of main
motions and lower-ranking subsidiary motions (*Postpone
Indefinitely, Amend, Commit, Postpone*), the adoption of one
motion limiting or extending debate in a certain way does   *15*
not cause another such conflicting motion to be out of order.
A motion to set different limitation(s) or extension(s), or
to change from one to the other, or to order the *Previous
Question* (**16**), can be made at any time that it is in order
under the order of precedence of motions, until the pending   *20*
questions affected have been finally disposed of. The reason
is that the two-thirds vote necessary for the adoption of any
motion to modify the limits of debate also fulfills the requirement for changing something previously adopted (see **35**).

25

CONDITIONS FOR EXHAUSTION OF ITS EFFECT.
An order limiting or extending limits of debate is *exhausted*:
(1) when all of the questions on which it was imposed have
been voted on; (2) when those questions affected by the
order and not yet voted on have been either referred to a   *30*
committee or postponed indefinitely; or (3) at the conclusion
of the session in which the order has been adopted—
whichever occurs first. If any of the questions to which the
order applies are postponed definitely or laid on the table,
and are taken up again later during the same session, the   *35*

1   unexecuted part of the order remains in effect. Any questions
affected by an order modifying limits of debate that in any
way go over to the next session—or that are referred to a
committee and reported back, even in the same session in
5   which committed—become open to debate under the regular
rules. An order limiting or extending limits of debate applies
to reconsiderations of the affected questions before, but not
after, exhaustion of the order.

10   **Form and Example**

The forms in which this motion may be made depend on
the desired object, as follows:

15   a) To fix the hour for closing debate and putting the question: "I move that at 9 P.M. debate be closed and the
question on the resolution be put to a vote."
b) To limit time spent in debate: "… that debate on the
pending amendment be limited to twenty minutes."
20   c) To reduce or increase the number or length of speeches:
"… that debate be limited to one speech of five minutes
for each member"; or "… that Mr. Lee's time be extended three minutes"; or "I ask unanimous consent that
Mr. Lee's time …" (see pp. 54–56).
25   d) To combine several of the above objects: "I move that
_____ and _____ [the leaders on the two sides]
each be allowed twenty minutes, which may be divided
between two speeches, and that other members be limited
to one speech of two minutes each, provided that all
30   pending questions shall be put to a vote at 4 P.M." (see
also example on p. 639).

The form of *stating* the question on this amendable but
undebatable motion is:

CHAIR: It is moved and seconded that no later than 9 P.M. debate be closed and the question on the resolution be put. The motion to limit or extend limits of debate is not debatable, but it can be amended. [Pause; or, "Are you ready for the question on ..."; or, "Are there any amendments to ..."] the motion to limit debate?

The words at the end of the last sentence, "... the motion to ...," can be varied depending on the particular form in which the motion was made.

Unless the motion to *Limit or Extend Limits of Debate* is adopted by unanimous consent (pp. 54–56), the chair puts it to a vote taken by rising, as in the example shown for a motion to postpone a question and make it a special order, on page 190. In announcing the result, the chair states the parliamentary situation as it then exists:

CHAIR (after taking a rising vote): There are two thirds in the affirmative and the motion is adopted. The resolution will therefore be put to a vote no later than 9 P.M. and debate cannot continue beyond that hour. The question is on [stating the immediately pending question].

§16. PREVIOUS QUESTION
(Immediately to close debate and the making of subsidiary motions except the motion to Lay on the Table)

The *Previous Question* is the motion used to bring the assembly to an immediate vote on one or more pending questions; its adoption does this with certain exceptions.

Adopting or "ordering" the *Previous Question*:

1) immediately closes debate on, and stops amendment of, the immediately pending question and such other pending questions as the motion may specify (in consecutive series; see Standard Characteristic 2); and

2) prevents the making of any other subsidiary motions except the higher-ranking (**5**) *Lay on the Table*.*

The adoption of an order for the *Previous Question* does not prevent the making of privileged or incidental motions (**6**) as applicable, and, strictly speaking, it does not prevent a special order set for a particular hour (**14, 41**) from interrupting the pending business (see also pp. 203–4).

The motion for the *Previous Question* has nothing to do with the last question previously considered by the assembly and has a long history of gradually changing purpose.

The *Previous Question* is not allowed in committees (**50**).

Standard Descriptive Characteristics

The subsidiary motion for the *Previous Question*:

1. Takes precedence over all debatable or amendable motions to which it is applied, and over the subsidiary motion to *Limit or Extend Limits of Debate*; and, if adopted, it supersedes the effect of an unexhausted order limiting or extending debate, with respect to the motions to which it is applied. It yields to the subsidiary motion to *Lay on the Table*, to all privileged motions, and to all applicable incidental motions.
2. Can be applied to any immediately pending debatable or amendable motion; to an entire series of pending debatable or amendable motions; and to any consecutive part

---

*In practice it is seldom appropriate to move to lay a pending question or series of questions on the table after the *Previous Question* has been ordered on them; but a legitimate need to do so may sometimes arise, particularly in a large assembly if the vote(s) are to be taken by a method such as by ballot, standing for a count, or roll call (see also **45**, and *Misuses of the Motion to Lay on the Table*, pp. 215–16).

of such a series, beginning with the immediately pending question. (Under this rule it can be applied to motions that are amendable but not debatable,* for the purpose of stopping amendment; see tinted p. 43.) It supersedes any earlier order for the closing of debate at a future time and can be applied while such an order is in effect. In practice, this motion usually is made in an unqualified form, such as "I move the previous question," and then it applies only to the immediately pending question. In its qualified form, however, it can be applied to include consecutively any series beginning with the immediately pending question. For example, the following motions might be pending: (a) a resolution; (b) an amendment to the resolution; (c) a motion to refer the resolution and its pending amendment to a committee; and (d) an immediately pending motion to postpone all of these questions to a definite time. In this case, an unqualified motion for the *Previous Question* will apply only to (d). Such a motion can be qualified to apply to (d) and (c); to (d), (c), and (b); or to (d), (c), (b), and (a). It cannot include only (d) and (b); only (d), (b), and (a); only (d), (c), and (a); or only (d) and (a); and no motion for the *Previous Question* excluding the immediately pending question (d) can be made until (d) has been voted on. No subsidiary motion can be applied to the *Previous Question*, except that when it is pending the main question can be laid on the table, carrying to the table also all adhering motions, including the motion for the *Previous Question*.

3. Is out of order when another has the floor.
4. Must be seconded.

---

*An example of such a motion is the motion to *Limit or Extend Limits of Debate* (**15**).

5. Is not debatable.

6. Is not amendable. However, it has a special characteristic that permits an effect similar to amendment when the motion is applied while a series of questions is pending. When a motion for the *Previous Question* is immediately pending in such a case, it can be made again with more or fewer pending questions included (subject to the restrictions shown in Standard Characteristic 2, above), *before* the first motion for the *Previous Question* is voted on. The procedure resembles filling blanks (see pp. 162–67) except that each of the motions must be made by a member who has obtained the floor, and each must be seconded.* For example, if one member has made this motion in the unqualified form when a series of questions is pending (so that it would apply only to the question immediately pending at that time), another member can move it on part of the series and still another can move it on *all* pending questions. The vote is taken first on the motion that would order the *Previous Question* on the largest number of motions; if this fails, then on the next smaller number, and so on, until one is adopted (by a two-thirds vote), or until all of the motions for the *Previous Question* are rejected.

7. Requires a two-thirds vote. (If a motion for the *Previous Question* fails to gain the necessary two-thirds vote, debate continues as if this motion had not been made.) In ordinary bodies, the requirement of a two-thirds vote for ordering the *Previous Question* is important in protecting the democratic process. If this rule were not observed, a temporary majority of only one vote could deny the re-

---

*For the form to be followed by the chair in granting limited recognition to a member who seeks the floor at such a time, see pages 208–9.

maining members all opportunity to discuss any measure *1*
that such a majority wished to adopt or kill.*

8. An affirmative vote on the motion for the *Previous Question* can be reconsidered before any vote has been taken
under the order of the *Previous Question*, but (in contrast *5*
to the motion to *Limit or Extend Limits of Debate*) it cannot be reconsidered after the order has been partly executed;** see also pages 205–6. A negative vote on the
motion for the *Previous Question* can be reconsidered only
until such time as progress in business or debate has been *10*
sufficient to make it essentially a new question—that is,
only until such time as it is reasonable to assume that debate or action on any of the motions involved may have
made more members desire to vote immediately on some
or all of the questions still pending. Thereafter, it can be *15*
renewed (see pp. 339–40).

---

*Although the rules of the United States House of Representatives per-
mit the *Previous Question* to be ordered by a majority vote, there are differences between the conditions in that body and in the ordinary organization
that should be understood. Because of another House rule, an order for the
Previous Question does not actually bring a measure to an immediate vote in
Congress unless it has already been debated. If no discussion of the measure
has taken place on the floor of the House, forty minutes' debate is allowed
after adoption of the *Previous Question*—twenty minutes for each of the opposing sides. These rules derive from the great volume of business and the
fact that under the two-party system of government by elected representatives,
opposing sides often become nearly equal. At the same time, this system creates special conditions that make it unlikely that there will be unfair use of the
power to curtail debate. The United States Senate does not admit the *Previous
Question*, although it permits debate to be limited by means of a motion for
cloture.

**When the *Previous Question* has been ordered on a number of motions,
the order is said to be partly executed (or partly carried out) if one or more,
but not all, of these motions have been voted on. When all of the motions
specified in the order have been voted on, it is fully executed.

Further Rules and Explanation

EQUAL APPLICATION OF RULES TO COLLO-
QUIAL FORMS SUCH AS "CALL FOR THE QUES-
TION." A motion such as "I call for [or "call"] the
question" or "I move we vote now" is simply a motion for
the *Previous Question* made in nonstandard form, and it is
subject to all of the rules in this section. Care should be taken
that failure to understand this fact does not lead to violation
of members' rights of debate.

Sometimes the mere making of a motion for the *Previous
Question* or "call for the question" may motivate unanimous
consent to ending debate. Before or after such a motion has
been seconded, the chair may ask if there is any objection to
closing debate. If member(s) object or try to get the floor,
he should ask if there is a second to the motion or call; or, if
it has already been seconded, he must immediately take a vote
on *whether to order* the *Previous Question*. But *regardless of the
wording of a motion or "call" seeking to close debate, it always
requires a second and a two-thirds vote, taken separately from
and before the vote(s) on the motion(s) to which it is applied, to
shut off debate against the will of even one member who wishes
to speak and has not exhausted his right to debate* (see pp. 44,
387–90).

EXEMPTION OF UNDEBATED PREAMBLE FROM
THE PREVIOUS QUESTION UNLESS SEPARATELY
ORDERED. When a resolution having a preamble (one or
more explanatory clauses beginning "Whereas, …") is pending, if the *Previous Question* is ordered on the resolution
before consideration of the preamble has been reached
(pp. 106ff., 139, 278–79), the order does not apply to debate
and amendment of the preamble, to which the assembly proceeds before voting on the resolution. After the chair has declared the preamble open to debate and amendment in such

a case, the entire resolution can be brought to an immediate   *1*
vote, if desired, by then ordering the *Previous Question* on the
preamble.

VOTING ON A SERIES OF MOTIONS UNDER   *5*
THE PREVIOUS QUESTION; INTERRUPTION OF
EXECUTION.   When the *Previous Question* is ordered on
a series of pending motions as explained above under Standard Characteristic 2, they are voted on in order of rank beginning with the immediately pending question—that is, in   *10*
reverse of the order in which they were made. If the series
includes motions to *Postpone Definitely*, to *Commit*, or to
Postpone Indefinitely and one of these motions is adopted,
further voting stops—regardless of how many of the remaining questions were, or were not, included under the order   *15*
for the *Previous Question*. But if voting is not stopped in
such a manner, then, when all of the motions on which the
Previous Question was ordered have been voted on, consideration of any questions still pending resumes under the regular
rules.   *20*
    If a question or series of questions (including motions
on which the *Previous Question* has been ordered) *ceases to be
the pending business* before all of the motions affected by the
order have been voted on, *execution* of the order is said to be
interrupted. Interruption of the execution of an order for the   *25*
Previous Question may occur as follows:

- If a motion to *Postpone*, to *Commit*, or to *Postpone Indefinitely* on which the *Previous Question* has been ordered is
  adopted (as in the preceding paragraph) in a case where   *30*
  one or more of the remaining questions *were also included*
  under the order, execution of the order is thus *interrupted
  after it has been partly carried out*.
- *Before or after* an order for the *Previous Question* has
  been *partly carried out*, as already noted, it is also possible   *35*

for its execution to be interrupted as a result of the question(s)'s being laid on the table, or by the intervention of a special order set for a particular hour (**14**, **41**), a question of privilege (**19**), a recess (**8**, **20**), or an adjournment (**8**, **21**). (If the hour set for a special order, a recess, or an adjournment has arrived and the *Previous Question* has been ordered on one or more pending motions, however, there usually will be no objection to the chair's putting them all to a vote in succession before he announces the matter that intervenes.)

EXHAUSTION OF THE PREVIOUS QUESTION. The *Previous Question* is said to be *exhausted* (in reference to a particular order for it) when all of the motions on which it was ordered have been finally disposed of, or when any motions not yet finally disposed of are no longer affected by the order. The conditions for exhaustion of the *Previous Question* are the same as for an order limiting or extending limits of debate—that is: (1) when all motions on which the *Previous Question* was ordered have been voted on; (2) when those not yet voted on have either been committed or postponed indefinitely; or (3) at the end of the session in which the *Previous Question* was ordered—whichever occurs first. After the *Previous Question* is exhausted, any remaining questions that come up again are open to debate and amendment just as if there had been no order for the *Previous Question*.

If the execution of an order for the *Previous Question* is interrupted and if the motion or motions that were pending come up again later, the rules in the foregoing paragraph apply as follows:

- If the questions were *referred to a committee* and are later reported, the *Previous Question* is *exhausted* and the motions are open to debate and amendment, even if it is during the same session.

- But if the interruption of execution occurred by any *other means than referral* and the questions come up again during the *same session*, the order *remains in effect*; all motions on which the *Previous Question* was ordered must be voted on immediately (unless a reconsideration of the order is possible and a motion to reconsider it has been made, or is then made; see below).

- If the questions do not come up again until a *later session*, the *Previous Question* is *always exhausted*, regardless of how the interruption of execution occurred.

RECONSIDERATION OF A VOTE THAT HAS ORDERED THE PREVIOUS QUESTION.   As noted in Standard Characteristic 8, a vote that has ordered the *Previous Question* can be reconsidered before, but not after, any of the motions affected by the order have been voted on. Consequently, it will frequently happen that a motion to reconsider an affirmative vote on the *Previous Question* itself can be made only in the brief moment after the vote ordering the *Previous Question* is completed and before the first vote is taken under the order (see also p. 209).

If the execution of an order for the *Previous Question* was interrupted before any vote was taken under the order, and if the questions come up again during the same session, a motion to reconsider the order (if not made earlier) can be made only in the moment after the chair has announced these questions as the pending business and before any of them are voted on. In addition, the regular time limits for making a motion to *Reconsider* apply (see **37**).

It should be noted that if a motion or series of motions that is under an order for the *Previous Question* comes up after having been *postponed*, there can never be a reconsideration of the order. The reason is that the motion to *Postpone* can only have been made before the *Previous Question* was ordered, so that the order for the *Previous Question* will

1   always have been partly executed by the vote that caused the postponement.

In practice, if a motion to reconsider an affirmative vote on the *Previous Question* prevails, the subsequent procedure 5 is abbreviated as follows: The vote that adopted the motion to *Reconsider* is also presumed to have carried out the reconsideration and to have reversed the vote that is reconsidered; that is, the *Previous Question* is now presumed to be rejected and is not voted on again, for this reason: In such a case, only 10 members opposed to the *Previous Question* would vote to reconsider it after it had been adopted; consequently, if a majority have voted for reconsideration, it will be impossible to obtain a two-thirds vote in favor of the *Previous Question*.

15 RECONSIDERATION OF A VOTE TAKEN UNDER THE PREVIOUS QUESTION. If a vote *ordered by* adopting a motion for the *Previous Question* is reconsidered before the *Previous Question* is exhausted, the motion to *Reconsider* is undebatable and the motion reconsidered cannot be de- 20 bated or amended. But if the reconsideration occurs after the *Previous Question* is exhausted, the motion to *Reconsider* and the question to be reconsidered are no longer affected by the *Previous Question*.

25 EFFECT ON APPEALS. An appeal is undebatable if it is made after the *Previous Question* has been moved or ordered and before the order is exhausted.

EFFECT ON SUBSEQUENT MOTIONS GENER- 30 ALLY. The general rules as to the effect of an unexhausted order for the *Previous Question* on subsequent motions that would normally be debatable or amendable are as follows:

- While one or more *motions on which the Previous Question* 35 *has been ordered remain pending*, the order also applies to any other motions that may take precedence over these

pending questions. (The rules stated in the two preceding   *1*
paragraphs—for motions to reconsider a vote taken under
the *Previous Question* and for appeals—are applications of
this principle.)

- But if a *question of privilege* is raised and is admitted   *5*
  for immediate consideration (see **19**), or if a special order
  set for a particular hour intervenes, these questions are
  independent of an unexhausted order for the *Previous
  Question* applying to business that they interrupt.

                                                   10

Form and Example

The forms used in making this motion include: "I move
the previous question" (to apply only to the immediately
pending question); "I move [or "demand," or "call for"] the   *15*
previous question on the motion to commit and its amendment"; "I demand the previous question on all pending questions"; and so on. Calls of "Question!" by members from their
seats are not motions for the *Previous Question* and are disorderly if another member is speaking or seeking recognition.   *20*

In stating the question on this undebatable, nonamend-
able motion, the chair does not pause or ask, "Are you ready
for the question?" but *puts* the question for a rising vote on
the motion for the *Previous Question* immediately as shown
below. Similarly, in announcing an affirmative result, he at   *25*
once states the question on the motion that is then immediately pending.

Assume that a series of several debatable and amendable
motions is pending.

                                                   30

MEMBER A (obtaining the floor): I move the previous question on
[specifying the motions, unless he desires that only the immediately
pending question be affected]. (Second.)

CHAIR: The previous question is moved and seconded on [naming
the motions, unless none was specified]. Those in favor of ordering the   *35*
previous question on [repeating the motions], rise. ... Be seated. Those

1   opposed, rise. … Be seated. There are two thirds in the affirmative and
    the previous question is ordered on [naming again the motions to which
    the order applies]. The question is now on the adoption of the motion
    to … [stating in full the immediately pending question]. Those in favor
5   [and so on, putting to vote in proper sequence all motions on which the
    Previous Question has been ordered].

    If there are less than two thirds in the affirmative, the
    chair announces the result of the vote on the motion for
10 the *Previous Question* as follows:

        CHAIR: There are less than two thirds in the affirmative and the mo-
    tion for the previous question is lost. The question is now on … [stating
    the question on the immediately pending motion.] Debate may now re-
15 sume. [The chair does not say, "Are you ready for the question?" here,
    since the assembly has just shown that it is not ready.]

    The following example shows the forms used in handling
    alternative motions for the *Previous Question* that specify dif-
20 ferent numbers of pending questions in a series, as described
    under Standard Characteristic 6.
        Assume that a resolution, an amendment to the resolu-
    tion, and a motion to *Commit* are pending (in which case the
    motion to *Commit* is the immediately pending question).
25
        MEMBER X (obtaining the floor): I move the previous question. (Sec-
    ond. In this case only the motion to *Commit* is affected.)
        CHAIR: The previous question is demanded. Those in favor of
    ordering …
30   MEMBER Y (quickly rising and interrupting the chair): Mr. President.
        CHAIR: For what purpose does the member rise?
        MEMBER Y: I move the previous question on all pending questions.
    (Second.)
        CHAIR: The previous question is also moved on all pending questions.
35 The question is now on the demand for the previous question on all
    pending questions. Those …

MEMBER Z (quickly rising): Mr. President.   *1*

CHAIR: For what purpose does the member rise?

MEMBER Z: I move the previous question on the motion to commit and on the amendment to the resolution. (Second.)

CHAIR: The previous question is also demanded on the motion to   *5*
commit and on the amendment to the resolution. The question is first, however, on the motion to order the previous question on all pending questions. Those in favor of ordering … [and so on. Alternative motions for the *Previous Question* are voted on in order beginning with the one that would apply to the largest number of pending questions. Therefore,   *10*
after admitting Member Y's motion, the chair starts to put the question on it first; but after admitting Member Z's, he returns to taking a vote on Member Y's. If one of these motions for the *Previous Question* is adopted, any remaining ones are ignored.]

15

If a member wishes to make a higher-ranking motion or to move a reconsideration while a motion for the *Previous Question* is pending or after the *Previous Question* has been ordered, he seeks limited recognition by rising and interrupting the chair just as in the example above.   *20*

§17. LAY ON THE TABLE
*(To interrupt the pending business so as to permit
doing something else immediately)*

25

The motion to *Lay on the Table* enables the assembly to lay the pending question aside temporarily when something else of immediate urgency has arisen or when something else needs to be addressed before consideration of the pending question is resumed, in such a way that: *30*

- there is *no set time* for taking the matter up again;
- but (until the expiration of time limits explained on p. 214) its consideration *can be resumed at the will of a majority* and in preference to any new questions that may   *35*
then be competing with it for consideration.

1   This motion is commonly misused in ordinary assemblies—
in place of the motion to *Postpone Indefinitely* (**11**), to *Post-*
pone to a Certain Time (**14**), or other motions. Particularly
in such misuses, it also is known as a motion "to table."

5   By adopting the motion to *Lay on the Table*, a majority
has the power to halt consideration of a question immediately
without debate. Such action violates the rights of the minority
and individual members if it is for any other purpose than the
one stated in the first sentence of this section. In ordinary as-
10 semblies, the motion to *Lay on the Table* is out of order if the
evident intent is to kill or avoid dealing with a measure. If a
time for resuming consideration is specified in making the
motion, it can be admitted only as a motion to *Postpone* (**14**),
in which case it is debatable (see also pp. 215–17).

15

Standard Descriptive Characteristics

The subsidiary motion to *Lay on the Table*:

20 1. Takes precedence over the main motion, over all other
subsidiary motions, and over any incidental motions that
are pending when it is made. It yields to all privileged motions, and to motions that are incidental to itself.

    2. Can be applied to main motions, with any other sub-
25   sidiary motions that may be pending; can be thus applied
to *orders of the day* (**14, 41**) or *questions of privilege* (**19**)
while they are actually pending as main motions, and such
an application is independent of, and does not carry to
the table, any other matter that they may have inter-
30   rupted; can be separately applied to debatable appeals that
do not adhere (p. 118) to the main question (or to nonadhering points of order referred by the chair to the
judgment of the assembly that are debatable when so referred), and this application has no effect on the status of
35   any other questions that may be pending; can be applied

to adhering appeals—whether debatable or undebatable—only by laying the main question on the table, in which case the appeal and all other adhering motions go to the table also; and can be applied to an immediately pending motion to *Reconsider* (**37**), whenever *Lay on the Table* would be applicable if the motion to be reconsidered were immediately pending, and in such a case, it carries to the table also the motion to be reconsidered, or the series of questions adhering to the latter motion. It cannot be applied to an undebatable appeal that does not adhere to the main question; and it cannot be applied to any subsidiary motion except in connection with application to the main question. No motion or motions can be laid on the table apart from motions which adhere to them, or to which they adhere; and if any one of them is laid on the table, all such motions go to the table together. The motion to *Lay on the Table* can be made while an order limiting debate or an order for the *Previous Question* is in force (see also below). No subsidiary motion can be applied to the motion to *Lay on the Table*.

Since the motion to *Lay on the Table* can be applied *only* to a question that is actually *pending*, a class or group of main questions such as orders of the day, unfinished business, or committee reports *cannot be laid on the table as a unit.* (An item of business can be reached in such a case, however, by methods that are explained on pp. 215, 363.)

3. Is out of order when another has the floor.
4. Must be seconded.
5. Is not debatable. It is proper for, and the chair can ask, the maker of this motion to state his reason first, however, as: "Our speaker must catch an early flight," or "Laying this question aside temporarily will ensure adequate time to consider the next item of business, which must be decided at this meeting." (The urgency and the legitimate

intent of the motion can thus be established; but mentioning its purpose imposes no requirement as to when or whether the assembly will take the question from the table. An essential feature of this motion is that it cannot be qualified in any way and that, so long as the question remains on the table, the decision as to when—or if—it will be taken up is left open. For the limitations on the length of time that a question can lie on the table, see p. 214.)

6. Is not amendable.

7. Requires a majority vote.

8. An affirmative vote on the motion to *Lay on the Table* cannot be reconsidered, because it is easier and more direct to move to take the question from the table (see below). A negative vote on the motion to *Lay on the Table* can be reconsidered only until such time as the motion can be renewed. As explained on pages 213–14, renewal of the motion to *Lay on the Table* is permitted only when either (a) progress in business or debate has been sufficient to make it essentially a new question, or (b) something urgent has arisen that was not known when the assembly rejected this motion; see pages 339–40.

Further Rules and Explanation

LAYING THE PENDING QUESTIONS ON THE TABLE AFTER DEBATE HAS BEEN CLOSED.   If debate has been closed by ordering the *Previous Question* or by the expiration of the time to which debate was limited, then up until the moment of taking the last vote under the order, the questions still before the assembly can be laid on the table. Thus, while a resolution and an amendment are pending, if the *Previous Question* is ordered on both motions, it is in order to lay the resolution on the table, carrying with it the adhering amendment. If the amendment had already been

voted on, it would likewise have been in order to lay the res- *1*
olution on the table.

TAKING A QUESTION FROM THE TABLE.   Rules
affecting the motion to *Lay on the Table* are closely related to *5*
the motion to *Take from the Table* (**34**). After a question has
been laid on the table, it can be taken from the table by a majority vote as soon as the interrupting business is disposed of
and whenever no question is pending, provided that business
of the same class as the question on the table, unfinished busi- *10*
ness, general orders, or new business is in order.

Any member can move to take a question from the table
in a *regular* meeting or in a meeting that is an adjournment
(**9**) of a regular meeting. A question can be taken from the
table at a *special* meeting only if it has been laid on the table *15*
at that meeting or if the intention that it be taken from the
table has been stated in the call of the meeting. When a question is taken from the table, everything is in the same condition, so far as possible, as it was when laid on the table, except
that if the motion is not taken up until the next session, the *20*
effect of an order limiting or extending the limits of debate
or the *Previous Question* is exhausted (pp. 195–96, 204–5).

RENEWAL OF THE MOTION TO LAY ON THE
TABLE; LAYING A QUESTION ON THE TABLE *25*
AGAIN.   A motion to *Lay on the Table* that has been voted
down can be renewed, or a question that has been taken from
the table can be laid on the table again, subject to the following condition in either case: A motion made the same day to
lay the same question on the table is in order only after ma- *30*
terial progress in business or debate has been made, or when
an unforeseen urgent matter requires immediate attention.
(This rule is a consequence of the fact that the rejection of a
motion to *Lay on the Table* or the taking of a question from
the table means that the assembly wishes to consider the *35*

1 matter at that time.) Motions to *Recess* (**20**) or to *Adjourn*
   (**21**) that have been made and lost do not justify a new motion to lay the same question on the table, but the renewal
   might be justified after a vote on an important amendment
5 or on a motion to *Commit*.

   PARTICULAR EFFECTS OF THE MOTION. The
   effects of the adoption of a motion to *Lay on the Table* are as
   follows:
10   It places on the table—that is, in the care of the secretary—the pending question and everything adhering to it.
   Thus, if a resolution with a proposed amendment and a motion to *Commit* are pending and the resolution is laid on the
   table, all of these questions go to the table at the same time
15 and, if taken from the table, all will return together. But a
   proposed amendment to anything previously adopted—
   existing bylaws, for example—is a main motion and when laid
   on the table does not carry with it what it proposes to amend.
       In cases in which the next regular business session will
20 be held before a quarterly time interval has elapsed (see
   pp. 89–90), a question laid on the table remains there until
   taken from the table or until the close of the next regular session; if not taken up by that time, the question dies. In cases
   in which the lapse of time between regular business sessions
25 is greater than a quarterly time interval (see pp. 89–90), a
   question laid on the table can remain there only until the end
   of the current session; and unless taken from the table earlier,
   the matter dies with the close of that session.
       Since a motion that has been laid on the table is still
30 *within the control of the assembly* (pp. 340–41), no other motion on the same subject is in order that would either conflict
   with, or present substantially the same question as, the motion that is lying on the table. To consider another motion
   on the same subject, it is necessary first to take the question
35 from the table and then to move the new proposal as a sub-

stitute, or to make whatever other motion is appropriate to the case. 1

Laying a question on the table with the idea of attending to something else does not suspend any rules or set aside an order of business that may interfere with doing the thing desired at the time. Taking up the desired business may require an additional motion after the question has been laid on the table (see *Suspend the Rules*, **25**). 5

MISUSES OF THE MOTION. As stated at the beginning of this section, the motion to *Lay on the Table* is subject to a number of incorrect uses that should be avoided.* 10

It is out of order to move to lay a pending question on the table if there is evidently no other matter requiring immediate attention. However, if members who command a majority wish to bring up a measure out of its order but lack the two thirds required to suspend the rules to do so, they may lay each intervening matter on the table in succession, until the desired matter is reached. This is proper because their evident object is not to suppress without debate the items laid on the table, but instead to advance consideration of something they consider more urgent (see p. 363). At a special meeting, it is dilatory (**39**) and out of order to move 15

20

---

*Some misuses of the motion to *Lay on the Table* probably arise from a misunderstanding of the practice of the United States House of Representatives, where this motion has gradually become converted to a special purpose that is not applicable in ordinary assemblies. The press of legislation in the House is so great that only a fraction of the bills introduced each year can be considered. With this volume of work under the two-party system in such a large body, the majority must be given power to suppress a measure without debate, and the agenda must be tightly regulated. The House rules therefore do not allow a question to be taken from the table without first suspending the rules by a two-thirds vote. Consequently, when a matter is laid on the table in the House it is virtually killed.

to lay on the table the matter for which the meeting has been called.

The motion to *Lay on the Table* is often incorrectly used and wrongly admitted as in order with the intention of either killing an embarrassing question without a direct vote, or of suppressing a question without debate. The first of these two uses is unsafe if there is any contest on the issue; the second is in violation of a basic principle of general parliamentary law that only a two-thirds vote can rightfully suppress a main question without allowing free debate.

If the majority were to lay a question on the table, erroneously supposing that it thereby becomes dead, some of those who voted with the majority might leave before the time of final adjournment and the minority might all stay. The real minority might thus become a temporary majority, take the question from the table, and act upon it in the absence of many interested parties. They also might take the question from the table at the next session in cases where that session is held at least within the next quarterly time interval (see pp. 89–90).

CORRECT PROCEDURES IN LIEU OF MISUSES. In the situations that give rise to improper use of the motion to *Lay on the Table*, the correct procedures are as follows:

If it is desired to dispose of a question without a direct vote, the suitable method is to use the motion to *Postpone Indefinitely*. If it is desired to do this without further debate, the motion to *Postpone Indefinitely* can be followed immediately by a motion for the *Previous Question*. A motion that has been indefinitely postponed is killed for the remainder of the session, but is no more difficult to renew at a later session than any other motion that is subject to such renewal (p. 337).

If it is believed that any discussion of a particular original main motion might do harm, the proper course is to raise

Objection to the Consideration of the Question (**26**) before its
consideration has begun. For cases where *Postpone* (**14**) is the
proper motion in lieu of an incorrectly used motion to *Lay
on the Table*, see "Form and Example," below.

Form and Example

Forms used in making this motion are: "I move to lay the
question on the table"; or "I move that the resolution be laid
on the table." (It is preferable to avoid moving "to table" a
motion, or "that the motion be tabled.")*

This motion, as explained earlier, is undebatable and cannot be qualified in any way. In moving it, a member can mention its intended purpose or name a time at which he plans
to move that the question be taken from the table, but he
cannot move to lay a question "on the table until after the
completion of …," or, "on the table until 2 P.M." Rather than
always ruling such a motion out of order, however, the chair
should properly treat it as a motion "to postpone the question
until …"; that is, he should state the motion as admitted in
that form unless the motion to *Postpone* is out of order at
the time.

Since the motion to *Lay on the Table* can be neither debated nor amended, the chair puts it to a vote immediately
after stating the question on it, as follows:

CHAIR: It is moved and seconded to lay the pending question(s) on
the table. As many as are in favor of laying the pending question(s)

---

*In the United States, the word "table" used as a verb often suggests the
improper application of the motion to *Lay on the Table*, as explained on
pages 215–16. In British usage, on the other hand, the same expression has
an entirely different meaning and refers not to a subsidiary motion but to the
introduction of a proposed resolution or document to be placed among items
of business waiting to be considered.

1 on the table, say *aye*. ... Those opposed, say *no*. ... [and so on, as in the examples already given for motions requiring a majority vote for adoption].

5 For certain limited purposes not involving debate or amendment—such as to make a privileged motion or a motion to *Reconsider* (**37**)—a member can claim the floor while the motion to *Lay on the Table* is pending. To do so, the member rises and interrupts the chair by calling out "Mr.
10 President!"—immediately *after* the chair has said, "It is moved and seconded to lay the pending question(s) on the table," and *before* the vote is taken. The chair grants the member limited recognition by answering, "For what purpose does the member rise?"
15 After a question has been laid on the table, if further action by the assembly is needed to reach the desired business, the chair immediately says, for example, "Is there a motion to suspend the rules that interfere with hearing the speaker at this time?" (Or, "The chair will entertain a motion to ...")

CHAPTER VII

PRIVILEGED MOTIONS

*See 6, pages 66ff., for a list of these motions and a
description of their characteristics as a class.*

§18. CALL FOR THE ORDERS OF THE DAY
(To demand to take up the proper business in order)

A *Call for the Orders of the Day* is a privileged motion by
which a member can require the assembly to conform to its
agenda, program, or order of business, or to take up a general
or special order that is due to come up at the time (**14, 41**),
unless two thirds of those voting wish to do otherwise.

Taking up business in the prescribed order is of substantial
importance, especially in conventions—which must follow a
closely regulated schedule with much of the underlying work
taking place off the convention floor in conferences and committees. For business to receive proper consideration, officers,
committee members, and the delegates who are principally
involved in major questions must be able to know the approximate times at which subjects will come up.

If the presiding officer consistently performs his duty of
announcing the business to come before the assembly in its
proper order, there will be no occasion for calling for the orders of the day. But the chair may fail to notice that the time

1   assigned for a general or special order has arrived, or he may
    skip an item in the order of business by mistake, or delay an-
    nouncing a special order set for that time because he thinks
    the assembly is so interested in the pending question that it
5   does not yet wish to take up the special order. In these cases,
    any member has the right to call for the orders of the day.
    The call must be simply "for the orders of the day" and not
    for a specified one, as this motion is only a demand that the
    proper schedule of business—whatever it is—be followed. In
10 other words, while the member may remind the chair of what
    is scheduled, he cannot by this call obtain consideration of an
    order of the day that does not have first priority for consider-
    ation at that time.

15   **Standard Descriptive Characteristics**

        The privileged *Call for the Orders of the Day*:

    1. Takes precedence over all motions except (a) other privi-
20   leged motions and (b) a motion to *Suspend the Rules* (**25**)
        that relates to the priority of business—although it can
        interrupt a *pending* question only if the neglect of a spe-
        cial order is involved (see below). It yields to all other
        privileged motions, and to any applicable incidental mo-
25   tions that may arise and that must be disposed of before
        it is disposed of. Except when a special order must be
        taken up, this call also yields to a motion to *Reconsider* or
        to the calling up (**37**) of a motion to *Reconsider* that has
        been made previously.
30 2. Is not applied *to* any motion, but is applicable as follows:
        (a) when the agenda, program, or order of business is
        being varied from; (b) when a general order that is in
        order at the time is not being taken up; or (c) when the
        time for considering a special order has arrived or passed
35   and it is not being taken up. (For a statement of the pre-

cise times at which a *Call for the Orders of the Day* is in
order, see below.) No subsidiary motion can be applied
to this call.

3. If in order at the time, is in order when another has the
floor, even if it interrupts a person speaking.

4. Does not require a second.

5. Is not debatable.

6. Is not amendable.

7. Upon a call by a single member the orders of the day must
be enforced, except that a two-thirds vote can set them
aside. (That is, the orders of the day can be set aside:
either by a vote of two thirds in the negative on a question
put by the chair as to the assembly's desire to proceed to
the orders of the day; or by a vote of two thirds in the
affirmative on a motion by a member to extend the time
for considering the pending question, or to suspend the
rules and take up the desired question; see below.)

8. Cannot be reconsidered.

Further Rules and Explanation

TIMES WHEN A CALL FOR THE ORDERS OF THE
DAY IS IN ORDER. The particular conditions under
which a *Call for the Orders of the Day* is in order are as
follows:

- Referring to cases (a) and (b) under Standard Characteristic 2, which do not involve the neglect of a special order:
As soon as it is evident that the agenda, program, or order
of business is being varied from, or that the time for the
consideration of a postponed motion has arrived or
passed, a *Call for the Orders of the Day* is in order whenever no question is pending. In such a case where no special order is involved, if a member starts to make a motion
departing from the correct order of business, or if the

1   chair announces a wrong item, the call must be made
     before any motion is stated by the chair; otherwise, it can-
     not be made until after the motion has been disposed of.

 •   Referring, on the other hand, to case (c) under Standard
5   Characteristic 2: If the chair does not immediately an-
     nounce a special order when the time set for its consider-
     ation has arrived, a *Call for the Orders of the Day* can be
     made at once—even while another question is pending,
     unless the pending question is itself a special order that
10   was made before the one set for the present time was
     made (see **14**, **41**). From the time when a particular
     special order becomes the proper order of business and
     until it is announced, a *Call for the Orders of the Day* is in
     order.

15

     A *Call for the Orders of the Day* cannot be made in a com-
     mittee of the whole (see **52**).

     STATUS OF AN ORDER OF THE DAY AS A MAIN
20   MOTION.   In contrast to the privileged *Call for the Orders
     of the Day*, an order of the day which such a call may bring
     before the assembly is itself invariably a main motion, and
     when it is announced and pending, it is debatable and amend-
     able, and all of the other rules governing main motions apply
25   to it. The orders of the day as a whole cannot be laid on the
     table or postponed, but an individual order of the day when
     actually pending can be so disposed of. As soon as the orders
     of the day that have interrupted business that was pending
     are completed, the interrupted business is taken up again at
30   the point at which it was discontinued.

     SETTING ASIDE THE ORDERS OF THE DAY.
     When the orders of the day are called for, the chair can, and
     ordinarily should, immediately announce as the newly pend-
35   ing business the subject that is then in order. But sometimes

the chair or a member may sense that the assembly would   1
prefer to continue consideration of the presently pending
question or take up another matter first. In such cases, the
assembly by a two-thirds vote can set aside the orders of
the day, as follows: 5

a) *At the initiative of the chair:* Instead of announcing the
orders of the day when they are called for, the chair can
put the question on proceeding to them: "The orders of
the day are called for. The orders of the day are [identify-   10
ing the business that is in order]. The question is: Will
the assembly proceed to the orders of the day? As many
as are in favor of proceeding to the orders of the day ...
[and so on, taking a rising vote]." Since to refuse to proceed to the orders of the day is an interference with the   15
order of business similar to suspending the rules, two
thirds in the *negative* are required to vote down this question and refuse to take up the orders of the day. Once the
assembly has refused to proceed to the orders of the day,
they cannot be called for again until the pending business   20
is disposed of.

b) *At the initiative of a member:* When the orders of the day
are called for or announced, a member can move (depending on the case) "that the time for considering the
pending question be extended" a certain number of min-   25
utes, or "that the rules be suspended and" the desired
question be taken up (see **25**). These motions require a
two-thirds vote in the *affirmative* for their adoption, since
they change the order of business, agenda, or program.

    30

Form and Example

The form of the motion is as follows: To call for the
orders of the day, a member rises and, addressing the chair
without waiting for recognition, says, "Mr. President, I call   35

for the orders of the day," or "Madam President, I demand the regular order." The member can, if necessary, remind the chair of the matter set for that time.

Assume that at yesterday's meeting of a convention, a resolution was postponed and made a special order for 11:30 A.M. today. That time has now arrived, but a member is speaking on a pending question.

MEMBER A (rising and addressing the chair): Madam President, I call for the orders of the day.

CHAIR: The orders of the day are called for. Yesterday the convention postponed the resolution relating to tax reform to 11:30 A.M. today, and made it a special order. It is now 11:30. The question is on the resolution, "*Resolved*, That ..."

After consideration of the resolution is completed, the former business is resumed where it was left off:

CHAIR: When the orders of the day were called for, the convention was considering the resolution "*Resolved*, That ..." Mr. Henley had the floor at that time. The chair recognizes Mr. Henley.

§19. RAISE A QUESTION OF PRIVILEGE

To *Raise a Question of Privilege* is a device that permits *a request or main motion relating to the rights and privileges of the assembly or any of its members* to be brought up for possible immediate consideration because of its urgency, while business is pending and the request or motion would otherwise be out of order. (For types and examples of questions of privilege,* see pp. 227–30.)

---

*The term *question of privilege* is applied to any request or motion relating to the rights and privileges of the assembly or its members, whether or not it is introduced by means of the device *Raise a Question of Privilege*.

This device operates as follows: A member rises and
addresses the chair saying that he "rises to a question of privilege ..." (as explained on p. 227), and the chair immediately
directs the member to state his question of privilege; the chair
must then rule (subject to appeal, **24**) whether the request
or motion is in fact a question of privilege and, if so, whether
it is urgent enough to interrupt the pending business.

It is important to understand the distinction between the
device *Raise a Question of Privilege* and the question of privilege itself. The point to be decided in connection with the
former is whether a certain question shall be admitted for consideration with the status and priority of the latter. The "raising" of a question of privilege is governed by rules appropriate
to the device's high rank in the order of precedence of motions. When a question of privilege is taken up after it has
been raised and has been admitted by the chair, however, depending on the form in which it was introduced, it is handled
as a *request* (**32, 33**), or it is treated as a main motion and is
debatable and amendable and can have any subsidiary motion
applied to it—regardless of whether it interrupted, or awaited
the disposal of, the pending business. Questions of privilege
can also be introduced while no motion is pending, either as
requests or by being moved and seconded just as any other
main motion; in that case, the device of "raising" a question
of privilege does not enter in.

Questions of privilege or motions growing out of them
should not be confused with "privileged motions" (or "privileged questions"). The latter comprise the five highest-ranking motions in the order of precedence, among which *Raise
a Question of Privilege* is assigned a position.

The eight characteristics below apply only to the device
of *raising* a question of privilege; that is, to a member's obtaining recognition to state his urgent motion or request while
business is pending, and to the chair's ruling on the question's
admissibility as noted above (and described on pp. 227–28).

Standard Descriptive Characteristics

The privileged device *Raise a Question of Privilege*:

1. Takes precedence over all other motions except the three higher-ranking privileged motions to *Recess*, to *Adjourn*, and to *Fix the Time to Which to Adjourn*. It yields to these three privileged motions, and to any applicable incidental motions that may arise and that *must* be disposed of before it is disposed of.
2. Cannot be applied to any other motion, and no subsidiary motion can be applied to it.
3. Is in order when another has the floor if warranted by the urgency of the situation. (In such cases, the raising of a question of privilege is in order after another has been assigned the floor and before he has begun to speak; it should not interrupt a member who is actually speaking unless the object of the question of privilege would otherwise be defeated—as it would be, however, in each of the two examples at the end of this section, pp. 228–30. The raising of a question of privilege cannot interrupt voting or verifying a vote.)
4. Does not require a second, as relates to *raising* the question of privilege; that is, no second is required at any step in the process unless (after the chair has directed the member to state his question of privilege) the member states it in the form of a motion; such a motion must be seconded.
5. Is not debatable; that is, there can be no debate as to admitting the request or motion that has been raised as a question of privilege. (But a main motion that is pending after having been admitted as a question of privilege is debatable.)
6. Is not amendable; that is, the motion to *Amend* is not applicable to the process of raising a question of privilege.

(But a main motion that is pending after having been   *1*
admitted as a question of privilege can be amended.)
7. Is ruled upon by the chair. No vote on the question's admissibility is taken unless the chair's ruling is appealed
(**24**).   *5*
8. The chair's ruling on whether to admit the request or motion that has been raised as a question of privilege cannot
be reconsidered.

Further Rules and Explanation   *10*

TYPES OF QUESTIONS OF PRIVILEGE.   Questions
of privilege are of two types: (1) those relating to the privileges of the assembly as a whole; and (2) questions of personal
privilege. If the two come into competition, the former take   *15*
precedence over the latter. Questions of the privileges of
the assembly may relate to its organization or existence;
to the comfort of its members with respect to heating, ventilation, lighting, and noise or other disturbance; to the conduct of its officers and employees, or of visitors; to the   *20*
punishment of its members; or to the accuracy of published
reports of its proceedings; etc. A motion to go into executive
session (**9**) is a question of the privileges of the assembly.
Questions of personal privilege—which seldom arise in ordinary societies and even more rarely justify interruption of   *25*
pending business—may relate, for example, to an incorrect
record of a member's participation in a meeting contained in
minutes approved in his absence, or to charges circulated
against a member's character.

  30

STEPS IN RAISING AND DISPOSING OF A QUES-
TION OF PRIVILEGE.   In raising a question of privilege,
a member rises, addresses the chair without waiting for recognition, and says, "I rise to a question of privilege affecting the
assembly," or "… to a question of personal privilege."   *35*

1   The chair, even if he has assigned the floor to another person, directs the member to state his question of privilege. Depending on the case, the member then either (a) describes the situation briefly and asks that it be remedied, or (b) if he believes that the matter will require formal action by the assembly, makes a motion covering his question of privilege, and another member seconds it. The chair at his discretion can ask a member to put into the form of a motion a question of privilege that the member has stated as a request. Unless the point is simple enough to be promptly adjusted (as in the first example, below) or unless it is in the form of a motion and is not seconded, the chair rules whether the question is a question of privilege, and, if so, whether it is of sufficient urgency to warrant interruption of the existing parliamentary situation. From this ruling an undebatable appeal can be taken.

     If the motion made as a question of privilege is seconded, and if the chair admits it as such and decides that it should be entertained immediately, he states the question on it and proceeds as with any other main motion. When the question of privilege has been disposed of, business is resumed at exactly the point at which it was interrupted. If a member had the floor when the question of privilege was raised, the chair assigns him the floor again.

Form and Example

     The forms used in raising a question of privilege include: "I rise to a question of privilege affecting [or "relating to"] the assembly" (or "to a question of the privileges of the assembly"), and "I rise to a question of personal privilege." The preceding forms should always be adhered to in cases where it is necessary to interrupt a person speaking. When a question of the privileges of the assembly is raised in a small meeting without interrupting a speaker, a variation such as "A question of privilege, Mr. President!" is permissible.

The following is an example of a question relating to
the privileges of the assembly that can be stated as an informal request and that can be routinely adjusted by the
chair:

Assume that, while an important speech is in progress at
a meeting in a large hall with upper windows, workmen begin
to operate jackhammers in an alley beside the building. Member A rises and interrupts, addressing the chair:

MEMBER A: Mr. President, I rise to a question of privilege affecting
the assembly.

CHAIR: The gentleman will state his question.

MEMBER A: Mr. President, I don't think we're going to be able to
hear unless some of the windows are closed.

CHAIR: Will one of the ushers ask the building engineer to have the
windows closed on the left side. May we have the sound turned up a little
until the windows are closed.

The next example illustrates a question of the privileges
of the assembly requiring a formal motion which interrupts
pending business. In an ordinary society these occasions are
rare, but in a convention or large assembly a situation of unforeseen complications may cause such a motion to become
appropriate.

Assume that, to hear a prominent speaker, an association
has opened one of its meetings to the public. Because of the
speaker's commitments at a later hour, his address was given
first, preceding the business meeting—which was expected to
be brief and routine. But Member X has surprised this meeting by introducing a resolution dealing with a delicate matter
of obvious importance that may call for prompt action by the
association.

Member Y, sensing that consideration of this question
should be kept within the organization, interrupts Member
X's speech on the pending resolution by rising "to a question

1 of privilege relating to the assembly." As directed by the president, he states the question of privilege:

MEMBER Y: Mr. President, I believe this is a question we should con-
5 sider in a closed meeting. With apologies to our guests, I move that the open portion of this meeting be declared ended and that our guests be excused. (Second.)

CHAIR: The chair rules that the question is one of privilege to be entertained immediately. It is moved and seconded that [stating the ques-
10 tion on the motion to go into executive session].

Debate or amendment follows, if needed; then the question is put to a vote. After announcing the result, the president expresses appreciation to guests. As soon as they have left, he
15 states the resolution that was interrupted by the question of privilege, and recognizes Member X, who had the floor.

§20. RECESS

20 A *recess* is a short intermission in the assembly's proceedings, commonly of only a few minutes, which does not close the meeting and after which business will immediately be resumed at exactly the point where it was interrupted.* A recess may be taken, for example, to count ballots, to secure infor-
25 mation, or to allow for informal consultation.

The privileged motion to *Recess* (or to *Take a Recess*) is a motion that a recess begin *immediately*, made *while another question is pending*.

A motion to recess that is made *when no question is pend-
30 ing* (whether the recess is to begin immediately or at a future time) is a *main motion*, and the eight characteristics given below do not apply to it. Consequently, a motion to recess is

---

*For an explanation of the distinction between *recess* and *adjournment*, see **8**, especially page 85.

privileged only when another question is pending; and a mo-   *1*
tion to take a recess at a future time is in order only when no
question is pending.

The eight characteristics below apply only to the *privileged* motion to *Recess*.   *5*

Standard Descriptive Characteristics

The privileged motion to *Recess*:

                                                              10

1. Takes precedence over the main motion, over all subsidiary and incidental motions, and over all privileged motions except those to *Adjourn* and to *Fix the Time to
   Which to Adjourn*. It yields to motions to *Amend* or for
   the *Previous Question* that are applied to it, and it yields *15*
   to the *privileged* motions to *Adjourn* and to *Fix the Time
   to Which to Adjourn* (but in the cases where motions to
   adjourn or to set a time for meeting again are "not privileged"—that is, are main motions—it takes precedence
   over these motions; see **21** and **22**). It also yields to any *20*
   applicable incidental motions that may arise and that *must*
   be disposed of before the motion to *Recess* is voted on.
2. Is not applied *to* any motion. Motions to *Amend* can be
   applied to it. The *Previous Question* can also be applied to
   it to prevent amendments being moved, although this sit- *25*
   uation rarely arises in ordinary societies. No other subsidiary motion can be applied to it.
3. Is out of order when another has the floor.
4. Must be seconded.
5. Is not debatable.   *30*
6. Is amendable as to the length of the recess; any such
   amendment is undebatable.
7. Requires a majority vote.
8. Cannot be reconsidered.

Further Rules and Explanation

DECLARING A RECESS WHEN IT HAS BEEN PROVIDED FOR IN THE AGENDA OR PROGRAM.   If a recess is provided for in the adopted agenda or program of a convention or other meeting, the chair, without further action by the assembly, announces the fact and simply declares the assembly in recess when the specified time arrives. If the chair does not announce the recess at the scheduled time, a member can call for the orders of the day (**18**), thereby demanding that the recess be declared.

POSTPONING THE TIME FOR TAKING A SCHEDULED RECESS.   The time for taking a scheduled recess can be postponed by a two-thirds vote if, when that time arrives, the assembly does not wish to recess. In the latter event, the taking of the recess is treated just as any other order of the day that is due to be taken up, and it can be set aside by any of the procedures described on pages 222–23.

Form and Example

Forms in which this motion may be made are: "I move that the meeting recess [or "take a recess"] until 2 P.M."; "I move to recess for ten minutes"; or "I move to recess until called to order by the chair."

If such a motion is adopted, the chair announces the result as follows:

CHAIR: The ayes have it and the meeting stands recessed [or, "in recess"] for fifteen minutes [rapping once with the gavel, if desired].

At the end of the specified time, the chair gains the attention of the assembly and begins:

CHAIR: The convention [or "meeting"] will come to order. The time   *1*
of recess has expired. The question is on the resolution … [Or, if the recess was taken following the vote on a question or an election but before
the result had been announced, the first business would be the announcement of the vote.]   *5*

§21. ADJOURN

To *adjourn* means to close the meeting (**8**). A motion to
adjourn may be a privileged or a main motion depending on   *10*
a number of conditions. The motion to adjourn that commonly occurs in meetings of ordinary societies is the privileged motion. The adoption of any motion to adjourn closes
the meeting immediately unless the motion specifies a later
time for adjourning (but if it does specify such a time it is not   *15*
a privileged motion).

The *privileged* motion to *Adjourn* (which is always moved
in an unqualified form with no mention of a time either for
adjourning or for meeting again) is a motion to close the
meeting immediately, made under conditions where some   *20*
other provision for another meeting exists (so that the adjournment will not have the effect of dissolving the assembly),
and where no time for adjourning the present meeting has
already been set. In such a case, regardless of whether business is pending, a majority should not be forced to continue   *25*
in session substantially longer than it desires, and even if no
business is pending, a decision as to whether to close the
meeting should not be allowed to consume time. For this reason, when there is provision for another meeting and no time
for adjourning is already set, an unqualified motion "to ad-   *30*
journ" is afforded sufficiently high privilege to interrupt the
pending question and, on adoption, to close the meeting before the pending business is disposed of. And for the same
reason, such a motion has the unique characteristic that, *even*

1 *if it is made while no question is pending*, it is not debatable or
amendable and it remains subject to all of the rules governing
the privileged motion to *Adjourn* (except those that relate to
making the motion while business is pending; see *Standard*
5 *Descriptive Characteristics*). Under the conditions just described, a motion to *Adjourn* is therefore said to be "privileged" or to be "a privileged motion" even when no question
is pending.

A motion to adjourn is always a privileged motion *except*
10 in the following cases:

1) When the motion is qualified in any way, as in the case of
   a motion to adjourn at, or to, a future time.
2) When a time for adjourning is already established, either
15   because the assembly has adopted a motion or a program
   setting such a time, or because the order of business, the
   bylaws, or other governing rules prescribe it.
3) When the effect of the motion to adjourn, if adopted,
   would be to dissolve the assembly with no provision for
20   another meeting, as is usually the case in a mass meeting
   or the last meeting of a convention.*

Under any of conditions (1) through (3) above, a motion to
adjourn is not privileged and is treated just as any other main
25 motion. Consequently, a motion to adjourn at or to a future
time is always out of order while business is pending in any
assembly; and any motion to adjourn at all is out of order
while business is pending under either of conditions (2) or
(3)—which, however, do not commonly apply to meetings
30 of ordinary societies.

---

*In state or national organizations where subordinate units choose del-
egates each time an annual or biennial convention is held, each convention is
a separate assembly, since it is made up of a different body of delegates.

In ordinary societies having bylaws that provide for several regular meetings during the year and having no fixed hour for adjournment, a motion "to adjourn," when unqualified, is always a privileged motion. In meetings of these organizations, such a motion to *Adjourn* is in order regardless of whether business is pending; and even when business is not pending, this motion is undebatable and is subject to the rules given below.

The following eight characteristics apply only to the *privileged* motion to *Adjourn*.

Standard Descriptive Characteristics

The privileged motion to *Adjourn*:

1. Takes precedence over all motions except the *privileged* motion to *Fix the Time to Which to Adjourn*; but it is not in order while the assembly is engaged in voting or verifying a vote, or before the result of a vote has been announced by the chair, except that, in the case of a vote taken by ballot, a motion to *Adjourn* is in order after the ballots have been collected by the tellers and before the result has been announced.* It yields to the *privileged* motion to *Fix the Time to Which to Adjourn* (but it takes precedence over a motion to set a time for meeting again in the cases where such a motion is "not privileged"— that is, is a main motion; see **22**). It also yields to any applicable incidental motions that may arise and that *must* be disposed of before the motion to *Adjourn* is voted on;

---

*When much time may be consumed in counting ballots, it is generally better to take a recess, but the assembly can adjourn if it has previously appointed a time for the next meeting. In any case, the result of the ballot vote should be announced as soon as business is resumed.

but an incidental motion that can wait should not be entertained after a motion to *Adjourn* has been made.

2. Is not applied *to* any motion, and no subsidiary motion can be applied to it.

3. Is out of order when another has the floor.

4. Must be seconded.

5. Is not debatable (see pp. 238–40, however).

6. Is not amendable.

7. Requires a majority vote.

8. Cannot be reconsidered (but see p. 240 regarding its renewal).

Further Rules and Explanation

EFFECT OF ADJOURNMENT ON PENDING BUSINESS OR ON AN UNCOMPLETED ORDER OF BUSINESS.   Except as the assembly may have adopted rules providing otherwise, the effect of an adjournment on a pending motion or an uncompleted order of business is as follows:

a) *When the adjournment does not close the session* (as when an adjourned meeting [9] has been set, or in any meeting of a convention except the last one): Business is immediately resumed at the next meeting at the point where it left off, except that there may first be brief opening ceremonies or reading of the minutes (see **41**).

b) *When the adjournment closes the session in an assembly having its next regular business session within a quarterly time interval (see pp. 89–90), and having no members whose terms of membership expire before the next regular session* (for example, in ordinary clubs and societies that hold frequent "regular meetings"): The complete order of business is followed at the next regular session. If a question was pending at the time of adjournment, it is taken up as the first item under unfinished business (or under special

orders, if it was a special order)—resuming the question   1
at exactly where it was previously interrupted. Any general or special order that was not reached is also taken
up under unfinished business or under special orders,
respectively (see **41**).   5

c) *When the adjournment closes a session in a body that will
not have another regular session within a quarterly time interval (see pp. 89–90), or closes a session that ends the term
of all or some of the members* (as may happen in an elected
legislative assembly or in a board): Matters temporarily   10
but not finally disposed of, except those that remain in
the hands of a committee to which they have been referred (see p. 90, l. 9 to p. 91, l. 16), fall to the ground.*
They can, however, be introduced at the next session, the
same as if they had never before been brought up.   15

ADJOURNMENT OF BODIES WITHOUT REGU-
LARLY SCHEDULED MEETINGS.   The adjournment of
a mass meeting or the last meeting of a convention dissolves
the assembly unless provision has been made whereby it will,   20
or may, be later reconvened. When adjournment would dissolve an assembly, the motion to adjourn is a main motion.
A motion to close the session in an assembly that will thereby
be dissolved, or will not meet again for a long time unless
called into authorized special session under the bylaws or   25
other governing rule, is often referred to as a motion to "adjourn sine die," which means to "adjourn without day" (see
also p. 83). If the bylaws of an organization provide for the
calling of a special convention after the regular convention
session has been held, this assembly should meet as a distinct   30
session with a body of delegates and alternates that must be

---

*In the case of an adopted motion which is the subject of a motion to
Reconsider that was not finally disposed of, it is only the motion to *Reconsider*
that falls to the ground, and the adopted motion then goes into effect.

chosen anew under provisions established in the bylaws. However, program items normally associated with conventions of the organization need not be provided for.

If a board or committee meeting is adjourned without any provision having been made for future meetings, the next meeting is held at the call of the chairman (see also pp. 499, 501). Consequently, since there usually is no fixed hour for adjournment, the unqualified motion to adjourn is usually privileged in boards or committees. When a special committee has completed the business referred to it, however, it "rises" and reports, which is equivalent to the main motion to adjourn.

PARLIAMENTARY STEPS THAT ARE IN ORDER WHILE THE PRIVILEGED MOTION TO ADJOURN IS PENDING, OR AFTER THE ASSEMBLY HAS VOTED TO ADJOURN.   Although the privileged motion to *Adjourn* is undebatable, the following parliamentary steps are in order while it is pending:

- to inform the assembly of business requiring attention before adjournment;
- to make important announcements;
- to *make* (but not to take up*) a motion to reconsider a previous vote;

---

*Because of time limits on moving a reconsideration, a motion to *Reconsider* is allowed to be *made* and recorded (but *not* to be *considered*) while a motion to *Adjourn* is pending, or even after it has been voted to adjourn and before the chair has declared the assembly adjourned. A motion to *Reconsider* that is made at such a time normally must wait to be *called up* at a later meeting, unless it is made before the motion to *Adjourn* is voted on and that motion is withdrawn or voted down. If the reconsideration is moved after it has been voted to adjourn and it appears to require immediate attention, however, the chair should retake the vote on the motion to *Adjourn* (see *unique characteristics* of the motion to *Reconsider*, pp. 315–17).

- to make a motion to *Reconsider and Enter on the Minutes* (pp. 332–35);
- to give notice of a motion to be made at the next meeting (or on the next day, in a session consisting of daily meetings) where the motion requires *previous notice* (see pp. 121–24); and
- to move to set a time for an adjourned meeting (**9, 22**) if there is no meeting scheduled for later within the same session.

Any of the above steps that are desired should be taken care of earlier, if possible; but there may sometimes be no such opportunity, particularly in a convention or a session of several meetings that is following an adopted agenda or program (**41**), or in cases where a meeting of an ordinary society adjourns before completing its regular order of business. If any matters of the types listed above arise after it has been moved to adjourn, the chair should state the facts briefly, or a member who rises and addresses the chair for the purpose should be allowed to do so—or to make the necessary motion or give the desired notice—before the vote is taken on the motion to *Adjourn*. If something requires action before adjournment, the member who moved to adjourn can be requested to withdraw his motion.

Regardless of the type of motion by which it is voted to adjourn, the meeting is not closed until the chair has declared that the meeting "is adjourned" (or "stands adjourned"), and members should not leave their seats until this declaration has been made. After it has been voted to adjourn but before the chair has declared the meeting adjourned, it is still in order to take any of the steps listed in the preceding paragraph, if necessary. In announcing an affirmative vote on a motion to adjourn, the chair should usually pause before declaring the meeting adjourned, saying: "The ayes seem to have it. [Pausing and resuming slowly:] The ayes have it, and the meeting

1 is adjourned." The pause affords time for members to demand a division (**29**) on the vote to adjourn, or to take any
of the other steps just described. If the chair learns, immediately after declaring the assembly adjourned, that a member
5 seeking the floor for one of these purposes had risen and addressed the chair before the adjournment was declared, then,
since the adjournment was improper and this breach was
promptly noted, the chair must call the meeting back to
order—but only long enough for the purpose for which the
10 member legitimately sought the floor.

LEGITIMATE RENEWAL OF THE PRIVILEGED
MOTION AND ITS ABUSES.   Since a motion to *Adjourn*
may be voted down because a majority wish to hear one
15 speech or take one vote, this motion must be renewable as
soon as there has been any progress in business or even material progress in debate. But this privilege of renewal and the
high rank of the motion are sometimes abused to the annoyance of the assembly. The chair should therefore refuse to
20 entertain a motion to *Adjourn* that is obviously made for ob-
structive purposes—for example, when a motion to *Adjourn*
has just been voted down and nothing has taken place since
to indicate that the assembly may now wish to close the meeting. If a member who has not properly obtained the floor calls
25 out, "I move to adjourn," such a call cannot be entertained
as a motion except by unanimous consent (see *Dilatory
Motions*, **39**).

CASES WHERE THE ASSEMBLY CAN ADJOURN
30 WITHOUT A MOTION.   If an hour for adjourning a
meeting within a convention or other session of more than
one meeting has been scheduled—either in an agenda or program or by the adoption of a motion setting a time—no motion to adjourn is necessary when that hour arrives. The chair
35 simply announces the fact and declares the meeting ad-

journed, as described for a recess on page 232. If the assembly   *1*
does not then wish to adjourn, the matter is handled as a case
of setting aside the orders of the day, as explained on pages
222–23 (see also p. 370). If such a meeting wishes to adjourn
earlier, it is done by a main motion, which, however, can be   *5*
adopted by a majority vote (see p. 234). The rules stated
above regarding parliamentary steps that are in order after it
has been voted to adjourn are applicable in this case also.

When it appears that there is no further business in a
meeting of an ordinary local society that normally goes   *10*
through a complete order of business (**41**) at each regular
meeting (**9**), the chair, instead of waiting or calling for a motion to adjourn, can ask, "Is there any further business?" If
there is no response, the chair can then say, "Since there is
no further business, the meeting is adjourned."   *15*

Form and Example

The following forms may be used for either a privileged
or a main motion: "I move to adjourn," or "I move that the   *20*
meeting ["now"] adjourn." Additional forms in order as a
main motion are: "I move that the club now adjourn to meet
at 8 P.M. on April 10," or "I move that the convention adjourn *sine die* [or "adjourn without day"]."

Assume that while a resolution is pending in a regular   *25*
monthly meeting of a local society, a member obtains the
floor and moves to adjourn, and the motion is seconded.
Since this motion is privileged and therefore undebatable, the
chair immediately puts the question.

30

CHAIR: It is moved and seconded to adjourn. Those in favor, say *aye*
[continuing to take the vote as described on pp. 45–46].

If the motion is adopted, the chair announces the result
and declares the meeting adjourned (first making sure that   *35*

no member is seeking the floor, as described on pp. 239–40). If the motion is lost, the chair, after announcing the result, immediately restates the resolution that was pending when the motion to *Adjourn* was made.

After the pending resolution has been disposed of, or if there has been sufficient debate to show that the assembly now wishes to adjourn, a new motion to adjourn is in order. If such a motion is made and seconded and there is no other business, the chair, if he senses a general desire to adjourn, can suggest unanimous consent (pp. 54–56), as follows:

CHAIR: If there is no objection, the meeting will now adjourn. [Pause.] Since there is no objection, the meeting is adjourned.

The adjournment may be signaled by a single rap of the gavel, if desired.

§22. FIX THE TIME TO WHICH TO ADJOURN

The object of the motion to *Fix the Time to Which to Adjourn* (also referred to as the motion to "fix the time for an adjourned meeting") is to set the time, and sometimes the place, for another meeting to continue business of the session, with no effect on when the present meeting will adjourn.

A motion to *Fix the Time to Which to Adjourn* is in order only if at the time it is offered there is no meeting scheduled for later within the same session. If there is such a meeting, additional meetings within the same session may be set by a motion either to *Suspend the Rules* (**25**) or to *Amend Something Previously Adopted* (**35**), namely, the previously adopted agenda or program for the session.

A motion to fix the time to which to adjourn is privileged only when it is made while a question is pending.

If a motion to fix the time to which to adjourn is made in any assembly when no question is pending, it is in order and is debatable and subject to all of the other rules applicable to

main motions. If feasible, any desired motion to fix the time
to which to adjourn should be made while no other question
is pending. But situations may arise in which immediate
establishment of the time for an adjourned meeting is important, yet there is no opportunity to make a main motion. The
privileged motion to *Fix the Time to Which to Adjourn* can
then be used.

The following eight characteristics apply only to the *privileged* motion to *Fix the Time to Which to Adjourn.*

Standard Descriptive Characteristics

The privileged motion to *Fix the Time to Which to
Adjourn*:

1. Takes precedence over all other motions. It yields to motions to *Amend* or for the *Previous Question* that are applied to it and yields to any applicable incidental motions
   that may arise and that must be disposed of before the
   motion to *Fix the Time to Which to Adjourn* is voted on.
   While it is pending, the motion to *Reconsider* can be
   made, but not considered (see **37**). The privileged motion
   to *Fix the Time to Which to Adjourn* can be moved even
   after the assembly has voted to adjourn, provided that the
   chair has not yet declared the assembly adjourned.
2. Is not applied *to* any motion. Motions to *Amend* can be
   applied to it. The *Previous Question* can also be moved on
   it to prevent amendments, although this seldom serves a
   useful purpose.
3. Is out of order when another has the floor.
4. Must be seconded.
5. Is not debatable.
6. Is amendable as to the date, hour, or place; such amendments are undebatable.
7. Requires a majority vote.
8. Can be reconsidered.

1   **Further Rules and Explanation**

PROVISIONS AS TO TIME AND PLACE.   In an organized society, the adjourned meeting scheduled by adop-
5   tion of this motion (privileged or main) must be set for a time
before that of the next regular meeting. When the assembly
has no fixed place for its meetings, the motion should include
the place as well as the time of the adjourned meeting.

If an assembly holding regularly scheduled business meet-
10   ings adjourns to meet "at the call of the chair," an adjourned
meeting called accordingly is a continuation of the same session; but, if no such meeting is held before the next regular
session, the adjournment of the previous session becomes
final retrospectively as of the date the last meeting adjourned,
15   and the chair's authority to call an adjourned meeting expires.

EFFECT OF THE MOTION.   Whether introduced as
a privileged or a main motion, the effect of this motion is to
establish an *adjourned meeting*—that is, another meeting that
20   will be a continuation of the session at which the motion is
adopted. Unlike a special meeting, an adjourned meeting
does not require notice, although it is desirable to give such
notice if feasible. An adjourned meeting should not be confused with a *special meeting*, which is a separate session called,
25   in ordinary societies, as prescribed by the bylaws.

Because of the nature of the situations that give rise
to use of the privileged motion to *Fix the Time to Which to
Adjourn*, adoption of this motion is often followed by immediate introduction of a motion to *Postpone*, or of the privi-
30   leged motion to *Adjourn*, depending on the purpose, as
shown in the examples below. At the adjourned meeting, except for the reading of the minutes, business will be taken up
from the point at which the previous meeting adjourned or
at which questions were postponed.

35   It should be noted that the adoption of this motion does
not adjourn the present meeting or set a time for its adjourn-

ment; thus, it has no direct effect on when the present meet- *1*
ing shall adjourn, and is very different from a motion to fix
the time *at* which to adjourn (which is always a main motion).

Form and Example *5*

Forms in which this motion may be made are: "I move
that when this meeting adjourns, it adjourn to meet at
2:00 P.M. tomorrow"; "I move that when this meeting adjourns, it stand adjourned to meet at 8:00 P.M. on Wednesday, *10*
April 2, at the Riggs Hotel"; or "I move that on adjournment, the meeting adjourn to meet at the call of the chair."

In announcing an affirmative result, the chair says, for instance, "The ayes have it. When the meeting adjourns this
evening, it will adjourn to meet at 2 P.M. tomorrow." *15*

As a first example, assume that a number of members wish
to set up an adjourned meeting to deal with an involved
pending question, so that the remaining order of business can
be completed now.

  20

MEMBER A (obtaining the floor): Madam President, I believe the
pending resolution will require longer discussion than we have time for
this evening. I move that when the meeting adjourns, it adjourn to meet
here next Tuesday at 8:15 P.M. (Second.)

  25

The chair states the question on this motion. Amendment
as to time and place is possible, but no debate is in order. The
chair then puts to vote the motion to *Fix the Time to Which
to Adjourn*. After announcing the result—whether adoption
or rejection—she says that the question is on the resolution, *30*
which she rereads or indicates by descriptive title. If the motion to *Fix the Time to Which to Adjourn* has been adopted,
Member A rises once more.

MEMBER A (obtaining the floor): I move to postpone the pending res- *35*
olution to the adjourned meeting set for next Tuesday evening. (Second.)

The motion to postpone is considered in the usual manner. If it is adopted, the chair continues:

CHAIR: The ayes have it and the resolution is postponed to the adjourned meeting. The next item of business is ...

As a second example, assume that the motion to *Fix the Time to Which to Adjourn* is to be made with a view to immediate adjournment to a specified time, when this purpose cannot be reached by a main motion:

At the annual meeting of a society, the hour is growing late. A controversial bylaw amendment is pending, on which a strong minority is determined to continue debate.

MEMBER X (obtaining the floor): I move that when this meeting adjourns, it adjourn to meet at the same time tomorrow evening. (Second.)

The motion is treated as in the first example. If it is adopted, Member X, after the question has been restated on the pending bylaw amendment, again rises and addresses the chair.

MEMBER X (obtaining the floor): I move that the club now adjourn. (Second.)

The chair states the question on the motion to *Adjourn* and immediately puts it to vote. If it is adopted, the chair announces the result, as follows:

CHAIR: The ayes have it and the club stands adjourned until eight o'clock tomorrow evening.

CHAPTER
VIII

INCIDENTAL MOTIONS

See 6, pages 69ff., for a list of these motions and a description of their characteristics as a class.

§23. POINT OF ORDER

When a member thinks that the rules of the assembly are being violated, he can make a *Point of Order* (or "raise a question of order," as it is sometimes expressed), thereby calling upon the chair for a ruling and an enforcement of the regular rules.

Standard Descriptive Characteristics

A *Point of Order*:

1. Takes precedence over any pending question out of which it may arise. It yields to all privileged motions and (if it adheres to pending question[s], p. 118) it yields to a motion to lay the main question on the table, in cases where these motions are in order at the time according to the order of precedence of motions. Except for yielding to the motion to *Lay on the Table* when it adheres to pending question(s) as just stated, it does not yield to any

subsidiary motion so long as it is handled in the normal manner—that is, by being ruled upon by the chair without debate. Consequently, under this normal procedure:

- If a point of order which adheres to pending question(s) is raised while any one of the six lower-ranking subsidiary motions is immediately pending, no other subsidiary motion except *Lay on the Table* can be made until the point of order is disposed of; but in such a case, *Lay on the Table* or any privileged motion can be moved and must be considered before the point of order is ruled upon.

- If a point of order which does not adhere to pending question(s) is raised while *any* subsidiary motion is immediately pending, *no* subsidiary motion can be made until the point of order is disposed of, but any privileged motion can be moved and must be considered first.

- With reference to either of the above cases, on the other hand, if a motion to *Lay on the Table* or a privileged motion is *pending* and a point of order arises out of the parliamentary situation existing then, the point of order is disposed of first, although it can be interrupted by a still higher-ranking privileged motion.

In cases where the chair, being in doubt, refers the point of order to the judgment of the assembly and where the point thereby becomes debatable (see Standard Characteristic 5, below), it—like a debatable appeal (**24**)—also: yields to the subsidiary motions to *Limit or Extend Limits of Debate* and for the *Previous Question*; yields to the motions to *Commit* and to *Postpone Definitely* provided that they are in order at the time according to the order of precedence of motions; and yields to incidental motions arising out of itself.

2. Can be applied to any breach of the assembly's rules. So long as it is handled in the normal manner by being ruled

upon by the chair, no subsidiary motion can be applied *1*
to it—except that, if it adheres to pending question(s),
then (unless the motion to *Lay on the Table* was already
pending when the point of order arose) the main question
can be laid on the table while the point of order is pend- *5*
ing, and the point of order also goes to the table with all
adhering motions. If the chair, being in doubt, refers the
point of order to the judgment of the assembly and it
thereby becomes debatable (see Standard Characteristic 5, below), the application of subsidiary motions to it *10*
is governed by the same rules as stated for debatable appeals under Standard Characteristic 2, pages 256–57.

3. Is in order when another has the floor, even interrupting
a person speaking or reading a report if the point gen-
uinely requires attention at such a time (see *Timeliness* *15*
Requirement for a Point of Order, below).

4. Does not require a second.

5. Is not debatable—but, with the chair's consent, a member
may be permitted to explain his point and knowledgeable
or interested members can be heard by way of explana- *20*
tion. If the chair submits the point to a vote of the assembly, the rules governing its debatability are the same as for
an *Appeal* (see p. 254; see also Standard Characteristic 5,
pp. 257–58).

6. Is not amendable. *25*

7. Is normally ruled upon by the chair. No vote is taken unless the chair is in doubt or his ruling is appealed.

8. Cannot be reconsidered.

Further Rules and Explanation *30*

GROUNDS FOR A POINT OF ORDER.   It is the
right of every member who notices a breach of the rules to
insist on their enforcement. If the chair notices a breach, he
corrects the matter immediately; but if he fails to do so— *35*

1 through oversight or otherwise—any member can make the appropriate *Point of Order*. The presiding officer may wish to engage in brief research or consult with the parliamentarian before ruling, and may allow the assembly to stand at ease *5* (see p. 82) while he does so. In any event, when the presiding officer has made a ruling, any two members can appeal (one making the appeal and the other seconding it), as described in **24.** *

If a member is uncertain as to whether there is a breach *10* on which a point of order can be made, he can make a parliamentary inquiry of the chair (see pp. 293–94). In ordinary meetings it is undesirable to raise points of order on minor irregularities of a purely technical character, if it is clear that no one's rights are being infringed upon and no real harm is *15* being done to the proper transaction of business.

TIMELINESS REQUIREMENT FOR A POINT OF ORDER.   If a question of order is to be raised, it must be raised promptly at the time the breach occurs. For example, *20* if the chair is stating the question on a motion that has not been seconded, or on a motion that is out of order in the existing parliamentary situation, the time to raise these points of order is when the chair states the motion. After debate on such a motion has begun—no matter how clearly out of order *25* the motion may be—a point of order is too late. If a member is unsure of his point or wishes to hear what the maker has to say on behalf of the motion before pressing a point of order, he may, with the chair's sufferance, "reserve a point of order" against the motion; but after the maker has spoken, he must *30* insist upon his point of order or withdraw it. Points of order regarding the conduct of a vote must be raised imme-

---

*There can be no appeal from a ruling on a point of order that is raised while an appeal is pending.

diately following the announcement of the voting result (see *1* pp. 408–9).

The only exceptions to the rule that a point of order must be made at the time of the breach arise in connection with breaches that are of a continuing nature, in which case a point *5* of order can be made at any time during the continuance of the breach. Instances of this kind occur when:

a) a main motion has been adopted that conflicts with the bylaws (or constitution) of the organization or assembly,* *10*
b) a main motion has been adopted that conflicts with a main motion previously adopted and still in force, unless the subsequently adopted motion was adopted by the vote required to rescind or amend the previously adopted motion, *15*
c) any action has been taken in violation of applicable procedural rules prescribed by federal, state, or local law,
d) any action has been taken in violation of a fundamental principle of parliamentary law (p. 263), or
e) any action has been taken in violation of a rule protecting *20* absentees, a rule in the bylaws requiring a vote to be taken by ballot, or a rule protecting a basic right of an individual member (pp. 263–64).

In all such cases, it is never too late to raise a point of order *25* since any action so taken is null and void.

PRECEDENT.   The minutes include the reasons given by the chair for his or her ruling (see p. 470, ll. 15–17). The ruling and its rationale serve as a precedent for future refer- *30* ence by the chair and the assembly, unless overturned on

---

*Unless the conflict is with a rule in the nature of a rule of order as described on page 17, lines 22–25, in which case a point of order must be timely.

appeal, the result of which is also recorded in the minutes and may create a contrary precedent. When similar issues arise in the future, such precedents are *persuasive* in resolving them— that is, they carry weight in the absence of overriding reasons for following a different course—but they are not binding on the chair or the assembly. The weight given to precedent increases with the number of times the same or similar rulings have been repeated and with the length of time during which the assembly has consistently adhered to them.

If an assembly is or becomes dissatisfied with a precedent, it may be overruled, in whole or in part, by a later ruling of the chair or a decision of the assembly in an appeal in a similar situation, which will then create a new precedent. Alternatively, adoption, rescission, or amendment (**35**) of a bylaw provision, special rule of order, standing rule, or other motion may alter the rule or policy on which the unsatisfactory precedent was based.

REMEDY FOR VIOLATION OF THE RIGHT TO VOTE.   If one or more members have been denied the right to vote, or the right to attend all or part of a meeting during which a vote was taken, it is never too late to raise a point of order concerning the action taken in denying the basic rights of the individual members—and if there is any possibility that the members' vote(s) would have affected the outcome, then the results of the vote must be declared invalid if the point of order is sustained. If there is no such possibility, the results of the vote itself can be made invalid only if the point of order is raised immediately following the chair's announcement of the vote. If the vote was such that the number of members excluded from participating would not have affected the outcome, a member may wish, in the appropriate circumstances, to move to *Rescind/Amend Something Previously Adopted* (**35**), to move to *Reconsider* (**37**), or to renew a motion (**38**), arguing that comments in debate by the excluded members

could have led to a different result; but the action resulting   *1*
from the vote is not invalidated by a ruling in response to the
point of order.

Form and Example   *5*

When a member notices a breach of order that may do
harm if allowed to pass, he rises and, without waiting for
recognition, immediately addresses the chair as follows:
                                                                  10
MEMBER A: I rise to a point of order. [Or, "Point of order!"]

Anyone who is speaking takes his seat. If the point relates
to a transgression of the rules of debate, the form used
may be: *15*

MEMBER A: Mr. President, I call the gentleman to order.

The chair then asks the member to state his point of
order, or what words in the debate he objects to.   *20*

MEMBER A: I make the point of order that ...

On completing his statement, the member resumes his
seat. The chair then rules whether "the point of order is well   *25*
taken" or "is not well taken," stating briefly his reasons,
which should be recorded in the minutes. If the chair desires,
he can review the parliamentary situation without leaving the
chair, but standing, before giving his ruling.

If the chair's decision requires any action and no appeal   *30*
is made, he sees that the necessary action is taken before proceeding with the pending business. Thus, if the point of order
relates to a breach of decorum in debate that is not serious,
the chair can allow the member to continue his speech. But
if the member's remarks are decided to be improper and   *35*

1   anyone objects, the member cannot continue speaking with-
    out a vote of the assembly to that effect (see pp. 645–46).

       Before rendering his decision, the chair can consult the
    parliamentarian, if there is one. The chair can also request
5   the advice of experienced members, but no one has the right
    to express such opinions in the meeting unless requested to
    do so by the chair.

       When the chair is in doubt as to how to rule on an im-
    portant point, he can submit it to the assembly for decision
10 in some such manner as:

       CHAIR: Mr. Downey raises a point of order that the amendment is
    not germane to the resolution. The chair is in doubt and submits the
    question to the assembly. The resolution is [reading it]. The proposed
15 amendment is [reading it]. The question is, "Is the amendment germane
    to the resolution?"

       Since no appeal can be made from a decision of the assem-
    bly itself, this question is open to debate whenever an appeal
20 would be—that is, the question submitted by the chair to the
    assembly for decision is debatable except when it relates to
    indecorum or transgression of the rules of speaking, or to the
    priority of business, or when an undebatable question is im-
    mediately pending or involved in the point of order. As in the
25 case of debate on an appeal (**24**), when a point of order that
    is submitted to a vote is debatable, no member can speak more
    than once in the debate except the chair, who can speak in
    preference to other members the first time, and who is also
    entitled to speak a second time at the close of debate.

30   In the example given above, the question may be put as
    follows:

       CHAIR: Those of the opinion that the amendment is germane, say
    aye. ... Those of the opinion that it is not germane, say *no.* ... The ayes
35 have it and the amendment is in order. The question is on the adoption
    of the amendment.

Or:

1

> CHAIR: ... The noes have it and the amendment is out of order. The question is on the adoption of the resolution.

5

When a point of order is submitted to a vote of the assembly and the point relates to stopping something from being done, it is usually best to put the question so that an affirmative vote will be in favor of allowing the proceedings to continue as if the point had not been raised. Thus, if a *10* point is made that the chair is admitting a motion which is out of order, the question should be put so that an affirmative result of the vote will mean that the motion is in order—as in the example above, or as follows: "... Those of the opinion that the motion is in order, say *aye*. ...; etc." When a member *15* has been called to order because of indecorum in debate, the corresponding form is: "... Those of the opinion that the member should be allowed to resume speaking, say *aye*. ..." If the foregoing principle has no clear application to the case, the question can be put so that an affirmative result will up- *20* hold the point of order: "... Those of the opinion that the point is well taken, say *aye*. ..."*

§24. APPEAL

25

By electing a presiding officer, the assembly delegates to him the authority and duty to make necessary rulings on questions of parliamentary law. But any two members have the right to *Appeal* from his decision on such a question. By

---

*It should be noted that the latter method of putting the question may often be the opposite of the first method in cases where the first method is applicable. Thus, in the example of a point of order that an amendment is not germane, as shown above, the question is put so that a vote of *aye* is a vote that the amendment *is* germane; but in that case, a vote of *aye* is a vote that the point is *not* well taken.

1 one member making (or "taking") the appeal and another
   seconding it, the question is taken from the chair and vested
   in the assembly for final decision.

   Members have no right to criticize a ruling of the chair
5 unless they appeal from his decision.

Standard Descriptive Characteristics

   An *Appeal*:

10

1. Takes precedence over any question pending at the time
   the chair makes a ruling from which the appeal is made.
   It yields to all privileged motions (provided that they are
   in order at the time according to the order of precedence
15   of motions), and it yields to incidental motions arising
   out of itself. If it is debatable (see Standard Characteristic
   5, below), it also yields to the subsidiary motions to *Limit
   or Extend Limits of Debate* and for the *Previous Question*,
   and yields to the motions to *Commit*, to *Postpone Defi-*
20   *nitely*, and to *Lay on the Table*, provided that they are in
   order at the time according to the order of precedence of
   motions. If it is undebatable and adheres to pending ques-
   tion(s), it does not yield to any subsidiary motion except
   to *Lay on the Table*; and if it is undebatable and does *not*
25   adhere to pending question(s), it yields to no subsidiary
   motion.

2. Can be applied to any ruling by the presiding officer except that:

   a) if a point of order is raised while an appeal is pending,
30   there is no appeal from the chair's decision on this
      point of order, although the correctness of the ruling
      can be brought up later by a motion covering the case;
      and

   b) when the chair rules on a question about which there
35   cannot possibly be two reasonable opinions, an appeal
      would be dilatory and is not allowed.

Rules governing the applicability of subsidiary motions to *debatable appeals* are as follows: A motion limiting or extending debate or a motion for the *Previous Question* can be applied to a debatable appeal without affecting any other pending question. Also:

- When a *debatable* appeal *does not adhere* to pending question(s)—that is, when the decision on it would in no way affect pending question(s)—such a debatable appeal can have any of the subsidiary motions applied to it except *Postpone Indefinitely* and *Amend*.

- But when a *debatable* appeal *adheres* to pending question(s)—as in the case of an appeal from a ruling that an amendment is not germane—the subsidiary motions, except the motions affecting debate, cannot be applied to the appeal alone. However, they can be applied to the main question, and if the latter is committed, postponed, or laid on the table, the appeal goes with this main question.

In the case of *undebatable* appeals:

- When an *undebatable* appeal *does not adhere* to pending question(s), no subsidiary motion can be applied to it; however,

- When an *undebatable* appeal *adheres* to pending question(s), no subsidiary motion can be applied to it alone; but the main question can be laid on the table, and the appeal then goes to the table with the main question and all adhering motions.

3. Is in order when another has the floor, but the appeal must be made at the time of the ruling. If any debate or business has intervened, it is too late to appeal.

4. Must be seconded.

5. Is debatable, unless it (a) relates to indecorum or a transgression of the rules of speaking; (b) relates to the priority of business; or (c) is made when an undebatable question is immediately pending or involved in the appeal. When

an appeal is debatable, no member is allowed to speak more than once except the presiding officer—who need not leave the chair while so speaking, but should stand. The first time the chair speaks in debate on the appeal, he is entitled to preference over other members seeking recognition. He can answer arguments against the decision or give additional reasons by speaking a second time at the close of the debate. He may announce his intention to speak in rebuttal and ask if there are others who wish to speak first. Even when the appeal is not debatable, the chair can, when stating the question on it, give the reasons for his decision without leaving the chair.

6. Is not amendable.

7. A majority or a tie vote sustains the decision of the chair on the principle that the chair's decision stands until reversed by a majority. If the presiding officer is a member of the assembly, he can vote to create a tie and thus sustain his decision.

8. Can be reconsidered.

Further Rules and Explanation

APPROPRIATENESS OF APPEAL.   If a member disagrees with a ruling of the chair affecting any substantial question, he should not hesitate to appeal. The situation is no more delicate than disagreeing with another member in debate. In the case of serious questions when proponents and opponents appear nearly equal, a presiding officer may welcome an appeal from his decision. By relieving the chair of responsibility in a strongly contested situation and placing it on the assembly itself, better relationships are often preserved.

APPLICABILITY LIMITED TO RULINGS.   As explained in Standard Characteristic 2, an appeal is applicable only to a *ruling* by the chair.

No appeal can be made from the chair's response to a par- *1*
liamentary inquiry or other query, since such a reply is an
opinion rendered by the chair, not a ruling on a question that
has actually arisen. For example, if, in answer to a parliamentary inquiry, the chair states that a certain motion would be *5*
out of order at the time, this reply is not subject to appeal.
But the point can be put at issue before the assembly by making the motion despite the chair's opinion and, when he *rules*
the motion out of order, appealing from the chair's decision.

The chair's judgment as to the more numerous side in a *10*
vote, or whether there are two thirds in the affirmative, also
is not a ruling and is not subject to appeal.* If a member
doubts the correctness of such an announced result, however,
he should call for a *Division* (see **29**) or move that the vote
be counted. *15*

Form and Example

A member desiring to appeal rises and, without waiting
to be recognized, addresses the chair as follows: *20*

MEMBER A: I appeal from the decision of the chair. (Second.)
CHAIR: The decision of the chair is appealed from.

The chair, after stating clearly the exact question at issue, *25*
and the reasons for his decision if he thinks an explanation
necessary, states the question on the appeal as follows:

CHAIR: The question is: "Shall the decision of the chair stand as the
judgment of the assembly [or "club," "society," "board," etc.]?" *30*

---

*If the chair made a procedural error in declaring a motion adopted or
lost, for example, in declaring that a motion which received a majority vote
but not a two-thirds vote was adopted when a two-thirds vote was required
under the rules, a point of order may be raised to that effect.

1   Or:

CHAIR: The question is, "Shall the decision of the chair be sustained?"

5   The question should not be on "sustaining the chair," because the *decision*, not the presiding officer, is in question.
     The vote is taken so that the affirmative will be in favor
of sustaining the chair's decision, as follows:

10   CHAIR: Those in favor of sustaining the chair's decision, say *aye*. ...
     Those opposed to sustaining this decision, say *no*. ...

     After the result of the vote is announced, business is
resumed in accordance with the situation existing after the
15   action on the appeal.

§25. SUSPEND THE RULES

     When an assembly wishes to do something during a meet-
20   ing that it cannot do without violating one or more of its regular rules, it can adopt a motion to *Suspend the Rules*
interfering with the proposed action—provided that the proposal is not in conflict with the organization's bylaws (or constitution), with local, state, or national law prescribing
25   procedural rules applicable to the organization or assembly,
or with a fundamental principle of parliamentary law.

Standard Descriptive Characteristics

30   The incidental motion to *Suspend the Rules*:

1. Can be made at any time that no question is pending.
    When business is pending, *Suspend the Rules* takes prece-
    dence over any motion if it is for a purpose connected
35 with that motion. It yields to the motion to *Lay on the*

Table and to all privileged motions when these motions are in order at the time according to the order of precedence of motions—except that if it relates to the priority of business it does not yield to a *Call for the Orders of the Day*. It also yields to incidental motions arising out of itself.

2. Can be applied to any rule of the assembly except bylaws* (or rules contained in a constitution or corporate charter). No subsidiary motion can be applied to *Suspend the Rules*.
3. Is out of order when another has the floor.
4. Must be seconded.
5. Is not debatable.
6. Is not amendable.
7. Usually requires a two-thirds vote (see below, however). In any case, no rule protecting a minority of a particular size can be suspended in the face of a negative vote as large as the minority protected by the rule.
8. Cannot be reconsidered (see below regarding its renewal).

Further Rules and Explanation

OBJECT AND EFFECT OF THE MOTION.　The object of this motion is to suspend one or more rules applicable to the assembly—such as rules contained in the parliamentary authority, special rules of order, or standing rules**—that interfere with proposed action during a meeting. A motion to "take up a question out of its proper order," or to consider one before a time to which it has been postponed, is an application of the motion to *Suspend the Rules* (see **14**, **41**).

---

*Regarding the suspendibility of rules in the nature of rules of order when placed within the bylaws, see page 17, lines 22–25.

For the classes of rules that an organization or an assembly may adopt, see **2.

1   In making the incidental motion to *Suspend the Rules*, the particular rule or rules to be suspended are not mentioned; but the motion must state its specific purpose, and its adoption permits nothing else to be done under the suspension.

5   Such a motion, for instance, may be "to suspend the rules and take up the report of the Building Committee," or "to suspend the rules and agree to [that is, to adopt without debate or amendment] the resolution ..." When the purpose of a motion to *Suspend the Rules* is to permit the making of an-

10   other motion, and the adoption of the first motion would obviously be followed by adoption of the second, the two motions can be combined, as in "to suspend the rules and take from the table (**34**) the question relating to ..." The foregoing is an exception to the general rule that no member

15   can make two motions at the same time except with the consent of the assembly—unanimous consent being required if the two motions are unrelated (see also pp. 110, 274–75).

      If a motion to *Suspend the Rules* is adopted and its object is to allow consideration of business that could not otherwise

20   have been considered at the time, the chair should immediately recognize the member who moved the suspension of the rules, to make the appropriate motion that will bring up the desired business. Or, if no further motion is necessary (for example, if the two motions were combined as indicated

25   above, or if the question is one that was postponed), the chair should announce the business as pending.

      RENEWAL OF THE MOTION.   If a motion to suspend the rules is voted down, it cannot be renewed by mov-

30   ing to suspend the rules for the same purpose at the same meeting, unless unanimous consent is given. It can, however, be renewed for the same purpose after an adjournment, even if the next meeting is held the same day. Any number of motions to suspend the rules for different purposes can be

35   entertained at the same meeting.

RULES THAT CANNOT BE SUSPENDED. Rules *1*
contained in the *bylaws* (or constitution) cannot be suspended—no matter how large the vote in favor of doing so
or how inconvenient the rule in question may be—unless the
particular rule specifically provides for its own suspension, or *5*
unless the rule properly is in the nature of a rule of order as
described on page 17, lines 22–25. A rule in the bylaws requiring that a vote—such as, for example, on the election of
officers—be taken by (secret) *ballot* cannot be suspended,
however, unless the bylaws so provide (see also *Voting by* *10*
Ballot, pp. 412–13).

No applicable *procedural rule prescribed by federal, state,*
or local law can be suspended unless the rule specifically provides for its own suspension.

Rules which embody *fundamental principles of parlia-* *15*
mentary law, such as the rule that allows only one question
to be considered at a time (p. 59), cannot be suspended, even
by a unanimous vote. Thus, since it is a fundamental principle
of parliamentary law that the right to vote is limited to
the members of an organization who are actually present *20*
at the time the vote is taken in a regular or properly called
meeting (p. 423), the rules cannot be suspended so as to give
the right to vote to a nonmember,* or to authorize absentee
(pp. 423–24) voting. Likewise, since it is a fundamental
principle that each member of a deliberative assembly is en- *25*
titled to one—and only one—vote on a question, the rules
may not be suspended so as to authorize cumulative voting
(pp. 443–44).

Rules *protecting absentees* cannot be suspended, even by
unanimous consent or an actual unanimous vote, because the *30*
absentees do not consent to such suspension. For example,
the rules requiring the presence of a quorum, restricting

---

*In contrast, the rules may be suspended to allow a nonmember to speak
in debate.

business transacted at a special meeting to that mentioned in the call of the meeting, and requiring previous notice of a proposed amendment to the bylaws protect absentees, if there are any, and cannot be suspended when any member is absent.*

Rules protecting a *basic right of the individual member* cannot be suspended. Thus, while generally applicable limits on debate and the making of motions may be imposed by motions such as the *Previous Question*, the rules may not be suspended so as to deny any particular member the right to attend meetings, make motions or nominations, speak in debate, give previous notice, or vote. These basic rights may be curtailed only through disciplinary proceedings.

At a regular meeting of an organization that has an established order of business, the assembly cannot, even unanimously, vote to *dispense with* that order of business (in the sense of voting, in advance of the time when it adjourns, that the order of business shall not be gone through at all at that meeting). If the assembly, by a two-thirds vote, adopts a motion "to dispense with the regular order of business and proceed to"** a certain subject, it has in effect voted to *pass* all classes in the order of business which normally would precede that subject (see pp. 363–64). In such a case, when the matter taken up out of its proper order has been disposed of, even if it has consumed as much time as the usual meeting, the chair must return to the regular order of business and call for the items in sequence, unless the assembly then votes to adjourn (see **21**).

Rules that have their application outside of the session which is in progress cannot be suspended. For example, a

---

*An elected or appointed body that lacks the authority to determine its own quorum may not suspend the quorum requirement, even if all members are present.

**This usage should be avoided.

policy prohibiting total contributions to any one charitable *1*
organization in excess of $500.00 in any one calendar year is
a rule which has its application outside of a meeting context,
and thus cannot be suspended so as to permit the adoption
of a motion to make a contribution in excess of the specified *5*
amount. (Such a rule can, however, be rescinded or amended;
see **35**.) Likewise, the rules cannot be suspended in order to
permit postponement of a motion to a future session that will
be held after the next regular business session or that will be
held after more than a quarterly time interval has elapsed. *10*

RULES WHOSE SUSPENSION REQUIRES A TWO-
THIRDS VOTE. The *rules of order* of a society, as contained in the manual established by the bylaws as the
parliamentary authority, or as included in any special rules of *15*
order adopted by the organization (see **2**), are rules of parliamentary procedure, the suspension of which requires a
two-thirds vote. Some societies call all their rules "standing
rules." But by whatever name a rule is called, if it relates to
parliamentary procedure, it requires either (a) previous notice *20*
and a two-thirds vote or (b) a vote of a majority of the entire
membership for its amendment; hence, it requires a two-
thirds vote for its suspension.

RULES THAT CAN BE SUSPENDED BY A MAJOR- *25*
ITY VOTE. An ordinary* *standing rule*, as the term is used
in this book, is a rule that does not relate to parliamentary
procedure as such and refers, for example, to such matters
as the use of recording devices at meetings (see p. 18). Standing rules are adopted, as any ordinary motion, by a majority *30*
vote, and they may be amended by a majority vote with previous notice (see p. 306, ll. 24–31); they therefore can be

---

*In conventions, the term *standing rule* is used in a special sense that
may include parliamentary rules adopted by the convention (see pp. 618ff.).

1 suspended by a majority vote as they do not involve the protection of a minority of a particular size. Through an incidental main motion adopted by a majority vote, a standing rule can be suspended for the duration of the current session.

5   SUSPENSION OF RULES BY UNANIMOUS CONSENT.   Frequently, when the matter is clearly not controversial, time may be saved by asking unanimous consent rather than by making a formal motion to suspend the rules.
10 A member who has obtained the floor can say, for example, "Madam President, I ask unanimous consent to offer the courtesy resolutions before we receive the report of the special committee." The chair then asks if anyone objects and, if so, proceeds to take a vote on suspending the rules, just as
15 if a formal motion had been made.

Form and Example

*   The usual form of this motion is:
20

    MEMBER A (obtaining the floor): I move that the rules be suspended [or "to suspend the rules"] which interfere with ... [stating the object of the suspension]. (Second.)

25 Or:

    MEMBER A (obtaining the floor): I move to suspend the rules and take up ... (Second.)

30   When the object is to adopt a motion without debate or amendment, the form is:

    MEMBER A (obtaining the floor): I move to suspend the rules and adopt [or "agree to"] the following resolution: "*Resolved*, That ..."
35 (Second.)

If such a motion does not receive the required two-thirds *1*
vote, the main motion can be taken up only in the normal
way. A member moving to suspend the rules can briefly give
sufficient information to enable the members to vote intelli-
gently on his undebatable motion. (For the manner of taking *5*
a two-thirds vote, see pp. 46–47, 50–51.) In announcing an
affirmative result, the chair says, for example,

CHAIR: There are two thirds in the affirmative and the rules are suspended for the purpose of ... The chair recognizes Mrs. Watkins. *10*

§26. OBJECTION TO THE CONSIDERATION OF A QUESTION

15

The purpose of an *Objection to the Consideration of a
Question* is to enable the assembly to avoid a particular original main motion altogether when it believes it would be
strongly undesirable for the motion even to come before the
assembly. *20*

Standard Descriptive Characteristics

An *Objection to the Consideration of a Question*:

25

1. Takes precedence over original main motions and over an
   unstated subsidiary motion except *Lay on the Table*. The
   objection can be raised only before there has been any debate or any subsidiary motion except *Lay on the Table* has
   been stated by the chair; thereafter, consideration of the *30*
   main question has begun and it is too late to object. It
   does not take precedence over any *pending* subsidiary motion. It yields to the motion to *Lay on the Table*, to all
   privileged motions, and to incidental motions arising out
   of itself. *35*

2. Can be applied to original main motions (p. 100) and to petitions and communications that are not from a superior body. It cannot be applied to incidental main motions. No subsidiary motion can be applied to it alone, but while it is pending the main question can be laid on the table, and the objection then goes to the table with the main question.

3. Is in order when another has the floor, until consideration of the question has begun, as indicated in Standard Characteristic 1, above.

4. Does not require a second.

5. Is not debatable.

6. Is not amendable.

7. A two-thirds vote *against consideration* is required to sustain the objection.

8. A negative vote—that is, a vote sustaining the objection—can be reconsidered, but not an affirmative vote.

Further Rules and Explanation

RESEMBLANCE TO POINT OF ORDER.   An *Objection to the Consideration of a Question* is similar in some ways to a *Point of Order*. The presiding officer, on his own initiative, can submit his objection of this kind to a vote, just as he can raise a question of order on his own accord. An *Objection to the Consideration of a Question* is not used if a main motion is outside the society's objects as defined in the bylaws or constitution, or outside the announced purpose for which a mass meeting has been called; such a motion should be ruled out of order (p. 113, ll. 10–13).

DIFFERENCE FROM OBJECTION IN OTHER CONTEXT.   *Objection to the Consideration of a Question* should not be confused with an objection to a request for unanimous consent (see pp. 54–56).

EFFECT OF THE OBJECTION. If an objection to consideration is sustained, the main motion is dismissed for that session and cannot be renewed during the same session except by unanimous consent or by reconsideration of the vote on the objection. If the objection is not sustained, consideration of the main motion proceeds as if no objection had been made. Even if the objection is sustained, the same main motion can be introduced at any succeeding session.

RECONSIDERATION OF A VOTE THAT HAS SUSTAINED THE OBJECTION. As noted in Standard Characteristic 8, a vote *sustaining* an objection to consideration can be reconsidered. The motion to reconsider such a vote is undebatable and requires a majority vote for its adoption, and it can be taken up or called up only when no other motion is pending. If the motion to *Reconsider* is adopted, it is also presumed to have overturned the objection, and the chair immediately states the question on the main motion whose consideration had been objected to, without again putting the objection to a vote. (The reason for this abbreviated procedure is that only the members who wish to consider the main question would vote to reconsider the objection to its consideration; consequently, if a majority have voted for reconsideration of the objection, this implies that there are less than two thirds who wish to prevent consideration of the main question.)

MANNER OF PUTTING THE QUESTION. When the objection is put to a vote in its correct form (see *Form and Example*, below), members are asked to vote for or against *consideration* of the question objected to (not for or against sustaining the objection). Therefore, those who wish to *prevent consideration* of the question *vote in the negative*. The objection is sustained if there are at least twice as many negative as affirmative votes.

Form and Example

A member rises, even if another has been assigned the floor, and without waiting to be recognized, addresses the chair as follows:

MEMBER A: Mr. President, I object to the consideration of the question [or "resolution," "motion," etc.].

The chair responds:

CHAIR: The consideration of the question is objected to. Shall the question be considered? Those in favor of considering it, rise. ... Be seated. Those opposed to considering the question, rise. ... Be seated. There are two thirds opposed and the question will not be considered.

Or, if the objection is not sustained, the announcement of the vote may be worded as follows:

CHAIR: There are less than two thirds opposed and the objection is not sustained. The question is on the resolution, "*Resolved*, That ..."

In putting the objection to vote, the chair must be careful *not* to say, "Shall the objection be sustained?" This would reverse the effect of affirmative and negative votes and might cause confusion.

§27. DIVISION OF A QUESTION

When a motion relating to a single subject contains several parts, each of which is capable of standing as a complete proposition if the others are removed, the parts can be separated to be considered and voted on as if they were distinct questions—by adoption of the motion for *Division of a Question* (or "to divide the question").

There are also certain motions which must be divided on
the demand of a single member, in which case a formal motion to divide is not used (see pp. 274–75). The eight characteristics below apply only to the incidental *motion* for *Division
of a Question*.

Standard Descriptive Characteristics

The incidental motion for *Division of a Question*:

1. Takes precedence over the main motion and over the subsidiary motion to *Postpone Indefinitely.* If applied to an
   amendment, it also takes precedence over that amendment; but a motion to divide the main question cannot
   be made while an amendment to the main question is
   pending. It yields to all subsidiary motions except *Postpone Indefinitely, Amend,* and *Limit or Extend Limits of
   Debate*; to all privileged motions; and to all applicable incidental motions. Although it is preferable to divide a
   question when it is first introduced, a motion to divide
   can be made at any time that the main motion, an amendment which it is proposed to divide, or the motion to
   Postpone Indefinitely is immediately pending—even after
   the *Previous Question* has been ordered.
2. Can be applied to main motions and their amendments,
   if they are susceptible to division (see below). No subsidiary motion can be applied to it alone except *Amend*
   and (for the purpose of stopping its amendment) the *Previous Question*; but while it is pending the main question
   can be committed, postponed, or laid on the table, and it
   then undergoes the same process with the main question.
3. Is out of order when another has the floor.
4. Must be seconded.
5. Is not debatable.
6. Is amendable.

7. Requires a majority vote.

8. Cannot be reconsidered.

Further Rules and Explanation

SPECIFICATION OF THE MANNER IN WHICH THE QUESTION IS TO BE DIVIDED.   The motion to divide must clearly state the manner in which the question is to be divided. While the motion to divide is pending, another member can propose a different division by moving an amendment. If several different proposals are made, they should be treated as filling blanks; that is, they should be voted on in the order in which they were proposed unless they suggest different numbers of questions, in which case the largest number is voted on first (pp. 162–67). Usually, however, little formality is involved in dividing a question, and it is arranged by unanimous consent.

MOTIONS THAT CANNOT BE DIVIDED.   A motion cannot be divided unless each part presents a proper question for the assembly to act upon if none of the other parts is adopted, and unless the effect of adopting all of the parts will be exactly the same—no more, no less—as adoption of the compound main question. Thus, if it is moved to establish a committee and give it instructions, this motion is indivisible because, should the part establishing the committee fail, the part giving the committee instructions would be absurd.

Another type of motion that cannot be divided is one whose parts are not easily separated. The division cannot require a rewriting of the resolution beyond an essentially mechanical separation of it into the required parts. If possible, the division should be carried out by no more than a renumbering of phrases or clauses, prefacing each part with the formal word(s), "That," "*Resolved*, That," or "*Ordered*, That,"

dropping conjunctions where necessary, or replacing pro-
nouns with the nouns for which they stand, with or without
the definite article "the," as required. Depending on how the
compound main motion or resolution is worded, however, it
may sometimes be necessary to repeat words in more than
one part which, in the main motion, appear only once and
apply to more than one element of the proposed division.
Also needed in this connection may be slight corrections in
syntax or phrase structure in order to render each part as a
complete grammatical sentence free of awkward wording.
These adjustments are permissible provided care is taken to
preserve exact logical equivalence of statement and no new
language is introduced.

For example, suppose that the following resolution is
pending: "*Resolved*, That the Society congratulate its member
Ernest Dunn on his novel *Crestwood*, and that three copies
be purchased for the Society's library." Suppose also that a
member wishes to divide the question so as to consider the
purchase of the books separately. The first divided part obviously would be, "*Resolved*, That the Society congratulate its
member Ernest Dunn on his novel *Crestwood*." The second
part, with the wording adjusted no more than necessary to
avoid awkwardness, would have to read, "*Resolved*, That three
copies of the novel *Crestwood* by the Society's member Ernest
Dunn be purchased for the Society's library." The phrasing
of the second part involves both types of modification described in the last three sentences of the preceding paragraph.

As indicated in this subsection, if separating the elements
of action in a proposed resolution would require recasting the
parts more than described above, the resolution cannot be
divided.

CONFORMING AMENDMENTS.   Sometimes several
changes throughout a motion or resolution are needed
in order to achieve one end, in which case these separate

amendments are proposed and adopted by a single subsidiary motion to *Amend*. For example, suppose a lengthy resolution is pending relating to the creation of a new standing committee, called the "Ways and Means Committee," to study and make recommendations concerning the society's financial circumstances and requirements, and this committee is referred to by name in a number of places scattered throughout the resolution. If it is desired to change the name of this committee from "Ways and Means Committee" to "Finance Committee," it is both necessary and in order to move "to amend the pending resolution by striking out 'Ways and Means Committee' wherever it appears and inserting 'Finance Committee' in lieu thereof." In such cases (where all of the individual amendments must be made, if any one of them is made, in order to leave a coherent resolution pending if the motion to amend is adopted), the proposed amendments are offered in a single motion, as in the example given. Such proposed amendments may not be divided.

STRIKING OUT PART OF AN INDIVISIBLE MOTION OR SERIES OF MOTIONS.   When a question is indivisible and a member is opposed to a portion of it, he can seek the desired result by moving to *strike out* (**12**) the part to which he is opposed. In like manner, when a series of resolutions is proposed as a substitute for another series, the substitute series is indivisible if the several resolutions are not completely parallel, but a motion can be made to strike out of the series any of the component resolutions before the vote is taken on whether to make the substitution.

MOTIONS THAT MUST BE DIVIDED ON DEMAND.   Sometimes a series of independent resolutions or main motions dealing with different subjects is offered in one motion. In such a case, one or more of the several resolutions must receive separate consideration and vote at the request of a single member, and the motion for *Division of a Question*

is not used. Such a demand (which should not be confused   1
with a demand for a division of the assembly—that is, for a
rising vote) can be made even when another has the floor, as
in, "Mr. President, I call for a separate vote on Resolution
No. 3." This demand must be asserted before the question   5
on adopting the series has actually been put to vote.

Similarly, a series of amendments to a main motion (or
conceivably to a primary amendment such as a substitute)
may be offered in one motion. Unless these amendments
meet the standard for conforming amendments given on   10
pages 273–74, any member may demand a separate vote
on one or more of them. After the others have been
voted on together, the amendment(s) on which separate votes
were requested are disposed of.

                                                              15

Form and Example

Referring to the example relating to Ernest Dunn's novel
Crestwood on page 273, a motion to divide the question may
be made either by stating the proposed parts in their entirety   20
or by using a shorter description of how the division is to be
made, if it is perfectly clear.

In the first instance, the motion would be made thus:

MEMBER A (obtaining the floor): Madam President, I move to divide   25
the resolution into two parts as follows: [repeating them as shown in the
example on p. 273]. (Second.)

The question as to whether to divide the resolution is
voted on first. In this case, the chair would doubtless use   30
unanimous consent.

Under the shorter form of the motion, it may be made
instead as follows:

MEMBER A (obtaining the floor): Madam President, I move to divide   35
the resolution so as to consider separately the question of purchasing the

1   books. [Or, "… so that the question of purchasing the books be considered separately."] (Second.)

The procedure is then the same as in the first case. If the
5   motion for the division prevails, the chair should state each
of the separated resolutions in full as it is considered.

§28. CONSIDERATION BY PARAGRAPH OR SERIATIM

10

A report or long motion consisting of a series of resolutions, paragraphs, articles, or sections that are not totally separate questions can be considered by opening the different
15   parts to debate and amendment separately, without a division
of the question. If the chair does not follow such a course of
his own accord and the assembly wishes to do so, the procedure can be ordered by adopting a motion to *Consider by
Paragraph* (or to *Consider Seriatim*). Several distinct main
20   motions *on different subjects* cannot be considered seriatim
if a single member objects (see Standard Characteristic 8,
below).

Standard Descriptive Characteristics

25

The incidental motion for *Consideration by Paragraph or
Seriatim*:

1. Takes precedence over the main motion and over the sub-
30   sidiary motion to *Postpone Indefinitely*. If applied to an
amendment, it also takes precedence over that amendment; but it cannot be applied to the main question while
an amendment to the main question is pending. It yields
to all subsidiary motions except *Postpone Indefinitely*,
35   *Amend*, and *Limit or Extend Limits of Debate*; to all privileged motions; and to all applicable incidental motions.

2. Can be applied to main motions and amendments of such *1*
   length and structure that the method is appropriate. No
   subsidiary motion can be applied to it alone except *Amend*
   and (for the purpose of stopping its amendment) the *Previous Question*; but while it is pending the main question *5*
   can be committed, postponed, or laid on the table, and it
   then undergoes the same process with the main question.
3. Is out of order when another has the floor.
4. Must be seconded.
5. Is not debatable. *10*
6. Is amendable.
7. Requires a majority vote.
8. Cannot be reconsidered. If it has been decided to consider divisible material seriatim, even if the material was
   divisible on the demand of a single member, it is too late *15*
   to move or demand a division of the question.

Further Rules and Explanation

EFFECT OF CONSIDERATION BY PARAGRAPH. *20*
The effect of considering a document by paragraph or seriatim is as follows: If a member exhausts his right to debate
under the usual rules on one part, his right to debate begins
over again as each succeeding part is opened to debate and
amendment; yet no vote on adoption is taken until there has *25*
been opportunity to perfect all the parts by amendment.
Keeping all subdivisions of the series open until one final vote
avoids the possibility of complications which would result—
especially in the case of bylaws—if amendments to later paragraphs necessitated changes in others that had already been *30*
adopted.

CASES IN WHICH THE CHAIR NORMALLY
APPLIES THE METHOD.   In adopting a set of bylaws or
the articles of a platform, consideration by paragraph is the *35*
normal and advisable procedure, followed as a matter of

1 course unless the assembly votes to do otherwise. The chair, on his own initiative, can apply this method to any elaborate proposition susceptible to such treatment, unless he thinks the assembly wishes to act on the question as a whole; or the
5 manner of consideration can be settled by unanimous consent. Should the chair neglect this, a member can move "that the resolution be considered by paragraph" (or "seriatim").

MOTION TO CONSIDER AS A WHOLE.   If the
10 chair suggests consideration by paragraph and a member feels that time could be saved by acting on it as a whole, the member can move "that it be considered as a whole." This motion is governed by rules identical to those for *Consideration by Paragraph or Seriatim.*

15
PROCEDURE FOR CONSIDERATION BY PARA-
GRAPH.   The procedure in considering by paragraph or seriatim is as follows: The member who moved the adoption of the document, the secretary, or the presiding officer (as the
20 chair may decide) reads the first subdivision, and it is explained by its proponent. The chair then asks, "Is there any debate or amendment to this paragraph [or "section," etc.]?" When there is no further debate or amendment to the first paragraph, each succeeding one is taken up. Amendments are
25 voted on as they arise, but no paragraph as amended is acted upon (as to final adoption or rejection) at that time. After all parts have been considered, the chair opens the entire document to amendment. At this time additional parts can be inserted, or parts can be struck out, or any one of them can be
30 further amended. It is not necessary to amend the numbers of articles, sections, or other subdivisions. It is the duty of the secretary to make all such corrections where they become necessary (see pp. 598–99).

If there is a preamble, it is treated in the same way before
35 the final vote. Then the entire document is acted upon in a

single vote. If the *Previous Question* is ordered before the pre-amble has been considered, it does not apply to the preamble unless expressly so stated.

APPLICATION OF SUBSIDIARY MOTIONS TO THE ENTIRE PROPOSITION DURING CONSIDERA-TION BY PARAGRAPH.   During the consideration of the separate paragraphs, any motion to *Postpone Indefinitely*, *Commit*, *Postpone*, or *Lay on the Table* can apply only to the entire series or proposition. If a motion to *Postpone Indefi-nitely* is made under these circumstances, it is stated by the chair, but is not debated or voted on until the paragraph-by-paragraph phase of consideration is completed and the entire document has been declared open to amendment. This rule is a consequence of two characteristics of the motion to *Post-pone Indefinitely*—that amendments take precedence over it, and that while it is pending the entire main question is open to debate. Motions to *Commit*, *Postpone* (definitely), or *Lay on the Table*, on the other hand, are taken up as they arise; and, if adopted, they affect the entire main question immedi-ately. If or when the main question comes before the assembly again later, the consideration by paragraph or seriatim is re-sumed at the point where it was interrupted. The *Previous Question* and *Limit or Extend Limits of Debate* can be applied to amendments or to the entire document but not to the in-dividual paragraphs.

Form and Example

When the chair does not initiate seriatim consideration, this form can be used:

MEMBER A (obtaining the floor): Mr. President, I move that the res-olution [or "the platform," etc.] be considered by paragraph [or "seri-atim"]. (Second.)

1   If the chair suggests consideration by paragraph and a member feels that the proposition could be acted upon as a whole, this form may be used:

5   MEMBER X (obtaining the floor): Madam President, I move that ... be considered as a whole. (Second.)

§29. DIVISION OF THE ASSEMBLY

10   Whenever a member doubts the result of a voice (viva-voce) vote or a vote by show of hands—either because the result appears close or because he doubts that a representative number of the members present have voted—he can call for a *Division of the Assembly*, thereby requiring the vote to be

15   taken again by rising.*

A voice vote retaken by a show of hands is not a *Division of the Assembly*, since in large assemblies it may be less accurate than a rising vote, and since—even in a small meeting—the rising vote may be more effective in causing a maximum num-

20   ber of members to vote.

On an inconclusive voice vote in a very small meeting where all present can clearly see one another, if, instead of calling for a *Division*, a member asks for a show of hands, this is in the nature of a request, and the chair can retake the vote

25   by this method unless a call for a *Division* is also made. Before or after the vote is thus retaken, however, any member still has the right to demand a *Division* if he believes it will obtain a more conclusive result.

---

*In the earliest forms of this procedure, members in favor of a measure and those opposed were asked to rise from their seats and proceed to the opposite sides of the meeting hall—hence the name, "division."

Standard Descriptive Characteristics   *1*

A *Division of the Assembly*:

1. Takes precedence over any motion on which a vote is   *5*
   being taken or has just been taken. It may be called for
   from the moment the negative votes have been cast until
   the announcement of the result is complete, or immediately thereafter (see pp. 408–9). It does not yield to any
   motion.   *10*
2. Can be applied to any motion on which the assembly is
   called upon to vote by voice or by a show of hands. No
   subsidiary motion can be applied to it.
3. Is in order when another has the floor and is called for
   without obtaining the floor.   *15*
4. Does not require a second.
5. Is not debatable.
6. Is not amendable.
7. Does not require a vote, since a single member can demand a division.   *20*
8. Cannot be reconsidered.

Further Rules and Explanation

PROCEDURE FOR RETAKING A VOTE.   When a   *25*
Division is demanded, the chair immediately takes the vote
again, first by having the affirmative rise, then by having the
negative rise. If it appears to the chair, when those in the affirmative rise, that the vote will be close, he can count the vote
or order it to be counted. If a member desires the vote on the   *30*
division to be counted, he must make a motion to that effect,
which requires a majority vote (see pp. 52, 410; **30**).

VOTE RETAKEN AT CHAIR'S INITIATIVE.   The
chair has the responsibility of obtaining a correct expression   *35*

1   of the will of the assembly. If he is uncertain of the result of
     a vote or if he feels that the vote is unrepresentative, the chair
     can of his own accord take the vote again by a rising vote.

5   DILATORY USE.   When it is clear that there has been
     a full vote and there can be no reasonable doubt as to which
     side is in the majority, a call for a *Division* is dilatory, and the
     chair should not allow the individual member's right of de-
     manding a *Division* to be abused to the annoyance of the
10   assembly.

Form and Example

     While, or immediately after, the chair announces the re-
15   sult of a vote, "The ayes [or "noes"] have it and ...," a mem-
     ber can call for a division from his seat, without obtaining the
     floor:

     MEMBER: Division!
20
     Or:

     MEMBER: I call for [or "demand"] a division.

25   Or:

     MEMBER: I doubt the result of the vote.

     To such a call in any of these forms, the chair responds:
30
     CHAIR: A division is called for [or "demanded"].

     The chair then proceeds to take the rising vote, as shown on
     pages 46–47.

§30. MOTIONS RELATING TO METHODS OF VOTING AND THE POLLS

1

The object of these motions is to obtain a vote on a question in some form other than by voice, by show of hands, or by *Division* (rising); or to close or reopen the polls. These motions include those that the vote be taken by ballot, that it be taken by roll call (the yeas and nays), and that a standing vote be counted (tellers). Similarly, unusual voting methods are included, such as the use of black and white balls or a signed ballot (see p. 420).

5

10

A motion prescribing the method of voting, or to close or reopen the polls, is an incidental motion—and subject to the rules given here—only when a motion or election is pending or the vote on it has just been taken; otherwise, it is an incidental main motion.

15

Standard Descriptive Characteristics

Incidental motions relating to methods of voting and the polls:

20

1. Take precedence over the motion being voted on or to be voted on. When applied to a vote which has just been taken, they can be moved from the moment the chair has reported the vote (see p. 48, ll. 18–23) until the announcement of the result is complete, or immediately thereafter (see pp. 408–9). They can be moved while an order for the *Previous Question* is in effect on the votes to which they apply. They yield to the privileged motions, and to a motion to *Lay on the Table* moved while the question to which they are applied is pending.

25

30

2. Can be applied to any motion on which the assembly is called upon to vote other than another motion relating to the method of voting, or a motion to close or reopen

35

1   the polls.* No subsidiary motion can be applied to them
       except *Amend.***

3. Are out of order when another has the floor; but, within
   the time limits specified in Standard Characteristic 1
5 above, a member can claim preference in being recognized for the purpose of making one of these motions
   when applied to a vote that has just been taken.
4. Must be seconded.
5. Are not debatable.
10 6. Are amendable.
7. Require a majority vote, except a motion to close the
   polls, which requires a two-thirds vote.
8. The vote on a motion ordering that the polls be closed
   or reopened at a specified time can be reconsidered at any
15 time before the order has been carried out. Otherwise,
   neither a vote to close the polls nor an affirmative vote to
   reopen the polls can be reconsidered; the same effect can
   be obtained by renewal or by the opposite motion. A negative vote on a motion to reopen the polls can be recon-
20 sidered within the period during which a motion to
   reopen the polls could be made originally. Other motions
   relating to methods of voting can be reconsidered.

   Further Rules and Explanation
25
   METHODS OF VOTING.   In practice, the method of
   taking a vote usually can be agreed upon informally. But when
   different methods are suggested, they are usually treated not
   as amendments but as filling blanks, the vote normally being

---

*However, a motion to take a counted vote can be applied to any motion
except to another motion to take a counted vote.

**In principle, the *Previous Question* can also be applied to them to stop
their amendment, though such a case will rarely arise in practice.

taken first on the one taking the most time. (For ways of vot- *1*
ing, see pp. 44–54; **45**.)

A member who believes that a secret vote will give a truer
expression of the assembly's will on a pending motion can
move that the vote on the motion be taken by ballot. An *5*
order that the vote on a main motion be taken by ballot also
applies to a vote on whether to postpone the main motion
indefinitely. (See also *Roll-Call Vote*, pp. 420ff.)

RETAKING A VOTE.   As explained in **4** (see pp. 44–54) *10*
and **45** (see pp. 409–10), the regular methods of initially taking a vote are by voice (*viva voce*), by rising (division), or by
show of hands—the latter two of which may also be called for
by any member as a means of verifying an inconclusive vote
that has just been taken (see **29**)—and the chair may order that *15*
a vote be counted or that an uncounted vote be retaken as a
counted vote. After a question has been voted on in any of
these ways, and within the time specified in Standard Characteristic 1 above, the assembly can still order that the vote be
taken again by some method other than any of the regular ones *20*
(see *Other Methods of Voting*, pp. 112ff.) or that an uncounted
vote be retaken as a counted vote. But after a vote has been
taken by one of those other methods, or after the assembly has
ordered that a counted vote be taken, it is not in order to move
that the vote be taken again. It is never in order to move that *25*
the vote on a question be taken a second time by the same
method.

EXHAUSTION OF AN ORDER PRESCRIBING THE
METHOD OF VOTING.   If the method of voting on a *30*
motion is ordered by the assembly (and not prescribed by
the assembly's rules), such an order is exhausted (1) when the
question on which it was imposed has been finally disposed
of, or (2) at the conclusion of the session in which the order
has been adopted—whichever occurs first. If, after such an *35*

1 order is exhausted, the motion to which it previously applied
comes to a vote (for example, during reconsideration or at a
subsequent session), the order is no longer in effect. Notwithstanding the exhaustion of this order, however, a motion
5 which has been voted on by ballot must also be voted on by
ballot during any reconsideration of it, since no action is in
order that would force the disclosure of a member's vote or
views on the matter (see p. 413, ll. 1–4). Likewise, if the
assembly adjourns after balloting for an office has begun
10 but before the election to that office is complete (p. 444),
any additional votes needed to complete the election must
also be taken by ballot, even if they are taken at a subsequent
session.

15   CLOSING OR REOPENING THE POLLS.   Motions
relating to opening and closing the polls are applicable only
with respect to ballot votes. It is usually better to leave it to
the chair to close the polls. When the vote is taken by ballot,
as soon as the chair thinks that all have voted who wish to,
20 he inquires if all have voted. If there is no response, he declares the polls closed, and the tellers proceed to count the
vote.
        If a motion is made to close the polls when the voting
has closed naturally, the chair can treat the motion as a
25 unanimous-consent request and declare the polls closed. In
any case, a formal motion to close the polls should not be
recognized until all have presumably voted. Like motions relating to the close of debate or nominations, the motion to
close the polls requires a two-thirds vote.
30   If members enter afterward and it is desired to reopen the
polls, this can be done by a majority vote.
        The time at which the polls shall be closed or reopened
can be specified in the motion, or added by amendment.

§31. MOTIONS RELATING TO NOMINATIONS

While an election is pending, a member may wish to offer a motion to determine the method of making nominations* (when it is not prescribed in the bylaws or rules of order). Members also may wish to offer motions to close or reopen nominations.

Standard Descriptive Characteristics

Incidental motions relating to nominations:

1. Take precedence over the pending election for which nominations are to be made. They yield to the privileged motions, and to the motion to *Lay on the Table*.
2. Apply to any pending election. No subsidiary motion except *Amend*** can be applied to them.
3. Are out of order when another has the floor or any member is attempting to make a nomination.
4. Must be seconded.
5. Are not debatable.
6. Are amendable.
7. Require a majority vote, except a motion to close nominations, which requires a two-thirds vote because (a) its adoption deprives members of a basic right—to nominate; and (b) the assembly must be protected against attempted abuse of the power to close nominations by a temporary majority.

---

*A motion prescribing the method of nominating is an incidental motion—and subject to the rules given here—only when the election is pending; otherwise, it is an incidental main motion (see **10**).

**See second footnote on page 284, which also applies to these motions.

8. Can be reconsidered, except the motion to close nominations, or an affirmative vote on a motion to reopen nominations. (In the latter cases, the same effect can be obtained by renewal or by the opposite motion.)

Further Rules and Explanation

MOTIONS TO PRESCRIBE METHODS OF NOMINATING.   If no method of making nominations is designated by the bylaws or rules and the assembly has adopted no order on the subject, anyone can make a motion prescribing the method of nomination for an office to be filled. When different methods are proposed, they can be moved as amendments, but are frequently treated as filling blanks (pp. 162–67). In that event, the vote is taken on the various suggested methods of nominating, in this order: (a) by the chair; (b) from the floor (sometimes called "open nominations"); (c) by a committee; (d) by ballot; and (e) by mail (see **46**). It should be noted that not all of these methods are appropriate or desirable in average societies.

MOTIONS TO CLOSE OR REOPEN NOMINATIONS.   In the average society, a motion to close nominations is not a necessary part of the election procedure and it should not generally be moved. When nominations have been made by a committee or from the floor, the chair should inquire whether there are any further nominations; and when there is no response, he declares that nominations are closed. In very large bodies, the formality of a motion to close nominations is sometimes allowed, but this motion is not in order until a reasonable opportunity to make nominations has been given; as noted above, it is out of order if a member is rising, addressing the chair, or otherwise attempting to make a nomination, and it always requires a two-thirds vote. When no one wishes to make a further nomination, the motion serves no useful purpose.

A legitimate use of the motion to close nominations would be, for example, to end delay of an election by numbers of nominations obviously intended only to honor persons who have no chance of being elected.

When for any reason it is desired to reopen nominations, this can be done by a majority vote.

The time at which nominations shall be closed or reopened can be specified in the motion, or added by amendment.

§32. REQUEST TO BE EXCUSED FROM A DUTY

Occasionally the bylaws of a society may impose specific duties on members beyond the mere payment of dues. Members may be obligated to attend a certain number of meetings, to prepare talks or papers, to serve on committees, or even to accept office if elected. In these cases, a member cannot, as a matter of right, decline such a duty or *demand* that he or she be excused from it, but the assembly—except as the bylaws may provide otherwise—can grant the member's *request* to be so excused. The request can be granted by unanimous consent, or a motion to grant it, which is debatable and amendable, can be offered.

Standard Descriptive Characteristics

A *Request to Be Excused from a Duty*:

1. Takes precedence over any motion with whose purpose it is connected and can also be made at any time when no

1   question is pending. A motion on a request that is pend-
     ing yields to all subsidiary motions except *Postpone Indefi-
     nitely*, to all privileged motions, and to other incidental
     motions.

5   2. Can be applied in reference to any motion or parliamen-
       tary situation out of which it arises. All subsidiary motions
       except *Postpone Indefinitely* can be applied to it.
    3. Is in order when another has the floor if it requires im-
       mediate attention.
10 4. Does not require a second except when moved formally
       by the maker of the request. A motion to *grant* the request
       of another member does not require a second since the
       maker of the request and the maker of the motion—two
       members—wish the question to be considered.
15 5. Is debatable.
    6. Is amendable.
    7. Requires a majority vote, but is frequently settled by
       unanimous consent.
    8. Where the member requesting to be excused from a duty
20   has learned of the action taken on his or her request, only
       a negative vote can be reconsidered.

Further Rules and Explanation

25   If a duty is not compulsory, a member can decline when
     he is first named to it or, if absent at that time, when he first
     learns of his election or appointment. At times other than
     during a meeting, such a notice of declination can be ad-
     dressed to the secretary or to the appointing power. Since in
30   these cases the duty is not compulsory, no motion to excuse
     the member is necessary.
        A member who remains silent when presumably aware
     that he has been named to a duty is regarded as accepting,
     and he thereby places himself under the same obligations as
35   if he had expressly accepted.

If a member who has accepted an office, committee assignment, or other duty finds that he is unable to perform it, he should submit his resignation. A resignation is submitted in writing, addressed to the secretary or appointing power; alternatively, it may be submitted during a meeting either orally or in writing.* By submitting a resignation, the member is, in effect, requesting to be excused from a duty. The chair, on reading or announcing the resignation, can assume a motion "that the resignation be accepted."

The duties of a position must not be abandoned until a resignation has been accepted and becomes effective, or at least until there has been a reasonable opportunity for it to be accepted.

A request to be excused from a duty *essential to the functioning of a society or assembly* is a question of privilege affecting the organization of the assembly; and so also is the filling of a vacancy created by the acceptance of a resignation. In such cases, the assembly can proceed immediately to fill the vacancy, unless notice is required or other provision for filling vacancies is made in the bylaws. In the case of a resignation *from office*, unless the bylaws provide otherwise, the assembly cannot proceed to fill the vacancy immediately since notice is a requirement. But if a member is elected and declines, no notice is required to complete the election immediately or at the next meeting (see p. 444).

RESIGNATION FROM MEMBERSHIP.   A member in good standing with his dues paid cannot be compelled to continue his membership so that additional obligations are incurred. His resignation should be accepted immediately, and if it is not, he incurs no obligation after his resignation has been sent in, provided he does not avail himself of the

---

*See pages 177, 467–68.

1 privileges of membership. It is different with members who
have not paid their dues up to the date of sending in their
resignations. Until they have settled their dues, the society is
under no obligation to accept their resignations, and thus ad-
5 ditional amounts may become due. If their dues are not paid
within a reasonable time, instead of accepting their resignations, the society may expel them. A resignation sent in to
escape charges need not be accepted. The charges may be preferred, and the trial should proceed the same as if the resig-
10 nation had not been sent in.

§33. REQUESTS AND INQUIRIES

In connection with business in a meeting, members may
15 wish to obtain information or to do or have something done
that requires permission of the assembly. Any member can
make the following types of inquiry or request: (a) *Parliamentary Inquiry*; (b) *For Information*; (c) *For Permission (or
Leave) to Withdraw or Modify a Motion*; (d) *To Read Papers*;
20 and (e) *For Any Other Privilege*.

Standard Descriptive Characteristics

With respect to the requests and inquiries growing out of
25 the business of the assembly that are listed above, the following rules apply:

1. All take precedence over any motion with whose purpose
    they are connected, and can also be made at any time
30   when no question is pending. A motion on a request that
    is pending yields to all privileged motions and to other
    incidental motions.
2. All can be applied in reference to any motion or parlia-
    mentary situation out of which they arise. No subsidiary
35   motion can be applied to any of them.

3. All are in order when another has the floor if they require *1*
   immediate attention.

4. A *Parliamentary Inquiry* and a *Request for Information*
   do not require a second. The other requests do not require a second, except when moved formally *by the maker* *5*
   of the request. A motion to *grant* the request of another
   member does not require a second, since two members
   already wish the question to come up—the maker of the
   request and the maker of the motion.

5. All are not debatable. *10*

6. All are not amendable.

7. No vote is taken on a *Parliamentary Inquiry* and a *Request
   for Information.* The other requests require a majority
   vote in order to be granted, and are frequently settled by
   unanimous consent. When it is too late for renewal, unan- *15*
   imous consent is *required* to grant permission to withdraw a motion to *Reconsider* (p. 317, ll. 11–15), or to
   withdraw previous notice of a proposed motion requiring
   such notice (pp. 121–24).

8. A *Parliamentary Inquiry* and a *Request for Informa-* *20*
   tion are not subject to reconsideration. The vote on a request *For Permission to Modify a Motion, To Read Papers,*
   and *For Any Other Privilege* can be reconsidered. On a
   request *For Permission to Withdraw a Motion,* only a negative vote can be reconsidered. *25*

Further Rules and Explanation (with Forms)

a. PARLIAMENTARY INQUIRY.   A *Parliamentary
Inquiry* is a question directed to the presiding officer to ob- *30*
tain information on a matter of parliamentary law or the rules
of the organization bearing on the business at hand. It is the
chair's duty to answer such questions when it may assist a
member to make an appropriate motion, raise a proper point
of order, or understand the parliamentary situation or the *35*

effect of a motion. The chair is not obliged to answer hypo-
thetical questions.

In making an inquiry, the inquirer arises, and without obtaining the floor, addresses the chair as follows:

MEMBER A: Madam President, I rise to a parliamentary inquiry. [Or,
"A parliamentary inquiry, please."]

CHAIR: The member will state the inquiry.

MEMBER A: Is it in order at this time to move the previous question?

The chair's reply to a parliamentary inquiry is not subject
to an appeal, since it is an opinion, not a ruling. A member
has the right to act contrary to this opinion, however, and if
ruled out of order, to appeal such a ruling. If an inquiry is
made when another member has the floor and an immediate
answer is not necessary, the chair can defer a reply until the
floor has been yielded.

b. REQUEST FOR INFORMATION. A *Request for
Information* (also called a *Point of Information*) is a request
directed to the chair, or through the chair to another officer
or member, for information relevant to the business at hand
but not related to parliamentary procedure.

It is treated like a parliamentary inquiry, as follows:

MEMBER A: Mr. President, I have a request for information. [Or, "A
point of information, please."]

CHAIR: The member will state his question.

MEMBER A: Will the convention delegates report at this meeting?

Or:

MEMBER A: This motion calls for a large expenditure. Will the treasurer state the present balance?

If information is desired of a member who is speaking,   *1*
the inquirer, upon rising, may use the following form instead:

MEMBER A: Madam President, will the member yield for a question?

5

Or:

MEMBER A: Mr. President, I would like to ask the gentleman [or "the
member"] a question.

10

If the speaker consents to the interruption, the time consumed will be taken out of his allowed time. The chair therefore asks if the speaker is willing to be interrupted, and if he
consents, directs the inquirer to proceed. Although the presiding officer generally remains silent during the ensuing ex-   *15*
change, the inquiry, the reply, and any resulting colloquy are
made in the third person through the chair. To protect decorum, members are not allowed to carry on discussion directly
with one another.

An inquiry of this kind may also be for the purpose of re-   *20*
minding a speaker of a point to be made in argument, or it
may be intended to rebut his position; but it must always be
put in the form of a question.

c. REQUEST FOR PERMISSION (OR LEAVE) TO   *25*
WITHDRAW OR MODIFY A MOTION.   Conditions for
withdrawing or modifying a motion depend upon how soon
the mover states his wish to withdraw or modify it. *Permission*
for him to do so is required only after the motion to which it
pertains has been stated by the chair as pending.   *30*

Before a motion has been stated by the chair, it is the property of its mover, who can withdraw it or modify it without
asking the consent of anyone. Thus, *in the brief interval between the making of a motion and the time when the chair*

1 *places it before the assembly by stating it*, the maker can withdraw it as follows:

   MEMBER A (who made the motion): Madam President, I withdraw
5 the motion.

   Or:

   MEMBER A (who made the motion): Mr. President, I wish to modify
10 the motion by striking out "demand" and inserting "urge."

   In the same interval also, another member can ask if the
   maker of the motion is willing to withdraw it or accept a
   change in it, which suggestion the maker can either accept or
15 reject. In such a case the chair either announces, "The motion
   has been withdrawn," or states the question on the modified
   motion. If a motion is modified, the seconder can withdraw
   his second. When the seconder withdraws his second to the
   modified motion, the member who suggested the modifica-
20 tion has, in effect, supplied a second.
       After a motion has been stated by the chair, it belongs to
   the meeting as a whole, and the maker must request the assembly's permission to withdraw or modify his own motion,
   according to the rules stated in Standard Characteristics 1–8,
25 above. In such cases the procedure is as follows.
       To *withdraw* a motion that is before the assembly, the
   member who made it may use this form:

   MEMBER A (who made the motion): Madam President, I ask permis-
30 sion [or "leave"] to withdraw the motion.

   The chair treats this first as a unanimous-consent request.
   That is, if no one objects, the announcement is:

35   CHAIR: Unless there is objection [pause] the motion is withdrawn.

If there is an objection, the chair of his own accord can put   *1*
the question on granting the request, or any member can
move "that permission to withdraw the motion be granted."
If a member other than the one making the request made the
motion, it does not require a second, since the maker of   *5*
the motion to grant permission and the maker of the request
surely both favor it.

A request for permission to withdraw a motion, or a motion to grant such permission, can be made at any time before
voting on the question has begun, even though the motion   *10*
has been amended, and even though subsidiary or incidental
motions may be pending. Any such motions that adhere to
the main motion cease to be before the assembly and require
no further disposition if the main motion is withdrawn. Any
member can suggest that the maker of a motion ask permis-   *15*
sion to withdraw it, which the maker can do or decline to do,
as he chooses.

After a question has been divided, one or more of the
parts can be withdrawn without affecting the other parts.
A motion to *Reconsider* (**37**), or a previous notice of a pro-   *20*
posed motion requiring such notice (pp. 121–24), cannot be
withdrawn after it is too late for renewal, unless unanimous
consent is given.

After a motion has been withdrawn, the situation is as
though it had never been made; therefore, the same motion   *25*
can be made again at the same meeting.

To *modify* a motion after it has been stated by the chair,
the maker asks permission to do so, as in the case of withdrawal of a motion. If there is no objection, the chair states
the question on the modified motion. If anyone objects, the   *30*
chair must then determine whether an amendment equivalent
to the requested modification would be in order. If not, the
modification may not be made unless a motion to suspend
the rules is made and adopted. If a motion for such an
amendment is in order, the chair can assume it or any member   *35*

1   can move it formally. The amendment requires a second if
moved by the member who originally made the request. The
rules governing consideration of amendments are followed
(see **12**). A pending motion can be amended only by vote or
5   unanimous consent of the assembly, even if the maker of the
motion states that he "accepts" the amendment. (See also
treatment of "Friendly Amendments," p. 162.)

d. REQUEST TO READ PAPERS.   If any member ob-
10   jects, a member has no right to read from—or to have the
secretary read from—any paper or book as a part of his speech
without permission of the assembly. This rule is a protection
against the use of reading as a means of prolonging debate
and delaying business. It is customary, however, to permit
15   members to read short, pertinent, printed extracts in debate
so long as they do not abuse the privilege. If a member wishes
to do so, he can, while speaking in debate, say, "If there is no
objection, I would like to read ... [indicating the nature and
length of the paper]." The member can then begin to read
20   unless another member objects.* In such a case, at any time
until the speaker has finished reading, another member can
interrupt him by an objection, which must be addressed to
the chair. Or, if the speaker desiring to read prefers, he can
formally request permission: "Mr. President, I ask permission
25   to read a statement ... [briefly describing it, as above]"; and
the chair then asks if there is objection. In either case, if there
is an objection, the chair can, of his own accord, put the question on granting permission, or any member can move "that
permission to read a paper in debate be granted." This mo-
30   tion requires no second unless moved by the member who
made the request. Action of the assembly granting a request

---

*The procedure of presuming permission to read until objection is raised
is applicable *only in debate on a pending question*.

to read a paper can be reconsidered at any time until the read-   *1*
ing has been concluded.

The foregoing paragraph applies only to papers or documents that are not before the assembly for action. When any
paper is laid before the assembly for action, it is a right of   *5*
every member that it be read once; and, if there is any debate
or amendment, that it be read again before members are
asked to vote on it. Except as just stated, no member has the
right to have anything read without permission of the assembly. But whenever any member requests that a document that   *10*
is before the assembly be read—obviously for information and
not for delay—and no one objects, the chair normally should
direct that it be read. If there is an objection, a majority vote
is required to order that it be read. If a member was absent
from the hall when the paper under consideration was read—   *15*
even though absent on duty—he cannot insist on its being
read again; in this case, the convenience of the assembly is
more important than that of a single member.

e. REQUEST FOR ANY OTHER PRIVILEGE.   When   *20*
a member desires to make a request not covered by one of
the four types explained above—as, for example, a request to
address remarks or make a presentation while no motion is
pending—he rises, addresses the chair, and, as soon as he
catches the presiding officer's attention, states his request.   *25*
Although he does not have to wait for recognition and can
make his request even though another member has been assigned the floor, he should never interrupt a member speaking unless sure that urgency justifies it. Generally, such
matters are settled by unanimous consent or informally, but   *30*
if there is an objection, a motion can be made to grant the
request. If explanation is required, it can be requested or
given, but this must not extend into debate. These requests
should be treated so as to interrupt the proceedings as little
as is consistent with the demands of justice.   *35*

CHAPTER

IX

MOTIONS THAT BRING
A QUESTION AGAIN
BEFORE THE ASSEMBLY

*See 6, pages 74ff., for a list of these motions and
a description of their characteristics as a group.*

§34. TAKE FROM THE TABLE

The object of the motion to *Take from the Table* is to
make pending again before the assembly a motion or a series
of adhering motions that previously has been laid on the table
(see **17**).

Standard Descriptive Characteristics

The motion to *Take from the Table*:

1. Takes precedence over no pending motion, and therefore
cannot be moved while any other question is pending;
but, subject to the conditions indicated in the next sentence, it takes precedence over a main motion that has
been made but has not yet been stated by the chair. Unless it is moved under a suspension of the rules (**25**) it
must be moved at a time when no program or rule interferes, and while business of the class to which the subject

300

question belongs, unfinished business, general orders, or new business is in order; and it cannot interrupt a series of motions connected with taking up a single item of business (see below). It yields to privileged and incidental motions but not to subsidiary ones.

2. Can be applied to any question or series of *adhering* motions that lies on the table as explained in the first paragraph under *Further Rules and Explanation*, below. This motion is not in order, however, until some business or interrupting matter has been transacted or dealt with since the question was laid on the table; and if it is moved and voted down, the motion to *Take from the Table* cannot be renewed until some further business has been transacted. No subsidiary motion can be applied to the motion to *Take from the Table*.

3. Is out of order when another has the floor; but a member can claim preference in being recognized for the purpose of making this motion ahead of a new main motion, or he can claim the floor for such a purpose after a new main motion has been made but before the new motion has been stated by the chair (see below).

4. Must be seconded.

5. Is not debatable.

6. Is not amendable.

7. Requires a majority vote.

8. Cannot be reconsidered. If the motion to *Take from the Table* is adopted, the question can be laid on the table again whenever it would be in order to do so, and if it is voted down, it can be renewed each time that any business has been transacted.

Further Rules and Explanation

TIME LIMITS ON TAKING A QUESTION FROM THE TABLE. A question that has been laid on the table remains there and can be taken from the table during the same session (**8**), or, if the next regular business session will be held before a quarterly time interval has elapsed (see pp. 89–90), also at the next session after it was laid on the table. If not taken from the table within these time limits, the question dies, although it can be reintroduced later as a new question.

RIGHT OF WAY IN PREFERENCE TO A NEW MAIN MOTION.   In ordinary assemblies a question is supposed to be laid on the table only temporarily, with the expectation that its consideration will be resumed after disposal of the interrupting matter or at a more convenient time. Consequently, as soon as the business or interrupting matter has been disposed of, any member can seek recognition for the purpose of moving to take the question from the table; or, so long as it remains on the table, he can do so at any time under the classes of business listed in Standard Characteristic 1 above— except while another motion is pending or while a series of motions connected with one question is being introduced, as explained in the next paragraph. If the chair recognizes someone else as having risen and addressed the chair first, a member who rose at about the same time to move to take the question from the table should remain standing and say that he rises for this purpose, and the chair should then assign him the floor. Or, even after a new motion has been made but before it has been stated by the chair, a member who quickly rises and says that he does so to move to take the question from the table should be assigned the floor. The principle is that, if the assembly so desires, a motion already within its control by being only temporarily disposed of (pp. 90–91, 340–41) has the right of way over a new main motion.

Even if no question is pending, a motion to *Take from the Table* cannot interrupt a series of motions connected with bringing up a single item of business, but must wait until the

complete series is disposed of. For example, such a series of
motions is in process of being dealt with:

- when the assembly has just voted to suspend the rules and
  permit a certain main motion to be introduced;
- when a question has just been laid on the table for the announced purpose of admitting another motion;
- when a previous action has just been rescinded (**35**) to
  enable a conflicting main motion to be made; or
- when a main motion has just been voted down after a
  member stated in debate that in that event he would offer
  a different motion covering the case.

In each of the above instances, until the main motion that
was specified has been made and disposed of, it is not in order
to move to take still another question from the table.

STATUS OF A QUESTION TAKEN FROM THE
TABLE. When a question is taken from the table, it is before the assembly, with everything adhering to it, exactly as it
was when laid on the table. If amendments and a motion to
Commit were pending when a resolution was laid on the
table, then when it is taken from the table the question is first
on the motion to *Commit*. The same would be true if a motion to *Postpone to a Certain Time* were adhering to a resolution, except that if the resolution is not taken from the table
until after the time of proposed postponement, the motion
to postpone is ignored. If the question is taken up on the
same day that it was laid on the table, members who had
exhausted their right of debate cannot speak on the question
again; but if on another day, no notice is taken of speeches
previously made. The *Previous Question* or a limitation or extension of debate is not exhausted, however, if the question
to which such an order was applied is taken from the table at
the same session, even on another day—as in a convention.

1   At the next session any such order is exhausted and the reg-
    ular rules of debate prevail.

    Form and Example
5
        The form used in making this motion is, for example, "I
    move to take from the table the resolution relating to ... and
    its amendment."
        If Member A, who has risen to seek the floor for the pur-
10 pose of making this motion, observes that the chair has rec-
    ognized another member who rose at about the same time
    and who apparently intends to make a new main motion, the
    procedure would be as follows:

15   MEMBER A (remaining standing and interrupting): Mr. President, I
    rise for the purpose of moving to take a question from the table.

        Upon recognition, Member A then would move "... to take
    from the table the motion relating to ..."
20   If Member A did not rise to claim the floor before the
    chair recognized another member who already has made a
    new motion, then before this question has been stated by the
    chair, Member A can quickly rise and address the chair, thus:

25   MEMBER A: Madam President.
        CHAIR: For what purpose does the member rise?
        MEMBER A: I rise for the purpose of moving ... [and so on, as in the
    case above].

§35. RESCIND; AMEND SOMETHING PREVIOUSLY ADOPTED

1

By means of the motions to *Rescind* and to *Amend Something Previously Adopted*—which are two forms of one 5 incidental main motion governed by identical rules—the assembly can change an action previously taken or ordered. *Rescind*—also known as *Repeal* or *Annul*—is the motion by which a previous action or order can be canceled or counter-manded. The effect of *Rescind* is to strike out an entire main 10 motion, resolution, order, or rule that has been adopted at some previous time. *Amend Something Previously Adopted* is the motion that can be used if it is desired to change only a part of the text, or to substitute a different version.

15

Standard Descriptive Characteristics

The motions to *Rescind* and to *Amend Something Previously Adopted*:

20

1. Take precedence over nothing, and can therefore be moved only when no other motion is pending. *Previous notice* (pp. 121–24) of intent to offer one of these motions at the next meeting can be given while another question is pending, however—provided that it does not interrupt 25 a speaker (see Standard Characteristic 7). These motions yield to subsidiary, privileged, and incidental motions.

2. Can be applied to anything (e.g., bylaw, rule, policy, decision, or choice) which has continuing force and effect and which was made or created at any time or times as 30 the result of the *adoption* of one or more main motions. (However, see below for actions that cannot be rescinded or amended.) All of the subsidiary motions can be applied to the motions to *Rescind* and to *Amend Something Previously Adopted*. 35

3. Are out of order when another has the floor; but previous notice of intent to offer one of these motions at the next meeting can be given after another member has been assigned the floor, provided that he has not begun to speak.

4. Must be seconded.

5. Are debatable; debate can go into the merits of the question which it is proposed to rescind or amend.

6. Are amendable, by the processes of primary and secondary amendment in any of the forms discussed in **12**, as applicable to the particular case. Thus, a motion to *Rescind* can be amended, for example, by substituting for it a motion to amend what is proposed to be rescinded. But if a motion to *Rescind* or to *Amend Something Previously Adopted* is amended so that the change proposed by the amended motion then exceeds the scope of a previous notice that was given, the effect of the previous notice is destroyed and the motion can no longer be adopted by a majority vote (see Standard Characteristic 7). When these motions *require* previous notice (as may be the case with respect to a motion to rescind or amend a provision of the bylaws or a special rule of order), such a motion cannot be amended so as to make the proposed change greater than that for which notice has been given.

7. In an assembly, except when applied to a constitution, bylaws, or special rules of order, require (a) a two-thirds vote, (b) a majority vote when notice of intent to make the motion, stating the complete substance of the proposed change, has been given at the previous meeting within a quarterly time interval or in the call of the present meeting, or (c) a vote of a majority of the entire membership—any one of which will suffice. The same vote is required for the assembly to rescind or amend an action taken by subordinate bodies, such as some executive boards, empowered to act on behalf of the assembly. In a committee, these motions require a two-thirds vote unless all committee members who voted for the motion to be

rescinded or amended are present or have received ample
notice, in which case they require a majority vote. A motion to rescind or amend provisions of a constitution or
bylaws is subject to the requirements for amendment as
contained in the constitution or bylaws (see **56, 57**). If
the bylaws or governing instrument contains no provision
relating to amendment, a motion to rescind or amend applied to a constitution or to bylaws is subject to the same
voting requirement as to rescind or amend special rules
of order—that is, it requires (a) previous notice as described above *and* a two-thirds vote or (b) a vote of a
majority of the entire membership.

8. A negative vote on these motions can be reconsidered,
but not an affirmative vote.

Further Rules and Explanation

RIGHT OF ANY MEMBER TO MAKE THE MO-
TIONS, WITHOUT TIME LIMIT.   In contrast to the case
of the motion to *Reconsider*, there is no time limit on making
these motions after the adoption of the measure to which
they are applied, and they can be moved by any member, regardless of how he voted on the original question. When previous notice has been given, it is usual to wait for the member
who gave notice of these motions to move them; but if he
does not, any member can do so.

PROPOSED AMENDMENTS BEYOND THE SCOPE
OF THE NOTICE.   As noted in Standard Descriptive
Characteristic 6 above, when previous notice is a *requirement*
for the adoption of a motion to rescind or amend something
previously adopted, no subsidiary motion to amend is in
order that proposes a change greater than that for which notice was given. This is always the case, for example, when the
bylaws of an organization require previous notice for their
amendment, which they should do (pp. 580–82). It will also

be the case, as a practical matter, whenever a majority of the entire membership is not in attendance at the time the vote is taken on a motion to rescind or amend a provision of the constitution or bylaws, or a special rule of order. In either of the situations described above, no subsidiary motion to amend is in order that proposes a change going beyond the scope of the notice which was given, for the reason that adoption of such a motion will destroy the effect of the notice, and the motion is thus tantamount to a motion to *Postpone Indefinitely.*

ACTIONS THAT CANNOT BE RESCINDED OR AMENDED.   The motions to *Rescind* and to *Amend Something Previously Adopted* are not in order under the following circumstances:

a) When it has previously been moved to reconsider the vote on the main motion, and the question can be reached by calling up the motion to *Reconsider* (**37**).

b) When something has been done, as a result of the vote on the main motion, that is impossible to undo. (The unexecuted part of an order, however, can be rescinded or amended.)

c) When a resignation has been acted upon, or a person has been elected to or expelled from membership or office, and the person was present or has been officially notified of the action. (The only way to reverse an expulsion is to follow whatever procedure is prescribed by the bylaws for admission or reinstatement. For the case of an election, see pp. 653–54 regarding removal of a person from office.)

Form and Example

When previous notice has been given, the motions to *Rescind* or to *Amend Something Previously Adopted* may be made as follows:

MEMBER A (obtaining the floor): In accordance with notice given at   *1*
the last meeting, I move to rescind the resolution that authorized additional landscaping of the grounds. [Or "… to amend the resolution …
by adding …"] (Second.)

                                                                          5
In such a case, a majority vote is sufficient.
    When no notice of the motion to *Rescind* or to *Amend
Something Previously Adopted* has been given, the motions
may be made as follows:

                                                                         10
MEMBER A (obtaining the floor): I move to rescind the motion relating to … adopted at the May meeting. [Or "… to amend the motion …
by inserting …"] (Second.)

Without previous notice, the motion requires a two-thirds   *15*
vote or a majority of the entire membership for its adoption.
    In a great many instances, the motion or resolution orig-
inally adopted is not referred to, and only the bylaw, rule,
or policy to be rescinded or amended is mentioned. For
example: *20*

MEMBER A (obtaining the floor): In accordance with the notice given
in the call of this meeting, I move to amend Article V, Section 3 of the
bylaws by striking out subparagraph (c) thereof. (Second.)

                                                                         25
To offer an amendment to change one form of the mo-
tion into the other:
    If the motion was made "to amend the motion relating
to … adopted at the May meeting … by inserting …":

                                                                         30
MEMBER A (obtaining the floor): I move to substitute for the pending
motion the following: "To rescind the motion relating to … adopted at
the May meeting."

If the motion was made "To rescind the resolution that   *35*
authorized additional landscaping of the grounds.":

1   MEMBER A (obtaining the floor): I move to substitute for the pending motion the following: "To amend the resolution that authorized additional landscaping of the grounds by adding 'at a cost not to exceed $100,000.'"

5

Rescind and Expunge from the Minutes

On extremely rare occasions when it is desired not only to rescind action but also to express the strongest disapproval, 10   a member may move to *Rescind and Expunge from the Minutes* (or *the Record*). Adoption of this motion requires an affirmative vote of a majority of the entire membership, and may be inadvisable unless the support is even greater. Even a unanimous vote at a meeting is insufficient if that vote is not 15   a majority of the entire membership. If such a motion is adopted, the secretary, in the presence of the assembly, draws a single line through or around the offending words in the minutes, and writes across them the words, "Rescinded and Ordered Expunged," with the date and his signature. In the 20   recorded minutes the words that are expunged must not be blotted or cut out so that they cannot be read, since this would make it impossible to verify whether more was expunged than ordered. In any published record of the proceedings, the expunged material is omitted. Rather than 25   expunging, it is usually better to rescind the previous action and then, if advisable, to adopt a resolution condemning the action which has been rescinded.

§36. DISCHARGE A COMMITTEE
30

By means of the motion to *Discharge a Committee* from further consideration of a question or subject, the assembly can take the matter out of a committee's hands* after refer-

---

*Or a committee can take it out of a subcommittee's hands.

ring it to the committee and before the committee has made   *1*
a final report on it, and the assembly itself can consider it.

So long as a question is in the hands of a committee, the
assembly cannot consider another motion involving practically the same question.   *5*

The rules governing this motion are similar to those
applying to the motion to *Rescind* or to *Amend Something
Previously Adopted*—of which it is a particular case in certain
applications, as explained on pages 313–14.

                                                                    10

Standard Descriptive Characteristics

The motion to *Discharge a Committee*:

1. Takes precedence over nothing, and therefore can be   *15*
   moved only when no other question is pending. *Previous
   notice* of intent to offer the motion at the next meeting
   can be given while another question is pending, however—provided that it does not interrupt a speaker. This
   motion yields to all subsidiary, privileged, and incidental   *20*
   motions.
2. Can be applied to any main motion, or any other matter,
   that has been referred to a committee and that the committee has not yet finally reported to the assembly. All of
   the subsidiary motions can be applied to it.   *25*
3. Is out of order when another has the floor; but previous
   notice of intent to offer this motion at the next meeting
   can be given after another member has been assigned the
   floor, provided that he has not begun to speak.
4. Must be seconded.   *30*
5. Is debatable; debate can go into the merits of the question
   in the hands of the committee.
6. Is amendable. For example, the motion can be amended
   as to the time at which the assembly is to consider
   the question; or an amendment to the effect that the   *35*

1 committee be instructed to report instead of being discharged can be moved as a substitute.

7. Since the motion would change action already taken by
   the assembly, requires (a) a two-thirds vote, (b) a majority
5 vote when notice of intent to make the motion has been
   given at the previous meeting within a quarterly time interval or in the call of the present meeting, or (c) a vote
   of a majority of the entire membership—any one of
   which will suffice. To prevent business from being delayed
10 by a committee, however, there are two special circumstances under which the motion requires only a majority
   vote (even without notice): (a) if the committee fails
   to report within a prescribed time as instructed, and
   (b) while the assembly is considering any partial report of
15 the committee.

8. A negative vote can be reconsidered, but not an affirmative vote.

Further Rules and Explanation
20

CIRCUMSTANCES JUSTIFYING THE MOTION;
ALTERNATIVE PROCEDURES. Action to discharge a
committee from further consideration of a question or subject
is generally advisable only when the committee has failed to
25 report with appropriate promptness or when, for some urgent
reason, the assembly desires to proceed on the matter without
further aid from the committee, or wishes to drop the matter.

If the committee to which the matter was referred has not
yet taken it up and if it is not too late to move to *Reconsider*
30 (the day of its committal or the next business-meeting day),
the appropriate motion is to reconsider the vote on the motion of referral, which requires only a majority vote. The
motion of referral may have been a subsidiary motion to
Commit (**13**) or a main motion, depending on the case, as
35 explained below.

Instead of discharging the committee, the assembly can   *1*
instruct it to report at a reasonable specified time. A motion
to do this can be moved as a substitute (see **12**) for a pending
motion to *Discharge a Committee*, or it can be introduced as
an incidental main motion when no question is pending. If   *5*
no instruction as to time of reporting has been given previously, this motion requires only a majority vote for adoption.
If it changes a previously specified reporting time before that
time has arrived, however, the vote required is the same as
for the motion to *Discharge a Committee*.   *10*

No motion to *Discharge a Committee* is needed when a
committee's final report on a referred question or subject has
been received by the assembly, since the committee is then
automatically discharged from further consideration of the
matter.   *15*

EFFECT OF DISCHARGING A COMMITTEE.
When a committee is discharged from considering a matter,
either by the adoption of a motion to discharge it or by the
submission of its final report, the committee continues in ex-   *20*
istence if it is a standing committee, but ceases to exist if it is
a special committee that was appointed to take up the matter.
In any case, when a committee is thus discharged, its chairman returns to the secretary of the society all papers relating
to the referred matter that were previously entrusted to him.   *25*

When a committee is discharged from further consideration of a question which was pending at the time of its referral
and which was referred by means of the subsidiary motion to
Commit, the question comes before the assembly automatically at that time (unless the committee is discharged by   *30*
means of a motion that includes the specification of a later
time for considering it). If no later time was specified in the
motion, the question can then be postponed, if desired; or if
the assembly wishes to drop the matter, the question can be
postponed indefinitely. If a motion to *Discharge a Committee*   *35*

1 specifies a later time for considering the question and does
not make it a special order, the question comes up under
the same conditions as if postponed to that time without
making it a special order—that is, it is a general order for
5 the time named. If the motion to *Discharge a Committee* includes a provision making the question a special order, it requires a two-thirds vote, just as any other motion to make a
special order. (See pp. 185–88 regarding the priority to which
a question is subject when it is due to come up after
10 postponement.)

On the other hand, a motion to discharge a committee
from further consideration of a subject that was referred to
the committee by means of a *main* motion is a particular case
of the motion to *Rescind* or to *Amend Something Previously*
15 *Adopted* (**35**). When such a motion to *Discharge a Committee*
has been adopted, another main motion is needed to bring
before the assembly the matter that was referred; otherwise
it dies.

20 **Form and Example**

The form used in making this motion, as applied to a
question being considered by a *standing committee*, may be:

25 MEMBER A (obtaining the floor): I move that the Finance Committee
be discharged from further consideration of the resolution relating to …
(Second.)

In the case of a *special committee*, the following form may
30 be used:

MEMBER A (obtaining the floor): I move that the committee to which
was referred the resolution relating to … be discharged. (Second.)

35 If it is desired to take up the question at a later time, there
may be added to either of the above forms, for example, the

words, "and that the resolution be considered at 4 P.M." (in   *1*
which case it is a general order for that time), or, "and that it
be made a special order for ..."

If the motion to discharge the committee is adopted and
includes no provision for consideration at a later time, and if   5
the question was referred while pending (by means of the
subsidiary motion to *Commit*), the chair announces the result
and immediately states the question brought out of committee. For example:

   10

> CHAIR: There are two thirds in the affirmative and the committee is
> discharged. The question is now on the resolution, "*Resolved*, ..."

§37. RECONSIDER

   15

Reconsider—a motion of American origin—enables a
majority in an assembly, within a limited time and without
notice, to bring back for further consideration a motion
which has already been voted on. The purpose of reconsidering a vote is to permit correction of hasty, ill-advised, or   *20*
erroneous action, or to take into account added information
or a changed situation that has developed since the taking of
the vote.

To provide both usefulness and protection against
abuse, the motion to *Reconsider* has the following *unique*   *25*
characteristics:

a) It can be made only by a member who voted with the pre-
     vailing side. In other words, a reconsideration can be
     moved only by one who voted *aye* if the motion involved   *30*
     was adopted, or *no* if the motion was lost. (In standing
     and special committees, the motion to *Reconsider* can be
     made by any member who did not vote on the losing
     side—including one who did not vote at all.) It should be
     noted that it is possible for a minority to be the prevailing   *35*
     side if a motion requiring a two-thirds vote for adoption

is lost. A member who voted by ballot may make the motion if he is willing to waive the secrecy of his ballot. Also, if the motion to be reconsidered was adopted by unanimous consent, all the members present at the time of the adoption are in the same position as if they had voted on the prevailing side and qualify to move to reconsider. This requirement for making the motion to *Reconsider* is a protection against its dilatory use by a defeated minority—especially when the motion is debatable (see Standard Characteristic 5, below) and the minority is large enough to prevent adoption of the *Previous Question* (**16**). When a member who cannot move a reconsideration believes there are valid reasons for one, he should try, if there is time or opportunity, to persuade someone who voted with the prevailing side to make such a motion. Otherwise, he can obtain the floor while no business is pending and briefly state his reasons for hoping that a reconsideration will be moved, provided that this does not run into debate; or, if necessary while business is pending, he can request permission to state such reasons (see *Request for Any Other Privilege*, p. 299).

b) The making of this motion is subject to time limits, as follows: In a session of one day—such as an ordinary meeting of a club or a one-day convention—the motion to *Reconsider* can be made only on the same day the vote to be reconsidered was taken. In a convention or session of more than one day, a reconsideration can be moved only on the same day the original vote was taken or on the next succeeding day within the session on which a business meeting is held. These time limitations do not apply to standing or special committees (see pp. 329–30).

c) The *making* of this motion has a higher rank than its *consideration*; that is, the motion can be made and seconded at times when it is not in order for it to come before the assembly for debate or vote. In such a case it can be taken up later, even after it would be too late to move it in the first place. If the motion to *Reconsider* is introduced at a time when it cannot be taken up, the chair does not state the question on it as pending, but asks the secretary to record the motion as made and seconded. This temporarily suspends any action growing out of the vote it is proposed to reconsider. While a motion to reconsider the vote on a main motion has this status, a member can bring the motion before the assembly at any time when its consideration is in order. When he does this, he is said to *call up* the motion to *Reconsider*. Except by unanimous consent, a motion to *Reconsider* that has not been finally disposed of cannot be withdrawn after it is too late to renew it; that is, it can be withdrawn only within the same time limits as for making the motion in the first place.

Standard Descriptive Characteristics

The motion to *Reconsider*:

1. a) With respect to *making* the motion, takes precedence over any other motion whatever and yields to nothing.* The making of this motion is in order when any other question is pending, and also after the assembly has voted to adjourn, if the member rose and addressed the chair before the chair declared the meeting adjourned. If a reconsideration appears to require immediate action in the latter case, the vote on adjourning should be retaken. Even while an order for the *Previous Question* is in effect on a motion which

---

*The motion to *Reconsider* has a special form known as *Reconsider and Enter on the Minutes*, however, which outranks the regular form of the motion (see pp. 332–35).

is immediately pending, until the chair actually begins to take the vote, the making of a motion to *Reconsider* an earlier vote on another question is in order.*

   b) With respect to its *consideration*, has only the same rank as that of the motion to be reconsidered, although it has the right of way in preference to any new motion of equal rank until such a motion has been stated by the chair as pending. (The procedure for calling up a motion to *Reconsider* in preference to a main motion just made by someone else, and relating to another matter, is similar to that described for moving to *Take from the Table*; see **34**.) Provided that no question is pending, the reconsideration of a vote disposing of a main motion, either temporarily or permanently, can be taken up even while the assembly is in the midst of taking up the general orders.

2. Can be applied to the vote on any motion except:
   a) a motion which can be renewed (see pp. 339–40);
   b) a negative vote on a motion which, at the time the motion to *Reconsider* is made, would be out of order because:
      i) it conflicts with a motion previously adopted and still in force,
     ii) it conflicts with a motion which has been temporarily but not finally disposed of and which remains within the control of the assembly, or
    iii) it would conflict with a pending motion if that motion were adopted;
   c) an affirmative vote whose provisions have been partly carried out;**

---

*The *Previous Question* itself can be reconsidered only before any vote has been taken under it.

**Exception (c) does not apply to a motion to *Limit or Extend Limits of Debate*, on which the vote can be reconsidered even if such an order has been partly carried out.

d) an affirmative vote in the nature of a contract when the party to the contract has been notified of the outcome;

e) any vote which has caused something to be done that it is impossible to undo;

f) a vote on a motion to *Reconsider*; or

g) when practically the same result as desired can be obtained by some other parliamentary motion.

In the case of subsidiary or incidental motions that adhered to a main motion, however, *Reconsider* can be applied only in such a way that the reconsideration takes place while the main motion to which they adhered is pending—either before the main motion is voted on or when it is being reconsidered at the same time. The same is true where one subsidiary or incidental motion adheres to another; for example, *Reconsider* can be applied to the vote on a secondary amendment only in such a way that the reconsideration takes place before the primary amendment involved is voted on or while the primary amendment is being reconsidered.

By application of these principles, it follows that certain motions cannot be reconsidered, while in the case of others only the vote on an affirmative result can be reconsidered, and with still others, only the vote on a negative result. (See tinted pp. 46–47 for a list of the motions in each of these categories; see also Standard Characteristic 8 in the sections on each individual motion.)

The motion to *Lay on the Table* can be applied to the motion to *Reconsider*. Motions to *Postpone to a Certain Time*, to *Limit or Extend Limits of Debate*, and for the *Previous Question* can also be applied to it when it is debatable (see Standard Characteristic 5). When a motion to *Reconsider* is postponed or laid on the table, all adhering questions are also postponed or go to the table. Motions to *Postpone Indefinitely*, *Amend*, or *Commit* cannot be applied to a motion to *Reconsider*.

3. Is in order (with respect to *making* the motion) even after another person has been assigned the floor, so long as he has not actually begun to speak. The *calling up* of a motion to *Reconsider* is out of order when another has the floor.

4. Must be seconded at the time it is made. Unlike the making of the motion, which must be done by a person who voted with the prevailing side, the seconding can be done by any member regardless of how he voted on the motion to be reconsidered. The *calling up* of the motion to *Reconsider* does not require a second.

5. Is debatable in all cases in which the motion proposed to be reconsidered is debatable, and when debatable, opens to debate the merits of the question whose reconsideration is proposed. (See pp. 327–28, however, regarding a series of motions proposed to be reconsidered, and the question that is opened to debate in such a case.) When the motion proposed to be reconsidered is not debatable—either because of its nature or because it is subject to an unexhausted order for the *Previous Question* (**16**)—the motion to *Reconsider* is undebatable. Similarly, if the *Previous Question* is in effect on a pending question or series of questions, and if a motion which is proposed to be reconsidered adheres to these pending question(s) in such a way that the reconsideration must be taken up before the *Previous Question* is exhausted, both the motion to *Reconsider* and the motion to be reconsidered are undebatable—even if the latter motion was open to debate as its earlier consideration and the *Previous Question* was ordered later.

6. Is not amendable.

7. Requires only a majority vote, *regardless of the vote necessary to adopt the motion to be reconsidered.* (But see pp. 329–30 for a different rule in the case of standing and special committees.)

8. Cannot be reconsidered. If it is voted on and lost, the
   motion to *Reconsider* cannot be renewed except by unanimous consent. By the same principle, no question can be
   reconsidered twice unless it was materially amended during its first reconsideration.

Further Rules and Explanation

SUSPENDING EFFECT OF MAKING A MOTION
TO RECONSIDER.   The effect of *making* a motion to
Reconsider is the suspension of all action that depends on the
result of the vote proposed to be reconsidered, either (a) until
the motion to *Reconsider* has been voted on and, if the motion is adopted, until the reconsideration is completed; or
(b) if the motion to *Reconsider* is not taken up, until the suspension terminates as follows: if no more than a quarterly
time interval (pp. 89–90) will elapse until the next regular
session, the suspension terminates with the adjournment of
the next regular session; but if more than a quarterly time interval will intervene before the next regular session, the suspension terminates with the end of the same session in which
the motion is made. If the motion to *Reconsider* is not called
up within these limits of time, the situation becomes the same
as if there had been no such motion, and the vote which it
was proposed to reconsider—and any other action held up
because of the proposed reconsideration—comes into full
force, as if in effect, so far as applicable, from the time the
vote was originally taken.

RECONSIDERATION OF A MOTION THAT IS NO
LONGER IN ORDER BECAUSE OF INTERVENING
ACTION.   It should be noted that, as a consequence of the
rule set forth in (b) of Standard Characteristic 2 above, action
taken by an assembly may preclude the making of a motion
to reconsider the vote on a previously rejected motion. For

1 an example, assume that a motion to spend all of an available
sum of money for library books is voted down, and thereafter
a motion to spend the same money for athletic equipment is
made and adopted. No motion to reconsider the vote on the
5 motion to purchase library books will thereafter be in order
because, if adopted, it would place before the assembly a motion which conflicts with a motion previously adopted and still
in force (see p. 343, ll. 17–20). In such a case, if it is desired
to reconsider the vote on the rejected motion, the subse-
10 quently adopted motion must first be rescinded (or amended
in some fashion so that it no longer conflicts), or the vote on
it must be reconsidered and reversed.

TAKING UP THE MOTION TO RECONSIDER AT
15 THE TIME IT IS MADE.   If a motion to *Reconsider* is
made at a time when it can be taken up—that is, when the
motion proposed to be reconsidered would be in order initially—the chair immediately states the question on the motion to *Reconsider* as pending before the assembly. In
20 proposing a reconsideration of the vote on a main motion, it
is usually better to make the motion to *Reconsider* when no
other business is pending and the motion can be taken up immediately—unless it appears that there may be no such opportunity or there is an important reason for doing otherwise.
25 Whenever the motion to *Reconsider* is taken up, as noted
in Standard Characteristic 5, it is debatable if the motion proposed to be reconsidered is debatable, and debate can go into
the merits of the question proposed to be reconsidered. The
right of each member to debate the motion to *Reconsider* is
30 separate from the original consideration of the motion proposed to be reconsidered. Therefore, even if a member exhausted his right to debate in the original consideration and
the motion to *Reconsider* is taken up on the same day, he still
has the right to speak the regular number of times (twice un-
35 less the assembly has a special rule providing otherwise) in

debate on the motion to *Reconsider*. (For rules affecting a member's right to debate in the reconsideration if the motion to *Reconsider* is adopted, see pp. 324–25.)

If a motion to *Reconsider* is voted on and lost, the vote which it proposed to reconsider, and any action held up because of the proposed reconsideration, comes into full force, effective from the time the first vote was taken.

CALLING UP THE MOTION TO RECONSIDER. If a motion to *Reconsider* that involves a main motion cannot be taken up when it is made, then as long as its suspending effect lasts it can be called up and acted upon during any regular meeting, or any special meeting called for that purpose, at any time that no question is pending and no other member has the floor. To call it up, a member obtains the floor and says, "Mr. President, I call up the motion to reconsider the vote on the motion … [identifying it]." No second is necessary, since the motion to *Reconsider* was seconded at the time it was made. When this motion is called up, the chair immediately states the question on it as pending (see *Form and Example*).

Privilege Accorded the Mover in Regard to the Time at Which Reconsideration Takes Place. Although any member can call up the motion to *Reconsider* as just described, usually no one but the mover of the reconsideration calls it up on the day the motion is made—at least in cases where the session is to last beyond that day and there is no need for immediate action. The reason is that the mover may wish time to assemble new information, or—if the reconsideration is moved on the same day the original vote was taken—he may want the unrestricted debate that will be allowable if the motion is taken up on another day (see below). So long as business is not unreasonably delayed and the mover of the reconsideration acts in good faith, he is entitled to have it take place at a time he feels will make for the fullest and fairest reexamination of the question.

1   *Duty of the Chair When Failure to Call Up the Motion May Do Harm.* In cases where a failure to call up a motion to *Reconsider* may do harm, the chair has the duty to point out the situation to the assembly. Suppose, for example, that in a
5 meeting of an ordinary society that will meet within a quarterly time interval (pp. 89–90), there has been a motion to *Reconsider* a vote to do something that can only be done before the next meeting. Should the present meeting adjourn without taking up the motion to *Reconsider*, the measure pro-
10 posed to be reconsidered would be killed unless an adjourned meeting or special meeting were held to consider it. Therefore, if this meeting seems on the point of adjourning before the motion to *Reconsider* has been taken up, the chair should explain the facts and suggest that someone call up the motion.
15 If it has been moved to adjourn under these circumstances, the motion to *Adjourn* can be withdrawn or voted down—or the time can be fixed for an adjourned meeting, which can be done either before or after the vote on adjournment has been taken (see *Fix the Time to Which to Adjourn*, **22**).
20

EFFECT OF ADOPTION OF THE MOTION TO RECONSIDER; RULES GOVERNING DEBATE ON THE RECONSIDERATION. The effect of the adoption of the motion to *Reconsider* is immediately to place before
25 the assembly again the question on which the vote is to be reconsidered—in the exact position it occupied the moment before it was voted on originally.

    Rules governing debate on the reconsideration of the vote are as follows:
30   *Reconsideration of a Vote on the Same Day.* A member's right to debate the reconsideration of a vote is independent of the extent to which he took part in debate on the motion to *Reconsider*. If the reconsideration takes place on the same day as the first consideration, however, anyone who exhausted
35 his right to debate in the first consideration will not be able

to speak on it again during the reconsideration, without per-   *1*
mission of the assembly. (But such a member can pursue an
equivalent purpose while the motion to *Reconsider* is pending, since the motion proposed to be reconsidered is also
open to discussion in debate on the motion to *Reconsider*.)   *5*

Reconsideration of a Vote on a Later Day.   Every member's right to debate in the reconsideration of a question begins over again, regardless of speeches made previously, if
reconsideration takes place on a day other than that on which
the vote to be reconsidered was taken.   *10*

*Reconsideration Under an Order Limiting or Extending
Limits of Debate.*   If a vote on one of a series of motions is
taken under an order *limiting* debate or for the *Previous Question*, and then is reconsidered before such an order is exhausted (as explained in the sections on those motions, **15**   *15*
and **16**), the same restrictions continue to apply to debate
both on the motion to *Reconsider* and on the reconsideration.
In the case of reconsidering a motion similarly covered by an
unexhausted order *extending* limits of debate, the extension
applies only to the reconsideration itself, not to debate on the   *20*
motion to *Reconsider*. When reconsideration takes place after
exhaustion of the *Previous Question* or a limitation or extension of debate, these orders do not come back into force, and
debate or amendment is subject to the ordinary rules.

25

RECONSIDERATION OF SUBSIDIARY, PRIVI-
LEGED, AND INCIDENTAL MOTIONS.   Conditions
under which subsidiary, privileged, or incidental motions can
be reconsidered depend on what other motions are pending
at the time the reconsideration is moved, as follows: *30*

*To Reconsider a Subsidiary, Privileged, or Incidental
Motion: Reconsideration Moved While the Main Question Is
Pending.*   When a main motion is pending (with or without
a series of adhering motions) and it is moved to reconsider
the vote on a related subsidiary, privileged, or incidental   *35*

1   motion, the motion to *Reconsider* becomes (a) immediately pending or (b) pending at a lower position in the series, depending on whether the motion proposed to be reconsidered would then be in order if moved for the first time.

5   Referring to case (a) above, the motion to *Reconsider* becomes the immediately pending question at once *if no other motions that would take precedence over the motion proposed to be reconsidered are also pending* (see **5** and **6**; see also the chart on tinted pp. 3–5). For example, assume that it is moved and
10 seconded to reconsider a negative vote on a motion to refer the pending main question to a committee. If the main question is now pending alone, or if no other questions are pending except motions to *Postpone Indefinitely* or to *Amend* (which rank below the motion to *Commit*), the chair at once
15 states the question on the motion to *Reconsider* as immediately pending.

      On the other hand, referring to case (b) above, if a series of motions is pending with the main question and *one or more of them would take precedence over the related motion whose re-*
20 *consideration is proposed*, the motion to *Reconsider* does not become the immediately pending question when it is moved, but it becomes pending as one of the series, at a position corresponding to the rank of the motion proposed to be reconsidered. In such a case, the motion to *Reconsider* is taken up
25 immediately after voting has been completed on all motions that would take precedence over the motion to be reconsidered if that were pending. For example, suppose that while a main motion, an amendment, and a motion to lay the pending questions on the table are pending, it is moved to recon-
30 sider a previous negative vote on referring the same main question and amendment to a committee. The order of rank, from highest to lowest, of the four motions is: (1) *Lay on the Table*, (2) *Commit*, (3) *Amend*, and (4) the main motion. This is the order in which these motions would be voted on,
35 and the reverse of the order in which they would be made.

The procedure in this instance is as follows: The chair takes *1*
note of the fact that the motion to *Reconsider* has been made
and seconded, instructing the secretary to record it. He then
proceeds to take the vote on the motion to *Lay on the Table*.
If that motion is lost, he automatically states the question on *5*
the motion to reconsider the vote on the referral to the committee, since the motion to *Commit* is next lower in rank. If
the motion to *Reconsider* is adopted, the motion to *Commit*
is then reconsidered and voted on again; and if this is lost,
the question is then stated on the amendment. (If the motion *10*
to *Lay on the Table* is adopted, then whenever the questions
are taken from the table, the immediately pending question
is the motion to *Reconsider*, and from this point the procedure is the same as above.)

If the reconsideration of a primary amendment is moved *15*
while another amendment of the same degree is pending, the
pending amendment is disposed of first. Then the chair states
the question on the motion to reconsider the amendment
previously acted upon.

When it is moved to reconsider a debatable subsidiary or *20*
incidental motion which relates to a pending main question
or a series of pending questions (in which case the motion to
Reconsider is debatable, as noted in Standard Characteristic 5), debate on the motion to *Reconsider* can go into the
merits of the motion *proposed to be reconsidered*, but not into *25*
the merits of any other pending question. For example, in the
debate on a motion to reconsider an amendment to the pending main question, the merits of the amendment are open to
discussion, but not those of the main question apart from the
amendment. *30*

*To Reconsider an Adhering Subsidiary or Incidental
Motion: Reconsideration Moved After the Main Question Has
Been Acted Upon.* If it is desired to reconsider the vote on a
subsidiary or incidental motion (an amendment, for example)
after the main question to which it adhered has been finally *35*

1   disposed of (by adoption, rejection, or indefinite postpone-
    ment), the vote on the main question, or on its indefinite
    postponement, must also be reconsidered (see also Standard
    Characteristic 2). In such a case, one motion to *Reconsider*
5   should be made to cover both the vote on the subsidiary
    or incidental motion whose reconsideration is desired, and
    the vote on the main question (or its indefinite postpone-
    ment). The member who makes this motion to *Reconsider*
    must have voted with the prevailing side in the original vote
10 on the subsidiary or incidental motion—that is, on the mo-
    tion which will be reconsidered first if the reconsideration
    takes place.

        The same principle applies to the reconsideration of a sec-
    ondary amendment after the related primary amendment has
15 been voted on. If such a reconsideration is desired while the
    main question is still pending, the primary amendment must
    also be reconsidered. If it is desired to reconsider the second-
    ary amendment after the main question has been finally
    disposed of, the secondary amendment, the primary amend-
20 ment, and the main question must all be reconsidered, and
    one motion to *Reconsider* should be made covering the votes
    of these three motions.

        When a motion to *Reconsider* covers the votes on two or
    more connected motions, not all of these questions can be
25 discussed in debate on the motion to *Reconsider*, but only the
    one that will be voted on first if the motion to *Reconsider* is
    adopted. Thus, if the motion is to reconsider the votes on a
    resolution, a primary amendment, and a secondary amend-
    ment, only the secondary amendment is open to debate in
30 connection with debate on the motion to *Reconsider*. If this
    motion to *Reconsider* is adopted, the chair states the question
    on the secondary amendment and recognizes the mover of
    the reconsideration as entitled to the floor. The question is
    now in exactly the same condition as it was just before the
35 original vote was taken on the secondary amendment.

If a main motion is included in a series covered by a single motion to *Reconsider*, as just described, the reconsideration is in order at the same times as if it had been moved to reconsider the main motion alone. If the motion to *Reconsider* is made at a time when it cannot be taken up, it suspends action in the way described on page 321 and stands until called up, subject to the same conditions as if it applied only to the main motion.

If a motion to reconsider the vote on an adhering subsidiary or incidental motion (an amendment, for example) is made after the main question to which it adheres has been either postponed to a certain time or laid on the table, the motion to reconsider is properly noted and is taken up in due course (pp. 326–27) if and when the main motion is again brought before the assembly. The same is true if the motion to reconsider the adhering subsidiary or incidental motion was made before, but was not called up before, the main question was postponed or laid on the table. On the other hand, if a main question is referred to a committee, no motion to reconsider the vote on an adhering subsidiary or incidental motion is in order while the question is in the hands of the committee, and any such motion to reconsider that was made but not taken up prior to referral is thereafter ignored.

RECONSIDERATION IN STANDING AND SPECIAL COMMITTEES.   Reconsideration in a standing or a special committee (**50**) differs from reconsideration in a meeting of the assembly in the following respects:

1) A motion to reconsider a vote in the committee can be made and taken up *regardless of the time that has elapsed* since the vote was taken, and there is no limit to the number of times a question can be reconsidered. Likewise, the rule requiring unanimous consent to renew a defeated motion to *Reconsider* does not apply in committees.

2) The motion can be made by any member of the committee who *did not vote with the losing side*; or, in other words, the maker of the motion to *Reconsider* can be one who voted with the prevailing side, or one who did not vote at all, or even was absent.

3) Unless all the members of the committee who voted with the prevailing side are present or have been notified that the reconsideration will be moved, it requires a *two-thirds vote* to adopt the motion to *Reconsider*.

In other respects, reconsideration in a committee is the same as in a meeting of the society or its board. A vote cannot be reconsidered in a committee of the whole.

Form and Example

This motion may be made in forms such as the following:

a) For the reconsideration of a main question: "I move to reconsider the vote on the resolution relating to the annual banquet. I voted for [or "against"] the resolution."

b) To move the reconsideration of a subsidiary, privileged, or incidental motion related to the main question, while the main question is pending: "I move to reconsider the vote on the amendment to strike out 'Friday' and insert 'Saturday.' I voted for [or "against"] the amendment."

c) When the reconsideration of a subsidiary or incidental motion is desired after the main question to which it adhered has been acted upon: "I move to reconsider the votes on the resolution relating to the annual banquet and on the amendment to strike out 'Friday' and insert 'Saturday.' I voted for [or "against"] the amendment."

If the maker of the motion to *Reconsider* fails to state which side he voted on, the chair, before making any other response, directs the member to do so:

CHAIR: The member moving the reconsideration must state how he *1* voted on the resolution ["motion," "amendment," etc.].

If the resolution was adopted by unanimous consent, the chair should ask whether the member was present at the time. *5* If the member did not vote with the prevailing side, another member who did so can make the motion to *Reconsider*, if he desires. The motion must be seconded.

If it is in order to take up the motion to *Reconsider* when it is made, the chair immediately states the question as *10* follows:

CHAIR: It is moved and seconded to reconsider the vote on the following resolution [reading it].

15

If it is not in order to take up the motion to *Reconsider* when it is moved, the chair says instead:

CHAIR: It is moved and seconded to reconsider the vote on the resolution relating to ... The Secretary will make a note of it. *20*

He then continues with the pending business.

When it is in order to call up the motion to *Reconsider* and a member wishes to do so, the member rises and addresses the chair: *25*

MEMBER A (obtaining the floor): I call up the motion to reconsider the vote [or "votes"] on ...

The chair proceeds: *30*

CHAIR: The motion to reconsider the vote [or "votes"] on ... is called up. The question is on the motion to reconsider ... [etc.].

If a reconsideration that could not be taken up when *35* it was moved is one that later comes before the assembly

1 automatically, then when that point is reached, the chair says, for example:

> CHAIR: The question is now on the motion to reconsider the vote
> 5 on the amendment to ...

After debate on a motion to *Reconsider*, assuming that this motion is adopted, the chair puts the question and states the result as follows:
10

> CHAIR: As many as are in favor of reconsidering the vote on the res-
> olution relating to the annual banquet, say *aye*. ... Those opposed, say
> *no*. ... The ayes have it and the vote on the resolution is reconsidered.
> The question is now on the resolution, which is ... [etc.].

15 Or:

> CHAIR: The ayes have it and the votes on the resolution and the
> amendment are reconsidered. The question is now on the amendment,
> 20 which is ... [etc.].

Note that if the result of the vote on the motion to *Reconsider* is negative, it is the only vote taken. But if the motion to *Reconsider* is adopted, this is followed—after any 25 debate—by the taking of the vote or votes that are consequently reconsidered.

Reconsider and Enter on the Minutes

30 *Reconsider and Enter on the Minutes* is a special form of the motion to *Reconsider* that has a different object from the regular motion. Its purpose is to prevent a temporary majority from taking advantage of an unrepresentative attendance at a meeting to vote an action that is opposed by a majority of 35 a society's or a convention's membership. The effect of this

form of the motion arises from the fact that when it is
moved—on the same day that the vote to be reconsidered
was taken—it cannot be called up until another day, even if
another meeting is held on the same day.* Thus, with a view
to obtaining a more representative attendance, it ensures reconsideration of a question on a different day from the one
on which the question was put to vote.

DIFFERENCES FROM THE REGULAR FORM OF
THE MOTION. *Reconsider and Enter on the Minutes*
differs from the regular form of *Reconsider* in the following
respects:

1) It can be moved only on the same day that the vote proposed to be reconsidered was taken. The regular form of
   the motion to *Reconsider* can be used on the next succeeding day within the session on which a business meeting is held.
2) It takes precedence over the regular motion to *Reconsider*.
   Also, this motion can be made even after the vote has
   been taken on the motion to *Reconsider*, provided that
   the chair has not announced the result of the vote. In this
   case the regular motion to *Reconsider* is then ignored. If
   it were not for the rule that the motion to *Reconsider and
   Enter on the Minutes* takes precedence over the regular
   motion to *Reconsider*, the motion to *Reconsider and
   Enter on the Minutes* would generally be forestalled by the
   regular motion, which would be voted down, and then
   Reconsider and Enter on the Minutes could not be moved.
3) It can be applied only to votes that finally dispose of main
   motions; that is, to: (a) an affirmative or negative vote on
   a main motion; (b) an affirmative vote on postponing indefinitely; or (c) a negative vote on an objection to the

---

*For an exception, see item (6) below.

consideration of a question, if the session extends beyond that day.

4) It cannot be applied to votes on motions whose object would be defeated by a delay of one day. For example, a motion asking a visitor to address a convention the following day cannot have this motion applied to it.

5) If more than a quarterly time interval (pp. 89–90) will intervene before the next regular business session, it cannot be moved at the last business meeting of the current session.

6) It cannot be called up on the day it is made, except that when it is moved on the last day—but not the last meeting—of a session of an organization that is not scheduled to meet again within a quarterly time interval (pp. 89–90), it can be called up at the last business meeting of the session.

After a motion to *Reconsider and Enter on the Minutes* has been called up, its treatment is the same as that of the regular motion to *Reconsider*. The name of this form does not imply that the regular motion to *Reconsider* is not also recorded in the minutes.

PROCEDURE FOR USE OF THE MOTION.   To illustrate the use of this form of the motion, suppose that at a long meeting of a county historical society, many members have left, unknowingly leaving a quorum composed mainly of a small group determined to commit the society to certain action that a few of those present believe would be opposed by most of the membership. A member in opposition can prevent the vote on such action from becoming final by moving "to reconsider and enter on the minutes the vote on …" To be in a position to do this, such a member—detecting the hopelessness of preventing an affirmative result on the vote—should vote in the affirmative himself. If the motion to

Reconsider and Enter on the Minutes is seconded, all action *1* required by the vote proposed to be reconsidered is suspended, and there is time to notify absent members of the proposed action.

If no member of the temporary minority voted on the *5* prevailing side and it is too late for anyone to change his vote (see pp. 408–9), notice can be given that a motion to rescind the assembly's action will be made at the next meeting. At this next meeting, provided that such notice has been given, the motion to *Rescind* can then be adopted by a majority vote. *10*

PROTECTING AGAINST ABUSES OF THE MOTION. The motion to *Reconsider and Enter on the Minutes* may occasionally be subject to attempted abuse, particularly in ordinary societies with single-meeting sessions, since it *15* gives any two members power to hold up action taken by a meeting. In the average organization this motion should generally be reserved for extreme cases, and should be regarded as in order only when final decision on the question could, if necessary, wait until the next regular meeting, or when an *20* adjourned or special meeting to take it up is a practical possibility.

If an actual minority in a representative meeting makes improper use of this motion by moving to reconsider and enter on the minutes a vote which requires action before the *25* next regular meeting, the remedy is to fix the time for an adjourned meeting (**9, 22**) on another suitable day when the reconsideration can be called up and disposed of. In such a case, the mere making of a motion to set an adjourned meeting would likely cause withdrawal of the motion to *Reconsider* *30* *and Enter on the Minutes*, since its object would be defeated.

RENEWAL OF MOTIONS; DILATORY AND IMPROPER MOTIONS

§38. RENEWAL OF MOTIONS

If a motion is made and disposed of without being adopted, and is later allowed to come before the assembly after being made again by any member in essentially the same connection, the motion is said to be *renewed*. Renewal of motions is limited by the basic principle that an assembly cannot be asked to decide the same, or substantially the same, question twice during one session—except through a motion to reconsider a vote (**37**) or a motion to rescind an action (**35**), or in connection with amending something already adopted (see also pp. 74–75). A previously considered motion may become a substantially different question through a significant change in the wording or because of a difference in the time or circumstances in which it is proposed, and such a motion may thus be in order when it could not otherwise be renewed.

The rules restricting renewal of motions do not apply to any motion that was last disposed of by being withdrawn. A motion that is withdrawn becomes as if it had never been made and can be renewed whenever it would be originally in order. The rules restricting renewal of motions also do not apply to any motion that dies for lack of a second. Although such a motion is not treated as if it had never been made, it too is a motion which the assembly was not called upon to decide, and thus it too may be renewed whenever it would originally be in order to make it.

Two general principles govern the renewal of motions:

1) *No motion can be renewed during the same session in which it has already been before the assembly, except where its renewal is permitted by a specific rule; and such a rule always implies circumstances under which the motion has in some respect become a different question.* (For a discussion of the rules growing out of this principle, see *Nonrenewability During the Same Session, and Exceptions,* below.) Whenever it is stated without qualification that a particular parliamentary motion "cannot be renewed," such a statement means that the motion cannot be renewed during the same session, or, in the case of a subsidiary or incidental motion, not during that session in connection with the same motion to which it directly adhered.

2) *Any motion that is still applicable can be renewed at any later session, except where a specific rule prevents its renewal; and such an impediment to renewal at a later session normally can exist only when the first motion goes over to that session as not finally disposed of, in which case the question can then be reached through the first motion* (see pp. 90–91, 340–41).

Nonrenewability During the Same Session, and Exceptions

The following rules are derived from the first principle stated above, by which a motion is not renewable at the same session unless the question has become somehow different.

1   PARTICULAR CASES OF THE GENERAL RULE
AGAINST RENEWAL.   Applications of the general rule
against renewal during the same session include the following:

5   • A main motion, or a motion for the same amendment to
a given motion, cannot be renewed at the same session
unless there is a change in wording or circumstances sufficient to present substantially a new question, in which
case this becomes technically a different motion. If a series
10   of resolutions voted on together is lost, however, one or
more of them can be offered again at the same session,
but enough resolutions must be left out to present a gen-
uinely different question from the viewpoint of probable
voting result; otherwise this procedure becomes dilatory.
15   • A motion to *Postpone Indefinitely* cannot be renewed
in connection with the same main question during the
same session, even if the main motion has been materially amended since the previous vote against indefinite
postponement. There will be another opportunity to ac-
20   complish the same object—that is, to defeat the main motion—when it comes up for a final vote.
• A motion to *Reconsider* that has been rejected cannot be
renewed in connection with the same vote. To be able to
be reconsidered a second time, the original question must
25   have been materially amended during the first reconsideration—in which case the proposal to reconsider a second time is a new question.
• A motion to *Rescind* that has been voted down cannot
be renewed at the same session unless the motion pro-
30   posed to be rescinded has meanwhile been amended sufficiently to present a new question.
• A motion to divide the same question in substantially the
same way cannot be renewed at the same session.
• When a *Question of Privilege* or a *Point of Order* has been
35   ruled on adversely by the chair, it cannot be raised again

at the same session unless an appeal is made and the chair's decision is reversed. After a decision of the chair has been sustained on an appeal, no point of order or appeal contrary to it can be made during that session.

MOTIONS THAT CAN BE RENEWED AT A LATER MEETING OF THE SAME SESSION. Following are two cases of motions which cannot be renewed at the same *meeting*, but which may have become different questions—and consequently are renewable—at another meeting of the same session (see **8**):

- Although the motion to *Suspend the Rules* for the same purpose cannot be renewed at the same meeting, such a motion can be renewed at the next meeting or any later meeting, even if the next meeting is held on the same day or is part of the same session. This renewal is allowable because by the time of the next meeting the attendance or situation may already have changed sufficiently to justify the renewal. The mere passage of time may make it a new question.
- The same motion to *Fix the Time to Which to Adjourn*—that is, a motion to set the same date, hour, and place for an adjourned meeting—cannot be renewed at the same meeting at which it is voted down; but if, after the first motion is rejected, the assembly decides to set an adjourned meeting for an earlier time than proposed in the first motion, then at that adjourned meeting it is in order to move to set a second adjourned meeting for the same time as originally considered for the first.

MOTIONS THAT CAN BE RENEWED AFTER MATERIAL PROGRESS IN BUSINESS OR DEBATE. The following motions are renewable if they become new questions as described, even within the same meeting:

- The subsidiary motions to *Commit*, to *Postpone to a Certain Time*, to *Limit or Extend Limits of Debate*, for the *Previous Question*, and to *Lay on the Table* can be renewed whenever progress in business or debate has been such that they are no longer practically the same questions. In addition, a motion to *Lay on the Table* can be renewed if something urgent has arisen that was not known when the assembly rejected this motion.

- A motion to *Take from the Table* that has failed can be renewed after disposal of the business that was taken up following rejection of the motion.

- A *Call for the Orders of the Day* can be renewed after disposal of the business that was taken up when the assembly refused to proceed to the orders of the day.

- A motion to *Adjourn* or to *Recess* can be renewed after material progress in business or in debate—such as an important decision or speech. A vote on a motion to *Recess* or to *Lay on the Table* is not business of a character to justify renewal of a motion to *Adjourn*; and a vote on any of these three motions is not sufficient business to allow renewal of either of the others.

- Motions to close nominations or the polls can be renewed after progress in nominations or voting has been such as to make them essentially new questions.

Conditions That May Impede Renewal at a Later Session

MAIN MOTIONS THAT GO OVER TO ANOTHER SESSION; MOTIONS WITHIN THE CONTROL OF THE ASSEMBLY, BECAUSE NOT FINALLY DISPOSED OF.   Referring to the second general principle stated on page 337, a main motion that was introduced but not adopted during one session can, except as noted in this paragraph, be renewed at any later session unless it has become

absurd. Such exceptions occur only through one of the
processes by which, from one session to another, a main
motion can remain *within the control of the assembly* (that is,
temporarily, but not finally, disposed of), so that *the same* motion can be considered at the later session. Four of these
processes (numbered 1 through 4 below) can arise only in
cases of organizations where no more than a quarterly time
interval (see pp. 89–90) will elapse until the next regular session. In such societies, a main motion cannot be renewed during the next session after a session at which it was:

1) postponed to, or otherwise set as a general or special
   order for, the next session (**14**);
2) allowed to go over to the next session as unfinished business or as an unfinished special order (see pp. 236–37,
   356–59);
3) laid on the table and not taken from the table (**17**, **34**);
   or
4) the subject of a motion to *Reconsider* (**37**) that was made
   but not finally disposed of.

Also, in any assembly:

5) a main motion that has been referred to a committee cannot be renewed until after the session at which the assembly finally disposes of the main motion—after the
   committee has reported it back or has been discharged
   from its consideration (**36**).

NONRENEWABILITY OF UNSUSTAINED OBJEC-
TION TO THE CONSIDERATION OF A QUESTION.
An unsustained *Objection to the Consideration of a Question*
(**26**) cannot be renewed in connection with the same main
motion—even at a later session if the main motion goes
over to that session through one of the processes stated

1   immediately above. By deciding to consider the question, the
assembly has already begun its involvement, and it is too late
to make an objection. But if an original main motion is finally
disposed of at one session without being adopted and is re-
5   newed at a later session, it is then a new motion and its consideration can be objected to, subject to the usual rules.

§39. DILATORY AND IMPROPER MOTIONS

10   ### Dilatory Motions

A motion is *dilatory* if it seeks to obstruct or thwart the
will of the assembly as clearly indicated by the existing parliamentary situation.
15   Parliamentary forms are designed to assist in the transaction of business. Even without adopting a rule on the subject,
every deliberative assembly has the right to protect itself from
the dilatory use of these forms.
Any main or other motion that is frivolous or absurd or
20   that contains no rational proposition is dilatory and cannot
be introduced. As further examples, it is dilatory to obstruct
business by appealing from a ruling of the chair on a question
about which there cannot possibly be two reasonable opinions, by demanding a division (**29**) on a vote even when there
25   has been a full vote and the result is clear, by moving to lay
on the table the matter for which a special meeting has been
called, by constantly raising points of order and appealing
from the chair's decision on them, or by moving to adjourn
again and again when nothing has happened to justify renewal
30   of such a motion. By use of such tactics, a minority of two or
three members could bring business to a standstill.
It is the duty of the presiding officer to prevent members
from misusing the legitimate forms of motions, or abusing the
privilege of renewing certain motions, merely to obstruct busi-
35   ness. Whenever the chair becomes convinced that one or more

members are repeatedly using parliamentary forms for dilatory
purposes, he should either not recognize these members or
he should rule that such motions are out of order—but he
should never adopt such a course merely to *speed up* business,
and he should never permit his personal feelings to affect his
judgment in such cases. If the chair only *suspects* that a motion
is not made in good faith, he should give the maker of the
motion the benefit of the doubt. The chair should always be
courteous and fair, but at the same time he should be firm in
protecting the assembly from imposition.

Improper Motions

Motions that conflict with the corporate charter, constitution, or bylaws of a society, or with procedural rules prescribed by national, state, or local laws, are out of order, and
if any motion of this kind is adopted, it is null and void. Likewise, motions are out of order if they conflict with a motion
that has been adopted by the society and has been neither rescinded, nor reconsidered and rejected after adoption. Such
conflicting motions, if adopted, are null and void unless
adopted by the vote required to rescind or amend the motion
previously adopted.

Motions are also improper when they present practically
the same question as a motion previously decided at the same
session. In addition, motions are improper that conflict with,
or present practically the same question as, one still within
the control of the society because not finally disposed of (see
pp. 90–91, 340–41). If a conflicting motion were allowed in
such cases, it would interfere with the freedom of the assembly in acting on the earlier motion when its consideration is
resumed.

No motion can be introduced that is outside the object
of the society or assembly as defined in the bylaws (see
p. 571), unless by a two-thirds vote the body agrees to its

1 consideration. Except as may be necessary in the case of a motion of censure or a motion related to disciplinary procedures
(**61, 63**), a motion must not use language that reflects on a
member's conduct or character, or is discourteous, unneces-
5 sarily harsh, or not allowed in debate (see **43**).

XI

QUORUM; ORDER OF BUSINESS AND RELATED CONCEPTS

§40. QUORUM

As indicated on page 21, a quorum in an assembly is the number of members (see definition, p. 3) who must be present in order that business can be validly transacted. The quorum refers to the number of members present, not to the number actually voting on a particular question.

Rules Pertaining to the Quorum

NUMBER OF MEMBERS CONSTITUTING A QUORUM. Depending on the organization and the provision it adopts in this regard, the number of members constituting a quorum may vary. As discussed below, most voluntary societies should provide for a quorum in their bylaws, but where there is no such provision, the quorum, in accordance with the common parliamentary law, is as follows:

1) In a mass meeting, the quorum is simply the number of persons present at the time, since they constitute the entire membership at that time.

2) In organizations such as many churches or some societies in which there are no required or effective annual dues and the register of members is not generally reliable as a list of the bona-fide members, the quorum at any regular or properly called meeting consists of those who attend.

3) In a body of delegates, such as a convention, the quorum is a majority of the number who have been registered as attending, irrespective of whether some may have departed. This may differ greatly from the number elected or appointed.

4) In any other deliberative assembly with enrolled membership whose bylaws do not specify a quorum, the quorum is a majority of all the members.

To accomplish their work, voluntary societies that have an enrolled membership generally need a provision in their bylaws establishing a relatively small quorum—considerably less than a majority of all the members. In most such organizations, it is rarely possible to obtain the attendance of a majority of the membership at a meeting. Sometimes the specification of a quorum is based on a percentage of the membership; but such a method has the disadvantage of requiring recomputation and may lead to confusion—for example, when the secretary, or other officer who is in a position to certify as to the current number of members for purposes of the percentage calculation, is absent. There is no single number or percentage of members that will be equally suitable as a quorum in all societies. The quorum should be as large a number of members as can reasonably be depended on to be present at any meeting, except in very bad weather or other exceptionally unfavorable conditions.

NOTE ON PROCEDURE IN CHANGING THE QUORUM PROVISION IN BYLAWS.   If it becomes necessary to change the quorum provision in a society's bylaws, care should be taken, because if the rule is struck out first, the quorum will instantly become a majority of the membership, so that in many cases a quorum could not be obtained to adopt a new rule. The proper procedure is to strike out the old provision and insert the new provision, which is moved and voted on as one question.

QUORUM IN BOARDS AND COMMITTEES.   In a committee of the whole or its variations (**52**), the quorum is the same as in the assembly unless the rules of the assembly or the organization (that is, either its bylaws or its rules of order) specify otherwise. In all other committees and in boards, the quorum is a majority of the members of the board or committee unless a different quorum is provided for: (a) by the bylaws, in the case of a board or standing committee that the bylaws specifically establish; or (b) by a rule of the parent body or organization or by the motion establishing the particular committee, in the case of a committee that is not expressly established by the bylaws.

PROCEEDINGS IN THE ABSENCE OF A QUORUM.   In the absence of a quorum, any business transacted (except for the procedural actions noted in the next paragraph) is null and void. But if a quorum fails to appear at a regular or properly called meeting, the inability to transact business does not detract from the fact that the society's rules requiring the meeting to be held were complied with and the meeting was convened—even though it had to adjourn immediately.

Even in the absence of a quorum, the assembly may fix the time to which to adjourn (**22**), adjourn (**21**), recess (**20**), or take measures to obtain a quorum. Subsidiary and incidental motions, questions of privilege, motions to *Raise a Question of Privilege* or *Call for the Orders of the Day*, and other motions may also be considered if they are related to

1   these motions or to the conduct of the meeting while it remains without a quorum.

A motion that absent members be contacted during a recess would represent a measure to obtain a quorum. A mo-
5   tion to obtain a quorum may be moved as a main motion
when no business is pending, or as a privileged motion that
takes precedence over a motion to *Recess* (**20**). Such motions
are out of order when another has the floor; must be seconded; are debatable except when privileged; are amendable;
10 require a majority vote; and can be reconsidered. Motions to
obtain a quorum are similar to a *Call of the House,* which can
be ordered in assemblies having the power to compel attendance (see below).

The prohibition against transacting business in the ab-
15 sence of a quorum cannot be waived even by unanimous consent, and a notice (pp. 121–24) cannot be validly given. If
there is important business that should not be delayed until
the next regular meeting, the assembly should fix the time for
an adjourned meeting and then adjourn. If, instead, the
20 members present take action informally in the absence of a
quorum, they do so at their own risk. Although the assembly
can later ratify their action (pp. 124–25), it is under no obligation to do so.

If a committee of the whole finds itself without a quorum,
25 it can do nothing but rise and report to the assembly, which
can then proceed as described above. A quasi committee of
the whole or a meeting in informal consideration of a question can itself take any of the actions permitted an assembly
in the absence of a quorum, but a quasi committee of the
30 whole is thereby ended (see **52**).

Manner of Enforcing the Quorum Requirement

Before the presiding officer calls a meeting to order, it is
35 his duty to determine, although he need not announce, that

a quorum is present. If a quorum is not present, the chair   *1*
waits until there is one, or until, after a reasonable time, there
appears to be no prospect that a quorum will assemble. If a
quorum cannot be obtained, the chair calls the meeting to
order, announces the absence of a quorum, and entertains a   *5*
motion to adjourn or one of the other motions allowed, as
described above.

When the chair has called a meeting to order after finding
that a quorum is present, the continued presence of a quorum
is presumed unless the chair or a member notices that a quo-   *10*
rum is no longer present. If the chair notices the absence of
a quorum, it is his duty to declare the fact, at least before taking any vote or stating the question on any new motion—
which he can no longer do except in connection with the
permissible proceedings related to the absence of a quorum,   *15*
as explained above. Any member noticing the apparent absence of a quorum can make a point of order to that effect at
any time so long as he does not interrupt a person who is
speaking. *Debate* on a question already pending can be
allowed to continue at length after a quorum is no longer   *20*
present, however, until a member raises the point. Because of
the difficulty likely to be encountered in determining exactly
how long the meeting has been without a quorum in such
cases, a point of order relating to the absence of a quorum is
generally not permitted to affect prior action; but upon clear *25*
and convincing proof, such a point of order can be given
effect retrospectively by a ruling of the presiding officer, subject to appeal (**24**).*

---

*What happens to a question that is pending when a meeting adjourns
(because of the loss of a quorum or for any other reason) is determined by
the rules given on pages 236–37. If such a question, however, was introduced
as new business and it is proven that there was already no quorum when it
was introduced, its introduction was invalid and, to be considered at a later
meeting, it must again be brought up as new business.

Call of the House

In legislative bodies or other assemblies that have legal power to compel the attendance of their members, a procedure that can be used to obtain a quorum, if necessary, is the motion for a *Call of the House*. This is a motion that unexcused absent members be brought to the meeting under arrest. A *Call of the House* is not applicable in voluntary societies.

Assemblies in which there may be occasion to order a *Call of the House* should adopt a rule governing this motion and providing that if one third, one fifth, or some other number less than a majority of the members or members-elect are present, they can order a *Call of the House* by a majority vote. When a quorum is not present, this motion should take precedence over everything except a motion to *Adjourn* (**21**). If the rule allows the call to be moved while a quorum is actually present (for the purpose of obtaining a *greater* attendance), the motion at such times should rank only with questions of privilege, should require a majority vote for adoption, and, if rejected, should not be allowed to be renewed while a quorum is present.

When a *Call of the House* is ordered, the clerk calls the roll of the members, then calls again the names of the absentees—in whose behalf explanations of absence can be made and excuses can be requested. After this, no member is permitted to leave, the doors are locked, and the sergeant-at-arms, chief of police, or other arresting officer is ordered to take into custody absentees who have not been excused from attendance and bring them before the house. He does this on a warrant signed by the presiding officer and attested by the clerk. When arrested members are brought in, they are arraigned separately, their explanations are heard, and, on motion, they can be excused with or without penalty in the form of pay-

ment of a fee. Until a member has paid such a fee assessed   1
against him, he cannot vote or be recognized by the chair for
any purpose.

After a *Call of the House* has been ordered, no motion is
in order, even by unanimous consent, except motions relating   5
to the call. Motions to adjourn or dispense with further proceedings under the call, however, can be entertained after a
quorum is present, or after the arresting officer reports that
in his opinion a quorum cannot be obtained. An adjournment
terminates all proceedings under the *Call of the House*.   10

§41. ORDER OF BUSINESS; ORDERS
OF THE DAY; AGENDA OR PROGRAM
                                                                 15

The terms *order of business, orders of the day, agenda,*
and *program* refer to closely related concepts having to do
with the order in which business is taken up in a session (**8**)
and the scheduling of particular business. The meaning of
these terms often coincides, although each has its own appli-   20
cations in common usage.

An *order of business* is any established sequence in which
it may be prescribed that business shall be taken up at a
session of a given assembly. In the case of ordinary societies
that hold frequent regular meetings, an order of business that 25
specifies such a sequence only in terms of certain general types
or classes of business and gives only the *order* in which they
are to be taken up is normally prescribed for all regular meetings by the rules of the organization. The typical order of
business of this kind is described on pages 353–60. In other   30
cases, such as in a convention, an order of business expressly
adopted for a particular session frequently assigns positions, and even times, to specific subjects or items of business;
and to this type of order of business the terms *agenda* and

1 *program** are applicable, as explained on pages 371–75.
Although the terms *order of business, agenda,* and *program* relate primarily to the business of an entire session, the same
terms are also applied to a part of the whole, in speaking of
5 "the order of business," "the agenda," or "the program"
of a meeting within a session.

An *order of the day* is an item of business that is scheduled
to be taken up during a given session, day, or meeting, or at
a given hour (unless there is business having precedence over
10 it that interferes). The methods by which orders of the day
can be made, their division into the classes of *general orders*
and *special orders,* and their treatment in cases where they
come into conflict are explained on pages 364ff. General orders and special orders are also discussed with particular ref-
15 erence to making them by means of the motion to *Postpone*
on pages 185–88 (see also *Call for the Orders of the Day,* **18**).
Unless designated for particular hours or assigned positions
item by item in an agenda or program formally adopted for a
given session, general orders and special orders are taken up
20 under assigned headings or in customary positions allotted to
each of these categories in the order of business. (Note such
headings in the "standard" order of business described
below.)

Within a meeting in which the only items of business that
25 are in order have been specified and set in sequence in advance—as might occur, for example, in a particular meeting
of a convention—the orders of the day are identical with the

---

*The term *program* has two senses in parliamentary usage. In the first
sense, as used here, it refers to a type of order of business that may be identical
with an agenda, or (in a convention) may include an agenda together with
the times for events outside of the business meetings (see also **59**). In the second sense, as used on page 362, the term refers to a heading, often included
within the order of business for meetings of ordinary societies, that covers
talks, lectures, films, or other features of informational or entertainment value.

order of business (which, in such a case, is in the form of an
agenda or program).

Usual Order of Business in Ordinary Societies

BASIC HEADINGS COVERING BUSINESS PROPER.
The customary or "standard" order of business comprises the
following subdivisions:

1) Reading and Approval of Minutes
2) Reports of Officers, Boards, and Standing Committees
3) Reports of Special (Select or Ad Hoc) Committees
4) Special Orders
5) Unfinished Business and General Orders
6) New Business

In organizations that have adopted this book as parliamentary authority and that have not adopted a special order of business, this series of headings is the prescribed order of business for regular meetings, unless the periods intervening between consecutive regular meetings are usually more than a quarterly time interval (see pp. 89–90). This standard order of business prescribes only the sequence of the headings, not the time to be allotted to each—which may vary with every meeting. Certain optional headings are also described following the detailed discussion of the regular headings below.

The presiding officer may find it helpful to have at hand a memorandum of the complete order of business, listing, under headings (2) and (3) as explained below, all known reports which are expected to be presented, and under headings (4) and (5), all matters which the minutes show are due to come up, arranged in proper sequence or, where applicable, listed with the times for which they have been set. The secretary can prepare, or assist the presiding officer to prepare, such a memorandum. In this connection, regarding the

1   practice in some societies or assemblies of providing each
    member with a copy of the expected agenda in advance of a
    meeting, see page 372.

         After the presiding officer has called the meeting to order
5   as described on page 25, and after any customary opening
    ceremonies (see *Optional Headings*, pp. 360–61), the meet-
    ing proceeds through the different headings in the order of
    business:

         1. Reading and Approval of Minutes.   The chair says,
10 "The Secretary will read the minutes." However, in organi-
    zations where copies of the minutes of each previous meeting
    as prepared by the secretary are sent to all members in ad-
    vance, the chair announces that this has been done, and the
    actual reading of them aloud is omitted unless any member
15 then requests that they be read. (For "dispensing" with the
    reading of the minutes—that is, not reading them for ap-
    proval *at the regular time*—see p. 474.) If for any reason there
    are minutes of other meetings in addition to the last meeting
    that have not been read previously, they are each read and
20 approved first, in order of date from earliest to latest. In all
    but the smallest meetings, the secretary stands while reading
    the minutes.

         A formal motion to approve the minutes is not necessary,
    although such a motion is not out of order. After the minutes
25 have been read (or after their reading has been omitted by
    unanimous consent as described in the previous paragraph),
    and whether or not a motion for approval has been offered,
    the chair asks, "Are there any corrections to the minutes?"
    and pauses. Corrections, when proposed, are usually handled
30 by unanimous consent (pp. 54–56), but if any member ob-
    jects to a proposed correction—which is, in effect, a subsidiary
    motion to *Amend*—the usual rules governing consideration
    of amendments to a main motion are applicable (see **12**).

         After any proposed corrections have been disposed of,
35 and when there is no response to the chair's inquiry, "Are

there any corrections [or "further corrections"] to the min-   *1*
utes?" the chair says, "There being no corrections [or "no
further corrections"] to the minutes, the minutes stand [or
"are"] approved [or "approved as read," or "approved as corrected"]." The minutes are thus approved without any for-   *5*
mal vote, even if a motion for their approval has been made.
The only proper way to object to the approval of the secretary's draft of the minutes is to offer a correction to it. It
should be noted that a member's absence from the meeting
for which minutes are being approved does not prevent the   *10*
member from participating in their correction or approval.

The practice of sending to all members advance copies of
the minutes as drafted by the secretary has both advantages
and disadvantages. It is natural for the members to prefer to
study the minutes beforehand to be better prepared to offer   *15*
corrections; and this procedure generally saves time when the
minutes come up for approval. On the other hand, the minutes do not become *the* minutes and assume their essential
status as the official record of the proceedings of the society
until they have been approved; and before this happens, the   *20*
secretary's draft may be materially modified in the correction
process. Members may miss some of the corrections or neglect to mark them on their copies—or may not get them right
unless the chair repeats them very carefully—with the result
that many inaccurate copies of the true minutes as finally ap-   *25*
proved are likely to remain in existence. Only the secretary's
corrected copy or a retyping of it is official in such a case.

2. *Reports of Officers, Boards, and Standing Committees.*
In most societies it is customary to hear reports from all
officers (**47**, **48**), boards (**49**), and standing committees (**50**)   *30*
only at annual meetings. At other meetings the chair calls only
on those who have reports to make, as by saying (in calling
upon the secretary), "Is there any correspondence?" Or,
"May we have the Treasurer's report." Or, "The chair recognizes Mr. Downey, Chairman of the Membership Committee,   *35*

1   for a report." If the chair is uncertain, he may ask, for example, "Does the Program Committee have a report?" *Standing committees* listed in the bylaws are called upon in the order in which they are listed.

5   If an officer, in reporting, makes a recommendation, he should not himself move its implementation, but such a motion can be made by another member as soon as the officer has concluded his report. In the case of a committee report, on the other hand, the chairman or other reporting member

10   should make any motion(s) necessary to bring the committee's recommendations before the assembly for consideration. A motion arising out of an officer's, a board's, or a committee's report is taken up immediately, since the object of the order of business is to give priority to the classes of business

15   in the order listed.

       If an item of business in this class is on the table (that is, if it was laid on the table at the present session, or at the preceding session if no more than a quarterly time interval has intervened [see pp. 89–90], and if the item has not been

20   taken from the table), it is in order to move to take such business from the table under this heading (see **17**, **34**).

       (For procedures to be followed in making reports and in handling recommendations arising from reports, see **51**.)

       3. Reports of Special Committees.   The special committees

25   (**50**) that are to report are called on in the order in which they were appointed. Only those special committees that are prepared, or were instructed, to report on matters referred to them should be called on. Business incident to reports of special committees that is on the table can be taken from the

30   table under this heading (**17**, **34**).

       4. Special Orders.   Under this heading (referring to the explanation of *Orders of the Day* beginning on p. 364) are taken up the following in the order listed:

35   a) Any unfinished special orders (that is, special orders that were not disposed of at the preceding meeting)—

taken in sequence beginning with the special order
that was pending when that meeting adjourned if it
adjourned while one was pending, and continuing with
the remaining unfinished special orders in the order in
which they were made (that is, were set by action of the
assembly).

b) Items of business that have been made special orders for
the present meeting* without being set for specific
hours—taken in the order in which they were made.

Regarding the interruption of business under this heading by
special orders that have been set for particular hours, see
pages 369–70.

Normally—unless an order of the day was made as a part
of an agenda for a session—no motion is necessary at the time
the order comes up, since the introduction of the question
has been accomplished previously, as will be seen from the
description of the methods by which orders of the day are
made, on page 365. When a special order that was so introduced comes up, the chair announces it as pending, thus: "At
the last meeting, the resolution relating to funds for a new
playground was made a special order for this meeting [or, if
the special order was made by postponement, ". . . was postponed to this meeting and made a special order."]. The resolution is as follows: '*Resolved,* That . . . [reading it].' The
question is on the adoption of the resolution."

Matters that the bylaws require to be considered at a particular meeting, such as the nomination and election of officers, may be regarded as special orders for the meeting and
be considered under the heading of *Special Orders* in the
order of business. If a special order is on the table, it is
in order to move to take it from the table under this heading
when no question is pending (**17**, **34**).

---

*But not *the* special order (see p. 371).

5. *Unfinished Business and General Orders.* The term *unfinished business,** in cases where the regular business meetings of an organization are not separated by more than a quarterly time interval (pp. 89–90), refers to questions that have come over from the previous meeting (other than special orders) as a result of that meeting's having adjourned without completing its order of business (pp. 236–37) and without scheduling an adjourned meeting (**9, 22**) to complete it.

A *general order* (as explained under *Orders of the Day,* below) is any question which, usually by postponement, has been made an order of the day without being made a special order.

The heading of *Unfinished Business and General Orders* includes items of business in the four categories that are listed below in the order in which they are taken up. Of these, the first three constitute "Unfinished Business," while the fourth consists of "General Orders":

a) The question that was pending when the previous meeting adjourned, if that meeting adjourned while a question other than a special order was pending.

b) Any questions that were unfinished business at the previous meeting but were not reached before it adjourned—taken in the order in which they were due to come up at that meeting as indicated under (a) and (c).

c) Any questions which, by postponement or otherwise, were set as general orders for the previous meeting, or for a particular hour during that meeting, but were not reached before it adjourned—taken in the order in which the general orders were made.

---

*The expression "old business" should be avoided, since it may incorrectly suggest the further consideration of matters that have been finally disposed of.

d) Matters that were postponed to, or otherwise made gen-   *1*
eral orders for, the present meeting—taken in the order
in which they were made.

Regarding the relationship between this heading in the order   *5*
of business and general orders for particular hours, see pages
367–69.

The chair should not announce the heading of *Unfinished
Business and General Orders* unless the minutes show that
there is some business to come up under it. In the latter case,   *10*
he should have all such subjects listed in correct sequence in
a memorandum prepared in advance of the meeting. He
should *not* ask, "Is there any unfinished business?" but should
state the question on the first item of business that is due to
come up under this heading; and when it has been disposed   *15*
of, he should proceed through the remaining subjects in their
proper order. If a question was pending when the previous
meeting adjourned, for example, the chair might begin this
heading by saying, "Under Unfinished Business and General
Orders, the first item of business is the motion relating to use   *20*
of the parking facilities, which was pending when the last
meeting adjourned. The question is on the adoption of the
motion 'That . . . [stating the motion].'" Later under the same
heading, in announcing a general order that was made by
postponing a question, the chair might say, "The next item of   *25*
business is the resolution relating to proposed improvement
of our newly purchased picnic grounds, which was postponed
to this meeting. The resolution is as follows: '*Resolved,* That
. . . [reading the resolution].' The question is on the adoption
of the resolution."   *30*

Any item of business (in whatever class) that is on the
table can be taken from the table under this heading at any
time when no question is pending (**17**, **34**). To obtain the
floor for the purpose of moving to take a question from
the table at such a time, a member can rise and address the   *35*

1   chair, interrupting him as he starts to announce the next item
      of business after the previous one is disposed of.

           It should be noted that, with the exception indicated in
      the preceding paragraph, a subject should not be taken up
5   under Unfinished Business and General Orders unless it has
      acquired such status by one of the formal processes (a), (c),
      or (d) listed on pages 358–59. If brief consultation during a
      meeting leads to an informal understanding that a certain
      subject should be "brought up at the next meeting," that
10   does not make it unfinished business. Instead, the matter
      should be introduced at the next meeting as new business, as
      explained below.

           6. *New Business.*   After unfinished business and general
      orders have been disposed of, the chair asks, "Is there any
15   new business?" Members can then introduce new items of
      business, or can move to take from the table any matter
      that is on the table (**17**, **34**), in the order in which they are
      able to obtain the floor when no question is pending, as ex-
      plained in **3** and **4**. So long as members are reasonably
20   prompt in claiming the floor, the chair cannot prevent the
      making of legitimate motions or deprive members of the right
      to introduce legitimate business, by hurrying through the
      proceedings.

25   OPTIONAL HEADINGS.   In addition to the standard
      order of business as just described, regular meetings of organ-
      izations sometimes include proceedings in the categories
      listed below, which may be regarded as optional in the order
      of business prescribed by this book.

30   After the call to order and *before the reading of the min-
      utes,* the next two headings may be included:

           Opening Ceremonies or Exercises.   Opening ceremonies
      immediately after the meeting is called to order may include
      the Invocation (which, if offered, should always be placed
35   first), the singing of the National Anthem, the reciting of the

Pledge of Allegiance to the flag, a ritual briefly recalling the objects or ideals of the organization, or the like.

Roll Call. In some organizations it is customary at meetings to call the roll of officers in order to verify their attendance—or, sometimes in very small societies, even to call the roll of members. If there is a roll call of this nature, it should take place at the end of the opening ceremonies unless a special rule of the organization assigns it a different position in the order of business. The chair announces it by saying, "The Secretary will call the roll of officers [or "will call the roll"]."

Consent Calendar. Legislatures, city, town, or county councils, or other assemblies which have a heavy work load including a large number of routine or noncontroversial matters may find a *consent calendar* a useful tool for disposing of such items of business. Commonly, when such a matter has been introduced or reported by a committee for consideration in the assembly, its sponsor, or, sometimes, an administrator, may seek to have it placed on the consent calendar. This calendar is called over periodically *at a point established in the agenda by special rule of order, at least preceding standing committee reports.* The matters listed on it are taken up in order, unless objected to, in which case they are restored to the ordinary process by which they are placed in line for consideration on the regular agenda. The special rule of order establishing a consent calendar may provide that, when the matters on the calendar are called up, they may be considered in gross or without debate or amendment. Otherwise, they are considered under the rules just as any other business, in which case the "consent" relates only to permitting the matter to be on the calendar for consideration without conforming to the usual, more onerous, rules for reaching measures in the body.

After the completion of new business—that is, when no one claims the floor to make a motion in response to the chair's query, "Is there any further new business?"—the chair may

1   proceed to one or more of the following headings, in an order
that may be subject to variation determined by the practice
of the organization.

Good of the Order, General Good and Welfare, or Open
5   *Forum.*   This heading, included by some types of societies
in their order of business, refers to the general welfare of the
organization, and may vary in character. Under this heading
(in contrast to the general parliamentary rule that allows discussion only with reference to a pending motion), members
10   who obtain the floor commonly are permitted to offer informal observations regarding the work of the organization,
the public reputation of the society or its membership, or the
like. Certain types of announcements may tend to fall here.
Although the Good of the Order often involves no business
15   or motions, the practice of some organizations would place
motions or resolutions relating to formal disciplinary procedures for offenses outside a meeting (**63**) at this point. In
some organizations, the program (see below) is looked upon
as a part of the Good of the Order.

20   *Announcements.*   The chair may make, or call upon other
officers or members to make, any necessary announcements;
or, if the practice of the organization permits it, members can
briefly obtain the floor for such a purpose. The placing of
general announcements at this point in the order of business
25   does not prevent the chair from making an urgent announcement at any time.

Program.   If there is to be a talk, film, or other program
of a cultural, educational, or civic nature, it is usually presented
before the meeting is adjourned, since it may prompt a desire
30   on the part of the assembly to take action. Although the program is commonly placed at the end of the order of business
in such cases, it can, by special rule or practice, be received
before the minutes are read; or, by suspending the rules (**25**),
it can be proceeded to at any time during the meeting. If, in
35   courtesy to a guest speaker who is present, the chair wishes

the talk to be located at an unscheduled point within the business portion of the meeting, he can usually obtain unanimous consent for a suspension of the rules by simply announcing, "If there is no objection, we will hear our speaker's address at this time."

Taking Up Business Out of Its Proper Order

Any particular item of business can be taken up out of its proper order by adopting a motion to suspend the rules (**25**) by a two-thirds vote, although this is usually arranged by unanimous consent (pp. 54–56). Hence, an important committee report or an urgent item of new business can be advanced in order to assure its full and unhurried consideration. If desired, before the completion of the advanced question the regular order of business can be returned to by a majority vote—by adopting a motion to lay the pending question on the table (**17**).

To take up a motion out of its proper order—for example, to introduce an item of new business before that heading is reached—a member who has obtained the floor can say, "I ask unanimous consent to introduce at this time a resolution on financing better schools." If there is any objection, or the member anticipates that there may be, he can say, "I move to suspend the rules that interfere with the introduction at this time of . . ." If unanimous consent is given or if this motion is adopted by a two-thirds vote, the member is immediately recognized to introduce the resolution. If only one or two items stand ahead of the item it is desired to reach, it may be just as simple to lay the intervening items on the table individually (**17**), or to postpone them as they arise (**14**). It is not in order to lay on the table or postpone a *class* of questions, like committee reports, or anything but the question that is actually before the assembly. (See pp. 184–85, 211, 215.)

1   The chair himself cannot depart from the prescribed order
of business, which only the assembly can do by at least a two-
thirds vote. This is an important protection in cases where
some of the members principally involved in a particular ques-
5 tion may be unable to be present through an entire meeting.
When such a departure from the order of business is justified,
however, it is usually easy for the chair to obtain the necessary
authorization from the assembly. He can say, for example,
"The chair will entertain a motion to suspend the rules, and
10 take up . . . "; or (for obtaining unanimous consent), "If there
is no objection, the chair proposes at this time to proceed to
take up . . . " (see also illustration under the heading *Program*
above).

15   **Orders of the Day**

An *order of the day,* as stated above, is a particular subject,
question, or item of business that is set in advance to be taken
up during a given session, day, or meeting, or at a given hour,
20 provided that no business having precedence over it interferes. In cases where more than a quarterly time interval
(pp. 89–90) will elapse before the next regular business session of the organization, an order of the day cannot be made
for a time beyond the end of the present session. If the next
25 regular business session will be held within a quarterly time
interval, an order of the day cannot be made beyond the end
of that next session. An order of the day cannot be taken up
before the time for which it is set, except by reconsidering
(**37**) the vote that established the order (so long as a recon-
30 sideration is possible), or by suspending the rules (**25**) by a
two-thirds vote.

Orders of the day are divided into the classes of *general
orders* and *special orders.* A special order is an order of the day
that is made with the stipulation that any rules interfering
35 with its consideration at the specified time shall be suspended

except those relating: (a) to adjournment or recess (**8, 20, 21**); (b) to questions of privilege (**19**); (c) to special orders that were made before this special order was made; or (d) to a question that has been assigned priority over all other business at a meeting by being made *the* special order for the meeting as described on page 371. An important consequence of this suspending effect is that, with the four exceptions just mentioned, a special order for a particular hour interrupts any business that is pending when that hour arrives. Since the making of a special order has the effect of suspending any interfering rules, it requires a two-thirds vote (except where such action is included in the adoption of an agenda or program for a session having no prescribed order of business). Any matter that is made an order of the day without being made a special order is a general order for the time named.

An item of business can be made an order of the day in the following ways:

1) While the question is pending, it can be postponed (**14**) to the specified time by a majority vote (in which case it is a general order); or, by a two-thirds vote, it can be postponed to that time and made a special order.

2) A question that has not yet been brought before the assembly can be made a special order for a future time by means of a main motion adopted by a two-thirds vote. Similarly, it is possible, although less common, to make a question that is not pending a general order for a future time by a majority vote.

3) An agenda or program assigning a specific position or hour to the item of business can be adopted. The subject is then a general order or a special order, depending on the form of the agenda or program (see p. 371). For the vote required to adopt an agenda, see *Procedure for Adoption*, page 372.

1   FORMS FOR MOTIONS TO MAKE GENERAL OR
SPECIAL ORDERS.   The forms in proposing to make
a *pending* question an order of the day for a future time
by means of the motion to *Postpone* are given on pages
5   189–90.
When a question that is *not pending* is made an order of
the day, it is usually made a special order. A main motion to
make a particular subject a special order can be introduced
whenever business of its class or new business is in order and
10   nothing is pending. It can be offered in this form: "I move
that the following resolution be made a special order for the
next meeting: '*Resolved,* That . . .'"; or, "I offer the following
resolution and move that it be made a special order for 3 P.M.:
'. . .'" In the case of a committee report, a resolution such as
15   this may be adopted: "*Resolved,* That the report of the committee on the revision of the bylaws be made the special order
for Wednesday morning and thereafter until it has been disposed of."
Motions in similar forms can also be used to make a ques-
20   tion that is not pending a general order. In this connection,
however, it should be noted that a majority can thus prevent
a matter from coming before the assembly until a future time,
but after a majority has taken such action, nothing less than
a two-thirds vote can change it unless it is reconsidered (**37**).
25   If a main motion to make a question that is not pending
an order of the day for a future time is introduced, any member who would prefer to consider the matter immediately
should speak in debate against the motion that would make
it an order of the day. If that motion is voted down, he can
30   then introduce the subject of the proposed order as a main
question.

RELATION OF ORDERS OF THE DAY TO THE
ESTABLISHED ORDER OF BUSINESS.   In assemblies
35   that follow the "standard" order of business explained above,

orders of the day for a given session, day, or meeting that are
not set for particular hours are taken up under the headings
of *Special Orders* and *Unfinished Business and General Orders*
(see pp. 356–60). In cases where an ordinary society has
adopted its own order of business for regular meetings, it usually includes similar headings covering such orders of the day.
Where an organization's order of business does not provide
such headings, special orders not set for particular hours are
taken up before unfinished business and general orders, or (if
there are neither of these), at all events before new business.
Under the same conditions, general orders are taken up after
any unfinished business (that is, business pending at the adjournment of the previous meeting, if any, and orders of
the day not disposed of at the time of its adjournment), and
before new business unless a later hour is specified (see
below).

The most common instances of orders of the day set for
particular hours occur in conventions.

In any type of assembly, in cases where orders of the
day have been set for particular hours, their consideration
at the proper time may cause interruption or modification
of the order of business as it exists apart from these orders of
the day; and different orders of the day may come into conflict. Rules governing such cases are as follows:

Rules of Precedence Affecting General Orders for Particu-
lar Hours.　　As stated above, a general order that has been
set for a particular hour cannot be considered before that
hour unless the rules are suspended by a two-thirds vote, or
unless the vote that made the general order can still be reconsidered. This is the principal effect of making a subject a
general order for a particular hour. Since the making of a general order does not suspend any rules, even if it is designated
for a particular hour, delay in its consideration when that hour
arrives may arise from a number of causes. Even though the
hour fixed for a general order has arrived, the order can be

1 taken up only when all of the following additional conditions
   are fulfilled:

   a) no other business is pending;
5 b) the category of General Orders in the prescribed order of
       business has been reached or passed;
   c) no special order interferes;
   d) no reconsideration (**37**) that may then be moved or called
       up interferes; and
10 e) no general order made before this order was made re-
       mains undisposed of, unless such other general order was
       set for a time that has not yet arrived.

   As soon after the designated hour as conditions (a), (b), (c),
15 and (e) are met, the chair should announce the general order
   as the pending business; but as he starts to do so, any member
   can rise and address the chair for the purpose of moving or
   calling up a reconsideration.
       The rule that a general order for a particular hour does
20 not interrupt a pending question when that hour arrives holds
   even when the pending question is a general order that was
   made later.* But if a general order for an earlier time is not
   reached by the time set for another general order that was
   made before it was, the general order that was made first is
25 taken up in preference to the one for the earlier time.
       Example.   A motion is postponed to 4:30 P.M. Later, an-
   other motion is postponed to 4:15 P.M. If the 4:15 motion is
   taken up at that time (or at least before 4:30) and is not disposed of by 4:30, it continues under consideration and is not
30 interrupted. But if the 4:15 motion is not reached by 4:30,
   the 4:30 motion, having been postponed first, has preference

---

*If it is desired to take up a general order at its specified hour and a pend-
ing question interferes, that pending question can, however, be laid on the
table (**17**) or postponed (**14**).

and will be taken up first. Unless something else affects the
situation, the 4:15 motion in such a case will be considered
after the disposal of the 4:30 motion.

If several general orders were made for the same time,
they are taken up in the order in which they were made. If
several general orders were made for the same time in the
same motion, they are taken up in the order in which they
are listed in the motion. If all of this business is not disposed
of before adjournment, it is treated as described on pages
236–37 and 358–59.

*Rules of Precedence Affecting Special Orders for Particular
Hours.*   A special order for a particular hour cannot be considered before that hour except by a two-thirds vote. But
when the designated hour arrives, the special order automatically interrupts any business that may be pending except:
(a) a motion relating to adjournment or recess; (b) a question
of privilege; (c) a special order that was made before the special order set for the present hour was made; or (d) *the* special
order for a meeting, as described below. The chair simply
announces the special order at the proper time, as shown on
page 191.

With the exception of *the* special order for a meeting,
when special orders that have been made at different times
come into conflict, the one that was made first takes precedence over all special orders made afterward, which rank in
the order in which they were made. This rule holds even
when special orders made later have been set for consideration
at earlier hours. No special order can interfere with one that
was made earlier than itself. If several special orders have been
made at the same time for the same hour, they rank in the
order in which they are listed in the motion by which they
were made. If they were made at the same time for different
hours, each has preference at the hour set for its consideration
and interrupts the pending question, even if that pending
question is a special order.

1   *Example.*   Assume that a special order has been made for 3 P.M. Thereafter, one is made for 2 P.M. Still later, one is made for 4 P.M. At two o'clock, the special order for that time is taken up, even if it interrupts a general order that is pending.

5   However, if the 2 P.M. special order is still pending at 3 P.M., the 3 P.M. special order is immediately taken up—interrupting the one that is pending—because it was made first. Also, because the 3 P.M. order was made first, if it is still under consideration at four o'clock, it continues regardless of the order

10   for that time. Even after the 3 P.M. order is disposed of, the 4 P.M. order must await completion of the prior-made 2 P.M. order, which is resumed first. Not until all of these special orders are disposed of, together with any others whose times are reached in the meantime, can the assembly return to its

15   regular order of business, first resuming consideration of any subject that may have been interrupted at 2 P.M. It is possible, of course, to rearrange these special orders by reconsidering the votes that made them, or, if reconsideration is no longer possible (**37**), by suspending the rules and taking up each one

20   of them in succession, only to postpone it and make it a special order for the desired new time. When a series of special orders has been made at the same time in one motion, it is implied that the vote on each one will be taken when the hour for the next special order arrives, but if this is not done the

25   pending special order is interrupted by its successor.

It should be noted that a special order does not interfere with a recess or adjournment that is scheduled for a particular hour. When such an hour arrives, the chair announces it and declares the assembly in recess or adjourned, even if a special

30   order is pending that was made before the hour of recess or adjournment was fixed. When the chair announces the hour, anyone can move to postpone the time for adjournment, or to extend the time of considering the pending question for a specified period. These motions are undebatable and require

35   a two-thirds vote (see also pp. 232, 240–41).

The Special Order for a Meeting. When it is desired to devote an entire meeting to a subject, or as much of the meeting as may be necessary, the matter can be made *the* special order for the meeting (as distinguished from *a* special order for the meeting; see pp. 356–57). *The* special order for the meeting will then be taken up as soon as the minutes have been approved, and the remainder of the order of business will not be taken up until this special order has been disposed of. Although *the* special order for a meeting takes precedence over all other forms of special orders, even if they were made before it was, the times of any such orders for particular hours that may come into conflict should be adjusted, as indicated on page 370, lines 16–21.

Agenda or Program

By a single vote, a series of special orders or general orders—or a mixture of both—can be made; such a series is called an *agenda*. When an hour is assigned to a particular subject in an agenda, that subject is thereby made a special order unless, by footnote or other means, it is stated that the time is intended merely for guidance, in which case the subject is only a general order. Subjects for which no hour is specified in an agenda are general orders.

In an agenda, often an hour is assigned only to such subjects as the calls to order, recesses, adjournments, and particularly important items of business where it is desired to give the members greater assurance that the matter will not be considered before that time. These, then, are special orders for the time stated, and a strict adherence to these times provides a protection to the members and invited speakers, who often come from great distances. Occasionally, a time is assigned for every item on the agenda. While this practice may be necessary in some cases, the resulting loss of flexibility often outweighs any benefits that may be gained.

1   ORGANIZATIONS AND MEETINGS IN WHICH
       ADOPTION OF AN AGENDA IS CUSTOMARY.   It is
       customary to adopt an agenda or program for each session in
       organizations that do not hold frequent regular meetings, and
5   at conventions and other sessions that may last for several days
       (see **59**). This is also frequently done when, for any reason,
       neither the standard order of business nor a special order of
       business established by rule of the organization is practical or
       applicable.
10

       PROCEDURE FOR ADOPTION.   In cases in which
       an agenda is adopted, usually this is done at the outset of a
       session and the agenda is intended to cover the entire session.
       At a session having no prescribed or adopted order of busi-
15   ness, such an agenda is followed as a guide by the chair pend-
       ing its formal adoption and can be adopted by majority vote,
       even if it contains special orders; it is then the order of busi-
       ness for that session. At a session that already has an order of
       business, an agenda can be adopted by a majority vote only if
20   it does not create any special orders and does not conflict with
       the existing order of business; otherwise, a two-thirds vote is
       required (see also p. 264, ll. 14–28).

       AGENDA PROVIDED IN ADVANCE.   In some or-
25   ganizations, it is customary to send each member, in advance
       of a meeting, an order of business or agenda, with some in-
       dication of the matters to be considered under each heading.
       Such an agenda is often provided for information only, with
       no intention or practice of submitting it for adoption. Unless
30   a precirculated agenda is formally adopted at the session to
       which it applies, it is not binding as to detail or order of con-
       sideration, other than as it lists preexisting orders of the day
       (pp. 364ff.) or conforms to the standard order of business
       (pp. 25–26, 353ff.) or an order of business prescribed by the
35   rules of the organization (pp. 16, 25).

CHANGING AN AGENDA.   When the adoption of a 1
proposed agenda is pending, it is subject to amendment by
majority vote. After an agenda has been adopted by the assembly, no change can be made in it except by a two-thirds
vote, a vote of a majority of the entire membership, or unan- 5
imous consent. (See also *Taking Up Business Out of Its Proper
Order*, pp. 363–64; cf. p. 630, ll. 12–17.) An affirmative vote
to adopt an agenda may not be reconsidered.

AGENDA IN THE FORM OF A PROGRAM.   In ref- 10
erence to an order of business specially adopted for a given
session, the term *program* is often used instead of *agenda*;
but while the latter technically includes only items of business,
the former may include also the times for speakers, meals, and
other nonbusiness matters. 15

TAKING UP TOPICS IN AN AGENDA.   When the
assigned time for taking up a topic in an agenda arrives,
the chair announces that fact. Then he puts to a vote any
pending questions without allowing further debate, unless 20
someone immediately moves to lay the question on the table,
postpone it, or refer it to a committee. If any of these subsidiary motions are moved, they are likewise put to a vote,
together with any amendment to them, without debate. Besides recognizing these subsidiary motions, the chair also 25
should recognize a motion to extend the time for considering
the pending question, if such a motion is made. While an extension under these conditions is seldom desirable and is
often unfair to the next topic, it is sometimes necessary, and
a motion for the extension can be adopted without debate 30
by a two-thirds vote (see also **18**). As soon as the business
that was pending has been disposed of as described, the chair
recognizes the member who is to offer the motion or resolution embodying the scheduled topic (unless the question has
previously been introduced and has come over from an earlier 35

1 time, in which case the chair announces it as the pending
business).

DECLARING A SCHEDULED RECESS OR AD-
5 JOURNMENT.   When a recess or adjournment has been
scheduled for a particular hour (either by provision in the
adopted agenda or program or by adoption of a motion setting the time) and that hour arrives, the chair announces it
and, unless a member promptly seeks the floor for one of the
10 purposes described below, declares the assembly in recess or
adjourned. (However, if the *Previous Question* has already
been ordered on one or more pending motions when the
hour for a recess or adjournment arrives, there usually will
be no objection to the chair's putting them all to a vote in
15 succession before declaring the assembly to be in recess or
adjourned.)

When the chair announces the hour, any member can
move to reschedule the time for recess or adjournment, or to
extend the time of considering the pending question for a
20 specified period. These motions are undebatable and require
a two-thirds vote; see also pages 232 and 241. Before declaring the meeting adjourned, the chair must allow, in addition
to the motions just described, any of the parliamentary steps
that would be in order when a privileged motion to *Adjourn*
25 is pending or has just been voted for (see pp. 238–40).

In the case of a recess, any pending business is interrupted
for the recess, and taken up again after the recess. In the case
of an adjournment, see *Carrying Over Unfinished Business*
below.

30

ADVISABILITY OF PROVIDING FOR UNFIN-
ISHED BUSINESS.   At intervals or near the end of the session, an agenda should include provision for unfinished
business. In agendas in which most or all of the items are spe-
35 cial orders for particular times, it may be necessary to provide

for unfinished business near the end of each day's sitting. *1*
Such provisions give the assembly a recourse whenever it
needs a little more time before voting on a question. It can
postpone a question to a time provided for unfinished business or, at all events, can conclude consideration of a question *5*
during such a period. Otherwise, a pending question that is
merely postponed until the disposal of the next item—since
it becomes only a general order—may be severely buffeted by
the remaining special orders. Its further consideration would
depend upon the next or some successive items taking less *10*
time than allotted, and it might soon be interrupted again by
the next subject for which a time was assigned.

CARRYING OVER UNFINISHED BUSINESS. In
sessions consisting of several meetings, if the time set for ad- *15*
journment of a meeting arrives before all of the matters
scheduled for that meeting have been considered, the remaining items of business are carried over to the next meeting.*
The unfinished items of business are taken first in their order
before the matters scheduled for the later meeting, provided *20*
that the agenda makes no special provision for unfinished
business that day and no conflict arises with a special order.
Therefore, when most items in the agenda are general orders,
it is wise to schedule the more important items of business at
a reasonably early meeting of a convention or to set them as *25*
special orders. (See also p. 628, ll. 24–35.)

---

*For the treatment of business unfinished at the end of a session, see
pages 236–37.

CHAPTER XII

ASSIGNMENT OF THE FLOOR; DEBATE

§42. RULES GOVERNING ASSIGNMENT OF THE FLOOR

The manner in which a member obtains the floor is described on pages 29–31, with an initial treatment of the principal rules governing the assignment of the floor under ordinary conditions in most business meetings. More complete rules affecting the assignment of the floor are contained in this section.

Recognition of a Member

Before a member in an assembly can make a motion or speak in debate, he must claim the floor by rising* and addressing the chair as described on page 29, and must be recognized by the chair. The chair must recognize any member

---

*In small boards and in committees, members generally need not rise to obtain the floor. See page 487.

who seeks the floor while entitled to it. The chair normally   1
recognizes a member (thereby assigning the floor to him) by
announcing, as applicable, the member's name or title, or the
place or unit that he represents. If necessary, the member—
either on his own initiative or at the request of the chair—   5
should state his name, with any appropriate additional
identification, as soon as the presiding officer turns toward
him after he has risen and addressed the chair. Variations in
the granting of recognition are as follows:

10

- If only one person is seeking the floor in a small meeting
  where all present can clearly see one another, the chair
  may recognize the member by merely nodding to him.
- If a speech is prearranged, or if several members are attempting to claim the floor at once in a large meeting, a   15
  wording frequently used by the chair in granting recognition is, "The chair recognizes Mr. Smith."

Whenever a member rises and addresses the chair at a time
when the floor can be granted only for limited purposes and   20
the chair is not certain that the member understands this
fact—for example, when an undebatable question is immediately pending as explained on page 380—the chair, before
recognizing the member, should ask, "For what purpose does
the member [or "the gentleman," or "the lady," or, as in   25
Congress, "the gentlewoman"] rise?" If members remain
seated around a conference table and do not rise, the chair
may ask, "For what purpose does the member address the
chair?"

Except by unanimous consent (pp. 54–56), a motion can   30
be made only by one who has been recognized by the chair
as having the floor. If a motion is called out by anyone who
has not obtained the floor, the chair should ignore it if another member, by rising promptly and claiming the floor,
shows that unanimous consent has not been given.   35

When assigned the floor, a member may use it for any proper purpose, or a combination of purposes; for example, although a member may have begun by debating a pending motion, he may conclude by moving any secondary motion, including the *Previous Question* (**16**), that is in order at the time.

Assignment of the Floor When More Than One Person Claims It

If two or more rise at about the same time to claim the floor, the general rule is that, all other things being equal, the member who rose and addressed the chair first *after the floor was yielded* is entitled to be recognized. A member who rises before the floor has been yielded is not entitled to the floor if any other member rises afterward and addresses the chair.*

Under a variety of particular conditions, however, when more than one member claims the floor at about the same time, the best interests of the assembly require the floor to be assigned to a claimant who was not the first to rise and address the chair. Such a claimant to the floor in these cases is said to be entitled to "preference in being recognized" or "preference in recognition." A member cannot rise to claim preference in recognition after the chair has actually recognized another member. However, there are a number of purposes for which a member who has been assigned the floor may be interrupted; see pages 383–85.

When the chair has just reported a vote, a member is entitled to preference in recognition to make an appropriate motion that the vote be taken again by another method (**30**). Other rules governing preference in recognition may be grouped as relating to cases when a debatable question is

---

*For modification of these rules in large assemblies, see page 383.

immediately pending, when an undebatable question is immediately pending, and when no question is pending.

PREFERENCE IN RECOGNITION WHEN A DEBATABLE QUESTION IS IMMEDIATELY PENDING.
While a motion is open to debate:

1) A member may rise to give previous notice of another motion (pp. 122–23).
2) If the member who made the motion that is immediately pending claims the floor and has not already spoken on the question, he is entitled to be recognized in preference to other members. Under some particular cases or variations of this rule, the members entitled to preference in recognition are:
   a) in the case of a motion to implement a recommendation in a committee's report, the reporting member (who presented the committee's report to the assembly);
   b) in the case of a question that has been taken from the table (**34**), the member who moved to take it from the table; and
   c) in the case of a motion to *Reconsider* (**37**), the member who *made* the motion to *Reconsider*, not necessarily the one who may have called it up (see pp. 316–17, 323).
3) No member who has already had the floor in debate on the immediately pending question is entitled to it again on the same day for debate on the same question so long as any member who has not spoken on that question claims the floor.
4) In cases where the chair knows that persons seeking the floor have opposite opinions on the question—and the member to be recognized is not determined by (1) through (3) above—the chair should let the floor

alternate, as far as possible, between those favoring and those opposing the measure. In large assemblies, various devices are sometimes used to assist the chair in following this rule, such as having members seeking recognition hold up cards of different colors, go to different microphones "for" and "against," or the like.

In the case of an *Appeal* (or a *Point of Order* that the chair has submitted to a vote) that is debatable, the chair is entitled to speak once in preference to any member seeking the floor and a second time at the close of the debate (see pp. 254, 257–58).

When a member has moved to reconsider the vote on a motion for the announced purpose of amending the motion, if the vote is reconsidered he must be recognized in preference to others in order to move his amendment. This rule also applies to reconsiderations of amendable motions that are not debatable (see list on tinted p. 43), as noted below.

PREFERENCE IN RECOGNITION WHEN AN UNDEBATABLE QUESTION IS IMMEDIATELY PENDING. When the immediately pending question is undebatable (tinted pp. 42–43), the floor can be assigned only to a member who wishes to give previous notice of a motion (pp. 121–24) or make a motion or raise a question that would take precedence over the immediately pending question. In such a case, the mover of the immediately pending question has no preference to the floor. When an undebatable motion that can be amended is reconsidered for that announced purpose, however, the maker of the motion to *Reconsider* (37) is entitled to preference in recognition, as explained in the preceding paragraph.

PREFERENCE IN RECOGNITION WHEN NO QUESTION IS PENDING. Cases where a member is

entitled to preference in recognition when no question is   *1*
pending occur as follows:

1) When a member has been assigned to offer a motion
   which a special meeting was called to consider, or an im-   *5*
   portant prearranged main motion at any meeting, that
   member is entitled to prior recognition and no other
   members should be permitted to intervene in an effort to
   offer another motion in competition.
2) When a desired object requires a series of motions, each   *10*
   of which is moved while no question is pending, and
   when the assembly has disposed of one motion in such a
   series, the next motion in the series has the right of way;
   and, for the purpose of making that motion, the chair
   should recognize the member who is presenting the   *15*
   series, even if another member has risen and addressed
   the chair first. For example:
   a) When a question has been laid on the table (**17**) for a
      legitimate purpose—to enable the assembly to take up
      a more urgent matter—the member who moved to   *20*
      lay on the table is entitled to preference in recognition
      to introduce the urgent business.
   b) When the rules have been suspended (**25**) to enable
      a certain motion to be made, the member who moved
      to suspend the rules is entitled to the floor to make   *25*
      the motion involved.
3) Similarly, when a motion has been voted down at the urg-
   ing of a member who stated in debate that in such event
   he would offer a different motion on the same subject (see p. 116), that member is entitled to preference   *30*
   in recognition so that he may introduce his alternative
   motion.
4) When no question is pending and no series of motions
   has been started, and a member has risen seeking the floor
   to make a main motion, another member is entitled to   *35*

preference in recognition if he addresses the chair and states that he rises for one of the following purposes:

a) to make a motion to *Reconsider and Enter on the Minutes* (pp. 332–35);

b) to move to reconsider a vote (**37**);

c) to call up a motion to *Reconsider* (in its regular or special form [**37**]) that has been made earlier;

d) to give previous notice (pp. 121–24); or

e) to move to take a question from the table (**34**) when it is in order to do so.

If members come into competition in rising for these purposes, they have preference in the order in which the five actions are listed above. Time limits on making the motion to *Reconsider*—and shorter limits on its special form, to *Reconsider and Enter on the Minutes*—account for first preference of these two motions in such cases.

ASSIGNMENT OF THE FLOOR BY VOTE; APPEALS.   If the chair is in doubt as to who is entitled to the floor, he can allow the assembly to decide the question by a vote, in which case the member receiving the largest vote is entitled to the floor.

If at any time the chair makes a mistake and assigns the floor to the wrong person when more than one member rose and addressed the chair promptly, a *Point of Order* can be raised. Except in a mass meeting, the decision of the chair in assigning the floor can be appealed from by any two members—one making the appeal and the other seconding it (**24**).*

---

*In a mass meeting, the chair's decision in assigning the floor is not subject to appeal. In a very large body other than a mass meeting, if the best interests of the assembly require that the chair be given greater power in assigning the floor, a special rule that there shall be no appeal from his decision in granting recognition can be adopted (see *Rules of Order,* pp. 15–17; see also, in regard to standing rules in a convention, pp. 618ff.).

VARIATIONS IN LARGE ASSEMBLIES. In large conventions or similar bodies, some of the rules applicable to the assignment of the floor may require adaptation, which, pending the adoption of appropriate convention standing rules or special rules of order, the chair may direct. For example, in a large hall where microphones are in use and members must walk some distance to reach one, members may be asked to line up at numbered microphones. They may be recognized in numerical order, or someone may list them for the chair in the order in which assistant sergeants-at-arms turned on lights affixed to the microphones. It may be provided that a member who has a priority matter, such as a point of order, may ask the assistant at the microphone to flash the light to so indicate. Should a member, called in whatever order is established, move an amendment or other debatable motion, others awaiting a turn should stand aside unless their debate is germane to the new motion. If the *Previous Question* or a motion to limit debate is moved, members who have been waiting in line cannot validly protest; as in all other cases, the chair cannot choose the occasions when such motions will be in order. He may advise the assembly that, if it wishes to continue debate and hear from those waiting in line, a minority greater than one third has this within its power.

If ushers are equipped with hand microphones and a microphone is carried to each member who is recognized, the standard rules on page 378, lines 11–17, can be followed.

Interruption of a Member Assigned the Floor

When a member has been assigned the floor and has begun to speak—unless he begins to discuss a subject when no motion is pending or speaks longer in debate than the rules of the assembly allow—he cannot be interrupted by another member or by the chair except for one of the following purposes, and then only when the urgency of the situation justifies it:

a) a *Call for the Orders of the Day* (**18**) when they are not being conformed to,
b) the raising of a question of privilege (**19**),
c) a *Point of Order* or the calling of the member who has the floor to order (**23, 61**)—or the chair's calling this member's attention to the fact that he is failing to observe the rules of speaking (pp. 645–46),
d) a call for a separate vote on one or more of a set of independent resolutions on different subjects, or a divisible set of amendments, that have been offered by a single motion (pp. 110, 274–75),
e) a request or inquiry (**32, 33**) that requires an immediate response;

or, in certain special circumstances, these additional purposes:

f) an *Appeal* (**24**),
g) an *Objection to the Consideration of a Question* (**26**), or
h) a *Division of the Assembly* (**29**).

After a member has been assigned the floor but before he has begun to speak, it is in order to take any of the steps listed above, and also, if there may be no other opportunity, to rise for the purpose of:

a) giving notice of intent to introduce a motion requiring such notice (pp. 121–24); or
b) making a motion to *Reconsider* (**37**) or to *Reconsider and Enter on the Minutes* (pp. 332–35).

If an interruption occurs for any of the reasons listed above, the member who had the floor does not lose it,

although he takes his seat while the interrupting matter is   *1*
being attended to. As soon as the interruption has been disposed of, the chair directs him to rise and proceed by saying,
for example, "Mr. Lewis has the floor."

If a member presenting a committee report or other doc-   *5*
ument to the assembly hands it to the secretary or a reading
clerk to be read, the member does not thereby yield the floor,
but has it again when the reading is finished.

When a member has risen to claim the floor or has been
assigned the floor, it is out of order for another to call out a   *10*
motion to adjourn, or a motion to lay the pending question
on the table. If someone does so, or if calls of "Question!"
are made, it is the duty of the chair to obtain order and protect the rights of the member who is entitled to the floor.

                                                                    15

§43. RULES GOVERNING DEBATE

Debate, rightly understood, is an essential element in the
making of rational decisions of consequence by intelligent
people. In a deliberative assembly, this term applies to discus-   *20*
sion on the merits of a pending question—that is, whether
the proposal under consideration should, or should not, be
agreed to. That the right of debate is inherent in such an
assembly is implied by the word *deliberative.*

Debatability is a characteristic of all main motions and of   *25*
certain other motions, depending on the parliamentary function they serve, according to principles summarized at the end
of this section; and from such principles are derived the specific rules stated under Standard Characteristic 5 in **11–37**.

While the amount of debate on a motion in actual practice   *30*
will depend on such factors as its importance, how strongly
it is contested, etc., every member of the assembly has the
right to speak to every debatable motion before it is finally
acted upon; and subject only to general limitations on debate
established by parliamentary law or the rules of the body as   *35*

1 explained below, this right cannot be interfered with except
by a two-thirds vote.

Summary of Procedures Incident to Debate

5

Until a matter has been brought before the assembly in
the form of a motion proposing a specific action, it cannot
be debated. As explained in **3** and **4**, the motion must be
made by a member who has obtained the floor while no ques-
10 tion is pending (or while the motion is in order, if it is not a
main motion), after which it must be seconded by another
member (unless it is made by direction of a board or committee), and must be stated by the chair. The chair may conclude his statement of the question on the debatable motion
15 by asking, "Are you ready for the question?" or, less formally,
"Is there any debate?" Alternatively, he may simply pause and
turn toward the maker of the motion to see if he desires the
floor first in debate. After the maker of the motion has had
the opportunity to speak first if he wishes, other members can
20 rise and address the chair to claim the floor for the purpose
of debate, as explained on pages 29ff. and in **42**.

While debate is in progress, amendments or other secondary (subsidiary, privileged, or incidental) motions can be introduced and disposed of—and can be debated in the process,
25 if they are debatable—as explained on pages 116–18. A member may both speak in debate and conclude by offering a
secondary motion, which is a particular application of the
principle that a member having been recognized for *any*
legitimate purpose has the floor for *all* legitimate purposes.

30 When debate appears to have concluded, the chair may
again ask, "Are you ready for the question?" (or "Is there any
further debate?") or if, after a reasonable pause, no one
rises to claim the floor, the chair may assume that no member wishes to speak and, standing, may proceed to put the
35 question.

It should be noted that, under legitimate parliamentary procedure, there is no such thing as "gaveling through" a measure. The right of members to debate or introduce secondary motions cannot be cut off by the chair's attempting to put a question to vote so quickly that no member can get the floor—either when the chair first states the question or when he believes debate is ended. Debate is not closed by the presiding officer's rising to put the question. If a vote has been taken or begun quickly and it is found that a member rose and addressed the chair with reasonable promptness after the chair asked, "Are you ready for the question?" or, by a pause or otherwise, indicated that the floor was open to assignment, then—even if the chair has announced the result of such a vote—the vote must be disregarded, the member is entitled to the floor, and debate begins or resumes. But if the chair gives ample opportunity for members to claim the floor before he puts the question, and no one rises, the right to debate cannot be claimed after the voting has commenced. If, because a member sought the floor in timely fashion, debate is resumed after voting has begun, the question must be put fully again— that is, both the affirmative and the negative votes must called for—regardless of how far the earlier vote had proceeded. When a vote is taken a second time for purposes of verification—as when a *Division* (**29**) is demanded—debate cannot be resumed except by unanimous consent (pp. 54–56).

Length and Number of Speeches

MAXIMUM TIME FOR EACH SPEECH.   In a nonlegislative body or organization that has no special rule relating to the length of speeches (**2**), a member, having obtained the floor while a debatable motion is immediately pending, can speak no longer than ten minutes unless he obtains the consent of the assembly. Such permission can be given by unanimous consent (pp. 54–56), or by means of a motion to

1   *Extend the Limits of Debate* (**15**), which requires a two-thirds vote without debate.

When a member's time is exhausted, the chair rises and—if the member does not immediately conclude his remarks—
5   calls his attention to the fact by an appropriate signal, or by interrupting him if necessary. The chair may appoint time-keepers to provide assistance in fulfilling this responsibility. If it appears that a minute more will afford sufficient time for the member to conclude more gracefully, the chair can ask
10 unanimous consent to extend the member's time for a short period, or any member can do so.

Rights in regard to debate are not transferable. Unless the organization has a special rule on the subject, a member cannot yield any unexpired portion of his time to another mem-
15 ber, or reserve any portion of his time for a later time—that is, if a member yields the floor before speaking his full ten minutes, he is presumed to have waived his right to the remaining time.* If a speaker yields to another member for a question (*Request for Information,* pp. 294–95), the time
20 consumed by the question is charged to the speaker.

A committee chairman or reporting member is not considered to be debating when presenting or reading the committee's report, but he is bound to obey the assembly's rules relating to debate in any speech made by him in support of
25 the motion offered on behalf of the committee.

NUMBER OF SPEECHES ON THE SAME QUESTION PER MEMBER PER DAY. Unless the assembly has

---

*This rule reflects the traditional parliamentary principles. The House of Representatives has a different rule which permits control of all time by a single member or the leaders of the opposing sides of the question. The House rule also prevents members to whom time has been yielded for debate from making motions. See form (d) on page 196 and, especially, the form on pages 639–40.

a special rule providing otherwise, no member can speak *1*
more than twice to the same question on the same day—
except that in the case of an *Appeal* (**24**), only the presiding
officer can speak twice (the second time at the close of the
debate), all other members being limited to one speech. *5*
Merely asking a question or making a brief suggestion is not
counted as speaking in debate; nor is the making of a secondary motion counted as speaking in debate,* so long as in making the motion the member makes no comment on the
then-pending question. It will be seen from this rule that if *10*
debate on a pending motion is continued at the next meeting,
and if that meeting is held on the same day, members who
have already made two speeches on a question are not allowed
to speak on it again without the assembly's permission. But
if the next meeting is held on another day, all members have *15*
their right to debate entirely renewed with reference to that
question. Under this rule, each debatable motion is a separate question with respect to members' rights to debate it.
Thus, if a series of debatable questions is pending and a member has, for example, spoken twice that day while the main *20*
motion is immediately pending, he has exhausted his right to
debate the main motion; but, even on the same day, he can
still speak twice on a motion to postpone the main question
indefinitely, and twice on each amendment that may be
moved, and so on. As noted under the rules for assigning the *25*
floor (**42**), however, a member cannot make a second speech
on the same question the same day until every member who
desires to speak on it has had an opportunity to do so once.

---

*Thus a member who has exhausted the number of speeches permitted
him on a main motion may still seek recognition to move its referral or amendment, for example. In such a case the chair should grant limited recognition
by saying, "The member has exhausted his right to debate. For what purpose
does he rise?"

1 If debate is closed before the member has an opportunity to make a second speech, none may be made.

Modification of General Limits of Debate
5

The general rules limiting the length and number of speeches in debate that are stated above can be modified to serve the assembly's needs as follows:

10 ADOPTING A SPECIAL RULE.   The rule allowing each member two speeches of ten minutes' length per day on each debatable question can be made either more restrictive or more liberal for all meetings of a society by adopting a special rule of order by a two-thirds vote after notice, or by a *15* vote of a majority of the entire membership (**2**; see also pp. 121–24). An example of a more restrictive rule might be one setting a limit of not more than one speech of five minutes' length on the same question on the same day for each member.
20

CHANGING THE LIMITS FOR A SESSION.   An assembly at any session can change the limits of debate, for that session only, by means of a main motion adopted by a two-thirds vote without notice. In a convention—where the limits *25* of debate generally need to be stricter than in a local society—such a modification is usually adopted in the form of a *standing rule of the convention* (**59**), requiring a two-thirds vote in such a case.

30 CHANGING THE LIMITS FOR THE PENDING QUESTION(S) ONLY.   While a debatable question is immediately pending, the allowed length or number of speeches can be reduced or increased, for that question only, by means of the subsidiary motion to *Limit or Extend Limits of Debate* *35* (**15**), adopted by a two-thirds vote. This motion can also be used to close debate at a specified future time. If two thirds

of those voting wish to close debate immediately, they can do   *1*
so by adopting the motion for the *Previous Question* (**16**). If
a series of adhering debatable questions (p. 118) is pending,
either of these motions can also be applied to the entire series
or any consecutive part of the series beginning with the   *5*
immediately pending question. (For forms, see pp. 196–97,
207–9, 639–40.) If it is desired to prevent any discussion
of a subject—even by the introducer of the motion, who has
the right to the floor first—the only way this can be done is
to raise an *Objection to the Consideration of the Question* (**26**)   *10*
before debate begins or any subsidiary motion (other than a
motion to *Lay on the Table*) is stated. If the objection is sustained by a two-thirds vote, the question cannot be considered in any way at that time or during that session.

On the other hand, if, in considering a particular ques-   *15*
tion, it is desired to retain the usual limit on the length of
speeches but remove restrictions on the total number of times
members can speak, the assembly by a majority vote can resolve itself into a committee of the whole or into quasi committee of the whole, or it can consider the question informally   *20*
(see p. 529, l. 30 to p. 530, l. 5). Speeches made under these
procedures do not count against a member's right to debate
the same question if it is further considered by the assembly
on the same day under the regular rules. If the question under
consideration is composed of a number of sections or para-   *25*
graphs—as in the case of bylaws, for example—the total number of speeches allowed each member can be greatly
increased, but not made unlimited, by considering the document seriatim (**28**), in which case each member can speak
twice on each paragraph, section, or unit that is taken up as a   *30*
separate part.

Decorum in Debate

The following practices and customs observed by speakers   *35*
and other members in an assembly assist the carrying on of

1   debate in a smooth and orderly manner. The paragraphs under the head *Pattern of Formality* on pages 22–25 should be read in connection with this subject.

5   CONFINING REMARKS TO THE MERITS OF THE PENDING QUESTION.   In debate a member's remarks must be germane to the question before the assembly—that is, his statements must have bearing on whether the immediately pending motion should be adopted (see also *Principles* 10 *Governing the Debatability of Motions,* pp. 396–99).

REFRAINING FROM ATTACKING A MEMBER'S MOTIVES.   When a question is pending, a member can condemn the nature or likely consequences of the proposed 15 measure in strong terms, but he must avoid personalities, and under no circumstances can he attack or question the motives of another member. The measure, not the member, is the subject of debate. If a member disagrees with a statement by another in regard to an event that both witnessed, he cannot 20 state in debate that the other's statement "is false." But he might say, "I believe there is strong evidence that the member is mistaken." The moment the chair hears such words as "fraud," "liar," or "lie" used about a member in debate, he must act immediately and decisively to correct the matter and 25 prevent its repetition (see **61**).

ADDRESSING ALL REMARKS THROUGH THE CHAIR.   Members of an assembly cannot address one another directly, but must address all remarks through the chair. 30 If, while a member is speaking in debate, another member wishes to address a question to him—which the person speaking can permit or not as he chooses, but which is taken out of his time if he does—the member desiring to ask the question should rise and address the chair, proceeding as explained 35 under *Request for Information* (pp. 294–95).

AVOIDING THE USE OF MEMBERS' NAMES.   As   *1*
much as possible, the use of names of members should be
avoided in debate. It is better to describe a member in some
other way, as by saying, "the member who spoke last," or,
"the delegate from Mason County." The officers of the soci-   *5*
ety should always be referred to by their official titles. There
is no need, however, to refer to oneself in debate in the third
person as by the use of such expressions as "this member." A
member's debate is expected and intended to be partial, and
the first person is quite acceptable.   *10*

REFRAINING FROM SPEAKING ADVERSELY ON
A PRIOR ACTION NOT PENDING.   In debate, a mem-
ber cannot reflect adversely on any prior act of the society that
is not then pending, unless a motion to reconsider, rescind,   *15*
or amend it is pending, or unless he intends to conclude his
remarks by making or giving notice of one of these motions.

REFRAINING FROM SPEAKING AGAINST ONE'S
OWN MOTION.   In debate, the maker of a motion, while   *20*
he can vote against it, is not allowed to speak against his own
motion. He need not speak at all, but if he does he is obliged
to take a favorable position. If he changes his mind while
the motion he made is pending, he can, in effect, advise the
assembly of this by asking permission to withdraw the motion   *25*
(pp. 295–97).

READING FROM REPORTS, QUOTATIONS, ETC.,
ONLY WITHOUT OBJECTION OR WITH PERMIS-
SION.   If any member objects, a member has no right to   *30*
read from—or to have the secretary read from—any paper or
book as part of his speech, without permission of the assembly. Members are usually permitted to read short, pertinent,
printed extracts in debate, however, so long as they do not
abuse the privilege (see also pp. 298–99).   *35*

BEING SEATED DURING AN INTERRUPTION BY THE CHAIR.   If at any time the presiding officer rises to make a ruling, give information, or otherwise speak within his privilege, any member who is speaking should be seated (or should step back slightly if he is standing at a microphone some distance from a seat) until the presiding officer has finished. At that time the member can resume his speech, unless he is denied the right as a disciplinary measure. (Questions of discipline arising from disorderly debate by members are treated in **61**.)

REFRAINING FROM DISTURBING THE ASSEMBLY.   During debate, during remarks by the presiding officer to the assembly, and during voting, no member should be permitted to disturb the assembly by whispering, walking across the floor, or in any other way. The key words here are *disturb the assembly.* This rule does not mean, therefore, that members can never whisper, or walk from one place to another in the hall during the deliberations of the assembly. At large meetings it would be impossible to enforce such a rule. However, the presiding officer should watch that such activity does not disturb the meeting or hamper the transaction of business.

Rule Against the Chair's Participation in Debate

If the presiding officer is a member of the society, he has—as an individual—the same *rights* in debate as any other member; but the impartiality required of the chair in an assembly precludes his exercising these rights while he is presiding. Normally, especially in a large body, he should have nothing to say on the merits of pending questions. On certain occasions—which should be extremely rare—the presiding officer may believe that a crucial factor relating to such a question has been overlooked and that his obligation as a member to call attention to the point outweighs his duty to preside at

that time. To participate in debate, he must relinquish the   *1*
chair; and in such a case he should turn the chair over:

a) to the highest-ranking vice-president present who has not
     spoken on the question and does not decline on the   *5*
     grounds of wishing to speak on it; or
b) if no such vice-president is in the room, to some other
     member qualified as in (a), whom the chair designates
     (and who is assumed to receive the assembly's approval
     by unanimous consent unless member(s) then nominate   *10*
     other person(s), in which case the presiding officer's
     choice is also treated as a nominee and the matter is de-
     cided by vote).

The presiding officer who relinquished the chair then should   *15*
not return to it until the pending main question has been disposed of, since he has shown himself to be a partisan as far as
that particular matter is concerned. Indeed, unless a presiding
officer is extremely sparing in leaving the chair to take part in
debate, he may destroy members' confidence in the impar-   *20*
tiality of his approach to the task of presiding.

     In debate on an appeal (**24**) or a point of order (**23**) that
the chair has submitted to the judgment of the assembly
(pp. 254–55), the foregoing rule does not apply, and the presiding officer does not leave the chair, since his participation   *25*
in the debate relates to the function of presiding.

Occasions Justifying Brief Discussion
Outside Debate

  30

INFORMAL CONSULTATION TO ASSIST THE
FRAMING OF A MOTION.   As already stated, debate is
permitted only while a debatable question is immediately
pending. Occasionally, however—in small assemblies when a
subject is not strongly contested—brief informal consultation   *35*

1   or discussion of a subject may assist a member in framing a
proper motion. If the chair permits such discussion, he generally should not allow it to continue more than a few mo-
ments or longer than is reasonably necessary to arrive at a
5   motion embodying the member's ideas.

In general, for a member to speak when no question is
pending, without promptly leading to a motion, implies an
unusual circumstance and requires permission *of the assembly*.
But occasionally, in very small bodies, a member who has
10   obtained the floor at such a time may state that, if there is no
objection, he would like to give some explanations dealing
with a specified subject and to conclude by offering a motion
on that subject. If no one objects, the member can then proceed; and the chair, knowing the subject, can hold him to it
15   as he would in debate on a motion (see also pp. 34–35).

ALLOWABLE EXPLANATION OF A PENDING
UNDEBATABLE MOTION.   Sometimes business may be
expedited by allowing a few words of factual explanation
20   while an undebatable motion is pending. The distinction between debate and asking questions or making brief suggestions should be kept in mind in this connection. The chair
should be careful not to allow this type of consultation to develop into an extended colloquy between members or to take
25   on the semblance of debate; and he should generally remain
standing while the consultation takes place, to show that the
floor has not been assigned.

30   **Principles Governing the Debatability of Motions**

Rules as to each motion's debatability or undebatability
are given under Standard Characteristic 5 in **10–37** and in
the Table of Rules Relating to Motions on tinted pages 6–29.
The following is a brief summary of these rules in relation to
35   the principles on which they are based.

Every main motion is debatable, from the nature of the *1*
deliberative assembly itself.

With the exception of the two subsidiary motions that
have to do with debate, the degree to which each of the subsidiary motions can be debated depends on the extent to *5*
which its adoption would restrict the assembly in dealing with
the main question.

- Since the motion to *Postpone Indefinitely* (**11**) will kill the
  main motion if it is adopted, it is fully debatable and leaves *10*
  the main question open to debate.
- A motion to *Amend* (**12**) is debatable when it is applied
  to the main question or to any other debatable motion,
  since it would alter the question it proposes to amend;
  but the debate is limited to the merits of the amendment, *15*
  and other pending questions can be brought into the discussion only as necessary in this connection. A motion to
  amend an undebatable motion is undebatable, because
  to allow debate on it would be contrary to the purposes
  of the other motion's undebatability. *20*
- In the case of the motions to *Commit* (**13**) and to *Postpone to a Certain Time* (**14**), debate is quite limited, because the main question will be open to further debate
  when the committee reports or when the time arrives to
  which the question was postponed. Hence, debate is con- *25*
  fined in the first instance to the wisdom of referring or to
  the choice of personnel of the committee and to the nature of its instructions, and in the latter instance to the
  wisdom of postponement and the choice of a time to
  which the question will be postponed. *30*
- Motions to *Limit or Extend Limits of Debate* (**15**) and for
  the *Previous Question* (**16**) are undebatable inasmuch as
  their very object is to alter the debatability of pending
  question(s), and their purpose would be defeated if they
  were debatable; they are also in the nature of specialized *35*

motions to suspend the rules, and any such motion made
while business is pending is undebatable.

- The motion to *Lay on the Table* (**17**) is undebatable because its legitimate purpose would be defeated if it were
debatable, and because its adoption in no way interferes
with the right of the majority to take the question from
the table (**34**) and resume debate.

The privileged motions are all undebatable because, if
they were debatable, their high privilege would allow them
to interfere with business. The right of debate is thus incompatible with high privilege. With reference to the two lowest-
ranking privileged motions, it is, of course, the "calling" for
the orders of the day (**18**) or the "raising" of a question of
privilege (**19**) that is undebatable. When the order of the day
or the question of privilege involved in such a case becomes
the pending main motion, it is debatable.

Except as noted in this paragraph, the incidental motions
are undebatable, because they have high privilege to interrupt
any motions or situations to which they are incidental. In the
case of an *Appeal* that relates to indecorum, the rules of debate, or the priority of business, it is assumed that debate
would be a hindrance to business, as it would be if the appeal
were made when an undebatable question is immediately
pending or involved in the appeal. At all other times, an appeal is fully debatable so long as the debate is germane to the
subject matter of the appeal. The incidental motion to create a proviso, like the corresponding subsidiary motion to
create a proviso by amending a motion's enacting words (see
p. 597, ll. 6–14), is debatable when the motion to which it
applies is debatable. A *Request to Be Excused from a Duty,* such
as a resignation, may require some discussion for its proper
decision, and for this reason it is debatable.

Rules as to the debatability of motions that bring a question again before the assembly may be summarized as follows:

- The motion to *Take from the Table* (**34**) is undebatable   *1* because debate would serve no useful purpose and would delay business, and because, if it is voted down, it can be renewed each time any business has been transacted.

- The motion to *Rescind* or to *Amend Something Previously*   *5* *Adopted* (**35**) is fully debatable, and it opens to debate the entire motion that it proposes to rescind or to amend. The same is true of the motion to *Discharge a Committee* (**36**).

- The motion to *Reconsider* (**37**) is debatable only to the   *10* extent that the motion proposed to be reconsidered is debatable, and it opens the merits of that question to debate. A motion to reconsider an undebatable motion is thus undebatable.

CHAPTER XIII

VOTING

1 ## §44. BASES FOR DETERMINING A VOTING RESULT

Majority Vote—the Basic Requirement

5   As stated on page 4, the basic requirement for approval of an action or choice by a deliberative assembly, except where a rule provides otherwise, is a *majority vote*. The word *majority* means "more than half"; and when the term *majority vote* is used without qualification—as in the case of the *10* basic requirement—it means more than half of the votes cast by persons entitled to vote, excluding blanks or abstentions, at a regular or properly called meeting. For example (assuming that there are no voters having fractions of a vote, as may occur in some conventions):

15

- If 19 votes are cast, a majority (more than 9½) is 10.
- If 20 votes are cast, a majority (more than 10) is 11.
- If 21 votes are cast, a majority (more than 10½) is 11.

20   Other bases for determining a voting result, as described below, are required under parliamentary law for certain procedures, or may be prescribed by the rules of the particular body—for decisions in general or for questions of a specified

400

nature (see also Standard Characteristic 7, pp. 103–4). Re- *1*
gardless of the basis required, a decision can be validly made
only when a quorum is present (unless otherwise specified in
the rules, as in the case of certain procedural actions); see **40**.

                                                                5

Two-Thirds Vote

A *two-thirds vote*—when the term is unqualified—means
at least two thirds of the votes cast by persons entitled to vote,
excluding blanks or abstentions, at a regular or properly called *10*
meeting. For example (assuming that there are no fractions
of votes):

- If 30 votes are cast, a two-thirds vote is 20.
- If 31 votes are cast, a two-thirds vote is 21.   *15*
- If 32 votes are cast, a two-thirds vote is 22.
- If 33 votes are cast, a two-thirds vote is 22.

As a compromise between the rights of the individual
and the rights of the assembly, the principle has been estab- *20*
lished that a two-thirds vote is required to adopt any motion
that: (a) suspends or modifies a rule of order previously
adopted; (b) prevents the introduction of a question for consideration; (c) closes, limits, or extends the limits of debate;
(d) closes nominations or the polls, or otherwise limits the *25*
freedom of nominating or voting; or (e) takes away membership. (For a list of motions that require a two-thirds vote, see
tinted pp. 44–45.)

In determining whether a question has obtained two
thirds of the votes cast, the chair should take a rising vote (or, *30*
in a very small assembly, if he prefers and no one objects,
a vote by show of hands), and he should obtain a count of
the vote whenever he is in doubt concerning the result.

The chair can obtain a count of the vote initially if it
appears—when those in the affirmative rise—that the result *35*

1 will be close; or he can retake it as a counted rising vote if
he is afterward in doubt. In an assembly that has no special
rule permitting a small fraction (that is, a specified fraction
somewhat less than one third) of the voters to require a two-
5 thirds vote to be counted, the chair, in judging whether to
obtain a count of the vote at his own instance, must be particularly careful to leave no room for anyone to doubt the result in cases where he finds that there *are* two thirds on the
side that thereby prevails. Without a count at the chair's in-
10 stance under these conditions, if he announces that a two-
thirds vote has been obtained and those on the losing side
doubt the result, they are powerless to have it verified should
those declared the winners choose to prevent a count. The
reason is that—whatever may be the true result in view of the
15 closeness of the vote in such a case—those declared the losers
are no more than approximately one third of those voting,
and therefore cannot command the majority necessary to
order the vote counted.

20   ## Modifications of Usual Bases for Decision

By modifying the concepts of a majority vote and a two-
thirds vote, other bases for determining a voting result can
be defined and are sometimes prescribed by rule. Two ele-
25 ments enter into the definition of such bases for decision:
(1) the proportion that must concur—as a majority, two
thirds, three fourths, etc.; and (2) the set of members to
which the proportion applies—which (a) when not stated, is
always the number of members *present and voting*, but (b) can
30 be specified by rule as the number of members present, the
total membership, or some other grouping.

Assume, for example, that at a meeting of a society with
a total membership of 150 and a quorum of 10, there are
30 members present, of whom 25 participate in a given
35 counted vote (taken by rising, by show of hands, by roll call,
or by ballot). Then, with respect to that vote:

A majority is	13	*1*
A majority of the members present is	16	
A majority of the entire membership is	76	
A two-thirds vote is	17	
A vote of two thirds of the members		*5*
present is	20	
A vote of two thirds of the entire		
membership is	100	

Regarding these bases for determining a voting result, the   *10*
following points should be noted:

- Voting requirements based on the number of members present—a majority of those present, two thirds of
  those present, etc.—while possible, are generally undesir-   *15*
  able. Since an abstention in such cases has the same effect
  as a negative vote, these bases deny members the right to
  maintain a neutral position by abstaining. For the same
  reason, members present who fail to vote through indif-
  ference rather than through deliberate neutrality may af-   *20*
  fect the result negatively. When such a vote is required,
  however, the chair must count those present immediately
  after the affirmative vote is taken, before any change can
  take place in attendance. (See p. 45, ll. 4–18.)
- A *majority of the entire membership** is a majority of the   *25*
  total number of those who are members of the voting
  body at the time of the vote. (Thus, in a society that has

---

*In the case of a body having a fixed membership—for example, a per-
manent board—it is also possible to define a voting requirement as a majority
of the fixed membership, which is greater than a majority of the entire membership if there are vacancies on the board. Thus, in a board whose membership is fixed at 12, if 2 members have died and their successors have not been
named, a majority of the entire membership is 6, and a majority of the fixed
membership is 7. Where a majority of the fixed membership is required for a
decision, the body cannot act if half or more of the membership positions are
vacant.

both a general membership and an executive board, a "majority of the entire membership" at a board meeting refers to a majority of the membership of the board, not of the society.) In a convention of delegates a majority of the entire membership means a majority of the total number of convention members entitled to vote as set forth in the official roll of voting members of the convention (pp. 7, 617). The vote of a majority of the entire membership is frequently an alternative to a requirement of previous notice, and is required in order to rescind and expunge from the minutes (see p. 310). Otherwise, prescribing such a requirement is generally unsatisfactory in an assembly of an ordinary society, since it is likely to be impossible to get a majority of the entire membership even to attend a given meeting, although in certain instances it may be appropriate in conventions or in permanent boards where the members are obligated to attend the meetings.

Whenever it is desired that the basis for decision be other than a majority vote or (where the normal rules of parliamentary law require it) a two-thirds vote or a vote of a majority of the entire membership, the desired basis should be precisely defined in the bylaws or in a special rule of order. Whatever voting basis is used, it is also possible to include a requirement of *previous notice* for specified types of action. Previous notice means that notice of intent to introduce the proposal must be given at the preceding meeting (in which case the notice can be oral), or in the call of the meeting at which it is brought up (for a discussion of *previous notice,* see pp. 121–24).

Plurality Vote

A *plurality vote* is the largest number of votes to be given any candidate or proposition when three or more choices are

possible; the candidate or proposition receiving the largest   *1*
number of votes has a plurality. A plurality that is not a majority never chooses a proposition or elects anyone to office
except by virtue of a special rule previously adopted. If such
a rule is to apply to the election of officers, it must be pre-   *5*
scribed in the bylaws. A rule that a plurality shall elect is unlikely to be in the best interests of the average organization.
In an international or national society where the election is
conducted by mail ballot, a plurality is sometimes allowed to
elect officers, with a view to avoiding the delay and extra   *10*
expense that would result from additional balloting under
these conditions. A better method in such cases is for the
bylaws to prescribe some form of preferential voting (see
pp. 425–28).

15

Tie Votes and Cases in Which
the Chair's Vote Affects the Result

If the presiding officer is a member of the assembly, he
can vote as any other member when the vote is by ballot (see   *20*
also p. 414, ll. 25–28). In all other cases the presiding officer,
if a member of the assembly, can (but is not obliged to) vote
whenever his vote will affect the result—that is, he can
vote either to break or to cause a tie; or, in a case where a two-
thirds vote is required, he can vote either to cause or to block   *25*
the attainment of the necessary two thirds. In particular:

- On a tie vote, a motion requiring a majority vote for
  adoption is lost, since a tie is not a majority. Thus, if there
  is a tie without the chair's vote, the presiding officer can,   *30*
  if he is a member, vote in the affirmative, thereby causing
  the motion to be adopted; or, if there is one more in the
  affirmative than in the negative without the chair's vote
  (for example, if there are 72 votes in favor and 71 opposed), he can vote in the negative to create a tie, thus   *35*
  causing the motion to be rejected.

1   • Similarly, in the case of a motion requiring a two-thirds
       vote, if, without the chair's vote, the number in the affir-
       mative is one less than twice the number in the negative
       (for example, if there are 59 in the affirmative and 30 in
5   the negative), the chair, if a member, can vote in the
       affirmative and thus cause the motion to be adopted; or,
       if there are exactly two thirds in the affirmative without
       his vote (for example, if there are 60 in the affirmative
       and 30 in the negative), the chair can vote in the nega-
10   tive, with the result that the motion is rejected.* Similarly,
       the chair's vote might affect the result in cases where a
       majority of the members can decide a question.

       The chair cannot vote twice, once as a member, then again
15   in his capacity as presiding officer.
       In an appeal from the decision of the chair, a tie vote sus-
       tains the chair's decision, even though his vote created the
       tie, on the principle that the decision of the chair can be re-
       versed only by a majority.
20

§45. VOTING PROCEDURE

Rights and Obligations in Voting

25   VOTING RIGHTS OF A MEMBER IN ARREARS.   A
       member of a society who is in arrears in payment of his dues,
       but who has not been formally dropped from the membership
       rolls and is not under a disciplinary suspension, retains the full
       rights of a voting member and is entitled to vote except as
30   the bylaws may otherwise provide. (See also pp. 6, 571–72.)

---

*It should be noted that if, without the chair's vote, the number of neg-
ative votes is one more than half the number of affirmative votes, the chair's
vote cannot affect the result. Thus, if there are 60 in the affirmative and 31
in the negative without the chair's vote, and he were to vote in the affirmative,
the resulting 61 in the affirmative would still fall short of two thirds of the
total vote of 92.

ONE PERSON, ONE VOTE.   It is a fundamental prin- *1*
ciple of parliamentary law that each person who is a member
of a deliberative assembly is entitled to one—and only one—
vote on a question. This is true even if a person is elected or
appointed to more than one position, each of which would *5*
entitle the holder to a vote. For example, in a convention, a
person selected as delegate by more than one constituent
body may cast only one vote. An individual member's right
to vote may not be transferred to another person (for example, by the use of proxies). *10*

RIGHT OF ABSTENTION.   Although it is the duty of
every member who has an opinion on a question to express
it by his vote, he can abstain, since he cannot be compelled
to vote. By the same token, when an office or position is to *15*
be filled by a number of members, as in the case of a committee, or positions on a board, a member may partially abstain by voting for less than all of those for whom he is
entitled to vote.
20

ABSTAINING FROM VOTING ON A QUESTION
OF DIRECT PERSONAL INTEREST.   No member
should vote on a question in which he has a direct personal
or pecuniary interest not common to other members of the
organization. For example, if a motion proposes that the or- *25*
ganization enter into a contract with a commercial firm
of which a member of the organization is an officer and
from which contract he would derive personal pecuniary
profit, the member should abstain from voting on the motion. However, no member can be compelled to refrain from *30*
voting in such circumstances.

VOTING ON QUESTIONS AFFECTING ONESELF.
The rule on abstaining from voting on a question of direct
personal interest does not mean that a member should not *35*
vote for himself for an office or other position to which

1 members generally are eligible, or should not vote when other members are included with him in a motion. If a member never voted on a question affecting himself, it would be impossible for a society to vote to hold a banquet, or for
5 the majority to prevent a small minority from preferring charges against them and suspending or expelling them (**61, 63**).

INTERRUPTION OF VOTES.   Interruptions during
10 the taking of a vote are permitted only before any member has actually voted, unless, as sometimes occurs in ballot voting, other business is being transacted during voting or tabulating. For points of order regarding the conduct of a vote, see below and pages 250–51.
15

RULE AGAINST EXPLANATION BY MEMBERS DURING VOTING.   A member has no right to "explain his vote" during voting, which would be the same as debate at such a time.
20

CHANGING ONE'S VOTE.   A member has a right to change his vote up to the time the result is announced; after that, he can make the change only by the unanimous consent of the assembly requested and granted, without debate, im-
25 mediately following the chair's announcement of the result of the vote (see below).

TIME LIMITS ON EFFORTS TO CHALLENGE, RE-TAKE, OR CHANGE A VOTE.   After the result of a vote
30 has been announced, members can still propose or demand certain actions that may change the result. A member may raise a point of order regarding the conduct of the vote, demand a division of the assembly, move to retake the vote under another method, move for a recapitulation of a roll-call vote,
35 or request unanimous consent to change his vote. With the exception of a point of order raised against a breach of a con-

tinuing nature (p. 251, ll. 3–23), if any of these actions is to apply to a vote after the result has been announced, it must be taken immediately after the chair's announcement, before any debate or business has intervened. For example, it is too late to take these actions after any member has been recognized and begun to speak in debate or to give a report or presentation, or after the chair has stated the question on a subsequently made motion, or after the chair has begun to take the vote and any member has voted on another motion that was pending. For the time limits on ordering that a counted rising vote, a ballot, or a roll-call vote be recounted, see pages 411 (ll. 19–21), 418–19, and 422 (ll. 30–33). See also *Contesting the Announced Result of an Election*, pages 444–46.

ASSEMBLY'S PREROGATIVE IN JUDGING VOTING PROCEDURES. The assembly itself is the judge of all questions arising that are incidental to the voting or the counting of the votes. In an election by ballot, for example, the tellers should refer to the assembly for decision all questions on which there is any uncertainty (see p. 416, ll. 12–19).

Regular Methods of Voting on Motions

In Chapter II are described the following methods of voting:

1) by *voice (viva voce)*—the normal method of voting on a motion;
2) by *rising*—used in verifying an inconclusive voice vote, and in voting on motions requiring a two-thirds vote for adoption; and
3) by *show of hands*—an alternative method that can be used in place of a rising vote in very small assemblies if no member objects. In some small groups, a vote by show of hands is also used in place of a voice vote as a normal method of voting.

1 Pages 44–54 should be read in connection with these three methods of voting.

Also described in Chapter II is the procedure of action by *unanimous consent*. Pages 54–56 should be read in reference
5 to this method of transacting business.

A characteristic that the three methods of voting listed above have in common is that in each case the chair calls first for those voting in the affirmative to indicate the fact in a specified manner ("say *aye*," "rise," or "raise the right hand"),
10 after which he calls for the negative vote, then judges and declares which side prevails.

VERIFYING A VOTE.   In connection with the methods of voting by voice, by rising, or by show of hands, as ex-
15 plained in Chapter II, if the chair is in doubt on a voice vote or a vote by show of hands, he should retake it as a rising vote and, if necessary to satisfy himself of the result, he should obtain a count of it. Any member, by demanding a *Division* (**29**), can require a voice vote or a vote by show of hands to
20 be retaken as a rising vote—but no individual member can compel it to be counted. If the chair does not obtain a count at his own instance and a member thinks one is desirable, he should move that the vote be counted; and if this motion is seconded, the chair must put the question on ordering the
25 count. Where no special rule has been adopted, a majority vote is required to order a count. In organizations where it is desired to allow less than a majority to order a count, a special rule of order establishing the required vote should be adopted. Such a rule is particularly desirable with reference
30 to motions that require a two-thirds vote for adoption (see also pp. 401–2). It should be noted that a vote is never retaken by the same form of voting, although, in a counted rising vote, a ballot, or a roll call, a recount of the votes or of the tellers' tabulations can be ordered to ensure that the
35 count is precisely correct as reported.

METHOD OF COUNTING A RISING VOTE. In small meetings, the chair can take such a count himself—with or without directing the secretary to make an independent count for verification. In a large assembly, the chair should appoint tellers to take the count. The count is taken by having those in the affirmative rise and stand until counted, then having those in the negative rise and stand until counted. The votes can also be counted by having the members pass between tellers, or having them count off by rows and be seated one at a time, although the latter process is particularly subject to confusion if great care is not exercised by the tellers. Those in the affirmative are always counted first. In all but small assemblies, the doors should be closed and no one should enter or leave the hall while a count is being taken. The form used in taking a count is as shown on page 47, ll. 4–10. In a meeting small enough that each member present can make his own verification of a count on a show of hands, the chair can take the count by this method, if he prefers and no one objects. If written records are prepared in counting the vote, such as tellers' tally sheets, they are subject to the same retention and recount rules as ballots (pp. 418–19).

VOTING CARDS. Some organizations like to use a brightly colored cardboard card, approximately three inches wide and a foot long, in voting on most or all occasions by raising it when asked to do so by the chair. The authorization of the use of these devices in voting, however, depends on expected conditions in the meeting. If the "voters' cards" have been distributed to the voters in advance, and the chair or a member thinks a simple division vote (as described on p. 46, l. 14 to p. 47, l. 3) is called for, the chair may say: "As many as are in favor of the motion, raise your voters' cards. . . . Down. Those opposed, raise your voters' cards. Down. . . ." If a count is desired, however, the chair or the assembly must authorize the count as in the case of a counted

1 division (as described on p. 47, ll. 4–10; see also **30**, *Motions Relating to Methods of Voting and the Polls*). If this method of voting is to be used, it must be authorized by a special rule of order or, in a convention, by a convention standing rule.

5

Other Methods of Voting

In contrast to the methods of voting mentioned in the preceding subsection, the voting methods described below
10 are used only when expressly ordered by the assembly or prescribed by its rules.

VOTING BY BALLOT.   Voting by *ballot* (slips of paper on which the voter marks his vote) is used when secrecy of
15 the members' votes is desired. The bylaws of the organization may prescribe that the vote be by ballot in certain cases, as in the election of officers and in admission to membership.* Any vote related to charges or proposed charges before or after a trial of a member or any officer should always be by ballot.
20 In cases in which there is no requirement that a vote be by ballot, a ballot vote can be ordered by a majority vote—which may be desirable whenever it is believed that members may thereby be more likely to vote their true sentiments.

When the bylaws require a vote to be taken by ballot, this
25 requirement cannot be suspended, even by a unanimous vote. A vote ordering a ballot vote on a particular question (see **30**) can, however, be reconsidered as long as the balloting has not yet begun.

---

*In some organizations—particularly secret societies—black and white balls, deposited in a box out of sight of all but the voter, are used in voting on the admission of candidates to membership—a white ball signifying a *yes* vote and a black one a *no* vote. This method is used principally where one or very few negative votes are to be sufficient to cause a candidate's rejection. This custom, however, is apparently declining.

When a vote is to be taken, or has been taken, by ballot, *1*
whether or not the bylaws require that form of voting, no
motion is in order that would force the disclosure of a member's vote or views on the matter. A motion to make unanimous a ballot vote that was not unanimous is thus out of *5*
order, unless that motion is also voted on by ballot—since
any member who openly votes against declaring the first vote
unanimous will thereby reveal that he did not vote for the
prevailing choice.

Whenever a vote is to be taken by ballot, it is out of order *10*
to move that one person—the secretary, for example—cast
the ballot of the assembly.

Form of the Ballot.   A ballot can consist of simply a small
slip of paper on which the voter writes his choice in a manner
directed by the chair; but if it is known ahead of time that a *15*
vote is to be by ballot and what the exact questions are, the
ballots should be prepared in advance for distribution at
the proper time. In such a case, each question to be voted on
appears on the ballot with a list of the possible answers beside
blank spaces or boxes, so that the voter can check the answer *20*
he desires. Two or more questions can be listed on the same
sheet, provided that each is marked in such a way that there
can be no confusion, as illustrated below.

Indicate vote with X.   *25*
1. Shall the National Headquarters be moved to
    Thresher City?
            Yes _____
            No _____
2. Meeting place of next convention: *30*
            Seattle_____
            New Orleans_____
            Other_____
                (Fill in name)

1   In elections, "for" and "against" spaces or boxes should not be used. They are applicable only with respect to votes on motions. In an election, a voter can vote against one candidate only by voting for another who has been nominated

5   or by writing in the name of another candidate.

Balloting Procedure.   In balloting in a meeting where the voting is in the same room as the meeting, the chair appoints tellers to distribute, collect, and count the ballots, and to report the vote. The number of tellers is dependent on the

10   number of voters, and the number of offices to be filled or questions to be answered, or the number of candidates. For a small group, two or three tellers are usually sufficient. The tellers should be chosen for accuracy and dependability, should have the confidence of the membership, and should

15   not have a direct personal involvement in the question or in the result of the vote to an extent that they should refrain from voting under the principle stated on page 407. Often their position with regard to the issue involved is well known, however, and they are frequently chosen to protect the inter-

20   ests of each opposing side. They normally vote themselves.

To ensure accuracy and to enable the tellers when unfolding the ballots to detect any error, each ballot should be folded in a manner announced in advance or stated on the ballot itself.

25   The presiding officer, if a member of the assembly, can always vote in the case of a ballot at the time other members do. Should he fail to vote before the polls are closed, he cannot then do so without the permission of the assembly.

When the balloting is completed, the chair directs the tell-

30   ers to collect the ballots. In collecting the ballots, it is the tellers' responsibility to see that no member votes more than once—for the assurance of which the assembly should adopt some reasonable and orderly method. For example: (a) In meetings where only voters are present, members can remain

35   in their seats and drop their ballots into a receptacle passed

by a teller, accompanied by another teller as watcher and   *1*
checker; (b) they can go to a central ballot box monitored by
at least two tellers and deposit their ballots; or (c) they can
hand their ballots to a teller—who judges by the thickness
and feel of the paper that only one ballot is being cast, and   *5*
who deposits them in a central ballot box. Whatever method
of collecting the ballots is followed, it—like other details
relating to voting—should be fixed by rule or custom in the
organization and should not be subject to haphazard variation from occasion to occasion.   *10*

After all have voted who wish to, the polls can be closed
on the motion of a member by a two-thirds vote (**30**); but it
is usually best to rely on the chair to close the polls. When
everyone appears to have voted, the chair inquires, "Have all
voted who wish to do so?" If there is no response, he says,   *15*
"If no one else wishes to vote . . . [pause], the polls are
closed," thus in effect declaring the polls closed by unanimous
consent. Thereafter, if other members arrive who wish to
vote, a majority vote is required to reopen the polls (**30**). The
tellers proceed to count the ballots—in a secluded location   *20*
or in another room if the meeting proceeds to other business
during the counting. Some small organizations have a custom
that ballots are counted in full presence of the meeting.

Recording the Votes. In recording the votes cast, the principle followed is that a choice has no mandate from the voting   *25*
body unless approval is expressed by more than half of those
entitled to vote and registering any evidence of having some
preference. Accordingly, the tellers ignore blank ballots and
other ballots that indicate no preference, treating them as
abstentions. (Blank ballots are sometimes cast by members to   *30*
conceal the fact that they do not wish to vote.)

All ballots that indicate a preference—provided they have
been cast by persons entitled to vote—are taken into account
in determining the number of votes cast for purposes of computing the majority. Each such ballot is credited to the voter's   *35*

1   preferred candidate or choice if the meaning of the ballot is
     clear and the choice is valid. Unintelligible ballots or ballots
     cast for an unidentifiable or ineligible candidate are treated
     instead as *illegal votes*—that is, they are counted as votes cast
5   but are not credited to any candidate or choice. Similarly, a
     ballot that contains votes for too many candidates for a given
     office is counted as one illegal vote cast for that office, be-
     cause it is not possible for the tellers to determine which can-
     didate(s) the voter prefers.
10   Technical errors, like the misspelling of a word or name,
     do not make a vote illegal if the meaning of the ballot is clear.
     If the meaning of one or more ballots is doubtful, they can
     be treated as illegal if it is impossible for them to affect the
     result; but if they may affect the result, the tellers report them
15   to the chair, who immediately submits to the assembly the
     question of how these ballots should be recorded. When re-
     porting doubtful ballots, the tellers must be careful whenever
     possible not to show how the decision would affect any of
     the candidates.
20   If, in unfolding the ballots, it is found that two or more
     filled-out ballots are folded together, they are recorded as
     illegal votes—that is, each set of ballots folded together is
     reported as one illegal vote, and is not credited. On the
     other hand, a blank ballot folded in with one that is properly
25   filled out is ignored and does not cause the rejection of the
     ballot with which it was folded.
          If one or more ballots are identifiable as cast by persons
     not entitled to vote, these ballots are excluded in determining
     the number of votes cast for purposes of computing the ma-
30   jority. If there is evidence that any unidentifiable ballots were
     cast by persons not entitled to vote, and if there is any possi-
     bility that such ballots might affect the result, the entire ballot
     vote is null and void, and a new ballot vote must be taken.
          On a ballot containing several questions or several inde-
35   pendent offices or positions to be filled, each section of the

ballot—that is, each portion that contains one question or   *1*
position to be filled, or one group of identical positions (such
as on a board or committee) to be filled—is treated for all
purposes as if it were a separate ballot, which is counted in
accordance with the rules given above. Therefore, the num-   *5*
ber of votes cast for purposes of computing the majority must
be tallied independently for each section. So, too, if a member
leaves one or more of the sections blank, the blank sections
in no way affect the validity of the sections that are filled; nor
do illegal votes on one section affect the validity of the re-   *10*
maining sections. Likewise, the folding together of two or
more ballots that contain multiple sections creates an illegal
vote only for each section that is filled out on more than one
of the folded-together ballots. (Regarding the election of
members of a board or committee in which votes are cast for   *15*
several identical positions on one section of the ballot, see
also p. 411, ll. 11–24)

Tellers' Report and the Chair's Declaration of the Result.
The chairman of tellers, standing, addresses the chair, reads
the tellers' report, and hands it to the chair without declar-   *20*
ing the result. In the case of an election, the report should
follow this form:

TELLERS' REPORT

Number of votes cast 97		*25*
Necessary for election (majority) 49		
Mr. Miller received 51		
Mr. Wilson received 24		
Mr. Strong received 14		
Illegal Votes		*30*
Mr. Friend (ineligible) 7		
Two ballots for		
Mr. Wilson folded together, rejected 1		

1   In the case of balloting on a motion, the tellers' report is as follows:

5   Number of votes cast 102
Necessary for adoption (majority) 52
Votes for motion 69
Votes against 32
Illegal votes
10   Two ballots against,
          folded together, rejected 1

The tellers' report should not include the number of members eligible to vote nor the number abstaining. In a
15   local society or other body in which membership continues on a long-term basis, only the officer responsible for maintaining the membership roll, and in a convention only an immediate updated report of the credentials committee, can validly determine the number of members eligible to vote if
20   this figure becomes needed. The reporting teller never declares the result of a ballot vote. The result is always declared by the chair, who also reads the tellers' report before he does so. In an election, the chair separately declares the election of each officer (see also **46**). In balloting on a motion, the chair
25   announces the result.
     The tellers' report is entered in full in the minutes, becoming a part of the official records of the organization. Under no circumstances should this be omitted in an election or in a vote on a critical motion out of a mistaken deference
30   to the feelings of unsuccessful candidates or members of the losing side.
     After completion of an election or balloting on a motion, unless the voting body directs otherwise, the tellers place the ballots and tally sheets in the custody of the secretary, who
35   keeps them under seal until the time within which a recount

may be ordered expires, and then destroys them. A re- *1*
count may be ordered by the voting body, by a majority vote,
at the same session at which the voting result was announced,
or at the next regular session if that session is held within a
quarterly time interval (see pp. 89–90). A recount may also *5*
be ordered at a special session properly called for that purpose, if held within a quarterly time interval of the session at
which the voting result was announced and before the next
regular session.

10

MACHINE OR ELECTRONIC VOTING.   The voting
process has been considerably changed in many organizations—especially in those comprising hundreds of voters—
by the use, instead of paper ballots, of voting machines such
as those used in political elections, or electronic devices similar *15*
to those used in the House of Representatives and many other
legislative bodies but set up to provide for secrecy of the vote
and the identity of the voters. It is important that the electronic device provided be programmed to comply with the
rule stated on pages 416–17 that each section of a ballot be *20*
treated as if it were a separate ballot and that the votes cast
for each office or issue be ascertained. Where such devices are
to be used, the following considerations are important:

- Preparations for the election should be made in consulta- *25*
  tion with the person in charge of installing the devices, so
  that all adjustments required by the particular conditions
  of the election can be provided for.
- Persons who are to tend the devices during voting must
  be carefully instructed in their duties, and must be able *30*
  to explain the use of the devices to voters.
- If there are likely to be many voters who have never
  used the devices, it may be advisable to have a device available for the voters' inspection on a day previous to the
  election. *35*

1   ROLL-CALL VOTE.   Taking a vote by *roll call* (or by *yeas and nays,* as it is also called) has the effect of placing on the record how each member or, sometimes each delegation, votes; therefore, it has exactly the opposite effect of a ballot

5 vote. It is usually confined to representative bodies, where the proceedings are published, since it enables constituents to know how their representatives voted on certain measures. It should not be used in a mass meeting or in any assembly whose members are not responsible to a constituency.

10   *Ordering a Roll-Call Vote.*   In a representative body, if there is no legal or constitutional provision specifying the size of the minority that can order a roll-call vote, the body should adopt a rule fixing the size of such a minority—for example, *one fifth of those present,* as in Congress, or some other portion

15 of those present that is less than a majority. In the absence of such a special rule, a majority vote is required to order the taking of a vote by roll call—in which case a motion to do so is likely to be useless, since its purpose is to force the majority to go on record. In local societies having a large membership

20 but relatively small attendance at meetings, a motion to take a vote by roll call is generally dilatory. It is in order, as one of the *Motions Relating to Methods of Voting,* however, to move "that a signed ballot be taken by tellers"; and if such a vote is ordered, the voter writes "yes" or "no" on the ballot and signs

25 it. The votes can be recorded in the minutes just as a roll call would be, but the names of all members need not be called. A roll-call vote cannot be ordered in committee of the whole.

    Procedure for Roll-Call Vote.   When a vote is to be taken by roll call (see **30** for the motion), the chair puts the ques-

30 tion in a form like the following:

> CHAIR: As many as are in favor of the adoption of the resolution will, as their names are called, answer *aye* [or "*yes,*" or "*yea*"]; those opposed will answer *no* [or "*nay*"]. The Secretary [or "the Clerk"] will call the

35 roll.

The roll is called in alphabetical order except that the pre-   1
siding officer's name is called last, and only when his vote will
affect the result. It is too late, after one person has answered
to the roll call, to renew the debate. Each member, as his name
is called, responds in the affirmative or negative as shown   5
above. If he does not wish to vote, he answers *present* (or *abstain*). If he is not ready to vote, but wishes to be called on
again after the roll has been completely called, he answers *pass*.

The secretary repeats each member's name and answer
aloud as it is given and notes the answers to the roll call in   10
separate columns. A convenient method of noting the answers is to write the number *1* to the left of the name of the
first member answering in the affirmative, the number *2* to
the left of the second name in the affirmative, and so on. The
negative answers are treated similarly in a column to the right   15
of the names; and those answering *present* are tallied in a third
column, to the far right or left. In this way, the last number
in each column shows how the vote stands at any given point
in the list.

At the conclusion of the roll call, the names of those who   20
failed to answer can be called again, or the chair can ask if
anyone entered the room after his or her name was called.
Each of these members who then responds can be assigned
the final number for his or her vote or abstention in the
proper column, continuing from the last number previously   25
in the column, although the member's number will appear in
a position out of sequence. Changes of vote are also permitted at this time, before the result is announced. When this
happens, the number beside the member's name is struck
through, the total for that column is adjusted accordingly,   30
and the next, final number in the proper column is entered.
Changes of vote may be limited when some electronic equipment is used.

The secretary gives the final number of those voting on
each side, and the number answering *present*, to the chair,   35

1 who announces these figures and declares the result. The chair, at his or her discretion, may direct, or the assembly may order, a "recapitulation"—a procedure in which the secretary calls out the names, first, of the members who voted in the

5 affirmative, second, of the members who voted in the negative, and third, of the members who answered *present*, with the chair calling for any necessary corrections to each category after the names in that category have been called.

In roll-call voting, a record of how each member voted,

10 as well as the result of the vote, should be entered in full in the journal or minutes. If those responding to the roll call do not total a sufficient number to constitute a quorum, the chair must direct the secretary to enter the names of enough members who are present but not voting to reflect the atten-

15 dance of a quorum during the vote.

In large conventions, the roll is sometimes called of entire delegations rather than of the individual members. The secretary, in calling for the votes of a delegation, should state the vote entitlement, as: "Local No. 145: 8 votes." In such cases,

20 the chairman or spokesman of each delegation, as it is called in alphabetical or numerical order, responds by giving its vote, as: "Local No. 145 votes 5 'for' and 3 'against.'" The secretary repeats this for confirmation and calls the next delegation. If any member of the assembly doubts the chairman's

25 announcement of the delegation's vote, he may demand a poll of the delegation, in which case each delegate's name is called by the secretary, and the delegation votes individually. When all delegates have voted, the secretary announces the totals for the delegation, which are recorded.

30 The same rules concerning the custody and preservation of tally sheets and the authority of the voting body to order a recount that govern ballot votes (see pp. 418–19) apply to a roll-call vote.

Electronic Roll-Call Vote Installation. Various forms of

35 electronic devices have become available to take the place of a roll-call vote. Any deliberative body can use such a sys-

tem with appropriate adjustments to conform as closely as possible with the rules given above for roll-call voting procedure. When used, there is usually a presumption of technical, mechanical accuracy of the electronic system if properly used by the members. Changes of votes after the result has been announced by the chair on the allegation of machine error are not entertained. On the same grounds, a recapitulation (see p. 422, ll. 1–8) is not permitted. Where electronic voting is used, it should be noted that, if it is impossible to erect a display board in the hall, members of the same delegation will not be able to ascertain how other members of the delegation vote. Also, steps must be taken to prevent members from being able to vote more than once by using a neighbor's keypad, or a member lending his keypad to a friend so that the friend can vote for him in his absence by "proxy."

ABSENTEE VOTING. It is a fundamental principle of parliamentary law that the right to vote is limited to the members of an organization who are actually present at the time the vote is taken in a regular or properly called meeting, although it should be noted that a member need not be present when the question is put. Exceptions to this rule must be expressly stated in the bylaws. Such possible exceptions include: (a) voting by postal mail, e-mail, or fax, and (b) proxy voting. An organization should never adopt a bylaw permitting a question to be decided by a voting procedure in which the votes of persons who attend a meeting are counted together with ballots mailed in by absentees. The votes of those present could be affected by debate, by amendments, and perhaps by the need for repeated balloting, while those absent would be unable to adjust their votes to reflect these factors. Consequently, the absentee ballots would in most cases be on a somewhat different question than that on which those present were voting, leading to confusion, unfairness, and inaccuracy in determining the result. If there is a possibility of any uncertainty about who will be entitled to vote, this

1   should be spelled out unambiguously and strictly enforced to
avoid unfairness in close votes.

A VOTE BY MAIL.   A vote by mail, when authorized
5   in the bylaws, is generally reserved for important issues, such
as an amendment to the bylaws or an election of officers—
on which a full vote of the membership is desirable even
though only a small fraction of the members normally attend
meetings. Situations of this kind frequently occur in scientific
10 societies or in alumni associations whose members may be in
many countries.

For a vote by mail—so that there may be no question of
the result in the event that the vote is close—it is important
that the mailing list used should exactly correspond to the cur-
15 rent official roll of voting members. For this purpose, the secretary should furnish to the chairman of tellers or other official
in charge of issuing the ballots a list of the names and mailing
addresses of record of all persons entitled to vote, which the
secretary should certify as corrected to the date as of which
20 the ballots are issued. Each nominee may be allowed to furnish for enclosure with the ballots a brief factual statement of
his service and qualifications, provided that all nominees are
accorded equal opportunity and space.

If the vote is not to be secret, the following items should
25 be sent to each qualified voter: (1) a printed ballot containing
a space for the voter's signature, to ensure against votes being
cast by persons not entitled to vote, together with full instructions for marking and returning by the required date; and
(2) a specially recognizable, self-addressed return envelope
30 with the name and address of the secretary, the chairman of
tellers, or other person designated to receive the marked ballot. E-mail and other means of electronic communication can
be tailored to comply with these requirements.

If the vote is to be secret, an inner return envelope—with
35 a space for the voter's signature placed on its face instead of

on the ballot—should be sent to the voter with the ballot, in 1
addition to the self-addressed outer return envelope described
above. The ballot sent to the voter should be prefolded a
sufficient number of times so that—when returned marked
and refolded in the same manner and sealed in the inner 5
envelope—there will be no chance of accidental observance
of the member's vote by the teller who removes the ballot
from the inner envelope. The person designated as addressee
for the returned ballots should hold them in the outer envelopes for delivery, unopened, at the meeting of the tellers 10
where the votes are to be counted. At that meeting all inner
envelopes are first removed from the outer envelopes. In the
procedure by which the tellers remove the ballots from
the inner envelopes, each envelope and ballot is handled
in the following manner: (1) the signature on the envelope 15
is checked against the list of qualified voters; (2) the voter is
checked off on the list as having voted; and (3) the envelope is opened and the ballot is removed and placed, still
folded, into a receptacle. When all inner envelopes have thus
been processed, the ballots are taken from the receptacle and 20
the votes are counted. In order to ensure the accuracy
and the secrecy of such a vote by mail, special care should be
taken in all phases of handling the ballots. The chairman of
tellers or other person responsible must be able to certify the
results from both of these standpoints. Should the recipient 25
of the ballots receive two evidently sent in by the same voter,
the above procedure permits the voter to be contacted for a
determination of which is the voter's true vote and, if both
are, which (the most recent) is to be counted. As with respect
to nonsecret ballots, e-mail and other means of electronic 30
communication may be able to be tailored to comply with
the above requirements for secret mail balloting.

Preferential Voting. The term *preferential voting* refers
to any of a number of voting methods by which, on a single
ballot when there are more than two possible choices, the 35

1   second or less-preferred choices of voters can be taken into account if no candidate or proposition attains a majority. While it is more complicated than other methods of voting in common use and is not a substitute for the normal proce-

5   dure of repeated balloting until a majority is obtained, preferential voting is especially useful and fair in an election by mail if it is impractical to take more than one ballot. In such cases it makes possible a more representative result than under a rule that a plurality shall elect. It can be used with respect

10   to the election of officers only if expressly authorized in the bylaws.

      Preferential voting has many variations. One method is described here by way of illustration. On the preferential ballot—for each office to be filled or multiple-choice question

15   to be decided—the voter is asked to indicate the order in which he prefers all the candidates or propositions, placing the numeral *1* beside his first preference, the numeral *2* beside his second preference, and so on for every possible choice. In counting the votes for a given office or question, the ballots

20   are arranged in piles according to the indicated first preferences—one pile for each candidate or proposition. The number of ballots in each pile is then recorded for the tellers' report. These piles remain identified with the names of the same candidates or propositions throughout the counting

25   procedure until all but one are eliminated as described below. If more than half of the ballots show one candidate or proposition indicated as first choice, that choice has a majority in the ordinary sense and the candidate is elected or the proposition is decided upon. But if there is no such majority, can-

30   didates or propositions are eliminated one by one, beginning with the least popular, until one prevails, as follows: The ballots in the thinnest pile—that is, those containing the name designated as first choice by the fewest number of voters— are redistributed into the other piles according to the names

35   marked as second choice on these ballots. The number of bal-

lots in each remaining pile after this distribution is again   *1*
recorded. If more than half of the ballots are now in one pile,
that candidate or proposition is elected or decided upon. If
not, the next least popular candidate or proposition is similarly eliminated, by taking the thinnest remaining pile and re-   *5*
distributing its ballots according to their second choices into
the other piles, except that, if the name eliminated in the last
distribution is indicated as second choice on a ballot, that
ballot is placed according to its third choice. Again the number of ballots in each existing pile is recorded, and, if nec-   *10*
essary, the process is repeated—by redistributing each time
the ballots in the thinnest remaining pile, according to the
marked second choice or most-preferred choice among those
not yet eliminated—until one pile contains more than half of
the ballots, the result being thereby determined. The tellers'   *15*
report consists of a table listing all candidates or propositions,
with the number of ballots that were in each pile after each
successive distribution.

   If a ballot having one or more names not marked with
any numeral comes up for placement at any stage of the   *20*
counting and all of its marked names have been eliminated,
it should not be placed in any pile, but should be set aside. If
at any point two or more candidates or propositions are tied
for the least popular position, the ballots in their piles are redistributed in a single step, all of the tied names being treated   *25*
as eliminated. In the event of a tie in the winning position—
which would imply that the elimination process is continued
until the ballots are reduced to two or more equal piles—the
election should be resolved in favor of the candidate or
proposition that was strongest in terms of first choices (by   *30*
referring to the record of the first distribution).

   If more than one person is to be elected to the same type
of office—for example, if three members of a board are to be
chosen—the voters can indicate their order of preference
among the names in a single list of candidates, just as if only   *35*

1   one was to be elected. The counting procedure is the same
as described above, except that it is continued until all but
the necessary number of candidates have been eliminated
(that is, in the example, all but three).

5   When this or any other system of preferential voting is
to be used, the voting and counting procedure must be precisely established in advance and should be prescribed in detail. The members must be thoroughly instructed as to how
to mark the ballot, and should have sufficient understanding
10   of the counting process to enable them to have confidence in
the method. Sometimes, for instance, voters decline to indicate a second or other choice, mistakenly believing that such
a course increases the chances of their first choice. In fact, it
may prevent any candidate from receiving a majority and re-
15   quire the voting to be repeated. The persons selected as tellers
must perform their work with particular care.

The system of preferential voting just described should
not be used in cases where it is possible to follow the normal
procedure of repeated balloting until one candidate or propo-
20   sition attains a majority. Although this type of preferential ballot is preferable to an election by plurality, it affords less
freedom of choice than repeated balloting, because it denies
voters the opportunity of basing their second or lesser choices
on the results of earlier ballots, and because the candidate or
25   proposition in last place is automatically eliminated and may
thus be prevented from becoming a compromise choice.

PROXY VOTING.   A *proxy* is a power of attorney given
by one person to another to vote in his stead; the term also
30   designates the person who holds the power of attorney. Proxy
voting is not permitted in ordinary deliberative assemblies unless the laws of the state in which the society is incorporated
require it, or the charter or bylaws of the organization provide
for it. Ordinarily it should neither be allowed nor required,
35   because proxy voting is incompatible with the essential char-

acteristics of a deliberative assembly in which membership is 1
individual, personal, and nontransferable. In a stock corporation, on the other hand, where the ownership is transferable,
the voice and vote of the member also is transferable, by use
of a proxy. But in a nonstock corporation, where membership 5
is usually on the same basis as in an unincorporated, voluntary
association, voting by proxy should not be permitted unless
the state's corporation law—as applying to nonstock corporations—absolutely requires it.

If the law under which an organization is incorporated 10
allows proxy voting to be prohibited by a provision of the
bylaws, the adoption of this book as parliamentary authority
by prescription in the bylaws should be treated as sufficient
provision to accomplish that result (cf. footnote, p. 580).

15

STRAW POLLS NOT IN ORDER.   A motion to take
an informal straw poll to "test the water" is not in order because it neither adopts nor rejects a measure and hence is
meaningless and dilatory. If the assembly wishes to discuss
and take a vote on a matter without the vote constituting final 20
action by the assembly, it may instead vote to go into a committee of the whole or a quasi committee of the whole (**52**).
Under these procedures, the assembly considers the matter
as would a committee, and its vote while in committee of the
whole (or quasi committee of the whole) serves only as a rec- 25
ommendation to the assembly, which the assembly is free to
reject just as would be the case with regard to the report of
any ordinary committee.

CHAPTER XIV

NOMINATIONS AND ELECTIONS

§46. NOMINATIONS AND ELECTIONS

Nominations

A nomination is, in effect, a proposal to fill the blank in an assumed motion "that _____ be elected" to the specified position. In choosing someone to fill an office or other elective position in a society or assembly, a more effective freedom of choice is maintained through the practice of nominating persons for the office, rather than moving that a given person be elected as in the older British procedure. Hence, a form of ballot on which provision is made for voting "for" or "against" a candidate or candidates, as distinguished from a motion, is not proper. Since such a ballot is improper, in order to defeat a candidate for an office it is necessary to vote for an opposing candidate, thus avoiding the anomaly of an assembly refusing to elect anyone to an office.

Strictly speaking, nominations are not necessary when an election is by ballot or roll call, since each member is free to vote for any eligible person, whether he has been nominated or not. In most societies, however, it is impractical to proceed

to an election without first making nominations. While mem-   1
bers are always free to "write in," on a ballot, the name of an
eligible person who has not been nominated, or to vote for
an eligible non-nominee during a roll-call vote, under normal
conditions it is likely that most members will confine their   5
choice to the nominees. Without nominations, voting might
have to be repeated many times before a candidate achieved
the required majority.

Methods of nomination are: (a) by the chair; (b) from the
floor (sometimes called "open nominations"); (c) by a com-   10
mittee; (d) by ballot; (e) by mail; and (f) by petition. If no
method of nominating has been specified in the bylaws and
if the assembly has adopted no rule on the subject, any member can make a motion prescribing the method (**31**).

As the following descriptions of the six methods of nom-   15
ination indicate, not all of them are appropriate or desirable
in average societies. The order in which they are listed corresponds to that in which they would be voted on if all six were
proposed in motions prescribing the method of nomination.

20

NOMINATIONS BY THE CHAIR.   At a mass meeting
it is a common practice to have the chairman nominated by
the person who was designated to call the meeting to order,
but an organized society should adopt other methods of
nominating for office. The chair, however, can make nomi-   25
nations for committee membership and similar positions (an
exception being made in the case of the nominating committee), as may be provided in the bylaws or by the adoption of
a motion.

30

NOMINATIONS FROM THE FLOOR.   Under the
procedure of nominations from the floor, the chair calls for
nominations at the time established by rule or custom of the
organization or assembly—which may be while the election
is pending or earlier, but in any case is subsequent to the   35

report of the nominating committee if there is such a committee. A member need not be recognized by the chair to make a nomination. In a large meeting or convention a member should rise when making a nomination from the floor, but in small assemblies nominations frequently are made by members from their seats. No second is required, but sometimes one or more members will second a nomination to indicate endorsement. Where more than one person is to be elected to an office, such as to a board of directors or trustees, or to a position, such as to a committee, no one may nominate more than one person for the office or position, if an objection is made, until every member wishing to nominate has had an opportunity to do so. In no event may a member nominate more persons than there are places to fill.

The same person can be nominated for more than one office, even if voting for all offices is to take place at the same time on a single ballot. If one person is elected to more than one office under these conditions, the case is resolved as described on page 440, lines 3–17.

If there is no nominating committee and nominations are to be from the floor, the chair calls for them by saying, for example, "Nominations are now in order for the office of President." If there is a nominating committee, the chair calls for nominations as shown on pages 435–36. When the presiding officer has called for nominations from the floor, a member rises and makes a nomination as follows:

MEMBER: I nominate Mr. A. [Or, in a large assembly, "Mr. President, I nominate Mr. A."]

CHAIR: Mr. A is nominated. Are there any further nominations [or "any further nominations for the office of President"]?

The chair repeats each nomination in this way until all nominations for the office have been made. (For the procedure for closing nominations, see p. 436.) Nominations for the different offices are thus called for in the order in which the offices are listed in the bylaws.   1

NOMINATIONS BY A COMMITTEE.   In the election of officers of an ordinary society, nominations often are   5
made by a nominating committee. Usually in such cases a nominating committee is chosen in advance to submit nominations for the various offices for which elections are to be held at the annual meeting.

Designation of the Nominating Committee.   The nomi-   10
nating committee should be elected by the organization wherever possible, or else by its executive board. Although in organizing a new society it may be feasible for the chair to appoint the nominating committee, in an organized society the president should not appoint this committee or be a   15
member of it—ex officio or otherwise. The bylaws may provide that "the President shall appoint all committees except the Nominating Committee . . ." and that "the President shall be ex officio a member of all committees except the Nominating Committee . . ."; the exception should not be   20
omitted in either case.

Nominees.   Although it is not common for the nominating committee to nominate more than one candidate for any office, the committee can do so unless the bylaws prohibit it. It is usually not sound to *require* the committee to nominate   25
more than one candidate for each office, since the committee can easily circumvent such a provision by nominating only one person who has any chance of being elected (see also p. 573).

Members of the nominating committee are not barred from becoming nominees for office themselves. To make such   30
a requirement would mean, first, that service on the nominating committee carried a penalty by depriving its members of one of their privileges; and second, that appointment or election to the nominating committee could be used to prevent a member from becoming a nominee.   35

1   It is desirable policy for the nominating committee, before making its report, to contact each person whom it wishes to nominate, in order to obtain his acceptance of nomination—that is, his assurance that he will serve in the speci-
5   fied office if elected. The bylaws can make such a practice mandatory.

Report of the Nominating Committee.   The time at which the nominating committee's report is made is a matter to be determined by rule or established custom of the particular or-
10   ganization—depending on its own conditions. In some societies this report is not formally presented to the voting body until the election is pending; but in any organization where advance interest in the election may develop, the nominations submitted by the committee should be made known to the
15   membership earlier. These nominations can be sent to all members, for example, several days before the regular meeting—usually the election meeting itself—at which the chair calls for additional nominations from the floor (see below). The report should always be formally presented at a regular
20   meeting, even if the names of the committee's nominees have been transmitted to the members of the society beforehand. Sometimes—in societies that hold frequent regular meetings—the nominating committee's report is presented at the regular meeting preceding the annual meeting (**9**) at which
25   the election is to take place.

When the nominating committee is called upon for its report at a meeting, its chairman rises and presents the report as follows:

30   NOMINATING COMMITTEE CHAIRMAN: Mr. President, the Nominating Committee submits the following nominations: For President, Mr. A [or "John A"]; for Vice President, Mr. B; for Secretary, Mr. C; . . . [and so on for each office to be filled, naming the nominees in the order in which the offices are listed in the bylaws].

A minority within a nominating committee, as a group,   *1*
may propose other nominees for some or all of the offices in
any case where nominations from the floor are permitted.

A nominating committee is automatically discharged
when its report is formally presented to the assembly, al-   *5*
though if one of the nominees withdraws before the election,
the committee is revived and should meet immediately to
agree upon another nomination if there is time.

Call by the Chair for Further Nominations from the Floor.
After the nominating committee has presented its report and   *10*
before voting for the different offices takes place, the chair
must call for further nominations from the floor. This is
another stage of nomination and election procedure for
which a number of details should be established by rule or
custom of the particular organization. In many organizations,   *15*
nominations from the floor are called for immediately after
the presentation of the nominating committee's report—
while the election is pending or earlier. When the calling for
nominations from the floor is about to begin, if some time
has elapsed since the presentation of the nominating commit-   *20*
tee's report, the complete list of the committee's nominations
should be read again before further nominations are called
for. In any case, if the nominating committee has for any reason failed to make its report at the appropriate time, this does
not prevent the assembly from proceeding to nominations   *25*
from the floor.

In some organizations all nominations from the floor are
completed and nominations are closed for each office before
voting for any office takes place. In other organizations, when
nominations for one office have been completed, votes are   *30*
cast for that office and the result is announced before the
chair calls for nominations for the next office (see also
pp. 439–41). A custom of the organization based on its own
conditions should determine which of the two procedures is

1   used. In either case, the different offices are taken in the order
in which they are listed in the bylaws. The chair, as he calls
for nominations, first repeats the name that was submitted by
the nominating committee, thus:

5

    CHAIR: For President, Mr. A is nominated by the Nominating Com-
mittee. Are there any further nominations for President? [If a member
nominates another person, the chair repeats the name of that nominee.]
Mr. N is nominated. Are there any further nominations?

10

    When it appears that no one else wishes to make a nom-
ination, the chair should again ask if there are any further
nominations; and if there is no response, he normally declares
that nominations (for that office) are closed, without waiting
15   for a motion to that effect, as follows:

    CHAIR: Are there any further nominations for President? . . . [Pause.]
If not . . . [pause], nominations are closed. [Or, "Without objection, . . .
nominations are closed."]

20

    (For use of the motion to close nominations, which requires
a two-thirds vote, see **31**.) After nominations have been
closed, a majority vote is required to reopen them.
    After nominations have been closed, voting for that office
25   takes place, or nominations for the next office are called for
by the chair, depending on the procedure being followed by
the particular organization.

    NOMINATIONS BY BALLOT.   The object of a nom-
30   inating ballot is to provide the members with an indication
of the sentiments of the voting body, which they may take
into account in voting in the election. The value of the nominating ballot is that it shows the preferences without electing
anyone. The nominating ballot is conducted in the same way

as an ordinary electing ballot except that everyone receiving
a vote is nominated; the tellers' report, therefore, does not
state the number of votes necessary for nomination. Since
each member has the opportunity to nominate on his ballot
a candidate for every office, he does not have the right then
to make nominations from the floor, unless the assembly by
a majority vote authorizes such nominations.

*Impropriety of Making the Nominating Ballot the Electing
Ballot.*   Sometimes a motion is made to declare the nominating ballot the electing ballot. Such action negates all the
advantages of a nominating ballot and is, in effect, the same
as having an electing ballot without any nominations. If there
is to be only one ballot, it should be the electing ballot, with
nominations from the floor, or by a nominating committee
and from the floor. A nominating ballot cannot take the place
of an electing ballot in an organization whose bylaws require
elections to be held by ballot.

*Impropriety of Limiting Voting in the Election to the Two
Leading Candidates.*   In some organizations using the nominating ballot, an attempt is made to limit the voting on the
electing ballot to the two nominees for each office receiving
the highest number of votes on the nominating ballot. This—
or any attempt to limit the number of candidates for an office
to two, by whatever method they are nominated—is an unfortunate practice and should be discouraged. Often the two
leading candidates for a position will represent two different
factions, and division within the organization may be deep-
ened by limiting the election to them. On the other hand, it
may be possible to unite the members if the assembly has the
choice of a compromise candidate.

NOMINATIONS BY MAIL.   In organizations whose
membership is widely scattered, the method of nominating
by mail is often adopted. In such a case a nominating ballot

can be prepared, deposited, and counted in the same way as
an electing ballot—with the secretary of the organization
mailing to every member a nominating ballot, plus instructions for completing and returning it as described on pages
424–25. Or, in some organizations, a blank on which each
member can submit the names of desired nominees, in a
signed ballot, is used instead of a secret nominating ballot.

NOMINATIONS BY PETITION.   The bylaws may
provide that a member shall be a nominee upon the petition
of a specified number of members. Sometimes, a nominating
petition blank is sent to the members with a copy of the list
of nominees submitted by a nominating committee. In large
state or national societies composed of local units, the blanks
are sometimes sent to these units with instructions for their
distribution or processing.

Elections

In an assembly or organization that does not have a rule
or established custom prescribing the method of voting in
elections, the voting can be by any of the accepted methods.
While some form of election by ballot is generally appropriate
in organized societies, each assembly should adopt—and each
society should prescribe in its bylaws—the procedure best
suited to its purposes and needs. Where there is no determining rule, a motion to fix the method of voting (or any other
detail of nomination or election procedure) is an incidental
main motion if made before the election is pending, or an incidental motion if made while the election is pending (**30,
31**). Such a motion can be offered containing a blank so that
different methods are voted on in succession; or the chair can
take votes on the methods in this way, assuming the motion,
if no member objects. In the absence of a rule establishing
the method of voting, the rule that is established by custom,

if any, should be followed, unless the assembly, by adoption   *1*
of an incidental motion or incidental main motion, agrees to
do otherwise.

BALLOT ELECTION.   Two alternative procedures for   *5*
the sequence of nominating and voting in elections by ballot
can be prescribed or adopted, as mentioned above. The first
method requires the least time, while the second affords
greater flexibility in choosing officers. These procedures are
as follows: *10*

1) All nominations can be completed before any balloting
takes place—in which case voting for all offices is commonly done by a single ballot. This method is suitable for
use in conventions where voting takes place at a "polling   *15*
place" apart from the convention meetings. It may also
be a preferred method in any large meeting where the
time required for balloting is an important consideration.
The elections should take place early in such a meeting,
to allow time for any necessary additional balloting for   *20*
any office for which no candidate receives a vote sufficient
for election. Votes can be cast for any person who is
eligible for election, even if he has not been nominated.
The procedure followed in balloting, in counting the
votes, and in reporting the results is described on pages   *25*
412–19. The tellers prepare a tellers' report for each
office involved, in the form shown on page 417. When
these reports are completed for all offices, the chairman
of tellers, after reading them to the assembly, submits
them to the chair, who, as he reads each one of them   *30*
again, declares the result for that office. In each case
where a candidate has a majority, the chair declares that
candidate elected. For offices for which no candidate has
a majority, the chair announces, "no election." When the
tellers' reports for all offices have thus been read, the chair   *35*

1   directs that new ballots be distributed for those offices for
     which no candidate attained a majority (see also below).

         When voting for multiple offices by a single ballot, the
     members are not able to take the result for one office into
5   account when voting for another office. For this reason, a
     candidate is never deemed elected to more than one office
     by a single ballot unless the motion or rules governing the
     election specifically provide for such simultaneous elec-
     tion. When there is no such provision, a candidate who
10   receives a majority for more than one office on a single
     ballot must, if present, choose which one of the offices he
     will accept; if he is absent, the assembly decides by vote
     the office to be assigned to him. The assembly then ballots
     again to fill the other office(s). (The assembly is free, how-
15   ever, to elect the same person to another office on a sub-
     sequent ballot, unless the bylaws prohibit a person from
     holding both offices simultaneously.)

2)   Under the usual form of the second election procedure,
     balloting for each office immediately follows nominations
20   from the floor for that office. The ballots are counted for
     one office and the result of that election is announced—
     after repeated balloting, if necessary—before the next
     office to be voted on is opened to nominations from the
     floor. The members are thus able to take into account
25   the results for the offices voted on first, in deciding upon
     both nominations and votes for the later offices. Under
     this method the ballots normally consist of small slips of
     blank paper handed out by the tellers as each ballot is
     taken—on which voters write the name of the candidate
30   of their choice (who need not have been nominated).
     This method is generally practical only in assemblies small
     enough that the votes from each balloting can be counted
     while the meeting briefly pauses—usually without recess-
     ing or proceeding to other business, although it can do
35   either of these things if it wishes.

Whichever one of the preceding methods of election is *1* used, if any office remains unfilled after the first ballot, as may happen if there are more than two nominees, the balloting is repeated for that office as many times as necessary to obtain a majority vote for a single candidate. When repeated ballot- *5* ing for an office is necessary, individuals are never removed from candidacy on the next ballot unless they voluntarily withdraw—which they are not obligated to do.* The candi- date in lowest place may turn out to be a "dark horse" on whom all factions may prefer to agree. *10*

In an election of members of a board or committee in which votes are cast in one section of the ballot for multiple positions on the board or committee, every ballot with a vote for one or more candidates is counted as one vote cast, and a candidate must receive a majority of the total of such votes *15* to be elected. In such a case, if more than the prescribed num- ber receive a majority vote, the places are filled by the proper number receiving the largest number of votes. If less than the proper number receive a majority vote, those who do have a majority are elected, and all others remain as candidates for *20* the necessary repeated balloting. Similarly, if some individuals receive a majority but are tied for the lowest position that would elect, all of them also remain as candidates on the next ballot.

If the bylaws require the election of officers to be by bal- *25* lot and there is only one nominee for an office, the ballot must nevertheless be taken for that office unless the bylaws provide for an exception in such a case. In the absence of the

---

*An organization could suspend the rules, or adopt a special rule of order, so that the nominee with the fewest votes is dropped from the list of nominees for succeeding ballots in the expectation that voters will then confine their choice to the remaining nominees. Only a bylaws provision, however, could make the dropped nominee ineligible for election so as to ren- der illegal any subsequent votes cast for that nominee. (See pp. 430–31.)

1 latter provision, members still have the right, on the ballot,
   to cast "write-in votes" for other eligible persons.

   An election by ballot can be conducted by mail if the
   bylaws so provide, as explained on pages 424–28. For such
5 an election, however—unless repeated balloting by mail is
   feasible in cases where no candidate attains a majority—the
   bylaws should authorize the use of some form of preferential
   voting or should provide that a plurality shall elect.

10   VIVA-VOCE ELECTION.   The viva-voce method of
   election finds application principally in mass meetings—or
   when an election is not strongly contested and the bylaws do
   not require election by ballot.

   When there is more than one nominee for a given office
15 in a viva-voce election—or in an election by rising vote or by
   show of hands—the candidates are voted on in the order in
   which they were nominated. When the nominations have
   ended, the chair repeats the nominations and continues:

20   CHAIR: As many as are in favor of Mr. A for President say *aye*. . . .
   Those opposed say *no*. . . . The ayes have it and Mr. A is elected President.

   If the noes are in the majority the wording is:

25   CHAIR: The noes have it and Mr. A is not elected. Those in favor of
   Mr. B [the next nominee] say *aye*. . . . Those opposed say *no*. . . .

   As soon as one of the nominees receives a majority vote, the
   chair declares him elected and no votes are taken on the re-
30 maining nominees for that office. The other officers are
   elected in the same way. When a number of members are to
   be elected to identical offices in the nature of a single office
   held by more than one person—as, for example, in electing
   four directors—the same procedure is followed; when four
35 have received a majority, the voting ceases.

It will be seen that, under the procedure just described,   1
it is necessary for members wishing to vote for a later nominee to vote against an earlier one. This fact gives an undue
advantage to earlier nominees and, accordingly, a voice vote
is not a generally suitable method for electing the officers of   5
organized societies.

If only one person is nominated and the bylaws do not
require that a ballot vote be taken, the chair, after ensuring
that, in fact, no members present wish to make further nominations, simply declares that the nominee is elected, thus   10
effecting the election by unanimous consent or "acclamation." The motion to close nominations cannot be used
as a means of moving the election of the candidate in such
a case.

The assembly cannot make valid a viva-voce election if the   15
bylaws require the election to be by ballot.

ROLL-CALL ELECTION.   Although unusual, an elec-
tion can be held by roll call. Either the first or second procedure described on pages 439–40 for election by ballot can be   20
generally followed, and the member (or the chairman of a
delegation, as the case may be), when called upon, declares
his vote or the votes of the members of his delegation for each
office to be filled. The secretary should record the vote(s) and
then repeat them to be sure of their accurate recordation.   25

CUMULATIVE VOTING.   For ballot or roll-call elections of boards, committees, delegates, or other positions
held by more than one individual, the bylaws may provide for
cumulative voting. In this form of voting, each member is   30
entitled to cast one vote for each position, so that, if, for
example, three directors are to be elected, each member may
cast three votes. These votes may all be cast for one, two, or
three candidates, as the voter chooses. A minority group, by
coordinating its effort in voting for only one candidate who   35

1   is a member of the group, may be able to secure the election
    of that candidate as a minority member of the board. How-
    ever, this method of voting, which permits a member to cast
    multiple votes for a single candidate, must be viewed with
5   reservation since it violates the fundamental principle of par-
    liamentary law that each member is entitled to one and only
    one vote on a question.

    PROVIDING FOR COMPLETION OF AN ELEC-
10 TION.   If an assembly wishes to adjourn when an election
    is incomplete, an adjourned meeting (**9**) should be provided
    for. If such an adjourned meeting is not provided for and the
    organization will hold another regular business session before
    a quarterly time interval has elapsed (see pp. 89–90), the elec-
15 tion is completed at the next regular meeting.

    TIME AT WHICH AN ELECTION TAKES EFFECT.
    An election to an office becomes final immediately if the can-
    didate is present and does not decline, or if he is absent but
20 has consented to his candidacy. If he is absent and has not
    consented to his candidacy, the election becomes final when
    he is notified of his election, provided that he does not im-
    mediately decline. If he does decline, the election is incom-
    plete, and another vote can be taken immediately or at the
25 next meeting without further notice. After an election has
    become final as stated in this paragraph, it is too late to
    reconsider (**37**) the vote on the election.
    An officer-elect takes possession of his office immediately
    upon his election's becoming final, unless the bylaws or other
30 rules specify a later time. If a formal installation ceremony is
    prescribed, failure to hold it does not affect the time at which
    the new officers assume office.

    CONTESTING THE ANNOUNCED RESULT OF
35 AN ELECTION.   Depending on the circumstances, the

voting body may be able to order a recount if an election was   *1*
conducted by ballot (see p. 419, ll. 1–9), roll-call vote (see
p. 422, ll. 30–33), or counted vote (see p. 411, ll. 19–21).
In the case of a roll-call vote, a recapitulation may be possible
(see p. 422, ll. 1–8). It may be possible, under some cir-   *5*
cumstances, to order that the election be voted on again by
another method (see *Retaking a Vote*, p. 285).

Otherwise, an election may be contested only by raising
a point of order. The general rule is that such a point of order
must be timely, as described on page 250, line 30 to page   *10*
251, line 2. If an election is disputed on the ground that a
quorum was not present, the provisions on page 349, lines
21–28, apply. Other exceptions to the general timeliness requirement are those that come within the five categories listed
on page 251, lines 9–23, in which cases a point of order can   *15*
be made at any time during the continuance in office of the
individual declared elected. For example:

- If an individual does not meet the qualifications for the
  post established in the bylaws, his or her election is tan-   *20*
  tamount to adoption of a main motion that conflicts with
  the bylaws.
- If there was a previously valid election for the same term,
  the subsequent election of another is the adoption of a
  main motion conflicting with one still in force.   *25*
- If the votes of nonmembers or absentees in the election
  affect the result, action has been taken in violation of the
  fundamental principle of parliamentary law that the right
  to vote is limited to the members of an organization who
  are actually present at the time the vote is taken.   *30*
- If an election to fill a vacancy is held without required
  previous notice, action has been taken in violation of a
  rule protecting the rights of absentees.
- If a number of members sufficient to affect the result are
  improperly prevented from voting in an election, action   *35*

1   has been taken in violation of a rule protecting a basic
     right of the individual member.

     Because the voting body itself is the ultimate judge of
5   election disputes, only that body has the authority to resolve
     them in the absence of a bylaw or special rule of order that
     specifically grants another body that authority. Thus, for ex-
     ample, when an election has been conducted at a membership
     meeting or in a convention of delegates, an executive board,
10   even one that is given full power and authority over the soci-
     ety's affairs between meetings of the body that conducted the
     election, may not entertain a point of order challenging, or
     direct a recount concerning, the announced election result.
     While an election dispute is immediately pending before the
15   voting body, however, it may vote to refer the dispute to a
     committee or board to which it delegates power to resolve
     the dispute.

CHAPTER XV

OFFICERS; MINUTES
AND OFFICERS' REPORTS

§47. OFFICERS

As stated on page 22, the minimum essential officers for the conduct of business in any deliberative assembly are a presiding officer and a secretary or clerk. The usual duties of these and other officers generally required in an organized society are summarized and discussed in this section. Every society should specify in its bylaws what officers it requires, how they shall be elected or appointed, their term of office, and any qualifications for holding office or any duties different from or in addition to those stated in the parliamentary authority.

Principles Applying to Holding of Office

In most societies it is usual to elect the officers from among the members; but in all except secret societies, unless the bylaws provide otherwise, it is possible for an organization to choose its officers from outside its membership. In many legislative bodies the presiding officer is not a member of the body. A large society with complex financial affairs may wish to employ a professional as treasurer.

An office carries with it only the rights necessary for executing the duties of the office, and it does not deprive a member of the society of his rights as a member. If a person holds an office in a society of which he is not a member and the bylaws make that officer an ex-officio member of the board, the nonmember is thereby a full-fledged board member with all the accompanying rights; but this does not make him a member of the society.

The bylaws may contain a provision that "No person shall be eligible to serve _____ consecutive terms in the same office." In filling vacancies for unexpired terms, an officer who has served more than half a term in an office is considered to have served a full term. As stated on page 444, the term of office begins as soon as the officer is elected, unless the bylaws establish a different time.

Elected Officers

CHAIRMAN OR PRESIDENT.   The presiding officer of an assembly ordinarily is called the *chairman** when no special title has been assigned, or in a body not permanently organized, such as a mass meeting (**53**). In organized societies the presiding officer's title is usually prescribed by the bylaws, that of *president* being most common. The term *the chair* refers to the person in a meeting who is actually presiding at the time, whether that person is the regular presiding officer or not. The same term also applies to the presiding officer's station in the hall from which he or she presides, which should not be permitted to be used by other members as a place from which to make reports or speak in debate during

---

*See page 23 regarding variations of this term which have come into use.

a meeting (see also p. 453, ll. 18–25). In assemblies where   *1*
committee chairmen or others will require a lectern for their
papers, another lectern on the side of the platform or on the
floor at the front should be provided so that the chair can
maintain his presiding location. For the manner in which the   *5*
chair should be addressed in a meeting, see pages 22–23.

The presiding officer of an assembly—especially of a large
one—should be chosen principally for the ability to preside.
This person should be well versed in parliamentary law and
should be thoroughly familiar with the bylaws and other rules   *10*
of the organization—even if he or she is to have the assistance of a parliamentarian. At the same time, any presiding
officer will do well to bear in mind that no rules can take the
place of tact and common sense on the part of the chairman.

Duties of the Presiding Officer of an Assembly.   The prin-   *15*
cipal duties of the presiding officer of an assembly under parliamentary law are listed below—with references, where
appropriate, to fuller descriptions elsewhere in this book.
Additional information relating to the duties of the chair in
particular cases will be found in the treatment of the sub-   *20*
jects involved. It is the duty of the presiding officer of an
assembly:

1) To open the meeting at the appointed time by taking the
   chair and calling the meeting to order (p. 25), having   *25*
   ascertained that a quorum is present (p. 21; **40**).
2) To announce in proper sequence the business that comes
   before the assembly or becomes in order in accordance
   with the prescribed order of business, agenda, or program, and with existing orders of the day (**41**).   *30*
3) To recognize members who are entitled to the floor
   (pp. 29–31; **42**).
4) To state and to put to vote all questions that legitimately
   come before the assembly as motions or that otherwise
   arise in the course of proceedings (except questions that   *35*

1   relate to the presiding officer himself in the manner noted
         below), and to announce the result of each vote (**4**); or,
         if a motion that is not in order is made, to rule it out of
         order. (For a discussion of the circumstances under which
5   the chair votes, see pp. 405–6. See also the discussion of
         unanimous consent, pp. 54–56.)

5) To protect the assembly from obviously dilatory motions
   by refusing to recognize them (**39**).

6) To enforce the rules relating to debate and those relating
10   to order and decorum within the assembly (pp. 22–25,
       42–44; **43**).

7) To expedite business in every way compatible with the
   rights of members.

8) To decide all questions of order (**23**), subject to appeal
15   (**24**)—unless, when in doubt, the presiding officer prefers
       initially to submit such a question to the assembly for
       decision.

9) To respond to inquiries of members relating to parliamentary procedure (*Parliamentary Inquiry*, pp. 293–94) or
20   factual information (*Request for Information*, pp. 294–95)
       bearing on the business of the assembly.

10) To authenticate by his or her signature, when necessary,
    all acts, orders, and proceedings of the assembly.

11) To declare the meeting adjourned when the assembly so
25   votes or—where applicable—at the time prescribed in the
       program, or at any time in the event of a sudden emer-
       gency affecting the safety of those present (**8**, **21**).

30 At each meeting, in addition to the necessary papers
      proper to that meeting's business, the presiding officer should
      have at hand:

- a copy of the bylaws and other rules of the organization;
- a copy of its parliamentary authority (that is, this book, if
35   it is prescribed in the bylaws);

- a list of all standing and special committees and their members; and
- a memorandum of the complete order of business listing all known matters that are to come up, shown in proper sequence under the correct headings—or with their scheduled times—as applicable.

Except in a small board or a committee, the presiding officer should stand while calling a meeting to order or declaring it adjourned, and while putting a question to vote. He should also stand—without leaving the chair—while explaining his reasons for a ruling on a point of order (if the explanation entails more than a few words) or when speaking during debate on an appeal or a point of order that he has submitted to the judgment of the assembly (**23**, **24**). When speaking for the first time during debate in either of the latter two cases, he can do so in preference to other members (see p. 254, ll. 24–29 and Standard Characteristic 5, pp. 249, 257–58). While a member is speaking in debate on any question, the presiding officer should remain seated—unless the view between him and the members would be obstructed, in which case he should step back slightly during the member's speech. At times other than those just mentioned, the presiding officer can stand or sit as he finds convenient for commanding the assembly's attention, preserving order, etc.— provided that his station is arranged so that even when seated he can see the entire hall and all present can see him (see also p. 22, ll. 9–20; p. 448, l. 29 to p. 449, l. 5).

Whenever a motion is made that refers only to the presiding officer in a capacity not shared in common with other members, or that commends or censures him with others, he should turn the chair over to the vice-president or appropriate temporary occupant (see below) during the assembly's consideration of that motion, just as he would in a case where he wishes to take part in debate (see also pp. 394–95). The chair, however, should not hesitate to put the question on a motion to elect officers or appoint delegates or a committee even if he is included.

Temporary Occupants of the Chair. If it is necessary for the president to vacate the chair during a meeting, or if the president is absent, the chair is occupied temporarily by another—who also must not be precluded from presiding by any of the impediments mentioned in the preceding paragraph—as follows:

1) *A vice-president.* If the president for any reason vacates the chair or is absent, the vice-president or first vice-president normally should take the chair unless he also, because of involvement in the debate or for any other reason, should disqualify himself from presiding in the particular case; and if the first vice-president is absent or must disqualify himself, the duty of presiding devolves on the other vice-presidents in order. For this reason, the bylaws should number the vice-presidencies if there are more than one, and persons should be elected to specific positions. It should be noted, however, that if the bylaws provide for a president-elect, they usually provide also that the president-elect shall precede the first vice-president in the right to preside.

2) *An appointed chairman pro tem.* If the president vacates the chair during a meeting and no vice-president is available, he can, subject to the approval of the assembly, as explained on page 395, appoint a temporary chairman who is called the *chairman pro tempore,* or *chairman pro tem.* The return of the president, the arrival of a vice-president, or the first adjournment puts an end to this appointment, and the assembly can terminate it even earlier by the adoption of a motion to "declare the chair vacant and proceed to elect a new chairman" (see pp. 651–52). The regular presiding officer, knowing that

he will be absent from a future meeting, cannot in ad- *1*
vance authorize another member to preside in his place.

3) *An elected chairman pro tem.* If neither the president nor
any vice-president is present, the secretary—or in the secretary's absence some other member—should call the *5*
meeting to order, and the assembly should immediately
elect a chairman pro tem to preside during that session.
Such office is terminated by the entrance of the president
or a vice-president, or by the adoption of a motion to
"declare the chair vacant and proceed to elect a new chair- *10*
man" (see pp. 651–52). If the assembly is to elect a chairman pro tem to hold office beyond the current session
(in the event that the president and the vice-presidents
are unable to perform their duties for that length of time),
notice must be given at the preceding meeting or in the *15*
call of the meeting at which such election is held.

The practice in some organizations of permitting the
chairman of a committee to preside over the assembly or put
questions to vote during the presentation and consideration *20*
of the committee's report violates numerous principles of parliamentary law relating to the chair's appearance of impartiality and the inappropriateness of his entering into debate, not
to speak of the regular presiding officer's duty to preside (see
pp. 448–49). *25*

Invited Temporary Presiding Officer. In certain instances
in an ordinary society—for example, if an adjourned meeting
or a special meeting (**9**) must deal with a problem that has
intensely divided the organization—it may be that such a
meeting can accomplish more under the chairmanship of an *30*
invited nonmember who is skilled in presiding. (Sometimes
this may be a professional presiding officer.) If the president
and vice-president(s) do not object, the assembly, by majority
vote, can adopt such an arrangement for all or part of a session. Alternatively, the rules may be suspended to authorize *35*

1   it, even over the objection of the president or a vice-president. Cf. pages 652–53.

Suggestions for Inexperienced Presiding Officers. The larger the assembly, the more readily it will detect the slightest

5   weakness in a presiding officer. Efforts to capitalize on any such failing may follow with sometimes disastrous results. It is often said that knowledge is strength, and certainly that is true in this case. The presiding officer should be thoroughly familiar with the "Duties of the presiding officer of an assem-

10   bly," as stated on pages 449–52, and should have with him the documents listed on pages 450–51. There is no accept-able alternative to parliamentary procedure for the conduct of business in a deliberative assembly; yet many presiding officers try to get along with a minimum of knowledge. This

15   approach inevitably results in signs of unsureness. A presiding officer should make every effort to know more parliamentary procedure than other members, and should at least become familiar with 1 through 9 of this book and memorize the list of ordinary motions in their order of precedence, on tinted

20   page 4. The chair should be able to refer to the table of rules relating to motions on tinted pages 6–29 quickly enough that there will be no delay in deciding all points con-tained there. These steps are simple and will enable a presi-dent to master parliamentary procedure more quickly. As

25   more difficult points arise, a careful reading of the detailed treatment of such points in the body of this book will make them readily understood and mastered.

    The presiding officer must not permit members to press on so rapidly that the parliamentary steps are abridged or go

30   unobserved. When a motion is made, he should not recog-nize any member or allow anyone to speak until the motion is seconded (where that is required) and he has stated the question.

    The chair should take special care to make sure that the

35   members always understand what is the immediately pending

business—the *exact* question to be voted on the next time a   1
vote is taken. Failure of presiding officers to do so is one of
the greatest causes of confusion in meetings. The chair should
carefully follow the directions for stating a question on a motion or resolution given on pages 37–39. Particularly in stat-   5
ing the question on an unwritten motion, the chair should
always say, "It is moved and seconded that" and then give the
precise words of the motion fully, no matter how clearly
the motion may have been framed when moved by its maker.
The chair should never try to avoid this critically important   10
duty by saying, "You have heard the motion" or by saying,
"The motion is moved and seconded" without repeating its
words. The chair must be careful to be exact in stating any
proposed amendment so as to make clear the effect its adoption would have on the motion to be amended. After the vote   15
on an amendment, he should fully restate that motion as it
stands as a result of the amendment's adoption or failure (see
pp. 142–44). Above all, just before the vote, the chair must
make clear the precise question the assembly is to decide. It
is far better to risk taxing the patience of an assembly by re-   20
peating the wording of a motion on which all may be clear,
than to risk taking a vote whose effect may be unclear to even
a few members.

When a vote is taken, the result should be announced and
also what question, if any, is then pending, before any mem-   25
ber who addresses the chair is recognized. In a large assembly
where a microphone is required, the chair should insist that
a member go to it and identify himself. This brief delay
is often very salutary in quieting heated feelings. Efforts to
abbreviate the requirements of parliamentary procedure often   30
signal an effort to substitute the member's will for the parliamentary leadership of the presiding officer. A not uncommon
instance of this kind is described on page 381, lines 4–9,
where a member attempts quickly to obtain the floor to offer
a motion in competition with one arranged by the officers to   35

1 be offered by another member. Firmness and, at the same
time, calm insistence on the regular order is a technique
essential to the development of a skilled presiding officer.

While a commanding presence and knowledge are essen-
5 tial in procedural matters, the president of an ordinary deliberative assembly, especially a large one, should, of all the
members, have the least to say upon the substance of pending
questions. While providing strong leadership, he should be
fair. He should never get excited; he should never be unjust
10 to even the most troublesome member, or take advantage of
such member's lack of knowledge of parliamentary law, even
though a temporary good might be accomplished thereby.
The president should never be technical or more strict than
is necessary for the good of the meeting. Good judgment is
15 essential; the assembly may be of such a nature, through its
unfamiliarity with parliamentary usage and its peaceable disposition, that strict enforcement of the rules, instead of
assisting, would greatly hinder business. But in large assemblies where there is much work to be done, and especially
20 where there is likelihood of trouble, the only safe course is to
require a strict observance of the rules.

Administrative Duties of the President of a Society. All
of the duties of the presiding officer described above relate
to the function of presiding over the assembly at its meetings.
25 In addition, in many organized societies, the president has
duties as an administrative or executive officer; but these
are outside the scope of parliamentary law, and the president
has such authority only insofar as the bylaws provide it. In
some organizations, the president is responsible for appoint-
30 ing, and is ex officio a member of, all committees (with the
exception of the nominating committee, which should be
expressly excluded from such a provision, and with the further possible exception of all disciplinary committees; see
pp. 579–80). But only when he is so authorized by the by-
35 laws—or, in the case of a particular committee, by vote of the

assembly—does he have this authority and status. As an *1*
ex-officio member of a committee, the president has the same
rights as the other committee members, but is not obligated
to attend meetings of the committee and is not counted in
determining the number required for a quorum or whether *5*
a quorum is present.

PRESIDENT-ELECT.   Some organizations desire to
elect their president one entire term in advance, and in such
cases, during the term following the election, the person cho- *10*
sen is called the *president-elect*. This office exists only if
expressly provided for in the bylaws, in which case the members never vote on any candidate for the office of president,
but elect a president-elect and the other officers of the organization. Accordingly, when a member has served his full term *15*
as president-elect, he automatically becomes president for a
full term. Once a person has been elected president-elect, the
assembly cannot alter its decision regarding the succession of
that person to the presidency, unless he vacates office during
his term as president-elect or unless ground arises for depos- *20*
ing him from that office (see pp. 653–54).

When the bylaws of an organization provide for a president-elect, it is usual to provide also that if the president
should be absent, or if the office of the president should
become vacant between elections, the president-elect shall *25*
preside, if present, or shall fill the vacancy. Unless such provision is made, the first vice-president would preside or complete the president's term. It is also customary to provide in
the bylaws for some method to fill a vacancy in the office of
president-elect, should one occur between elections. It is *30*
important to consider these provisions with great care. The
bylaws can assign the president-elect specific responsibilities.

VICE-PRESIDENT.   In the absence of the president,
the vice-president serves in his stead; thus, it is important to *35*

1 elect a vice-president who is competent to perform the duties
of president. When a vice-president is presiding, he or she
should be addressed as "Mr. or Madam President" (unless
confusion might result—for example, when the president is
5 also on the platform—in which case the form "Mr. or Madam
Vice-President" should be used).

Some societies elect several vice-presidents in an order of
precedence: first, second, third, and so on. In case of the resignation or death of the president, the vice-president (if there
10 is only one) or the first vice-president (if there are more than
one) automatically becomes president for the unexpired term,
unless the bylaws *expressly* provide otherwise for filling a
vacancy *in the office of president*. The second vice-president,
if there is one, then becomes first vice-president, and so
15 on, with the vacancy to be filled occurring in the lowest-
ranking vice-presidency. Sometimes the bylaws provide that
the different vice-presidents shall have administrative charge
of different departments.

Although in many instances the vice-president will be
20 the logical nominee for president, the society should have the
freedom to make its own choice and to elect the most prom-
ising candidate at that particular time.

SECRETARY.   The secretary is the recording officer of
25 the assembly and the custodian of its records, except those
specifically assigned to others, such as the treasurer's books.
The recording officer is sometimes called the *clerk*, the *recording secretary* (when there is also, for example, a corresponding
secretary or financial secretary), the *recorder*, or the *scribe*.
30 *Duties of the Secretary*. The duties of the secretary are:

1) To keep a record of all the proceedings of the organization—usually called the *minutes*.
2) To keep on file all committee reports.

3) To keep the organization's official membership roll (un-   *1*
   less another officer or staff member has this duty); and to
   call the roll where it is required.
4) To make the minutes and records available to members
   upon request (see p. 460, ll. 13–17).   *5*
5) To notify officers, committee members, and delegates of
   their election or appointment, to furnish committees with
   whatever documents are required for the performance of
   their duties, and to have on hand at each meeting a list
   of all existing committees and their members.   *10*
6) To furnish delegates with credentials.
7) To sign all certified copies of acts of the society.
8) To maintain record book(s) in which the bylaws, special
   rules of order, standing rules, and minutes are entered,
   with any amendments to these documents properly   *15*
   recorded, and to have the current record book(s) on hand
   at every meeting.
9) To send out to the membership a notice of each meeting,
   known as the *call* of the meeting, and to conduct the general correspondence of the organization—that is, corre-   *20*
   spondence that is not a function proper to other offices
   or to committees (see also *Corresponding Secretary* and
   Executive Secretary, below).
10) To prepare, prior to each meeting, an order of business
    (**41**) for the use of the presiding officer, showing in their   *25*
    exact order, under the correct headings, all matters known
    in advance that are due to come up and—if applicable—
    the times for which they are set.
11) In the absence of the president and vice-president, to call
    the meeting to order and preside until the immediate   *30*
    election of a chairman pro tem.

   In the absence of the secretary, a secretary pro tem should
be elected; the corresponding, financial, or executive secretary

1   in organizations having such officers is not an automatic replacement. If, under "Reports of Officers" in the order of
business, correspondence of an official character is to be read,
it is normally read by the recording secretary and not by the
5   corresponding secretary.

Records of the Secretary.   When written reports are received from boards or committees, the secretary should
record on them the date they were received and what further
action was taken on them, and preserve them among his
10   records. It is not necessary for an assembly to vote that a
board or committee report be "placed on file," as that should
be done without a vote.

Any member has a right to examine these reports and the
record book(s) referred to on page 459, lines 13–16, includ-
15   ing the minutes of an executive session, at a reasonable time
and place, but this privilege must not be abused to the annoyance of the secretary. The same principle applies to
records kept by boards and committees, these being accessible
to members of the boards or committees but to no others
20   (but see p. 487, ll. 13–20). When a committee requires certain records for the proper performance of its duties, the
secretary should turn them over to the committee chairman—after consulting with the president in any cases where
he or she is in doubt. The corporation law of each state fre-
25   quently provides for the availability of records of any group
incorporated in that state.

CORRESPONDING SECRETARY.   In larger societies,
the duties of issuing notices of meetings and conducting the
30   general correspondence of the organization as described
under item (9) on page 459 are frequently assigned to a separate elected officer, usually called the *corresponding secretary.*
When there is a corresponding secretary, the unqualified
word *secretary* used alone refers to the recording officer.

TREASURER, AND FINANCIAL SECRETARY.   The *1*
treasurer of an organization is the officer entrusted with the
custody of its funds. The treasurer, and any other officers who
handle funds of the society, should be bonded for a sum sufficient to protect the society from loss. The specific duties of   *5*
the treasurer will vary depending on the size and complexity
of the society; but this officer cannot disburse funds except
by authority of the society or as the bylaws prescribe. The
treasurer is required to make a full financial report annually
or as the bylaws may prescribe, and to make such interim re-   *10*
ports as the assembly or the executive board may direct. (For
the suggested form of this annual report in simple cases, see
pp. 477–79.)

In ordinary societies, tasks incident to the collection of
dues from members are a part of the treasurer's duties unless   *15*
the bylaws provide otherwise. Much clerical work may be
attached to this function, however, in large organizations,
in societies where dues are payable in frequent installments,
or in societies that suspend the voting-membership rights
of members who fall in arrears in dues payments (see pp. 6,   *20*
406, 571–72). In such cases some organizations have, in addition to the treasurer, a *financial secretary*—an officer whose
usual duties are to bill members for their dues and to receive
payment of them, to maintain a ledger of each member's account, and to turn over to the treasurer and obtain his receipt   *25*
for moneys received.

OTHER OFFICERS.   In addition to the officers described above, an organization can provide in its bylaws for
any other officers it may wish—including assistant officers.   *30*
Officers sometimes included, and their usual duties, are:

- *Directors* (or *trustees,* or *managers*), who sit as members
  of the executive board (**49**)—usually in addition to the

other officers—and perform such duties as the bylaws may require. In some organizations the term *trustees* refers to officers who perform the duties of elected auditors (see pp. 479–80).

- A *historian,* who prepares a narrative account of the society's activities during his or her term of office, which, when approved by the assembly, will become a permanent part of the society's official history.

- A *librarian,* who, if the society possesses a collection of books or other written or printed matter, has custody of these items, and—subject to the society's direction—control over members' access to them.

- A *curator,* who serves as custodian of any objects of value that may belong to the society (other than library holdings).

- A *chaplain,* who recites or leads invocations and benedictions where such prayers are offered at the opening and closing of meetings or other events, and who—if a clergyman—serves the organization in that capacity in such manner as it may require.

- A *sergeant-at-arms* (or *warden,* or *warrant officer,* as sometimes called), who, on the floor of the meeting hall, assists in preserving order as the chair may direct. In a convention or large meeting this officer may have charge of the ushers. He may handle certain physical arrangements in the hall as well, such as being responsible in some cases for seeing that the furnishings are in proper order for each meeting. In a legislative or public body that has the power to penalize or compel the attendance of its members, the sergeant-at-arms may have the duty of serving warrants or notices of fines, or of arresting absent members in the event of a *Call of the House* (pp. 350–51).

- A *doorkeeper* or *guard,* who, in meetings where only members or some other limited category of persons are permitted to enter, checks the credentials or eligibility of those arriving, and denies entrance to unauthorized persons.

Directors should always be elected. The other officers mentioned above are usually elected also, but the bylaws can provide for their appointment.

HONORARY OFFICERS (AND MEMBERS). An honorary office is in fact not an office but—like honorary membership—a complimentary title that may be bestowed on members or nonmembers. When it is desired to honor a nonmember, it is more usual to elect such a person to honorary membership. An honorary officer—for example, an honorary president or an honorary treasurer—is often elected at the time of retirement from the corresponding actual office, particularly when the person has filled it creditably for a long time. If there are to be honorary officers or honorary members, they must be authorized by the bylaws. Like an honorary degree conferred by a college or university, an honorary office or membership is perpetual—unless rescinded or unless its duration is limited by the bylaws. Rights carried with the honor include the right to attend meetings and to speak, but not to make motions or vote unless the person is also a regular member, or unless the bylaws provide full membership rights.* Honorary presidents and vice-presidents should sit on the platform, but they do not preside. An honorary office entails no duties and in no way conflicts with a member's holding a regular office or being assigned any duty

---

*Some societies provide in the bylaws for electing to "honorary life membership"—or even its automatic conferment upon—a person who has been an active member for a specified long period of years, sometimes with the added requirement that he shall have attained a certain age. The bylaws may prescribe that such an honorary member shall pay no dues but shall retain full voting privileges.

1 whatever. It is not improper to include in the published list
of honorary officers the names of those who are deceased, if
that fact is clearly indicated.

5 ## Appointed Officers or Consultants

EXECUTIVE SECRETARY.   The term *executive secre-
tary,* or *executive director,* is usually applied to a salaried officer who devotes full time to the position of administrative
10 officer and general manager of an organization, especially at
the national, regional, or state level; and unless otherwise
indicated the term is used in that sense in this book. In most
organizations, the executive secretary is employed by the
board of directors under contract, but in some this officer is
15 elected by the convention.

Duties of the Executive Secretary.   The executive secretary
is in charge of the central office of the society and acts under
the immediate direction of the board and the executive committee, if there is one (see p. 485). He is sometimes ex officio
20 the secretary of the executive committee (and sometimes
of the board) and is responsible for seeing that the committee's instructions are carried out. He is expected to recommend plans of work and to conduct the day-to-day business
of the organization. He is often responsible for the work that
25 would otherwise be carried out by an elected corresponding
secretary. He usually hires, fires, and determines the salaries
of other staff members with the approval of the board or
executive committee, which may regulate this function by
adopting personnel policies. The bylaws should specify the
30 duties of the executive secretary and should describe the manner in which he is to be selected, and for how long a term.

Relationship to the President.   The relationship between
the office of executive secretary and that of president depends
on the duties and authority of these officers as defined in the
35 bylaws. In some organizations, the executive and managerial

function that would otherwise be exercised by the president *1*
is entirely split off and vested in the executive secretary. This
arrangement leaves the president his duties as presiding officer and spokesman for the organization. In any case, the president should not attempt to give orders to the executive *5*
secretary independently unless the bylaws so authorize; in the
absence of such a provision, the executive secretary receives
his direction from the board or executive committee.

PARLIAMENTARIAN.   The parliamentarian is a con- *10*
sultant, commonly a professional, who advises the president
and other officers, committees, and members on matters of
parliamentary procedure. The parliamentarian's role during
a meeting is purely an advisory and consultative one—since
parliamentary law gives to the chair alone the power to rule *15*
on questions of order or to answer parliamentary inquiries.

A small local organization should rarely require the services of a parliamentarian, unless it undertakes a general revision of its bylaws; but for large assemblies and conventions
or organizations where the transaction of business is apt to *20*
be complex, it is advisable to engage one. Some state or
national organizations find it advisable to employ a parliamentarian throughout the year to assist with any questions
that may arise in interpreting bylaws and rules, or in connection with the work of the board and of officers or committees. *25*
In such a case, the parliamentarian's duties extend beyond
giving opinions to the presiding officer during meetings, and
may include assisting in the planning and steering of business
to be introduced.

Appointment of the Parliamentarian.   If a parliamentar- *30*
ian is needed by an organization, the president should be free
to appoint one in whom he has confidence. The board or
society must approve any fee that will be required, however.
If needed for only one meeting, a parliamentarian should be
appointed as far as possible in advance of the meeting at *35*

1　which he is to serve, since his main work should be done outside the meeting.

　　Duties of the Parliamentarian.　The president, knowing
in advance the business to come before the assembly, should
5　confer with the parliamentarian before the meetings open,
and during recesses, in order to anticipate any problems that
may arise and to avoid, as much as possible, frequent consultation during the meetings. There is no set rule for the number of additional functions a parliamentarian may be asked to
10　perform as a permanent appointee, such as teaching classes,
holding office hours during conventions, and the like.

　　During a meeting the work of the parliamentarian should
be limited to giving advice to the chair and, when requested,
to any other member. It is also the duty of the parliamentar-
15　ian—as inconspicuously as possible—to call the attention of
the chair to any error in the proceedings that may affect the
substantive rights of any member or may otherwise do harm.
There should be an understanding between the parliamentarian and the presiding officer that there will probably be
20　occasions when it may be essential for the chair to listen to
suggestions being made by the parliamentarian, even if it
means momentarily not giving full attention to others or asking the assembly to *stand at ease* during the consultation (see
p. 82; p. 250, ll. 2–5). This practice will enable the chair to
25　be in a position to act promptly at the correct time and be
fully informed. In advising the chair, the parliamentarian
should not wait until asked for advice—that may be too late.
An experienced parliamentarian will often see a problem
developing and be able to head it off with a few words to the
30　chair. Only on the most involved matters should the parliamentarian actually be called upon to speak to the assembly;
and the practice should be avoided if at all possible. The parliamentarian should be assigned a seat next to the chair, so as
to be convenient for consultation in a low voice, but the chair
35　should try to avoid checking with the parliamentarian too

frequently or too obviously. After the parliamentarian has   *1*
expressed an opinion on a point, the chair has the duty to
make the final ruling and, in doing so, has the right to follow
the advice of the parliamentarian or to disregard it. But if the
parliamentarian's advice on important procedural issues is   *5*
habitually disregarded, he may find it necessary, at the end of
the present engagement or session, to resign.

A member of an assembly who acts as its parliamentarian
has the same duty as the presiding officer to maintain a position of impartiality, and therefore does not make motions,   *10*
participate in debate, or vote on any question except in the
case of a ballot vote. He does not cast a deciding vote, even
if his vote would affect the result, since that would interfere
with the chair's prerogative of doing so. If a member feels
that he cannot properly forgo these rights in order to serve   *15*
as parliamentarian, he should not accept that position. Unlike
the presiding officer, the parliamentarian cannot temporarily
relinquish his position in order to exercise such rights on a
particular motion.

Regarding the duties of the parliamentarian in connection   *20*
with a convention, see also pages 608–9.

Vacancies

The power to appoint or elect persons to any office or   *25*
board carries with it the power to accept their resignations,
and also the power to fill any vacancy occurring in it, unless
the bylaws expressly provide otherwise. In the case of a society whose bylaws confer upon its executive board full power
and authority over the society's affairs between meetings of   *30*
the society's assembly (as in the example on p. 578, ll. 11–15)
without reserving to the society itself the exclusive right to
fill vacancies, the executive board is empowered to accept resignations and fill vacancies between meetings of the society's
assembly. For particular vacancies, see page 457, lines 22–30   *35*

1 (president-elect), page 458, lines 7–18, and page 575, lines 6–17 (president and vice-presidents). See also page 177 (vacancies in a committee).

5 Notice of filling a vacancy in an office (including a vacancy in an executive board or executive committee) must always be given to the members of the body that will elect the person to fill it, unless the bylaws or special rules of order clearly provide otherwise.

10

§48. MINUTES AND REPORTS OF OFFICERS

Minutes

The official record of the proceedings of a deliberative
15 assembly is usually called the *minutes,* or sometimes—particularly in legislative bodies—the *journal.* In an ordinary society, the minutes should contain mainly a record of what was *done* at the meeting, not what was *said* by the members. The minutes should never reflect the secretary's opinion, favorable
20 or otherwise, on anything said or done. The minutes should be kept in a substantial book or binder.

CONTENT OF THE MINUTES.   The *first paragraph* of the minutes should contain the following information
25 (which need not, however, be divided into numbered or separated items directly corresponding to those below):

1) the kind of meeting: regular, special, adjourned regular, or adjourned special;
30 2) the name of the society or assembly;
3) the date and time of the meeting, and the place, if it is not always the same;
4) the fact that the regular chairman and secretary were present or, in their absence, the names of the persons who
35 substituted for them; and

5) whether the minutes of the previous meeting were read   *1*
   and approved—as read, or as corrected—and the date of
   that meeting if it was other than a regular business meeting. Any correction approved by the assembly is made
   in the text of the minutes being approved; the minutes of   *5*
   the meeting making the correction merely state that the
   minutes were approved "as corrected," without specifying
   what the correction was (see form, p. 472, ll. 8–9).

The body of the minutes should contain a *separate para-*   *10*
graph for each subject matter, and should show:

6) all main motions (**10**) or motions to bring a main question again before the assembly (pp. 74–79; **34–37**) that
   were made or taken up—except, normally, any that were   *15*
   withdrawn*—stating:
   a) the wording in which each motion was adopted or
      otherwise disposed of (with the facts as to whether
      the motion may have been debated or amended be-
      fore disposition being mentioned only parentheti-   *20*
      cally); and
   b) the disposition of the motion, including—if it was
      temporarily disposed of (pp. 90–91, 340–41)—any
      primary and secondary amendments and all adhering
      secondary motions that were then pending;   *25*

---

*There may be certain instances in which a main motion is withdrawn
under circumstances that require some mention in the minutes. In such a case,
only as much information should be included in the minutes as is needed to
reflect the necessary details clearly. For example, if, at one meeting, a main
motion was made *the* special order for the next meeting (p. 371), or a
main motion was postponed after lengthy consideration to a meeting at which
it was withdrawn by consent, action at the first meeting should always be
recorded, and the withdrawal at the second meeting should be stated for completeness of the minutes.

7) secondary motions that were not lost or withdrawn, in cases where it is necessary to record them for completeness or clarity—for example, motions to *Recess* or to *Fix the Time to Which to Adjourn* (among the privileged motions), or motions to *Suspend the Rules* or grant a *Request to Be Excused from a Duty* (among the incidental motions), generally only alluding to the adoption of such motions, however, as ". . . the matter having been advanced in the agenda on motion of . . ." or ". . . a ballot vote having been ordered, the tellers . . .";

8) the complete substance of oral committee reports that are permitted to be given in small assemblies in particular cases as provided on pages 525–27;

9) all notices of motions (pp. 121–24); and

10) all points of order and appeals, whether sustained or lost, together with the reasons given by the chair for his or her ruling.

The *last paragraph* should state:

11) the hour of adjournment.

Additional rules and practices relating to the content of the minutes are the following:

• The name of the maker of a main motion should be entered in the minutes, but the name of the seconder should not be entered unless ordered by the assembly.

• When a count has been ordered or the vote is by ballot, the number of votes on each side should be entered; and when the voting is by roll call, the names of those voting on each side and those answering "Present" should be entered. If members fail to respond on a roll-call vote, enough of their names should be recorded as present to

reflect that a quorum was present at the time of the vote.   *1*
If the chair voted, no special mention of this fact is made
in the minutes.

- The proceedings of a committee of the whole, or a quasi
  committee of the whole, should not be entered in the   *5*
  minutes, but the fact that the assembly went into committee of the whole (or into quasi committee) and the
  committee report should be recorded (see **52**).

- When a question is considered informally, the same information should be recorded as under the regular rules,   *10*
  since the only informality in the proceedings is in the
  debate.

- When a committee report is of great importance or
  should be recorded to show the legislative history of a
  measure, the assembly can order it "to be entered in the   *15*
  minutes," in which case the secretary copies it in full in
  the minutes.

- The name and subject of a guest speaker can be given,
  but no effort should be made to summarize his remarks.

- The declaration by the chair in "naming" an offending   *20*
  member as a part of disciplinary procedures—as well as
  any disorderly words that led to such naming and that the
  chair directed the secretary to take down—is entered in
  the minutes (see pp. 646–47).

25

The use by the secretary of a recording device can be of
great benefit in preparing the minutes, but a transcription
from it should never be used as the minutes themselves.

THE SIGNATURE.   Minutes should be signed by the   *30*
secretary and can also be signed, if the assembly wishes, by
the president. The words *Respectfully submitted*—although
occasionally used—represent an older practice that is not
essential in signing the minutes.

1   FORM OF THE MINUTES. The principles stated
above are illustrated in the following model form for
minutes:

5   The regular monthly meeting of the L.M. Society
was held on Thursday, January 4, 20__, at 8:30 P.M., at
the Society's building, the President being in the chair
and the Secretary being present. The minutes of the last
meeting were read and approved as corrected.
10   The Treasurer reported the receipt of a bill from
the Downs Construction Company in the amount of
$5,000 for the improvements recently made in the Soci-
ety's building. The question put by the chair "that the
bill be paid" was adopted.
15   Mr. Johnson, reporting on behalf of the Membership Committee, moved "that John R. Brown be admitted to membership in the Society." The motion was
adopted after debate.
          The report of the Program Committee was received
20   and placed on file.
          The special committee that was appointed to inves-
tigate and report on suitable parking facilities near the
Society's building reported, through its chairman,
Mrs. Smith, a resolution, which, after debate and
25   amendment, was adopted as follows: "*Resolved,*
That . . . [its exact words immediately before being
acted upon, incorporating all amendments]."
          The resolution relating to the use of the Society's
library by nonmembers, which was postponed from the
30   last meeting, was then taken up. This motion and a
pending amendment were laid on the table after the
chair announced that the guest speaker had received a
phone message which would require his early departure.
          The President introduced the guest speaker, Mr.
35   James F. Mitchell, whose subject was _____.

At the conclusion of Mr. Mitchell's talk, the res-   *1*
olution relating to the use of the Society's library by
nonmembers was taken from the table. After amendment and further debate, the resolution was adopted
as follows: "*Resolved,* That . . . [its exact wording imme-   *5*
diately before being finally voted on]."

Mr. Gordon moved "that the Society undertake the
establishment of a summer camp for boys on its lake-
front property." Mrs. Thomas moved to amend this
motion by inserting the word "underprivileged" before   *10*
"boys." On motion of Mr. Dorsey, the motion to establish the camp, with the pending amendment, was referred to a committee of three to be appointed by the
chair with instructions to report at the next meeting.
The chair appointed Messrs. Flynn, Dorsey, and Fine   *15*
to the committee.

The meeting adjourned at 10:05 P.M.

Margaret Duffy, Secretary

READING AND APPROVAL OF THE MINUTES.   *20*
When the next regular business session will be held within a
quarterly time interval (see pp. 89–90), *when the session does*
not last longer than one day, and when there will be no change
or replacement of a portion of the membership before the next
session, procedures relative to the reading and approval of   *25*
minutes are as follows:

• The minutes of the meeting are normally read and
  approved at the beginning of the next regular meeting,
  immediately after the call to order and any opening cere-   *30*
  monies. An adjourned meeting of an ordinary society
  approves the minutes of the meeting that established
  the adjourned meeting; its own minutes are approved
  at the next adjourned or regular meeting, whichever
  occurs first. A special meeting does not approve minutes;   *35*

its minutes should be approved at the next regular meeting.

- Corrections, if any, and approval of the minutes are normally done by unanimous consent. The chair calls for the reading of the minutes, asks for any corrections, then declares the minutes approved, as shown on pages 354–55.

- If the assembly does not wish to carry out the reading and approval of the minutes at the regular time, it may, by majority vote without debate, "dispense with the reading of the minutes." The minutes can then be taken up by majority vote without debate at any later time during the meeting while no business is pending. If the minutes are not thus taken up before adjournment, they are read and approved at the following meeting, before the later minutes are taken up. A motion to "dispense with the reading of the minutes" is not a request to omit their reading altogether.

- A draft of the minutes of the preceding meeting can be sent to all members in advance, usually with the notice. In such a case, it is presumed that the members have used this opportunity to review them, and they are not read unless this is requested by any member. Correction of them and approval, however, is handled in the usual way. It must be understood in such a case that the formal copy placed in the minute book contains all corrections that were made and that none of the many copies circulated to members and marked by them is authoritative (see also p. 355).

When the next regular business session will not be held within a quarterly time interval (see pp. 89–90), and the session does not last longer than one day, or in an organization in which there will be a change or replacement of a portion of the membership, the executive board or a committee appointed for the

purpose should be authorized to approve the minutes. The *1*
fact that the minutes are not then read for approval at the
next meeting does not prevent a member from having a relevant excerpt read for information; nor does it prevent the
assembly in such a case from making additional corrections, *5*
treating the minutes as having been previously approved (see
third paragraph below).

In sessions lasting longer than one day, such as conventions,
the minutes of meetings held the preceding day are read and
are approved by the convention at the beginning of each day's *10*
business after the first (and minutes that have not been approved previously should be read before the final adjournment)—except as the convention may authorize the executive
board or a committee to approve the minutes at a later time.

When the minutes are approved, the word *Approved,* with *15*
the secretary's initials and the date, should be written below
them.

If the existence of an error or material omission in the
minutes becomes reasonably established after their approval—
even many years later—the minutes can then be corrected by *20*
means of the motion to *Amend Something Previously Adopted*
(**35**), which requires a two-thirds vote, or a majority vote
with notice, or the vote of a majority of the entire membership, or unanimous consent.

25

PUBLICATION OF AN ASSEMBLY'S PROCEED-
INGS.   Sometimes a society wishes to have a full record
of its proceedings made available to the public, and when
such a record of the proceedings is to be published (in which
case it is often called "proceedings," "transactions," or the *30*
like), it frequently contains, in addition to the information
described above for inclusion in the minutes, a list of the
speakers on each side of every question, with an abstract or
the text of each address. In such cases the secretary should
have an assistant. When it is desired, as in some conventions, *35*

1   to publish the proceedings in full, the secretary's assistant
should be a stenographic reporter or recording technician.
The presiding officer should then take particular care that
everyone to whom he assigns the floor is fully identified.
5   Under these conditions it is usually necessary to require members to use a public address system. Reports of committees
should be printed exactly as submitted, the record showing
what action was taken by the assembly in regard to them; or
they can be printed with all additions in italics and parts
10   struck out enclosed in brackets, in which case a note to that
effect should precede the report or resolution. Any such
record or transcript of the proceedings prepared for publication, however, does not take the place of the minutes, and
it is the minutes which comprise the official record of the
15   assembly's proceedings.

Reports of Officers

In principle, all reports of officers in a society are incident
20   to administrative duties that these officers have by virtue of
provisions in the bylaws or other rules. Strictly speaking, in a
purely deliberative assembly, the officers make no reports.

In an organized society, the bylaws may require each of
the principal officers to make a report of the year's work
25   at the annual meeting (**9**). At any meeting at which officers'
reports are made, they immediately follow the reading and
approval of the minutes.

REPORTS OF EXECUTIVE OFFICERS.   In addition
30   to their annual reports, the president and vice-president from
time to time may wish or need to report on their activities in
connection with administrative duties. Such reports are usually for purposes of information only, but may sometimes contain recommendations calling for action by the assembly. In
35   either case, the reports should generally conform to the rules

as to form, substance, and disposition that govern committee   *1*
reports (**51**). Motions to adopt or implement any recommendations should be made from the floor by a member *other
than the reporting officer.*

5

REPORTS BY THE TREASURER.   At each meeting of
a society, the chair may ask for a "Treasurer's report," which
may consist simply of a verbal statement of the cash balance
on hand—or of this balance less outstanding obligations.
Such a report requires no action by the assembly.   *10*

In addition, the treasurer is required to make a full financial report annually, and in some societies more often. Such
an annual report should always be audited. It is compiled and
dated as of the last day of the fiscal year, if there is one, or
December 31 if no different financial year is stated in the   *15*
bylaws.

Form and Content of the Financial Report.   The best
form for the financial report depends on particular conditions, such as the kind and size of the society, the nature of
its activities, the frequency of reporting, and so on. The form   *20*
used should be patterned after reports in similar organizations. In any case, since the financial report is made for the
information of the members, it should not contain details of
dates and separate payments, which are a hindrance to the report's being understood.   *25*

The brief model report on page 478 is in a form suitable
for most small societies whose financial affairs are simple and
primarily involve cash. In organizations whose finances are
more involved, a double-entry set of books may be advisable
or required. Such a system should be set up with the assis-   *30*
tance of an accountant, and the report would normally consist
of a balance sheet showing the society's assets, liabilities, and
fund balance (or members' equity) as well as an income statement similar to the report on page 478 without the opening
and closing cash balances. Other statements may be included   *35*

REPORT OF THE TREASURER OF THE L.M. SOCIETY
FOR THE YEAR ENDING DECEMBER 31, 20___

Balance on hand January 1, 20___ $1,253.25

Receipts
   Members' Dues $630.00
   Proceeds from Spring Barbecue   296.75
   Fines   12.00

    Total Receipts   938.75

    Total $2,192.00

Disbursements
   Rent of Hall $500.00
   Custodial Service Fees   175.00
   Stationery and Printing   122.40
   Postage   84.00

    Total Disbursements $ 881.40

Balance on hand December 31, 20___   1,310.60

    Total $2,192.00

                                   Richard Larson, Treasurer

Audited and found correct.
   Colleen Burke
   Randolph Schuler
    Auditing Committee

as needed, such as a statement of changes in members' equity,   *1*
a statement of sources and application of funds, and a cash
forecast. This system may be on a cash or an accrual basis and
will usually require review or audit by an accountant.

Action on the Financial Report.   No action of acceptance   *5*
by the assembly is required—or proper—on a financial report
of the treasurer unless it is of sufficient importance, as an
annual report, to be referred to auditors. In the latter case it
is the auditors' report which the assembly accepts. The treasurer's financial report should therefore be prepared long   *10*
enough in advance for the audit to be completed before the
report is made at a meeting of the society.

When the amounts involved are very large and the reports
complicated, or the organization's contributors or others require it, it is desirable to have the audits made by indepen-   *15*
dent certified accountants. But in ordinary societies and those
in which the expense of a professional cannot be justified,
it is practical to have the financial reports audited by an auditing committee of two or more members of the society—
appointed in advance if there is not a standing auditing   *20*
committee. In some organizations the financial reports are
audited by elected officers known as "trustees." Where professional examination is desired but the organization does not
require a full audit, a "review" (as distinct from a mere "compilation") by an accountant may supply sufficient testing and   *25*
verification to satisfy the organization. If the auditors' report
consists only of an endorsement on the financial report—to
the effect that it has been found correct, as shown in the
model above—the treasurer can simply read out this certifi-
cation as he concludes the presentation of his own report.   *30*
After the treasurer has made his report to the assembly (and
after any detailed report presented by the chairman of the
auditing committee, if it is needed), the chair states the question on adopting the *auditors'* report. The adoption of the
auditors' report has the effect of relieving the treasurer of   *35*

1   responsibility for the period covered by his report, except in
case of fraud.

If the treasurer presents an unaudited annual report or
other financial report that the bylaws require to be audited,
5   and if there is a standing auditing committee or if auditors
have already been chosen in some other manner, the chair,
without waiting for a motion when the treasurer has finished reading his report, immediately says, "The report is
referred to the Auditing Committee [or "to the auditors," or
10   "to the Trustees for audit"]." If no auditors have been chosen, the proper procedure is to adopt a motion to refer the
report to an auditing committee to be appointed by one of
the methods described in **50**.

15   REPORTS OF OTHER OFFICERS.   Other officers as
may be prescribed in the bylaws, such as a historian or a
librarian, may also have occasion to report to the assembly.
These reports are usually made annually and, like those of the
executive officers, are generally for purposes of information
20   only. They can, however, contain recommendations upon
which it is hoped the assembly will act. If the report is to
become a permanent official document of the organization,
it should be formally adopted by the assembly. Thus, for example, historical accounts prepared by the historian do not
25   become part of the official history of the society until the
assembly formally adopts them, with any desired changes,
after their presentation by the historian.

CHAPTER
XVI

BOARDS AND COMMITTEES

§49. BOARDS

1

The essential characteristics of a *board* are stated on pages 8–9. All of the material under the heading *Types of Deliberative Assembly* on pages 5–9 should be read in connection with this section.

5

The authority by which a board is constituted commonly prescribes the times at which it shall hold regular meetings, and the procedure by which special meetings of the board can be called; or the board can establish such provisions to the extent that it has the authority to adopt its own rules (see p. 486).

10

The Executive Board of an Organized Society

15

Except in the simplest and smallest local societies, or those holding very frequent regular meetings, it is generally found advisable to provide in the bylaws for a board to be empowered to act for the society when necessary between its regular meetings, and in some cases to have complete control over certain phases of the society's business. Such a board is usually

20

1   known as the *executive board,* or—in organizations where
there is an executive committee within and subordinate to
the board as described below—the *board of directors, board of
managers,* or *board of trustees.* Any such body is referred to
5   in this book as an executive board, however—regardless of
whether there is an executive committee—in cases where the
distinction is immaterial.

If a society is to have an executive board, the bylaws
should specify the number of board members and how they
10   are to be determined, should define the board's duties and
powers, and should make provision for meetings of the board
as stated above. An executive board commonly consists of
those of the society's officers (**47**) who also have duties apart
from the board, together with a number of directors, man-
15   agers, or trustees who may or may not have other duties
such as the chairmanship of important standing committees
(**50**). (See sample bylaws, Art. IV, Sec. 1, and Art. VI, Sec. 1,
pp. 585, 586.) The directors usually should be elected in the
same way and at the same time as the other officers of the so-
20   ciety. Frequently it is provided that a specified percentage of
the directors shall be chosen periodically in such a way that
their terms of office overlap those of the others—as when, for
example, there are six directors and it is provided that two
shall be elected at each annual meeting for three-year terms.

25   A society has no executive board, nor can its officers act
as a board, except as the bylaws may provide; and when so
established, the board has only such power as is delegated to
it by the bylaws or by vote of the society's assembly referring
individual matters to it. The amount of regular power dele-
30   gated to an executive board under the bylaws varies considerably from one organization to another. If the society as a
whole meets less often than within quarterly time intervals
(pp. 89–90), or if its main purpose is other than to transact
business, the entire administrative authority of the society is
35   best left to the board between the society's meetings. Usually

in organizations meeting monthly or oftener, and some-   *1*
times in those meeting quarterly, the board is not given so
much power, since the society can attend to much of its business at its regular meetings. (For appropriate wordings for
the governing provision in the bylaws in each of these two   *5*
cases, see pp. 578, 586.) In any event, no action of the board
can alter or conflict with any decision made by the assembly
of the society, and any such action of the board is null and
void (see p. 577, ll. 23–33). Except in matters placed by the
bylaws exclusively under the control of the board, the soci-   *10*
ety's assembly can give the board instructions which it must
carry out, and can rescind or amend any action of the board
if it is not too late (see **35**). It should be noted, however, that
exactly the opposite condition prevails in connection with
boards of business corporations, in which the board has ex-   *15*
clusive power and authority to operate the business.

Ex-Officio Board Members

Frequently boards include ex-officio members—that is,   *20*
persons who are members of the board by virtue of an office
or committee chairmanship held in the society, or in the parent state or national society or federation or some allied
group; or—sometimes in boards outside of organized societies—by virtue of a public office. In the executive board of   *25*
a society, if the ex-officio member of the board is under the
authority of the society (that is, if he is a member, an employee, or an elected or appointed officer of the society),
there is no distinction between him and the other board
members. If the ex-officio member is not under the authority   *30*
of the society, he has all the privileges of board membership,
including the right to make motions and to vote, but none
of the obligations—just as in a case, for example, where the
governor of a state is ex officio a trustee of a private academy.
The latter class of ex-officio board member, who has no   *35*

obligation to participate, should not be counted in determining the number required for a quorum or whether a quorum is present at a meeting. Whenever an ex-officio board member is also ex officio an officer of the board, he of course has the obligation to serve as a regular working member.

When an ex-officio member of a board ceases to hold the office that entitles him to such membership, his membership on the board terminates automatically.

Concerning ex-officio members of committees, including the president, see page 497, lines 20–29.

Officers of Boards

A board that is not an instrumentality of a parent assembly or membership body is organized as any deliberative assembly, with a chairman* or president, a secretary, and other officers as may be needed. In general, such a board elects its own officers if the authority under which the board is constituted makes no other provision as to how the officers are to be determined. A board that is to elect its officers should meet for this purpose as soon as possible after the selection of its members (see also p. 489, ll. 10–14). In ordinary societies having executive boards, on the other hand, the president and the secretary of the society serve in the same capacities within the board (and the executive committee, if there is one), unless the bylaws provide otherwise.

Bodies Subordinate to a Board

As a general principle, a board cannot delegate its authority—that is, it cannot empower a subordinate group to act independently in its name—except as may be authorized by the bylaws (of the *society*) or other instrument under which

---

*See page 23 regarding variations of this term that have come into use.

the board is constituted; but any board can appoint commit-   *1*
tees to work under its supervision or according to its specific
instructions. Such committees *of the board* always report *to
the board*.

   5

EXECUTIVE COMMITTEE. In a society where the
board is large or its members must travel from a distance to
meet, it is usual for the bylaws to establish an *executive committee* composed of a specified number of board members,
which shall have all or much of the power of the board be-   *10*
tween meetings (just as the board has all or much of the
power of the society between the society's meetings), but
which cannot alter any decision made by the board (just as
the board cannot alter any decision made by the society). The
executive committee is thus in reality a "board within a   *15*
board" and operates under the rules in this book applicable
to boards rather than those applicable to committees. Usually
the membership of the executive committee is specified in the
bylaws, rather than being left to the choice of the full board.
It is advisable that the executive committee be small and, un-   *20*
less it has been authorized to conduct electronic meetings
(see pp. 97–99), that its members live near enough to each
other to be able to hold frequent regular meetings and also
special meetings when necessary. The executive secretary, if
there is one, should work closely with the executive commit-   *25*
tee, but should be appointed by the parent body or at least
by the board. A board cannot appoint an executive committee
unless the bylaws so authorize.

COMMITTEES OF A BOARD. Where an organiza-   *30*
tion is local—for example, a society for sustaining a fos-
ter home for children—the executive board usually divides
itself into committees having charge of different branches of
the work during the interval between the monthly or quarterly meetings of the board. At the board meetings these   *35*

1   committees report on the fulfillment of their assigned respon-
    sibilities. In such cases the committees are genuinely subor-
    dinate to the board and must ordinarily report back to it for
    authority to act (in contrast to an executive committee, which
5   usually has power to act as the board, and in contrast to
    standing committees of the *society*, which are not subordinate
    to the board unless made so by a provision in the bylaws).
    Any board can appoint committees of the kind just described
    without authorization in the bylaws.
10

Conduct of Business in Boards

    GENERAL PROCEDURE.   The executive board of an
    organized society operates under the society's bylaws, the so-
15 ciety's parliamentary authority, and any special rules of order
    or standing rules of the society which may be applicable to it.
    Such a board may adopt its own special rules of order or
    standing rules only to the extent that such rules do not con-
    flict with any of the rules of the society listed above. It may
20 protect itself against breaches of order by its members during
    board meetings, and against annoyance by nonmembers, by
    employing the procedures outlined on pages 645–49, but the
    maximum penalty which may be imposed upon a disorderly
    member of the board is that he be required to leave the meet-
25 ing room during the remainder of the meeting. A board that
    is not a part of a society can adopt its own rules, provided
    that they do not conflict with anything in the legal instrument
    under which the board is constituted.
        Under the general parliamentary law, business is trans-
30 acted in large boards according to the same rules of procedure
    as in other deliberative assemblies. In smaller boards, these
    rules apply as far as practicable, with the exceptions noted
    below. In any case, a board can transact business only in a reg-
    ular or properly called meeting of which every board member
35 has been notified—or at an adjournment of one of these

meetings (pp. 93–94)—and at which a quorum (a majority *1* of the total membership unless otherwise specified in the by-laws or established by the constituting power) is present. (See also *Electronic Meetings*, pp. 97–99.) The personal approval of a proposed action obtained separately by telephone, by *5* individual interviews, or in writing, even from every member of the board, is not the approval of the board, since the members lacked the opportunity to mutually debate and decide the matter as a deliberative body. If action is taken on such a basis, it must be ratified (pp. 124–25) at a regular or properly *10* called board meeting in order to become an official act of the board.

A record of the board's proceedings should be kept by the secretary, just as in any other assembly; these minutes are accessible only to the members of the board unless the board *15* grants permission to a member of the society to inspect them, or unless the society by a two-thirds vote (or the vote of a majority of the total membership, or a majority vote if previous notice is given) orders the board's minutes to be produced and read to the society's assembly. *20*

At regular board meetings the executive committee, if there is one, should be required to make a report of its activities since the last board meeting. No action need be taken on this report, which is generally intended as information only.

25

PROCEDURE IN SMALL BOARDS. In a board meeting where there are not more than about a dozen members present, some of the formality that is necessary in a large assembly would hinder business. The rules governing such meetings are different from the rules that hold in other *30* assemblies, in the following respects:

• Members may raise a hand instead of standing when seeking to obtain the floor, and may remain seated while making motions or speaking.

35

- Motions need not be seconded.
- There is no limit to the number of times a member can speak to a debatable question.* Appeals, however, are debatable under the regular rules—that is, each member (except the chair) can speak only once in debate on them, while the chair may speak twice.
- Informal discussion of a subject is permitted while no motion is pending.
- When a proposal is perfectly clear to all present, a vote can be taken without a motion's having been introduced. Unless agreed to by unanimous consent, however, all proposed actions must be approved by vote under the same rules as in larger meetings, except that a vote can be taken initially by a show of hands, which is often a better method in small meetings.
- The chairman need not rise while putting questions to a vote.
- If the chairman is a member, he may, without leaving the chair, speak in informal discussions and in debate, and vote on all questions.**

EFFECT OF PERIODIC PARTIAL CHANGE IN BOARD MEMBERSHIP.   In cases where a board is constituted so that a specified portion of its membership is chosen periodically (as, for example, where one third of the board is

---

*However, motions to close or limit debate (**15, 16**), including motions to limit the number of times a member can speak to a question, are in order even in meetings of a small board (but not in meetings of a committee; see p. 500), although occasions where they are necessary or appropriate may be rarer than in larger assemblies.

**Informal discussion may be initiated by the chairman himself, which, in effect, enables the chairman to submit his own proposals without formally making a motion as described on pages 33–35 (although he has the right to make a motion if he wishes).

elected annually for three-year terms), it becomes, in effect, *1*
a new board each time such a group assumes board membership. Consequently, when the outgoing portion of the board
vacates membership, all matters temporarily but not finally
disposed of (see pp. 90–91), except those that remain in the *5*
hands of a committee to which they have been referred, fall
to the ground under provision (c) on page 237. (See also
p. 502, l. 26 to p. 503, l. 2, regarding the continuity of matters that have been referred to a special committee appointed
by the board.) If the board is one that elects its own officers *10*
or appoints standing committees, it chooses new officers and
committees as soon as the new board members have taken up
their duties, just as if the entire board membership had
changed. The individual replacement of persons who may
occasionally vacate board membership at other times, how- *15*
ever, does not have these effects.

§50. COMMITTEES

A committee, as understood in parliamentary law, is a *20*
body of one or more persons, elected or appointed by (or by
direction of) an assembly or society, to consider, investigate,
or take action on certain matters or subjects, or to do all of
these things. Unlike a board, a committee is not itself considered to be a form of assembly. *25*

Although the term *committee* commonly implies a relatively small number of persons appointed to give a task more
detailed attention than is possible in a body the size of the
assembly, this characteristic more accurately describes what
are known as *ordinary committees.* An assembly can also des- *30*
ignate all of its members present to act as a committee, which
is called a *committee of the whole* and is distinguished from an
ordinary committee. In large assemblies, the use of a committee of the whole is a convenient method of considering a
question when it is desired to allow each member to speak an *35*

1 unlimited number of times in debate. Committees of the whole are treated separately in **52**. The statements in this section apply principally to ordinary committees.

5 Ordinary committees are of two types—*standing committees* (which have a continuing existence) and *special committees* (which go out of existence as soon as they have completed a specified task).

Generally the term *committee* implies that, within the area of its assigned responsibilities, the committee has less authority to act independently for the society (or other constituting power) than a board is usually understood to have. Thus, if the committee is to do more than report its findings or recommendations to the assembly, it may be empowered to act for the society only on specific instructions; or, if it is given standing powers, its actions may be more closely subject to review than a board's, or it may be required to report more fully. Also, unlike most boards, a committee in general does not have regular meeting times established by rule; but meetings of the committee are called as stated on pages 499 and 501–502. Some standing committees, however—particularly in large state or national organizations—function virtually in the manner of boards, although not designated as such.

When a committee is appointed "with power," this means with power to take all the steps necessary to carry out its instructions.

In large assemblies or those doing a great volume of business, much of the preliminary work in the preparation of subjects for consideration is usually done by committees. In many such bodies, in fact, it is advisable to have every main question go to a committee before final action on it is taken by the assembly.

Standing committees are constituted to perform a continuing function, and remain in existence permanently or for the life of the assembly that establishes them. In an ordinary society, the members of such a committee serve for a term

corresponding to that of the officers, or until their successors have been chosen, unless the bylaws or other rules
otherwise expressly provide. Thus, a new body of committee
members is normally appointed at the beginning of each
administration.

A standing committee must be constituted by name (a) by
a specific provision of the bylaws or (b) by a resolution which
is in effect a special rule of order and therefore requires for
its adoption either previous notice and a two-thirds vote or a
vote of a majority of the entire membership, if any of the following conditions are to apply:

- if the committee is to have standing authority to act for
  the society on matters of a certain class without specific
  instructions from the assembly;
- if all business of a certain class is to be automatically referred to the committee; or
- if some other rule of parliamentary procedure is affected
  by the committee's assigned function.

If a standing committee's assigned function does not
affect a rule of parliamentary procedure in any of these three
ways, it can be established by a standing rule adopted by a
majority vote without notice, although, even in such a case,
the committee is frequently constituted by name in the bylaws
as indicated above. If certain standing committees are enumerated in the bylaws, an inference arises that there shall be
no others unless the bylaws also include a provision authorizing their appointment; and without such a provision, no
standing committee aside from those enumerated can be
established unless the bylaws are amended to include it (see
also pp. 578–80). A standing committee of a society reports
to the assembly of the society, and not to the executive board
or board of directors, unless the bylaws provide otherwise. In
some societies, standing committees in effect have charge of

certain branches of the organization's work, in which case these committees are really in the nature of boards.

A *special* (*select,* or *ad hoc*) *committee* is a committee appointed, as the need arises, to carry out a specified task, at the completion of which—that is, on presentation of its final report to the assembly—it automatically ceases to exist. A special committee may not be appointed to perform a task that falls within the assigned function of an existing standing committee.

Appointment of Committees

METHODS OF APPOINTMENT.   In an assembly or organization that has not prescribed in its bylaws or rules how the members of its committees shall be selected, the method can be decided by unanimous consent or by majority vote at the time the committee is appointed, as described on page 174, lines 11–20; or (in the case of a special committee) the method can be specified in the motion to establish the committee. The power to appoint a committee carries with it the power to appoint the chairman and to fill any vacancy that may arise in the committee. The two paragraphs headed *Designating the Committee Chairman* on pages 175–76 should be read in connection with the five methods of appointing a committee described below.

It is possible for persons who are not members of the assembly or the society to be appointed to committees—even to the position of committee chairman—but control over each such appointment is reserved to the assembly in the individual case. From this principle, it follows that, referring to these five methods of appointment, non–assembly members may be appointed to committees by methods (a), (b), (c), and (e), as listed below. When method (d) is used and the chair appoints either a standing or a special committee, however, the governing rule regarding the appointment of non–assembly members is as stated under *Naming Members to a Special Committee*, on pages 174–75.

Methods by which committees can be appointed are as follows:

a) *Election by ballot.* This method is principally applicable to important standing committees having extensive powers. Under this procedure, nominations for committee membership can be made by any of the methods described in **46**; then the nominees are voted on by ballot just as in an election of a board, a majority vote being necessary to elect. In the event that more, or less, than the required number receive a majority, places on the committee are filled as explained on page 441, lines 11–24. If it is the assembly's practice—or its wish in the particular case—to select the committee chairman (rather than leave it to the committee to do so as explained on p. 176, ll. 11–15), the chairmanship can be treated as a separate position to be voted for on the same ballot with the other committee members; or, in a smaller assembly, if preferred, the chairman can be elected from among the committee's members on a second ballot, after their names have been announced.

b) *Nominations from the floor (open nominations) with viva-voce election* (usually called simply "nominations from the floor"). This is a common method of appointing members to a committee when the assembly wishes to reserve the selection to itself without requiring secrecy in the voting. When this method has been decided upon, the chair says, "Members will please nominate," or, "Nominations for the committee are now in order." The chair announces each nomination as he hears it, as shown on page 432. No one has a right to nominate more than one person to membership on the committee until every other member has had an opportunity to nominate a candidate; and thus the nomination of more than one person at a time by a single member can be entertained only by unanimous consent. If no more than the prescribed number of committee members are nominated, a vote is unnecessary since the fact that no more than the required number are nominated shows that there is unanimous consent that the committee should consist of these persons, which the chair declares as follows: "Messrs. A, B, and C, Mrs. D, and Mrs. E are nominated. Are there any further nominations? . . . Since there are no further nominations, the committee is composed of the persons just named [or he repeats the names if he feels it advisable]." If there are more nominees than the required number of committee members, then, when there are no further nominations, the chair repeats all of the names in the order in which they were nominated, and in the same order puts the question on the election of each nominee—one at a time until the proper number have been elected—as described for viva-voce elections (**46**). For reasons explained on pages 442–43, those nominated last in such a case have less chance of being elected. After the selection of committee members has been completed, the assembly can elect a committee chairman from among them, if desired; or a chairman can be elected separately, first.

c) *Nominations by the chair* (with confirmation by voice vote). This method is used when the assembly wishes to take advantage of the chair's knowledge and judgment as to suitable appointees, yet wishes to have veto power. In this case, the chair names the same number of persons as there are to be members of the committee, always naming his choice of committee chairman first, thus: "The chair nominates Mr. X as chairman, Mrs. Y, and Mr. Z.* The

---

*The first person that the chair names is automatically chairman of the committee unless the assembly rejects that person as a committee member or unless he or she declines the chairmanship; but it is good practice for the chair to mention him or her as chairman (see pp. 175–76).

question is: Shall these persons constitute the committee?" *1*
Any member can then move to strike out one or more
names—but not to insert new ones, which the chair must
do if such a motion to strike out is adopted. After any
changes in the original names have thus been made, the *5*
chair repeats the proposed names as they stand and puts
the question on the entire list: "Mr. X, Mrs. Y, and
Mr. W are nominated. Those in favor of these persons
constituting the committee, say *aye*. . . . Those opposed,
say *no*. . . . , etc." *10*

d) *Appointment by the chair.* In the absence of special conditions, appointment of committees by the chair, or by
the regular presiding officer, is usually the best method
in large assemblies, and it is the ordinary procedure in
many smaller societies as well. The president cannot *15*
assume such power, however, unless it is given to him by
the bylaws or by action of the assembly in the individual
case (pp. 171, 174, 579–80). When the bylaws provide
that the *president* shall appoint all committees, this power
does not transfer to the *chair* if someone else presides. A *20*
clause in the bylaws assigning to the president the duty
of appointing all committees should therefore contain
appropriate provision for its own suspension if necessary
(for example, if there is occasion to appoint a special committee during a meeting from which the president is ab- *25*
sent). In addition, a clause conferring on the president
such power of appointment should exclude the nominating committee, and it may be advisable for such a clause
also to exclude all disciplinary committees. Whenever it
is stated in the bylaws (with or without the proper excep- *30*
tions just noted) that the president "shall appoint all committees," this means that the president shall select the
persons to serve on such committees as the bylaws prescribe to be established or the assembly may direct to be
appointed; it does not mean that the president can himself *35*
decide to appoint and assign a task to a group and thereby

give it the status of a committee of the society. When
the chair appoints a committee, no vote is taken on the
appointees, except any who are not members of the
assembly in cases where there is no prior authorization
for the chair to appoint non–assembly members to the
committee—either in the bylaws or in a motion directing
the appointment of the particular committee (see also
pp. 174–75). But the chair must announce the names of
the committee members to the assembly, naming the
chairman of the committee first, as in (c) above; and until
such announcement is made the committee cannot act.
If the assembly orders the appointment of a special committee and it is desired to let the chair select the committee members after adjournment, this delay must be
authorized by the assembly; the names of the committee
members must then be announced at the next meeting
and recorded in the minutes.

e) *Appointment by adoption of a motion naming members of
a committee.* This method finds use in the case of special
committees when the rules or particular conditions do
not dictate the use of another procedure. The names of
the proposed committee members can be included in the
motion proposing to appoint the committee, either as it
is originally offered or by way of an amendment. Or, if
the motion to appoint the committee is adopted without
prescribing the manner of appointment, a second motion
can be made "That the committee be composed of Mr. X,
Mr. Y, . . ." In either case, the motion naming the committee members can specify the committee chairman or
not as the assembly wishes. If other names (intended to
replace one or more of those in the motion) are proposed
while the motion is pending, all such names and those
in the motion should be treated as nominations and
should be voted on as in the case of an election (see also
pp. 171ff.).

Unless the bylaws or other governing rules expressly provide that committee members shall serve ". . . *and* until their successors are chosen" or for a fixed period, as ". . . for a term of two years" (in which case the procedure for their removal or replacement is the same as that for officers described on p. 654), committee members (including the chairman) may be removed or replaced as follows: If appointment was as provided in paragraphs (a), (b), (c), or (e) above, the removal or replacement of a committee member requires the same vote as for any other motion to *Rescind* or *Amend Something Previously Adopted.* If appointment was by the president acting alone under paragraph (d), he may remove or replace committee members by his own act (see p. 177).

A committee (except a committee of the whole, **52**) can appoint subcommittees, which are responsible to and report to the committee and not to the assembly. Subcommittees must consist of members of the committee, except when otherwise authorized by the society in cases where the committee is appointed to take action that requires the assistance of others.

The rules affecting ex-officio members of committees are the same as those applying to ex-officio members of boards (pp. 483–84). When the bylaws provide that the president shall be ex officio a member of all committees (or of all committees with the stated exception of those from which the president is best excluded; see pp. 579–80), the president is an ex-officio member who has the right, but not the obligation, to participate in the proceedings of the committees, and he is not counted in determining the number required for a quorum or whether a quorum is present at a meeting.

The resignation of a member of a committee should be addressed to the appointing power, and it is the responsibility of that power to fill the resulting vacancy (see also pp. 467–68).

PROPER COMPOSITION OF COMMITTEES. The members of a standing committee should be chosen so as to provide the strongest possible group for the handling of any task that may arise within the province of the committee. In the case of a special committee, the purpose for which it is appointed affects the desirable size and composition, as follows:

- When a special committee is appointed to implement an order of the assembly, it should be small and should consist only of those in favor of the action to be carried out. If anyone not in sympathy with the action is appointed, he should ask to be excused.
- When a special committee is appointed for deliberation or investigation, however, it should often be larger, and it should represent, as far as possible, all points of view in the organization, so that its opinion will carry maximum weight. When such a committee is properly selected, its recommendations will most often reflect the will of the assembly. By care in selecting committees, debates on delicate and troublesome questions in ordinary societies can be mostly confined to the committees. The usefulness of the committee will be greatly impaired, on the other hand, if any important faction of the assembly is not represented.

INFORMATION, INSTRUCTIONS, AND REFERRED PAPERS. Upon the appointment of a committee, the secretary of the society should see that all persons appointed are notified, and should furnish a list of the members of the committee to its chairman or, in the chairman's absence, to some other authorized committee member. When a subject or item of business is referred to the committee (normally at the time of its appointment if it is a special committee, or at any time if it is a standing committee), the secretary should provide the committee chairman or his representative with copies of the papers, motion, or other

matter formally referred to it, and whatever instructions the   *1*
assembly has given. Upon the committee's request, any other
papers or books necessary for the proper performance of its
duties should be made available to it by the appropriate officers of the society, who can first consult with the president if   *5*
in doubt.

A committee should take care to preserve the papers referred to it from the society, since, after its assignment is completed, they must be returned in the same condition as when
received. If the committee wishes to write on copies of the   *10*
documents, therefore, it must obtain its own photocopies,
unless it has been provided with extra copies specified in its
instructions as for that purpose. In any case, amendments prepared for recommendation to the assembly when the committee reports should be drawn up on a separate sheet.   *15*

Conduct of Business in Committees

COMMITTEE MEETINGS.   When a committee has
been appointed, its chairman (or first-named member tem-   *20*
porarily acting—see p. 176) should call it together.* If its
chairman fails to call a meeting, the committee must meet
on the call of any two of its members, unless (for very large
committees) the assembly's rules prescribe, or empower the
assembly or the committee to require, a larger number. It is   *25*
the responsibility of the person or persons calling a committee
meeting to ensure that reasonable notice of its time and place
is sent to every committee member. The quorum in a committee is a majority of its membership unless the assembly has

---

*For cases in which it is impractical to bring the members of a committee
together for a meeting, the report of the committee can contain what has
been agreed to by every one of its members (see p. 503). Also, committees
are sometimes authorized to hold "electronic meetings"; see pages 97–99,
especially the paragraph *Electronic Meetings in Committees*.

1   prescribed a different quorum (**40**). All of the meetings of a
     special committee constitute one session (**8**).

     COMMITTEE PROCEDURE.   In small committees,
5   the chairman usually acts as secretary, but in large ones and
     many standing committees, a secretary may be chosen to keep
     a brief memorandum in the nature of minutes for the use of
     the committee.
     The informalities and modifications of the regular rules
10   of parliamentary procedure listed on pages 487–88 for use in
     small boards are applicable during the meetings of all standing
     and special committees, unless the committee is otherwise in-
     structed by the society (see next paragraph below); also, the
     rules governing the motions to *Rescind*, to *Amend Something*
15   *Previously Adopted*, and to *Reconsider* are modified as stated
     on page 306, line 34 to page 307, line 2, and pages 329–30.
     In committees, the chairman is usually the most active partic-
     ipant in the discussions and work of the committee. In order
     that there may be no interference with the assembly's having
20   the benefit of its committees' matured judgment, motions to
     close or limit debate (**15, 16**) are not allowed in committees.*
     Committees of organized societies operate under the by-
     laws, the parliamentary authority, and any special rules of
     order or standing rules of the society which may be applicable
25   to them. A committee may not adopt its own rules except as
     authorized in the rules of the society or in instructions given

---

*If a member abuses his privilege of speaking an unlimited number of
times in debate in order to obstruct the business of the committee, such dilatory behavior should be reported to the committee's parent, which may then
remove that member from the committee, adopt an order limiting or closing
debate in the committee, or take such other action as it deems advisable.
However, *if there will be no opportunity for this to occur* within the time needed
to effectively resolve the problem, it is the duty of the committee chairman
to deny such a member any further recognition to speak in debate on the
pending question.

to the committee by its parent assembly in a particular case. *1*
If a standing or special committee is so large that it can function best in the manner of a full-scale assembly, it should be
instructed that the informalities and modifications of the regular rules of parliamentary procedure listed for small boards *5*
on pages 487–88 are not to apply to its proceedings.

When a committee is to make substantive recommendations or decisions on an important matter, it should give
members of the society an opportunity to appear before it
and present their views on the subject at a time scheduled by *10*
the committee. Such a meeting is usually called a *hearing.*
During actual deliberations of the committee, only committee members have the right to be present.

A standing or special committee may protect itself against
breaches of order by its members during committee meetings, *15*
and against annoyance by nonmembers, by employing the
procedures outlined on pages 645–49, but the committee,
instead of itself imposing any penalty on a disorderly member,
can only report such behavior to the committee's parent
body, which may then take such action as it deems advis- *20*
able. However, *if there will be no opportunity for this to occur*
within the time needed to effectively resolve the problem and
enable the committee to complete its assigned tasks, the committee may protect itself against such disruptive behavior by
requiring the disorderly member to leave the meeting room *25*
during the remainder of the meeting.

ADJOURNMENT; PROVISION FOR FUTURE
MEETINGS. When a committee intends to reconvene, it
can simply adjourn, or adjourn to meet at a later time. In the *30*
first case—when it adjourns without appointing a time for
another meeting—the next meeting is held at the call of the
chairman, who must ensure that reasonable notice of its time
and place is sent to every committee member (see p. 499).
In the second case—when it sets an adjourned meeting— *35*

1 notice of the adjourned meeting is not required (although
it is desirable to give such notice if feasible), but reasonable
efforts must be made to inform absent members of its time
and place.

5   When a special committee has finished with the business
assigned to it, a motion is made for the committee to "rise"—
which is equivalent to the motion to adjourn sine die (or
without day)—and for the chairman or some other member
to make its report to the assembly. The motion to rise is never
10 used in standing committees, or in special committees until
they are ready to go out of existence.

CONTINUITY AND CONCLUSION OF COMMIT-
TEE ASSIGNMENT.   Since members of standing com-
15 mittees in ordinary societies are appointed for a term
corresponding to that of the officers, such a committee is
generally required to report at least once a year, usually at the
annual meeting, on its activities and everything referred to it
during the year. When a standing committee submits such a
20 report at the conclusion of its members' term, the *committee*
is not discharged from further consideration of referred matters on which it reports partially at that time, unless the
assembly so votes (**36**); thus such matters normally go over
to the new committee. The members of the old committee
25 continue their duties until their successors are chosen.

A special committee—since it is appointed for a specific
purpose—continues to exist until the duty assigned to it is
accomplished, unless discharged sooner (see **36**); and it ceases
to exist as soon as the assembly receives its final report. The
30 fact that an annual meeting intervenes does not discharge a
special committee. But in a body which ceases to exist or in
which the terms of some or all of its members expire at a definite time, like a convention of delegates, a city council, or a
board of directors, a special committee expires with the body
35 that appointed it, unless it is appointed expressly to report at

a later time. If it does not report, its life expires with that of   *1*
the body to which it was to report.

§51. REPORTS OF BOARDS AND COMMITTEES   *5*

A report of a subordinate board or a committee is an
official statement formally adopted by, and submitted in the
name of, the reporting body, informing the parent assembly
of action taken or recommended, or information obtained.

10

General Considerations Affecting Board and Committee Reports

LIMITATION OF REPORT CONTENT TO WHAT
HAS BEEN PROPERLY AGREED TO.   Except as noted   *15*
in this paragraph, a report of a board or committee can contain only what has been agreed to by a majority vote at a regular or properly called meeting of which every member has
been notified (or at an adjournment of one of these meetings,
pp. 93–94)—where a quorum of the board or committee was   *20*
present. A presentation of facts or recommendations made
merely upon separate consultation with every member of a
board must be described thus to the parent assembly, and not
as an official report of the board (see also pp. 486–87). In
the case of a committee, however, if it is impractical to bring   *25*
its members together for a meeting, the report of the committee can contain what has been agreed to by every one of
its members. (See also *Electronic Meetings*, pp. 97–99.)

TYPES OF REPORTS.   For convenience in the discus-   *30*
sions in this section, reports may be divided into two general
categories as follows:

a) *Annual or periodic reports of boards or standing committees*
    are usually submitted in accordance with requirements in   *35*

1   the bylaws, are primarily for information, and should sum-
     marize important work done by the board or committee
     during the year or other period covered by the report.
     They may also contain recommendations—which may re-
5   late to general policy to be followed by the organization,
     or may propose specific action by its assembly (see next
     paragraph).

   b) *Reports relating to single items of business arising during
      the year* fall into a number of particular forms—which are
10   described for the case of committees beginning on page
     514. As will be seen from examples in the text on those
     pages, these reports can often be quite brief unless special
     circumstances or instructions to the reporting body call
     for a detailed presentation of facts.

15

     RECOMMENDATIONS IN A REPORT.   In any re-
   port of a subordinate board or a committee (of type [a] or [b]
   above), specific recommendations for immediate action by the
   parent assembly should be grouped at the end—repeating
20 them if they have already been noted at separate places in
   the report—and should generally be cast in the form of one
   or more proposed resolutions. Although it is possible for a
   report, in the circumstances just described, to present recommendations which are not in the form of resolutions or
25 motions, the "adoption" of such recommendations by the
   parent assembly may, depending on their wording or that of
   the motion to adopt, lead to confusion as to whether their
   adoption *authorizes action,* or only has the force of a declaration of intent (requiring the adoption of subsequent resolu-
30 tions for implementation). A board or committee is usually
   best fitted to prepare resolutions to carry out its recommendations, and it should never leave this responsibility to others.
     When a report is made for the purpose of presenting rec-
   ommendations on a single subject—especially if it is the report
35 of a committee to which the subject was referred—it is often

best for the formal report to be confined as much as possible   *1*
to the recommendations, whether they are in the form of resolutions or otherwise (see examples, pp. 514ff.). If this approach is followed and it is desired to bring supporting reasons
to the attention of the assembly, the reporting member (that   *5*
is, the person who presents the report) can include brief oral
explanations with his presentation. Or, supporting reasons can
be explained at greater length during debate on the report—
by the reporting member, who has the right to the floor first
in debate, and also by other members of the board or com-   *10*
mittee, if appropriate, as the debate progresses.

In the foregoing connection, it should be noted that
under parliamentary conditions the inclusion of supporting
facts or reasoning in a report proposing certain action may
tend to work against the taking of that action, since some   *15*
members who might otherwise have been willing to accept
the proposals may be led to vote against them if they disagree
with the factual background as reported or the reasoning of
the reporting body.

20

FORM OF DETAILED REPORT.   If special conditions
dictate that a report devoted to a single subject and presenting recommendations should include a full account of the details involved in the case, the body of the report is best
organized according to the following topics, as applicable: *25*

1) a description of the way in which the reporting body (usually a committee in such cases) undertook its charge;
2) the facts uncovered or information obtained;
3) the findings or conclusions derived from the facts or in-   *30*
   formation; and
4) resolutions or recommendations.

If for any reason one or more resolutions or recommenda-
tions are placed within this type of detailed report before its   *35*

1 conclusion, they should be repeated at the end, as stated
above. In this way they can be more easily dealt with apart
from any implied endorsement of reported facts and reasoning which some members may not accept.

5   PRESENTATION AND RECEPTION OF REPORTS.
A report of a board or committee to an assembly is presented
at the proper time by a "reporting member" of the board or
committee. For the report of a board whose chairman is also
10 the presiding officer of the assembly, the secretary or another
one of its members acts as reporting member. In the case of
a committee, the committee chairman is the reporting member unless—because he does not agree with the report or for
any other reason—he does not wish to give it, in which event
15 the committee chooses another one of its members.

A reporting member *makes* or *presents* a report on behalf
of a board or a committee when, having been assigned the
floor for such a purpose in a meeting, he does one of the following things (depending on the nature of the report and
20 other conditions): (a) renders the report orally, if it is not in
writing; (b) reads the report to the assembly and passes it to
the chair or the secretary; or (c) announces that he is submitting it and passes it to one of these officers to be read by a
reading clerk. When the assembly hears the report thus read
25 or orally rendered, it *receives* the report. The terms *presentation* and *reception* accordingly describe one and the same
event from the respective viewpoints of the reporting member
and the assembly.

30   MOTIONS FOR ACTION ON REPORTS.   Immediately after receiving a board's or a committee's report—unless
it is a report containing only information on which no action
is taken (p. 525)—an assembly normally considers whatever
action may be recommended in or arise out of the report. In
35 the remaining pages of this section, it is explained how such

action under various conditions may involve the introduction
of motions—to implement recommendations or, occasionally,
to adopt the entire report.

Motions to Implement Recommendations. When a report
contains recommendations—except in cases where the recommendations relate only to the adoption or rejection of
question(s) that were referred while pending (**13**) and consequently become pending again automatically when reported
(pp. 516–19)—the reporting board or committee member
usually makes the necessary motion to implement the recommendations at the conclusion of his presentation, provided
he is a member of the assembly (see examples, pp. 514–16
and 519ff., in which it is generally assumed that the "reporting member" is a member of the assembly). If the report is
read by the secretary or a reading clerk in such a case, the
reporting member resumes the floor for the purpose of making the motion immediately after the reading is completed.
No second is required in these cases, since the motion is made
on behalf of the board or committee (see p. 36, ll. 15–23).

If the person presenting the report is not a member of
the assembly or for any other reason does not make the required motion to implement the recommendations as just
described, any member of the assembly can do so; but the
motion should then be seconded. Or, when the proper motion is a matter of clear-cut procedure and must necessarily
be introduced to resolve the case, the chair may sometimes
expedite matters by *assuming* the motion—that is, stating the
question on it without waiting for it to be made—*provided
that the assembly is accustomed to this method.**

Motion to Adopt an Entire Report. In rare instances after
an assembly has received a report, it may have occasion to

---

*Such a practice is justified by the fact that more than one person must
have voted for the recommendation within the board or committee and must
therefore wish it to come before the assembly.

1   adopt the (entire) report; an affirmative vote on such a motion has the effect of the assembly's endorsing every word of
the report—including the indicated facts and the reasoning—
as its own statement (see also p. 124). Unlike motions to
5   take the action recommended in a report as described above,
a motion "to adopt the report" should be made by someone
other than the reporting member and requires a second.
Adoption of an entire report is seldom wise except when
it is to be issued or published in the name of the whole
10 organization.

     EQUIVALENCE OF TERMS; INCORRECT MO-
TIONS. As applied to an assembly's action with respect
to board or committee reports or any of their contents, the
15 expressions *adopt, accept,* and *agree to* are all equivalent—that
is, the text adopted becomes in effect the act or statement of
the assembly. It is usually best to use the word *adopt,* however, since it is the least likely to be misunderstood.
     A common error is to move that a report "be received"
20 after it has been read—apparently on the supposition that
such a motion is necessary in order for the report to be
taken under consideration or to be recorded as having been
made. In fact, this motion is meaningless, since the report has
already been received. Even before a report has been read, a
25 motion to receive it is unnecessary if the time for its reception
is established by the order of business, or if no member
objects (see also below).
     Another error—less common, but dangerous—is to
move, after the report has been read (or even before the read-
30 ing), that it "be accepted," when the actual intent is that of
the mistaken motion to receive, as just explained, or of a
legitimate motion to receive made *before* the report is read.
If a motion "to accept" made under any of these circumstances is adopted and is given its proper interpretation, it im-
35 plies that the assembly has endorsed the complete report.

APPLICABILITY OF REGULAR RULES TO QUES-   *1*
TIONS ARISING OUT OF REPORTS.   When a board or
committee report has been received and the chair has stated
the question on the adoption of the motion, resolution(s),
recommendation(s), or report—whether the question became   5
pending automatically, or the proper motion was made or was
assumed by the chair as explained above—the matter is treated
as any other main question, is open to debate and amendment, and can have any of the subsidiary motions applied to
it. Similarly, if a committee to which the main question was   10
referred has recommended that it be amended or definitely
or indefinitely postponed, the motion to take such action is
debatable and (for primary amendment or definite postponement) amendable, under the regular rules for these motions.

In the foregoing connection it should be noted that the   15
consideration of a matter *that was referred* to a board or committee cannot be objected to (**26**) when it is reported on—
regardless of whether the matter was referred as a pending
question (**13**) or as a subject on which no question was pending. The reason is that an *Objection to the Consideration of a*   20
Question can be raised only against an original main motion
at the time of its introduction; and the reported matter in no
case has this status since (a) if it was referred as a pending
question, it was introduced at an earlier time, or (b) if it was
referred as a subject on which no question was pending, the   25
main question introduced following the report is an incidental main motion (see pp. 101–2).

CONDITIONS FOR AMENDMENT OF A REPORT
BY THE ASSEMBLY BEFORE ITS ADOPTION.   An as-   30
sembly that is to adopt an entire report which it has received
can amend the report, but the text as published or recorded
must not make the reporting board or committee appear to
say anything different from the wording that was actually
reported. For this reason, the published or recorded text   35

1 should show clearly the reported version and the changes that the assembly has made—for example, by enclosing in brackets all that was struck out and underlining or putting in italics all that was inserted, and including a note explaining this nota-
5 tion at the beginning of the report (see also p. 507, l. 30 to p. 508, l. 4 and p. 510, l. 31 to p. 511, l. 8).

Board Reports

10 OCCASION AND MANNER OF PREPARATION. The executive board (or board of directors) of a society reports to the assembly annually on the work done during the year, and at such other times and upon such subjects as the bylaws may prescribe or the society's business may
15 require.
     A board report is usually drafted by the president or secretary, and this draft often passes through the executive committee first, if there is one, before it comes up for con- sideration and adoption by the board at one of its meetings
20 (see also pp. 503–4). A board report should be signed by the president or chairman of the board and its secretary only.

RECEPTION AND DISPOSITION OF BOARD RE- PORTS.   In meetings at which the executive board is to
25 make a report, the chair calls for it at the time provided in the order of business, or, if there is no such provision, before committee reports are received or unfinished business is taken up. After the reading of the report, the reporting member moves the adoption of any resolutions included in it, which,
30 as indicated above, should be grouped or repeated at the end. If the annual report of the board is to be formally adopted by the society before being published, an appropriate wording for the minutes in such a case is the following: "The Executive Board [or "Board of Directors," etc.] submitted its report,

which, after debate and amendment [if any], was adopted as   *1*
follows, the words in brackets having been struck out and
those underlined [or, "in italics"] having been inserted before
the report was adopted." A society need not endorse the report of its board, and can even decline to allow the report to   *5*
be printed, or it can adopt only a part; but whatever it prints
or records from the report must show any changes clearly
marked.

Committee Reports   *10*

GENERAL FORM OF COMMITTEE REPORTS.   All
committee reports should be submitted in writing, except as
noted (for particular types of brief reports in a small assembly)
on pages 525–27. In the case of such exceptions, a report can   *15*
be given orally only if it is brief enough that the secretary
can record its complete substance in the minutes on hearing
it given—which he must do if no written copy is submitted
for file.

Usually a written committee report is not addressed or   *20*
dated. It is understood to be addressed to the assembly, and
its date is that on which it is presented in a meeting of the
assembly as recorded in the minutes.

A committee report should always be worded in the third
person—that is, as shown in the next paragraph (not "I report   *25*
. . ." or "We recommend . . . "). Similarly, in an assembly a
committee report is always spoken of by the chair and others
as, for example, "the report of the Finance Committee" or
"the report of the committee to which was referred . . . [stat-
ing the subject]." It should never be spoken of as "the report   *30*
of the chairman of the Finance Committee" and never as
"Mr. Smith's report," even though it is usually presented by
the committee chairman and even if he may have personally
drafted it or done most of the work reported.

A committee report should begin with an identification of the committee submitting it—the name of the committee in the case of a standing committee, or the subject that was referred in the case of a special committee; thus:

> [*For a standing committee:*] The Committee on . . . wishes to report [or, "reports"] that . . . [or, "submits the following report: . . ."].

Or:

> Report of the Committee on . . . :

> [*For a special committee:*] The committee to which was referred [stating the subject] reports [or "recommends"] that . . .

Or:

> The committee appointed to [stating the purpose] reports that . . . [or, "submits the following report: . . ."].

If a written committee report is of considerable importance, it should be signed by all the members concurring.* Otherwise, the committee can authorize its chairman to sign the report alone, in which case he adds the word *Chairman* after his signature. By so signing, the committee chairman certifies that the report has been adopted by the committee as explained on page 503. When all concurring members sign the report, it is customary for the chairman to sign first, but this is not obligatory. In any case, he should not place the word *Chairman* after his name except when he signs alone on behalf of the entire committee. The use of the words *Respectfully submitted* preceding the signature(s) on a committee report is unnecessary and no longer customary.

---

*Regarding signature with an expression of disagreement in a certain particular, see page 529.

RECEPTION OF COMMITTEE REPORTS.   Reports   *1*
of committees are called for or can be presented in a meeting
as follows:

- If, as is usually the case, a place has been provided in the   *5*
  order of business for the reports of committees, the chair
  calls for the reports of standing committees first, in the
  order in which they are listed in the bylaws or other rules;
  after that he calls for the reports of the special committees,
  in the order of their appointment. (The chair omits calling   *10*
  for the report of any committee that he knows has no report to make; see also pp. 355–56.) As each report is
  called for, the committee chairman or other reporting
  member rises, addresses the chair, and presents the report.
- Or, if the order of business makes no provision for com-   *15*
  mittee reports, the committee chairman or other reporting member should obtain the floor when no business is
  pending and, addressing the chair, inform the assembly
  that the committee has agreed upon a report which he is
  prepared to submit. If the chair thinks that the assembly   *20*
  wishes to hear the report, the chair directs the member
  to proceed. If anyone objects to the report's reception
  or if the chair is in doubt as to whether the report should
  be received at that time, he puts the question to the
  assembly: *25*

> CHAIR: The question is, "Shall the report be received now?"
> Those in favor of receiving the report now, say *aye*. . . . Those
> opposed say *no*. . . ., etc.

30

This question requires a majority vote. If the vote is in
the negative, a later time for the reception of the report
should be set, either by a vote or by unanimous consent.
The manner of presenting the report is the same as described above.   *35*

1   (For the reception of "minority reports," see pp. 528–29.)

MANNER OF PRESENTATION AND DISPOSITION
5 OF COMMITTEE REPORTS IN PARTICULAR CASES.
The proper method of presenting and disposing of different types of committee reports is explained below, with sample reports being given in certain cases. Whenever a motion by the reporting member is a normal part of the procedure
10 in the examples, it is assumed that this member actually makes the motion rather than leaving it to the chair to state the question without a formal motion (see pp. 506–8).

A Report at the Initiative of a Standing Committee Recommending Action.   If a standing committee wishes on its
15 own initiative to recommend action by the assembly on a matter within the committee's concern, it is generally desirable, as stated above, for the report to consist of or conclude with one or more proposed resolutions embodying the committee's recommendations. Such resolutions should always
20 be in writing. Although the reporting member in a small assembly may sometimes give accompanying explanations orally, it is usually better to submit a formal written report if it is to contain anything other than the resolutions themselves. In any event, after giving or reading the report, the re-
25 porting member moves the adoption of the resolution(s). He may make such a presentation, for example, as follows:

REPORTING MEMBER (reading written report):
The Buildings and Grounds Committee wishes to report that the
30 clubhouse roof was extensively damaged by the hurricane last week. The committee therefore recommends the adoption of the following resolution: "*Resolved*, That the Buildings and Grounds Committee be authorized to request bids for repair of the clubhouse roof and to award a contract for the same, provided that, without further authorization, the
35 cost shall not exceed $5,000."

George Wilson, Chairman

Mr. President, by direction of [or "on behalf of"] the committee, I *1*
move the adoption of the resolution just read.

The chair then states the question on the resolution, and
it is considered just as any other main motion. If the report *5*
contains more than one resolution, the reporting member
makes a single motion for the adoption of them all, and the
rules given on page 110 apply.

Although it is not generally the best procedure, a report
may sometimes contain recommendations not in the form of *10*
motions or resolutions. In any case, as stated above, the recommendations should be placed at the end of the report even
if they have been given separately before. Sometimes also, in
this connection, it is moved "to adopt the committee's rec-
ommendation(s)," although, as noted on page 504, lines *15*
22–30, this can lead to confusion as to the precise effect of the
motion. A better method of treating a committee recommendation that is not in the form of a resolution—in a case, for
example, where the recommendation is to authorize a $2,000
expenditure for a personnel consultant's fee—is to offer a mo- *20*
tion like this: "In accordance with the recommendation in the
committee's report, I move that the expenditure of $2,000
for a personnel consultant's fee be authorized." The reporting
member can make such a motion after reading the report, or
another member can obtain the floor to do so. In cases where *25*
the committee has offered no resolutions embodying its recommendations and the drafting of satisfactory resolution(s)
covering them is likely to require the further attention of a
committee, another member can move to refer the matter to
the same or another committee for this purpose.* *30*

*A Report on a Referred Subject on Which No Resolution or
Motion Was Pending.*   If a subject on which no resolution or

---

*The motion to refer in such a case is a main motion, since the matter
being referred is not a pending question (see p. 168, ll. 29–35).

motion was pending has been referred to a committee for recommendations, the report usually should conclude with one or more resolutions, unless the committee recommends that no action be taken. The committee's report on the subject referred to it may be presented, for example, thus:

> REPORTING MEMBER (reading written report):
> The committee that was appointed to recommend a suitable recreational facility for the Club to donate to the new Runnymede Park project finds that no provision has been made for tennis courts. The committee therefore recommends the adoption of the following resolution: "*Resolved*, That the Club underwrite the cost of two tennis courts to be constructed in Runnymede Park."
>
> Howard Ford, Chairman
>
> Mr. President, on behalf of the committee, I move the adoption of the resolution just read.

The resolution is treated as any other main question, just as in the preceding case dealing with the recommendation of a standing committee. Recommendations not in the form of resolutions are also handled as described in the preceding case.

A Report on a Resolution Previously Referred to a Committee.   When a committee reports on a resolution or other main question which was referred to it (**13**) or which the rules require to be considered by it before coming before the assembly with the committee's recommendation, the form of the report and the type of action depends on the nature of the case, as follows:

• *Recommending adoption, or rejection, or (when a majority of the committee fail to agree) making no recommendation.* Such a report in a small assembly can be given orally (provided that the secretary records it in the minutes); for example, thus:

REPORTING MEMBER: The committee to which was referred the   *1*
resolution, "*Resolved,* That the Federation endorse the so-called
Farnsworth Plan for financing the proposed new school construction
program," recommends that the resolution be adopted [or "not be
adopted"].   *5*

Or:

The committee to which was referred . . . has been unable to
arrive at a recommendation.   *10*

If the resolution is too long to fit into the form given
above, a form such as the following may be used:

REPORTING MEMBER: The committee to which was referred the   *15*
resolution relating to governmental reorganization reports it with
the recommendation that it be adopted as referred.

The reporting member should then hand to the chair
or the secretary the copy of the resolution that was turned   *20*
over to the committee.

When the presentation of the report is concluded
in each of the above cases, the resolution or main question becomes pending automatically and the chair states
the question accordingly, no motion being necessary.   *25*
If the committee recommends adoption or makes no
recommendation, the chair, as soon as the reporting
member has resumed his seat, proceeds:

CHAIR: The committee to which was referred the resolution on   *30*
. . . recommends its adoption [or, "is unable to arrive at a recommendation"]. The resolution is . . . [reading it]. The question is on
the adoption of the resolution.

The question is always stated and put on the *adoption*   *35* of the resolution (that is, so that a vote of *aye* is a vote in favor of it). Thus, when the committee's recommendation is in the negative, the chair states the question as follows:

CHAIR: The committee to which was referred . . . recommends that it not be adopted. The resolution is . . . [reading it]. The question is on the adoption of the resolution, the recommendation of the committee to the contrary notwithstanding. [Or, simply, "The question is on the adoption of the resolution," in which case the chair may add, "The committee recommends that the resolution be rejected."]

- *Recommending action on a resolution and an amendment that were pending when referred.* If an amendment was pending when the resolution was referred, the report can be given orally in a small assembly provided that it is recorded in the minutes; and it should first state the committee's recommendation as to the disposition of the amendment, then as to the disposition of the resolution. For example:

REPORTING MEMBER: The committee to which was referred the resolution, "*Resolved,* That the proposed expansion of the yacht basin be authorized," together with the pending amendment, "to add the words, 'at a cost not to exceed $150,000,'" recommends that the amendment be adopted and that the resolution as thus amended be adopted.

As in the preceding case, no motions are necessary, and the chair states the question first on the amendment, and after it is voted on, then on the resolution. The same principles apply if a primary amendment and a secondary amendment were pending when the resolution was referred. The report should state the committee's recommendations first on the secondary amendment, then on

the primary amendment, and finally on the resolution; and *1*
the chair states the questions in that order.

- *Recommending definite or indefinite postponement.* If a resolution or other main question is referred to a committee *5*
while a motion to postpone it indefinitely is pending, that
motion to *Postpone Indefinitely* (**11**) is ignored by the
committee and by the assembly when the committee reports. But whether or not such a motion was pending at
the time of referral, the committee can report the main *10*
question with a recommendation that it be postponed indefinitely or that it be postponed to a certain time (**14**).
Thus, if (a) no amendment was pending at the time of
referral, or if (b) an amendment was pending and the
committee recommends postponement to a certain time, *15*
the reporting member makes a motion for the postponement at the conclusion of his presentation. But if (c) an
amendment was pending and the recommendation is for
indefinite postponement, the motion to *Postpone Indefi-*
nitely cannot be made until after the amendment has been *20*
voted on (see *Order of Precedence of Motions,* **5**). In each
of the three cases, the report can be given orally in a small
assembly, provided that it is recorded in the minutes, as
follows:

 a) If no amendment was pending at the time of referral: *25*

   REPORTING MEMBER: The committee to which was referred
  the resolution, "*Resolved,* That . . . ," recommends, and on behalf
  of [or "by direction of"] the committee I move, that the resolution be postponed until . . . [or "be postponed indefinitely."].
                            30

  The chair then states the question first on the postponement, and if that is voted down, next on the
  resolution.

 b) If an amendment was pending and the recommendation is for postponement to a certain time: *35*

REPORTING MEMBER: The committee to which was referred the resolution, "*Resolved,* That . . . ," together with the pending amendment [stating the amendment], recommends, and by direction of the committee I move, that the resolution be postponed until . . .

The chair states the question first on the postponement as in (a); but if that is voted down, the question in this case is next on the amendment, and then on the resolution.

c) If an amendment was pending and the recommendation is for indefinite postponement (in which case the motion to *Postpone Indefinitely* is not in order when the report is made):

REPORTING MEMBER: The committee to which was referred the resolution, "*Resolved,* That . . . ," together with the pending amendment, [stating the amendment], recommends that the resolution be postponed indefinitely.

The reporting member resumes his seat without making a motion, and the chair immediately states the question on the amendment. After it has been voted on, he can state the question on the indefinite postponement (thus assuming this motion), or he can recognize the reporting member to move it by direction of the committee, and the procedure is then as in (a) above.

• *Recommending amendments.* When a committee reports back a resolution or paper with amendments that it proposes, the amendments, at least, should be in writing unless they are very simple. In a small assembly, depending on the complexity of the case, the amendments can be written out on a separate sheet that is handed to the chair

or the secretary at the conclusion of an oral presentation,   *1*
or a more formal written report can be submitted; the latter procedure should be followed in a large body. In the
report, the resolution can be included in full and be followed by a statement of the proposed amendments as in   *5*
the example below; or, if the resolution or document is
long and copies are available to the members, the report
can contain only the amendments with enough of the context of the resolution to make them understood. If no
amendment was pending at the time of referral, the report-   *10*
ing member at the conclusion of his presentation moves
the adoption of the amendments proposed by the committee, making a single motion covering them all. But if
an amendment was pending at the time of referral, the
chair (unless the committee recommends a secondary   *15*
amendment, whose adoption the reporting member would
first move) states the question on the referred amendment
first—the reporting member making no motion until after
that amendment has been voted on. The following exam-
ple (although equally suitable for treatment by the method   *20*
of reporting a substitute as on pp. 523–24) illustrates the
presentation of a written report proposing amendments to
a resolution short enough to be read in full, in a case where
no amendment was pending at the time of referral.

25

REPORTING MEMBER (reading written report):
   The committee to which was referred the resolution relating to
a proposed scholarship in journalism hereby submits its report. The
resolution is the following: "*Resolved,* That the Guild establish a
four-year scholarship in journalism at the State University, to be open   *30*
to sons and daughters of Guild members, the recipient to be chosen
annually by the Board of Directors of the Guild."
   The committee recommends that the resolution be amended as
follows:

1) by striking out the words "four-year scholarship" and inserting the words "scholarship covering the last three under-
graduate years";

2) by striking out the words "to be open to sons and daughters
of Guild members"; and

3) by adding the words "upon the recommendation of the
Dean of the School of Journalism";

and the committee further recommends that, as thus amended, the
resolution be adopted.

Milton Roth, Chairman
[Or (see p. 512):]
Milton Roth
John Harley
Elizabeth Norton
Elwood Quinn

Mr. President, by direction of the committee, I move the adoption of the amendments contained in the report.

After the chair states the question on the adoption of
the amendments proposed by the committee, the procedure is by one of the following methods:

a) Normally the chair immediately rereads or calls for a
rereading of the first of these amendments, after which
it is open to debate and secondary amendment. A vote
is then taken on the adoption of the first committee
amendment, after which the next one is read, and so
on. Until all of the committee's amendments have
been voted on, no other primary amendments are in
order, but only secondary amendments as each committee amendment comes up. After all of the committee's amendments have been acted upon, other
amendments which are not precluded by action taken
on the committee amendments can be proposed from
the floor. When these have been voted on, the chair

    puts the question on adopting the resolution or paper *1*
    as amended.*

  b) Alternatively, the chair puts a single question on all of
    the committee's amendments together, except those
    for which a member asks for a separate vote,** thus: *5*
    "Those in favor of adopting the amendments recom-
    mended by the committee, except those for which a
    separate vote has been asked, say *aye*. . . . Those op-
    posed, say *no*. . . ." This is called putting the question
    on the amendments *in gross*. He then takes up the re- *10*
    maining amendments separately in their order. This
    alternative, although it is in order whenever a com-
    mittee reports multiple amendments to a referred res-
    olution, may be most advisable when the amendments
    may be expected not to occasion debate or secondary *15*
    amendment—for example, if they are reported from a
    committee of the whole (**52**) where they have already
    been open to debate and amendment.

  c) By unanimous consent (pp. 54–56), the assembly can
    allow the introduction of a motion to adopt all recom- *20*
    mendations in the report, without considering the
    amendments separately.

 • *Recommending a substitute.* If a committee reports back
  a resolution with a substitute that it recommends for *25*
  adoption, at least the substitute should be in writing, just
  as in the case of any other report proposing amendments.

---

*The step of taking a vote on the adoption of the entire paper applies
only to cases where that paper is *pending*. This step does not apply in the case
of a report on a series of amendments to something previously adopted (**35**),
such as bylaws that are in effect (see also **57**).

**Separate votes may not be demanded on conforming amendments.
See pages 273–74.

1   If no amendment was pending when the resolution was
referred, the reporting member concludes his presentation
by making the motion to substitute; for example, thus:

5   REPORTING MEMBER: The committee to which was referred the
resolution, "*Resolved,* That the proceeds from the recent bequest
to the Association from the Asquith estate be invested in stock of
the Consolidated Development Corporation," recommends that,
for the resolution, the following substitute be adopted: "*Resolved,*
10   That the Executive Board be authorized to retain reputable investment counsel with a view to determining appropriate investment of
the proceeds from the Asquith bequest." On behalf of the committee I move that the resolution last read be substituted for the referred
resolution.

15   The chair then states the question on the motion to
substitute. But if amendment(s) were pending when the
resolution was referred, then, before the motion to substitute can be made, the question is first on the second-
20   ary amendment if one was pending, then on the primary
amendment that was pending. When these amendments
have been voted on, the reporting member makes the
motion to substitute and the chair states the question on
it (or the chair can state the question assuming the mo-
25   tion). In any event, the substitute proposed by the committee is treated as in the case of any other motion to
substitute (see pp. 153ff.). If the motion to substitute is
lost, the "original" resolution is open to further amendment; but if the motion to substitute is adopted, the res-
30   olution thus substituted can be amended only by *adding.*
(Regarding substitutes proposed by committees, see also
pp. 156–57.)

In regard to referred questions reported back, see also
35   *Resolutions Committee,* pages 633–36, 638–40.

A Report Containing Only Information.   Even if a report 1
contains only an account of work done or a statement of fact
or opinion for the assembly's information, it should be in
writing. Apart from filing such a report, however, no action
on it is necessary and usually none should be taken. (See also 5
Motion to Adopt an Entire Report, pp. 507–8, and *Conditions
for Amendment of a Report by the Assembly Before Its Adoption,*
pp. 509–10.)

*Membership and Nominating Committee Reports; Reports
of Other Kinds of Committees.*   When a membership commit- 10
tee reports on names of persons referred to the committee as
applicants for society membership, the report can be rendered
orally, but a list of the names of the persons recommended
for membership should be submitted in writing. When such
a report is made, the chair at once states the question on the 15
admission to membership of the candidates recommended by
the committee.

The report of the nominating committee consists of a
written list of candidates for office, just as in the case of the
membership committee's report. No vote on the nominating 20
committee's report should be taken, however; the procedure
is as described in **46**.

For the handling of the report of an auditing committee,
see pages 479–80.

For the report of a committee on bylaws, see **54** and **56**. 25

For the reports of the three principal committees that
perform parliamentary functions in the organization of a convention—the Credentials Committee, the Committee on
Standing Rules, and the Program Committee—see **59**.

For the report of an investigating committee appointed 30
under disciplinary procedures, see **63**.

SUMMARY OF TYPES OF REPORTS THAT CAN BE
RENDERED ORALLY IN A SMALL ASSEMBLY.   As
stated on page 511, committee reports should be submitted 35

in writing, with the following permissible exceptions that apply to very brief reports in a small assembly, provided that the secretary records the complete substance of the report in the minutes as it is given orally:

- With respect to a resolution or main question that was referred while pending:

  1) If the committee report consists only of a recommendation as to the disposition of the referred resolution or motion, the report can be given orally if implementation of the recommendation involves:

     a) no further motion, as when the committee recommends that the referred resolution or motion be adopted, or rejected; or

     b) the introduction of a subsidiary motion that can be made orally, as when the committee recommends that the referred resolution be postponed definitely or indefinitely, or be amended by the change of only a few words.

  2) If an amendment or a primary and a secondary amendment were pending with a resolution or main question that was referred and the committee has no new amendments to propose, the report can also usually be oral, in which case the reporting member simply states the committee's recommendation as to the adoption or rejection, first, of the secondary amendment, and then of the primary amendment, and finally its recommendation as to the disposition of the resolution or main motion—all before any of the referred questions are voted on.

  3) When the committee wishes to propose amendments, the amendments themselves should always be in writing if they involve more than a few words; but the complete report—that is, the declaration on behalf of the committee that it recommends the amend-

ments—can be oral or written depending on the com-   *1*
plexity of statement required by the resulting parliamentary situation.

- If a subject that was not in the form of a pending resolu-   *5*
tion or motion was referred to a committee for recommendations, and if the committee in its report presents
the recommendations in one or more resolutions offered
with no comment, only the resolutions need be in writing
and the statement that the committee recommends their   *10*
adoption can be given orally.

ACTION REQUIRED BY A PARTIAL REPORT.   A
partial report of a committee is handled in the same way as
the final report. If it is a progress report only, with no rec-   *15*
ommendations or conclusions, it is treated as any other report
for information only, and no action need be taken. But if the
partial report recommends action, the question is put on
adopting its proposed resolutions, or its recommendations,
or the report itself, just as if it were the final report. A com-   *20*
mittee can be discharged (**36**) by a majority vote at the time
at which it makes a partial report.

FORMAL EXPRESSION OF MINORITY VIEW
("MINORITY REPORT"). The formal presentation of a   *25*
so-called "minority report"—that is, the presentation of an
expression of views in the name of a group of committee
members not concurring with the committee report—is usually allowed by the assembly when such permission is requested, as explained below. Regardless of whether a minority   *30*
report is submitted, however, the report adopted by vote of
a majority in the committee should always be referred to as
"the committee report," never "the majority report."

*Nature of Committee Minority's Rights with Respect to
Reports.* As indicated above, the formal presentation of a   *35*

1 "minority report" is a privilege that the assembly may accord,
   not a matter of right—since the appointment of the committee implies that the assembly is primarily interested in the
   findings of the majority of the committee's members. But in
5 debate on any written or oral report in the assembly, any
   member of the reporting committee who does not concur
   has the same right as any other member of the assembly to
   speak individually in opposition. No one can make allusion
   in the assembly to what has occurred during the deliberations
10 of the committee, however, unless it is by report of the committee or by unanimous consent.
       Form of Minority Report; Minority Recommendations.   A
   "minority report" in writing may begin:

15   The undersigned, a minority of the committee ap-
           pointed to . . . , not agreeing with the majority, desire
           to express their views in the case. . . .

   If the committee report concludes with a proposed reso-
20 lution, the minority can (a) recommend rejection of the resolution; (b) recommend amendment of it; or (c) recommend
   adoption of some other suitable motion designed to dispose
   of the resolution appropriately.
       If the committee report is for information only, the views
25 of the minority may be similarly constructed or may conclude
   with a motion.
       Reception of Minority Report.   When the minority of a
   committee wishes to make a formal presentation of its views,
   it is customary, unless the assembly refuses permission, to re-
30 ceive its report immediately after the report of the committee.
   In such a case, the member presenting the committee report
   can properly notify the assembly that the minority wishes to
   submit its views in a separate report. As soon as the chair has
   stated the appropriate question on the committee report, he
35 should call for the minority presentation unless someone objects, in which case he should put the question on the report's

being received. A majority vote is required to receive a mi-   *1*
nority report; the question is undebatable.

When the minority report is presented, it is for information, and it cannot be acted upon except by a motion to substitute it for the report of the committee. Whether the views   *5*
of the minority are formally presented or not, however, any
member can move that resolutions proposed by the committee be amended, or that they be postponed indefinitely, or
that some other appropriate action be taken.

10

INDICATING AGREEMENT WITH A REPORT
EXCEPT IN A SPECIFIED PARTICULAR.   If a written
report of a committee is signed by all who concur and a committee member is in agreement with the report except in one
particular, he can, after all who agree to the report have   *15*
signed, add a statement that he concurs with the report except the part that he specifies, and then sign the statement—
regardless of whether a minority report is to be submitted.
Similarly, a committee member who agrees with most of a
minority report can sign it with an added note indicating   *20*
what he does not agree with, just as in the case of a committee
report. If the committee members in the minority do not
agree, the assembly can allow more than one minority report
to be submitted.

25

§52. COMMITTEE OF THE WHOLE
AND ITS ALTERNATE FORMS

The *committee of the whole* and its two alternate forms, the   *30*
quasi committee of the whole (or *consideration as if in committee of the whole*) and *informal consideration,* are devices that
enable the full assembly to give detailed consideration to
a matter under conditions of freedom approximating those
of a committee. Under each of these three procedures,   *35*
any member can speak in debate on the main question or

1   any amendment—for the same length of time as allowed by
the assembly's rules—as often as he is able to get the floor.
As under the regular rules of debate, however, he cannot
speak another time on the same question so long as a member
5   who has not spoken on it is seeking the floor.

Each of these three devices is best suited to assemblies of
a particular range in size and provides a different degree
of protection against disorderliness and its possible consequences—which are risked when each member is allowed to
10   speak an unlimited number of times in debate, such risk
increasing in proportion to the size of the assembly. With
respect to this type of protection, the essential distinctions between the three procedures may be summarized as
follows:

15

- In a *committee of the whole*, which is suited to *large assemblies*, the results of votes taken are not final decisions of
  the assembly, but have the status of recommendations
  which the assembly is given the opportunity to consider
20   further and which it votes on finally under its regular
  rules. Also, a chairman of the committee of the whole is
  appointed and the regular presiding officer leaves the
  chair, so that, by being disengaged from any difficulties
  that may arise in the committee, he may be in a better po-
25   sition to preside effectively during the final consideration
  by the assembly.
- In the *quasi committee of the whole*, which is convenient
  in *meetings of medium size* (about 50 to 100 members),
  the results of votes taken are reported to the assembly for
30   final consideration under the regular rules, just as with
  a committee of the whole. But in this case the presiding
  officer of the assembly remains in the chair and presides.
- *Informal consideration*, which is suited to *small meetings
  of ordinary societies*, simply removes the normal limitations
35   on the number of times members can speak in debate, as

stated in the first paragraph of this section. The regular presiding officer remains in the chair; and the results of votes taken during informal consideration are decisions of the assembly, which are not voted on again.

The complete rules governing committees of the whole, proceedings in quasi committee of the whole, and informal consideration are given below.

Committee of the Whole

Although the committee of the whole is not used extensively except in legislative bodies, it is the oldest of the three devices described above and is the prototype from which the other two are derived. Unlike the processes of quasi committee of the whole and informal consideration, a committee of the whole is a real committee in the parliamentary sense. Therefore, during the time that a meeting is "in committee of the whole," even though the committee consists of the entire body of members in attendance at the assembly's meeting, it is technically not "the assembly."

The parliamentary steps in making use of a committee of the whole are essentially the same as those involved in referring a subject to an ordinary committee. The assembly votes to go into a committee of the whole (which is equivalent to voting to refer the matter to the committee), and a chairman of the committee is appointed. The committee considers the referred matter, adopts a report to be made to the assembly, then votes to "rise and report." Finally, the committee chairman presents the report and the assembly considers the committee's recommendations—all as in the case of an ordinary committee.

GOING INTO COMMITTEE OF THE WHOLE. As implied above, the motion to go into a committee of the

1 whole is a form of the motion to commit (**13**). The motion is made as follows:

5   MEMBER (obtaining the floor): I move to go into a committee of the whole [or, "I move that the assembly now resolve itself into a committee of the whole"] to consider the pending question [or "to take under consideration . . . (stating the subject)"]. (Second.)

Instructions to the committee of the whole can be included
10 in this motion of referral.

    If the motion of referral to the committee of the whole is adopted, the presiding officer immediately calls another member to the chair—frequently, but not necessarily, the vice-president—and takes his place as a member of the com-
15 mittee. In large assemblies, the secretary may also leave his seat, the committee chairman may preside from that position, and an assistant secretary may act as secretary of the committee. For the committee's use until it reports, its secretary should keep a temporary memorandum of the business it
20 transacts, but the committee's proceedings are not entered in the minutes of the assembly. Those minutes should carry only the same kind of record of the referral to a committee of the whole, the committee's report, and the assembly's action on the report, as if the committee had been an ordi-
25 nary one.

    CONDUCT OF BUSINESS.   Like ordinary committees, a committee of the whole cannot alter the text of any resolution referred to it; but it can propose amend-
30 ments, which it must report in the form of recommendations to the assembly. Amendments to a resolution *originating in the committee* are in order, however; and if such amendments are adopted within the committee, they are incorporated in the resolution before it is reported to the assembly
35 for action.

A committee of the whole is under the rules of the assembly, except as follows:

1) The only motions that are in order in a committee of the whole are to adopt (within the committee, for inclusion in its report), to amend (what it is proposed to report), and to "rise" or "rise and report"*—except that, among the incidental motions, a point of order (**23**) can be raised, an appeal from the decision of the chair (**24**) can be made, a division of the assembly (**29**) can be called for, and applicable requests and inquiries (**32, 33**) can be made.

2) In debate on motions to adopt or amend, unless a limit is prescribed by the assembly before it goes into committee of the whole as explained below, each member can speak an unlimited number of times under the rules given in the first paragraph of this section.**

If the committee of the whole wishes action to be taken which requires the adoption of any motion other than those that are in order in the committee as listed in (1) above, it must vote to rise and report a recommendation that the assembly take the desired action (see below). The motion to

---

*As applied to committees in general, the word *rise* simply describes the parliamentary step of ceasing to function as a committee, preparatory to making a report. As stated on page 502, lines 5–11, the motion to rise is not used in ordinary standing committees, and in ordinary special committees it is used only when the committee is ready to make its final report and go out of existence. In a committee of the whole, on the other hand, the word *rise* applies to any case of the committee's returning to the status of the assembly—whether it is expected to be temporarily or permanently.

**Appeals in committee of the whole are debatable under the same rules as in the assembly—that is, each member (except the chair) can speak only once in debate on them.

1   rise is undebatable and cannot be amended, and it is always
    in order in committee of the whole, except during voting or
    verifying a vote and when another member has the floor.
        Among the consequences of the rules stated in the pre-
5   ceding paragraph are the following:

    • A committee of the whole cannot appoint subcommittees
      or refer a matter to another (ordinary) committee.
    • An appeal from the decision of the chair must be voted
10   on directly, since it cannot be postponed or laid on the
      table in the committee.
    • The only way for debate to be closed or limited in the
      committee is for the assembly to specify such conditions
      before going into committee of the whole. If the com-
15   mittee develops a desire to have debate limited, it can only
      do so by rising and requesting the assembly to impose the
      desired limits, as explained below. If debate has been
      closed at a particular time by order of the assembly, the
      committee does not have the power, even by unanimous
20   consent, to extend the time.
    • A roll-call vote or a vote by ballot cannot be ordered in a
      committee of the whole, nor can a counted rising vote be
      ordered except by the chair.
    • A committee of the whole has no power to impose disci-
25   plinary measures on its members, but can only report the
      facts to the assembly. If the committee becomes disorderly
      and its chairman loses control of it, the presiding officer
      of the assembly should take the chair and declare the com-
      mittee dissolved.
30 • A committee of the whole cannot adjourn or recess, but
      must rise in order that the assembly may do so.

    RISING AND REPORTING.   When a committee of
    the whole has completed its consideration of the matter re-
35 ferred to it, or when it wishes to bring the meeting to an end,

or wishes the assembly to take any other action requiring the *1*
adoption of a motion which is not in order in the committee,
the committee rises and reports.

If the committee originates a resolution, it concludes by
voting to report the resolution, as perfected. If a resolution *5*
was referred to the committee, however, it votes only on any
amendments that it will recommend, not on the resolution,
which it reports back to the assembly with the recommended
amendments. On a motion, or by unanimous consent, the
committee rises and the presiding officer of the assembly re- *10*
sumes the chair. The committee chairman returns to a place
in the assembly in front of the presiding officer, at which,
standing, he addresses the chair:

COMMITTEE CHAIRMAN: Mr. President, the committee of the whole *15*
has had under consideration . . . [describing the resolution or other mat-
ter] and has directed me to report the same as follows: . . .

The sample reports in the subsection *Manner of Presentation and Disposition of Committee Reports in Particular* *20*
Cases (pp. 514ff.) may be used as guides for reporting similar
cases from a committee of the whole, and the procedures for
disposing of such reports as described in the same pages are
likewise applicable. If no amendments are reported, the chair
states the question on the resolution that was referred to the *25*
committee or that it recommends for adoption; and this question is then open to debate and amendment in the assembly. If amendments proposed by the committee are reported,
the committee chairman reads them and hands the paper
to the chair, who reads them again or has the secretary do *30*
so. The chair then states and puts the question on all of the
committee's amendments in gross (that is, taken together),
unless a member asks for a separate vote on one or more of
them. If so, a single vote is taken on all of the other amendments, and then the question is stated separately on each of *35*

1   the amendments for which a separate vote was asked. These
    amendments can be further debated and amended in the
    assembly, as can the main question after action on all the com-
    mittee's amendments—under the same rules as when any
5   other committee reports.

    If the committee, to facilitate completion of its work,
    wishes the assembly to take an action outside the commit-
    tee's powers that requires the adoption of an undebatable
    motion—for example, to limit debate in the committee—
10 a motion to rise should be made in a form like the following:

>   MEMBER (obtaining the floor): I move that the committee rise and
>   request that debate be limited . . . [specifying the desired limitation].
>   (Second.)
15

    If this motion is adopted, the committee chairman reports to
    the assembly as follows:

>   COMMITTEE CHAIRMAN: Mr. President, the committee of the whole
20 has had under consideration . . . [describing the referred matter] and has
>   come to no conclusion thereon, but asks permission [or "leave"] to con-
>   tinue sitting with debate limited . . . [specifying the limitation].

    The presiding officer then puts the question on granting the
25 request, and if the result is affirmative, the committee chair-
    man resumes the chair.

    A committee of the whole can also rise, before completing
    its work, to request instructions, in which case the nature or
    wording of the request should be agreed to before the mo-
30 tion to rise is made.

    If the committee wishes to bring its proceedings to an
    end because it believes the matter can be better handled
    under the assembly's rules, or because it wishes the meeting
    to be adjourned, the motion to rise can be made in this
35 form:

MEMBER (obtaining the floor): I move that the committee rise. *1*
(Second.)

If this motion is adopted, the committee chairman then
reports: *5*

COMMITTEE CHAIRMAN: The committee of the whole has had under
consideration . . . [describing the matter] and has come to no conclusion
thereon.

10

With such a report, the committee passes out of existence unless the assembly directs it to sit again. In this connection,
however, the committee in reporting can "ask permission to
sit again," with or without specifying a time; and in granting
such a request, the assembly can make the sitting a general *15*
order or a special order (**41**) for a particular time. If the assembly grants the committee permission to sit again without
specifying a time, the sitting is unfinished business. A committee of the whole cannot itself arrange a future meeting.

If an hour for adjournment has been preset in the assem- *20*
bly and it arrives while the meeting is in committee of the
whole, the committee chairman announces, "The hour for
adjournment of the assembly has arrived and the committee
will rise." The committee chairman then reports that the
committee has come to no conclusion on the referred matter, *25*
as described in the preceding paragraph.

QUORUM IN COMMITTEE OF THE WHOLE.
The quorum of a committee of the whole is the same as that
of the assembly unless the bylaws provide, or the assembly *30*
establishes, a different quorum for the committee. If the bylaws do not provide a different quorum for the committee,
the assembly can establish one in the particular case before
going into committee of the whole, regardless of the quorum
that the bylaws require for the assembly. If at any time the *35*

committee finds itself without a quorum, it must rise and report the fact to the assembly. If the assembly itself is thereupon without a quorum, it must then adjourn or take one of the other courses that are open in the absence of a quorum (pp. 347–48).

Quasi Committee of the Whole
(Consideration As If in Committee of the Whole)

A somewhat simpler version of the committee of the whole, in effect, is the procedure of consideration in quasi committee of the whole (or consideration as if in committee of the whole), which is convenient in assemblies of medium size. In contrast to a committee of the whole, the quasi committee of the whole is not a real committee, but is "the assembly acting as if in committee of the whole."

GOING INTO QUASI COMMITTEE OF THE WHOLE.   The motion for consideration in quasi committee is made in a form like this:

MEMBER (obtaining the floor): I move that the resolution be considered in quasi committee of the whole [or "be considered as if in committee of the whole"]. (Second.)

This motion is debatable as to the desirability of going into quasi committee, just as any other motion to *Commit*. If it is adopted, the chair concludes his announcement of the result of the vote as follows:

CHAIR (after declaring the voting result): The resolution is before the assembly as if in committee of the whole.

The presiding officer of the assembly does not appoint a chairman of the quasi committee, but remains in the chair himself throughout its proceedings. The assembly's secretary

should keep a temporary memorandum of the business trans- *1*
acted in quasi committee; but, just as in the case of a real
committee of the whole, the minutes of the assembly should
carry only a record of the report from quasi committee and
the action thereon, as shown below. *5*

CONDUCT OF BUSINESS.   In the quasi committee
of the whole, the main question and any amendments that
may be proposed are open to debate under the same rules as
in a real committee of the whole—each member being *10*
allowed to speak an unlimited number of times as explained
on pages 529–30. In contrast to the case of a real committee
of the whole, however, any motion that would be in order in
the assembly is also in order in the quasi committee, where it
is debatable only to the extent permitted under the assembly's *15*
rules. But if any motion except an amendment is adopted, it
automatically puts an end to the proceedings in quasi committee. Thus, for example, if a motion to refer the main question to an ordinary committee is made in quasi committee
of the whole, such a motion to *Commit* would be equivalent *20*
to the following series of motions if the matter were being
considered in a real committee of the whole: (1) that the committee of the whole rise; (2) that the committee of the whole
be discharged from further consideration of the subject; and
(3) that the question be referred to an ordinary committee. *25*

REPORTING.   The motion to rise is not used in quasi
committee of the whole. If the quasi committee is not
brought to an end as described in the preceding paragraph,
then, when no further amendments are offered in response *30*
to the chair's call for them, the presiding officer immediately
proceeds to report to the assembly and to state the question
on the amendments as follows:

CHAIR: The assembly, acting as if in committee of the whole, has had *35*
under consideration . . . [describing the resolution] and has made the

1 following amendments . . . [reading them]. The question is on the adoption of the amendments.

5 The proceedings in a quasi committee of the whole are thus concluded, and from this point the procedure is the same as in disposing of the report of a real committee of the whole (p. 535, l. 19 to p. 536, l. 5)—the chair putting the question on the reported amendments in gross, except those for which a separate vote may be asked, and so on.

10

Informal Consideration

As explained above, if a question is considered in either a real committee of the whole or in quasi committee of the
15 whole, the recommendations of the committee or quasi committee must be reported to the assembly and then the assembly must take action on these recommendations. In ordinary societies whose meetings are not large, a much simpler method is to consider the question informally, which in effect
20 only suspends the rule limiting the number of times a member can speak in debate on the main question and any amendments to it.

When it is desired to consider a question informally, a member makes the motion that this be done:

25

MEMBER (obtaining the floor): I move that the question be considered informally. (Second.)

This is a variation of the motion to *Commit,* and can be de-
30 bated only as to the desirability of considering the question informally. If the motion is adopted, the chair announces the result thus:

CHAIR (after declaring the voting result): The question is now open
35 to informal consideration. There is no limit to the number of times a member can speak on the question or any amendment.

The "informal" aspect of the consideration applies only *1*
to the number of speeches allowed in debate on the main
question and its amendments; all votes are formal, and any
other motion that is made is under the regular rules of debate.
In contrast to the case of a committee of the whole or quasi *5*
committee of the whole, the proceedings under informal consideration are recorded in the assembly's minutes, just as they
would be if the consideration were formal. While considering
a question informally the assembly can, by a two-thirds vote,
limit the number or length of speeches, or in any other way *10*
limit or close debate. As soon as the main question is disposed
of, temporarily or permanently, the informal consideration
automatically ceases without any motion or vote.

Before the main question is disposed of, the informal consideration can be brought to an end, if desired, by adopting *15*
by majority vote a motion "that the regular rules of debate
be in force," or "that the question be considered formally."

Aids to the Crystallization of Opinion
20

The more traditional aids to the crystallization of opinion
in societies have been, simply, to take a *Recess* or to refer the
matter to a committee—often a large committee composed
of members representing differing views in the society, such
as a committee of the whole or one of its alternate forms. In *25*
more recent years, a practice has developed of establishing
breakout groups with every member in attendance being
urged to participate in a group. Each breakout group, of
which there may be many, is usually kept small—frequently
ten or twelve persons—and a moderator is appointed for each *30*
group. Often, the groups meet during a recess or adjournment of the assembly. Sometimes, the conclusions reached by
the various breakout groups are conveyed to a committee that
assembles them and attempts to report a consolidated response to the assembly. At other times, the breakout groups *35*
report through their moderators directly to the assembly after

1   it has been reconvened and the matter under consideration is
again pending. These reports are in the nature of debate.
Whatever method is used, in the end, the pending measure
must be returned to the full assembly for final consideration
5   under normal parliamentary procedure—just as in the case of
a referred question reported back by a committee—and the
assembly must make the final decision, if whatever is to purport to be a product of the assembly is to be valid as the
assembly's act.

XVII

MASS MEETINGS; ORGANIZATION OF A PERMANENT SOCIETY

§53. MASS MEETINGS

Distinguishing Characteristics of a Mass Meeting

A *mass meeting*, as understood in parliamentary law, is a meeting of an unorganized group, which in a publicized or   *5* selectively distributed notice known as the *call* of the meeting—has been announced:

- as called to take appropriate action on a particular problem or toward a particular purpose stated by the meeting's   *10* sponsors, and
- as open to everyone interested in the stated problem or purpose (or to everyone within a specified sector of the population thus interested).

15

To the extent that persons in the invited category are clearly identifiable—as, for example, registered voters of a particular political party, or residents of a certain area—only such persons have the right to make motions, to speak, and to vote at the meeting, and none others need be admitted if the sponsors so choose. In any event, a mass meeting is convened—and those who attend are admitted—upon the implied understanding that the sponsors (who have engaged the hall and assumed the expenses of promoting the meeting) have the right to have the proceedings confined to the overall object they have announced; but that the entire assembly (which is made up of persons whose help the sponsors are seeking) has the right to determine the action to be taken in pursuit of the stated object. With respect to this limitation of the right of attendance—or, at least, of participation—to persons in general sympathy with the announced object of the meeting, a mass meeting differs from a "town meeting," a public forum, a "lecture-and-discussion-period" type of meeting, or an open hearing held by an instrumentality of government.

Organization of a Mass Meeting

CALL OF THE MEETING.   The call or announcement of a mass meeting should specify the date, hour, and place of the meeting, its purpose, and—where applicable—who is invited to attend. It may also carry an identification of the sponsorship. Depending on the funds available and the people to be reached, the call can be given the desired publicity or distribution by whatever means are expected to be most effective—announcements in the newspapers or by radio or television, a web site, mailings, posters, handbills or flyers, or the like.

PREPARATION.   While a mass meeting should be conducted so as to accord the assembly its proper role in determining the outcome as described above, at the same time, a certain amount of planning by the sponsors is advisable to avoid the risk of the meeting's foundering.

Before the meeting, the sponsors should agree on the *1*
following:

* whom they prefer for its chairman;
* who shall call the meeting to order and nominate their *5*
  choice of chairman;
* who shall be nominated for secretary and by whom;
* what rules—if any—shall be proposed for adoption; and
* who shall make the initial talk explaining the purpose of
  the meeting. *10*

(See also the detailed discussion of these steps below.)

The person chosen as chairman should be competent as a
presiding officer and in sympathy with the object of the meeting, and it is an advantage if he personally knows many of the *15*
people who may attend. Depending on conditions, it is sometimes good policy to have a set of resolutions drafted in advance to submit to the meeting. Provision should also be
made for occupying the time of the gathering in the event
that resolutions are referred to a committee—or a committee *20*
is assigned to draft them (see below).

THE "MEMBERSHIP" OF A MASS MEETING. At
a mass meeting, the "membership" consists of all persons in
the invited category who attend. If no qualification was placed *25*
in the call, anyone who attends is regarded as a member and
has the same rights as members in other assemblies—to make
motions, to speak in debate, and to vote. If the call specified
only a particular category of persons as invited and if no
attempt is made to screen the attendance at the door, anyone *30*
attending is presumed to be entitled to participate as a member, subject only to his subsequent identification to the contrary. If only those invited are admitted, anyone legitimately
admitted has the rights of a member, and a person who is dis-
covered to have entered fraudulently can be asked to leave. *35*

1   RULES IN A MASS MEETING.   Mass meetings frequently operate with no formally adopted rules, upon the assumption that the meeting will proceed according to the
common parliamentary law—or that any differences of opin-
5 ion on procedural questions can be resolved by citing a
recognized parliamentary manual as persuasive (see pp. 3,
16–17). Depending on the probable character of the assembly, however, it may be wise to adopt a standard parliamentary
authority, which can be done by a majority vote on the mo-
10 tion of a member—made, as prearranged by the sponsors, immediately after the election of the secretary (see below).
Other rules are seldom necessary at a mass meeting unless it
is desired to modify the general rules (pp. 387–90) as to the
allowable length and number of speeches. If such a modifi-
15 cation is desired, the assembly can adopt a standing rule
covering the desired provisions at the same time as it adopts
the parliamentary authority, or at a later time. In regard
to the vote required for their adoption, or suspension, standing rules of a mass meeting (or a series of mass meetings) are
20 similar to standing rules of a convention as described on pages
619–21.

In any event, without adoption at a mass meeting and regardless of what rules the meeting may adopt, the provisions
of the call, specifying the meeting's purpose and those invited
25 to attend it, have a force equivalent to bylaws of an organized
society; that is, they define the subject matter within which
motions or resolutions are in order, and determine who
have the right to participate as members (see also pp. 545,
548–49). This effect is a consequence of the sponsors' rights
30 as explained in the first paragraph of this section.

Any person at a mass meeting who, after being advised,
persists in an obvious attempt to divert the meeting to a different purpose from that for which it was called, or who
otherwise tries to disrupt the proceedings, becomes subject
35 to the disciplinary procedures described in **61**.

OPENING OF THE MEETING; ELECTION OF *1*
OFFICERS.   A chairman and a secretary are in general the
only officers required by a mass meeting. Their election takes
place immediately after the meeting is called to order, a convenient method of electing them being by voice vote. As ex- *5*
plained in **46**, the first person nominated is voted on first
under this method. In the interest of electing competent persons, it is therefore advisable that a name chosen by the sponsors be placed in nomination first for each office. Additional
nominations can be made from the floor and the assembly can *10*
elect anyone it wishes, but except under unusual circumstances
it is likely to elect the apparent choices of the sponsors.

Although the person who calls the meeting to order can
call for nominations for chairman, and another can nominate
the sponsors' choice, it is proper—and simpler—for one per- *15*
son to perform both functions (see *Nominations by the Chair,*
p. 431). In the latter case, at the scheduled hour or shortly
thereafter, this person steps to the chair and, after waiting or
signaling for quiet, says, "The meeting will come to order. I
nominate Mr. A for chairman of this meeting." After any *20*
additional nominations from the floor, the chair puts the
question on each name in succession, beginning with the one
he placed in nomination himself, as described under *Viva-
Voce Election,* pages 442–43.

When the chairman of the meeting has been elected, he *25*
takes the chair and may say a few words of acknowledgment
if he wishes, after which he says, "Nominations are now in
order for secretary of this meeting." The person agreed upon
to nominate the sponsors' choice for secretary should
promptly place that name in nomination; members can also *30*
make additional nominations. The secretary is elected viva
voce in the same manner as the chairman. When the secretary
has been elected, he should take his seat near the chairman
and keep a record of the proceedings. If additional officers
are desired, they can be elected in the same way. *35*

Transaction of Business Specified in the Call

EXPLANATION OF THE MEETING'S PURPOSE. When the elections are completed, the chair says, "The Secretary will now read the call of this meeting." This reading of the call should include the names of the sponsors. The chair then recognizes the person who is to explain the purpose of the meeting more fully, or the chairman gives this presentation himself if he has been selected to do so.

RESOLUTIONS TO ACCOMPLISH THE PURPOSE. After the purpose of the meeting has been explained, it is in order for a member to offer a resolution, or a series of resolutions, to accomplish this purpose; or, if believed more suitable to the conditions, it can be moved that a committee be appointed to draft such resolution(s).

If the plan is for the resolution(s) to be offered immediately after the initial explanation, they can have been prepared in advance—with double-spaced reproduced copies for distribution to those in attendance—and a preselected member can now move their adoption. (For considerations to be observed in the drafting of resolutions, see *The Framing of Main Motions,* pp. 104–10.) After another member has seconded the resolution(s), the chair states the question on them, they are open to debate and amendment, and the assembly proceeds to consider them, the entire procedure being as described in **4** and (for a series of resolutions) on page 110.

In stating the question, the chair should make sure that those present understand the means by which the assembly can modify the proposals contained in the resolutions, and should provide such explanations as he believes necessary (see pp. 114–16). With reference to the proposal of substitutes or other amendments—or alternative resolutions if those first

introduced are rejected—any motion within the scope of the   1
meeting's purpose as announced in the call is in order; but
any motion outside of or contrary to that purpose is out
of order. For example, if the announced purpose of a mass
meeting is to oppose the construction of a proposed airport   5
in a particular location, any motion or resolution directed
toward preventing the airport's construction can be brought
up at the meeting; but a motion whose effect would be to
endorse the airport construction project is out of order.

The rules governing the assignment of the floor and de-   10
bate, as given in **42** and **43**, are generally applicable. In a mass
meeting, however, there is no appeal from the chair's decision
in assigning the floor. The rule requiring the assembly's permission to speak for longer than ten minutes at a time in debate on pending questions applies if the meeting has adopted   15
no other rule.

RESOLUTIONS DRAFTED BY A COMMITTEE
APPOINTED AT THE MEETING.   If resolutions have not
been prepared in advance, a committee should be appointed   20
at the meeting to draft them. Such a procedure is appropriate
when it is believed advisable to obtain expressions of opinion
from persons who attend the meeting, before attempting to
frame resolutions. In a small mass meeting, the chair at his
discretion can permit those present to make brief statements   25
of this nature after the initial explanation of the meeting's
purpose and before the motion to appoint the committee
is made. In that case, the chair should specify the time to be
allowed each member—which is a matter entirely under the
chair's control unless the meeting has adopted a special rule,   30
since the procedure is in effect a relaxation of the general parliamentary rule prohibiting speeches when no question is
pending (see pp. 34–35). In any event, the same kind of discussion can also take place in regular debate on the motion

1   to appoint the committee, since it is relevant to the committee's instructions to draft resolution(s) "expressing the sense of the meeting" on the specified subject, as explained below.

5   The person who is to make the motion to appoint the committee should be agreed upon by the sponsors in advance, as well as the matter of whether preliminary discussion is to be permitted before the motion is made. The motion may be made in a form such as the following:

10

> MEMBER (obtaining the floor): I move that a committee of five be appointed by the chair to draft resolutions expressing the sense of this meeting on . . . [the subject for which the meeting was called]. (Second.)

15   This is a main motion, since it is made when no question is pending. It is debatable and amendable and can have any subsidiary motion applied to it.

    In a mass meeting it is usually advisable to have all committees appointed by the chair—assuming that the chairman
20 has been well chosen. If the assembly prefers a different method of appointment, however, the procedures that can be followed are as described in **50**. When the committee has been appointed, it should immediately retire and prepare the resolution(s).

25   During the committee's absence from the hall, the assembly can attend to any other business related to the object of the meeting; or it can occupy the time in listening to talks, in engaging in forums or seminar-type discussions, or in watching a relevant film; or it can recess (**20**).

30   If the assembly does not recess and the chair sees the committee return to the room, he should ask, as soon as the pending business is disposed of (or as soon as the person giving a talk closes, etc.), "Is the committee that was appointed to draft resolutions prepared to report?"

When the committee chairman has answered affirmatively, the chair says, "If there is no objection, the meeting will now hear the committee's report. [Pause.] The chair recognizes the chairman of the committee appointed to draft resolutions." (See treatment of *unanimous consent,* pp. 54–56.)

If the chair does not notice the committee's return, the committee chairman, at the first opportunity, obtains the floor and says, "The committee appointed to draft resolutions is prepared to report." Unless objection is then made, the chair directs the committee chairman to proceed. If anyone objects, the chair puts the question on the report's being received (see p. 513).

The committee chairman, addressing the presiding officer of the assembly, presents the report as follows:

COMMITTEE CHAIRMAN: Madam President, the committee appointed to draft resolutions recommends, and on behalf of the committee I move, the adoption of the following resolution(s) . . . [reading them].

On the presentation of this report, the committee is discharged automatically. The chair then states the question on the resolutions, and they are considered in the same way as summarized above for the case in which resolutions are offered by a member from the floor (see also **51**).

Adjournment

In a mass meeting, unless a time for another meeting has already been set (by adopting a motion to *Fix the Time to Which to Adjourn,* **22**, or by adopting temporary rules as described below), a motion to adjourn is not in order while business is pending (see pp. 233–34).

When the business for which the mass meeting was called has apparently been completed and no question is pending,

1 someone should move "to adjourn," or the chair can call for such a motion. Unless a time has been set for another meeting, the adoption of this motion dissolves the assembly—so that, as explained in **21**, it is a main motion and can be 5 debated and amended just as any other main motion. An example of an amendment to a main motion "to adjourn" might be "to add the words 'until eight o'clock Wednesday evening,'" which would thereby include in the motion a provision to set a time for another meeting.

10 In cases where it is desired to close the meeting before its business has been completed, the rules are as follows:

a) If the time for another meeting has already been set, the motion to adjourn is privileged, just as in a meeting of an 15 ordinary permanent society, and is subject to the rules given in **21**.

b) If no time has been set for another meeting and a question is pending, a motion to *Fix the Time to Which to Adjourn* (**22**) should first be moved and adopted, after 20 which the privileged motion to *Adjourn* (**21**) is in order; the procedure is as shown on page 246, lines 7–31.

c) If no time has been set for another meeting and no question is pending, any member can move, for example, "to adjourn until eight o'clock Wednesday evening," which 25 is a main motion.

When a motion to adjourn a mass meeting has been adopted and no time is set for another meeting, the chair should say, "The ayes have it and the meeting is adjourned." 30 This announcement in effect declares the assembly dissolved. If a time for an adjourned meeting has been set, on the other hand—either previously or by means of a provision included in the motion to adjourn—the chair announces the result by saying, "The ayes have it and this meeting is [or "stands"] 35 adjourned until eight o'clock Wednesday evening." Before

declaring the adjournment, or even taking a vote on adjourn-   1
ing, the chair should make sure that all necessary announcements have been made.

Series of Mass Meetings; Temporary Society   5

If more than one mass meeting is necessary to achieve a
certain objective, or if the group is working toward the formation of an organized society, a temporary organization to
continue beyond a single mass meeting may become neces-   10
sary. If so, the officers elected at the first meeting are designated *chairman pro tem* and *secretary pro tem*—although the
words *pro tem* are not used in addressing these officers. If
a permanent society is the aim of the group, the temporary
officers serve until the election of permanent officers. If spe-   15
cial rules were not adopted at the first meeting, a committee
on rules can be appointed to recommend a few rules, providing for the hour and place for holding the meetings, the number and length of speeches allowed (if the general rules given
on pp. 387–90 are not satisfactory), and a work on parlia-   20
mentary law to be used as parliamentary authority. If such
rules specify periodic dates on which meetings are to be held,
each meeting is a separate session (**8**) as in an ordinary society; but if the time of each succeeding meeting is set at
the previous meeting or is "at the call of the chair," the entire   25
series of meetings constitutes a single session.

§54. ORGANIZATION OF A
PERMANENT SOCIETY   30

When it is desired to form a permanent society, the organizers proceed in much the same way as for a mass meeting,
except that the meetings while the organization is being
formed should usually be carefully limited to persons whose   35

1 interest in the project is known. For this reason, it may be desirable to solicit attendance for these meetings by personal contact or by letter, rather than by public announcement.

First Organizational Meeting

The first meeting, at which the business portion should be kept brief, sometimes follows a luncheon or dinner. At these meetings for purposes of organization, the call to order
10 can be delayed a few minutes beyond the scheduled time, if desired.

ELECTION OF TEMPORARY OFFICERS, AND INTRODUCTORY TALKS.   When the person designated for
15 the purpose has called the meeting to order, he announces, "the first business is the election of a chairman." As in a mass meeting, the one who calls the meeting to order can either nominate a chairman pro tem or immediately call for nominations from the floor, and the nominees are voted on
20 by voice. After the chairman pro tem has taken the chair, a secretary is elected, also as in the case of a mass meeting (see p. 547).

The chair then calls on the member most interested in the formation of the society to provide background information,
25 or he himself can make the talk. Others can also be asked to give their opinions on the subject, but the chair should not permit any one person to monopolize the meeting.

ADOPTION OF A RESOLUTION TO FORM A
30 SOCIETY.   After a reasonable time for such informal discussion, someone should offer a resolution proposing definite action. Those who planned the meeting should have prepared in advance a suitable resolution, which may be in a form essentially as follows:

Resolved, That it is the sense of this meeting that a   *1*
society for . . . [the object of the proposed society] now
be formed [or "shall now be formed"].

This resolution, when seconded, is stated by the chair, and is   *5*
then open to debate and amendment. Such a resolution, it
should be noted, is only a declaration of intention; its adoption
does not bring the organization into being, which is accomplished by the adoption of bylaws and the signing of the
membership roll by those who initially join the society, as de-   *10*
scribed below. If the meeting is a large one, it is usually better
that, except for a brief statement of purpose, the resolution be
offered before the introductory talks mentioned above.

FURTHER BUSINESS RELATING TO ORGANIZA-   *15*
TION. After the resolution to organize the society is
adopted, the succeeding steps generally are:

1) Introduction and adoption of a motion that a committee
   of a specified number be appointed by the chair to draft   *20*
   bylaws* for the society—and, where incorporation may
   be necessary, to consult an attorney as described below.
2) Introduction and adoption of a motion to fix the date,
   hour, and place of the next meeting (**22**), at which the
   report of the bylaws committee will be presented. If it is   *25*
   impractical to set a time and place for the next meeting,
   the motion can be that "when the meeting adjourns, it
   adjourn to meet at the call of the chair."
3) Introduction and adoption of a motion authorizing the
   committee on bylaws to provide reproduced copies of   *30*

---

*Called the *constitution* or *constitution and bylaws* in some organizations
(see pp. 12–15). For factors affecting the appropriate size of this committee,
see pages 566–67.

the completed draft for distribution to all who attend the next meeting. In this connection, persons seeking to form a society should take into account the fact that expenses may be involved, whether or not an organization materializes. Initiation fees or dues cannot be collected or received in the name of the society until its organization, as described in this section, is completed. Expenses advanced can be reimbursed.

Other business before adjournment may include informal discussion of aims and structure of the proposed society—which may serve to guide the bylaws committee (see also below).

When the business of the first meeting is concluded and a motion to adjourn is adopted (see pp. 551–53), the chair says either: (1) "The meeting stands [or "is"] adjourned to meet again at . . . [the date, hour, and place of next meeting]"; or (2) "The meeting is adjourned to meet again at the call of the chair."

Work of the Bylaws Committee

General principles for guidance in the drafting of bylaws are given in **56**. The drafting committee may find it helpful to procure and study copies of the bylaws of other organizations similar to the one being formed, although the possible applicability of their provisions must be carefully evaluated in the light of expected conditions within the new society. The committee may also find it advisable to consult a professional parliamentarian.

If it is expected that the society will own real estate, become a beneficiary under wills, engage employees, or the like, it may need to be incorporated according to the laws of the state in which it is situated (see pp. 11–12). In such a case,

the bylaws committee should be authorized to have one or
more of its members consult an attorney to secure information and advice regarding the legal requirements that must
be taken into account in drawing up the society's bylaws. If
the society is to be incorporated, the same attorney should
draft the charter or other instrument of incorporation, which
the committee submits for approval at the second organizational meeting, before the bylaws are considered, unless there
is some reason for delay (see below).

As indicated above, it is advisable to prepare double-
spaced reproduced copies of the proposed bylaws—as drawn
up by the committee—for distribution to each person entering the hall for the second organizational meeting. If desired,
such copies can be sent in advance to everyone who attended
the first meeting.

Second Organizational Meeting

READING AND APPROVAL OF THE MINUTES.
With the temporary officers elected at the first organizational
meeting serving until the regular officers are elected, the first
item of business at the second meeting is the reading and
approval of the minutes of the first meeting, with corrections
if necessary.

CONSIDERATION AND ADOPTION OF PRO-
POSED BYLAWS.   After the minutes are approved, the report of the bylaws committee normally is received. If there is
a proposed corporate charter, that document is presented
first. The assembly can amend the draft of the charter, but
any resulting modification should be checked by the attorney,
to whom the charter is returned after its adoption, for processing under the legal procedure for incorporation in the
particular state.

1   If there is no proposed corporate charter, the bylaws committee chairman, when recognized for the purpose of presenting the report, begins somewhat as follows:

5   COMMITTEE CHAIRMAN: Mr. Chairman, the committee appointed to
draw up proposed bylaws has agreed upon the following draft and has
directed me to move its adoption. [Reads proposals in full—members
following on their own copies—unless the first reading is dispensed with;
then moves the adoption of the document, as follows:] Mr. Chairman,
10 by direction of the committee, I move the adoption of the bylaws.

No second is necessary, since the motion is offered by a committee of more than one person. Since a complete set of bylaws is commonly considered *by article or section* (see **28**), the
15 chair states the question as follows:

      CHAIR: The question is on the adoption of the bylaws as proposed
by the committee. The committee chairman [or "the Secretary"] will
now read the proposed bylaws, one article or section at a time. After each
20 article or section is read, it will be open to debate and amendment. When
amendment of one article or section is completed, the next one will be
read and considered. No section or article will be adopted until all have
been opened to amendment.

25   Each article or section is read separately, each provision
being carefully explained by the chairman of the bylaws committee, as described above; and after the last one has been
completed, the chair gives opportunity to insert additional
paragraphs or sections and to correct any inconsistency or
30 oversight that may have arisen during the process of amendment, as follows:

      CHAIR: The entire set of bylaws is now open to amendment. Are
there any further amendments?

If, at any point during the consideration of the bylaws, it develops that important additions or amendments are desirable but will require time or investigation to prepare, it is in order to move to recommit (**13**) the proposed bylaws, with instructions that the committee report at another meeting for which the time can be fixed. Or, further consideration of the bylaws can simply be postponed (**14**) to such a meeting. This third meeting in forming an organization, although in many cases unnecessary, in others often pays dividends in increased understanding and a larger membership. In any event, at the second or third meeting, when there are no further amendments, the question is put on adopting the bylaws:

CHAIR: The question is on the adoption of the bylaws as amended. Those in favor of adopting the bylaws, say *aye*. . . . Those opposed, say *no*. . . . [and so on, taking a voice vote in the regular manner].

In case of doubt, the chair should call for a rising vote and, if necessary, direct that a count be made; or a member can call for a division (**29**), and can move that the vote be counted, as described on pages 51–52. Unlike the case of amending or revising the bylaws of an organization already established (**57**), the adoption of the bylaws through which a society is brought into being requires only a majority vote. The bylaws take effect immediately upon their adoption. A negative vote on their adoption can be reconsidered, but not an affirmative one.

RECESS TO ENROLL MEMBERS.   After the adoption of the bylaws, only those who join the society are entitled to vote in further proceedings. At this point, therefore, the meeting recesses to enroll initial members. Immediate admission to membership is contingent upon signing a permanent record sheet provided in advance by the secretary pro tem—

1 to be filed with the original papers of the organization. This
signature constitutes agreement to abide by the bylaws, and
is a commitment to prompt payment of the initiation fee (if
there is one) and dues for the first year or other period pre-
5 scribed by the bylaws. Persons thus signing become "charter
members."* The secretary pro tem should record and give
receipt for payments received from members until the treasurer is elected and takes office.

10   READING OF THE ROLL AND ELECTION OF
PERMANENT OFFICERS.   After the recess the chairman
pro tem calls for the reading of the roll of members, and the
secretary pro tem does so. The chair then says, "The next
business in order is the nomination and election of the per-
15 manent officers as prescribed in the bylaws."

The nomination and election processes are as described
in **46**, the election being by ballot if the bylaws so prescribe,
which they usually should. The members for whom one can
vote are not limited to nominees, since each member is free
20 to vote for any member who is not made ineligible by the bylaws. After the election is completed, the chair declares the
results. Unless a proviso attached to the bylaws (pp. 597–98)
prescribes otherwise, the newly elected officers immediately
replace the temporary ones.

25

ANY OTHER ESSENTIAL BUSINESS.   When the offices have been filled and the new president has taken the
chair, he should call for any business requiring immediate
attention. In a new society it is generally important that the
30 president have time to give careful thought to committee

---

*Sometimes, in forming a society, all who join before a specified date
after the actual establishment of the organization are included in the roll of
charter members.

appointments after examining the list of members. It is therefore often advisable to provide for an adjourned meeting to
complete the organization before the first regular meeting.
The president may find it essential, however, to name the
chairmen of certain committees, such as the membership or
program committees, immediately.

When the business of the meeting has been completed,
or when an adjourned meeting has been provided for, a
motion to adjourn is in order. If it is adopted, the chair
announces the result and declares the meeting adjourned.

Subsequent meetings of the society are conducted as described in **3** and **4**. For additional information regarding the
organization of a federation by a convention of delegates
from prospective member societies, see **60**.

§55. MERGER, CONSOLIDATION, AND DISSOLUTION OF SOCIETIES

Combining of Societies

DISTINCTION BETWEEN MERGER AND CON-
SOLIDATION.   In cases where two existing societies wish
to combine, there are two possible procedures, which are
legally distinct:

- In the case of a *merger,* one of the two organizations continues, while the other loses its independent identity and
  ceases to exist, since it is merged—that is, absorbed—into
  the former.
- In the case of a *consolidation,* two or more organizations
  each discontinue their independent existence, and a new
  entity is formed that includes the memberships of the
  consolidating organizations, continues their work, and
  assumes their assets and liabilities.

In either a merger or a consolidation, the resulting organization may be given a new name, which may include, for example, elements of the names of each of the combining organizations.

CASES INVOLVING INCORPORATED SOCIETIES. If one or more of the organizations involved in a merger or a consolidation are incorporated, an attorney should be consulted to draw up the proper papers and advise as to all steps necessary to fulfill the legal requirements.

CASES INVOLVING UNINCORPORATED SOCIETIES. If none of the organizations involved in a merger or a consolidation is incorporated, the respective procedures are as follows:

- In the case of a merger, the organization that is giving up its independent identity should adopt a resolution substantially as follows: "*Resolved,* That the A Society be, and hereby is, merged into the B Society as of [date] or when such merger shall be accepted by the B Society." For its adoption, such a resolution requires the same notice and vote as for amending the bylaws (see pp. 580–82). This resolution should be joined with, or its adoption should be followed by the adoption of, resolutions transferring all of the assets and liabilities to the organization into which it is merging, and providing for whatever other administrative details will be required in the mechanics of transition. The society into which the first organization is being merged should adopt a resolution accepting the merger, and this motion similarly requires the same notice and vote as to amend the accepting organization's bylaws, because it so greatly alters the per-capita interest of each member. Often, resolutions authorizing and approving mergers contain stipulations and qualifications, sometimes

even to the extent of naming the officers who will serve   *1*
during the first year after the merger. Usually these resolutions are the work of a joint committee of the two
organizations and form a part of its recommendations.

- In the case of a consolidation, the two or more con-   5
solidating organizations adopt resolutions authorizing
the consolidation, similar to the resolutions described
in the preceding item relating to merger. Often—but not
necessarily—these meetings are held simultaneously in the
same building. As in the case of a merger, the resolutions   *10*
containing details relating to the mechanics of transition
are usually drafted by a joint committee. After the consolidating organizations have each adopted resolutions
which are substantially identical and which provide for
consolidation as of a stated date, a joint meeting of the   *15*
members of the consolidating groups is held for the purpose of organizing the new society that is to emerge. In
contrast to the case of a merger, a new set of bylaws must
be drawn up and adopted. The procedure is similar to that
for the original establishment of a society as described in   *20*
54, except that the necessary resolutions and motions
normally are worded so that the date on which the new
organization is established, its bylaws take effect, and its
officers assume office coincides with the date on which
the consolidating groups discontinue separate existence.   *25*

Dissolution of a Society

It may sometimes happen over a period of time that the
needs which led to the formation of a society have largely dis-   *30*
appeared, and the organization may wish formally to disband
or dissolve.

DISSOLUTION OF AN INCORPORATED SOCIETY.
If a society is incorporated, the laws of the state in which it is   *35*

1 incorporated provide in some detail the legal requirements for the dissolution of the corporation. An attorney should be consulted to draw up the necessary papers and advise the society as to the procedure to be followed.

5   DISSOLUTION OF AN UNINCORPORATED SOCIETY.   In the case of an unincorporated society, a resolution should be prepared, such as: "*Resolved,* That the X Society be dissolved as of March 31, 20__." This resolution
10 may be preceded by a preamble setting forth the reasons for the dissolution. It is in effect a motion to rescind the bylaws, and therefore requires for its adoption the same notice and vote as to amend them (see pp. 580–82). The required notice must be sent to all members of record.

15   Such a resolution can be coupled with other resolutions stating the manner in which the society's assets shall be disposed of and attending to other administrative details—or these can be adopted separately. In certain tax-exempt organizations of a charitable or educational character, federal and
20 state tax laws must be adhered to in the disposal of the organization's assets. Often such assets are distributed to societies with similar objectives, or to a superior body.

CHAPTER
XVIII

BYLAWS

§56. CONTENT AND COMPOSITION OF BYLAWS

Nature and Importance of Bylaws

The constitution and/or bylaws of a society, as explained in **2**, contains its own basic rules that relate to itself as an organization, except for what must be included in the corporate charter of an incorporated society. Under the preferred practice for ordinary societies today, the constitution and the bylaws—once usually separate—are now combined in a single instrument, referred to in this book as the *bylaws* (although in some organizations called the *constitution,* or—even though only one document—the *constitution and bylaws*). A precise statement of the essential characteristics of bylaws, in the sense of the combination-type instrument, and their relation to the other kinds of rules that an organization may have is given in **2**, which should be read in connection with this chapter. Because bylaws in this sense are the most important rules which an organization must compose for itself, and because certain considerations must be taken into account

1 that affect their construction as a unified document rather than a series of separate rules, bylaws are given more detailed treatment below.

5   The content of a society's bylaws has important bearing on the rights and duties of members within the organization—whether present or absent from the assembly—and on the degree to which the general membership is to retain control of, or be relieved of detailed concern with, the society's business. Except as the rules of a society may provide otherwise, its assembly (that is, the members attending one of its regular or properly called meetings) has full and sole power to act for the entire organization, and does so by majority vote. Any limitation or standing delegation of the assembly's power with respect to the society as a whole can only be by provision in the bylaws—or in the corporate charter or separate constitution, if either of these exists.

Committee to Draw Up Bylaws

20   APPOINTMENT OF COMMITTEE. A committee to draw up proposed bylaws is usually appointed at the first organizational meeting when a new society is being formed, as described in **54**; or, if an existing society wishes to undertake a general revision of its bylaws, a committee to draw up the proposed revision can be appointed at any regular meeting, just as any other special committee.

    A committee to draw up proposed bylaws should generally be large, and should include the most judicious persons available, those who have a special interest in the rules of the society, and those who would otherwise be likely to consume much time in discussing the bylaws when they come before the assembly for adoption. Persons having writing ability of the kind required should also be included, unless a professional parliamentarian is to do the actual drafting of the bylaws. Even if the drafting is to be done by members of the committee, a parliamentarian can often be of great assistance as a consultant.

The committee should consult an attorney with reference to the considerations indicated on pages 556–57 if there is any possibility that the society should be incorporated. If it is to be incorporated, the committee works with the attorney to provide him with the necessary information for drafting an appropriate corporate charter, to which the bylaws must conform. The committee should review the draft of the charter before submitting it to the assembly.

INITIAL DISCUSSIONS; FACTORS INFLUENCING CONTENT OF BYLAWS.   The committee normally begins its work—with the entire committee present—in general discussion of the desired content of the bylaws. Besides reviewing the existing bylaws (in the case of a revision), it is well for the committee to study the bylaws of a number of similar organizations, or—if applicable—of other subordinate units within the same state or national society. Before any provisions from other documents are used as a pattern, however, possible differences between the conditions in the other organizations and the one for which the bylaws are being prepared should be carefully analyzed.

If the unit for which the bylaws are to be drawn up is subject to a parent organization or superior body, such as a state or a national society (or both), or a federation, the bylaws governing at these higher levels should be studied for provisions which are binding upon subordinate units in a way that must be taken into account. The bylaws of a subordinate unit need to conform to those of a superior body only on clearly requisite points. For example, if the superior body limits the size of its subordinate units to 200 members, the bylaws should contain this limit or one that is lower. But the subordinate unit should not adopt provisions from the other document that have no local application,

1   and the bylaws of the superior body should not require it
to do so.

In order to give the organization the greatest freedom to
act within its object, bylaws should be made no more restric-
5   tive nor more detailed in specification than necessary.

The description of the basic bylaw articles beginning on
page 570 provides a brief indication of the framework within
which the particular needs of the society should be considered
in determining the content of its bylaws. A sample set of by-
10   laws of the type that might be adopted by a small and independent local society is shown beginning on page 583. Such
a model can only illustrate how a typical document of this
kind is put together, however; and the provisions must be varied, additional ones inserted, or inapplicable ones omitted, as
15   appropriate to the individual organization.

DRAFTING OF BYLAWS; APPOINTMENT OF
SUBCOMMITTEE(S).   After conferences on the topics described above, the committee should appoint a drafting sub-
20   committee, or several of them for various articles if the bylaws
are expected to be long and complex. Another subcommittee
may be needed in the latter case to eliminate inconsistencies,
make the style uniform, and make sure that, as far as possible,
everything relating to a single subject is placed in the same
25   or adjacent articles.

The composition of bylaws is somewhat different from
ordinary expository writing, in that it places greater demand
on a "tight" clarity and precision in word choice, sentence
structure, and punctuation. In bylaws, every punctuation
30   mark may have an important effect; and what is omitted may
carry as much significance as what is included. Indisputability
of meaning and application is a more important consideration
than "readability," and the latter must be sacrificed when
both cannot be achieved. Each sentence should be written so
35   as to be impossible to quote out of context; that is, either its
complete meaning should be clear without reference to sen-

tences preceding or following, or it should be worded so as   *1*
to compel the reader to refer to adjoining sentences—as by
beginning, "Any member so elected . . ." Exceptions or qualifications to statements should be included, as far as possible,
within the sentence to which they apply—which can often be   *5*
accomplished by ending sentences with clauses beginning
"except that . . ." or "provided, however, that . . ." Where
such a technique is impractical, a sentence should contain at
least an allusion or reference to any exceptions to its own
applicability—as in "Except as provided in Article VI, Sec-   *10*
tion 2 of these bylaws, officers shall . . ."

Provisions of a temporary nature or relating to the mechanics of transition from old to revised bylaws should not
be included within bylaws (see pp. 597–98).

Regarding the inclusion of provisions in the nature of   *15*
rules of order within bylaws, see page 17, lines 11–27.

CRITICAL REVIEW BY FULL COMMITTEE.   After
the first draft of the bylaws has been completed, it should be
given thorough critical examination in discussions by the full   *20*
committee. The probable long-range effect of each provision
should be weighed, and particular care taken to detect and
eliminate any remaining inconsistencies or ambiguities. It is
much better to take a good deal of time in consideration of
bylaws before their adoption than to find an early need for   *25*
extensive amendment.

PRESENTATION OF REPORT.   After the proposed
bylaws are approved by the committee, the report of the
committee is presented to the assembly and is considered   *30*
seriatim—article by article and, whenever an article consists of more than one section, section by section. The procedure is as described on pages 557–59 and in **28**—except
that:

35

a) especially in the case of a revision of bylaws, the motion to adopt them may include provisos relating to transition, as explained on pages 597–98; and

b) a revision of bylaws is adopted by the vote required to amend the existing ones (pp. 580–82), rather than by a majority vote as in the case of bylaws that bring a society into being.

In presenting the report of the bylaws committee to the assembly, the committee chairman should explain each section and—in the case of a proposed revision of bylaws—make clear what is new about each provision or how it differs from the corresponding provision of the existing bylaws.

Content of Bylaw Articles

BASIC BYLAW ARTICLES.   While the number of bylaw articles will be determined by the size and activities of the organization adopting them, and more than those listed below will be needed in some cases, the average society will find it sufficient to include articles on the following numbered headings. The description of appropriate provisions in these articles, while in no sense exhaustive, should prove of help in framing bylaws. Articles are commonly designated with Roman numerals, and sections with Arabic numerals (see also sample bylaws beginning on p. 583). For ready reference, it may be helpful to precede lengthy bylaws with a table of contents when they are printed or copied for distribution.

Article I: Name.   In unincorporated societies, the full, exact, and properly punctuated name of the society should be given. In incorporated societies or those with separate constitutions, however, the bylaws can omit this article, since the official name of the organization is then stated in the corporate charter or constitution. If the name is in both locations, conflicts may creep in, and it is the name as stated in the superior document that is official.

Article II: Object. In unincorporated societies, the object   *1*
of the society should be concisely expressed in a single sentence, the various aspects or phases being written in sequence,
set off by semicolons, or in lettered subparagraphs, also set
off by semicolons. The statement should be general in its   *5*
application, since it sets boundaries within which business can
be introduced at the society's meetings—a two-thirds vote
being required to allow the introduction of a motion that falls
outside the society's object. For the same reason stated above
in reference to the society's name, this article also can be   *10*
omitted from the bylaws in incorporated societies or in those
having a separate constitution. Some societies prefer to set
forth the object in a preamble to the bylaws rather than in an
article, in which case the preamble precedes Article I, and the
numbering of the remaining articles described below is mod-   *15*
ified as necessary. This device is especially useful in societies
incorporated many years before, whose charter no longer
states its object in modern terms or with the specificity now
desired.

Article III: Members. Usually the article on members   *20*
consists of several sections, covering, for example: (1) classes
of members—as "active," "associate," and the like—with any
distinctions between them being set forth, and, as applicable,
the rights of each, and any limitation on their number; and
(2) qualifications or eligibility for membership, with appli-   *25*
cation and acceptance procedures, including the method of
reviewing and voting on applications. Unless the financial
obligations of members are especially complicated, a section
of this article should also state: (3) the required fees and dues,
the date(s) when payable (whether annually, semiannually,   *30*
quarterly, etc.), the time and prescribed procedure for notifying members if they become delinquent in payment, and
the date thereafter on which a member will be dropped for
nonpayment of dues. Before a member in arrears has been
finally dropped under such a provision, his voting rights   *35*

1 cannot be suspended unless the bylaws so provide. (See also pp. 6, 291–92, 406, 461, 584.) Members cannot be assessed any additional payment aside from their dues unless it is provided for in the bylaws. If the necessary provisions relating to

5 the financial obligations of members to the society are too complex to be included in this article, such provisions can be set out in a separate article immediately following.

Some organizations require attendance at a certain proportion of the meetings or a specified minimum participation

10 in the society's activities as a requirement for continued membership; this also can be done only by provision in the bylaws.

Sometimes this article also contains provisions for: (4) resignations; and (5) honorary members (see pp. 463–64).

In a state or national body or a federation, local units or

15 constituent clubs, rather than individuals, may be the "members" referred to in this article.

Article IV: Officers. As stated in **47**, every society should specify in this article of its bylaws the officers it requires, including honorary ones, and how they shall be elected or

20 appointed. The officers rank in the order listed, so that the president should be named first, the vice-president or first vice-president next (unless there is to be a president-elect; see p. 457), and so on. Directors should be classed as officers.

Normally all that need be said about the duties of offi-

25 cers (apart from occasional references in other articles, under the topics to which specific duties relate) can be included in the section designating the officers, to the effect that "These officers shall perform the duties prescribed by these bylaws and by the parliamentary authority adopted by the So-

30 ciety." In cases where the extraordinary duties of officers are numerous, however, a separate article titled "Duties of Officers" may sometimes follow this article, and treat the duties for each office in a separate section. Such a procedure is advantageous in collecting related information in one place, but

35 it results in repetition and may occasion problems of inter-

pretation. Great care must be taken in the writing of the
article not to omit any duty, since an implication that the duty
is not required could be read into the omission. For this reason, if such an article is to be included, it is well to conclude
the section on each office with a clause such as ". . . and such
other duties applicable to the office as prescribed by the parliamentary authority adopted by the Society."

A method of nominating officers (see **46**) may be prescribed in a section of this article; in the absence of such a
provision or any rule adopted by the society, nominations are
made in accordance with established custom (if any) or as
otherwise directed by vote of the society at the time of each
election (see also **31**). If the bylaws provide for a nominating
committee and prescribe that the committee shall nominate
"candidates for each office," the committee is not limited to
one candidate for each office. If it is desired to impose such
a limitation, the provision should state that the committee
shall nominate "a candidate for each office."

Election by ballot should usually be prescribed in the section pertaining to elections and terms of office—often with
additional details of election procedure as discussed in **46**. A
provision can be included to dispense with the ballot when
there is only one candidate for an office, although this deprives members of the privilege of voting for "write-in" candidates in such a case. If it is desired to elect by mail, by
plurality vote, by preferential voting, or by cumulative voting,
this must be expressly stated, and necessary details of the procedure should be prescribed (see **45**). The length of the terms
of office should be prescribed; and unless the terms are to
begin at the instant the chair declares each officer elected, the
time when they are to begin must be specified. (In either
case, the terms of the outgoing officers end when those of
the incoming officers begin.) To ensure the continued services of officers in the event, for example, of public emergency
or of difficulty in obtaining a nominee for an office, the

1   unqualified wording "for a term of . . . year(s)" should be
avoided, because at the end of that time there would be no
officers if new ones had not been elected. The exact wording
that instead ought to be used depends on a further consider-
5   ation, namely, the manner in which the organization wants
to make it possible to remove officers before the expiration
of their normal term.

Careful thought should be given to whether, given the
circumstances of the particular organization, it is preferable
10   (1) to permit removal of officers only for cause, through disciplinary proceedings that may involve a formal trial (see
p. 654, ll. 4–13), or (2) instead to permit their removal at
the pleasure of the membership by a two-thirds vote, a majority vote when previous notice has been given, or a vote of
15   a majority of the entire membership—any one of which will
suffice (see p. 653, l. 27 to p. 654, l. 3).

To accomplish the first alternative, the bylaws may provide that officers "shall hold office for a term of _____
year(s) *and* until their successors are elected." To accomplish
20   the second alternative, the bylaws may provide that officers
"shall hold office for a term of _____ year(s) *or* until their
successors are elected." (Emphases added.) Because the significant difference in effect between the use of "and" and
"or" is unlikely to be clear to most members, it may be desir-
25   able (although it is not essential) to add an explanatory sentence, such as:

• For the first alternative: "Officers may be removed from
  office for cause by disciplinary proceedings as provided in
30   the parliamentary authority."
• For the second alternative: "Officers may be removed
  from office at the pleasure of the membership as provided
  in the parliamentary authority."

35   Since a reasonable rotation in office is desirable in almost
all organizations, a section of this article may well provide

that "No person shall be eligible to serve . . . consecutive   1
terms [specifying the number] in the same office." For purposes of determining eligibility to continue in office under
such a provision, an officer who has served more than half a
term is considered to have served a full term in that office.   5

   The method of filling vacancies may also be provided (cf.
pp. 467–68). Unless the bylaws clearly provide otherwise, notice of filling a vacancy in office must always be given to the
members of the body that will elect the person to fill it. If
the bylaws are silent as to the method of filling a vacancy   10
in the specific case of the presidency, the vice-president or first
vice-president automatically becomes president for the remainder of the term, and the vacancy to be filled arises in the
vice-presidency or lowest-ranking vice-presidency; if another
method of filling a vacancy in the presidency is desired, it   15
must be prescribed and specified as applying to the office of
president in particular.

   Article V: Meetings. The first section of the article on
meetings should fix the day on which regular meetings
of the society are to be held—as by specifying, for example,   20
"the first Friday of each month." If the words "unless otherwise ordered by the Society [or "Executive Board"]" are
added, the date can be changed in an unusual circumstance,
but only for that single meeting on that particular occasion,
and not for a period of time including several meetings. To   25
change the general rule fixing the time for meetings would
require amendment of the bylaws. The hour and place at
which meetings are to be held should not be specified in
the bylaws, but should be established by a standing rule
(2) adopted by the society or, if it is empowered to do so, by   30
the executive board.

   Some organizations prefer to schedule meetings by resolution. If so, the bylaws should provide for the number of
days' notice required before regular meetings, since under
such a practice members cannot determine the meeting dates   35
by consulting the bylaws.

1   In a separate section it should be provided that "The regular meeting . . . [specifying which one, as "on the last Tuesday
in May"] shall be known as the annual meeting." As explained
in **9**, this meeting is conducted in the same way as any regular
5   meeting, except that officers are elected and annual reports
are received from officers and standing committees.

A section authorizing the calling of special meetings should
state by whom such meetings can be called—such as the president, the board, or a specified number of members nearly
10 equal to a quorum—and the number of days' notice required.
It may be well to provide that no business shall be transacted
except that mentioned in the call (that is, the notice) of the
special meeting, although this rule would apply even if not
expressly stated (see pp. 91–93). If the bylaws do not authorize
15 the calling of special meetings, such meetings are not permitted—except when authorized by the assembly itself, as part
of formal disciplinary procedures, for purposes of conducting
a trial and determining a punishment (see p. 660, l. 28 to
p. 661, l. 1).

20   The quorum for all meetings should be established in a
section of this article (see **40**).

In state or national bodies where one session—usually
called a *convention*—is held annually, biennially, or at less frequent intervals—the article on meetings is titled "Conven-
25 tions." While much that is stated above would be generally
applicable to such an article, considerable adaptation is
needed, as described on pages 601–2.

Article VI: Executive Board (or Board of Directors). As
explained on pages 481–83, all but the smallest societies usu-
30 ally find it advisable to establish a board whose members are
the officers of the society, such a body being entrusted with
administrative authority and responsibility to a degree that
varies with the organization. If there is to be such a board,
sections of this article should:

35

• specify the board's composition;

- delineate the powers of the board; and
- set forth any special rules by which the board is to conduct its business, such as when and how often it is to meet, its quorum, and the like.

In most societies this body is called the *Executive Board* unless there is to be a smaller body within it to act for the board between its meetings, in which case the full board is usually designated the *Board of Directors* and the smaller body is called the *Executive Committee* (see p. 485). The Executive Committee is then established in a separate article following the one on the complete board, with similar provisions. The bylaws may provide for how the presiding officer and the secretary of the board, and those of the Executive Committee, are to be determined. In the absence of such provisions in the bylaws, however, the president and the secretary of the society also serve in the same capacities within these bodies. Organizations may sometimes give varied names to their full boards, such as *Board of Managers, Board of Trustees, Board of Governors, Administrative Council,* etc. In such cases, the nature of the particular body as one of the types described above can be determined from the bylaw article that establishes it.

A board may never alter a decision of the society's assembly (and an executive committee may never alter a decision of either the assembly or the board), even by a motion to *Rescind or Amend Something Previously Adopted* or by adoption of a proposal which has been rejected, unless expressly authorized by the superior body or by the bylaws (see p. 483, ll. 6–13). Thus, for example, if it is desired that the assembly adopt an annual budget but that the board be empowered to alter it to deal with contingencies that may develop, the bylaws (or the budget resolution) must specifically confer this power on the board.

Article VI, Section 2 of the sample bylaws (p. 586) shows an appropriate wording for defining the board's powers so that the board's authority will be limited to the power to

1 supervise, and to determine the details of, implementation of
the decisions of the society's assembly and, in a manner not
inconsistent with such decisions, to attend to any business of
the society that cannot wait until the next meeting.

5   If the organization desires to leave the entire administrative authority of the society to the board between the society's
meetings—as may occur, for example, in organizations that
meet infrequently or whose main purpose is other than to
transact business—the same section might read:

10
       The Executive Board [or "Board of Directors," etc.]
       shall have full power and authority over the affairs of
       the Society except . . . [specifying classes of business
       over which the assembly of the society is to retain sole
15   authority].

       Article VII: Committees.   The article on committees
should provide for the establishment of each of the standing
committees (**50**) that it is known will be required. A separate
20 section devoted to each of these committees should give its
name, composition, manner of selection, and duties. If this
article names certain standing committees, no other standing
committees can be appointed without amending the bylaws,
unless a provision is included—usually in a separate section
25 of the article as described below—permitting the establishment of such other standing committees as are deemed necessary to carry on the work of the society. In any event, if a
standing committee is to have standing authority to act for
the society without specific instructions, if business of a cer-
30 tain class is to be automatically referred to it, or if some other
rule of parliamentary procedure is affected by the committee's
assigned function, such procedure must be prescribed in a
provision of the bylaws or in a special rule of order, establishing the committee by name.

35   The number and nature of the standing committees that
may be named in individual sections of this article will depend

on the size and object of the organization. The standing com- *1*
mittees most frequently established by local societies are few
in number; they may include a committee on membership, a
program committee, and sometimes a finance committee. (A
section relating to the nominating committee, when included, *5*
is usually located not in this article but in the article on officers, where nomination and election procedures are usually
prescribed.) In national or state bodies more committees may
be needed, but local units should not try to establish a committee to correspond to each one in the superior body, and *10*
the superior body generally should not require them to do so.

Appointment of special committees is usually provided for
in a separate section that may also, as indicated above, provide for the appointment of additional standing committees.
When this section empowers the president to appoint such *15*
special committees or additional standing committees as the
society or the board shall direct, he is not thereby authorized
to appoint other committees on his own initiative. If the president is to appoint committees and it is desired that he
have standing authority to appoint non–assembly members *20*
to positions on the committees without submitting these persons' names to the assembly for approval, this section should
contain a provision to that effect (see pp. 174–75, 492–93,
496). This section may also provide that certain officers—for
example, the president—"shall be ex officio a member of all *25*
committees except the Nominating Committee." In that
case, the president has the right, but not the duty, of participating in the work of the committees (see also pp. 483–84,
497). Without such a provision, he has no vote within the
committees, nor can he attend their meetings except as in- *30*
vited by a particular committee. The nominating committee
should always be expressly excluded in a provision making the
president an ex-officio member of committees. It may also
be advisable to exclude all disciplinary committees—such as
trial and investigating committees—both from a provision *35*
making the president an ex-officio member of committees

1   and from a provision authorizing the president to appoint
     committees.

        If no article on committees is included in the bylaws,
     standing and special committees are established as directed
5   by the society (see **13, 50**).

        Article VIII: Parliamentary Authority. The parliamentary
     authority—through the adoption of which a society estab-
     lishes its rules of order—should be prescribed in a one-
     sentence article reading: "The rules contained in the current
10   edition of . . . [specifying a standard manual of parliamentary
     practice, such as this book] shall govern the Society in all cases
     to which they are applicable and in which they are not incon-
     sistent with these bylaws and any special rules of order the
     Society may adopt."* Societies can adopt special rules of
15   order as they are needed to supplement their parliamentary
     authority, as explained in **2**. It should be noted that the bylaw
     language recommended above does not authorize the adop-
     tion of a special rule of order that would supersede a rule that
     the parliamentary authority states can be altered only by a
20   provision in the bylaws. When a particular work is adopted as
     the parliamentary authority, what any other book may say on
     any point is of no authority if in conflict with the adopted
     work. In other cases, it may be persuasive but is not binding
     upon the society.

25   *Article IX: Amendment of Bylaws.* The bylaws should
     always prescribe the procedure for their amendment, and

---

*Where a particular type of organization is subject to local, state, or na-
tional law containing provisions relating to its procedure—as for certain procedures in a labor organization, in condominium associations, or in an
incorporated association—it may be desirable to add at this point a phrase
such as, "and any statutes applicable to this organization that do not authorize
the provisions of these bylaws to take precedence." However, such statutes
(those that do *not* authorize bylaws to take precedence) supersede all rules of
the organization which conflict with them, even if no mention is made of it
in the bylaws.

such provision should always require at least that advance   *1*
notice be given in a specified manner, and that the amendment be approved by a two-thirds vote. If the bylaws contain
no provision for their amendment, they can be amended by
a two-thirds vote if previous notice (in the sense defined on   *5*
p. 121) has been given, or they can be amended by the vote
of a majority of the entire membership. In making a requirement that notice be given by submitting the amendment at a
meeting in advance of the one at which it is to be considered,
the provision should always specify submission at "*the* previ-   *10*
ous meeting," and not "a" previous meeting, since the latter
would permit indefinite delay and would defeat the object of
giving notice—namely, to alert the members to the proposed
amendment so that all those interested can arrange to be present at its consideration. The requirement of notice restricts   *15*
amendment of the proposed bylaw amendment to changes
within the scope of the notice, as explained on pages 594–96
(see also Standard Characteristic 6, p. 306).

The manner prescribed for giving notice should suit the
needs of the particular assembly. For some, oral notice is suf-   *20*
ficient; others may require written notice. Some may require
only a general statement of the purport of the amendment;
others may require that the exact wording of the amendment be given. If the bylaws require only previous notice of
an amendment without limitation of the period within which   *25*
it must be acted upon, and a committee is appointed to revise
the bylaws and report at a specified meeting, the appointing
action is all the notice required, and the amendments can be
immediately acted upon at the time the committee reports.
But if it is required that the amendment itself, or "notice of   *30*
such amendment," be submitted at the previous regular
meeting, the revision cannot be taken up until the meeting
following the meeting at which the committee submitted its
report. In societies having very frequent regular meetings primarily for presentation of a program, and also monthly or   *35*

quarterly business meetings (p. 89), it is well to permit action on amendments to the bylaws only at a quarterly or annual meeting or their adjournments. Where assemblies meet regularly only once a year, instead of requiring amendments to be submitted at the previous annual meeting, the bylaws should provide for both notice and copies of the proposed amendment to be sent to the member delegates or constituent societies.

If there is a constitution separate from the bylaws, the requirement for amendment of the constitution should be made more difficult than that for amendment of the bylaws; otherwise there would be no purpose in having separate documents. In either case, however, the necessary vote should be at least two thirds.

In prescribing the vote necessary for the adoption of an amendment, the expression "a vote of two thirds of the members" should never be used in ordinary societies, especially in large organizations. In such societies two thirds of the entire membership would rarely, if ever, be present at a meeting. It is more reasonable to require "a two-thirds vote" (see pp. 401–2).

The wording of this article should avoid redundant phraseology such as "amend, alter, add to, or repeal," or "alter or amend," or "amend or in any way change." The word *amend* covers any change, whether a word or a paragraph is to be added, struck out, or replaced, or whether a new set of articles is to be substituted for the old one. Efforts to define the meaning of such expressions as "two-thirds vote" should also be avoided in the wording of this article, since these definitions are found in the parliamentary authority.

ADDITIONAL BYLAW ARTICLES.   Some societies may have cause to include additional bylaw articles, such as those mentioned above, bearing on the subjects of finance, duties of officers, and an executive committee of the board

of directors. In a national organization, an article providing
for constituent societies or units at regional, state, or local
levels and establishing their relationships within the organizational structure may be required. In associations divided
into departments, the article establishing them—titled "Departments"—follows the article establishing committees. In
professional and some other societies there may be an article
on disciplinary procedure; and such an article can be simple
or very elaborate. Most such provisions, however, are generally unnecessary in ordinary societies, at least at the local level
(see **61–63**).

Sample Bylaws

Regarding the applicability of the following model, see
page 568, lines 6–15. Titles of sections are optional, but
they may be felt to be desirable, particularly if the bylaws become elaborate, as may be the case, for example, in a complex
national organization.

BYLAWS

OF THE _____ SOCIETY

OF _____

ARTICLE I

Name

The name of this Society shall be _____.

ARTICLE II

Object

The object of this Society shall be to _____;
to _____; and to _____.

ARTICLE III

Members

Section 1. Maximum Membership. The membership of this Society shall be limited to two hundred members.

Section 2. Membership Eligibility and Admission Procedure. Any adult resident of _____ shall be eligible for membership, provided that such resident shall be proposed by one member and seconded by another member of the Society. A proposal for membership, signed by the two endorsers, shall be sent to the Recording Secretary, who shall report it, together with the names of the sponsors, at the next regular meeting of the Society. Voting upon the admission shall take place at the next regular meeting thereafter. A two-thirds vote shall elect to membership. A person so elected shall be declared a member of the Society upon payment of the initiation fee and the annual dues for the first year.

Section 3. Initiation Fee and Dues. The initiation fee shall be _____ dollars. The annual dues shall be _____ dollars, payable in advance on or before _____ of each year. The Treasurer shall notify members _____ months in arrears, and those whose dues are not paid within _____ thereafter shall be automatically dropped from membership in the Society.

Section 4. Resignation from Membership. Any member desiring to resign from the Society shall submit his resignation in writing to the Recording Secretary, who shall present it to the Executive Board for action. No member's resignation shall be accepted until his dues are paid.

Section 5. Honorary Life Membership. Upon the signed recommendation of one member, seconded by another member, and by a three-fourths vote by ballot at the annual meeting, honorary life membership may be conferred upon an adult resident of _____ who shall

have rendered notable service to the Society. An honorary
member shall have none of the obligations of membership
in the Society, but shall be entitled to all of the privileges
except those of making motions, of voting, and of holding office.

ARTICLE IV

Officers

Section 1. Officers and Duties. The officers of the Society shall be a President, a First Vice-President, a Second
Vice-President, a Recording Secretary, a Corresponding
Secretary, a Treasurer, and four Directors. These officers
shall perform the duties prescribed by these bylaws and
by the parliamentary authority adopted by the Society.

Section 2. Nomination Procedure, Time of Elections.
At the regular meeting held on the second Tuesday in
February, a Nominating Committee of five members shall
be elected by the Society. It shall be the duty of this committee to nominate candidates for the offices to be filled
at the annual meeting in April. The Nominating Committee shall report at the regular meeting in March. Before the election at the annual meeting in April, additional
nominations from the floor shall be permitted.

Section 3. Ballot Election, Term of Office, Removal
from Office. The officers shall be elected by ballot to
serve for one year or until their successors are elected, and
their term of office shall begin at the close of the annual
meeting at which they are elected. Officers may be removed from office at the pleasure of the membership as
provided in the parliamentary authority.

Section 4. Office-Holding Limitations. No member
shall hold more than one office at a time, and no member shall be eligible to serve three consecutive terms in
the same office.

ARTICLE V

Meetings

Section 1. Regular Meetings. The regular meetings of the Society shall be held on the second Tuesday of each month from September to May inclusive unless otherwise ordered by the Society.

Section 2. Annual Meetings. The regular meeting on the second Tuesday in April shall be known as the annual meeting and shall be for the purpose of electing officers, receiving reports of officers and committees, and for any other business that may arise.

Section 3. Special Meetings. Special meetings may be called by the President or by the Executive Board and shall be called upon the written request of ten members of the Society. The purpose of the meeting shall be stated in the call, which shall be sent to all members at least three days before the meeting.

Section 4. Quorum. Fifteen members of the Society shall constitute a quorum.

ARTICLE VI

The Executive Board

Section 1. Board Composition. The officers of the Society, including the Directors, shall constitute the Executive Board.

Section 2. Board's Duties and Powers. The Executive Board shall have general supervision of the affairs of the Society between its business meetings, fix the hour and place of meetings, make recommendations to the Society, and perform such other duties as are specified in these bylaws.

Section 3. Board Meetings. Unless otherwise ordered by the Board, regular meetings of the Executive Board shall be held on the first Tuesday of each month from

September to June, inclusive. Special meetings of the   *1*
Board may be called by the President and shall be called
upon the written request of three members of the Board.

ARTICLE VII   *5*

Committees

Section 1. Finance Committee. A Finance Committee
composed of the Treasurer and four other members shall
be appointed by the President promptly after each annual   *10*
meeting. It shall be the duty of this committee to prepare
a budget for the fiscal year beginning the first day of April,
and to submit it to the Society at its regular meeting in
March. The Finance Committee may from time to time
submit amendments to the budget for the current fiscal   *15*
year, which may be adopted by a majority vote.

Section 2. Program Committee. A Program Committee of five members shall be appointed by the President
promptly after the annual meeting, whose duty it shall
be to plan the annual program of the Society. This com-   *20*
mittee's report shall be submitted to the Society for its
approval at its regular meeting in September.

Section 3. Auditing Committee. An Auditing Committee of three members shall be appointed by the President at the Society's March meeting, whose duty it shall   *25*
be to audit the Treasurer's accounts at the close of the fiscal year and to report at the annual meeting.

Section 4. Other Committees; President's Ex-Officio
Committee Membership. Such other committees, stand-
ing or special, may be established by the Society as it shall   *30*
from time to time deem necessary to carry on its work.
Their members shall be appointed by the President unless
this rule is suspended by a two-thirds vote before their
appointment. The President shall be ex officio a member
of all committees except the Nominating Committee and   *35*
any disciplinary committees.

ARTICLE VIII

Parliamentary Authority

The rules contained in the current edition of *Robert's Rules of Order Newly Revised* shall govern the Society in all cases to which they are applicable and in which they are not inconsistent with these bylaws and any special rules of order the Society may adopt.

ARTICLE IX

Amendment of Bylaws

These bylaws may be amended at any regular meeting of the Society by a two-thirds vote, provided that the amendment has been submitted in writing at the previous regular meeting.

Some Principles of Interpretation

In preparing bylaws and interpreting them, the following principles of interpretation—which have equal application to other rules and documents adopted by an organization—may be of assistance.

1) *Each society decides for itself the meaning of its bylaws.* When the meaning is clear, however, the society, even by a unanimous vote, cannot change that meaning except by amending its bylaws. An ambiguity must exist before there is any occasion for interpretation. If a bylaw is ambiguous, it must be interpreted, if possible, in harmony with the other bylaws. The interpretation should be in accordance with the intention of the society at the time the bylaw was adopted, as far as this can be determined. Again, intent plays no role unless the meaning is unclear or uncertain, but where an ambiguity exists, a majority

vote is all that is required to decide the question. The   *1*
ambiguous or doubtful expression should be amended as
soon as practicable.

2) *When a provision of the bylaws is susceptible to two mean-*
ings, one of which conflicts with or renders absurd another   *5*
bylaw provision, and the other meaning does not, the latter
must be taken as the true meaning. For example, assume
the bylaws define the officers as "a president, a vice-
president, a secretary, a treasurer, and five other members,
all of whom shall serve as members of the Board . . ."   *10*
Assume also that elsewhere the bylaws speak of "Directors" being board members. A suggestion that the "Directors" are not officers and are additional members of
the board would create a conflict within the bylaws and
cannot be taken as the true meaning. The "other mem-   *15*
bers" are the same as the "Directors."

3) *A general statement or rule is always of less authority than*
a specific statement or rule and yields to it. It is not practical
to state a rule in its full detail every time it is referred to.
General statements of rules are seldom strictly correct in   *20*
every possible application. The specific statement of the
rule that gives the details applying to the particular case
must always be examined. For instance: in the Sample Bylaws, Article III, Section 2 (p. 584), it is provided that
any "adult resident" shall, by a two-thirds vote, be elected   *25*
to membership. This is a general statement which yields
to the proviso stated in Section 1 of the same article that
restricts membership to two hundred. Thus, the Society
is not empowered to elect a two-hundred-and-first
member by a two-thirds vote. No one has a right to quote   *30*
a general statement as of authority against a specific
statement.

4) *If the bylaws authorize certain things specifically, other*
things of the same class are thereby prohibited. There is a
presumption that nothing has been placed in the bylaws   *35*

1   without some reason for it. There can be no valid reason
     for authorizing certain things to be done that can clearly
     be done without the authorization of the bylaws, unless
     the intent is to specify the things of the same class that
5   may be done, all others being prohibited. Thus, where
     Article IV, Section I of the Sample Bylaws (p. 585) lists
     certain officers, the election of other officers not named,
     such as a sergeant-at-arms, is prohibited.

5)   *A provision granting certain privileges carries with it a*
10   *right to a part of the privileges, but prohibits a greater priv-*
     ilege. The Sample Bylaws, in Article VI, Section 2 (p. 586)
     provide that the executive board may "fix the hour and
     place of meetings" of the society. The board may, there-
     fore, change the time or the place, or both, of a society's
15   meeting. But it may not change the day for which the
     meeting is scheduled.

6)   *A prohibition or limitation prohibits everything greater*
     than what is prohibited, or that goes beyond the limitation;
     but it permits what is less than the limitation, and also
20   *permits things of the same class that are not mentioned*
     in the prohibition or limitation and that are evidently
     not improper. The Sample Bylaws, Article IV, Section 4
     (p. 585) limits a member to holding one office at a time.
     This limitation carries with it, of course, the prohibition
25   of holding more than two or three offices as well. The
     next clause in Article IV, Section 4 (p. 585) prohibits
     officers from serving three consecutive terms in the same
     office. Hence, an officer cannot serve four consecutive
     terms, but may serve two consecutive terms. Article IX of
30   the Sample Bylaws (p. 588) limits amendments to the by-
     laws to those of which notice has been given and which
     are adopted by a two-thirds vote. Thus, the change of a
     single word is prohibited unless these conditions are met,
     and a revision of the entire bylaws requires that the same
35   steps be taken.

7) *The imposition of a definite penalty for a particular action prohibits the increase or diminution of the penalty.* If the bylaws state that a member shall be dropped from membership on a board if he misses three consecutive regular meetings of the board, he cannot be retained by vote of the board, nor can more severe penalties be imposed, such as a fine in addition. If, for example, it is desired to allow the board to diminish or waive the penalty, or increase it, the bylaw must not make it definite or must specifically provide for diminution, waiver, or enlargement.

8) *In cases where the bylaws use a general term and also two or more specific terms that are wholly included under the general one, a rule in which only the general term is used applies to all the specific terms.* Where the bylaws provide in the basic enumeration of the classes of membership that "members may be active, associate, or honorary," the general term "member" is used to apply to all three classes of members. But if, in the article on Members, it is stated that members may be either active or associate members, or if that article simply describes "members" without classification, as in the Sample Bylaws, Article III (pp. 584–85), the term "member" applies only to those classes or that class of members, even if honorary members are provided for elsewhere—in which case honorary membership is not real membership. Similarly, if the bylaws provide for "elected officers" and "appointed officers," the word "officers" or the expression "all officers," used elsewhere in establishing the term during which office shall be held, applies to both the elected and the appointed officers.

§57. AMENDMENT OF BYLAWS

A motion to amend the bylaws is a particular case of the motion to *Amend Something Previously Adopted* (**35**); it is therefore a main motion, and it is subject to the same rules as other main motions with the following exceptions:

1) Special requirements for this motion's adoption should be specified in the bylaws, and they should always include at least notice *and* a two-thirds vote, which (with a vote of a majority of the entire membership as an allowable alternative) are the requirements for its adoption if such specification in the bylaws is neglected (see pp. 580–82).
2) Permissible primary and secondary amendment of the motion to amend the bylaws is usually limited by the extent of change for which notice was given, as explained below.
3) An affirmative vote on the motion to amend the bylaws cannot be reconsidered (**37**).
4) The rule that, when a main motion is adopted, no other conflicting main motion is thereafter in order is not applicable to the motion to amend the bylaws, since several notices of proposals representing different approaches to the same problem may have been given, and all such bylaw amendments are entitled to be considered (see p. 593, l. 35 to p. 594, l. 27).

Method of Handling Bylaw Amendments

The extensiveness of amendments to the bylaws will determine the method of handling them, as follows:

ISOLATED CHANGES.   If only an isolated change is to be made in the bylaws, it can be treated as any motion to *Amend Something Previously Adopted* (**35**), subject to the par-

ticular rules indicated immediately above. Sometimes a more
extensive change is proposed involving the substitution of an
entire section, group of sections, or article. In such a case,
often only a few separated passages are actually involved in
the changes, and they are offered in the form of a single proposed substitute in order to avoid time-consuming separate
action on each change. The text of the substitute should then
be given with the notice of proposed amendment, or the notice should delineate each of the actual changes, and only
changes within the scope of those contained in the substitute can be considered. Portions of the substitute which remain as in the existing version cannot be amended, since they
involve areas for which no notice of proposed change was
given.

GENERAL REVISIONS.   Changes of the bylaws that
are so extensive and general that they are scattered throughout the bylaws should be effected through the substitution
of an entirely new set of bylaws, called a *revision*. Notice of
such a revision is notice that a new document will be submitted that will be open to amendment as fully as if the society
were adopting bylaws for the first time. In other words, in
the case of a revision, the assembly is not confined to consideration of only the points of change included in the proposed
revision as submitted by the committee that has drafted it.
The revision can be perfected by first-degree and second-
degree amendments, but as in the case of any other bylaw
amendment, the old document is not pending; and therefore,
while the revision can be rejected altogether, leaving the old
bylaws intact, the old document cannot be altered with a view
to retaining it in a changed form.

PROCEDURE OF CONSIDERATION.   A revision of
bylaws or a lengthy amendment involving more than one
section should be considered seriatim as described in **28**. If

1   notice is given of several amendments which conflict so that
all cannot be given effect, the chair should arrange them in a
logical order, much as in the case of filling blanks (**12**), generally taking the least inclusive amendment first and the most
5   inclusive last so that the last one adopted is given effect. Such
arrangement of the amendments can be altered by the assembly by a majority vote without debate. Adoption of such an
arrangement by unanimous consent or a formal vote is not
subject to a motion to *Reconsider,* nor may a later, separate
10 amendment be offered as a substitute for a pending one.
However, as already stated on page 592, all bylaw amendments of which notice was given should be considered, as a
matter of the rights of their proposers, and a bylaw amendment is not dropped simply because it would conflict with
15 one previously adopted. This procedure does not violate the
normal parliamentary rule as might appear, because when any
bylaw amendment is adopted, that amendment becomes a
part of the bylaws immediately; and it is the bylaw language
as thus amended, rather than the previous language, which
20 any bylaw amendments subsequently considered would now
propose to modify. If an amendment that has not been considered no longer presents a rational proposition because it
was applicable only to language which has disappeared from
the bylaws in this process, such a bylaw amendment must, of
25 course, be dropped; but this situation should generally not
arise if the amendments are taken up in proper order as indicated above.

The final vote on a bylaw amendment should be counted
and recorded in the minutes unless it is nearly unanimous.
30

Amending a Proposed Amendment to the Bylaws

While amendments to a proposed bylaw amendment can
be made in both the first and the second degrees (as appli-
35 cable) and can be adopted by a majority vote without notice,

they are subject to restrictions on the extent of the changes   *1*
they propose.

If the bylaws require previous notice for their amendment
(as they should), or if they do not but notice *has* been given
and a majority of the entire membership is not present, no   *5*
amendment to a bylaw amendment is in order that increases
the modification of the article or provision to be amended
(see Standard Characteristic 6, p. 306). This restriction prevents members from proposing a slight change and then taking advantage of absent members by moving a greater one as   *10*
an amendment to the amendment. Thus, if the bylaws place
the annual dues of members at $10 and an amendment is
pending to strike out 10 and insert 25, an amendment to
change the 25 to any number between 10 and 25 would be
in order, but an amendment to change the number to less   *15*
than 10 or greater than 25 would be out of order, even with
unanimous consent. Had notice been given that it was proposed to increase the dues to more than $25 or to reduce
them below $10, members who opposed such a change
might have attended the meeting to vote against the amend-   *20*
ment. The same principle applies to an amendment in the
nature of a substitute for sections or articles (short of a revision), as already indicated above; the proposed substitute is
open to amendments that diminish the amount of change,
but not to amendments that increase it or that introduce new   *25*
changes. Thus, if an amendment is pending to substitute a
new rule for one that prescribes the initiation fee and the
annual dues, and the substitute proposes to alter the initiation
fee but does not propose any change in the annual dues, then
an amendment which recommends changing the annual dues   *30*
would be out of order.

Amendments to strike out a sentence, paragraph, or section deserve special care. In such cases, the existing bylaw is
not itself open to consideration, but only the amendment. If
notice is given to strike out a provision of the bylaws and   *35*

some members feel it should be retained with certain changes whose substance would be outside the scope of that notice, those members should immediately give notice of the amendments to the existing provisions which they think are advisable. Otherwise, friends of the existing provision will be cut off from opportunity to work out compromises for its partial retention by perfecting the existing language.

Giving Notice of Amendments

Notice of a bylaw amendment should be formally worded in a form such as "To amend Article IV, Section 2, by striking out 'March' and inserting 'April' after the words 'second Tuesday in.'" When the bylaws do not place a limitation on those who can give notice of a bylaw amendment, any member is entitled to do so. If notice is to be given at a meeting, this is usually done under new business, although it can be done at any time, even after it has been voted to adjourn if the chair has not actually declared the meeting adjourned. A bylaws committee can give notice in that part of the order of business set aside for committee reports. If notice is to be sent with the call of the meeting at which the amendment will be introduced, the society is responsible for paying the cost of sending such notice, not the member proposing the amendment. When notice has been given of a bylaw amendment, it becomes a general order for the meeting at which it is to be considered. The notice should fairly inform the members of the changes contemplated. Showing the existing bylaw and the bylaw with the proposed changes in parallel columns is a good device so long as the exact amendment, stated in a formal manner, is set out at the top across both columns. When notice of a bylaw amendment is given in open meeting, it cannot be considered at that time, except to be discussed informally and briefly at the discretion of the presiding officer (see also pp. 395–96).

Time at Which a Bylaw Amendment Takes Effect

An amendment to the bylaws goes into effect immediately upon its adoption unless the motion to adopt specifies another time for its becoming effective, or the assembly has set such a time by a previously adopted motion. While the amendment is pending, a motion can be made to amend the enacting words of the motion to amend by adding a clause such as this: ". . . with the proviso that [or, ". . . provided, however, that"] this amendment shall not go into effect until after the close of this annual meeting." Or, while the amendment is pending, an incidental motion can be adopted that, in the event of the amendment's adoption, it shall not take effect until a specified time. Either method requires only a majority vote. It is a mistake to encumber the bylaws themselves with provisions which have effect for only a limited time. If the mechanics of transition to operation under a revised set of bylaws will be complicated in ways for which the act of adoption must provide temporarily, such provisions can be numbered and attached to the revision draft on a separate sheet headed "Provisos Relating to Transition." The motion to adopt the revision can then be made in this form: "I move the adoption of the revised bylaws with the provisos attached thereto."

Amendments to the article on officers may raise difficulties in relation to the time at which adopted changes take effect, unless special care is taken. A society can, for example, amend its bylaws so as to affect the emoluments and duties of the officers already elected, or even to abolish an office; and if it is desired that the amendment should not affect officers already elected, a motion so specifying should be adopted before voting on the amendment, or the motion to amend can have added to it the proviso that it shall not affect officers already elected. There is virtually a contract between a society and its officers, and while to some extent action can be taken by either party to modify or even terminate the

1 contract, such action must be taken with reasonable consideration for the other party.

It is important to note that, although the time when a bylaw amendment *takes effect* can be delayed by the assembly, 5 the amendment becomes part of the bylaws immediately upon adoption. If the amended bylaws are printed, a footnote or similar device should indicate that the amended language is not yet in effect and, if language was removed by the amendment, the text of that provision should be given if it is 10 still applicable in the organization.

Captions, Headings, and Article and Section Numbers

15 It was formerly customary to permit the secretary to fill in captions, headings, and article, section, or paragraph numbers or letters, and the like, after the assembly had adopted bylaws or other long documents. Such designations were treated as mere marginal notations which could be clerically 20 modified. It is now the usual practice to include these subtitles or identifying numbers or letters as an integral part of what is adopted by action of the assembly.

In the process of amending previously adopted documents of this kind, indisputably necessary changes in designation 25 by number or letter may be presumed to have been included in the assembly's action even if they were not mentioned. For example, if an assembly adopts a motion "to insert after Article III a new Article IV reading as follows: . . . ," the secretary or a committee should, of course, raise the numerical 30 designation of each of the later articles by one, even if the enacting motion made no reference to doing so. Only the assembly can amend captions or headings under the rules applicable to bylaws or other papers if such change could have any effect on meaning, and this authority may not be dele-35 gated. Corrections of article or section numbers or cross-

references that cannot result in a change of meaning can be   *1*
delegated, however, to the secretary or, in more involved
cases, to a committee. An assembly may delegate its authority
in this connection in a particular case, by adopting, for example, a resolution such as the following: *5*

> *Resolved*, That the secretary [or, "the . . . commit-
> tee"] be authorized to correct article and section desig-
> nations, punctuation, and cross-references and to make
> such other technical and conforming changes as may be   *10*
> necessary to reflect the intent of the Society in connec-
> tion with . . .

CHAPTER
XIX

CONVENTIONS

§58. CONVENTIONS OF DELEGATES

As commonly understood in parliamentary law and as used in this book, the word *convention* refers to an assembly of *delegates* (other than a permanently constituted public lawmaking body), who are usually chosen specially for each session as representatives of the constituent units or subdivisions within a larger group of people, to sit as a single deliberative body acting in the name of the entire group. The most common type of convention is that of an established state or national society—in which the delegates are selected by, and from among, the members of each local unit. Other terms by which such a convention may be described in some organizations include *congress, conference, convocation, general assembly, house of delegates,* and *house of representatives.*

The term *house of delegates,* or *house of representatives,* is often applied particularly in the case of learned or professional associations, to distinguish the voting body of delegates from large numbers of other members of the constituent units, who come to the convention to attend seminars, workshops, educational or social activities, or the like. In some societies, also, *house of delegates* or *house of representatives* may describe a body of delegates who, instead of being elected only for a

convention session, are elected for a fixed term during which   1
they hold sessions from time to time as the bylaws may
prescribe.

Conventions vary in size, duration, and complexity of
operation. A relatively small state society may hold a one-day   5
convention consisting of two or three meetings at which all
delegates are present. A week's convention of a national scientific or educational association, on the other hand, may be
divided into a number of specialized sections meeting separately at the same time, with only a few meetings when the   10
entire body of delegates gathers in one hall.

In addition, a convention is sometimes called for the purpose of forming an association or federation; or (like a mass
meeting, **53**) it may be convened to draw interested parties
or representatives of interested organizations together in act-   15
ing upon a particular problem.

This chapter is limited to the features common to most
conventions and relates principally to the convention of an
established society. (For variations of procedure applying to
other types of conventions, see **60**.)   20

Basic Provisions in Bylaws

In the case of an established state, regional, or national society composed of constituent units, the bylaws (see   25
pp. 12–15, 575–76) or other governing instrument of the
association or parent body should:

- authorize a periodic convention;
- define its powers and duties;   30
- fix its quorum;
- specify its voting members;
- prescribe the qualifications of its delegates and alternates,
  the basis of determining their number, and the method
  of electing them; and   35

1   • make such provision as the particular convention may re-
       quire for its organization and operation.

     Basic provision for the voting body of members may be
5   worded in the bylaws as appropriate to the particular orga-
     nization—for example, as follows:

           The voting members of the State Convention shall
           be the state officers (including members of the Execu-
           tive Board of the State Association), the president (or,
10   in his absence, the vice president) of each club within
           the Association, and the elected delegates of each club.

     In addition, the bylaws at the level on which the conven-
     tion is held should prescribe: (1) the conditions for a con-
15   stituent unit to be in good standing for purposes of the right
     to representation—commonly including a minimum mem-
     bership requirement; and (2) the number of delegates to
     which a unit shall be entitled depending on its size—usually
     by specifying, for example, that each unit shall be represented
20   by its president, plus one additional delegate if the unit has
     more than a certain number of members, or two additional
     delegates if the unit has more than twice that number of
     members, and so on.
     The bylaws at the level at which the convention is held
25   should also provide for the election of alternates as described
     on page 604.
     To avoid a change of officers during the convention, the
     bylaws should provide that newly elected officers shall take
     up their duties at the close of the convention (see p. 573,
30   ll. 28–33).

Convention Members and Alternates

     WAYS IN WHICH VOTING MEMBERSHIP COMES
35   ABOUT.   Voting membership in a convention of an estab-

lished society generally comes about in one of the following
ways:

1) through being an accredited delegate elected by a constituent body especially to act as its authorized representative (or one of several representatives) in a particular
   convention;
2) through provision in the bylaws, as in many organizations, that the president or chief officer (or, in his absence,
   the vice-president) of each constituent local unit shall
   be the delegate or one of the delegates;
3) through being an incumbent elective officer of the organization on the level at which the convention is held—for
   example, an officer of a state society in a state convention,
   where the officers of the state society as listed in the bylaws are ex officio the officers of the convention as well
   as members of it, irrespective of the number of delegates
   that the local unit to which an officer belongs is entitled
   to elect; or
4) through being an accredited elected alternate and replacing, at the time of the convention, a delegate who is unable to attend or who withdraws from registered status.

FILLING OF VACANCIES ARISING IN A DELE-
GATION. If the president of a constituent unit is unable
to be present at the convention of an established society, his
place there is taken by the vice-president (or by the second,
third, or ranking available vice-president if necessary and if
there are such officers), just as for any other duty in which
the vice-president acts in the president's place. If the vice-
president is himself an elected delegate but takes the president's place, the vice-president's original position as an
elected delegate is filled by an elected alternate in the manner
explained below—just as when any other elected delegate
does not serve.

Provision for Alternates. To ensure as complete representation at the convention as possible, the bylaws at the convention level should provide that each unit shall elect a certain number of alternates—frequently equal to the number of delegates. To maintain a uniform standard of representation, the qualifications for election as an alternate—which may include membership in good standing for a prescribed number of years—are made the same as for a delegate.

Alternates normally are elected with a designated order, in which they will be called to serve, if available, as vacancies arise in the delegation of their constituent unit. When a unit has more than one delegate, an elected alternate (other than the vice-president) is not associated with any particular delegate. The vacancy that occurs first in point of time (except one involving the president when the vice-president is able to serve in his stead) is filled by the first elected alternate or the ranking one available, and so on.

In cases where the individual delegates within a unit's delegation represent particular areas or groups, it may sometimes be desirable to make exception to the foregoing rule by providing, in the bylaws at the convention level, for the pairing of each alternate with a specific delegate. The disadvantage of such a system arises when both a particular delegate and his only alternate are unable to attend the convention—thus depriving a constituent unit of part of the representation to which it is entitled.

Status and Seating of Alternates; Replacement Procedure. Alternates registered as such are usually provided with badges of a different color or shape from those of delegates and are seated in sections apart from them. (In large conventions, assigned seats in the assembly hall ordinarily can be guaranteed only to the voting body.) When an alternate is officially registered by the Credentials Committee (pp. 610ff.) as taking the place of an elected delegate, however, he is supplied with a delegate's badge and becomes a voting delegate with the same duties and privileges as if originally so elected.

If an alternate is to replace a delegate who has registered, *1*
proper evidence of that delegate's withdrawal from such status must be presented to the Credentials Committee, and the
alternate must be reregistered as the new delegate before he
can sit or vote as a member of the convention. It is the duty *5*
of any registered delegate who ends his presence at the convention to see that his departure is promptly reported to the
Credentials Committee, and to whatever authority is concerned with locating the proper accredited alternate if one is
available. Unless the rules of the body provide otherwise, no *10*
alternate or other person can "substitute" for a delegate who
remains registered. In other words, a delegate's temporary
absence from the convention hall does not entitle an alternate
to make motions, speak in debate, or cast the delegate's
vote—even with the delegate's authorization—unless a rule *15*
of the body permits this procedure.

DUTIES OF DELEGATES.   When a member of a constituent unit has accepted election as a delegate, he has the
obligation to attend the convention, with such expense *20*
allowance as the unit may provide; he should not leave it to
an alternate to serve in his place except for serious reason. At
the convention, the delegate has the duty to be present at the
business meetings, and to be prepared on returning from
the convention to present to his unit an information report *25*
of what transpired. A delegate is free to vote as he sees fit on
questions at the convention, except as his constituent unit
may have instructed him in regard to particular matters
scheduled for consideration.

30

Caucuses

Prior to or during a convention, members of a delegation
may need or wish to meet as a group to decide how they
will act with reference to certain matters to come before the *35*
convention; a meeting of this kind is usually called a *caucus*.

1 Unless instructed otherwise by its parent society or unit, such a caucus is governed by the rules of procedure applicable to committees (**50**), since the delegation is in effect a committee to represent and act at the convention for the constituent so-

5 ciety or unit that chose it. If the president of a constituent society (or in his absence the vice-president) is automatically a delegate to a convention, he usually acts as chairman of his delegation; otherwise the delegation chairman is selected as outlined for the case of any other committee (pp. 175–76).

10   Sometimes caucuses are held of different groupings of delegates, as, for example, all delegates from a certain district, territory, or other geographic area as defined by the organization; and they are similarly governed by the rules generally applicable to committees.

15   As in the case of any committee, in the absence of a superior rule to the contrary a constituent society or unit can instruct its delegation, although this is not always a good practice in ordinary societies. Such instructions are binding upon the delegation to the extent that the convention's pre-

20 siding officer and other officials should enforce instructions of which they have been properly and officially notified. Such instructions, for example, frequently require a delegation to take a position for or against a measure expected to come before the convention, or to vote for certain candidates. As stated

25 above, the delegates are free to vote as they see fit except where an instruction has been given; but a society can, by instructing its delegation, bind it to vote as a unit (that is, to cast all of its votes in accord with the decision of the majority of the delegation) on all issues, on a particular class of business,

30 or on certain matters to be acted on by the convention.

    The term *caucus* is also sometimes applied to a similar meeting of all the known or admitted partisans of a particular position on an important issue—in a convention or any other deliberative assembly—who meet to plan strategy toward a

35 desired result within the assembly. Such a meeting may be

held on the presumed informal understanding that those who attend will follow the decisions of the caucus.

§59. ORGANIZATION OF A CONVENTION OF AN ESTABLISHED SOCIETY

Most conventions must operate on a closely controlled schedule and transact a large amount of business quickly—often with rented facilities available only for a prearranged length of time and with each added day of meetings entailing considerable expense both to the association and to the delegates personally. Maximum effort toward a well-organized convention is therefore essential.

Advance Preparation

The work of organizing and preparing for a convention normally begins weeks or months in advance and involves many committees, under the general direction of the officers and the board of the association.

The principal parliamentary functions most directly connected with the formal organization of the convention itself are performed by three committees, each of which has been appointed by the president or the board as prescribed in the bylaws. These three committees are: (1) the Credentials Committee, which prepares and certifies to the convention the list of officers, delegates, and alternates that it has registered after finding them entitled to accreditation; (2) the Committee on Standing Rules, which drafts rules of operating procedure specially required for the particular convention; and (3) the Program Committee, which works out a convention program combining a suitable *order of business* (**41**) with special features designed to promote and develop the association or society as a whole. Because the duties of these committees are exacting, a member should never be appointed to one of them for any other reason than his ability in the field involved.

In addition, depending on the size of the convention, one or more committees concerned with the necessary physical arrangements, such as securing the hall, hotel accommodations, and related services, should be appointed. If a single committee is responsible for all of these matters, it may be known as the Convention Arrangements Committee.

Another important committee that usually works before as well as during the convention is the Resolutions Committee. This committee screens and recommends appropriate action on resolutions and original (as distinct from incidental) main motions to come before the convention.

The duties of the convention committees are more fully explained in the succeeding pages of this chapter.

Each of the regular standing committees of the association—in consultation with the presiding officer, the executive body or board, and the Program Committee—should also carefully plan the presentation and management of the convention business that is the particular committee's concern.

A preconvention meeting of the board of the association is often held in the convention city a day or more in advance of the convention opening. A number of decisions bearing on business to come before the convention may be made at this meeting.

Services of a Parliamentarian

A key consultant in the preparation for a convention should be the parliamentarian, *who should be engaged well in advance*. It is desirable that this person be a professional—the more seasoned in actual operating experience within organizations, the better. Although he has the duty of giving parliamentary advice and opinions (see pp. 465–67) at con-

vention meetings (where he should be seated next to the pre-   *1*
siding officer), the parliamentarian's most important work
may well be performed before the convention opens. During
the period of preparation and while the convention is in
progress, he should serve as the principal adviser to the pres-   *5*
ident, the officers, and the committee chairmen regarding
management of the convention as it relates to the actual transaction of business. The chairmen of the Credentials Committee, the Committee on Standing Rules, the Program
Committee, the Resolutions Committee, the Elections Com-   *10*
mittee if there is one, and the standing committees who are
to present business to the convention should all consult with
the parliamentarian during this time; and it may be advisable
that he should attend certain meetings of these committees.
The parliamentarian should always be present at the precon-   *15*
vention board meetings mentioned above.

Formal Organization Procedure at the Convention

Before a convention can transact any other business, it   *20*
must officially form itself into a single voting body—which is
done at the first *business* meeting. Preliminary ceremonies—
whether at the commencement of the convention or at the
beginning of each day—are not regarded as business. A separate formal opening of inspirational nature can be held, if   *25*
desired, before the convention is officially organized. When
the assembly of delegates of an established society has been
so organized in accordance with the bylaws or other governing rules as described below, it then acts as and in
the name of the whole society and may be referred to as   *30*
"The Tenth Annual Convention of the National Society of
_____" or, as common formerly, "The National
Society of _____ in convention assembled."

The official organization of the convention is brought
about by the separate consideration and adoption of the   *35*

reports of three committees mentioned above—the Credentials Committee, the Committee on Standing Rules, and the Program Committee, in that order.

As each report comes up for consideration, it is presented to the convention by a reporting member, normally the respective committee chairman. This person should conclude his report with a statement that "by direction of the committee" he moves its adoption—unless he is not a voting member of the convention, in which case anyone who is such a voting member can make this motion; a convenient practice is for the recording secretary of the convention or a qualified member of the committee to do so. No second is required if the motion is made by a member of the committee. If no one offers the motion promptly, the chair can call for it, or can assume it by stating, for example, "The question is on the adoption of the report of the Program Committee."

Each of these committee reports is debatable and amendable. In an ordinary convention of a society, however, debate or proposals for amendment of any of them seldom occur, and the reports are likely to be adopted without dissenting vote—if the committees have done their work well. (The vote *required* for their adoption is a majority for the reports of the Credentials Committee and the Program Committee, and normally a two-thirds vote for that of the Committee on Standing Rules, as explained on pp. 619–20.) With the adoption of these three separate reports, the convention is officially organized for conducting business.

Credentials Committee

RESPONSIBILITIES.   The specific duties of the Credentials Committee are listed below. Items (1) through (4) must of necessity be spread over a considerable period of time in advance of the convention. Items (5) and (6) must be performed at the convention location during the period leading up to the convention opening. Items (7) and (8) relate to the committee's duties during the convention.

1) Distribution well in advance, to each constituent body entitled to representation, of (a) information, in accordance with the bylaws, as to the authorized number of representatives and alternates, eligibility requirements, and the time and manner of their election;* and (b) credentials forms with instructions that they are to be returned by a specified date after having been filled in with the names of the representatives and alternates designated by the constituent unit, and having been signed by the unit's secretary and sometimes also by its president. A single form can be used for all representatives and alternates, or a separate form in the form of a card can be used for each delegate and each alternate, with different colors to distinguish delegates from alternates. If alternates are paired with specific delegates as described on page 604, lines 18–22, double cards can be used.

2) (a) Examination of all forms returned, to verify the eligibility of each member listed; and (b) notification to the proper constituent unit whenever an elected delegate or alternate is found ineligible (through nonpayment of dues, insufficient duration of membership, etc.), advising the unit of its right to designate one of the elected alternates named on its credentials form to take the place of any ineligible delegate (unless replacement is automatic because of pairing of alternates with individual delegates).

3) Compilation of the list of members entitled to register and the basis of this right (officer who is a convention member ex officio, unit president, elected delegate,

---

*Some organizations include this information in a printed, general "Call to Convention."

alternate, etc.) arranged for quick reference—as alphabetically by districts, clubs, sections, or as may be suitable.

4) Arrangements for registration to take place at the convention—beginning one or two days before the convention
opens (see p. 613).

5) Registration—which normally includes these steps:

   a) Submission, by the member intending to register, of
   evidence that he is entitled to do so;

   b) Verification by the committee, or a subcommittee of
   it, that the member's credentials are correct;

   c) Recording of the member as officially registered,
   upon his paying the registration fee (which is sometimes sent in in advance) and signing the list of registrations; and

   d) Issuing of the particular badge to which the member
   is entitled, the official program, and additional necessary information, such as time and place of individual
   section or committee meetings or workshops.

6) Preparation of the committee's first report to the convention, which can include registrations only to such an hour
as will enable the chairman of the Credentials Committee
to present this initial report as the first item of official
business of the convention.

7) Continuation of the committee until the convention
ends—to record changes in the registration rolls occa-
sioned by: (a) additional registrations (which the bylaws
or the convention's standing rules [pp. 618ff.] may require to be closed at a specified time slightly earlier than
the final adjournment); or (b) the departure of delegates
and the reregistration of alternates who replace them.

8) Submission of a supplementary credentials report—at the
beginning of the first business meeting each day and at
other times when required—as resulting from changes in
the registration rolls.

In societies that maintain a permanent administrative
headquarters, most of the clerical duties required of the
Credentials Committee in advance of the convention usually
develop into a routine technique preserved from year to year
and performed largely by the regular paid staff; but the
authority and responsibility for general direction of this work
remain with the Credentials Committee.

TIMES AND PLACE OF REGISTRATION.   The
times and the place of registration should be announced in
the printed convention program. In a convention of any size
lasting for a number of days, registration may begin one or
two days before the convention opens, and provision should
be made to handle a heavy volume of registrations during the
afternoon and evening before the opening business meeting,
as well as on the morning of that meeting. This registration
normally takes place in a separate room or hall whose size and
equipment depend on the probable total number of registrants. Throughout the convention, a registration desk of the
Credentials Committee in a convenient location should be
manned a reasonable time before each business meeting begins, and should always remain open during meetings. Near
the end of the convention, usually only one or two committee
members stay on duty.

METHOD OF REGISTRATION.   The method used
by the Credentials Committee to register the delegates and
alternates will vary according to the size of the convention.
A procedure in common use is outlined as follows: The entire
association holding the convention is divided into parts, such
as states, districts, or counties, and a separate section of the
register—often prepared in triplicate, as noted below—is set
up for each subdivision. Each section of the register contains—arranged in an appropriate logical order—the typed

1   names of the constituent societies or units located within the
     corresponding geographical area; and under each unit's name
     are typed alphabetically the names of the delegates and alter-
     nates that have been sent in on the unit's credentials blanks,
5   provided that these persons have been found eligible by the
     committee. During the initial period when the bulk of reg-
     istrations take place, usually two committee members are
     assigned to a separate and conspicuously marked table or sta-
     tion for each section of the register. In a large convention,
10   ushers may be helpful in guiding delegates and alternates to
     the proper section, where they present their credentials and
     sign the register to the right of their typewritten names. At
     least one, and frequently two, duplicate registers (or photo-
     copy-reproduced sets of the register pages) are desirable in
15   addition to the Credentials Committee's master copy—one
     duplicate list to be submitted as an attachment to the com-
     mittee's report, the other for later use by election tellers
     in verifying the eligibility of voters. By use of the latter
     copy, counting procedure in an election can be expedited by
20   dividing the tellers into subcommittee groups for each sec-
     tion of the register, according to the same pattern as in the
     case of the Credentials Committee members during regis-
     tration. The delegates' badges can also be correspondingly
     labeled or numbered to facilitate identification with the cor-
25   rect section.

         Cases of contested seats in a delegation will seldom arise
     except in political conventions. In the rare event of a contest
     between two delegates or groups of delegates and serious
     doubt as to which is entitled to be seated, the committee
30   should omit both from the list and report the fact of the con-
     test to the convention as explained below. If, on the other
     hand, after hearing the facts, the committee thinks the contest
     is not justified, it should enter on the list only the names of
     the delegates whose claim it finds to be legitimate. The same
35   rules apply to the more common case of delegates chosen by

a local unit that is not entitled to representation or has chosen   *1*
delegates in excess of its entitlement.

ADOPTION OF REPORT.   Before the Credentials
Committee report is adopted, since the membership has not   *5*
been established, the only motions that are in order are those
related to its consideration or to the conduct of the meeting
before its adoption, as well as those that are in order in the
absence of a quorum (pp. 347–48).* Even, for example, a
motion relating to the validity of the holding of the conven-   *10*
tion is not in order at such a time. It is, therefore, essential
that the committee establish and hold itself to a deadline for
registrations to be included in its first report, which will leave
it time to prepare that report. The opening ceremonies will
afford some opportunity for this work, and, while it is in   *15*
process, delegates can continue to register—but not to be included in the committee's initial report. If the report is not
ready in time, the convention may continue with other nonbusiness matters, such as speakers, or may stand at ease or
take a recess.   *20*

The Credentials Committee report, which is read by the
committee's chairman, should state in substance that, "Attached is the list of the names of the voting members of the
convention and their alternates who have been registered up
until . . . [indicating the hour to which the list is corrected]."   *25*
This statement should be followed by whatever statistical summary is customary in the particular organization (frequently
including a breakdown according to basis of voting membership as indicated in item [3] on pp. 611–12), and should
always give the total number of convention members *entitled*   *30*
to vote and the number of registered alternates. Normally the

---

*But see pages 640–42 for necessary variations in the case of conventions
not of a permanent organization.

list of delegates and alternates is not read unless a portion of it is read upon request, for information. If there is an unresolved contest between delegates, the particulars should be stated, as well as the fact that the names of the contesting or contested delegates do not appear on the roll. The committee chairman concludes the report by saying, "On behalf of the committee, I move that the roll of delegates hereby submitted be the official roll of the voting members of the convention." The report with the attached list of names should then be handed to the chair or to the secretary.

Unless there is debate or proposed amendment, the chair, before taking the vote on the adoption of the report, asks, "Are there any questions on the report?" If seat(s) are contested, an amendment can be offered substantially in this form: "To amend by adding 'provided that the name of George J. Morse be added to the roll of delegates as submitted, as a delegate from the state of Missouri.'" The name of the rival delegate can then be offered in a secondary amendment, for example, "to strike out 'George J. Morse' and insert 'Frank Norton.'" Whether or not a contest is reported, it is in order to move such amendments or even to move to substitute an entirely different set of delegates for any delegation in the reported list, but no such amendment is permitted to include more names than those of a single challenged delegate or delegation all of whom are challenged on the same grounds, together with any claimants involved. On an amendment proposing changes in the list of delegates, none of the delegates involved in the case can vote. Those seated by the committee, though contested in a case not yet reached, can vote on all cases except their own. On the question of adopting the Credentials Committee's report or on motions connected with its consideration, only those persons whose names are on the list of voting members reported by the committee (as this list stands after any amendment already approved by the convention) are entitled to vote.

ROLL OF VOTING MEMBERS; SUPPLEMENTARY   *1*
REPORTS.   When the report of the Credentials Committee
is adopted, it is thereby ratified as the official roll of voting
members of the convention—subject to changes through
later reports. A voting member who registers after the sub-   *5*
mission of the first report assumes his full status as soon as he
has done so, if his status is not questioned; if it is, it must
await a decision by the committee or the convention itself.
Although the Credentials Committee normally makes a supplementary report only at the beginning of each day, it may   *10*
be called upon to do so at other times, such as immediately
before an important vote. If there has been no change in the
roll of registered delegates since the last report, no motion
or vote is required; but if there are changes, the committee
chairman should conclude his report by saying, "On behalf   *15*
of the committee, I move that the revised roll of delegates
hereby submitted be the official roll of voting members of
the convention." Although this motion might appear to be
one to amend something previously adopted (**35**), it requires
only a majority vote for its adoption, since it is always under-   *20*
stood that the roll will be added to and subtracted from as
delegates arrive late or leave early, and alternates may thereby
be shifted in status.

The Credentials Committee's master roll of currently registered voting members of the convention should be main-   *25*
tained at all times in such a way that their exact number can
be promptly determined. Accuracy of the list of registrants is
essential, since it may affect the outcome of elections or
closely contested issues. If the bylaws or the convention's
standing rules do not prescribe a quorum (**40**)—which they   *30*
should do—the quorum is a majority of the number of voting
members who have actually registered, irrespective of whether
some may have departed.

1   **Committee on Standing Rules**

RESPONSIBILITIES.   The Committee on Standing
Rules drafts and submits for consideration a group of rules
5 known as "The Standing Rules of the Convention," which,
as adopted, will apply to that one convention only. These
rules must in no way conflict with the bylaws of the society,
but (in contrast to ordinary standing rules in a local society) they can involve modifications of rules contained in the
10 parliamentary authority prescribed by the bylaws. The standing rules of a convention usually contain both "parliamentary" rules relating to the conduct of business, and
nonparliamentary rules, so that in some ways they resemble
a combination of special rules of order and ordinary standing
15 rules (**2**). Since their effect expires at the close of the session
that adopts them, however, they differ from either of the latter types of rules in certain respects.

The standing rules of successive conventions held by a
society often become developed to a point where little change
20 in the rules adopted by the preceding convention is necessary.
On the other hand, the work of this committee may sometimes require extensive research into past proceedings of
the organization. In any case, the parliamentarian should
always be consulted regarding the convention's standing
25 rules, and he often prepares a first draft for submission to this
committee.

A copy of the "Proposed Standing Rules of the Convention" that the committee is to recommend—usually printed
in the official program—should be handed to each person
30 when he registers. Until the proposed standing rules are
adopted, the convention is governed by the rules in the organization's parliamentary authority, such as those concerning
the seating of delegates and alternates (see pp. 604–5 and
p. 607, ll. 18–21) and assignment of the floor (see especially
35 p. 383).

PRESENTATION AND ADOPTION OF CONVEN- *1*
TION STANDING RULES.   The report of the Committee
on Standing Rules is presented to the convention immediately
after the adoption of that of the Credentials Committee by
offering a motion in a form similar to item 9, tinted page 31, *5*
and by reading the proposed rules in their entirety—regardless of their previous distribution—unless, in cases where
every delegate has been provided with a copy and the rules
generally do not change from year to year, a firmly established
custom of the organization permits this reading to be omit- *10*
ted. After debate or amendment (if any), a single vote normally is taken on the complete body of rules. It should be
understood that seriatim consideration (**28**) is not applicable
because, although the rules may be organized to have the appearance of being a single document, they are, in fact, a group *15*
of separate main motions being offered by the committee
under one enacting motion. By the demand of a voting member of the convention, a separate vote can be required on any
individual rule (see pp. 274–75), although such a demand is
advisable only if a serious matter appears to be at stake. If such *20*
a demand is made, the remainder of the rules are acted on
first, and then those separated out are acted on individually.
Under the usual procedure of voting on the standing rules as
a "package," a two-thirds vote is required for their adoption—because, if they are to fill the needs of the convention, *25*
they nearly always include provisions which can be imposed
only by a two-thirds vote. If a new rule is proposed, either
during the consideration of the committee's proposed rules
or later during the convention, it should be acted on separately after the adoption of the committee's proposals as dis- *30*
cussed below.

VOTE REQUIRED FOR ADOPTION OF AN INDI-
VIDUAL RULE.   If a standing rule of a convention is voted
on individually, the vote necessary for its adoption is in some *35*

1   cases two thirds and in others a majority, depending on the
    nature of the rule:

    1) Convention standing rules requiring a two-thirds vote
5   for adoption (even individually) are, in principle, distin-
       guished by the same characteristics as provisions which,
       in an ordinary local society or assembly, would need a
       two-thirds vote to be placed in effect for the duration
       of a meeting or session, or would require adoption as a
10   *special rule of order* to continue in force from session to
       session (see **2**). An example would be a rule limiting the
       time allowed for debate. Rules in this class are described
       by the term *parliamentary standing rules in a convention*
       as used in this book.
15 2) A standing rule is individually adoptable by a majority
       vote in a convention if it does not fall in class (1) above,
       and consequently could be adopted in a local assembly as
       an *ordinary standing rule* (see **2**). Examples of such con-
       vention rules would be those relating to the wearing of
20   badges or to the format in which written reports or reso-
       lutions shall be submitted.

    VOTE REQUIRED TO AMEND OR RESCIND A
    CONVENTION STANDING RULE.   To amend or re-
25 scind a standing rule of a convention requires a two-thirds
    vote or the vote of a majority of all the delegates or other
    "voting members" of the convention who have been regis-
    tered, except that a rule individually adoptable by a majority
    vote can be amended or rescinded by a majority vote after
30 notice on at least the preceding day.

    SUSPENSION OF A CONVENTION STANDING
    RULE.   Any standing rule of a convention (except one pre-
    scribing the parliamentary authority) can be suspended for a

particular specified purpose by a majority vote, even if the rule   *1*
required a two-thirds vote for its adoption. Under such a suspension, however, the applicable rules in the parliamentary
authority prescribed by the bylaws (or by a rule of the convention) come into force—as if the standing rule had not   5
been adopted. To suspend a convention standing rule and
also the general parliamentary rule normally applying to the
same situation requires a two-thirds vote, just as to suspend
the general rule when no standing rule is involved (**25**).* No
standing rule of a convention can be suspended for the re-   10
mainder of the session, and no standing rule which has only
a single application can be suspended, since this would be
equivalent to rescinding the rule, and the case would have to
be treated accordingly.

   15

SAMPLE SET OF CONVENTION STANDING
RULES.   The standing rules of a convention must vary with
its size, type, and responsibilities. While it is not possible to
name model rules which are universally applicable, the following sample set illustrates the nature of the standing rules   20
adopted by many conventions.

---

*The reason why a parliamentary standing rule of a convention can be
suspended by a majority vote even though it requires a two-thirds vote for its
adoption is as follows: In a convention, parliamentary standing rules—which
are in the nature of suspensions of the regular rules of order for the duration
of the convention session—generally arise from a need to give the majority
more power to transact business with minimum delay, even when the majority is not large enough to command a two-thirds vote. Since it is thus likely
to reduce the protection of a minority greater than one third, a parliamentary
standing rule of a convention requires a two-thirds vote for its adoption; but
since the same rule tends to protect a majority of less than two thirds, such a
majority should have the right to suspend the rules for a particular purpose
and allow the regular rules of order to come into force.

1

STANDING RULES OF THE _____ CONVENTION
OF _____

Rule 1. (a) The Credentials Committee, directly
5 after the opening ceremonies of the first business meeting,* shall report the number of delegates and alternates
registered as present with proper credentials, and shall
make a supplementary report after the opening exercises
at the beginning of each day that business continues.
10 (b) A member registered as an alternate may, upon
proper clearance by the Credentials Committee, be
transferred from alternate to delegate at any time during
the continuance of business meetings.

Rule 2. For admission to the assembly hall, to facili-
15 tate identification and seating, members, alternates, and
others shall be required to wear the badge issued by the
Credentials Committee upon registration.

Rule 3. A resolution offered by an individual member shall be in writing, signed by the maker and the sec-
20 onder—each of whom shall be a voting member of the
convention—and shall be sent directly to the desk of
the Recording Secretary.

Rule 4.** (a) All resolutions except those proposed
by the Executive Board [or "Board of Directors,"
25 "Board of Managers," etc.] or by committees, and all
recommendations made in reports of officers or committees of the convention that are not in the form of resolutions, shall be referred without debate to the Resolutions
Committee; resolutions proposed by the Executive
30 Board or by committees shall be presented by the Board
or proposing committee directly to the convention.

---

*See pages 609–10.

**Regarding variations in the rules and practices of societies relating to
the handling of resolutions at a convention, see pages 633–36.

(b) Each member who offers a resolution shall be given an opportunity to explain it to the Resolutions Committee if he so requests.

(c) The Resolutions Committee shall prepare suitable resolutions to carry into effect recommendations referred to it, and shall submit to the convention, with the Committee's own recommendation as to appropriate action, these and all other resolutions referred to the Committee, except questions which the Committee by a vote of two thirds of its members may decide not to report.*

(d) The convention by a majority vote may suspend this Rule 4 and may immediately consider a question, or may order the Resolutions Committee to report a question at a certain time, even if the Committee has voted not to report it.

Rule 5. No member shall speak in debate more than once on the same question on the same day, or longer than two minutes, without permission of the convention granted by a two-thirds vote without debate.

Rule 6. All reports and other material for the permanent record or printed proceedings shall be in typing and, immediately on presentation, shall be sent to the Recording Secretary.

Rule 7. Nominations for each office to be filled by the convention shall be limited to one nominating speech of three minutes and one seconding speech of one minute for each nominee.

Rule 8. Notices for announcement to the convention shall be in writing, signed by the person (or a proper representative of the persons) under whose authority the announcement is issued, and shall be sent to the desk of the Recording Secretary.

*See pages 635–36.

1   Rule 9.* The rules contained in the current edition
of *Robert's Rules of Order Newly Revised* shall govern
the convention in all cases to which they are applicable
and in which they are not inconsistent with the bylaws
5   of the Society [or "Federation," "Association," etc.]
and these standing rules.

Program Committee

10   The Program Committee plans and submits the proposed
schedule of meetings, proceedings, and special events of the
convention. When the program is adopted by the voting
body, with or without amendment, it becomes the *order of
business* of the entire convention session (**41**). The program
15   also commonly includes—interwoven throughout the convention timetable—a series of addresses, forums, workshops,
exhibits, tours, and other activities designed for membership-
training, motivational, or entertainment value.

20   RESPONSIBILITIES.   The nature of a convention Program Committee's responsibilities is considerably more complex than for a committee of the same name in a local society
that includes a "program" as a part of each meeting. The
overall program must cover all aspects of the society's work
25   and commitments on the level at which the convention is
held (district, state, national, etc.)—reviewing the period
since the preceding convention and anticipating the course
of the society until the next convention. In addition to en-
abling the convention to handle all business that it should

---

        *A rule on "Parliamentary Authority" is included in the standing rules
of a convention only if the bylaws of the organization do not prescribe the
authority. If this rule is included, it cannot be suspended as such, although a
particular rule stated in the parliamentary authority can be suspended by a
two-thirds vote.

consider within the time available, the program should be of
such nature as to stimulate each delegate to an evaluation
of the society's policies, accomplishments, and opportunities,
inasmuch as benefit from the convention to the general membership may depend largely on the impression that each local
president or delegate transmits to the unit he represents.

The Program Committee usually begins work soon after
the preceding convention closes, and its duties continue
throughout the convention that it plans—so that it functions as virtually a standing committee of the organization.
The Program Committee should work in close contact with
the president and the parliamentarian.

PLANNING THE PROGRAM.   Although the program
must come before the convention for adoption and can be
amended by it, many details must be decided far ahead. Prior
to the convention, the Program Committee must have the
authority (sometimes with designated members of the executive committee or board as advisers, and often acting in
cooperation with a Convention Arrangements Committee)
to engage outside speakers or entertainers, to work out an
order of business allotting appropriate amounts of time to
each subject, and to make all necessary advance arrangements.

Some societies send a tentative skeleton program to the
constituent units several weeks beforehand as part of a printed
"Call to Convention." The complete program that the committee expects to recommend should be printed at the latest
practical time for handing to each person as he registers at
the convention.

The order of business for the complete series of a convention's business meetings normally includes, in expanded form,
the elements of the one followed in ordinary meetings of the
society's constituent units (**41**). In the case of the convention,
however, greater detail and precision are necessary for two
principal reasons: (1) Adherence to a prearranged schedule is

imperative if the convention is to complete its work—timing being an especially important factor if there are to be features carried by radio and television at particular hours, addresses by government officials, or appearances by professional artists.

(2) Each member has the right to know at which meeting and at what approximate time a particular matter can be expected to come before the convention, so that he may avoid absence from the hall during important debates or votes.

Some organizations divide the printed convention program into two parts, the first of which gives the times and places of special events and—for each business meeting—only the hours of the call to order, adjournment, and any scheduled recesses. The second part, listing the items or classes of business set for each meeting, is then known as the *agenda* (**41**). Use of this term does not alter the fact that the items must be brought before the convention in the order named, and not until the meeting or hour for which they are set.

While it is not possible to set out a model program that would be suitable for all conventions, the following principles are commonly applicable:

- Notice of the times of registration should be given early general distribution by mail or other means, and should also be printed in the convention program. Handing out—with the program—a schedule of preconvention meetings of the board and of committees is often advisable, although the persons directly concerned with these meetings may need to be separately informed at an earlier time.
- When the invocation is offered, the national anthem is played or sung, and the pledge of allegiance is recited in opening ceremonies, they should always be in that order—that is, the invocation first and the pledge last.
- If there is an address of welcome—often given by a local public official at the opening of the convention—it should, as a matter of courtesy, be followed by remarks

of acknowledgment and appreciation by the presiding   *1*
officer or his designee on behalf of the organization.

- For each meeting, the program should specify the hour
of opening and closing, and the program or the agenda
should specify the order in which the subjects or classes   *5*
of subjects assigned to that meeting are to come up. The
extent to which such classes are subdivided should be
guided by the particular conditions and probable timing
problems of the individual convention. Sufficient time
should be allotted for thorough consideration of each im-   *10*
portant policy question that is expected to come before
the convention. For such an item of business, it is frequently advisable to set a particular hour—which *auto-*
matically makes the matter a *special order* unless otherwise
specified (see p. 371). Listed subjects for which no hour   *15*
is specified are general orders for the meeting to which
they are assigned.

- Reports of officers are commonly presented in the order
in which the officers are listed in the bylaws, the president reporting first, unless it is the desire or practice of   *20*
the organization to vary from such an order. Action on
the report of the auditors should immediately follow the
treasurer's report. Often reports of officers that are for
information only and do not require action by the convention are printed and distributed in advance. In such a   *25*
case it may not be necessary to have the report read; the
chair can simply pause for any questions by delegates to
the reporting officer, and the reporting officer can make
additional comments on his report at that time. The report of the board, if any, usually should follow the reports   *30*
of officers.

- Reports of committees that are for information only and
that do not require action by the convention should, as
far as possible, be brought up in succession at the same
point in the order of business. Time can frequently be   *35*

saved by reproducing and distributing these reports in advance, in which case it may be unnecessary to read them aloud to the convention. The chair can then simply call the name of each committee in sequence, pausing for any questions. The chairman of any committee can be permitted to make additional comments upon his committee's report at that time.

- The report of a committee having a resolution or other motion to offer can be received at any appropriate time, but it should usually be before the report of the Resolutions Committee.

- A time for announcements should immediately precede the adjournment of each meeting of the convention.

- Beginning with the second day of the convention (unless a rule or resolution is adopted providing for the approval of the minutes of the entire convention by the board or a committee), the minutes of the preceding day's meetings should be read immediately after any opening ceremonies at the first meeting of each day. Authority to approve such minutes is then usually delegated to the board or to a special committee, by means of a standing rule of the convention or an adopted resolution introduced by the Resolutions Committee.

- Business unfinished at the end of a day normally is taken up after the reading of the minutes (or after the opening of the meeting, if the minutes are not read) at the resumption of business the next day—provided that the program makes no special provision for unfinished business on that day and there is no conflict with a special order. If unfinished business is not listed as such in the program each day, the planned timing should nevertheless allow for it; a listed heading of "Unfinished Business" should then be provided near the end of the last business meeting, and at any point where it is advisable because special orders have been scheduled early in the day (see also **41**).

- Nominations and the election of officers should take place   *1*
  relatively early in the convention, if possible, so that there
  will be time to complete balloting if more than one ballot
  must be taken.
- If there is to be a formal installation of officers, this cere-   *5*
  mony is often made a part of a closing banquet meeting,
  at which any presentations of gavels, pins, awards, or the
  like are also made.

It is often advisable to schedule a meeting of the executive   *10*
body or board of the association a day after the close of the
convention, asking the board members and other necessary
personnel to remain in the convention city for this purpose.
If such a meeting is to be held, its time and place may be
announced in the printed convention program.   *15*

ADOPTION OF THE CONVENTION PROGRAM.
The program is the president's guide as to the order of
business during the initial proceedings, even before it has
been formally adopted by the convention. Directly after the   *20*
adoption of the standing rules, the report of the Program
Committee is presented—normally by the committee chairman—somewhat as follows: "Mr. President, a printed copy
of the program as proposed by the Program Committee is in
the hands of each registrant for the convention. By direction   *25*
of the committee I move the adoption of the program as
printed." (If the chairman or other person presenting the
report is not a voting member of the convention, he omits
the motion for adoption. For procedure in such a case, see
p. 610, ll. 4–16.)   *30*

If last-minute changes in the program have become necessary, the chairman can make his report by saying: "Mr. President, because of . . . [briefly indicating reasons], the Program
Committee recommends the following modifications in its
proposed program which has been printed and placed in the   *35*

1   hands of each registrant for the convention: . . . [clearly stat-
     ing each change, with reference to page and line in the
     printed program]. By direction of the Program Committee,
     I move that, with these changes, the printed program be
5   adopted." This motion is debatable and amendable. A major-
     ity vote adopts the program—even if it contains special
     orders. While the making of a special order requires a two-
     thirds vote under ordinary circumstances, the situation is dif-
     ferent in the case of a convention program, where the special
10   order is part of a complete order of business being adopted
     for the current session.

     To change the program after its adoption requires a two-
     thirds vote or the vote of a majority of all the delegates or
     other "voting members" of the convention who have been
15   registered—or unanimous consent, which can usually be ob-
     tained with no difficulty in cases where a departure from the
     program is justified. Thus, an affirmative vote to adopt
     the program cannot be reconsidered. (See pp. 54–56; see also
     Program and *Taking Up Business Out of Its Proper Order,*
20   pp. 362–64). Changing the program to add additional meet-
     ings within the same session requires such a vote except that
     during the last meeting scheduled by the program an addi-
     tional meeting may be set by majority vote through the use of
     the motion to *Fix the Time to Which to Adjourn* (**22**). Any
25   proposed changes except those to which there is obviously no
     reasonable alternative are best referred to the Program Com-
     mittee. The committee can recommend changes if and when
     needed while the convention is in progress, but neither the
     presiding officer nor the Program Committee is free to alter
30   the program as adopted—which only the convention can do.

     (For parliamentary rules applying at the expiration of the
     time allotted to a subject, and procedure at scheduled times
     of adjournment, see pp. 222–23, 238–40, 370, ll. 21–35,
     373–74.)

Convention Arrangements Committee

The complex arrangements necessary to a convention generally require the coordination of many additional details that are outside the province of any of the other committees mentioned in this chapter. In the simplest case a Convention Arrangements Committee is appointed—usually by the board at the convention level. Most often the committee's membership is largely made up of members of the constituent society or societies acting as convention hosts; it should, however, include persons who have had experience in similar work at prior conventions. In cases where there has been competition between cities for the convention site, it is often well to place on this committee local members who were instrumental in obtaining the selection of their city.

The Convention Arrangements Committee may be empowered to consult experts, who may include professional convention managers. Assistance frequently is obtainable also from staff members of hotels where conventions are held, and from convention bureaus in many cities.

Depending on the size and duration of the convention, duties ordinarily assigned to the Convention Arrangements Committee are sometimes delegated to subcommittees or even distributed among separate committees. At the outset, the convention headquarters must be selected and advance arrangements made concerning room accommodations in as many hotels or motor inns as may be necessary. The committee may work with the Credentials Committee in coordinating room reservations for delegates with their registration for the convention. While the Program Committee may arrange for all speakers and entertainment, details relating to the overnight and other accommodations for these guests are usually a responsibility of the Convention Arrangements Committee. Ensuring that dignitaries and honored guests are met at the airport or other point of arrival may also be one of the latter committee's functions.

Printed or reproduced material assembled in cooperation with the Program Committee for distribution to the delegates in advance of the convention should include directions for getting to the convention by the various means of transportation available, and information about the locality, points of interest, restaurants, entertainment, tours arranged by the Program Committee, and parking facilities for those driving to the convention.

Careful attention should be given to seating arrangements within the hall, voting members always being located in a separate section if other persons are assigned seating space on the convention floor. Pages, messengers, ushers, and doorkeepers—who are essential to the good order of all but the smallest conventions—should be trained to perform their duties in a calm and courteous manner. During the convention, liaison should be maintained with the Program Committee to ensure, for example, proper seating on the platform, as the needs may change from meeting to meeting.

The staffing of an information desk throughout the convention may lie within the province of the Convention Arrangements Committee, together with additional functions in the areas of communications and public relations. If the meetings are to be covered by the press, the representatives of the various media must be kept informed of developments and provided with an area on the floor near the platform, or in some other point of vantage in the hall. It is often helpful to have facilities for typing and copying close at hand, as well as for the distribution of literature. In very large conventions it is wise to investigate existing telephone and other communication facilities and to provide for their augmentation if necessary.

Resolutions Committee

The Resolutions Committee—also sometimes called the *Reference Committee* or, in certain cases described below, the *Platform Committee*—has as its basic purpose the screening of all original main motions (**10**) that have not been screened by another committee and that come—or are to come—before the convention. It is usually not intended to require purely formal or incidental main motions to be submitted to the Resolutions Committee, or to refer to it resolutions reported to the convention by other committees (see also **51**).

VARIATIONS IN RULES RELATING TO THE RESOLUTIONS COMMITTEE.   The establishment of a Resolutions Committee in a convention represents a limitation on the ordinary right of members to propose any number of motions from the floor without notice—such limitation arising from the need for keeping within a schedule and disposing of a large amount of business within a short time. The degree of limitation imposed and the manner in which the committee functions vary considerably, depending on the organization, in particulars such as the following:

Variations in the Time When a Resolution Can Be Introduced.   In the simplest situation a resolution is offered from the floor of the convention in the way it would be in an ordinary meeting. Such an arrangement is outlined in Standing Rules 3 and 4(a) on page 622. A place in the program or agenda should then be provided at each meeting, under a heading such as "New Business," for the introduction of resolutions. Under this system, the proposer of the resolution says, "Mr. President, I move the adoption of [or "I offer"] the resolution which I have sent to the Secretary's desk." The secretary reads the resolution, announcing the names of the mover and the seconder, and the chair says,

1 "Under the rules the resolution is referred to the Resolutions Committee."

To save even this time in a convention, an arrangement can be made whereby resolutions are submitted to the record-
5 ing secretary without being formally moved and read in open meeting, and the secretary then must promptly deliver them to the chairman of the Resolutions Committee. The convention can suspend such a rule at any time, however—by a majority vote if it is a standing rule of the convention,
10 or by a two-thirds vote if it is a higher-ranking rule (p. 17, ll. 19–27)— and can thus take up a resolution without sending it to the Resolutions Committee.

If many resolutions are customarily proposed by members, a permanent rule or provision in the bylaws can be
15 adopted by the organization requiring all resolutions to be submitted to the committee, or to the executive secretary for delivery to the committee, a number of days, weeks, or even months in advance of the convention. This system can be arranged to allow time for sending copies of all resolutions
20 considered by the Resolutions Committee to the constituent societies and their delegates in advance of the convention, thereby giving time for consultation and, possibly, instruction of delegates. In such cases it is advisable to provide that resolutions can also be introduced at the convention if permitted
25 by a two-thirds vote in the individual case.

Variations in Permitted Origin of Resolutions. In the ordinary case only the members of the convention—that is, the delegates—are allowed to introduce resolutions for consideration by the assembly, and other members of constituent
30 societies (who are not convention members) are allowed to speak for the purpose of suggesting motions only with the consent of the convention. Such consent can be granted in an individual case, or a rule can be adopted specifying persons who, in addition to the delegates, can submit resolutions;
35 the latter practice has particular value when resolutions are

required to be submitted in advance of the convention meetings.

In some cases any member of a constituent society, whether he is a delegate or not, is permitted to offer a resolution. In other organizations a resolution is required to have the sponsorship of a constituent society itself. A number of organizations require even the resolutions offered by standing and special committees of the organization to be screened and reported by the Resolutions Committee. In some types of organizations the Resolutions Committee originates and drafts its own resolutions for submission to the assembly. In any society, when an officer or committee simply makes one or more recommendations, the Resolutions Committee is customarily assigned the task of putting the recommendation(s) in the form of resolution(s).

Variations in the Power of the Resolutions Committee.   In the simplest arrangement, the Resolutions Committee has only the power to put resolutions in proper form, eliminate duplication where similar resolutions are offered, and ensure that all resolutions relating to a specific subject will be offered in a logical sequence. In other cases the committee is given the authority to make substantive alterations in a resolution, but only with the sponsor's consent; while in still others, by vote of the committee—sometimes a two-thirds vote—the substance of the resolution can be altered and the resolution can be reported to the assembly in the altered form as though the committee had originated it.

Except as the rules may provide otherwise, the Resolutions Committee is required to report all resolutions referred to it; but the committee can, if it wishes, report a resolution with "no recommendation." If the committee is given the power "not to report" a resolution—thus withholding it from consideration by the convention—a requirement of an unusually high vote within the committee (such as a three-fourths vote or a vote of two-thirds of the committee's

1   members) should always be imposed; and the convention
      should always be given power to override such a decision
      of the Resolutions Committee and order the committee to
      report the resolution, by a majority vote (see Rule 4(d) in the
5   sample standing rules of a convention, p. 623). In this con-
      nection, it should be noted that voting "not to report" a
      resolution, reporting it with "no recommendation," and re-
      porting it with the recommendation that it be rejected by the
      convention are each quite different.
10
          PLATFORMS OR POLICY STATEMENTS.   In polit-
      ical and certain other types of organizations, the Resolutions
      Committee is required to prepare and report a platform for
      adoption by the organization, setting forth its views, aims,
15   and aspirations. Other associations occasionally require the
      committee to draft statements of policy or similar documents
      that take the form of a platform rather than of a resolu-
      tion. In such a platform or statement, many of the principles
      applicable to drafting resolutions are followed.
20   If there is a preamble, instead of beginning each paragraph
      with the word "Whereas," a participle is used; thus, "Believ-
      ing in the . . . , [etc.]." Each paragraph is terminated by a
      semicolon and, in the case of the next-to-the-last paragraph,
      the word "and." The last paragraph of the preamble may be
25   followed by the word "therefore." Each new paragraph of the
      preamble begins with another participle. In the body of the
      paper, each paragraph, instead of opening with the enacting
      words "*Resolved,* That," begins with a verb denoting an atti-
      tude or position—for example, "Affirms . . . ," "Assures . . . ,"
30   "Condemns . . . ," "Calls upon . . . ," and the like. As in a
      resolution, no paragraph should contain a period within its
      structure. The paragraphs of the body of the document can
      be linked by a semicolon and the word "and," as in the pre-
      amble, or a semicolon only can be used. The first paragraph
35   of the body of the statement is often somewhat general. The

preamble and the body of the statement may be connected
by words such as "Issues this statement of . . . ; and. . . ." The
full name of the organization can precede these words, or it
can be placed before the preamble; for example, thus:

> Believing . . . ;
> Recalling . . . ; and
> Noting . . . ;
> The Phoenix Improvement Association issues this
> statement of its basic governing principles; and
> Affirms . . . ;
> Assures . . . ; and
> Condemns . . .

Or:

> The Phoenix Improvement Association,
> Believing . . . ; and
> Holding . . . ; therefore
> Issues this statement of its basic governing prin-
> ciples; and
> Affirms . . . ;
> Assures . . . ; [and so on].

COURTESY RESOLUTIONS.   In addition to its duties
in regard to the resolutions which are referred to it and
which usually relate to policy matters, the Resolutions Committee is often charged with the duty of drafting and presenting to the assembly any courtesy resolutions that may
seem appropriate. Ordinarily, courtesy resolutions express the
appreciation of the convention to those who arranged accommodations for its physical needs or rendered it service.

MEETINGS OF THE COMMITTEE.   Ordinarily the
Resolutions Committee should make known, through the

1   program or announcements, the times and places it will meet.
It is best to allow any sponsor of a resolution to appear before
the committee to explain it and answer any questions about
it; and interested delegates also may be allowed to attend and
5   even participate in discussion. Many times such free discussion reduces friction that may have developed concerning a
resolution, and the convention as a result goes more
smoothly. After any open "hearings" of this type, the committee meets in executive session (**9**) to review each resolu-
10   tion and prepare its report. The parliamentarian may be asked
to attend the committee's meetings.

REPORT OF THE RESOLUTIONS COMMITTEE.

In reporting, the Resolutions Committee follows the proce-
15   dure of any committee reporting back a resolution referred
to it, as described in **51**. Even when resolutions are submitted to the committee before the opening of the convention,
the report on each resolution is treated as if it had been
moved and seconded in the assembly before being referred
20   to the committee. It is never necessary for the Resolutions
Committee chairman or reporting member to move the
adoption of a resolution being reported—unless the committee itself originated it, as in the case of courtesy resolutions.

    When the committee recommends amendments to a res-
25   olution, in cases where it is not empowered to incorporate
them itself, its chairman reports as follows:

RESOLUTIONS COMMITTEE CHAIRMAN: Mr. President, the Resolutions
Committee recommends that the resolution relating to . . . [or "Resolu-
30   tion No. 6," etc.] be amended by striking out the words ". . ." and
inserting the words ". . . ," and that, as thus amended, the resolution be
adopted. By direction of the Resolutions Committee, I move the adoption of the recommended amendment.

35   If the convention members do not have reproduced copies

of the resolution, the chair should read it before stating the
question on the amendment. He then proceeds:

> CHAIR: The Resolutions Committee recommends the adoption of
> the resolution with the following amendment . . . [rereading the amend-
> ment]. The question is on the amendment.

In instances where it is advisable for a resolution of overriding importance to be considered as a special order rather
than as a part of the main body of resolutions reported by the
Resolutions Committee, this is arranged through liaison with
the Program Committee. The chairman of the Resolutions
Committee then reports the resolution at the time prescribed
for it in the agenda. If desired, the committee's report can
include a preliminary motion establishing special rules for the
consideration of the resolution, similar to the practice of
the U.S. House of Representatives. The following is an example of such a rule:

> *Resolved,* That at the time prescribed in the agenda
> the resolution relating to _____ be considered
> as a special order, the general debate to be limited to
> two hours and equally divided between, and controlled
> by, Mr. A, the leader for the affirmative, and Mr. B, the
> leader for the negative; that at the expiration of general
> debate the resolution shall be open to amendment, de-
> bate on said amendment(s) to be limited to two min-
> utes for each member.

Under such a rule, the leaders for the two sides are recognized alternately by the presiding officer and can speak
themselves or yield the floor to other member(s) for a portion of the time at their disposal. The leaders are usually the
more ardent or persuasive advocates of the two positions, and
frequently they speak first and save themselves enough time

so that at the end they can close debate for their side. An alternative procedure is to assign a longer period of debate to Mr. A and Mr. B, and require other members to adhere to a shorter limit. Often it is helpful to require general debate to be conducted first before amendments are allowed, but this provision can be dispensed with.

§60. CONVENTIONS NOT OF A PERMANENT SOCIETY

A convention called only for a specific purpose not involving a permanent organization, or one called to form a state or a national society or a federation, is similar to a mass meeting as described in **53** in that when called to order it has no bylaws or officers. Because it has no bylaws, added difficulty may be encountered in determining who are the properly appointed delegates.

The group sponsoring the convention should appoint a Convention Arrangements Committee, as described above, to secure the hall and accommodations for the delegates, make the preliminary arrangements for the convention, and perform the other coordinating and arranging duties assigned to it.

Someone designated by the sponsoring group—sometimes the chairman of the Convention Arrangements Committee—should call the meeting to order and preside during any opening exercises and the election of a temporary chairman. The sponsoring group's choice for temporary chairman and the person who is to nominate him should be agreed upon in advance. After the elected temporary chairman has taken the chair, a temporary secretary is elected. Next should come the appointment of the Credentials, Rules, and Program Committees, or the ratification of the prior selection of these committees. In a convention of this type, if these committees have not been appointed in advance, all committees should be appointed by the chair. Until the report of the Credentials Committee is adopted, no business other than its adoption or the other preliminary actions described in this paragraph may be considered, except that any motions related to the consideration of such business or to the conduct of the meeting before the report is adopted, as well as those that are in order in the absence of a quorum (pp. 347–48), are in order.

If the Credentials Committee and other organizing committees were not appointed in advance and are not, therefore, ready to report, the time they need to prepare their reports is usually spent in listening to talks, perhaps on various phases of the convention's object. Otherwise the reports of the organizing committees are received in the same manner as that described for organizing a convention of an established association. If a permanent organization is not contemplated, a permanent chairman and secretary can, but need not, be elected at this time, after which the convention proceeds with the business for which it was called together. The principal purpose in electing a temporary chairman first and a permanent chairman later in a convention of this kind is to enable the temporary chairman to preside over the convention while it acts upon any matters relating to contested seats (see pp. 614–16), so that the permanent chairman can be elected by the delegates on the permanent roll of the convention as it is finally determined after all such contests have been resolved.

If the convention is called to form a permanent organization, permanent officers are not elected until later (after the adoption of the bylaws), but a resolution should be adopted at this point in the proceedings expressing an intention to form such a permanent association, as in the case of forming a permanent local society (see **54**). A set of bylaws should have been carefully drawn up before the meeting of the convention, either by a Bylaws Committee appointed by the organizing group, with the appointments being ratified by the convention, or by members of the sponsoring group who thereafter hand them to a Bylaws Committee appointed at the convention. In the latter case some of those who drafted the bylaws should be appointed to the committee to avoid delay in reporting them.

After adoption of the bylaws, a Nominating Committee, selected in a manner as close as possible to that prescribed in the bylaws, nominates candidates for office, and those elected to these permanent offices take up their duties immediately, unless other provision is made.

CHAPTER

XX

DISCIPLINARY PROCEDURES

§61. DISCIPLINE OF MEMBERS AND GUESTS

In most societies it is understood that members are required to be of honorable character and reputation, and certain types of associations may have particular codes of ethics *5* to enforce. Although ordinary societies seldom have occasion to discipline members, an organization or assembly has the ultimate right to make and enforce its own rules, and to require that its members refrain from conduct injurious to the organization or its purposes. No one should be allowed to *10* remain a member if his retention will do this kind of harm.

Punishments that a society can impose generally fall under the headings of censure,* fine (if authorized in the bylaws), suspension, or expulsion. The extreme penalty that an organization or society can impose on a member is expulsion. *15*

If there is an article on discipline in the bylaws (p. 583, ll. 6–11), it may specify a number of offenses outside meetings for which these penalties can be imposed on a member

---

*It is also possible to adopt a motion of censure without formal disciplinary procedures.

of the organization. Frequently, such an article provides for their imposition on any member found guilty of conduct described, for example, as "tending to injure the good name of the organization, disturb its well-being, or hamper it in its work." In any society, behavior of this nature is a serious offense properly subject to disciplinary action, whether the bylaws make mention of it or not.

Formal disciplinary procedures should generally be regarded as a drastic step reserved for serious situations or those potentially so. When it appears that such measures may become necessary, proper and tactful handling of the case is of prime importance. It is usually in the best interests of the organization first to make every effort to obtain a satisfactory solution of the matter quietly and informally.

Cases of conduct subject to disciplinary action divide themselves into: offenses occurring in a meeting; and offenses by members outside a meeting.

Dealing with Offenses in a Meeting

PRINCIPLES GOVERNING DISCIPLINE AT MEETINGS.   A society has the right to determine who may be present at its meetings and to control its hall while meetings are in progress; but all members have the right to attend except in cases where the bylaws provide for the automatic suspension of members who fall in arrears in payment of their dues, or where the society has, by vote and as a penalty imposed for a specific offense, forbidden attendance.

Nonmembers, on the other hand—or a particular nonmember or group of nonmembers—can be excluded at any time from part or all of a meeting of a society, or from all of its meetings. Such exclusion can be effected by a ruling of the chair in cases of disorder, or by the adoption of a rule on the subject, or by an appropriate motion as the need arises— a motion of the latter nature being a question of privilege

(**19**). A motion to exclude all nonmembers (except absolutely necessary staff, if any) is often referred to as a motion to "go into executive session" (see **9**).

All persons present at a meeting have an obligation to obey the legitimate orders of the presiding officer.* Members, however, can appeal from the decision of the chair (**24**), move to suspend the rules (**25**), or move a reconsideration (**37**)—depending on the circumstances of the chair's ruling. A member can make such an appeal or motion whether the order involved applies to him or not.

In dealing with any case of disorder in a meeting, the presiding officer should always maintain a calm, deliberate tone—although he may become increasingly firm if a situation demands it. Under no circumstances should the chair attempt to drown out a disorderly member—either by his own voice or the gavel—or permit himself to be drawn into a verbal duel. If unavoidable, however, proper disciplinary proceedings to cope with immediate necessity can be conducted while a disorderly member continues to speak.

BREACHES OF ORDER BY MEMBERS IN A MEETING.   If a member commits only a slight breach of order—such as addressing another member instead of the chair in debate, or, in a single instance, failing to confine his remarks to the merits of the pending question—the chair simply raps lightly, points out the fault, and advises the member to avoid it. The member can then continue speaking if he commits no further breaches. More formal procedures can be used in the case of serious offenses, as follows:

Calling a Member to Order.   If the offense is more serious than in the case above—as when a member repeatedly questions the motives of other members whom he mentions

---

*See, however, *Remedies for Abuse of Authority by the Chair in a Meeting*, pages 650–53.

1   by name, or persists in speaking on completely irrelevant matters in debate—the chair normally should first warn the member; but with or without such a warning, the chair or any other member can "call the member to order." If the

5   chair does this, he says, "The member is out of order and will be seated." Another member making the call rises and, without waiting to be recognized, says, "Mr. President, I call the member to order," then resumes his seat. If the chair finds this point of order (**23**) well taken, he declares the offender

10   out of order and directs him to be seated, just as above. If the offender had the floor, then (irrespective of who originated the proceeding) the chair should clearly state the breach involved and put the question to the assembly: "Shall the member be allowed to continue speaking?" This question is

15   undebatable.

     "Naming" an Offender.   In cases of obstinate or grave breach of order by a member, the chair can, after repeated warnings, "name" the offender, which amounts to preferring charges and should be resorted to only in extreme circum-

20   stances. Before taking such action, when it begins to appear that it may become necessary, the chair should direct the secretary to take down objectionable or disorderly words used by the member. This direction by the chair, and the words taken down pursuant to it, are entered in the minutes only if

25   the chair finds it necessary to name the offender.

     Although the chair has no authority to impose a penalty or to order the offending member removed from the hall, the assembly has that power. It should be noted in this connection that in any case of an offense against the assembly

30   occurring in a meeting, there is no need for a formal trial provided that any penalty is imposed promptly after the breach (cf. pp. 250–51), since the witnesses are all present and make up the body that is to determine the penalty.

     The declaration made by the chair in naming a member

35   is addressed to the offender by name and in the second per-

son, and is entered in the minutes. An example of such a dec-   *1*
laration is as follows:

> CHAIR: Mr. J! The chair has repeatedly directed you to refrain from
> offensive personal references when speaking in this meeting. Three times   *5*
> the chair has ordered you to be seated, and you have nevertheless
> attempted to continue speaking.

If the member obeys at this point, the matter can be
dropped or not, as the assembly chooses. The case may be suf-   *10*
ficiently resolved by an apology or a withdrawal of objectionable statements or remarks by the offender; but if not, any
member can move to order a penalty, or the chair can first ask,
"What penalty shall be imposed on the member?" A motion
offered in a case of this kind can propose, for example, that   *15*
the offender be required to make an apology, that he be cen-
sured, that he be required to leave the hall during the remainder of the meeting or until he is prepared to apologize, that
his rights of membership be suspended for a time, or that he
be expelled from the organization.   *20*
The offending member can be required to leave the hall
during the consideration of his penalty, but he should be
allowed to present his defense briefly first. A motion to require the member's departure during consideration of the
penalty—which may be assumed by the chair if he thinks it   *25*
appropriate—is undebatable, is unamendable, and requires a
majority vote.
If the member denies having said anything improper, the
words recorded by the secretary can be read to him and, if
necessary, the assembly can decide by vote whether he was   *30*
heard to say them. On the demand of a single member—
other than the named offender, who is not considered to be
a voting member while his case is pending—the vote on imposing a penalty must be taken by ballot, unless the penalty
proposed is only that the offender be required to leave the   *35*

1   hall for all or part of the remainder of the meeting. Expulsion
    from membership requires a two-thirds vote.
        If the assembly orders an offending member to leave the
    hall during a meeting as described above and he refuses to do
5   so, the considerations stated below regarding the removal of
    offenders apply; but such a member exposes himself to the
    possibility of more severe disciplinary action by the society.

    PROTECTION FROM ANNOYANCE BY NON-
10 MEMBERS IN A MEETING; REMOVAL OF AN
    OFFENDER FROM THE HALL.   Any nonmembers
    allowed in the hall during a meeting, as guests of the organ-
    ization, have no rights with reference to the proceedings
    (pp. 644–45). An assembly has the right to protect itself from
15 annoyance by nonmembers, and its full authority in this
    regard—as distinguished from cases involving disorderly
    members—can be exercised by the chair acting alone. The
    chair has the power to require nonmembers to leave the hall,
    or to order their removal, at any time during the meeting;
20 and the nonmembers have no right of appeal from such an
    order of the presiding officer. However, such an order may
    be appealed by a member. That appeal is undebatable (see
    Standard Descriptive Characteristic 5[a], p. 257). At a mass
    meeting (**53**), any person who attempts to disrupt the pro-
25 ceedings in a manner obviously hostile to the announced pur-
    pose of the meeting can be treated as a nonmember under
    the provisions of this paragraph.
        If a person—whether a member of the assembly or not—
    refuses to obey the order of proper authority to leave the hall
30 during a meeting, the chair should take necessary measures
    to see that the order is enforced, but should be guided by
    a judicious appraisal of the situation. The chair can appoint a
    committee to escort the offender to the door, or the sergeant-
    at-arms—if there is one—can be asked to do this. If those
35 who are assigned that task are unable to persuade the offender

to leave, it is usually preferable that he be removed by   *1*
police—who may, however, be reluctant to intervene unless
representatives of the organization are prepared to press
charges.

The sergeant-at-arms or the members of the appointed   *5*
committee themselves may attempt to remove the offender
from the hall, using the minimum force necessary. Such a step
should generally be taken only as a last resort, since there may
be adverse legal consequences; and a person who would refuse to leave upon legitimate request may be the type most   *10*
likely to bring suit, even if with little justification. In cases
where possibly serious annoyance by hostile persons is anticipated—in some mass meetings, for example—it may be advisable to arrange in advance for the presence of police or
guards from a security service agency.   *15*

Offenses Elsewhere Than in a Meeting; Trials

If improper conduct by a member of a society occurs
elsewhere than at a meeting, the members generally have no   *20*
first-hand knowledge of the case. Therefore, if disciplinary
action is to be taken, charges must be preferred and a formal
trial held before the assembly of the society, or before a committee—standing or special—which should be required to
report its findings and recommendations to the assembly for   *25*
action. In addition, even when improper conduct occurs at
a meeting, in order for disciplinary action to be taken *other*
than promptly after the breach occurs, charges must be preferred and a formal trial held. However, the only way in which
a member may be disciplined for words spoken in debate is   *30*
through the procedure described on pages 645–48, which
may be employed only promptly after the breach occurs. In
some societies (depending on particular provisions of the bylaws, as explained in **62**), the same steps must also be employed if an officer of the society is to be deposed from office.   *35*

1 The procedures governing all such cases are described in detail in **63**.

5 ## §62. REMOVAL FROM OFFICE AND OTHER REMEDIES FOR DERELICTION OF DUTY IN OFFICE OR MISCONDUCT

The presiding officer and other officers have the duties
10 set forth in this manual (see **47**) and in the organization's by-laws. This section covers procedures available if they neglect those duties, abuse their authority, or engage in other misconduct that calls into question their fitness for office. This section also covers removal from office at the pleasure of the
15 assembly when the bylaws permit such removal.

Remedies for Abuse of Authority by the Chair in a Meeting

20 ENFORCING POINTS OF ORDER AND APPEALS. If the chair at a meeting acts improperly (for example, fails to recognize a member entitled to the floor, see **42**, or ignores a motion properly made and seconded that is not dilatory, see **39**, and neither states the question on the motion nor rules
25 it out of order), a *Point of Order* (**23**) may be raised, and from the chair's decision an *Appeal* (**24**) may be taken. This procedure enables the majority to ensure enforcement of the rules unless the chair ignores the point of order, ignores the appeal, or fails to act in accordance with the assembly's
30 decision on the appeal.

If the chair ignores a point of order that is not dilatory, the member can repeat the point of order a second and third time and if the chair still ignores it, the member, standing in his place, can immediately put the point of order to a vote
35 without debate. The question may be put as, "Is the point of

order that . . . well taken?" If the point of order was that the   1
chair improperly ignored another motion, the member may,
instead of repeating the point of order, repeat the original
motion, and if it is seconded and the chair still ignores it, may,
standing in his place, put the ignored motion to a vote with-   5
out debate.

Likewise, if the chair ignores an appeal appropriately made
and seconded,* a member can repeat the appeal and if, despite its being seconded, the chair ignores it again, the member can repeat it a third time and if it is again seconded but   10
still ignored by the chair, the member can immediately, standing in his place, put the appeal to a vote without debate. The
question may be put as: "Shall the decision of the chair be
sustained?"

15

REMOVAL OF PRESIDING OFFICER FROM CHAIR
FOR ALL OR PART OF A SESSION.   If the chair fails to
act in accordance with the assembly's decision on an appeal
(or on a point of order submitted to a vote of the assembly)
or otherwise culpably fails to perform the duties of the chair   20
properly in a meeting, the assembly may employ measures
temporarily to replace the chair with another presiding officer
expected to act in accordance with the will of the assembly.

If the offending occupant of the chair is an appointed or
elected chairman pro tem (see pp. 452–54), a motion can be   25
made to "declare the chair vacant and proceed to elect a new
chairman." Such a motion is a question of privilege affecting

---

*An appeal is not allowed from the chair's ruling on a question about
which there cannot possibly be two reasonable opinions (p. 256, ll. 34–36)
and is out of order in certain other circumstances (p. 256, ll. 29–32; p. 258,
l. 33 to p. 259, l. 15), but in such cases the chair must announce that the appeal is out of order for the relevant reason, not simply ignore the appeal (unless the appeal is dilatory as explained at pp. 342–43).

1   the assembly (**19**) and is an incidental main motion requiring
     a majority vote for its adoption.*

     If the chair is not an appointed or elected chairman pro
     tem, a motion to declare the chair vacant is not in order.
5   However, a motion can be made to *Suspend the Rules* so as
     to take away from him the authority to preside during all or
     part of a given session.** When such a motion is made and
     seconded, after stating the motion he must turn the chair over
     to another following the procedure described on page 395,
10   and the remedy for refusal or failure to do so is that the mo-
     tion may be put to a vote by its maker.

     Any one motion to *Suspend the Rules* that might limit the
     authority or duties of the presiding officer during a meeting
     can remain in effect, at most, for one session. (See p. 87,
15   ll. 6–11 and p. 88, ll. 26–35.) Therefore, in order to prevent
     the regular presiding officer from presiding during subse-
     quent sessions, the motion to *Suspend the Rules* would have

---

*Once such a motion is made and seconded, the chair must state it, and
then, since it refers to the presiding officer in a capacity not shared in common
with other members, the chair must be turned over to the secretary or secretary pro tem. The new occupant of the chair then presides during consideration of the motion to declare the chair vacant and proceed to elect a new
chairman. The new occupant continues to preside until the result of the vote
on that motion is announced and, if it is adopted, until the election of the
new chairman is completed.

If the presiding officer refuses or fails to turn the chair over as required,
and ignores a point of order on the issue (or ignores, or does not abide by
the decision on, an appeal of a ruling on the point of order) the motion to
declare the chair vacant may be put to a vote by its maker as explained on
pages 650–51. In such a case, the motion is undebatable.

**This is true even if the bylaws contain a provision to the effect that the
president shall preside at all meetings, since such a provision is clearly in the
nature of a rule of order, which may be suspended even if in the bylaws. See
page 17, ll. 22–25.

to be renewed and separately adopted at each of the sessions. Moreover, since *Suspend the Rules* applies only when "an assembly wishes to do something *during a meeting* that it cannot do without violating one or more of its regular rules" (p. 260, ll. 19–21, emphasis added), the motion cannot be used to remove from the presiding officer (even temporarily) any administrative duties—those related to the role of an executive officer that are distinct from the function of presiding over the assembly at its meetings. (Cf. p. 456, ll. 22–23.)

If the motion to suspend the rules is adopted by a two-thirds vote, then, unless the motion names a new occupant of the chair, the ranking vice-president (or, in the absence of the vice-president, an elected temporary presiding officer, pp. 453–54) has the duty of presiding through the end of the session (or any shorter period specified by the motion to suspend the rules).

A permanent removal of the presiding officer, and removal of authority to exercise administrative duties conferred by the bylaws, requires the procedure described below.

Removal from Office

Except as the bylaws may provide otherwise, any regularly elected officer of a permanent society can be removed from office by the society's assembly as follows:

- If the bylaws provide that officers shall serve "for __ years *or* until their successors are elected," the officer in question can be removed from office by adoption of a motion to do so. The vote required for adoption of such a motion is (a) a two-thirds vote, (b) a majority vote when previous notice (as defined on p. 121) has been given, or (c) a vote of a majority of the entire membership—any one of which will suffice. A motion to remove an officer from office is a question of privilege (**19**) affecting the organization of the assembly, and so also is the filling of any vacancy created by the adoption of such a motion.*

- If, however, the bylaws provide that officers shall serve *only* a fixed term, such as "for two years" (which is not a recommended wording; see p. 573, l. 33 to p. 574, l. 3), or if they provide that officers shall serve "for __ years *and* until their successors are elected," an officer can be removed from office only for cause—that is, neglect of duty in office or misconduct—in accordance with the procedures described in **63**; that is, an investigating committee must be appointed, charges must be preferred, and a formal trial must be held.

§63. INVESTIGATION AND TRIAL

As explained in **61** and **62**, the removal of an officer for cause, or the discipline of a member for improper conduct, may require that charges be preferred and that a formal trial be held. The full procedure for such cases is described in this section.**

---

*The assembly normally cannot proceed to fill the vacancy created by removal of an officer immediately, since notice is a requirement (see p. 291, ll. 20–23). If the president is removed from office, the vice-president thereby succeeds to the presidency, creating a vacancy in the vice-presidency which requires notice to fill. If it is desired to fill a vacancy that may be created by removal, previous notice may be given in advance of the meeting at which removal is contemplated that, should removal of the officer occur, the resulting vacancy may be filled at that meeting.

**It is possible for a disciplinary proceeding to affect an individual's status both as an officer and as a member, and a resolution preferring charges (see pp. 659–60) may combine notice to show cause both why the accused should not be removed from office and why he should not be expelled from membership. If the bylaws make membership a required qualification for office (see p. 447, ll. 16–19), then expulsion from membership necessarily results in removal from office.

Rights of the Society and the Accused

1

A society has the right to investigate the character of its members and officers as may be necessary to the enforcement of its own standards. But neither the society nor any member *5* has the right to make public any information obtained through such investigation; if it becomes common knowledge within the society, it should not be revealed to any persons outside the society. Consequently, a trial must always be held in executive session, as must the introduction and considera- *10* tion of all resolutions leading up to the trial.

If (after trial) a member is expelled or an officer is removed from office, the society has the right to disclose that fact—circulating it only to the extent required for the protection of the society or, possibly, of other organizations. Nei- *15* ther the society nor any of its members has the right to make public the charge of which an officer or member has been found guilty, or to reveal any other details connected with the case. To make any of the facts public may constitute libel. A trial by the society cannot legally establish the guilt of the *20* accused, as understood in a court of law; it can only establish his guilt as affecting the society's judgment of his fitness for membership or office.

Ordinarily it is impossible for the society to obtain *legal* proof of facts in disciplinary cases. To get at the truth under *25* the conditions of such a trial, hearsay evidence has to be admissible, and judgment as to the best interests of the society may have to be based on it. Witnesses are not sworn. The persons with first-hand knowledge may be nonmembers, who probably will decline to testify, and may be willing only to re- *30* veal the facts privately to a single member on condition that their names in no way be connected with the case. Even members may be reluctant to give formal testimony against the accused. A member can be required to testify at a trial on pain of expulsion, but it is very seldom advisable to force such an issue. *35*

A member or officer has the right that allegations against his good name shall not be made except by charges brought on reasonable ground. If thus accused, he has the right to due process—that is, to be informed of the charge and given time to prepare his defense, to appear and defend himself, and to be fairly treated.

If a member or officer is guilty of a serious offense and knows that other members are in possession of the facts, he may wish to submit his resignation. When the good of the society appears to demand the departure of an offender, it is usually best for all concerned to offer him the opportunity to resign quietly before charges are preferred. The society has no obligation to suggest or accept such a resignation at any stage of the case, however, even if it is submitted on the offender's own initiative.

Steps in a Fair Disciplinary Process

Most ordinary societies should never have to hold a formal trial, and their bylaws need not be encumbered with clauses on discipline. For the protection both of the society and of its members and officers, however, the basic steps which, in any organization, make up the elements of fair disciplinary process should be understood. Any special procedures established should be built essentially around them, and the steps should be followed in the absence of such provisions. As set forth below, these are: (1) confidential investigation by a committee; (2) report of the committee, and preferral of charges if warranted; (3) formal notification of the accused; (4) trial; and (5) the assembly's review of a trial committee's findings (if the trial has been held in a committee instead of the assembly of the society).

CONFIDENTIAL INVESTIGATION BY COMMITTEE. A committee whose members are selected for known integrity and good judgment conducts a confidential inves-

tigation (including a reasonable attempt to interview the   1
accused) to determine whether to recommend that further
action, including the preferring of charges if necessary, is
warranted.

Accordingly, if the rules of the organization do not other-   5
wise provide for the method of charge and trial, a member
may, at a time when nonmembers are not present, offer a resolution to appoint an investigating committee. This resolution is to be in a form similar to the following:
                                                              10
> *Resolved,* That a committee of . . . [perhaps "five"]
> be elected by ballot to investigate allegations of neglect
> of duty in office by our treasurer, J.M., which, if true,
> cast doubt on her fitness to continue in office, and that
> the committee be instructed, if it concludes that the al-   15
> legations are well-founded, to report resolutions cover-
> ing its recommendations.

To initiate disciplinary proceedings involving a member, a
suitable resolution would be: 20

> *Resolved,* That a committee of . . . [perhaps "five"]
> be appointed by the chair [or "be elected by ballot"] to
> investigate rumors regarding the conduct of our mem-
> ber, Mr. N, which, if true, would tend to injure the good   25
> name of this organization, and that the committee be in-
> structed, if it concludes the allegations are well-founded,
> to report resolutions covering its recommendations.

For the protection of parties who may be innocent, the   30
first resolution should avoid details as much as possible. An
individual member may not prefer charges, even if that member has proof of an officer's or member's wrongdoing. If a
member introduces a resolution preferring charges unsup-
ported by an investigating committee's recommendation,   35
the chair must rule the resolution out of order, informing the

1   member that it would instead be in order to move the appointment of such a committee (by a resolution, as in the example above). A resolution is improper if it implies the truth
of specific rumors or contains insinuations unfavorable to an
5   officer or member, even one who is to be accused. It is out
of order, for example, for a resolution to begin, "Whereas, It
seems probable that the treasurer has engaged in graft, . . ."
At the first mention of the word "graft" in such a case, the
chair must instantly call to order the member attempting to
10   move the resolution.

An investigating committee appointed as described above
has no power to require the accused, or any other person, to
appear before it, but it should quietly conduct a complete
investigation, making an effort to learn all relevant facts. In-
15   formation obtained in strict confidence may help the committee to form an opinion, but it may not be reported to the
society or used in a trial—except as may be possible without
bringing out the confidential particulars. Before any action is
taken, fairness demands that the committee or some of its
20   members make a reasonable attempt to meet with the accused
for frank discussion and to hear his side of the story. It may
be possible at this stage to point out to the accused that if he
does not rectify the situation or resign, he probably will be
brought to trial.
25

REPORT OF THE INVESTIGATING COMMITTEE;
PREFERRAL OF CHARGES.   If after investigation the
committee's opinion is favorable to the accused, or if it finds
that the matter can be resolved satisfactorily without a trial,
30   it reports that fact.* But if the committee from its investiga-

---

*If the investigating committee submits a report that does not recom-
mend preferral of charges, it is within the power of the assembly nevertheless
to adopt a resolution that does prefer charges. It is also possible for the assembly to adopt instructions to the committee specifying when it is to report,
or even to adopt a motion to *Discharge a Committee* (**36**) and thereafter to

tions finds substance to the allegations and cannot resolve the
matter satisfactorily in any other way, it makes a report in
writing—which is signed by every committee member who
agrees—outlining the course of its investigation and recommending in the report the adoption of resolutions preferring
charges, arranging for a trial, and, if desired, suspending the
rights of the accused, as in the following example:

> *Resolved,* That when this meeting adjourns, it ad-
> journ to meet at 8 P.M. on Wednesday, November 15,
> 20__. [For variations depending on conditions, see the
> first paragraph following these resolutions, below.]
>
> *Resolved,* That J.M. is hereby cited to appear at said
> adjourned meeting for trial, to show cause why she
> should not be removed from the office of treasurer on
> the following charge and specifications:
>
> > *Charge.* Neglect of duty in office.
> >
> > *Specification 1.* In that J.M. has failed to ac-
> > count for at least $10,000 of the Society's funds
> > known to have been given into her custody.
> >
> > *Specification 2.* In that J.M. has repeatedly
> > failed to provide the financial records of
> > her treasurership for review by the auditing
> > committee.
>
> *Resolved,* That from the time official notification of
> this resolution is delivered to J.M.'s address until dispo-
> sition of the case, all of J.M.'s authority, rights, and du-
> ties pertaining to the office of treasurer are suspended.
>
> *Resolved,* That members S and T act as managers for
> the Society at the trial. [See below.]

consider a resolution preferring charges; but in order to provide due process
to the accused, any such instructions must allow the investigating committee
a reasonable and adequate time to investigate and prepare a report, and the
committee may be discharged only if it has had such time yet has failed to
complete its report.

1   In a disciplinary proceeding against a member, an example of
     the second and third resolutions is:

5   *Resolved,* That Mr. N is hereby cited to appear at
            said adjourned meeting for trial, to show cause why he
            should not be expelled from the Society on the follow-
            ing charge and specifications:
                 Charge. Conduct tending to injure the good
            name of this organization.
10   *Specification 1.* In that Mr. N has so con-
            ducted himself as to establish among a number
            of his acquaintances a reputation for willfully
            originating false reports against
            innocent persons.
15   *Specification 2.* In that on or about the
            evening of August 12, 20__, in the Matterhorn
            Restaurant, Mr. N was seen by patrons to be
            the apparent provoker of a needless and violent
            disturbance, causing damage to the furnishings.
20   *Resolved,* That from the time official notification
            of this resolution is delivered to Mr. N's address until
            disposition of the case, all of Mr. N's rights as a member
            (except as relate to the trial) are suspended pending
            disposition of the case.

25
          With reference to an appropriate date for which to set
     the trial, thirty days is a reasonable time to allow the accused
     to prepare his defense. When a trial is to be before the assem-
     bly of the society, it is generally a good policy to hold it
30   at a meeting devoted exclusively to the matter, such as
     an adjourned meeting as in the example above. To devote
     a meeting to the trial when there is to be another regular
     meeting between the date of adoption of these resolutions
     and the date desired for the trial, the first resolution would
35   establish a special meeting instead of an adjourned meeting

(see **9**).* If believed advisable—and particularly when the trial
is likely to be delicate, involve potential scandal, or be long
and troublesome, or when the assembly of the organization
is large—the resolutions reported by the investigating committee, instead of providing for trial before the entire assembly, can be worded so as to establish a committee to hear
the trial and report its findings and recommendations to the
assembly for action. In such a case, the first two of the resolutions above would be worded as follows:

> *Resolved,* That a trial committee consisting of Mr. H
> as chairman and members A, B, C, D, E, and F be ap-
> pointed to try the case of J.M. and report its findings
> and recommendations. [A special committee appointed
> to hear a trial must be composed of persons different
> from those on the preliminary investigating committee.
> This resolution can either be offered with the names of
> the members of the proposed trial committee specified
> as in the example, or it can contain a blank so as to leave
> the manner of their selection to the assembly.]
>
> *Resolved,* That J.M. is hereby cited to appear before
> the said trial committee at the Society hall at 8 P.M. on
> Wednesday, November 15, 20__, to show cause why she
> should not be removed from the office of treasurer on
> the following charge and specifications: . . . [setting
> them forth, as above.]

The remaining resolutions would be the same whether the
trial is to be before the assembly or before a special committee
(see above).

---

*The assembly of a society may call a special meeting for purposes of con-
ducting a trial and determining a punishment, even if the bylaws fail to provide
for special meetings or the designation in the bylaws of those who can call
special meetings does not include the assembly.

1   A *charge* sets forth an *offense*—that is, a particular kind of
act or conduct that entails liability to penalty under the governing rules—of which the accused is alleged to be guilty. A
specification states *what the accused is alleged to have done*
5   which, if true, constitutes an instance of the offense indicated
in the charge. An accused officer or member must be found
guilty of a *charge* before a penalty can be imposed. If the bylaws of the society provide for the imposition of penalties for
offenses defined in the bylaws or an adopted code of conduct
10   or similar set of rules, a charge may consist of such a defined
offense. If such particular offenses are not defined or are not
applicable, a member may be charged with "conduct tending
to injure the good name of the organization, disturb its well-
being, or hamper it in its work," or the like, and an officer
15   may be charged with misconduct of the type just mentioned
or with "misconduct in office," "neglect of duty in office,"
or "conduct that renders him [or "her"] unfit for office."

Each separate charge contained in the resolutions must
be accompanied by at least one specification, unless the inves-
20   tigating committee and the accused agree in preferring that
this information not be disclosed outside the trial. It is best
if each specification is carefully worded so as to make no
broader allegation than is believed sufficient to establish the
validity of the charge if the specification is found to be true.

25   A resolution preferring charges may (although it need
not) be accompanied by one suspending all or some specified
portion of the accused's authority, rights, and duties as an
officer or rights as a member (except those rights that relate
to the trial) pending disposition of the case, effective from
30   the time official notification of the resolution is delivered
to the accused's address.

The "managers" at the trial—referred to in the fourth resolution of the complete set shown above—have the task of
presenting the evidence against the accused, and must be
35   members of the society. Their duty, however, is not to act as

prosecutors—in the sense of making every effort to secure   *1*
conviction—but rather to strive that the trial will get at the
truth and that, in the light of all facts brought out, the outcome will be just.

5

FORMAL NOTIFICATION OF THE OFFICER OR
MEMBER.   If the society adopts resolutions ordering trial
before the assembly or a committee, the secretary immediately sends to the accused, by a method providing confirmation of delivery to his address (such as registered mail with   *10*
delivery confirmation), a letter notifying him of the date,
hour, and place of the trial, containing an exact copy of the
charge(s) and specifications with the date of their adoption,
and directing him to appear as cited—even if the accused
officer or member was present when the resolutions were   *15*
adopted. The secretary's letter of notification can reproduce
the resolutions in full and can be worded as follows:

Dear Mr. N:
        Your attention is called to the fact that the . . .   *20*
Society, at its meeting on October 14, 20__, adopted
the following resolutions:
        . . . [Text of resolutions].
        Kindly be present at the Society hall at the time
indicated above.   *25*
                                        Sincerely,
                                        John Clark, Secretary

It is the duty of the secretary to have at hand at the trial
a photocopy, printout, or other direct reproduction of the   *30*
letter of notification with the delivery confirmation attached,
as proof that it was delivered to the accused's address.

TRIAL PROCEDURE.   The trial is a formal hearing on
the validity of the charges. At the trial, the evidence against   *35*

1   the accused officer or member is presented by the managers
    for the society, and the officer or member has the right to be
    represented by counsel and to speak and produce witnesses
    in his own defense. If the charges are found to be true, a
5   penalty may be imposed or recommended; but if the charges
    are not substantiated, the officer or member is exonerated
    and any authority, rights, duties, and privileges of office or
    membership that had been suspended are automatically re-
    stored. The managers, as previously stated, must be members
10 of the society. Defense counsel can be attorney(s) or not, but
    must be member(s) of the society unless the trial body (that
    is, the assembly or the trial committee as the case may be) by
    vote agrees to permit attorney(s) who are not member(s) to
    act in this capacity. Nonmembers who consent to testify can
15 be brought in as witnesses at the trial, but such a witness
    should be allowed in the room only while testifying.
        If the accused fails to appear for trial at the appointed time
    as directed, the trial proceeds without him.
        At any time before the commencement of the trial with
20 the first of the "preliminary steps" described below, the as-
    sembly may, by majority vote, adopt a resolution to govern
    the trial specifying details not inconsistent with the proce-
    dures described here.* The resolution may include an agenda
    that establishes times for portions of the trial, such as time
25 limits for opening and closing statements. If time limits are
    imposed, they must allow the defense at least equal time for
    each element of the trial as that allowed the managers, and
    this rule may not be suspended without the consent of the
    defense.
30   At the trial, in calling the meeting to order, the chair
    should call attention to the fact that the meeting is in execu-

---

*The assembly may vary the procedures described here through adoption
of special rules of order for disciplinary proceedings either by previous notice
and a two-thirds vote or by a vote of a majority of the entire membership.

tive session (**9**), and to the attendant obligation of secrecy. Preliminary steps then include the secretary's reading from the minutes the resolutions adopted by the society relating to the trial, the chair's verification—by inquiring of the secretary—that the accused was furnished with a copy of the charges, the chair's announcement of the names of the managers for the society, and the chair's inquiry of the accused as to whether he has counsel. The trial then proceeds as follows:

a) The chair directs the secretary to read the charge and specifications.
b) The chair asks the accused how he pleads—*guilty* or *not guilty*—first to each of the specifications in order, and then to the charge.
c) If a plea of *guilty* is entered to the charge, there need be no trial, and the meeting can proceed directly to the determination of the penalty after hearing a brief statement of the facts.
d) If the plea to the charge is *not guilty*, the trial proceeds in the following order, the chair first explaining all the steps, then calling for each of them in sequence: (1) opening statements by both sides—the managers first; (2) testimony of witnesses produced by the managers for the society; (3) testimony of defense witnesses; (4) rebuttal witnesses on behalf of the society; and then on behalf of the defense, if any; and (5) closing arguments by both sides. Up until the completion of the closing arguments, no one is entitled to the floor except the managers and the defense; and they must address the chair except when questioning witnesses. Cross-examination, re-direct-examination, and re-cross-examination of witnesses is permitted, and witnesses can be recalled for further testimony as the occasion may dictate.

　　From the first of the "preliminary steps" described above up until the completion of the closing arguments:

1   i) Subject to the relevant rules and the provisions in any resolution governing the trial, the presiding officer, similarly to a judge at a trial, directs the proceedings and rules on all questions of evidence and any objec-

5   tions or requests by the managers or the defense, the merits of which may first be argued by the managers and the defense. From any such direction or ruling, a member of the assembly may take an undebatable appeal, or the presiding officer may in the first instance

10   submit any such question to a vote, without debate, by the assembly. Any motion to alter a resolution previously adopted to govern the trial, which may be proposed only by the managers or defense, or a proposal by the chair to do the same, is submitted without de-

15   bate to a vote by the assembly; its adoption requires the vote necessary to *Amend Something Previously Adopted.*

   ii) If a member of the assembly who is not a manager or with the defense wishes a question to be put to a wit-

20   ness, a manager, or the defense, the question must be delivered in writing to the presiding officer, who at an appropriate point puts it, unless he rules it out of order of his own accord or upon an objection by the managers or the defense, which ruling, like any other

25   in the trial, is subject to an undebatable appeal.

   iii) The only motions in order are the five privileged motions and those motions that relate to the conduct of the meeting or to the trial itself. Any member who is not a manager or with the defense may offer such a

30   motion, subject to the limitation in (i) above, only in writing delivered to the presiding officer,* who at an appropriate point reads the motion aloud, inquires whether there is a second (if required), and either

---

*However, any member may address the chair to appeal a ruling.

rules upon it or puts the motion to a vote without *1*
debate.

e) When the closing arguments have been completed, the
accused must leave the room. If the trial is before the assembly rather than a trial committee, the managers, de- *5*
fense counsel (if members of the society), and member
witnesses for both sides remain, take part in discussion,
and vote as any other members. The chair then states the
question on the finding as to the guilt of the accused, as
follows: "The question before the assembly [or "the com- *10*
mittee"] is: Is Mr. N guilty of the charge and specifications preferred against him?" Each of the specifications,
and then the charge, is read, opened to debate, and voted
on separately—although the several votes can be delayed
to be taken on a single ballot. *15*

The specifications or the charge can be amended to
conform to facts brought out in the trial—but not in such
a way as to find the accused guilty of a charge not wholly
included within charge(s) for which he has been tried.

If the accused is found guilty of none of the specifica- *20*
tions relating to a charge, he is automatically found not
guilty of the charge, and no vote is taken on it (or, if the
vote on the charge was already taken on the same ballot
as the vote on the specifications, the vote on the charge
is ignored). If the accused is found guilty of one or more *25*
of the specifications but not of the charge, and if a lower
degree or level of the offense charged is defined in the
organization's bylaws, adopted code of conduct, or similar set of rules, then such a lesser charge may be moved
and voted on. *30*

If the accused is found guilty, the chair announces that
the next item of business is the determination of the
penalty. One of the managers for the society usually makes
a motion for a penalty the managers feel appropriate, although any member may move that a specific penalty be *35*

1 imposed; this motion is debatable and amendable. On the demand of a single member both the question of guilt and the question of the penalty must be voted on by ballot.

5 The usual possible penalties for an officer are censure or removal from office, although in special circumstances others may be appropriate (for example, to repay into the society's treasury funds that the officer has been found guilty of misappropriating, perhaps with an added fine). For all of these, including removal from office, a majority 10 vote is required. Penalties appropriate in disciplinary proceedings against members are discussed on page 643. For expulsion, a two-thirds vote is required.

 f) After voting is completed, the accused is called back into the hall and advised of the result.

15 A member who votes for a finding of guilt at a trial should be morally convinced, on the basis of the evidence he has heard, that the accused is guilty.

20 ASSEMBLY'S REVIEW OF A TRIAL COMMITTEE'S FINDINGS. If the trial has been held before a trial committee instead of the assembly of the society, this committee reports to the assembly in executive session (9) the results of 25 its trial of the case, with resolutions—in cases where its finding is one of *guilty*—covering the penalty it recommends that the society impose. The report is prepared in writing and includes, to the extent possible without disclosing confidential information which should be kept within the committee, a summary of the basis for the committee's finding.

30 Unless the report exonerates the accused, he is then permitted—personally, through counsel, or both, as he prefers—to make a statement of the case, after which the committee is given the opportunity to present a statement in rebuttal. The accused—and defense counsel if not member(s)—then leave 35 the room, and the assembly acts upon the resolutions submitted by the committee. The members of the committee

remain and vote on the case the same as other members of the society.

Under this procedure, the assembly can decline to impose any penalty, notwithstanding the trial committee's recommendation; or it can reduce the recommended penalty; but it cannot increase the penalty. The assembly cannot impose a penalty if the trial committee has found the accused not guilty.

Committee on Discipline

In some professional societies and other organizations where particular aspects of discipline are of special importance, the handling of such matters is simplified by providing in the bylaws for a standing Committee on Discipline (see **50**, **56**). Its prescribed duties are normally to be alert to disciplinary problems, to investigate them, to introduce all necessary resolutions, and—in event of a trial—to manage the case for the society.

This committee may also have the duty of hearing the actual trial, in which case it should be large enough that a subcommittee can perform the confidential investigation as described on pages 656–58. Under the latter practice, the full Committee on Discipline adopts the charge and specifications, and the chairman of the committee sends the citation to the accused and presides at the trial, which is conducted just as it would be if held before the assembly. It is generally best not to empower the committee to *impose* a penalty, however, but to require it to report its recommended disciplinary measures to the society for action, just as in the case of a special committee to hear a trial.

In organizations where disciplinary matters may arise with some frequency, the system of having a Committee on Discipline has the advantages of not unduly inconveniencing the society, and of promoting the avoidance of scandal and the settlement of disciplinary problems without an actual trial.

CHARTS, TABLES,
AND LISTS

I. CHART FOR DETERMINING WHEN EACH SUBSIDIARY OR PRIVILEGED MOTION IS IN ORDER

In the chart on the two following pages, the privileged, subsidiary, and main motions are listed in order of rank, the motion at the top taking precedence over all the others, and each of the remaining ones taking precedence over all those below it. A main motion is in order only when no other motion is pending.

When a given one of the motions listed is immediately pending, then: (a) any other motion appearing *above* it in the list is *in order*, unless a condition stated opposite the other motion causes that motion to be out of order; and (b) motions listed *below* the given motion which are not already pending are *out of order* (except for the application of *Amend* or the *Previous Question* to certain motions ranking above them as noted in the next paragraph; see also Standard Characteristic 2, pp. 132 and 198–99).

With respect to arrowed lines in the chart, (————) indicates applicability of all of the subsidiary motions to the main motion; (▬▬▬), applicability of *Amend* to certain other motions in the order of precedence; (▬ ▬ ▬), applicability of *Limit or Extend Limits of Debate* to debatable motions in the order of precedence; and (▬ ▬ ▬), applicability of the *Previous Question* to the motions that are debatable or amendable.

I. CHART FOR DETERMINING WHEN EACH SUBSIDIARY OR PRIVILEGED MOTION IS IN ORDER (cont.)

Order of Precedence of Motions

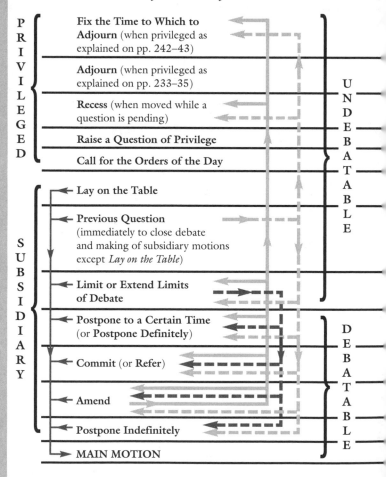

P R I V I L E G E D

Fix the Time to Which to Adjourn (when privileged as explained on pp. 242–43)

Adjourn (when privileged as explained on pp. 233–35)

Recess (when moved while a question is pending)

Raise a Question of Privilege

Call for the Orders of the Day

U N D E B A T A B L E

S U B S I D I A R Y

← **Lay on the Table**

← **Previous Question** (immediately to close debate and making of subsidiary motions except *Lay on the Table*)

← **Limit or Extend Limits of Debate**

← **Postpone to a Certain Time** (or **Postpone Definitely**)

← **Commit** (or **Refer**)

← **Amend**

← **Postpone Indefinitely**

→ **MAIN MOTION**

D E B A T A B L E

Other Conditions Affecting Admissibility
MOTION DIRECTLY TO LEFT ON FACING PAGE IS OUT OF ORDER WHEN:

- a motion to *Suspend the Rules* relating to priority of business is pending

- a *Point of Order*, undebatable *Appeal*, or one of the five *Requests and Inquiries*—not adhering to main question—is pending

- a motion which cannot be debated or amended is immediately pending

- any undebatable question is immediately pending; also when motion(s) under an order for the *Previous Question* remain to be voted on

- any undebatable question except *Division of the Question* or *Consider by Paragraph or Seriatim* is immediately pending; also when motion(s) under an order for the *Previous Question* remain to be voted on

- a motion to *Reconsider* is pending, or any undebatable question except *Division of the Question* or *Consider by Paragraph or Seriatim* is immediately pending; also when motion(s) under an order for the *Previous Question* remain to be voted on

- the application would be to the main question, and any motion except *Postpone Indefinitely* is pending; also, in any application, when motion(s) under an order for the *Previous Question* remain to be voted on

- any motion except the main question is pending; also when the *Previous Question* has been ordered

- any motion is pending

II. TABLE OF RULES RELATING TO MOTIONS

MOTION	CLASS[1]	IN ORDER WHEN ANOTHER HAS THE FLOOR	MUST BE SECONDED[2]
1. Main motion or question (**10**)	M	No	Yes
2. Adjourn, ordinary case in societies (**21**)	P	No	Yes
3. Adjourn at or to a future time, or in advance of a time already set, or when the assembly will thereby be dissolved (**8, 10, 21**)	M	No	Yes
4. Adopt, accept, or agree to a report (**10, 51**)	M	No	Yes
5. Adopt bylaws or constitution, initially in forming a society (**10, 54, 56**)	M	No	Yes[3]
6. Adopt revised bylaws or constitution (**35, 56, 57**)	M/B	No	Yes[3]
7. Adopt special rules of order (**2, 10**)	M	No	Yes
8. Adopt ordinary standing rules (p. 18) (**2, 10**)	M	No	Yes

[1]Key to classification symbols: M—main motions; S—subsidiary motions; P—privileged motions; I—incidental motions; B—motions that bring a question again before the assembly; M/B—incidental main motions classed with motions that bring a question again before the assembly (see pp. 74ff.).

(For forms used in making motions, see Table III.)

DEBATABLE	AMENDABLE	VOTE REQUIRED FOR ADOPTION	CAN BE RECONSIDERED
Yes	Yes	Majority, except as explained on pages 103–4	Yes
No	No	Majority	No
Yes	Yes	Majority	No
Yes	Yes	Majority	Yes
Yes	Yes	Majority	Negative vote only
Yes	Yes	As provided in existing bylaws. (In absence of such provision, same as in next line)	Negative vote only
Yes	Yes	(a) Previous notice *and* two-thirds; or (b) majority of entire membership	Negative vote only
Yes	Yes	Majority	Yes

[2]Motions listed as requiring a second do not need to be seconded when made by direction of a board or committee.

[3]In practice, motion is usually made by the reporting member of a committee, in which case it does not require a second.

II. TABLE OF RULES RELATING TO MOTIONS (cont.)

MOTION	CLASS[1]	IN ORDER WHEN ANOTHER HAS THE FLOOR	MUST BE SECONDED[2]
9. Adopt parliamentary standing rules in a convention (**10, 59**)	M	No	Yes[3]
10. Adopt agenda or program (**10, 41, 59**)	M	No	Yes[3]
11. Amend a pending motion (**12**)	S	No	Yes
12. Amend an amendment of a pending motion (**12**)	S	No	Yes
13. Amend Something Previously Adopted, general case, including ordinary standing rules (**35**)	M/B	No	Yes
14. Amend parliamentary standing rules in a convention, when they are not pending (**35, 59**)	M/B	No	Yes
15. Amend adopted agenda or program with reference to items not yet reached (**35, 41, 59**)	M/B	No	Yes[3]

[1]Key to classification symbols: M—main motions; S—subsidiary motions; P—privileged motions; I—incidental motions; B—motions that bring a question again before the assembly; M/B—incidental main motions classed with motions that bring a question again before the assembly (see pp. 74ff.).

[2]Motions listed as requiring a second do not need to be seconded when made by direction of a board or committee.

(For forms used in making motions, see Table III.)

DEBATABLE	AMENDABLE	VOTE REQUIRED FOR ADOPTION	CAN BE RECONSIDERED
Yes	Yes	Two-thirds	Negative vote only
Yes	Yes	Majority; but in session with existing order of business, two-thirds if in conflict with it or sets special order	Negative vote only
If motion to be amended is debatable[4]	Yes	Majority	Yes
If motion to be amended is debatable[4]	No	Majority	Yes
Yes	Yes	(a) Majority with notice; or (b) two-thirds; or (c) majority of entire membership	Negative vote only
Yes	Yes	Two-thirds; or majority of all having convention voting rights who have been registered	Negative vote only
Yes	Yes	As immediately above, though often by unanimous consent after Program Committee's recommendation	Negative vote only

[3]In practice, motion is usually made by the reporting member of a committee, in which case it does not require a second.

[4]Debate on motion must be confined to *its* merits only, and cannot go into the main question except as necessary for debate of the immediately pending question.

II. TABLE OF RULES RELATING TO MOTIONS (cont.)

MOTION	CLASS[1]	IN ORDER WHEN ANOTHER HAS THE FLOOR	MUST BE SECONDED[2]
16. Amend bylaws or constitution, when not pending (**35, 57**)	M/B	No	Yes
17. Amend special rules of order, when not pending (**2, 35**)	M/B	No	Yes
18. Appeal, general case (**24**)	I	Yes, at time of appealed ruling	Yes
19. Appeal, relating to indecorum or transgression of rules of speaking, or to the priority of business, or if made when an undebatable question is immediately pending or involved in the appeal (**24**)	I	Yes, at time of appealed ruling	Yes
20. Ballot, to order the vote on pending question to be taken by (**30, 45**)	I	No	Yes
21. Blank, to create by striking out (**12**)	I	No	Yes
22. Blanks, proposals for filling (**12**)	—	Can be called out when chair asks for them	No

[1]Key to classification symbols: M—main motions; S—subsidiary motions; P—privileged motions; I—incidental motions; B—motions that bring a question again before the assembly; M/B—incidental main motions classed with motions that bring a question again before the assembly (see pp. 74ff.).

(For forms used in making motions, see Table III.)

DEBATABLE	AMENDABLE	VOTE REQUIRED FOR ADOPTION	CAN BE RECONSIDERED
Yes	Yes	As provided in bylaws or constitution. (In absence of such provision, same as in No. 17, following)	Negative vote only
Yes	Yes	(a) Previous notice *and* two-thirds; or (b) majority of entire membership	Negative vote only
Yes,[4] under rules stated on pages 257–58	No	Majority in negative required to reverse chair's decision	Yes
No	No	Majority in negative required to reverse chair's decision	Yes
No	Yes	Majority	Yes
No	No	Majority	No
If filling a blank in a debatable motion[4]	No	Majority	Yes

[2]Motions listed as requiring a second do not need to be seconded when made by direction of a board or committee.

[4]Debate on motion or proposal must be confined to *its* merits only, and cannot go into the main question except as necessary for debate of the immediately pending question.

II. TABLE OF RULES RELATING TO MOTIONS (cont.)

MOTION	CLASS[1]	IN ORDER WHEN ANOTHER HAS THE FLOOR	MUST BE SECONDED[2]
23. Change or depart from adopted convention agenda or program, immediately to take up a matter out of its proper order (**25, 35**)	I	No	Yes
24. Commit, Refer, or Recommit a pending question (**13**)	S	No	Yes
25. Committee, to refer a matter that is not pending to (**10, 13**)	M	No	Yes
26. Consider informally (**13, 52**)	S	No	Yes
27. Consider by Paragraph or Seriatim (**28**)	I	No	Yes
28. Continue speaking after indecorum, to grant permission to (**23, 61**)	I	No	Yes, if in form of a motion
29. Debate and amendment, to obtain immediate closing of	(See *Previous Question*, No. 65)		
30. Debate, to Limit or Extend Limits of, on a pending question (**15**)	S	No	Yes

[1]Key to classification symbols: M—main motions; S—subsidiary motions; P—privileged motions; I—incidental motions; B—motions that bring a question again before the assembly; M/B—incidental main motions classed with motions that bring a question again before the assembly (see pp. 74ff.).

[2]Motions listed as requiring a second do not need to be seconded when made by direction of a board or committee.

(For forms used in making motions, see Table III.)

DEBATABLE	AMENDABLE	VOTE REQUIRED FOR ADOPTION	CAN BE RECONSIDERED
No	No	Two-thirds; or majority of all having convention voting rights who have been registered	No
Yes[4]	Yes	Majority	If committee has not begun consideration of the question[5]
Yes	Yes	Majority	If committee has not begun work on the matter
Yes[4]	Yes	Majority	Negative vote only
No	Yes	Majority	No
No	No	Majority	Yes
No	Yes	Two-thirds	Yes; but if vote was affirmative, only unexecuted part of order[5]

[4]Debate on motion must be confined to *its* merits only, and cannot go into the main question except as necessary for debate of the immediately pending question.

[5]A negative vote on this motion can be reconsidered only until such time as progress in business or debate has made it essentially a new question.

II. TABLE OF RULES RELATING TO MOTIONS (cont.)

MOTION	CLASS[1]	IN ORDER WHEN ANOTHER HAS THE FLOOR	MUST BE SECONDED[2]
31. Debate, to Limit or Extend Limits of, for the duration of a meeting (**10, 15**)	M	No	Yes
32. Discharge a Committee (**36**)	B or M/B[6]	No	Yes
33. Discharge a Committee, when it has failed to report at prescribed time, or while assembly is considering partial report of committee (**36**)	B or M/B[6]	No	Yes
34. Division of the Assembly (call for verification of a voting result by an uncounted rising vote) (**29**)	I	Yes	No
35. Count of vote on Division, to order, if chair does not do so (**4, 29, 30, 45**)	I	Yes	Yes
36. Division of a Question (**27**)	I	No	Yes

[1]Key to classification symbols: M—main motions; S—subsidiary motions; P—privileged motions; I—incidental motions; B—motions that bring a question again before the assembly; M/B—incidental main motions classed with motions that bring a question again before the assembly (see pp. 74ff.).

(For forms used in making motions, see Table III.)

DEBATABLE	AMENDABLE	VOTE REQUIRED FOR ADOPTION	CAN BE RECONSIDERED
Yes	Yes	Two-thirds	Yes
Yes; debate can go into question in hands of the committee	Yes	(a) Majority with notice; or (b) two-thirds; or (c) majority of entire membership	Negative vote only
Yes; debate can go into question in hands of the committee	Yes	Majority	Negative vote only
No	No	Demand of single member compels Division	No
No	Yes	Majority	No
No	Yes	Majority	No

²Motions listed as requiring a second do not need to be seconded when made by direction of a board or committee.

⁶B if committee is discharged from consideration of question that was pending at time of referral and was referred by subsidiary motion to *Commit*; M/B if subject was referred by a main motion (see pp. 313–14).

II. TABLE OF RULES RELATING TO MOTIONS (cont.)

MOTION	CLASS[1]	IN ORDER WHEN ANOTHER HAS THE FLOOR	MUST BE SECONDED[2]
37. Call for a separate vote on a resolution which is one of a series *on different subjects* offered by a single motion (pp. 110, 274–75) (**10, 27**)	I	Yes	No
38. Duty, to be excused from (**32**)	I	Yes	Yes, if motion is made by member to be excused; no, if made by another member
39. Effect, fix time for taking (**10, 12, 57**)	M, S, or I[7]	No	Yes
40. Extend time for consideration of pending question, or time until announced or scheduled adjournment or recess (**18**)	I	Yes, when orders of the day are announced or called for	Yes
41. Fix the Time to Which to Adjourn, if moved while a question is pending (**22**)	P	No	Yes
42. Fix the Time to Which to Adjourn, if moved while no question is pending (**10, 22**)	M	No	Yes

[1]Key to classification symbols: M—main motions; S—subsidiary motions; P—privileged motions; I—incidental motions; B—motions that bring a question again before the assembly; M/B—incidental main motions classed with motions that bring a question again before the assembly (see pp. 74ff.).

(For forms used in making motions, see Table III.)

DEBATABLE	AMENDABLE	VOTE REQUIRED FOR ADOPTION	CAN BE RECONSIDERED
No	No	Demand of single member compels specified separate vote	No
Yes	Yes	Majority	Negative vote only
Yes	Yes	Majority	Yes[8]
No	No	Two-thirds	No
No	Yes	Majority	Yes
Yes	Yes	Majority	Yes

[2]Motions listed as requiring a second do not need to be seconded when made by direction of a board or committee.

[7]See p. 597. This motion can be made as a main motion, as an amendment to enacting words, or as an incidental motion, and the same rules apply.

[8]See, however, Standard Characteristic 2, pp. 318–19 and pp. 327ff.

II. TABLE OF RULES RELATING TO MOTIONS (cont.)

MOTION	CLASS[1]	IN ORDER WHEN ANOTHER HAS THE FLOOR	MUST BE SECONDED[2]
43. Information, Request for (**33**)	I	Yes	No
44. Lay on the Table (**17**)	S	No	Yes
45. Minutes, to approve (when proposed by a motion) (**10, 41, 48**)	M	No	Yes
46. Minutes, to correct before adoption (when done by a motion) (**12, 41, 48**)	S	No	Yes
47. Minutes, to correct after approval	(See *Amend Something Previously Adopted*, No. 13.)		
48. Minutes, to dispense with reading of (**48**)	I	No	Yes
49. Nominations, to make (**46**)	—	No	No
50. Nominations, to close (**31**)	I	No	Yes
51. Nominations, to reopen (**31**)	I	No	Yes
52. Nominations, motions relating to (except to close or reopen nominations) made while election is pending (**31**)	I	No	Yes

[1]Key to classification symbols: M—main motions; S—subsidiary motions; P—privileged motions; I—incidental motions; B—motions that bring a question again before the assembly; M/B—incidental main motions classed with motions that bring a question again before the assembly (see pp. 74ff.).

[2]Motions listed as requiring a second do not need to be seconded when made by direction of a board or committee.

(For forms used in making motions, see Table III.)

DEBATABLE	AMENDABLE	VOTE REQUIRED FOR ADOPTION	CAN BE RECONSIDERED
No	No	Is not voted on	No
No	No	Majority	Negative vote only[9]
Yes	Yes	Is not voted on (see pp. 354–55)	Yes
Yes	Yes	Majority	Yes
No	No	Majority	No
Yes	No	Majority for election unless bylaws provide otherwise	Election cannot be reconsidered after person elected learns of it, and has not declined
No	Yes	Two-thirds	No
No	Yes	Majority	Negative vote only
No	Yes	Majority	Yes

[9]A negative vote on this motion can be reconsidered only until such time as either (a) progress in business or debate has made it essentially a new question, or (b) something urgent has arisen that was not known when the assembly rejected the motion.

II. TABLE OF RULES RELATING TO MOTIONS (cont.)

MOTION	CLASS[1]	IN ORDER WHEN ANOTHER HAS THE FLOOR	MUST BE SECONDED[2]
53. Nominations, motions relating to, made while election is not pending (**10, 46**)	M	No	Yes
54. Objection to Consideration of a Question (**26**)	I	Yes, until debate has begun or a subsidiary motion other than *Lay on the Table* has been stated by the chair	No
55. Order, to make a special, when question is not pending (see No. 63) (**10, 41**)	M	No	Yes
56. Orders of the Day, to Call for (**18**)	P	Yes	No
57. Orders of the day, to proceed to (**18**)	—	Chair at his discretion puts this question when orders of the day are due to be taken up or are called for	—
58. Orders of the day, when pending (**10, 18, 41**)	M	—	—
59. Order, Point of, Question of, or Calling a Member to (**23**)	I	Yes	No
60. Parliamentary Inquiry (**33**)	I	Yes	No

[1]Key to classification symbols: M—main motions; S—subsidiary motions; P—privileged motions; I—incidental motions; B—motions that bring a question again before the assembly; M/B—incidental main motions classed with motions that bring a question again before the assembly (see pp. 74ff.).

(For forms used in making motions, see Table III.)

DEBATABLE	AMENDABLE	VOTE REQUIRED FOR ADOPTION	CAN BE RECONSIDERED
Yes	Yes	Majority	Yes
No	No	Two-thirds against consideration sustains objection	Negative vote (sustaining objection) only
Yes[4]	Yes	Two-thirds	Yes
No	No	Must be enforced on demand of one member unless set aside by a two-thirds vote (see pp. 222–23)	No
No	No	Two-thirds in negative required to refuse to proceed to orders of the day	No
Yes	Yes	Majority, except as explained on pages 103–4	Yes
No (but chair can permit full explanation and can submit question to assembly, in which case rule is as for *Appeal*; see No. 18)	No	Is ruled upon by chair (unless he submits question to judgment of majority in assembly)	No
No	No	Is not voted on, but is responded to by chair	—

[2]Motions listed as requiring a second do not need to be seconded when made by direction of a board or committee.

[4]Debate on motion must be confined to *its* merits only, and cannot go into the main question except as necessary for debate of the immediately pending question.

II. TABLE OF RULES RELATING TO MOTIONS (cont.)

MOTION	CLASS[1]	IN ORDER WHEN ANOTHER HAS THE FLOOR	MUST BE SECONDED[2]
61. Postpone Indefinitely (**11**)	S	No	Yes
62. Postpone to a Certain Time, or Definitely, applied to a pending question (**14**)	S	No	Yes
63. Postpone a pending question to a certain time and make it a special order (see No. 55) (**14**)	S	No	Yes
64. Postpone an event or action previously scheduled (**35**)	M/B	No	Yes
65. Previous Question (immediately to close debate and the making of subsidiary motions except the motion to Lay on the Table) (**16**)	S	No	Yes
66. Proviso (**10, 12, 57**)	M, S, or I[7]	No	Yes
67. Question of Privilege, to Raise while regular introduction as main motion is not in order (**19**)	P	Yes, but should not interrupt a person who has begun to speak, unless unavoidable	No; but if the question of privilege thereby raised is in the form of a motion, the motion must be seconded

[1]Key to classification symbols: M—main motions; S—subsidiary motions; P—privileged motions; I—incidental motions; B—motions that bring a question again before the assembly; M/B—incidental main motions classed with motions that bring a question again before the assembly (see pp. 74ff.).

[2]Motions listed as requiring a second do not need to be seconded when made by direction of a board or committee.

(For forms used in making motions, see Table III.)

DEBATABLE	AMENDABLE	VOTE REQUIRED FOR ADOPTION	CAN BE RECONSIDERED
Yes; debate can go into main question	No	Majority	Affirmative vote only
Yes[4]	Yes	Majority, unless it makes question a special order	Yes[5]
Yes[4]	Yes	Two-thirds	Yes[5]
Yes	Yes	(a) Majority with notice; or (b) two-thirds; or (c) majority of entire membership	Negative vote only
No	No	Two-thirds	Yes; but if vote was affirmative, only before any vote has been taken under it[5]
Yes	Yes	Majority	Yes
No	No	Admissibility of question is ruled upon by chair	No

[4]Debate on motion must be confined to *its* merits only, and cannot go into the main question except as necessary for debate of the immediately pending question.

[5]A negative vote on this motion can be reconsidered only until such time as progress in business or debate has made it essentially a new question.

[7]See p. 597. This motion can be made as a main motion, as an amendment to enacting words, or as an incidental motion, and the same rules apply.

II. TABLE OF RULES RELATING TO MOTIONS (cont.)

MOTION	CLASS[1]	IN ORDER WHEN ANOTHER HAS THE FLOOR	MUST BE SECONDED[2]
68. Question of privilege in the form of a main motion, whether introduced when an ordinary main motion is in order or admitted by raising a question of privilege (**10, 19**)	M	Floor should be obtained in usual manner if question is brought up while main motion is in order	Yes
69. Ratify, or Confirm (**10**)	M	No	Yes
70. Read Papers, to grant permission to (**33**)	I	If not granted by unanimous consent, can be moved by person requesting permission or by another while the former has the floor	Yes, if motion is made by person requesting permission; no, if made by another member
71. Recess, to take a, if moved while business is pending (**20**)	P	No	Yes
72. Recess, to take a, if moved while no question is pending (**10, 20**)	M	No	Yes
73. Reconsider (**37**)	B	When another *has been assigned* the floor, but not after he has begun to speak	Yes

[1]Key to classification symbols: M—main motions; S—subsidiary motions; P—privileged motions; I—incidental motions; B—motions that bring a question again before the assembly; M/B—incidental main motions classed with motions that bring a question again before the assembly (see pp. 74ff.).

(For forms used in making motions, see Table III.)

DEBATABLE	AMENDABLE	VOTE REQUIRED FOR ADOPTION	CAN BE RECONSIDERED
Yes	Yes	Majority, except as explained on pages 103–4	Yes
Yes	Yes	Majority, except as explained on pages 103–4	Yes
No	No	Majority	Yes
No	Yes	Majority	No
Yes	Yes	Majority	No
If motion to be reconsidered is debatable, in which case debate can go into that question	No	Majority	No

[2]Motions listed as requiring a second do not need to be seconded when made by direction of a board or committee.

II. TABLE OF RULES RELATING TO MOTIONS (cont.)

MOTION	CLASS[1]	IN ORDER WHEN ANOTHER HAS THE FLOOR	MUST BE SECONDED[2]
74. Reconsider, in a committee (**37**)	B	Cannot interrupt a person speaking	No
75. Reconsider, call up motion to (**37**)	—	No	No
76. Rescind and expunge from minutes (**35**)	M/B	No	Yes
77. Rescind, Repeal, or Annul (**35**)	M/B	No	Yes
78. Refer	(See *Commit, Committee*, Nos. 24 and 25.)		
79. Substitute	(See *Amend a pending motion*, No. 11.)		
80. Suspend the Rules (as applied to rules of order) (**25**)	I	No	Yes
81. Suspend ordinary standing rules, or standing rules in a convention (**25, 59**)	I	No	Yes
82. Take from the Table (**34**)	B	No	Yes
83. Take up a question out of its proper order	(See *Suspend the Rules [as applied to rules of order]*, No. 80; cf. also No. 23)		

[1]Key to classification symbols: M—main motions; S—subsidiary motions; P—privileged motions; I—incidental motions; B—motions that bring a question again before the assembly; M/B—incidental main motions classed with motions that bring a question again before the assembly (see pp. 74ff.).

(For forms used in making motions, see Table III.)

DEBATABLE	AMENDABLE	VOTE REQUIRED FOR ADOPTION	CAN BE RECONSIDERED
As in No. 73, preceding	No	Two-thirds; but majority if every committee member who voted with prevailing side is present or was notified	No
—	—	—	—
Yes	Yes	Majority of entire membership	Negative vote only
Yes	Yes	(a) Majority with notice; or (b) two-thirds; or (c) majority of entire membership	Negative vote only
No	No	Two-thirds—except where rule protects a minority of less than one third (see p. 261)	No
No	No	Majority	No
No	No	Majority	No

[2]Motions listed as requiring a second do not need to be seconded when made by direction of a board or committee.

II. TABLE OF RULES RELATING TO MOTIONS (cont.)

MOTION	CLASS[1]	IN ORDER WHEN ANOTHER HAS THE FLOOR	MUST BE SECONDED[2]
84. Voting, motions relating to, if made while subject is pending (**30**)	I	No	Yes
85. Voting, motions relating to, if made while no question is pending (**10, 30, 45, 46**)	M	No	Yes
86. Withdraw or Modify a Motion, to grant maker permission to, after motion has been stated by the chair (**33**)	I	If not granted by unanimous consent, can be moved by person requesting permission, or by another while the former has the floor	Yes, if motion is made by person requesting permission; no, if made by another member

[1]Key to classification symbols: M—main motions; S—subsidiary motions; P—privileged motions; I—incidental motions; B—motions that bring a question again before the assembly; M/B—incidental main motions classed with motions that bring a question again before the assembly (see pp. 74ff.).

(For forms used in making motions, see Table III.)

DEBATABLE	AMENDABLE	VOTE REQUIRED FOR ADOPTION	CAN BE RECONSIDERED
No	Yes	Majority, except two-thirds for motion to close polls	To close polls, no; to reopen polls, negative vote only;[10] all others, yes
Yes	Yes	Majority	Yes
No	No	Majority	As to withdrawal, negative vote only; as to modification, yes

[9]Motions listed as requiring a second do not need to be seconded when made by direction of a board or committee.

[10]The vote on a motion ordering that the polls be closed or reopened at a specified time can be reconsidered at any time before the order has been carried out.

III. SAMPLE FORMS USED IN MAKING MOTIONS

1. Main motion or question (original)
   [For forms see pp. 33, 104–10]

2. Adjourn, ordinary case in societies
   • I move to adjourn.

3. Adjourn at or to a future time, or in advance of a time already set, or when the assembly will thereby be dissolved
   • I move to adjourn at 4 P.M.
   • I move that the meeting adjourn to meet at 8 P.M. Tuesday.
   • I move to adjourn.
   • I move to adjourn sine die.

4. Adopt, accept, or agree to a report
   • I move that the report be adopted.

5. Adopt bylaws or constitution, initially in forming a society
   • On behalf of the committee appointed to draw up bylaws, I move the adoption of the bylaws submitted by the committee.

6. Adopt revised bylaws or constitution
   • On behalf of the committee on revision of the bylaws, I move that, as a substitute for the present bylaws, the bylaws submitted by the committee be adopted with the following provisos: ...

7. Adopt special rules of order
   • In accordance with notice given at the last meeting, I move that the following resolution be adopted as a special rule of order: "*Resolved*, That ... "

8. Adopt ordinary standing rules
   • I move that the following resolution be adopted as a standing rule: "*Resolved*, That ... "

9. Adopt parliamentary standing rules in a convention
   • By direction of the Committee on Standing Rules, I move the adoption of the Standing Rules of the Convention as just read.

10. Adopt convention agenda or program
    • By direction of the Program Committee, I move the adoption of the Convention Program as printed.

11. Amend a pending motion
    • I move to amend by adding …
    • I move to amend by inserting the word … before the word …
    • I move to amend by striking out the second paragraph.
    • I move to amend by striking out "concrete" and inserting "blacktop."
    • I move to substitute for the pending resolution the following resolution: "*Resolved*, That … "
    [For manner in which above forms are varied in the particular case, see subsections under *Rules for the Different Forms of Amendment* in 12.]

12. Amend an amendment of a pending motion
    • I move to insert in the pending amendment the word … before the word …
    • I move to amend the pending amendment by … [varying form to fit particular case, as under *Amend a pending motion*, No. 11].

13. Amend Something Previously Adopted, general case, including ordinary standing rules
    • I move to amend the resolution relating to … , adopted at the September meeting, by …

14. Amend parliamentary standing rules in a convention, when they are not pending
    • I move to amend Standing Rule No. 6 by …

III. SAMPLE FORMS USED IN MAKING MOTIONS (cont.)

15. Amend adopted convention agenda or program with reference to items not yet reached
    • I move to amend the agenda [or "program"] by ...

16. Amend bylaws or constitution, when not pending
    • In accordance with notice given, I move the adoption of the following amendment to the bylaws ...

17. Amend special rules of order, when not pending
    • In accordance with notice given, I move to amend Special Rule of Order No. 3 by ...

18. Appeal, general case
    • I appeal from the decision of the chair.

19. Appeal, relating to indecorum or transgression of rules of speaking, or to the priority of business, or if made when an undebatable question is immediately pending or involved in the appeal
    [Same form as No. 18]

20. Ballot, to order the vote on a pending question to be taken by
    • I move that the vote on the pending question be taken by ballot.

21. Blank, to create by striking out
    • I move to create a blank by striking out "$10,000."

22. Blanks, proposals for filling
    • I suggest $20,000.

23. Change or depart from adopted convention agenda or program, immediately to take up a matter out of its proper order
    • I move to suspend the rules and take up ...

24. Commit, Refer, or Recommit a pending question
- I move to refer the motion to the Program Committee.
- I move that the motion be referred to a committee of three to be appointed by the chair.

[For additional variations see p. 178]

25. Committee, to refer a matter that is not pending to
- I move that a committee [stating number and manner of selection] be appointed to conduct a survey relating to …

26. Consider informally
- I move that the question be considered informally.

27. Consider by Paragraph or Seriatim
- I move that the resolution be considered by paragraph.

28. Continue speaking after indecorum, to grant permission to
- [Chair usually puts question without a motion. When done by a motion:] I move that the member be permitted [or "allowed"] to continue speaking.

29. Debate and amendment, to obtain immediate closing of
[See *Previous Question*, No. 65]

30. Debate, to Limit or Extend Limits of, on a pending question
- I move that debate be limited to one speech of three minutes for each member.

[For variations in particular cases see p. 196.]

31. Debate, to Limit or Extend Limits of, for the duration of a meeting
- I move that during this meeting debate be limited to five minutes for each member.

III. SAMPLE FORMS USED IN MAKING MOTIONS (cont.)

32. Discharge a Committee
   - [For a standing committee:] I move that the Finance Committee be discharged from further consideration of the resolution relating to ...
   - [For a special committee:] I move that the committee to which was referred ... be discharged.

33. Discharge a Committee, when it has failed to report at prescribed time, or while assembly is considering partial report of committee
   [Same forms as No. 32]

34. Division of the Assembly (call for verification of a voting result by an uncounted rising vote)
   - Division!
   - I call for a division.

35. Count of vote on Division, to order, if chair does not do so
   - I move that the vote be counted.
   - I move for [or "demand"] tellers.
   - I move that the vote on this motion be by counted division.

36. Division of a Question
   - I move to divide the resolution so as to consider separately ...

37. Call for a separate vote on a resolution which is one of a series *on different subjects* offered by a single motion
   - I call for a separate vote on the third resolution.

38. Duty, to be excused from
   - I move [or "ask"] that I be excused from ...
   - I move that the resignation be accepted.

39. Effect, fix time for taking
   - I move that the amendment to the ... take effect as of ...

40. Extend time for consideration of pending question, or time until scheduled adjournment or recess
- I move that the time for consideration of the pending resolution be extended for twenty minutes.
- I move to suspend the rules which interfere with continuing the consideration of the motion.
- I move that the time until the recess be extended ten minutes.

41. Fix the Time to Which to Adjourn, if moved while a question is pending
- I move that when this [or, "the"] meeting adjourns, it adjourn to meet next Tuesday at 8 P.M.

42. Fix the Time to Which to Adjourn, if moved while no question is pending
  [Same form as No. 41]

43. Information, Request for
- I have a request for information.
- A point of information, please.
- Will the member yield for a question?

44. Lay on the Table
- I move that the motion be laid on the table.

45. Minutes, to approve
- [Normally done by unanimous consent. When proposed by a motion:] I move that the minutes be approved as read [or "as corrected"].

46. Minutes, to correct before adoption
- [Usually suggested informally and done by unanimous consent except in cases of disagreement. When done by a motion:] I move to amend the minutes by ...

47. Minutes, to correct after approval
  [See *Amend Something Previously Adopted*, No. 13.]

III. SAMPLE FORMS USED IN MAKING MOTIONS (cont.)

48. Minutes, to dispense with reading of
   • I move that the reading of the minutes be dispensed with.

49. Nominations, to make
   • I nominate George Beall.

50. Nominations, to close
   • I move that nominations be closed.

51. Nominations, to reopen
   • I move that nominations for ... be reopened.

52. Nominations, motions relating to (except to close or reopen nominations) made while election is pending
   • I move that candidates for service on the committee be nominated from the floor.

53. Nominations, motions relating to, made while election is not pending
   [Same form as No. 52]

54. Objection to Consideration of a Question
   • I object to the consideration of the question.

55. Order, to make a special, when question is not pending
   • I move that the following resolution be made a special order for 3 P.M.: "*Resolved,* That ... "

56. Orders of the Day, to Call for
   • I call for the orders of the day.

57. Orders of the day, to proceed to
   [Chair at his discretion puts this question when orders of the day are due to be taken up or are called for.]

58. Order of the day, when pending
   [Will have been introduced earlier as a main motion.]

59. Order, Point of, Question of, or Calling a Member to
   - Point of order!
   - I rise to a point of order.
   - I call the member to order. [Applying to indecorum]

60. Parliamentary Inquiry
   - I rise to a parliamentary inquiry.
   - Parliamentary inquiry, Mr. President!

61. Postpone Indefinitely
   - I move that the resolution be postponed indefinitely.

62. Postpone to a Certain Time, or Definitely, applied to a pending question
   - I move to postpone the question to the next meeting.

63. Postpone a pending question to a certain time and make it a special order
   - I move that the resolution be postponed until 3 P.M. and made a special order.

64. Postpone an event or action previously scheduled
   - I move that the dinner previously scheduled for September 15 be postponed until October 17.

65. Previous Question (immediately to close debate and the making of subsidiary motions except the motion to Lay on the Table)
   - I move the previous question.
   - I demand the previous question.
   - I move the previous question on the motion to commit and the amendment.

66. Proviso
   - I move to add the following to the motion: provided that this shall not take effect until … .

III. SAMPLE FORMS USED IN MAKING MOTIONS (cont.)

67. Question of Privilege, to Raise while regular introduction as main motion is not in order
    • I rise to a question of privilege.

68. Question of privilege, to offer as a main motion when an ordinary main motion is in order or after being raised as in No. 67 above
    [Is moved as a main motion.]

69. Ratify, or Confirm
    • I move that the action of the Executive Board on ... be ratified.

70. Read Papers, to grant permission to
    • [Usually done by unanimous consent. When done by a motion:] I move that the member [or "I"] be permitted [or "allowed"] to read ...

71. Recess, to take a, if moved while business is pending
    • I move to recess for five minutes.

72. Recess, to take a, if moved while no question is pending
    [Same form as No. 71]

73. Reconsider
    • I move to reconsider the vote on the motion relating to ...
    • I move to reconsider the vote on the amendment striking out ... and inserting ...

74. Reconsider, in a committee
    [Form similar to No. 73]

75. Reconsider, call up motion to
    • I call up the motion to reconsider the vote ...

76. Rescind and expunge from the minutes
    • I move that the entry relating to ... be rescinded and expunged from the minutes.

77. Rescind, Repeal, or Annul
  • I move that the resolution relating to ... adopted on [date] be rescinded.

78. Refer
  [See *Commit, Committee*, Nos. 24 and 25.]

79. Substitute
  • I move to substitute for the pending resolution the following resolution: "*Resolved*, That ... "

80. Suspend the Rules (as applied to rules of order)
  • I move to suspend the rules which interfere with ...

81. Suspend ordinary standing rules, or standing rules in a convention
  [Form similar to No. 80]

82. Take from the Table
  • I move to take from the table the motion relating to ...

83. Take up a question out of its proper order
  • I move to suspend the rules and take up ...

84. Voting, motions relating to, if made while subject is pending
  • I move that the vote on this question be taken by rising and be counted.

85. Voting, motions relating to, if made while no question is pending
  [Form similar to No. 84]

86. Withdraw or Modify a Motion, to grant maker permission to, after motion has been stated by the chair
  • [Usually done by unanimous consent. When done by a motion, for the case of withdrawal:] I move that the member [or "I"] be permitted [or "allowed"] to withdraw the motion. [For the case of modification by a motion, see *Amend a pending motion*, No. 11.]

IV. MOTIONS AND PARLIAMENTARY STEPS

- **Which Are in Order When Another Has the Floor
and Do Not Require a Second**

Can interrupt a person speaking in debate if urgency requires it.	Calling a member to order (pp. 645–46)
	Call for the Orders of the Day (**18**)
	Call for Division of the Assembly (**29**)
	Call for separate vote(s) on one or more of a series of unrelated resolutions that have been offered by a single motion (pp. 110, 274–75), or on one or more of a series of amendments on which the chair has stated the question in gross (pp. 523, 535–36, 540)
	Parliamentary Inquiry (pp. 293–94)
	Point of Order (**23**)
	Raise a Question of Privilege (**19**)
	Request for Information (pp. 294–95)
	Requests, or motions to grant the request of another member, as follows:
	  For Permission to Withdraw or Modify a Motion (pp. 295–98)
	  For Permission to Read Papers (pp. 298–99)
	  For Any Other Privilege (p. 299)
	Request to Be Excused from a Duty (**32**)

In order when another has been assigned the floor but has not begun to speak. (See particular rules under references given.)	Notice of intent to introduce a motion requiring such notice (pp. 121–24) Objection to the Consideration of a Question (**26**)

- **Which Are in Order When Another Has the Floor but Must Be Seconded**

Can interrupt a person speaking in debate if urgency requires it.	Appeal (**24**) Formal motion to grant maker's own request, if it is not granted by unanimous consent (**32**; pp. 295–99)
In order when another has been assigned the floor but has not begun to speak. (See particular rules under references given.)	Reconsider (to *make* the motion, but not to have it considered at that time; **37**) Reconsider and Enter on the Minutes (to *make* the motion; pp. 332–35)

- **Which Are Out of Order When Another Has the Floor but Do Not Require a Second**

Call up a motion to Reconsider or a motion to Reconsider and Enter on the Minutes (**37**)
Nominations* (**46**)
Proposals for filling blanks* (pp. 162–67)

---

*When chair calls for them, can be offered without obtaining the floor.

V. MOTIONS AND PARLIAMENTARY STEPS

- ## Which Are Not Debatable and Not Amendable

  Adjourn (when privileged; **21**)

  Appeal, if it: (a) relates to indecorum or a transgression of the rules of speaking; (b) relates to the priority of business; or (c) is made when an undebatable question is immediately pending or involved in the appeal (**24**)

  Amend an amendment to an undebatable motion (**12**)

  Calling a member to order (pp. 645–46)

  Call for the Orders of the Day (**18**)

  Call for Division of the Assembly (**29**)

  Call for separate vote(s) on one or more of a series of unrelated resolutions which have been offered by a single motion (pp. 110, 274–75), or on one or more of a series of amendments on which the chair has stated the question in gross (pp. 523, 535–36, 540)

  Call up a motion to Reconsider, or a motion to Reconsider and Enter on the Minutes (**37**)

  Dispense with reading of the minutes (p. 474)

  Grant permission to continue speaking after indecorum (pp. 645–46)

  Lay on the Table (**17**)

  Objection to the Consideration of a Question (**26**)

  Parliamentary Inquiry (pp. 293–94)

  Point of Order (except one referred to assembly by chair on which appeal would be debatable, or one where debate is permitted at chair's discretion by way of explanation; **23**)

  Previous Question (**16**)

  Raise a Question of Privilege (**19**)

  Reconsider an undebatable motion (**37**)

  Request for Information (pp. 294–95)

  Requests or motions to grant requests, in these cases:
  - For Permission to Withdraw a Motion (pp. 295–97)
  - For Permission to Read Papers (pp. 298–99)
  - For Any Other Privilege (p. 299)

  Request for Permission to Modify a Motion (pp. 295–98)

  Suspend the Rules (**25**)

  Take from the Table (**34**)

  Take up a question out of its proper order (**25**; pp. 363–64)

- **Which Are Not Debatable but Are Amendable**

  Amend an undebatable motion (**12**)
  Consider by Paragraph or Seriatim (**28**)
  Division of a Question (**27**)
  Fix the Time to Which to Adjourn (when privileged; **22**)
  Limit or Extend Limits of Debate (**15**)
  Motions relating to methods of voting and the polls (**30**)
  Motions relating to nominations (**31**)
  Recess (when privileged; **20**)

- **Which Are Not Amendable but Are Debatable**

  Amend an amendment to a debatable motion (**12**)
  Appeal, in all cases except those listed at the top of the facing page as undebatable (**24**)
  Blank in a debatable motion, proposals for filling (pp. 162–67)
  Nominations, to make (**46**)
  Postpone Indefinitely (**11**)
  Question of Order, when it has been referred to the assembly by the chair and an appeal on the same point would be debatable (see above, and **23**)
  Reconsider a debatable motion (**37**)

- **On Which Debate Can Go into Merits of the Main Question or the Question Which Is the Subject of the Proposed Action**

  Amend Something Previously Adopted (**35**)
  Discharge a Committee (**36**)
  Fix the time at which a motion shall take effect (**10, 12, 57**)
  Postpone Indefinitely (**11**)
  Ratify (pp. 124–25)
  Reconsider a debatable motion (**37**)
  Rescind (**35**)

VI. MOTIONS WHICH REQUIRE A TWO-THIRDS VOTE

Motions marked † may also be adopted by a vote of a majority of the entire membership, even if previous notice has not been given.

Adopt agenda or program at a session already having an order of business, if it contains special orders or conflicts with the existing order of business (**10, 41, 59**)

† Adopt parliamentary authority in an organized society if the bylaws do not designate one, previous notice also being required (**2, 10**)

Adopt parliamentary standing rules in a convention (**10, 59**)

† Adopt special rules of order, previous notice also being required (**2, 10**)

† Amend an adopted agenda or program (**41, 59**)

† Amend or Rescind adopted parliamentary standing rule in a convention (**35, 59**)

† Amend or Rescind adopted non-parliamentary standing rule in a convention, if notice has not been given on at least the preceding day (**35, 59**)

† Amend or Rescind adopted constitution or bylaws containing no provision for own amendment, previous notice also being required (**35, 57**)

† Amend or Rescind adopted special rules of order (**2, 35**), previous notice also being required

† Amend or Rescind Something Previously Adopted (general case, including ordinary standing rules), when previous notice has not been given (**35**)

Amend or Rescind Something Previously Adopted, in a committee when someone who voted for the motion to be rescinded or amended is absent and has not been notified of the motion to Amend or Rescind (**35**)

Close nominations (**31**)

Close suggestions for filling a blank (**12**)

Close the polls (**30**)

† Depose from office where trial is not required (see pp. 653–54), and previous notice has not been given

† Discharge a Committee, if previous notice, or a partial report, has not been given (**36**)

Extend time for consideration of pending question (**18**), or time until scheduled adjournment or recess (**20, 21**)

Expel from membership, notice and a trial being also required unless the offense is committed in a meeting of the assembly (**61**)

Limit or Extend Limits of Debate (**15**)

Make a special order (**14, 41**)

Objection to the Consideration of a Question (**26**) (two-thirds against consideration sustains the objection)

Previous Question (**16**)

Reconsider in committee, when someone who voted with the prevailing side is absent and has not been notified that the reconsideration will be moved (pp. 329–30)

Refuse to proceed to the orders of the day (**18**)

Suspend the Rules (**25**)

Take up a question out of its proper order, or take up an order of the day before the time for which it has been set (**14, 25, 41**)

VII. MOTIONS WHOSE RECONSIDERATION IS PROHIBITED OR LIMITED

- **Cannot be reconsidered at all:**

  Adjourn (**21**)
  Close nominations (**31**)
  Close the polls immediately (**30**)
  Consider by Paragraph or Seriatim (**28**)
  Create a blank (pp. 163–64)
  Dispense with the reading of the minutes (p. 474)
  Division of the Assembly, or ordering a rising vote counted (**29**)
  Division of a Question (**27**)
  Extend time for consideration of pending question (**18**), or time until scheduled adjournment or recess (**20, 21**)
  Parliamentary Inquiry (pp. 293–94)
  Point of Order (**23**)
  Proceed to the orders of the day (**18**)
  Raise a Question of Privilege (**19**)
  Recess (**20**)
  Reconsider (**37**)
  Request for Information (pp. 294–95)
  Suspend the Rules (**25**)
  Take from the Table (**34**)
  Take up a question out of its proper order (**14, 25, 41**; pp. 363–64)

- **A negative vote cannot be reconsidered (although an affirmative vote can be):**

  Postpone Indefinitely (**11**)

- **An affirmative vote cannot be reconsidered (although a negative vote can be):**

  Accept resignation or grant Request to Be Excused from a Duty, if person was present or has been notified (**32**)
  Adopt or amend agenda or program (**41, 59**)

Adopt or amend bylaws or constitution, rules of order, or any other rules that require previous notice for their amendment (**2, 54, 57, 59**)

Amend Something Previously Adopted (**35, 57**)

Commit, if committee has begun work on referred matter (**13**)

Consider informally (**13, 52**)

Discharge a Committee (**36**)

Election, if person elected was present and did not decline, or was absent but had consented to candidacy, or had not consented to candidacy but has been notified and has not declined (**46**)

Expulsion from membership or office, if person was present or has been officially notified (p. 308)

Grant Permission to Withdraw or Modify a Motion (pp. 295–98)

Lay on the Table (**17**)

Objection to the Consideration of a Question (**26**)

Previous Question, after any vote has been taken under it (**16**)

Reopen nominations (**31**)

Reopen the polls immediately (**30**)

Rescind (**35**)

VIII. TABLE OF RULES FOR COUNTING ELECTION BALLOTS

(See pp. 415–17 and p. 441, ll. 11–24)

TYPE OF BALLOT	CREDITED TO CANDIDATE(S)	COUNTED TOWARD NUMBER OF VOTES CAST
Ballots That Indicate Preference, Cast by Member		
— if meaning of ballot is clear, and ballot indicates eligible candidate	Yes	Yes
— if ballot indicates ineligible candidate	No	Yes
— if meaning of ballot is unclear, but can't affect result	No	Yes
— if meaning of ballot is unclear, and may affect result	Submit to assembly for decision	Yes
— two or more filled-out ballots, folded together	No	Yes, but counted as one vote
— one filled-out ballot, folded together with one or more blank ballots	Yes	Yes
Blank Ballots, Ballots That Indicate No Preference	No	No
Ballots Cast by Nonmember	No	No[1]
Ballots for Multiple Positions on a Board or Committee		
— with votes for full number of positions to fill	Yes	Yes (one vote)[2]
— with votes for less than full number	Yes	Yes (one vote)[2]
— with votes for too many candidates	No	Yes (one vote)[2]

[1] If there is evidence that any ballots were cast by persons not entitled to vote but those ballots cannot be identified, and if there is any possibility that such ballots might affect the result, the entire ballot vote is null and void and a new ballot vote must be taken.

[2] When votes are cast in one section of the ballot for multiple positions on a board or committee, every ballot with a vote in that section for one or more candidates is counted as one vote cast.

INDEX

References are to page numbers, with **boldface page numbers** indicating definitions. (Top-level headings appear in **boldface text**, as a visual aid.)

Page numbers followed by *n* refer to footnotes. Page numbers preceded by *t* refer to the separately numbered "tinted pages" found between page 670 and this index.

Names of specific motions appear in *italic text*, and *italic page numbers* refer to their Standard Descriptive Characteristics (explained on pp. 79–80), the content of which is generally not indexed. Key facts with regard to the SDCs of motions are summarized in Chart I (t3–t5) and Table II (t6–t29).

The content of Tables II–VII (t6–t47), in which motions can be located alphabetically by category, is not indexed.

A

absentees, li, 2, 14, 566
  Call of the House, 350–351
  candidates, 444
  delegates, 605
  election, 445
  president, 152
  rights, 4, 14, 566
  rules protecting, 251, 263–264, 364, 595
  secretary, 459
  vote, 263, 423–424
abstention, 15, 400, 401
  blank ballots, 415
  chair, 53–54
  negative vote, when a. same effect, 403
  not called for in taking vote, 45
  oneself, questions affecting, 407–408
  right of, 403, 407
  roll call, 421–422
absurd motion, 172, 342
Accept. See *Adopt* report or recommendations
acclamation, xxx, 443
accused. See disciplinary proceedings
accused, rights
  due process in disciplinary proceedings, 656
  in investigation, 658–659
  investigation resolution without details, 657–658
  notice, 662–663

  in review of trial committee findings, 668
  in trial, 664–667
ad hoc committee. See special committee
add a paragraph. See insert (or add) a paragraph
add words. See insert (or add) words
Addison, Wesley, Longman, xlviii
address, how
  chair, 22–23, 29, 119
  presiding officer, 22–23
  vice-president, 23, 458
adhering motions, 75–76, **118**
  Commit or Refer, effect on, 177
  Lay on the Table, effect on, 214
  Limit or Extend Limits of Debate, effect on, 391
  Postpone to a Certain Time, effect on, 188
  Reconsider, effect on, 319, 325–329
  Take from the Table, effect on, 303
  withdrawn motion, effect on, 297
Adjourn, **adjournment**, 68, **82–83**, **233–242**, *235–236*. See also adjourn sine die (without day); adjourned meeting; *Chart I (t4–t5)*
  adjourned meeting called "adjournment," 94
  in agenda, 371, 374
  call meeting back to order after, 240
  Call of the House, 350, 351